THE AMERICAN CAR SINCE 1775

AN AUTOMOBILE QUARTERLY LIBRARY SERIES BOOK

Book Trade Distribution by E. P. Dutton & Co., Inc.
201 Park Avenue South, New York, N.Y. 10003

THe american

SECOND EDITION

Typesetting by Kutztown Publishing Co., Kutztown, Pa.

SECOND PRINTING

Published simultaneously in Canada by Clarke, Irwin & Company Limited, Toronto and Vancouver
Library of Congress Catalog Card Number: 76-158590
SBN-0-525-05300-X

Car since 1775

THE MOST COMPLETE SURVEY OF THE AMERICAN AUTOMOBILE EVER PUBLISHED

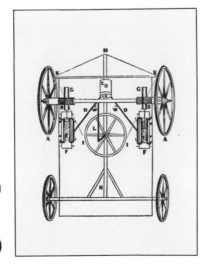

BY THE EDITORS OF AUTOMOBILE *Quarterly*

The Connoisseur's Magazine of Motoring Today, Yesterday and Tomorrow

MCMLXXI

PUBLISHER,
● L. SCOTT BAILEY ●

STAFF FOR THIS BOOK

EDITORIAL STAFF

Publisher: L. Scott Bailey
Senior Editor: Beverly Rae Kimes
Book Editor: Sue Ellen Johnson
Art Director: Theodore R. F. Hall
Production Manager: Chester DeTurk
Editorial Assistant: Roberta Schottland
Director of Research : Henry Austin Clark, Jr.

AUTOMOTIVE HISTORIANS AND CONSULTANTS

Donald H. Berkebile, Curator, Division of Transportation, Smithsonian Institution
James J. Bradley, Head of the Automotive Section, Detroit Public Library
Mary M. Cattie, Librarian-in-Charge, Automobile Reference Collection, Free Library of Philadelphia
John Conde, Automotive Historian

Ralph Dunwoodie, Harrah's Automobile Collection
Leslie R. Henry, Curator, Transportation Collection, Henry Ford Museum and Greenfield Village
William Jackson, former Editor, *Antique Automobile*
Dr. Alfred S. Lewerenz, Research Historian, Horseless Carriage Club of America
Walter O. MacIlvain, Editor, *The Bulb Horn*

Don Vorderman, Editor, AUTOMOBILE *Quarterly*

CONTRIBUTING EDITORS

Richard M. Langworth
Keith Marvin
John Montville
Jan P. Norbye
Hugo Pfau
Michael Sedgwick
Herman L. Smith
Frank T. Snyder, Jr.

Stanley K. Yost

RESEARCH CONTRIBUTORS

Henry Blommel
Hermann C. Brunn
Hugh Durnford
Henry E. Edmunds
Warren Fitzgerald
Otto H. Klausmeyer

Joseph Klima, Jr.
Cliff Lockwood
John R. Lyman
Harold E. McClelland
George Moffitt
Lord Montagu of Beaulieu
Earl D. Beauchamp, Jr.

George E. Orwig II
G. H. Rideout
Stanley G. Reynolds
Myron E. Scott
Robert F. Scott
Ruth Franklin Sommerlad
Donald J. Summar

Robert E. Turnquist
Michael E. Ware
Peter Weatherhead
Bernard J. Weis
Jack R. White
R. Perry Zavitz

ACKNOWLEDGEMENTS

We are indebted to numerous libraries, museums and historians for their help in searching out illustrative material during our preparation of this book. Credit for each photograph or drawing used in the book appears at the end of the illustration's caption, coded parenthetically by an alphabetical letter. The code for the various letters appears below. The absence of a code letter indicates that the illustration is from the files of AUTOMOBILE *Quarterly*.

PHOTO CREDITS—SECTIONS I THROUGH XII

American Motors Corporation historical collection, (A) Detroit, Michigan

John Montville Collection, Bronx, New York (B)

Chrysler Historical Collection, Detroit, Michigan (C)

Detroit Public Library, Automotive History Collection (D)

White Motor Company, Cleveland, Ohio (E)

Ford Archives & Henry Ford Museum, Dearborn, Michigan (F)

General Motors Corporation, Detroit, Michigan (G)

Thomas H. Hubbard Collection, Tucson, Arizona (H)

John de Bondt Collection, Ottawa, Ontario (I)

John A. Conde Collection, Bloomfield Hills, Michigan (J)

Library of Congress, Washington, D.C. (K)

Long Island Automotive Museum, Southampton, New York (L)

George A. Moffitt Collection, New York, New York (M)

Henry Davis Nadig, Norwalk, Connecticut (N)

Ontario Motor League, Toronto, Ontario (O)

Free Library of Philadelphia, Automobile Reference Collection (P)

Howard L. Applegate Collection, Syracuse, New York (Q)

(R) Richard M. Langworth Collection, Hopewell, New Jersey

(S) Syracuse University, George Arents Research Library

(T) Robert Turnquist Collection, Morristown, New Jersey

(U) Reynolds Museum, Wetaskiwin, Alberta

(V) H. W. Motors, Ltd., Walton-on-Thames, Surrey, England

(W) Waverly Hall Collection, Cold Spring, New York

(X) *The Reflector*, Antique and Classic Car Club of Canada, Toronto, Ontario

(Y) Montagu Motor Museum, Beaulieu, Hampshire, England

(Z) R. Perry Zavitz Collection, London, Ontario

(AA) Ford Motor Co., Ltd., Dagenham, Essex, England

(BB) Lytton P. Jarman Collection, Rugby, Warwickshire, England

(CC) Anthony Harding Collection, London, England

(DD) Trident Cars Ltd., Ipswich, Suffolk, England

(EE) G. N. Georgano Collection, London, England

(FF) Trojan, Ltd., Croydon, Surrey, England

(GG) T.V.R. Engineering, Blackpool, Lancashire, England

(HH) Ginetta Cars Ltd., Witham, Essex, England

PHOTO AND OWNER CREDITS—SECTION XIII

Photos by James G. Fitchett. All license plates illustrated are from the collection of Robert N. Tuthill, save for the following. From the collection of Keith Marvin: District of Columbia 1957 and 1965, Florida 1962, New Hampshire 1930, New York 1962, Prince Edward Island 1962 and Baja, California, Mexico 1958-59. The following license plates are from the collection of James G. Fitchett: Maryland 1957, Utah 1959 and 1966, New York Historical Plate and Idaho 1965. From a private collection are the license plates for Georgia 1941, Colorado 1920, South Dakota 1913, Arizona 1917, Hawaii 1926, Kansas 1918, Mississippi 1935 and North Carolina 1939.

CONTENTS

II: A pioneer of "The Neighboring Industry."

III: Front runners of "The Race to Produce."

IV-VI: A Weyman-designed Duesenberg SJ.

I: A pioneer of "The Other Revolution"—one Oliver Evans from Delaware.

VII-VIII: One of the "Cars of Both Worlds"—
the American-engined, Swiss-built Monteverdi hai.

XI-XII: The Columbia electric from Hartford,
one of America's early "Titans of the Road."

XIV: One of the one hundred seventy.

IX: One of the "5000 Marques."

X: One that didn't make it.

XIII: "Licensing the Motorcar"—New York, 1904.

XV: One of the eighty.

PREFACE

THE AMERICAN CAR SINCE 1775 is, we think, particularly appropriate as the first book of AUTOMOBILE *Quarterly*'s Library Series. For years we have wanted to do a book of this kind—presenting between two covers a panoramic survey of the American automobile. We were anxious, first of all, to record the thousands of automobiles which have been built in North America, the "5000 Marques" of our Section IX—and to similarly present the "Titans of the Road," those many scores of motor trucks which have played so vital a role in American commerce. An era past is that of the American coachbuilder—the more than one hundred firms contributing to that glorious age are recorded, as well as the more than a hundred firms abroad who have used the American automobile or its components as a basis for their own cars. Further listings include the production figures for automobile manufacturers in the United States from the year 1896—and those clubs and museums dedicated to the automobile which have proliferated in recent decades in the United States and Canada.

These various listings have been brought together in this book in an effort to present as comprehensive a look as possible at the automobile in America. To tell the story behind those listings there is included a series of historical sections. The first traces the development of the American automobile from its Eighteenth Century conception to 1895; another picks up the story at that point to examine a peculiar American phenomenon, the automobile production race, which is still going strong after seventy-odd years. Canada's industry is dwelt upon in another section, in another history of the American motor truck is presented. Elsewhere a British historian looks at "The Hybrids" and the American influence in foreign automobiles, and a designer who participated in it relives "The Golden Age of the Coachbuilder in America." Then

there's that oft-neglected adjunct to the automobile—the license plate. Its story, too, is told.

There's more, as the reader will discover. This delineation of the scope of the book has been given only to emphasize that THE AMERICAN CAR SINCE 1775 owes its existence to many hands. The book was a considerable undertaking—and without the help of the numerous writers and researchers who freely gave of their time and talent and knowledge, it would not have been possible at all. As the staff page indicates, we are indebted to many. Our appreciation for their efforts shall ever remain boundless.

Soon AUTOMOBILE *Quarterly* will celebrate its tenth anniversary. It's been an enormously rewarding decade for us, as it would be for any group of individuals engaged in doing that which they so much enjoy. The automobile is an extreme passion with us. It was this fascination with the automobile—the glory of its past, the challenge of its present, the promise of its future—which prompted the founding of AUTOMOBILE *Quarterly*. Since that date our magazine has garnered a number of tributes, among them the Thomas McKean Award for outstanding research in automobile history, the Benjamin Franklin Gold Medal for color lithography and printing, as well as a plethora of awards for editorial art and design. All that has been satisfying, to be sure. But more important—and clearly a source of delight to us—is the fact that AUTOMOBILE *Quarterly* has succeeded, for the very idea of the magazine was quite unconventional: a hard-bound, book-like magazine carrying no advertising and sold only through subscription. There aren't many magazines like that, on any subject, in the world—and it is, we think, significant that a magazine like ours, devoted solely to the automobile, is in that select company. Clearly it indicates that

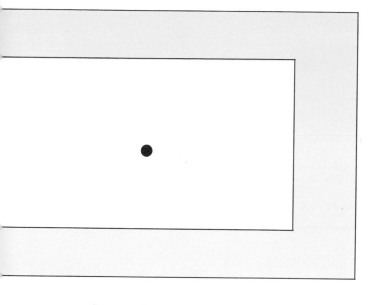

our concern for automobile history and its presentation in a manner commensurate with its past is shared by many others. Simply put, AUTOMOBILE *Quarterly* is a measure of the sophistication of the automobile enthusiast.

There can be no questioning that automobile history is gathering onto itself devotees in ever-increasing numbers. The success of AUTOMOBILE *Quarterly*'s Book Society—wherein recent and hard-to-find books in the automotive field, as well as automotive art and prints are made available to subscribers—has amply demonstrated that. The automobile enthusiast is obviously a voracious reader, and the range of his automotive interests is all-encompassing. It was recognition of this happy fact which led us to the inauguration of AUTOMOBILE *Quarterly*'s Library Series, which will be distributed to book stores and libraries through the publishing house of E. P. Dutton & Co., Inc. of New York. The Library Series is a venture to broaden the literature in the automotive field, a series of books—in the same size and format as this one—dedicated to various aspects of automobile history. The subject range of the series will be as wide as the automobile enthusiast's interest—already scheduled in the series are marque histories of Cadillac, Packard, Ford and Corvette, as well as pictorial surveys of all the various facets—racing, design, engineering—of the world of the automobile. Readers whose introduction to the world of the automobile may be recent and who may wish to know more about AUTOMOBILE *Quarterly* are invited to write our editorial offices: 40 East 49th Street, New York, New York 10021.

Herewith THE AMERICAN CAR SINCE 1775. To the many hands who helped bring it into being, our everlasting thanks. And to the memory of the man who started it all, a salute.

Eng⁴ by W.G. Jackman

1755-1819

THE OTHER REVOLUTION

BY L. SCOTT BAILEY

I

INTRODUCTION

Decades ago this writer fell in love with the automobile—and it's been an affair made more passionate as year passes year. An automobile is, after all, so much more than an object. The character of its parts can intrigue the mind, the look of it can delight the eye, and the operating of it can bring untold hours of pleasure. Even in this day when the automobile has come under attack from various quarters—much of the criticism being of merit—there still can be no denying the automobile's appeal. It's a personal appeal, and for those whose interest in the automobile transcends the merely practical, even the technical and aesthetic, there's the fascination of its history.

Every enthusiast of the automobile who delves at all into its history is time and again confronted by varied tales of its invention. Who was first with what and when, who invented the automobile? There are no easy answers, though a good many suggestions have been provided through the years. Back in the early Fifties, in an effort to dispel some rather outlandish claims being made on behalf of the Duryea motor wagon, J. Frank Duryea wrote the state legislature of Massachusetts: "If any single person invented the automobile . . . that man was Carl Benz of Mannheim, Germany." Mr. Benz has been accorded that honor by others; Mr. Daimler has his followers—and then there is the Siegfried Marcus controversy. There are no easy answers.

But what is spoken of in this regard is the gasoline automobile, the automobile as we know it today. Yet it's been with us for less than a hundred years. Decades before its arrival men were pursuing the automotive idea quite differently, and who's to say that decades hence the automobile might not have evolved into something altogether contrary to the limited parameters of the automobile as a gasoline-powered vehicle.

What is an automobile then?—defined not by its motive force. Actually the word "automobile" itself says it quite well, as does the antiquated expression "horseless carriage" and the cumbersome but accurate "self-propelled passenger-carrying road vehicle." In this context it is impossible to name one individual as the inventor or one country as the birthplace of the invention. The automobile, as has been said before, was born in many places and in many times.

What is distressing, however, to the American historian is how readily some European scholars dismiss the automobile's development in the United States. So often the view is taken that the automobile was virtually nonexistent in America until it was introduced to these shores from Europe; America did not develop the automotive idea, she merely borrowed it. This simply is not true.

The study that follows traces the birth of the automotive idea in America through six score years to 1895 and an event which established clearly that the automobile was here to stay. There has been no attempt to draw any parallels between European and American development, although certainly parallels do exist. Instead presented herein is the American automobile only, from its very beginning. The idea of an automobile was rather revolutionary then, but so, too, were a lot of the ideas about this country.

The Birth and Development
of the American Automobile

●

OLIVER EVANS: 1772-1792

In December of 1772 a young man in the Crown colony of Delaware had an idea, an idea which would challenge him the rest of his life, the ultimate reality of which would be the American automobile. It happened quite simply, as Oliver Evans himself wrote of the incident in 1772:

> ". . . But one of my brothers informing me, on a Christmas evening, that he had that day been in company with a neighboring black smith's boy, who, for amusement, had stopped up the touch-hole of a gun-barrel, then put into it about a gill of water, and rammed down a tight wadding; after which they put the breech-end of it into the smith's fire, when it discharged itself with as loud a crack as if it had been loaded with gunpowder. It immediately occurred to me that there was a power capable of propelling any waggon, provided that I could apply it; and I set myself to work to find out the means of doing so. I laboured for some time without success; at length, a book fell into my hands, describing the old atmospheric engine. I was astonished to observe that they had so far erred as to use the steam only to form a vacuum, to apply the mere pressure of the atmosphere, instead of applying the elastic power of steam, for original motion; a power which I supposed was irresistible. I renewed my studies with increased ardour, and soon declared that I could make steam waggons, and endeavoured to communicate my ideas to others; but, however practicable the thing appeared to me, my object only excited the ridicule of those to whom it was known. But I persevered in my belief, and confirmed it by experiments that satisfied me of its reality."

It is not hard to understand why Evans' best efforts were frustrated for so long. Even if he had stumbled upon a practical plan for his steam engine at once, he could not have found in all the Colonies the necessary tools, materials or skilled labor to execute his plans. His family were farmers. He was the fifth of eight sons, the only one who, very early, revealed a scientific interest and inventive talent. When he injured his hand with a scythe, Evans spent the idle hours of his recuperation making a small wooden model of a self-propelled land carriage. Amused and slightly annoyed, his father — and indeed his entire family — refused to take seriously what they termed his "visionary schemes." Undaunted, he took his model engine to a blacksmith — who refused to build it. A disappointed Evans later recalled:

> "There are witnesses living, to whom I communicated my intentions of applying my improved Steam Engine to propel carriages, as early perhaps as 1773, and to boats by means of paddle wheels, as early as 1778, certainly prior to 1781."

The range of Evans' interests was remarkably wide for so young a man. While pondering his land carriage idea, he turned his attention elsewhere as well, and by the time he was twenty-two he had successfully solved the knotty problem of making fine wire from American bar iron. There were other distractions as well — the American colonists had chosen to revolt, and in 1778 when the Revolutionary War raged south into the middle colonies, the twenty-three-year-old Evans enlisted in Captain William Robson's company of militia. Little is known about Evans' activities in the Continental Army; the documents remaining testify only to his willingness to serve. By Evans' own account, it was during the war years that he began formulating ideas for a flour mill which would carry grain from a wagon and through all milling operations without the use of manual labor. Ideas such as these would later gain for Evans considerable fame as a master millwright —

and they were among many he harbored and developed in this area. They, of course, cannot all be delineated here, but it should be said that the extent of Oliver Evans' inventiveness is truly awe-inspiring. For those interested in pursuing his multi-faceted career, a fascinating study is provided in *Oliver Evans: A Chronicle of Early American Engineering* by Greville and Dorothy Bathe, published by the Historical Society of Pennsylvania in 1935.

With the coming of peace, and the borning years of a new nation, Oliver Evans sought public recognition — and protection — for his inventions. In 1786 he petitioned the legislature of Pennsylvania for exclusive rights to those improvements he had devised for milling flour — as well as for the building of steam wagons. Those portions of his petition concerning the manufacture of flour were approved. Ignored completely was his request for exclusive rights for a steam wagon. In 1787 he tried again. On May 28th of that year he submitted to the state legislature of Delaware a petition requesting a patent for a high pressure steam engine and carriage, as follows:

> "To the Honourable the Representatives of the Freemen of the Delaware State in General Assembly met
> The petition of Oliver Evans of the County of New Castle respectfully Sheweth
> That your Petitioner hath long had in Contemplation the very great Power of Steam and the Pressure of the Atmosphere and hath at great expence of Study Time & Labour in Various Experiments made for the Purpose, Invented an entire New Plan of applying said Powers to Propelling land Carriages to travel with heavie Burdens up and Down hills without the aid of Animal fource with such Velocity as may be Convenient, and be guided by a person siting therein Secure from the Inclemency of the weather—But to Execute said Plan Compleatly, will require more Time, Labour & Money than your Petitioner Can think prudent to expend, without hopes of Considerable profit in Case of Compleat Success—Therefore your Petitioner prays your Honours to grant to him his Heirs and Assigns an exclusive Right of Propelling all land Carriages by the Power of Steam and the Pressure of the Atmosphere for the Term of Fifteen years and your Petition as in duty bound will ever Pray &c
> May 28, 1787   Oliver Evans

Regarding this petition, Greville Bathe has noted that "we believe though this was considered in committee the application was refused." Fortunately Oliver Evans had approached the state of Maryland with a similar request at about the same time — and that state's legislature was more congenial. Armed with drawings and specifications and a model steam engine, Evans effectively demonstrated his principles before the legislative committee, and on May 19th, 1787, the Maryland House of Delegates approved his patent, the state Senate concurring two days later. Interestingly, Evans indicated that he planned to apply his steam engine only to land vehicles, not to water vessels. Given the reality of that day — and the apparently more immediate and profitable application of steam power to water transport — it was perhaps a peculiar choice. An explanation, however, was provided in *Patent Right Oppression Exposed, or Knavery Detected*, a book written by Oliver Evans, under a pseudonym, in 1813: ". . .he did not include steam boats, because Rumsey and Fitch were at that time contending about their originality of invention in the application of such engines as were then known, besides, he entertained an opinion, that the western waters were those only where steam boats would be highly useful." No doubt Evans did not wish to lay claim to something he had

not invented, and it would appear, in any case, that he felt a steam road carriage would have a wider practical application.

The state of Maryland was, thus, the first to provide Evans patent protection for the development of his steam wagon. In recommending that Evans' petition be granted, committeeman Jesse Hollingsworth had argued that no harm could possibly come from it because to his knowledge no man in the world had ever thought of such a thing before, and there was every possibility of Evans producing something useful from his idea. Not all members of the committee were similarly enthused, however. During the course of his interview and demonstration before the Maryland group, Evans was baited repeatedly by one rudely skeptical committeeman. How, he scoffed, would Evans' self-propelled vehicle get out of the way of other wagons? The inventor's reply came quickly: "Why Sir, were you the waggoner, and did not give room for me to pass, I would crush you and your waggon to the earth." The resulting laughter quieted the antagonist, and the hearing resumed.

While awaiting the decision of his Maryland patent application, Evans made the acquaintance of Thomas Masters. Masters, a retired sea captain, was an inventor himself — of a machine to draw up trees by their roots — and conceivably he may also have had a patent petition pending before the Maryland legislature at that time. During the course of their discussions, Masters indicated that an engine on the Evans' high pressure principle could be successfully applied aboard ships crossing the Atlantic. Fired by the idea, Masters volunteered to introduce Evans' principles to prospective investors in England, and to lay the groundwork for obtaining a patent in that country. Accordingly, Evans prepared drawings and specifications for Masters to take with him on his forthcoming trip to England — and perhaps the model of his steam engine which he had demonstrated before the Maryland committee. But the English scheme was doomed before it started, for the British inventor James Watt, designer of an extremely economic and reliable rotative engine, had rejected the idea of applying steam engines to wagons. Furthermore, he was adamant in his belief that the application of steam pressures higher than two or three pounds to a square inch would present a very real and dangerous threat to the public good. Coming from so eminent and reputable a source as Watt, the condemnation of an obscure American's plan to apply 100 pounds of pressure per square inch seemed entirely proper to British scientists — to say nothing of potential investors.

Despite the rather chilly reception to his ideas in England, Evans remained convinced that securing an English patent was important to his work — and he was to try again. An English patent, he reasoned, would both attract investors and make available to him the technological advances available in that country. Nonetheless he pressed his course at home as well. In May of 1789 he visited Jonathon Ellicot and his brothers, the largest mill owners in the state of Maryland, to urge them to join him in a steam wagon enterprise. According to his diary, Evans explained the plans for his steam engine, but his audience was less than enthusiastic. Of Jonathon Ellicot, he wrote, "he thinks the power will be sufficiently applied, but is doubtful of its duration in good order." As Evans later recalled the visit:

> ". . . I tarried here a few days, using my best efforts to convince

AN Act to grant to Oliver Evans, for a Term of years, the sole and exclusive right of making and selling within this State the Machines herein described. —

Whereas Oliver Evans of the County of New-Castle in the State of Deleware, Miller, hath represented to this General Assembly that he hath invented, discovered, and introduced into exercise, two Machines for the use of Merchant Mills, one of which, denominated by the said Oliver Evans an Elevator; is calculated by its own motion to hoist the wheat or grain from the lower floor, and the Meal or Flour from the Stones of any Mill to the upper floor or loft of such Mill the other denominated an Hopper = Boy so constituted as to spread the Meal over the floor of a Mill to cool, gather it up again to the boultling hopper, and attend the same regularly without the assistance of Manual Labor, also one other Machine denominated a Steam Carriage so constructed as to move by the Power of Steam and the pressure of the atmosphere, for the purpose of Conveying burthens without the aid of Animal Force. And as the said Inventions of the said Oliver Evans will greatly tend to Simplify and render Cheap the Manufacture of Flour which is one of the principal Staples of this State, as also render the use of Land Carriages more convenient and less expencive, in order to make adequate Compensation to the said Oliver Evans for his ingenuity trouble and expence in the said Discoveries. —

Be it enacted, by the General Assembly of Maryland that from and after the passing this Act the said Oliver Evans, his Heirs and Assigns shall have the Sole and exclusive right of making and Selling within this State the said Machines above described, agreeably to his new method of constructing and making the same for and during the full Space and Term of fourteen Years from thence next ensuing as aforesaid and so toties quoties. —

Patent granted to Evans, from the General Assembly of Maryland, 1787. (D)

By the House of Delegates
May 19th 1787 —
Read and assented to

W Smallwood

By the Senate May 26th 1787
Read and assented.
By Order

14

them of the possibility and practicability of propelling waggons, on good turnpike roads, by the elastic power of steam. But they also feared the expense and difficulty of the execution, and declined the proposition."

Thwarted though he was in attracting investors to his steam wagon idea, Evans could at least console himself with the knowledge that his invention was protected by patent, by now in several states — until the second session of the first Congress convened on January 8, 1790, and enacted legislation which resulted in the establishment of a federal patent office shortly thereafter. With the institution of the United States Patent Office, all states were required to relinquish their patents to the jurisdiction of the federal government. Evans immediately applied for a federal patent covering his milling improvements, but, interestingly, did not include a petition for his steam principles as well. There were probably a number of reasons for this, more of which later, but conceivably one of them might have been the confusion that surrounded the establishment of a federal patent office. As indicated in the notice filed November 23, 1790, by federal clerk Henry Remsen, Jr. in Philadelphia:

"Some of the claims of patents founded on the supposed discovery of new applications for steam for useful purposes, not having been stated so precisely as to be satisfactory to the board and it being their wish to hear all those claims together, order that the first Monday in February next be appointed for the hearings of all parties interested; that notice be given to John Fitch, James Rumsey, Nathan Read, Isaac Briggs, and John Stevens of this order and that each of them be required to transmit in writing to the board the precise statement of their civil intentions and thereof."

EVANS' CONTEMPORARIES

Before discussing Evans' application for a federal patent for his steam engine, we should look first to those American inventors who preceded him in petitioning the new Patent Office for rights to similar inventions.

The distinguished career of Nathan Read of Warren, Massachusetts, included graduation from Harvard, a professorship at his alma mater, a judgeship and, later, a term in Congress. He is believed to have been the first to receive a patent from the new office. According to family records — all patents having been destroyed in a fire which swept through the patent record office in 1836 — Read's patent for a high pressure boiler and improved cylinder was signed by George Washington and Thomas Jefferson on August 26, 1791. Most of the year previous he had spent in New York drawing plans and making models of a steam boat and a land carriage. That year, too, he had gained an audience with George Washington, via a letter of introduction from General Benjamin Lincoln. On April 23rd he had petitioned the Secretary of State and the Secretary of Defense and the Secretary from the Department of War to show that he had "a simple method of moving land carriages by the power of steam, directing them principally by the same agent that I have invented, and improved method of propelling vessels in water against the currents of rapids in rivers by wheels." This discovery was soon applied to his plan for a steam wagon, "using two double acting engines, one driving each wheel for power and convenience of turning. Each engine would respond to the slower or faster movement of the wheel."

Presumably these experiments had culminated in the improved steam cylinder and boiler which he submitted to the patent office in 1791. The cylinder and boiler were not only lightweight and portable — he called it his "portable furnace boiler" — but convenient for an inclined or horizontal position as well. The mechanism was simple: The piston had two stems or rods, one coming out of each end of the cylinder alternately, acting with equal force in contrary directions. But like so many inventors of the automobile, Read found his ideas were a bit too radical for ready acceptance. As he wrote later:

"When my petition to Congress was read in the Congress Hall by the clerk of the House of Representatives . . . [and] . . . when he came to the part which related to the application of steam to land carriages a general smile was excited among the members and the idea was considered there and at Salem where I had the model of the steam carriage constructed as perfectly visionary."

Embittered, Read summed up his work with a judgment that, sadly, seems all too true in retrospect: "I was too early with my steam projects, and the country was then too poor and I have derived neither honor nor profit from the time and money extended."

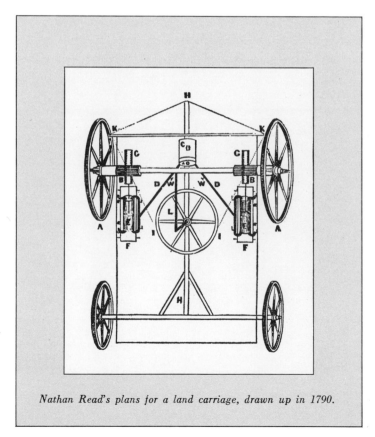

Nathan Read's plans for a land carriage, drawn up in 1790.

Much the same ultimate experience was dealt James Rumsey of Maryland and John Fitch of Windsor, Connecticut — the first Americans to propel boats by steam. It is believed that Rumsey obtained encouragement for his steam boat idea from his friend Benjamin Franklin, upon Franklin's return from France in 1785. At that time Franklin, whose wide-ranging interests are legendary, laid before the Philosophical Society of Philadelphia a plan for a practical steam boat. Certainly Rumsey had been thinking along the same lines since 1774, when he began work on an engine which utilized a pump-like device that drew in water and forced it from the stern of the boat, thereby propelling it forward. In 1786 he demonstrated the principle before President George Washington, enriched by Franklin's ideas and the experience of having constructed a vessel similar to Franklin's specifications. Emigrating to England to take advantage of that country's technological facilities and to pursue his studies of steam power, Rumsey was stricken by apoplexy in Liverpool and died before his projects could be completed.

A foreshortened career was also the fate of John Fitch. A prosperous jeweler and watchmaker from Camden, New Jersey, Fitch spent the Revolutionary War years manufacturing arms in Bethlehem, Pennsylvania. His was a mechanical genius, flawed, unfortunately, by stubbornness, an excitable temper, a panoramic range of personal problems, and a spectacular talent for driving away his friends, associates and prospective investors. But his grasp of the intricacies of steam propulsion was total. In 1785 he invented a steam boat, claiming priority over Rumsey's initial effort by blithely assuring all concerned that he had never heard of such a boat until he himself dreamed it up. When the dream materialized, it became apparent that Fitch's boat, crude though it was, surpassed the experiments of his predecessors, and a patent for it was granted by the federal patent office in 1791. Nor was a steam boat the only concern of the inventor Fitch. He was the first American entrepreneur to organize a company for the purpose of building steam engines, forming a partnership with Henry Voight—a watchmaker — for that purpose in 1786, with a capital of $300. No doubt he meant at least some of these engines to propel road wagons, for he built a scale model of a self-propelled road vehicle at this time. Unfortunately, his personal problems weighed heavy, and soon after moving to Bardstown, Kentucky, to develop his road-wagon idea, he committed suicide.

OLIVER EVANS: 1792-1804

In 1792 Oliver Evans petitioned the United States Patent Office for a

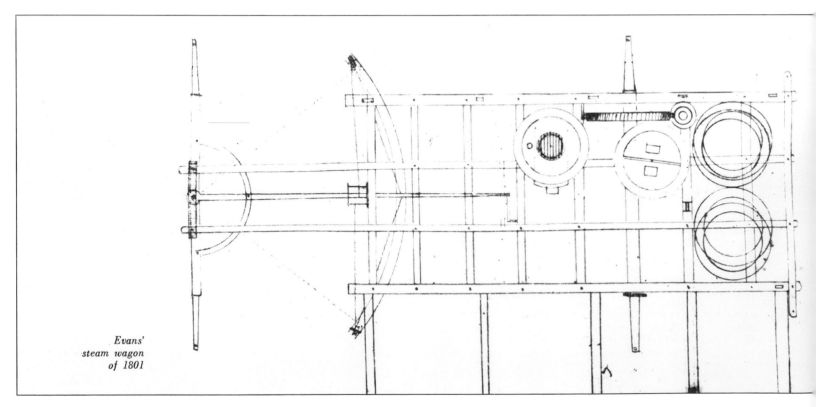

*Evans'
steam wagon
of 1801*

patent on his steam engine. Possibly his mill-work development was partially responsible for the two-year delay in applying once the new federal office had been opened, and the additional time, too, had allowed him to fully organize his ideas for a steam engine into a cohesive presentation. His drawings and specifications were deposited with the United States Patent Office on October 1st. Copies of that presentation exist today in the Transportation Library of the University of Michigan — the originals perished in the 1836 patent office fire — and they prove conclusively that Evans had developed by 1792 a reciprocating engine, both horizontal and vertical plus a rotary engine and a boiler enclosing a furnace. The rotary engine went unpatented, and perhaps this fact played some small part in his decision to abandon the circular configuration some time later. In Evans' papers survives a copy of his patent specifications, prefaced with the notation: "Specification of Oliver Evans' inventions and improvements on the application of steam as a power to give motion to engines and in particular to land carriages." One must admire the inventive theories proposed in this document, crude as they are in the light of modern technology. It must be remembered that Evans did not enjoy the exchange of scholarly knowledge available in the sophisticated scientific centers of Europe, nor did he have access to the tools and technology necessary to translate his concepts into reality. He was working under the most

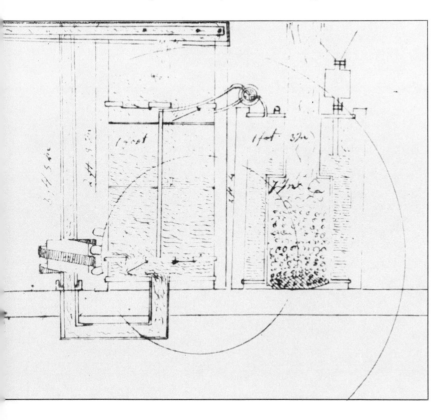

primal of conditions, in a country as new as many of his ideas. What he was able to accomplish is all the more remarkable because of it.

Significantly, with only the few books available in the United States that could help him formulate his theories, Evans himself was able to publish several widely read and appreciated books. In 1795 he wrote *The Young Mill-wright and Miller's Guide*, which clearly demonstrated his mastery of the entire process of flour and meal manufacture. It was a complete guide for the building of mills, laying down a regular system of mechanics and hydraulics explaining the principles of water-wheel power and regulating this power according to its various applications. Not only did he detail with calculations and tables those practices and theories previously held but which were irreconcilable in practice, but he verified his own new theories by comparing them and proving their agreement in actual practice. This book went through fifteen editions and a French translation, and as late as 1860 it was still considered the indispensable guide for millwrights. His principles of mechanics and hydrostatics remain sound today, although continuous improvement in milling machinery has rendered the portion of his book devoted to milling long since obsolete. His writings on thermodynamics, too, demonstrate his very real grasp of that subject.

A decade later Evans was to follow his first book with a second, entitled *The Abortion of a Young Steam Engineer's Guide*. Aside from its technical significance in the propounding of Evans' principles of high pressure steam, it is interesting for its account of the inventor's second attempt to introduce his theories to England:

> ". . . In 1794-95 I sent drawings, specifications and explanations to England to be shown to the steam engineers there, to induce them to put the principles into practice and to take out a joint patent for the improvement, in their names, which they declined and they could not understand the project and had no faith in it."

In this case the papers were sent to England via a Mr. Joseph Stacey Sampson of Boston. Unfortunately Sampson died in London; conceivably the papers might have survived, but to date they have not been found. This is unfortunate, because their discovery might decide the question of whether or not one Richard Trevithick utilized Evans' theories. Scholars have presented arguments on both sides. It is possible that Trevithick did indeed see Evans' papers since he was in London the year they were being shown around by Sampson, and it can be proved that Trevithick had not considered the development of high pressure steam until 1797 — well after the time that Evans' theories had been propounded in England. On the other hand, Trevithick's approach to the steam problem differed markedly from Evans' — despite the fact that a definite similarity exists between the two inventors' oscillating plugcock for the distribution of steam and the firing of the boiler by means of an internal furnace and flue. Perhaps the fact that neither of these details of construction was in any sense new at this time dictates that the question cannot really be resolved one way or the other. It is only important to note that it was Oliver Evans who first realized the vast potential of high pressure steam and desired to apply it to a self-propelled vehicle. Interestingly, in England, it was not until after the death of Watt in 1819 that British high pressure steam advocates could generate any support. Earlier Watt had told John Isaac Hawkins that Trevithick "deserved hanging for bringing into use the high-pressure engine."

The publication of his millwright's guide had earned for Evans a considerable reputation, and his store and millstone factory were prosperous enough to allow him to provide comfortably for his family. Still, he could find no investors willing to join him in the development of his steam engine principles and his steam wagon idea. It must have been particularly galling to him when, in 1799, the city of Philadelphia embarked upon a steam project which would altogether ignore his theories of high pressure steam and the practical advantages thereto. Work began that year on a plan by the City Council to lay down water pipes for the principal streets, both for the convenience of householders and to protect against fire. The Council had accepted the plan of one Benjamin Henry Latrobe which used two low pressure rotative steam engines built after the Boulton and Watt designs. These engines were of tremendous size, the first having a forty-inch bore and six-foot stroke, and the second a thirty-two-inch bore and six-foot stroke, theoretically capable of pumping 962,520 gallons every twenty-four hours — both powerful machines expected to perform fairly well for ten years. Contrasting sharply with Evans' concept, both of these engines utilized gargantuan boilers nine feet square by fourteen feet long, made of five-inch pine planks drawn together by long stay bolts. Moreover they depended upon vacuum, using only two or three pounds of pressure apiece.

As the Philadelphia project progressed, steam power became a general topic of conversation throughout Pennsylvania and neighboring states. Its merits and demerits were debated endlessly — and nowhere more vigorously than in the regional press, which most often condemned steam power as a public nuisance, unsafe and far too expensive. Stimulated by the controversy, Evans applied himself anew to the task of championing the concept. In 1800 he wrote that, although he was in full health, he might suddenly be carried off by Yellow Fever which had often visited Philadelphia. And, he added:

"I had not yet discharged my debt of honor to the State of Maryland by producing the steam waggons; I was determined, therefore, to set to work the next day to construct one."

First he consulted with Robert Patterson, professor of mathematics at the University of Pennsylvania, and with Mr. Charles Taylor, a steam engineer from England. Both listened to the explanation of his steam power principles and pronounced them completely sound and worthy of further experimentation. "They both advised me," said Evans of the first two men to offer him unqualified encouragement, "to prove them [his principles] without delay in hopes that I might produce a more simple, cheap and powerful steam engine than any in use." Less fortuitous, however, were the results of a similar attempt to explain his steam principles to Latrobe, of the Philadelphia water pipe project, who, for reasons best known to himself, pronounced them unworkable. In his report to the Philosophical Society of Pennsylvania Latrobe took his disapproval one step further by libelling Evans to such an extent that his remarks were removed from the final printing of the report. It should be added that Latrobe's vitriol was dictated by the obligations of old friendships and political associations, in addition to professional pique. Evans was hardly deterred by the encounter, but in fact left it more resolved than ever to build a steam-engined road wagon.

The project was Evans' alone. He hired the workers and paid them himself. But as the steam wagon began to take shape, he had an entirely new idea. As he said:

". . . the thought struck me that . . . I could obtain a patent for it and apply it to the mills, more profitably than to waggons; for until now I apprehended that, as steam mills had been used in England, I could only obtain a patent for waggons and boats. I stopped work immediately, and discharged my hands, until I could arrange my engine for mills; having laid aside my steam waggon for a time for more leisure."

One can only surmise that the kind of engine Evans had been considering for his steam wagon was his "rotary number 3" engine. And if such an engine was tested, it is certain that Evans later abandoned it in favor of a reciprocating type, or, as he called it, a "vibrating engine."

A short time later Evans completed a small engine with a cylinder six inches in diameter and a stroke of eighteen inches. He invested a total of $3700 in its development — an incredible investment if one considers that in those days the average pay per day for blacksmiths and millwrights was ninety cents. In terms of technical achievement, the engine paid off, and he turned his perfected machine to the task of breaking and grinding 300 bushels or twelve tons of plaster of paris — a highly regarded fertilizer at the time — in a brief twenty-four hour span. So pleased was he with the efficiency of his new engine that he staged a public demonstration in 1801 to show that the engine, driving twelve saws in heavy frames, could saw through 100 feet of marble in twelve hours, an exhibition which garnered a good deal of public attention for its inventor. Among those who approached him during the demonstration was the chairman of the Pennsylvania legislative committee who fifteen years earlier had presided during the patent hearing for Evans' steam engine. There was a memorable exchange. "Sir!" cried Oliver Evans, saluting the committee chairman, "this steam engine goes on the principles which I have intended to propel my steam carriages when I petitioned the legislature in 1786, in which I endeavored to explain to the committee that had they granted me then the exclusive rights for twenty-five years, I might have been driving my boats and my mills years ago." "To tell the truth, Mr. Evans," replied the chairman quietly, "we thought you were deranged when you spoke of making a steam waggon."

If potential investors came, saw, approved yet politely wandered away, the marble-cutting demonstration was nonetheless at least a partial success. Evans was satisfied that thousands of spectators had seen the utility of his discovery. The experiments continued. Evans' engine utilized a small boiler of cedar wood twelve inches in diameter by twenty inches in height, strongly hooped with iron. Inside this cylinder was a cast iron furnace seven inches in diameter at the lower and three inches in the upper end, with a flange of twelve inches diameter at each end serving as heads for the wooden cylinder. He fixed a safety valve and cock in the upper end, while the space between the furnace and the wooden cylinder contained the water which surrounded the fire. The small fire in the furnace soon raised the power of the steam to such a degree as to lift the safety valve pre-loaded at 152 pounds per inch. Finally, he opened the cock, regulating it so as to keep the valve just lifting.

In 1802 Evans constructed a similar engine for the purpose of powering a steam boat — a project which might have succeeded had the boat not been stranded inland by a flood near New Orleans before the trial. Her engine was removed and put to work in a saw mill where it ran flawlessly for a solid year. "Nothing in the engine broke out or got out of order nor stopped the mill for a single hour," marveled a Mr. Stackhouse, the engine man at the mill. If this afforded the engine's inventor a measure of self-esteem, the results of the Latrobe-inspired water system in Philadelphia must have provided Evans even greater satisfaction. The first water was delivered through the pipes on January 27, 1802, to be sure, but the cost of the system had exceeded the estimates by a staggering $93,000.

In February of 1803 Evans placed an advertisement in the *Aurora* newspaper of Philadelphia to notify the public that his own high pressure steam engines would soon be available for sale. During this year, too, he made a third attempt to introduce his high pressure

engines and boilers to England — with the same dismal results that had greeted the first two attempts. It is of interest, however, to learn through Greville Bathe's book that the courier this time was Mr. Humphrey Edwards, a British engineer who returned to England with Oliver Evans' plans, to join Arthur Woolf in partnership in an engineering works on Mill Street, Lambeth, London. It was there that the partners built their first high pressure compound engine, and in 1803 Woolf obtained an English patent for cast iron boilers. Just seven years later he patented a new type of steam engine in England along with a different method of preventing steam leakage past the pistons. To some, the Woolf engine bears some similarity to the one that Evans described in his 1792 patents and later abandoned as impractical. But no Trevithick-like controversy has sprung up in this regard. Greville Bathe believes that whatever similarity there was resulted from an innocent duplication of ideas.

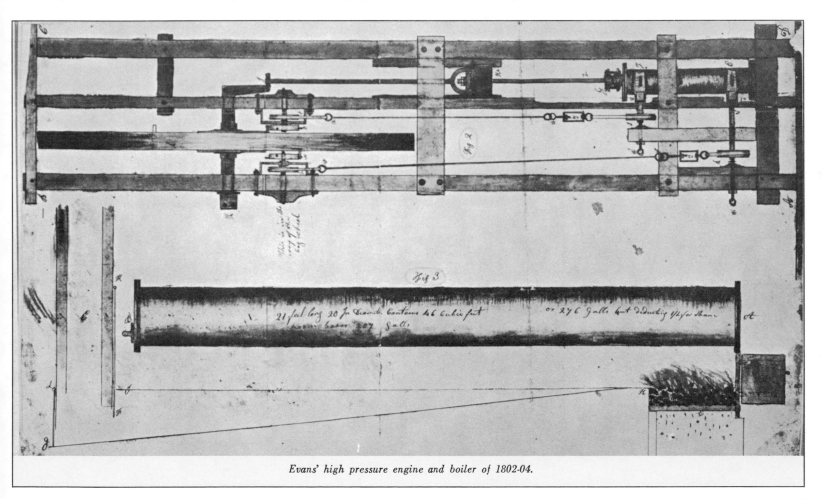

Evans' high pressure engine and boiler of 1802-04.

On February 14, 1804, Evans received a new patent from the United States Patent Office covering his latest high pressure steam engine "to propel boats and land carriages." One month later he utilized the pages of the *Aurora* press once again to call to the public's attention his entire catalogue of inventions, from steam engines to mill burr stones. The advertisement had a two-fold purpose; to announce his patent rights and to make known the availability of his inventions to prospective customers. And if his advertisement attracted the attention of investors willing to underwrite some of the cost of his engine building, that would have been fine too, for it was becoming an increasingly more expensive proposition. Evans' 1804 engines, also with a six-inch bore by eighteen-inch stroke, ran at 35 rpm with a pressure cut-off at one-third of the stroke and worked with a steam pressure of 50 pounds per inch or more. Evans estimated the cost of building one such engine to be $886.60, that price including a boiler having 8100 square inches of surface to produce 11,865 cubic inches of steam. His experiments only made him more determined to build a practical, lightweight, high pressure and relatively inexpensive steam engine — to power a road wagon.

The first toll road and superhighway in America was the sixty-two mile long Lancaster Turnpike which connected Columbia, Pennsylvania, and Philadelphia. Realizing the potential of this privately-owned highway, Evans — on September 26, 1804 — presented before the Lancaster Turnpike Road Company an analysis of the cost and profits between steam road wagons and horse-drawn wagons. Specifications and drawings of the steam wagons he proposed to run along the Turnpike have been lost, but his analysis survives. He proposed to build a steam wagon to carry 100 barrels of flour and to travel at three miles per hour on level road and one mile an hour up and downhill, making about forty miles in twenty-four hours between the two cities. This totalled two days for travel the entire length of the highway. In contrast, five wagons pulled by five horses apiece were required to transport the same number of barrels from the beginning to the end of the highway, taking three days to complete the trip. Evans calculated the cost and reported that the steam wagon would require $2500 as opposed to $804.15 for the horse-drawn wagons, but that didn't tell the whole story. Profit differential did, and the steam wagon was shoulders above the horse-drawn wagons in this regard — netting $50 a day, whereas the five horse-drawn wagons would clear only $18.30. Evans concluded his presentation thus:

> ". . . Add to all this that the steam waggon consumes nothing while standing, will roll and mend the roads, while the horse waggons will cut them up. Upon the whole it appears that no competition could exist between the two. The steam waggons would take all the business on the turnpike roads."

He went on to say that the project as he conceived it was too massive for him to undertake as an individual, and he hoped the directors of the turnpike company would come to see the value of the proposition. Possibly they did, but after due consideration, Evans' proposal was turned down.

Evans' overtures to the Lancaster Turnpike Company were accompanied by a suggested prospectus for a company he wanted to organize. The venture proceeded as far as a name — Evans called it the Experiment

One of the earliest recorded drawings (below) of the Orukter, as it appeared in The Mechanic magazine of July, 1834— and often thereafter reprinted. Of it, Greville Bathe has noted: "From what inspired source the artist drew upon for this picture is not known, but his imagination was wholly unequal to his task. The obvious defect in this drawing of the Orukter is that there could be no steering possible while the two axles were connected by a belt. Also as a steamboat it would be a failure because the paddle-wheel shaft is below the water line when the scow is afloat." From Evans' written accounts of the Orukter, Bathe built the model at right, which quite effectively shows its construction. It is on display at the Smithsonian Institution in Washington, D.C.

Company — and a proposal to sell 115 shares at $30 each to raise sufficient capital to go into the business of building steam wagons. And there it died — certainly a pity, for the development of the American automobile and railroad would have commenced far earlier than it did had the company succeeded.

THE ORUKTER SAGA

But neither Evans' stillborn Experiment Company nor the Lancaster Turnpike proposal can be termed complete failures, as they both brought him to the attention of the members of the Philadelphia Board of Health who provided him with an excellent opportunity to demonstrate the power of his small, high pressure steam engine to move great burdens over the road. In 1805 the now fifty-year-old Evans was contracted by that board to build a steam dredge for the City of Philadelphia. He called this self-propelled steam vehicle by the scholarly if somewhat awkward name of "Orukter Amphibolos," or "Amphibious Digger."

The engine for the Digger was entirely new. Aptly termed the

"grasshopper" because of its erratic motion pattern, the Orukter engine represented a great step in the development of the steam engine, because the thrust of its piston was transmitted almost directly to the crankshaft and the steam entered the cylinder at a pressure of 120 pounds/inch. When the Orukter's dredge and machinery were completed, he had them placed on wheels. On his first attempt to move the vehicle by steam the wheels broke down under the machine's weight. His workmen, excited by the project, volunteered to donate their own time to build a new set of wheels and axle trees for the amphibian. A second attempt to move the vehicle was made during the second week of July, and for the first time a vehicle moved by its own power across the streets of an American city. A public demonstration of the device was announced by Evans on July 13, 1805, in *Relf's Philadelphia Gazette*. The amphibian remained on exhibition for several days, circling the water works at Centre Square (now the site of the Philadelphia City Hall) where the ponderous Watt-Boulton-type engines recommended by Latrobe did their job in striking contrast to the little high pressure engine that moved the squeaking wheels of the amphibian. During the days of public display, a contribution box was passed so that "every generous person" could donate twenty-five cents

apiece for the privilege of seeing the vehicle perform.

At last the Orukter Amphibolos made its final run down to the river which stood at low tide. A paddle wheel was then fixed over the stern and connected by a belt to the engine shaft, while a temporary rudder was provided by means of a long oar. The mechanism that drove the wheels was disconnected and, fortunately, we have a fair idea of how it worked: The connection between the engine and the road vehicle was accomplished by a simple train of gearing, a method detailed in *The Abortion of a Young Steam Engineer's Guide*:

> ". . . it will answer well to drive a land carriage with a heavy burden . . . A pinion on the shaft of the fly-wheel to gear into a cog-wheel, which is afixed on the axle of the two wheels, will give them motion forward or backwards at pleasure, and enable the engineer to turn his carriage on a small space of ground."

The Oruckter story itself is best told in its inventor's words:

> "I constructed for the Board of Health of Philadelphia a machine for cleaning docks, called the Orukter Amphibolos or the Amphibious Digger. It consisted of a heavy flat bottomed boat, 30 feet long and 12 feet broad, with a chain of buckets to bring up the mud, and hooks to clear away sticks, stones and other obstacles. These buckets are

wrought by a small steam engine set in the boat, the cylinder of which is 5 inches diameter and the length of stroke 19 inches. The machine was constructed at my shop, 1½ miles from the river Schuylkill where she was launched. She sunk 19 inches, displacing 551 cubic feet of water, which at 62.5 pounds, the weight of a cubic foot, gives the weight of the boat 34,437 pounds, which divided by 213, the weight of a barrel of flour, gives the weight of 161 barrels of flour that the boat and the engine is equal to. Add to this the heavy pieces of timber and the wheels used in transporting her, and the number of persons generally in her [12] will make the whole burden equal to at least 200 barrels of flour. Yet this small engine moves so great a burden, with a gentle motion up Market-street and around the Centre Square; and we concluded from the experiment, that the engine was able to rise any ascent allowed by law on the turnpike roads, which is not more than 4 degrees.

When she was launched we fixed a simple wheel at her stern to propel her through the water by the engine. Although she is square at each end and illy constructed for sailing, (excepting that she is turned up short at the bottom) and drew 19 inches water, yet we concluded that if the power had been applied to give the paddle wheel the proper motion we could have stemmed the tide of Delaware."

The amphibian's estimated rate of travel around Philadelphia was approximately three to four miles per hour. This resulted in some criticism, many an onlooker implying that Evans' proposed steam road wagon would be too slow for turnpike travel. The critics missed the point, however. As Evans retorted to one jibe, "If you will amongst your jockies make up a purse of $3000, I will make a steam carriage that will outrun the swiftest horse you can produce on a smooth level hard bottom!" Interestingly, the monetary figure Evans mentioned was nearly equal to the money he needed — and had been unable to raise — to start his Experimental Company for building of steam wagons.

With the exception of his early steam wagon models — of these, the plans for his 1801 wagon survive — the Orukter was the only steam wagon Evans ever built. Some scholars have, unfortunately, adopted a rather patronizing attitude toward this vehicle, regarding it as an historical fluke, a fortuitous happenstance which because it was destined for the water plays little or no part in the history of the American automobile. That simply is not true. The Orukter was built because Evans was able to procure the financing for its building, and it was an amphibious digger because that is what he was directed to build. For twenty years prior to the Orukter and for the nearly fifteen years which followed it until his death in 1819, Oliver Evans remained convinced of the possibility and value of the steam road wagon. That he could not so convince potential investors — and thus could not bring his idea to full reality — should not negate his place in the history of the American automobile. Evans did, of course, build, sell and license his high pressure steam engines — and quite successfully — but that is another story. What is pertinent here is that Evans' Orukter was not a chance-happening, but was the logical extension of the steam road vehicle principles he had been nurturing and espousing since 1772. Even in its own day, the Orukter enjoyed the sincerest form of flattery — imitation. Some years after the amphibian's ride through the streets of Philadelphia, two brothers of that city by the name of Johnson put together a steam wagon of their own. Lacking Evans' technical accomplishment, the brothers fared not at all well. They lost control during a trial run, and reportedly caused considerable damage to the City of Philadelphia and complete destruction of their vehicle.

To the public.—In my first attempt to move the *Orukter Amphibolos* or *Amphibious Digger*, to the water, by power of steam, the axletrees and wheels proved insufficient to bear so great a burden, and having previously obtained permission of the board of health, (for whom this machine is constructed) to gratify the citizens of Philadelphia, by the sight of this mechanical curiosity, on the supposition that it may lead to useful improvements. The workmen who had constructed it, voluntarily offered their labor to construct without wages, other wheels and axletrees of sufficient strength, and to receive as their reward one half of the sum that may be received from a generous public for the sight thereof, the other half to be at the disposal of the inventor, who pledges himself that it shall be applied to defray the expence of other new and useful inventions and improvements which he has already conceived and arranged in his mind, and which he will put in operation only when the money arising from the inventions he has already made, will defray the expence.

The above machine is now to be seen moving round the centre square at the expence of the workmen, who expect 25 cents from every generous person that may come to see its operation, but all are invited to come and view it as well those who cannot, as those who can conveniently spare the money.

OLIVER EVANS.

From the Aurora General Advertiser, July 15, 1805. (κ)

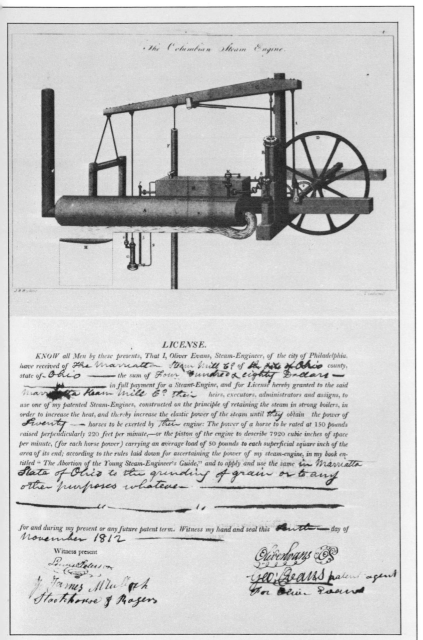

The Columbian Steam Engine.

LICENSE.

KNOW all Men by these presents, That I, Oliver Evans, Steam-Engineer, of the city of Philadelphia, have received of *The Marriatta Steam Mill Co. of the State of Ohio* county, state of *Ohio* ————— the sum of *Four hundred & eighty Dollars* ————— in full payment for a Steam-Engine, and for License hereby granted to the said *Marriatta Steam Mill Co. their* heirs, executors, administrators and assigns, to use one of my patented Steam-Engines, constructed on the principle of retaining the steam in strong boilers, in order to increase the heat, and thereby increase the elastic power of the steam until *they* obtain the power of *Seventy* ————— horses to be exerted by *their* engine: The power of a horse to be rated at 150 pounds raised perpendicularly 220 feet per minute,—or the piston of the engine to describe 7920 cubic inches of space per minute, (for each horse power) carrying an average load of 50 pounds to each superficial square inch of the area of its end; according to the rules laid down for ascertaining the power of my steam-engine, in my book entitled "The Abortion of the Young Steam-Engineer's Guide," and to apply and use the same *in Marriatta State of Ohio to the grinding of grain or to any other purposes whatever* ————— " ————— " ————— for and during my present or any future patent term. Witness my hand and seal this *tenth* day of *November 1812* —————

Witness present

Lemuel Peterson
James Mulloch
Stackhouse & Rogers

Oliver Evans
Geo. Pearss patent agent
for Oliver Evans

License granted by Oliver Evans in November of 1812 to the Marriatta Steam Mill Company of Ohio for use of his steam engine. (F)

Oliver Evans died April 15, 1819 in New York City. After being interred twice, his final resting place was the Trinity Cemetery, Broadway at 157th Street. His plot is known simply as No. 1641. The only memorial to Evans, a marble tablet erected almost eighty-five years ago in the Woods family burial lot in Woodland Cemetery of Philadelphia, bears the inscription:

"In memory of Oliver Evans, the inventor of the high pressure steam engine in general use as a motor on land and sea. Sometimes now used on railroads to accomplish locomotion by steam, on which system of travelling he was the original projector. Died 1819, age 64 years, buried elsewhere."

In closing his account of Oliver Evans' accomplishments in his 1821 translation of *The Abortion of the Young Steam Engineer's Guide* into French, Mr. I. Doolittle said:

". . . few men have been as useful to society as Oliver Evans. Very few have displayed any hopeful perseverance in rendering these services to their fellow men, that is to say, in spite of their fellow men. His contemporaries never appreciated him and his true value; but an understanding prosperity will place his name among those men who are most truly distinguished for their eminent services rendered to their country and humanity."

If America is to have a father of the automobile, it must surely be Oliver Evans.

STEAM DEVELOPMENT: 1800-1825

Obviously Oliver Evans was not alone in envisioning self-propelled travel in the United States. While his experimental work with steam engines for milling and road wagons advanced, Colonel John H. Stevens, an important figure during the Revolutionary War, began thinking along similar lines. As early as 1790 he was pondering the self-propelled vehicle idea, and in 1802 he built his first steam engine. His enthusiasm for steam power was boundless, as the following anecdote indicates. One morning in bed, he awoke with an idea for a new type of steam engine and busily sketched a plan for it with his finger nail upon the back of his wife, Rachel Cox Stevens, a woman of great beauty and good humor. Startled, she moved. He commanded her to "Hold still! Don't you know what figure I am making?" "Yes, Mr. Stevens," she replied demurely, "—the figure of a fool."

Stevens was hardly that, of course. Perhaps just a bit exuberant. His ideas were sound, and his ambition was a network of steam carriages running on rails. The virtual non-existence of adequate roads in the United States dictated his thinking along these lines, as did his negative reaction to the value of canal systems. In 1812, some years after the Amphibious Digger was demonstrated in Philadelphia, Colonel Stevens published a pamphlet entitled "Tending to Prove the Superior Advantages of Rail-Ways and Steam Carriages over Canal Navigation." This work approached the question of steam carriage transportation from a number of angles, but in the main it dealt with a cost comparison between the building of roads and canals. Author Stevens found that road transportation, with its unlimited advantages of expansion, would provide a greater source of revenue than canals limited by the dictates of geography. A system of steam wagons on rails or planks, moreover, would cost less to build, less to maintain and

23

We the undersigned, having for a long time been concerned in works requiring great power, have been led to examine the principles and powers of the Steam Engine, patented by the late Messrs. Bolton and Watt, in England ; and also the one constructed by Mr. Oliver Evans of Philadelphia, and after satisfactory investigation, we gave Mr. Evans' the preference, and have had it* a sufficient time at work to prove its real worth, durability, and cheapness, compared with others. We are convinced his Engine requires not more than one-third the fuel to produce the same power, as one on the principle of Bolton and Watt, and works with perfect safety. His late improvement of the inexhaustible principle, enables him to supply the boilers in any situation with pure water, where water can be obtained, either pure or impure, or impregnated with saline or argillaceous matter. These advantages, together with his method of keeping in reserve, any quantity of strong steam he may deem necessary to overcome occasional resistances, render his engines greatly superior (in our opinion) to all others for boat navigation, where foul waters, rapids or strong currents abound. In addition to all these, his engines require less water, are far less complex, more durable, and easily understood. than and others within our knowledge. His method of warming apartments, by the heat of the steam of the engine. we consider a new and valuable discovery, consequently the expense of fuel chargeable to the engine, is proportionably lessened.

(Signed) EDWD. MASON, jr.
DANIEL BATES,
HERCULES WHITNEY,
HENRY Y COFFIN,
ISAAC STANFORD.
* Two Steam Engines at Providence, Rhode-Island, driving manufactories.

One of many testimonials alluding to the superiority of the Evans' high pressure engine over the Watt low pressure design. This statement appeared in the March 18, 1815, issue of the Daily National Intelligencer, Washington, D.C. (κ)

would be of inestimable value in time of war. A steam-powered railroad would, in time, pay for itself; a canal, he concluded, could not.

The particular canal he was opposing was built. The State of New York appropriated five million dollars for its construction — and when the Erie Canal was finally opened in 1825, its cost had exceeded the estimate by two million dollars. Today, without tolls, the New York canal system is supported at a tremendous cost to the taxpayer, to the almost exclusive benefit of the large oil companies which use it regularly. And ironically it competes, quite inequitably, with the railroads.

Stevens stood almost alone in his campaign to halt construction of the Erie Canal. And though his efforts were a failure, he did, in 1815, receive a charter from the state of New Jersey to build the first American railway. By 1826 he had completed a circular track not far from the modern Stevens Institute in Hoboken. It was here that he exhibited the first steam locomotive to run on rails in the United States.

As the Nineteenth Century progressed, more inventors latched on to the steam wagon idea. In 1819 Benjamin Dearborn of Boston announced his intention to construct, by following Evans' plans or using one of his actual engines, what he called a "wheel carriage." Nothing further is known of this project. In 1825 Thomas Blanchard of Springfield, Massachusetts, built — if we discount the plans and models of Fitch, Rumsey and Read — what was probably the third operable steam carriage in the United States, with Evans and the ill-fated Johnson brothers running first and second respectively. The successful Blanchard machine was patented and although the original records were destroyed in the 1836 patent office fire, a description of the vehicle may be reconstructed from three newspaper accounts of the day. *The Republican* of Springfield, Massachusetts (November 26, 1826), the *Hampton Journal* also of Springfield (December 27, 1826), and the *Poughkeepsie Journal* of New York (December 27, 1826) carried complete accounts based on the observations of their reporters. According to one version, Blanchard's land carriage "could run forward and backwards, steer properly and climb hills, aided by a set of interchangeable gears which would transmit the driving force to the rear axle in two speeds." Weighing about half a ton, the steam carriage carried an additional 1500 pounds — representing approximately eight passengers — up a gentle slope. Its engine carried a two-inch cylinder and the stroke of the piston was eleven inches; its boiler, which burned pine wood for fuel, was calculated at about three gallons. Significantly, the Massachusetts State Legislature wholly endorsed Blanchard's work.

On the first of April, 1826 — the same year Blanchard demonstrated his steam vehicle in Springfield, Massachusetts — Samuel Morey of Oxford, New Hampshire, obtained a patent for a "gas and vapor engine." It was a two-cycle explosive engine with poppet valves, a primitive carburetor, electric spark and water cooling, and was described thus:

> ". . . the vacuum in the cylinder is produced by firing an explosive mixture of atmospheric air and vapor from common proof spirits, mixed with a small mixture of turpentine. A working model has been set in motion . . . and should no unfortunate difficulties present themselves in its operation on a large scale, it will be the greatest improvement which has been made for many years, particularly in its application to locomotive engines."

Two years earlier a Mr. M. Isnard of New York had received a patent for a similar internal combustion engine, but it was a crude design, displaying none of the refinements of Morey's engine, which might be regarded as the first successful application in America of internal combustion principles. Morey, an erstwhile lumberman and son of General Israel Morey, had previously been a steam exponent, having built his first steam boat in 1793, and his last in 1820. His steam principles were patented, and his work was known by Oliver Evans.

Most of this early experimentation was conducted, as we've seen, in the eastern United States, most particularly New England. Gradually the self-propelled vehicle idea moved westward. Between 1824 and 1825 a Mr. T. W. Parker is said to have built a steam wagon in Edgar County, Illinois. Unfortunately, as is so often the case with these early experiments, no verification exists beyond contemporary press reports, which identify only the inventor and the object of his invention. The history of the American automobile has many such half-told stories. For example, ten years later, in 1835, a steam wagon was reported built in Brattleboro, Vermont, and latter day published reports carried an extensive description of it. Apparently it resembled a single-horse wagon fitted with a boiler and two-cylinder engine. The boiler was fashioned of U-shaped tubes one and a half inches in diameter, so placed that the lower ends of these tubes served as a grate, while the flame followed them toward the top. Apparently, too, it was demonstrated successfully. Indeed the only fact missing from these accounts is the name of the man who built it.

STEAM DEVELOPMENT: 1825-1851

If one might fault the press of the day for providing sometimes sketchy accounts, one must acknowledge, too, that generally the regional press was attentive to steam car experimentation, and as the concept of self-propelled road transport became of increasing interest a technical press evolved as well. In 1825 the *American Mechanics Magazine*, headed by the enterprising science enthusiast J. B. Seaman, was launched, and began at once to vigorously discuss the prospects for both rail and highway travel. Perhaps that periodical's most interesting competitor was the *American Rail-Road Journal*, launched in 1832 by D. Kimball Minor. Although it was identified by title with the railroad, the magazine's editorial policy gave as much encouragement to the road machine as it did to the locomotive; indeed, the term "locomotive" in those days did not pertain exclusively to railed engines, but was applied indiscriminately to any vehicle driven by steam boiler and piston engine. The *American Rail-Road Journal* championed the cause of early highway improvement, and indeed it might be called the first automotive publication in this country. Aptly, its standing slogan was "Steam Carriages for Common Roads." During its first year of publication it featured seventeen articles on steam carriages, and, influenced by the study of English steam wagons undertaken by the United States Congress in 1831, its editors included descriptions of the various English steamers of such inventors as Hancock, Ogle and Sommers, together with a descriptive account of the John Louden McAdam roadbuilding system. The success of these two technical magazines doubtlessly encouraged the founding of others: *Scientific American* was launched in 1845, *The American Artisan* in 1864, *The American Inventor* in 1875 and *The American Machinist* in 1877.

Model of Samuel Morey's 1826 internal combustion engine, now on exhibit at the Long Island Automotive Museum, Southampton, New York.

The attention paid to roadbuilding by the technical press in America during the late 1820's and 1830's was well grounded, for it was a subject of concern to all who believed that steam carriages could be a viable means of transportation. According to an August 4, 1832, account in the Fredericksburg Area newspaper (Virginia), the officials of the Fredericksburg and Potomac Creek Rail-road had decided to build a road bed without rails for its new locomotive, one of the first attempts by a railroad to introduce steam carriages for travel on turnpike or common road. In the same year a Troy, New York, newspaper announced that plans were being made to improve a wagon road from Schenectady to Troy, in order to run steam carriages in competition with the Hudson Mohawk Rail-road. And later an effort was reported to have been made to introduce a steam carriage to run the common roads between Cambridge and Boston, as well as Salem and Boston.

The concept of steam transport was by now finding increasing favor on both sides of the Atlantic. Among its many advocates was John Ericcson, a Swiss who, after a precocious childhood, became an engineering officer in the army where he rose to captaincy. To further his interest in steam power, he obtained a discharge from the army to go to England to develop a steam engine. It was there that he built a locomotive engine for the famous Rainhill Trials in which George Stephenson won world fame with his locomotive "Rocket," triumphing over Ericcson, his sole opponent. Seemingly, Ericcson lost the contest only because he understood its rules differently; thus, he built a light locomotive intended for speed rather than endurance, and set a remarkable record of 30 mph. The winner Stephenson interpreted the rules to require a show of strength, and had geared his engine to sustain power many times greater than his opponent's machine could muster. But Ericcson's defeat was somewhat relieved when the railroad builders of England retained his services for further experimentation. As a direct result Ericcson built a steam fire engine which, after it extinguished an 1829 fire in the Argyle Rooms was described thusly in the British press: "For the first time, fire was extinguished by the mechanical power of fire."

Ericcson left England after unsuccessfully trying to introduce a twin-screw ship for ocean navigation, at a time when England was interested only in paddle-wheeled propulsion. Arriving in New York, he made plans to build a self-propelled fire engine for that city, but also began work on a hot-air engine in 1833, which he eventually marketed for a period of ten years. Ericcson was a most prolific patentee, securing five patents for his engines between 1851 and 1860, and a whopping total of forty in the following twelve years. Among his most interesting powerplants was a hot air engine he built for use in a ship. Because of its tremendous size, it must have been impressive to view: Its cylinders were fourteen feet in diameter and the stroke was eight feet. But problems were inherent in its very size, for it required such a large volume of heated air that it was almost impossible to generate sufficient external heat quickly enough. Consequently, he reduced the size of the cylinders, and the engine did power one ocean-going ship. Still, the voyage was unsuccessful, and Ericcson turned once again to steam. During the Civil War, as an officer for the Union Navy, he built the *Monitor*, which saw legendary sea battle with the *Merrimack*, the latter ship incidentally having been inspired by plans developed earlier by Colonel John H. Stevens. After the war, in 1870, Ericcson built a small experimental steam condensing engine which worked by solar power, intensifying the heat of the sun through optical glass. For this idea he had drawn from the past; a similar scheme had been proposed by Oliver Evans to run a steam engine.

The potential of compressed air power was explored by many an American inventor, and its tantalizing possibilities still intrigue engineers today. Its major drawback, then as now, is the enormous expense of its development. One of the first to experiment in this field was Lemuel W. Wright, who proposed that in a compressed air carriage, for the sake of economy, the air should be heated before being used, or used in combination with steam, a practice which became common eighty years later. In 1833 Wright is reported to have built an engine, curiously, a non-compression explosion type featuring a water-cooling system.

Steam power, however, still held center stage in America, and there is sufficient documentation to show that a considerable number of steam land carriages had been built and driven in the United States prior to 1850. In 1851 a company was launched in New York City for their

Advertisement appearing in an 1833 issue of the Philadelphia Gazette for the American Steam Carriage Company of Philadelphia. (K) Right: Front page of a prospectus for the American Steam Carriage Company, organized in New York, New York, during the year 1851. (D)

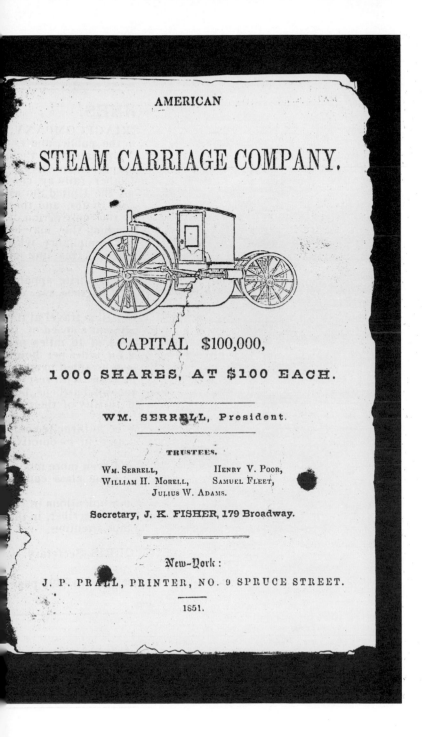

manufacture: the American Steam Carriage Company. It was not the first company of its kind. Even discounting Oliver Evans' Experiment Company, there was an earlier American Steam Carriage Company formed by one William Norris in 1833, in Philadelphia. When Norris obtained the rights to certain improvements on Colonel Stephen H. Long's locomotive engine, he organized at once, announcing that his company had in its possession the requisite apparatus for constructing engines weighing four, five and six tons, which could attain speeds of 15, 18 and 22½ mph. Moreover, Norris guaranteed that his company's engines would be equal to the best English engines of the same class. Nothing, apparently, came of the venture, and no more was heard of the American Steam Carriage Company until eighteen years later when its name was resurrected for the new carriage-building enterprise.

The prospectus for the 1851 company gave full credit for pioneer work in steam vehicles to the various English inventors, Oliver Evans, a Mr. Dyer of Boston, a Mr. Porter and a Mr. James of New York and Mr. J. K. Fisher: Of Messrs. Dyer and Porter, alas, we know nothing. William James, however, is known to have built several steam wagons, the first of which was a two-cylinder affair that ran along the streets of New York City at "great speed" in 1829. This vehicle utilized a reciprocating engine, but its inventor was soon achieving more power from a rotative type. In 1830 he built a three-wheeler with the drive to the rear wheels and a year later he entered a contest sponsored by the Baltimore and Ohio Rail-road with his own locomotive. Although his engine did not win first prize, he was offered an engineering position by the duly impressed officials of the railroad company — in much the same fashion that John Ericcson was retained by England's railroad officials. One had much to gain, it seems, by losing a railroad contest in those days.

With the American Steam Carriage Company of 1851 came the services of John Kenrick Fisher — a man with eleven years of first-hand knowledge of steam carriages. Fisher's first steam land carriage may have been built in 1840, and some years later he proudly displayed a steam car model to committees of the American Institute and the Mechanics Institute of New York. Reports by both these committees were reprinted in the American Steam Carriage Company's prospectus. The first, the American Institute's report, dated September 4, 1851 noted:

> "The carriage presented by Mr. Fisher embodies a number of new and important improvements, both in regards to its general arrangement and the application of steam. He had introduced a new method of working steam expansively, by means (we do not give the description, as it might prejudice the inventor's interest in foreign countries). We think it highly successful and effective. The arrangement for cutting off steam at different points of the stroke is equally effective as is the main movement. The combination of radius and parallel rods to afford steadiness to the machine at high velocities is certainly a great improvement—particularly if the machinery and carriage are sustained on easy springs as in the arrangement presented in the model. By this arrangement, it should be observed, all the weight of the heavy framing hereto used is dispensed with, thereby giving greater capacity for carrying all passengers. The whole of the machinery, including the apparatus for steering is so planned that only one person will be required to maintain the carriage. We consider the model presented by Mr. Fisher capable with some slight modifications of affording a very superior plan for steam carriages to run on good level roads. (signed) James Renwick, chairman.

27

The Mechanics Institute's committee on arts and sciences, chaired by Charles W. Copeland, submitted the following appraisal on September 9, 1851:

> "The committee . . . have had referred to them an improvement in steam-carriages for common or plank roads by Mr. J. K. Fisher: they appear to possess several advantages over those formerly experimented upon. The cut-off to work the steam expansively is a very ingenious contrivance, and is so arranged to cut off the steam at any part of the stroke: and it would answer for fixed engines as well as carriages. The backing or reversing motion appears to be very well arranged. The attaching the engines outside the wheels as done in some locomotives instead of cranking the axle tree as was done in most English carriages, is, we think, a decided improvement; and taking the arrangement altogether your committee think it is worthy of favorable consideration of the mechanics institute."

Unfortunately, the American Steam Carriage Company failed to make a go of it, despite its attractive installment plan of five dollars per payment for $100 worth of stock. Fisher himself built another steam carriage in 1853, which ran for about two years, and boasted a top speed of 15 mph. Thereafter his thoughts turned to fire engines, but that is a story to be related in due course.

ELECTRICITY AND INTERNAL COMBUSTION: 1830-1850

In the midst of experiments with steam, gas and compressed air power, there was another method of propulsion available to the would-be wagon builder which would eventually enjoy considerable popularity — electricity. It was Samuel F. B. Morse of New England who conceived of the electric telegraph in 1832 and was by 1837 exhibiting the apparatus to interested onlookers. In that latter year, too, was patented the first electric motor, incorporating the earliest form of the commutator. It was the invention of Thomas Davenport, an uneducated blacksmith from Brandon, Vermont. Four years earlier, in 1833, on a trip to the Penfield and Hammond Iron Works in Crown Point, New York, Davenport had chanced to see a large electromagnet, powered by primitive batteries and powerful enough to lift a blacksmith's anvil. (It had been built by Joseph Henry of Albany, New York, who was later the first secretary of the Smithsonian Institution.) So fascinated was Davenport by this strange new source of power that he insisted that his brother, a peddler, sell his horse and wagon immediately and buy it. Curiously, his brother agreed — and so for $75 Davenport had his electromagnet. By 1835, after intensive study, he had developed his electric motor. His patent application and model were destroyed in the fire that raged through the United States Patent Office in 1836, delaying the issuance of his patent to February 25, 1837. Thereafter Davenport founded the first electric company in America, issued the first newspaper, *The Electromagnet*, devoted exclusively to electricity news and printed on presses powered by one of his electric motors using zinc and copper plates and blue vitriol solution plus a walking beam apparatus. Davenport would build more than a hundred electric motors during his lifetime, and his further inventions would include a "rail" car powered by his motor and run on a circular railway. Sadly, though, his company and his newspaper failed, and Davenport died a disappointed man at the age of forty-nine. The patent models of his inventions can be seen today at the Smithsonian Institution.

A. DRAKE.
EXPLOSIVE GAS ENGINE.
No. 12,715. Patented Apr. 17. 1855.

Patent drawings of Dr. Alfred Drake's engine of 1855.

Inventive minds everywhere were charged by electric power, and it hadn't taken long for someone to discover a way to attach an electric motor to a set of wheels to propel a land carriage. In 1847 in Massachusetts Moses G. Farmer did it, exhibiting a locomotive driven by forty-eight Grove cells of one-pint capacity each. It ran on an eighteen-inch track and carried two people. Next came Professor Charles G. Page of Washington D.C. (later inventor of the Page ignition coil), whose vehicle, using a 16 hp motor driven by 100 Grove cells, was capable of carrying twelve or more people at 19 mph along the W & B Rail-road between Washington and Bladensburg. But the most imaginative electrical invention of the period had to be the system of controlling an electric car from a battery station developed by Lilly and Colton of Pittsburgh, Pennsylvania, in 1847. This "remote control" procedure transmitted current to the car on one rail, allowing it to flow back to the station on another — not unlike some toy trains of today.

There seems to have been a lapse of more than thirty years in electric car development after this period, during which considerable advances

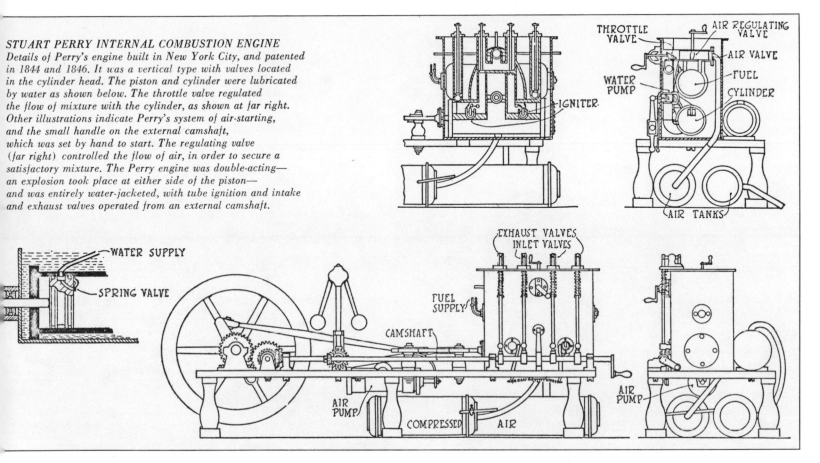

STUART PERRY INTERNAL COMBUSTION ENGINE
Details of Perry's engine built in New York City, and patented in 1844 and 1846. It was a vertical type with valves located in the cylinder head. The piston and cylinder were lubricated by water as shown below. The throttle valve regulated the flow of mixture with the cylinder, as shown at far right. Other illustrations indicate Perry's system of air-starting, and the small handle on the external camshaft, which was set by hand to start. The regulating valve (far right) controlled the flow of air, in order to secure a satisfactory mixture. The Perry engine was double-acting— an explosion took place at either side of the piston— and was entirely water-jacketed, with tube ignition and intake and exhaust valves operated from an external camshaft.

THROTTLE VALVE · AIR REGULATING VALVE · AIR VALVE · WATER PUMP · FUEL · CYLINDER · IGNITER · AIR TANKS

WATER SUPPLY · SPRING VALVE · EXHAUST VALVES · INLET VALVES · FUEL SUPPLY · CAMSHAFT · AIR PUMP · COMPRESSED AIR · AIR PUMP

were made in experiments with internal combustion principles. Among the most persistent experimenters was Dr. Alfred Drake of Philadelphia, who devoted more than twenty years, beginning in 1835, to the development of his engine, for which he ultimately secured several patents. His approach was generally similar to Lenoir's, but differed in at least one respect. Instead of the Lenoir jump spark, Drake's engine ignited by internally placed hot tubes, these tubes being kept hot by a flame blown into them via a pipe which entered from the outside and igniting the mixture which surrounded them by their red heat. One of these engines, exhibited at the Crystal Palace in New York in 1857, was viewed by a number of people who, later learning of Lenoir's engine, assumed it — erroneously — to be the same as Drake's.

But it was the mechanical genius of Stuart Perry that eclipsed the best efforts of his contemporaries in the area of internal combustion engine development. As early as 1844 this New Yorker constructed an engine similar to Morey's efforts of 1826, using turpentine for fuel. Patented in 1844 and 1846, this internal combustion engine was constructed

somewhat like a steam engine, a two-cycle affair similar to the engine Lenoir was to build some years later but for the fact that the air and vapor of the Perry machine were forced into the working cylinder by pumps instead of being drawn in by the piston movement. The new charge exploded by flame-ignition when the stroke had travelled about 1/8 of its distance, with a considerable length of stroke yet remaining for expansion. There was an economical value to this, and Perry's engine did have the advantage of Lenoir's in this respect; Lenoir did not ignite his new charge until well into the center of the piston movement. Furthermore, Perry was open to the question of whether or not to use sliding or other valves, although his patents show that he used rotating cylindrical valves with ports cut into their sides like those which later appeared on the 1906 Duryea and 1907 Darracq cars. Perry's turpentine fuel was vaporized by heat of the cylinder and the exhaust gas after the engine was started, and engine cooling was provided by a fan blowing air over the cylinders. Later he patented a water-cooled engine which allowed water to surround the cylinder and to lubricate the piston and insides of the cylinder to prevent wear and

Richard Dudgeon's first steam vehicle, completed in 1857, was destroyed in the Crystal Palace fire that year. His 1866 vehicle, pictured here in the yard of his Columbia Street home, is in the collection of George H. Waterman, Jr. and Kirkland H. Gibson of Providence, Rhode Island.

overheating. This second, water-cooled engine was also distinguished by the use of a platinum ignition.

One of the most important features of Perry's 1846 patented engine was the "employment of a receiver containing (compressed) atmospheric air for starting the engine, in combination with another received and with an air pump . . . said pump being operated by the engine." In other words, a primitive self-starter had been incorporated into the engine, testimony to the sophistication of engineering thought at the time. Perry's engine has been acclaimed as a milestone in the history of the American automobile, but, since the internal combustion engine remained to be invented and reinvented for many years to come, it is doubtful that his findings were acknowledged in his own day. The steam engine, easily built and easily incorporated into carriages, was the method of propulsion most favored at the time.

THE STEAM VEHICLE: 1850's

In New York Richard Dudgeon began work on a steam carriage in 1853 "to end the fearful horse murder and numerous other ills inseparable from their use." By 1857 the vehicle was finished and successfully tested. Exhibited at the Crystal Palace, it perished when that building burned to the ground on October 5, 1857. Only Dudgeon's plans and drawings of the vehicle remain. In 1866 the inventor constructed yet another steam wagon. Today this vehicle exists in the automobile collection of George H. Waterman and Kirkland H. Gibson of Providence, Rhode Island, as one of the earliest surviving self-propelled vehicles in America.

By this time steam power, of course, was giving birth to a soon-to-be-gigantic railroad industry. In the 1850's the idea would find still

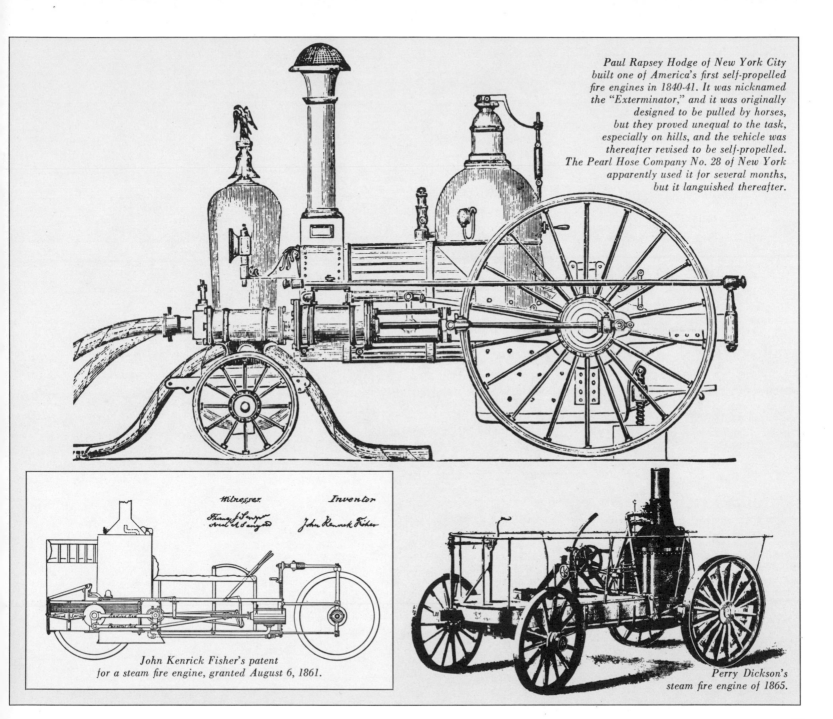

Paul Rapsey Hodge of New York City built one of America's first self-propelled fire engines in 1840-41. It was nicknamed the "Exterminator," and it was originally designed to be pulled by horses, but they proved unequal to the task, especially on hills, and the vehicle was thereafter revised to be self-propelled. The Pearl Hose Company No. 28 of New York apparently used it for several months, but it languished thereafter.

John Kenrick Fisher's patent for a steam fire engine, granted August 6, 1861.

Perry Dickson's steam fire engine of 1865.

New York's self-propelled steam fire engine of 1855.

another use — once the good citizens of Cincinnati, Ohio, decided that something had to be done about the boisterous inefficiency of their fire department. Fire houses in those days were for the most part club houses, whose membership comprised bullies, brawlers, ruffians, and loafers — all anxious for a good fight. Insurance companies provided them ample reason, awarding cash prizes to the first company to reach a fire or the first crew to actually get water to the flames. Sabotage and skullduggery became the order of the day. Companies raced each other to the fire, the more daring travelling along the smooth sidewalks, to the obvious peril of pedestrians. To be overtaken on the way to a fire was a disgrace no company wanted to suffer; the result was often a collision, accidental or engineered. It all usually ended in a street fight. Cincinnati suffered the ultimate outrage. In 1851 a planing mill caught fire in that city and an unusually fierce battle occurred between two of the Cincinnati companies answering the call. As the battle raged, so did the fire. Another company was summoned to the scene from across

the river in Covington, Kentucky, not to fight the fire, but to help out the losing side. Eventually ten companies were involved in the melee. Even Cincinnati's mayor could not restore order. Meanwhile the mill burned — completely to the ground.

That was simply too much for the citizens of Cincinnati—and the city's chief engineer set out to find a way to fight fires more efficiently. By reducing the number of men required to put out a fire, he concluded, also reduced would be the chance of a massive brawl. He engaged Moses Latta, a local manufacturer and mechanic of considerable genius, to build a steam engine to do the job. Latta found the assignment fraught with peril — the volunteer firemen sent spies to find out what he was doing, and on finding out, suggested rather emphatically that Latta declare such a steamer to be an impossibility. Latta didn't; the job was finished. The engine was set on three wheels, the foremost of which was used for steering. The piston rods of the

A New York steamer answering a fire call, mid-1860's.

steam cylinders were continued to form rods of the pumps; when required, these rods could also be coupled to the driving wheels. From one to six streams of water could be thrown with a total capacity of 2000 barrels per hour. The vehicle was not self-propelled, however. Four men and four horses were required to get it out of the fire house and to the fire. But there was no arguing with the fact that the new engine could take the place of twelve firemen manning the handpumps. Each handpumper had previously required the services of fifty to seventy-five firemen and runners. It was an unqualified success.

Generally speaking, fire apparatus would remain horse-drawn until the beginning of the Twentieth Century. It took longer to raise steam than it did to get a team of horses out of the fire house, and thus horse power was deemed more appropriate than steam power in this regard. Nonetheless self-propelled steam fire engines were tried — sometimes successfully. The first on record had been built in 1840-41 by Paul

Rapsey Hodge of New York. It was called the "Exterminator," and was tried for several months but was thereafter abandoned as impractical by the New York firemen. Cincinnati's first experience with steam power had proved so successful, however, that Latta soon thereafter built a second fire fighter, it being self-propelled. By 1853 Cincinnati had organized America's first professional paid fire department, and by 1860 the city could boast of eight steamers in service. In 1855 New York City had its first two steamers, built by Lee and Larned. That year, too, the fire insurance underwriters of New Orleans bought a Latta pumper, and in Philadelphia a citizens group bought a pumper from A. Shawk of Cincinnati, a former partner of the Lattas. Gradually the successful Cincinnati experience with steam power in fire fighting reached into numerous other metropolitan communities.

Once the steam-powered fire engine had proved workable, inventors set to work to improve and refine it. John Kenrick Fisher — of the 1851

Sylvester Hayward Roper, seated in one of his earliest steam carriages, probably built prior to 1863. (F)

American Steam Carriage Company — turned his attention to fire engines and submitted an application for a patent on December 4, 1860. His steam fire engine was approved August 6th, 1861. So proud was he of his new invention that he feuded with another inventor, Perry Dickson of Erie, Pennsylvania, over whose engine could get up steam the quickest to answer a fire call. Foremost among other noted fire engine and pumper builders was the Amoskeag Machine Shop of Manchester, New Hampshire. The shop's chief engineer, Neaomia Beane, built the company's first steam pumpers and later saw one of his creations shipped to Vienna and another to Paris. The largest of his fire fighters, named "Jumbo," weighed eight tons and was operated in Hartford, Connecticut, in the late 1860's.

THE STEAM VEHICLE: 1860's-1870's

By the 1860's the idea of a self-propelled land vehicle had garnered many more proponents in America — and most were experimenting along the high-pressure-steam/lightweight-boiler principles earlier advocated by Oliver Evans. In this decade and the two following, the steam car in America reached a peak in its development. No longer could there be any doubting — among the knowledgeable, at least — that here was a viable mode of transportation. Among those responsible for bringing the steam car idea to this plateau were Sylvester Hayward Roper, Frank Curtis, James S. Batchelder and William H. Writner, Henry Seth Taylor, Enos Merrill Clough, Dr. J. W. Carhart, George Alexander Long, Lucius D. Copeland, E. F. Fields and Frank Cranshaw.

In the vanguard of the movement was Sylvester Hayward Roper of Roxbury, Massachusetts. Although he began his experiments as early as 1859, public attention was not drawn to them until 1863, when the March 14th issue of *Scientific American* announced that Roper had invented and completed a 25 mph steam carriage weighing 650 pounds. It was a two-passenger four-wheeled carriage powered by a 2 hp engine, with a sixteen-inch boiler and a water tank fitted at the rear. Its fuel was coal, carried under the seat, and the cost per mile was estimated at a penny. Only fifteen to twenty pounds of steam pressure were needed to operate the little machine, but as much as sixty pounds of pressure could be generated if needed.

Roper would build more than ten vehicles in the next two decades, among them a four-wheeler driven by a hot air engine. But steam power remained his forte, and during the Velocipede craze of the 1860's he fitted a number of bicycles with steam motors. Roper built his last four-wheeled steam buggy in 1894 and sold it to William Holmes, a Boston brick manufacturer. Thereafter he confined his talent to two-wheeled steam vehicles, and it was while testing one of these in 1896 at the Charles River Track at Boston that he crashed, was thrown from the vehicle and died instantly. He was doing at the time a mile in slightly over two minutes. Two years earlier the Charles River Track had seen another fatal accident. W. W. Austen was killed after colliding with another steamer during a test drive — probably the first two-car collision in American history.

For years it was assumed that among the steam car builders of this period was the aforementioned W. W. Austen of Lowell, Massachusetts.

But the steam car he was reported to have built in 1868 was no doubt the one he bought from Roper that year. Indeed it would appear that Austen was Roper's agent, and if one might question his ethics in frequently omitting Roper's name from handbills advertising exhibitions of the car — substituting, of course, his own name — it should also be remembered that Austen did bring the steam car idea to the attention of a good many people who might otherwise not have seen it successfully demonstrated. Mr. Austen — or Professor Austen, as he later styled himself — was an exhibitor in the best medicine-man tradition who displayed Roper's cars extensively in New England and the eastern United States, at county fairs and race track circuits. Undoubtedly the technical significance of Roper's achievement was less important to Austen than the sale of admissions tickets, for the handbills promoting "the greatest wonder of the world" made little note of mechanical specifications. Promoted instead was the fact that the car could steam ". . . noiselessly and unwarily 30 mph on the highways. It halts and turns deviously or proceeds at a funeral pace at the bid of its driver." Since the car often led a circus parade in these exhibitions, one must allow for a certain margin of circus-type exaggeration in its promotion.

Apparently these exhibitions were enormously successful. Austen could always insure a sell-out by pitting the Roper machine against a horse in a match race around a track. Sometimes the last horse laugh went to the car's opponent. In June of 1865 in New Haven, Connecticut, the vehicle refused to budge; the race was called off and the disgruntled spectators were refunded their money. But in Poughkeepsie several weeks later the Roper beat a walking contestant named Rensley and

Another Roper steam carriage, this one built in 1863, now in the collection of the Henry Ford Museum in Dearborn, Michigan.

A typical advertising handbill for the Roper "Family Steam Carriage" as promoted by the self-styled Prof. W. W. Austen.

went on to triumph in a second contest against a horse. The local newspaper reported the time it took each contestant to complete the mile: The steam buggy made it in 2:20 minutes, the horse in 2:37.5 and Rensley on foot, 5:20. Results such as these were not always popular. In Anderson, Indiana, a representative body of citizens greeted the arrival of the Roper with a terse and succinct description of what they would do to the car — and probably to Austen as well — if the horse didn't win. After a period of thoughtful reflection, Austen cut an opening in the fairground fence the night before the race and capped his triumph the next day by escaping to a police house through this open hatch before the enraged spectators could lay hands on him.

One wonders what sort of contest might have been promoted for a device patented by Z. P. Dederick and I. Grass of Newark, New Jersey, in 1868. This bit of ingenuity allowed a walking man, attached to a wagon, to be propelled by steam power. Years later Charles E. Duryea claimed to have seen the walking steam-man perform.

Most of the steam experimentation of this period was certainly more serious than that, and the practical applications of steam power in transport was a subject of wide interest. Not all the experiments succeeded, of course; but the attempts are often worthy of note. Consider, for example, the plans of Major General Joseph Renfrew Brown of Minnesota. As an Indian agent, no one knew better than he the hardships involved in crossing the plains to the West. Consequently, in 1858 he contracted J. A. Reed of New York City to build a steam wagon capable of pulling covered wagons from the Mississippi river to Colorado. Steam power, he concluded, could pull more freight economically as well as reduce the time necessary for the trip from seven to four days. The vehicle was built and shipped from New York by rail and river to Nebraska City, where a gala reception was held during which the steamer was demonstrated, pulling about a dozen wagons filled with guests. Its next run, however, hauling freight between Nebraska City and Denver in 1862 was not so successful; seven miles outside of Nebraska the steamer's crankshaft broke. The machine was stored in Arbor Lodge, forgotten in the midst of the Civil War and the building of the Union Pacific Railroad. Eventually its boiler and engine were removed and sold for $200 to a mill. In 1915 Nebraska City erected a monument on the site of the vehicle's embarkation. It reads:

> Steam Wagon
> Invented and Owned by
> Joseph R. Brown of Minnesota
> Manufactured by
> John A. Reed of New York
> Landed at Nebraska City from Steamer
> "West Wind" July 12, 1862
> Started for Denver, Self-Propelled, July 22, 1862
> Disabled and Abandoned Seven Miles Out

It is possible that when the war ended in 1865 Brown envisioned new plans for the wagon route. *The American Artisan* reported on July 26, 1865, that J. K. Fisher was expected to build a steam wagon for hauling freight between "Missouri and Denver City." Whether the project was under the aegis of Brown is not known, but, in any case, it did not materialize.

Roper's steam velocipede, believed to have been built in 1869, now on exhibit at the Smithsonian Institution, Washington, D.C.

Miss Betsy Carr, seated in Frank Curtis' steam carriage of 1866. (D)

Others fared better. Around 1862-64 a New Englander named C. M. Spencer built at least two — possibly more — steam carriages which he ran successfully through local public streets and highways. Another, Henry House, with 130 patents to his credit, was decorated by Napoleon III at the Paris Exhibition of 1867 for his invention of a button-hole machine. The year previous, in Bridgeport, Connecticut, he had developed a steam car with a claimed 4 hp engine, which propelled the vehicle at 30 mph. The 1800-pound machine, which eventually ran over 1000 miles, featured a three-speed transmission, with reverse; its steel boiler had a capacity of 300 pounds of pressure per square inch. His development work continued for several decades thereafter, and by 1897 he was experimenting with liquid fuel for steam engines.

Equally significant was the work of Frank Curtis of Newburyport, Massachusetts. As an engineer at the local fire department, he had built a self-propelled fire engine in the mid-1860's. Subsequently, in 1866, he attracted the attention of a local citizen who commissioned him to build a steam car. It was built, the client couldn't pay Curtis' $1000 fee and the inventor repossessed the car. But Curtis had inherited a headache: So disliked was his steam car by some of the townspeople that one of them swore out a warrant for his arrest. When the sheriff attempted to serve the arrest papers, Curtis made his getaway in the car, leaving the lawman to pursue on foot. Not all of Curtis' neighbors resented his invention, however, and his admirers included the vast majority of Newburyport children who modeled their scooters after the Curtis machine, painting the words "Curtis Steam Wagon" on the hoods. Subsequently, Curtis built a second steam wagon.

The aforementioned Amoskeag company of Manchester, New Hampshire, produced a number of men dedicated to the development of the self-propelled vehicle. Neaomia Beane was one of them, as noted earlier. Two others are worthy of note as well: James S. Batchelder and William S. Writner. By the end of the Civil War they had built a steam car after their own design which was described in the July 9, 1868, issue of the *Manchester Mirror* as needing, ". . . some 15 minutes to feed, fire up and get into motion, but once in action will go 'like a bird'." The *Manchester Union*, a competing paper, reported a few days later that "we don't see exactly who has use or need for a carriage of this sort in New England." Apparently no one else did either, for Manchester historian Ashton Thorp reports that the vehicle made its longest trip to Goff's Falls and was then sold to a travelling salesman who used the boiler and engine in a launch.

To Canadian Henry Seth Taylor belongs the honor of having built the Dominion's first car, a steam buggy planned in the early 1860's, begun in 1865 and finished in 1867. For many years historians believed that the Taylor buggy was built in Derbyline, Vermont, but it was instead a Canadian vehicle, built in Stanstead, Quebec, and exhibited at that town's fair in 1867. The vehicle weighed 500 pounds; its boiler measured thirty inches high with a sixteen-inch diameter, containing 207 five-eighths-inch flues of nine-inch length. It operated with sixty pounds of pressure. It is not known if Taylor met any of his Yankee steam compatriots but it seems likely that he was at least familiar with their inventions. The Taylor buggy bears a resemblance to Roper's vehicle, and it is known that the Roper car was exhibited extensively throughout New England during this period. (Stanstead is only about twenty miles across the Canadian border from Newport, Vermont.) Both vehicles display the same arrangement of cylinders, connecting rods, rear axle and steering gear, as well as placement of the ratchet mechanism on the rear wheels. The major difference is the location of the boiler; Taylor put his behind the passengers, Roper situated his under them. Ultimately Taylor wrecked his car on a trial run; brakes had not been incorporated into the design of his vehicle, and a long downhill was his undoing. The car was stored and forgotten for many years until it was discovered in 1960 by Richard M. Stewart of the Anaconda American Brass Company, an automobile collector with a keen sense of history who bought and restored the vehicle. Today the Taylor Steam Buggy is on exhibition at the Ontario Science Centre in Toronto.

Enos Clough's "Faerie Queene"
built in 1869.

Back across the border, in Sunapee, New Hampshire, one Enos Merrill Clough put the finishing touches on his steam carriage in 1869. The vehicle comprised a reported — and obviously exaggerated — 5463 individual parts. It took fourteen years to build. Dubbing it the "Faerie Queene" he took the steamer for trial spins between his home and the neighboring villages of Newport, Laconia and Johnsbury before displaying it to the public at the Newport County Fair in 1869. Finally, when he was ordered to keep his invention off the public highways he traded the Faerie Queene to Richard Grove of Laconia, New Hampshire, for a valuable gold watch. Mr. Grove demolished the vehicle the first time he drove it. A likely epitaph for the car might be found in the poem for which it was named:

"It was an auncient worke of antique fame
And wondrous strong by nature, and by skilfull frame."
—Edmund Spenser, The Faerie Queene, II.ii.12

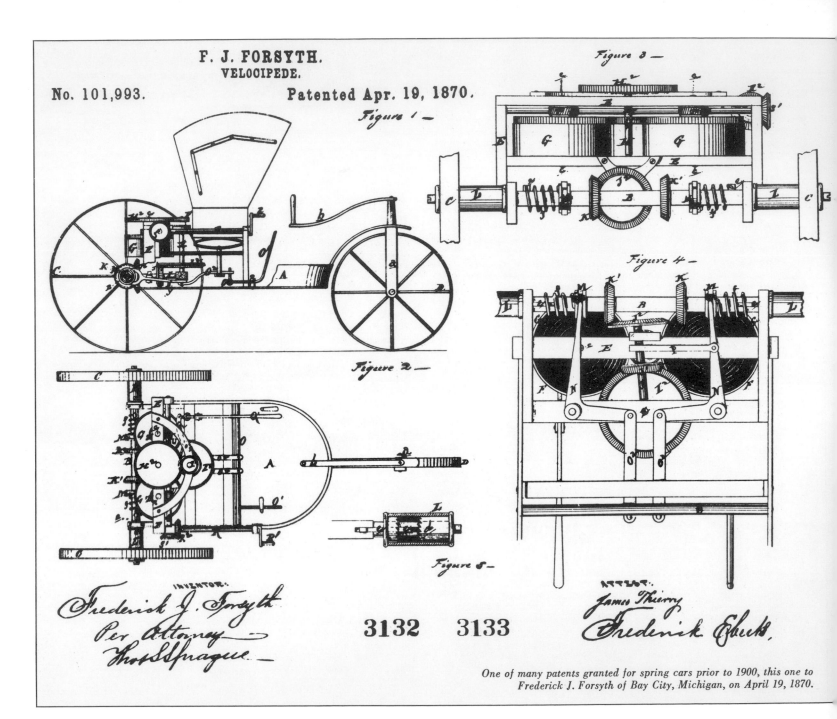

Steam power was but one of several motive agents being considered by inventors of that day. As we have already seen, the merits of the internal combustion engine, compressed air power and electricity were also being explored. But that wasn't all. Spring power came to the fore — as delightfully eccentric a means of propelling a vehicle as might be imagined. Frederick J. Forsyth of Bay City, Michigan, has been credited with the invention of a spring-powered car. And similarly whimsical fribbles were reported to have been demonstrated in Richmond, Virginia, and Manchester, Vermont. Among the most successful — using that word lightly, of course — must have been the spring-powered omnibus built in New Orleans in 1870, which carried ten people on a demonstration run. Weighing 1000 pounds, it employed eight springs formed of a strip of steel eight feet long by eighteen inches wide by 3/32 inches thick. Each spring developed two horsepower, for a grand total of sixteen, and a selective mechanism allowed the driver to increase or decrease the speed. Its speed capabilities, however, were not reported. Between 1866 and 1897 the United States Patent Office received a flood of applications for spring-powered automobiles, and more than fifty attempts were made to build them. Among them was a vehicle built by A. B. Andrews of Center Point, Iowa. Constructed on a baby carriage chassis, Andrews designed a system of springs wound with levers which would "wind its self up while going down hill . . . winding up six times as fast as it runs down . . . there being one spring to wind all the time and five to wind one up and pull the load." Andrews envisioned entering such a vehicle in the 1895 *Times-Herald* contest, but was unable to raise the necessary money to build the spring mechanism. Of spring cars, then, the New Orleans vehicle was probably the most propitious of the lot.

The steamer built in 1871 in Racine, Wisconsin, by the Rev. J. W. Carhart, with the assistance of his brother, Prof. H. S. Carhart.

Real success remained the preserve of the steam vehicle during these years. On December 14, 1914, J. D. Donald, Secretary of the State of Wisconsin, certified the fact that his state's first self-propelled vehicle was a steamer designed and operated in 1871 by the Rev. J. W. Carhart of Racine. The Rev. Carhart was assisted by his brother, H. S. Carhart, professor of physics at Northwestern University and later of the University of Michigan. He also solicited the help of the J. I. Case Company of Racine to make some of the parts and the engine, and the Button Steam Fire Engine Co. of Watertown, New York, for the car's body. "The Spark," as its inventor called it, was seen by Mr. George Slausen in 1942 resting in a barn on South Wisconsin Avenue in Racine, but the vehicle's whereabouts cannot be accounted for after that date. In its day, The Spark enjoyed a considerable reputation. So impressed was the Wisconsin legislature with the machine that to stimulate interest in land vehicles to ship produce to rail centers, Chapter 137 of the Laws of 1875 proposed a reward of $10,000 to be paid:

"to any citizen of Wisconsin who shall invent and after five years of continued trial and use shall produce a machine propelled by steam or other motive agent which will be a cheap and practical substitute for use of horses and other animals on the highway and farm."

As a test of the vehicle's ability, the Laws went on to require that it perform a journey of at least 200 miles on common road in a continuous line north and south in the state, totally propelled by its own internal power at an average rate of at least 5 mph working time. Other requirements of the document made it mandatory that the vehicle's construction conform to run in the ordinary track of the common wagon or buggy and that the new vehicle be able to run backwards and turn out of the road to accommodate other vehicles in passing. Further, the self-propelled vehicle had to be able to ascend or descend a grade of at least 200 feet to a mile in order to qualify for the competition.

If this made Wisconsin one of the first states to subsidize the development of the automobile, the resulting trials might well qualify as the first American automobile race as well. The competition was scheduled to take place between June 10 and July 30 of 1878. Of the seven registrants who had filed for the contest, only two started; a third, Mr. J. E. Baker of Madison failed to arrive even though the race was held up a few days to accommodate repairs on his steamer. At last, at 11 a.m. on Tuesday, July 16th, the race between the two remaining contestants began. Both drove two-cylinder steam vehicles. "The Green Bay Machine" belonging to E. P. Cowles of Wequiock weighed a reported 14,255 pounds, sported three speeds forward and reverse and was built for maximum speed. Its rival, "The Oshkosh" built by F. A. Shomer, J. F. Morse, A. Gallinger and A. M. Farriand, had but one forward speed and reverse, weighed 9875 pounds, and was designed for practicality — it could run for ten miles without refueling and taking on water. Soon after the race began, The Green Bay Machine broke through a culvert and was obliged to remain behind for repairs. Although it was quickly back on the road, it lost the race to The Oshkosh in the best tortoise-and-hare tradition; the winner covered the entire run of 201 miles in 33 hours and 27 minutes at an average and stately pace of slightly more than 6 mph.

In his report to the Wisconsin legislature, the Commissioner noted:

> "Although neither machine [steam road wagon] complied with the requirements of the law in that they did not prove to be 'a cheap and practical substitute for the use of horses' the prize of $10,000 should be awarded to the owners of the 'Oshkosh'."

It was further felt that, by making the full award, the legislature would greatly encourage continued efforts in the development of automotive road and farm machinery. After a period of spirited debate on the subject, the legislature finally awarded half the prize — $5000 — to the builders of The Oshkosh.

But for every effort by an enlightened legislature to encourage the development of self-propelled road transport, there was a corresponding effort by other lawmakers to quash the movement in its infancy. In 1871 one Elijah Ware is reported to have built a steam road wagon in San Francisco, California, presumably without dire repercussions. But five years earlier in Fleetwood, Pennsylvania, James F. Hill's building of a similar vehicle led to official retribution which rather dampened his enthusiasm for further experimentation. Initially, his car was a steamer, but Hill, fearing a boiler explosion, rebuilt it later to accommodate a gasoline engine. In this guise it ran until 1908, when it was rebuilt again with yet another gasoline engine. It should be noted that Charles E. Duryea, who saw the car, doubted that it was built as early as claimed. What does appear to have happened, however, is that the Fleetwood governing council passed an ordinance against the car in 1885, as reported in the Fleetwood Diamond Jubilee commemorative book published in 1948.

The Elijah Ware steam car of 1871. Apparently it was built in San Francisco, California, although there are some references indicating its birthplace was Bayonne, New Jersey.

Despite the frequent tribulations of the steam car inventor, many pioneers of the day managed to survive. One who did so with a tenacity was George Alexander Long, a man who lived to be one hundred years old. Having seen Roper's vehicle at a fair in Brattleboro, Vermont, Long went to work building his own three-wheeled steam carriage. It was patented in 1883. Today the Long steamer — which appears on the dust jacket of this book — resides in the Smithsonian collection of automobiles in Washington, D. C. One would think that tracing the history of this particular vehicle would be a simple task, since its inventor was available for interview until 1950. Not so. The task is made infinitely more difficult because Long's letters and interviews are

contradictory and his memory proved unreliable — not because of age, but because of the same syndrome that affects small boys who wish to be older than they are, mature women who push back their ages and, in the case of almost all inventors, a desire to take credit for an accomplishment earlier than was actually realized. A case in point is a letter written by Long in which he states that 500 people gathered to watch his first run in 1875. Still another document indicates that the run — when it was made — took place at 1 a.m.; one might suspect that fewer than 500 good citizens of Northfield, Massachusetts, would have been willing to give up their beds at that hour to watch Long's steam car perform. It was an unspectacular performance — according to its inventor, during its first outing the steamer stopped, and was started again but eventually had to be pushed back home. In yet another document, Long indicates that his vehicle's maiden trial was in 1876, and that — here there is a peculiar ring of truth — a Selectman of the neighborhood tried to have the steamer outlawed.

Regarding the Long, however, historians have generally since concurred that the engine was designed and built in 1879 in Northfield, Massachusetts. A year or so later Long constructed the framework and running gear in Colonel A. A. Pope's Columbia bicycle plant at the factory of the Weed Sewing Machine Company in Hartford, Connecticut. Long attached his 90° vee engine to a framework-mounted steel plate which moved to and fro via a lever in front of the seats. Of the two crankshaft pulleys, the larger was splined and moveable lengthwise along the shaft; thus, with the engine plate moved rearward, one of the driving pulleys came in contact with the rear wheel. The disparity in pulley diameters provided two driving ratios. The vehicle was driven by a five-foot rear wheel, while the front wheels with their spoon brakes stopped it. Solid tires were provided, and the complete vehicle weighed 350 pounds. Most interesting is the fact that Long intended his vehicle to be handled by two drivers and provided two handlebars and two brake levers for this purpose. He applied for a patent on this vehicle in 1882. It was granted the following year.

THE STEAM VEHICLE: 1870's-1895

As the century progressed, high-pressure steam-powered vehicles became increasingly more sophisticated — self-condensing, engines soon with automatic control, lightweight vehicles now reasonably safe and not outrageously expensive to build. To be sure, not everyone agreed that steam was the way to go. George B. Selden, who later became involved in a history-making patent dispute, considered building a steam carriage in 1873 but abandoned the project as "impractical." To the fore stepped Lucius D. Copeland, of Phoenix, Arizona, who began his work with steam engines in 1881. His first powered a Columbia bicycle; later a Safety Star bike could travel a good road at 15 mph wearing the same engine — a very creditable showing for a small powerplant. In 1884 he exhibited his steam-powered bicycle at the Maricopa County Fair at Phoenix and, anxious to obtain financial assistance for his experiments, he took the same vehicle to the Mechanics Pavillion in San Francisco during the same year. Initially the engine was reported to be just a quarter horsepower, weighing — water included — just eighteen pounds. According to a later report, however, the engine was one horsepower, capable of 1000 rpm and 12

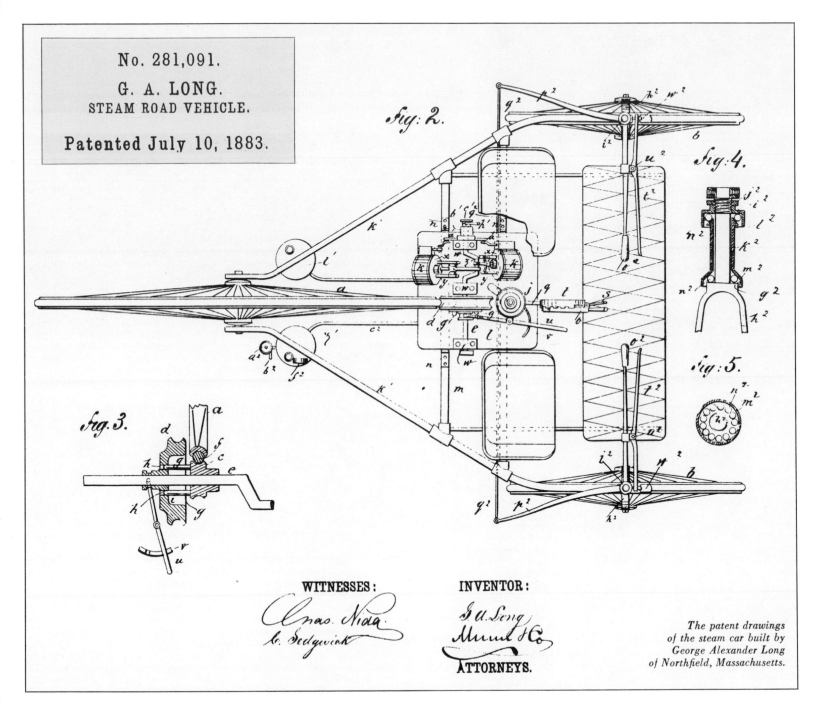

No. 281,091.

G. A. LONG.
STEAM ROAD VEHICLE.

Patented July 10, 1883.

Fig: 2.

Fig: 4.

Fig: 5.

Fig: 3.

WITNESSES:
Chas. Nida.
C. Sedgwick

INVENTOR:
G. A. Long
Munn & Co
ATTORNEYS.

The patent drawings of the steam car built by George Alexander Long of Northfield, Massachusetts.

43

Lucius Copeland is believed to have exhibited this steam bicycle built in 1883 at the Maricopa County Fair in Phoenix the following year. (D)

anticipating the modern sidecar by a good score of years. The Moto-cycle Manufacturing Company of Philadelphia controlled Copeland's patents and in 1890 the vehicle was produced, wearing heavy rubber tires instead of the usual bicycle wheels. Its safety boiler could get up steam in five minutes and could run for three hours or approximately thirty miles with only one filling of water. Steering was accomplished with one hand, while the other controlled the throttle.

Ingenious as they were, it is not known how many of these vehicles were sold. In one of Copeland's letters, now on file at the Automotive History Section of the Detroit Public Library, the inventor said that he became discouraged because he ". . . found that people would not pay more than $500 for a motor vehicle and to sell at such a price, there would be little profit." (That $500 figure, incidentally, was the one later considered by Charles E. Duryea as a projected reasonable price for any automobile.) Today, one of Copeland's vehicles, built in 1886, also may be found on exhibit at the Smithsonian Institution.

Working concurrently with Copeland was one John Clegg, an English-trained mechanic who, with his son Thomas, built a steam carriage in Memphis, Michigan. Years later Thomas Clegg described the steamer as a single-cylinder vehicle with seating room for four including the driver and stoker. Leather belts were used to transmit power, and spring adjustments on them provided enough play to turn corners. This clever vehicle took its longest ride — a journey of fourteen miles — in 1884.

Perhaps the American steam car of this era owed more to James H. Bullard than to any other single inventor. His first steamer — built in Springfield, Massachusetts, in 1885-6 — was the first steam vehicle of any kind to have automatic control of its essential functions. It was designed to carry a cylindrical boiler with fire tubes placed lengthwise through it. The two-cylinder engine was over the horizontal boiler and positioned at the rear of the driving axle. The cylinders were small, 3 x 4½ inches and angled at 90 degrees. Oscillating-type valves were used. There was no provision for reversing in this first Bullard car. A bevel gear differential was used and a clutch was provided around it so that the vehicle could coast without turning the engine. The wheelbase was about four feet and the track two and a half feet; the vehicle sported 50-inch diameter bicycle wheels controlled, at the rear, by handlebar steering.

But the vehicle's most interesting feature was its flash boiler, which used a liquid fuel rather than the conventional solid fuel. The boiler was heated by a continuously lit pilot light from kerosene wick lamps which made it possible to generate steam quickly once the pump began supplying water. Later Bullard experimented with a porcupine-type of tubular boiler holding about one to one and a half gallons of water, but found that he could not force an increased amount of heat from his fire wicks with this type boiler. He even tried alcohol, but discarded this idea for the same reason: insufficient heat and, worse, an embarrassing tendency to catch his vehicle on fire. Bullard was one of the first to atomize fuel oil with a small, spray type atomizer similar to today's perfume spray. This produced a very hot flame free of smoke which was all the inventor needed to forge ahead with the final details of the tank burners and other regulating devices that supplied the oil, compressed air and water. Ultimately he automated all of these in such a

mph. In either case, the entire engine could be easily removed and transferred to another bicycle, making it highly adaptable both in weight and size.

Fortune smiled upon Copeland. Where other inventors had seen their projects fail solely because they could not attract risk capital, he found a willing investor in Sanford Northrup of Camden, New Jersey. Within three months he put a running steam tricycle on the streets of Camden; it featured an automatic water level control and an automatic fire control which depended on the boiler pressure. The vehicle was demonstrated in Fairmount Park, Philadelphia, and, for additional publicity, Copeland took the tricycle on a 120-mile round-trip journey to Atlantic City, accompanied by a Dr. Starkey, one of the directors in the newly-formed Northrup Manufacturing Company. Copeland applied for a patent in October of 1886 — the specifications for which included the use of the frame tubing as a storage for oil and exhaust steam pre-heating the feed water and fuel oil. It was granted April 5, 1887.

Meanwhile Copeland was kept busy developing another motor vehicle designed along safety bicycle lines. To this bicycle, he attached a wheel at one side on an adjustable reach so it could be fitted to any gauge of the road — and on this reach he placed a seat for a third passenger, manner that the driver was free to devote his attention to the road — and to the pure pleasure of driving. The annoying task of stoking the engine was rendered unnecessary, for the steam pressure regulated the amount of fire, shutting it off automatically at just the right point, and the pilot fire burned constantly, ready to light the fire again if steam pressure fell below a certain level. The result of all of these pains-taking details was the first fully-automated steam engine, light enough to be lifted by two men, but strong enough to run successfully through-out the state of Massachusetts during 1886. Bullard secured patents covering all of the vehicle's unusual and advanced features, and turned his attention to adapting his process for burning oil to many other in-ventions until 1898, when he again took up the problem of a steam vehicle in partnership with A. H. Overman.

History looks upon the inventiveness of men such as Bullard rather more kindly than did his contemporaries. As we have seen many times before, the prophets of steam power went without honor in their own country. Consider, the case of E. F. Field of Lewiston, Maine, who in partnership with Frank Cranshaw developed a steam car in 1886. In-terestingly, an article about the vehicle in the August 27, 1887, issue of the *Lewiston Journal* dealt less with the mechanics of the machine itself than with the problems its inventor experienced in testing it. Ac-cording to the article, so strong was the public sentiment against such self-propelled vehicles that the early hours of dawn were often required for road tests. Moreover, inventors like Field were loath to test their vehicles upon public roads and highways for fear of incurring the wrath of their neighbors and because of the very real danger of accidents presented by startled, runaway horses.

Still, there were others who enjoyed actual encouragement — and from such close quarters as their own families: Ransom Eli Olds, for ex-ample, a second generation steam pioneer employed by his father's

A Copeland tricycle, photographed at the Smithsonian, circa 1888.

Plans of a three-passenger moto-cycle developed by Lucius Copeland in 1887 and produced for sale in 1890. Many of Copeland's vehicles used third and fourth wheels to serve as balance when the machine was at rest. This particular model had two adjustable idler wheels. (D)

Drawing of the first steam car (top) built by Ransom Eli Olds, completed in 1887 at the Lansing (Michigan) shops of P. F. Olds and Sons. Below it is Olds' second steam car, this one built in 1890-91. (D)

company, P. F. Olds and Sons. In 1880 his father was engaged in building small portable steam engines of one and two horsepower. These engines were simple, yet sturdy, and steam was generated by ordinary gasoline stove burners. A one-gallon gasoline tank was elevated at one end of the boiler causing the fuel to run down and, after the burner was lit, steam was up within five to ten minutes from cold. Because of the advantage of their cheap fuel and faster firing, the Olds engines were so successful that between 1887 and 1892 more than 2000 of them were built. Challenged by the possibility of adapting his father's engine to a steam carriage, young Ransom Olds began work on a three-wheeled buggy driven by steam engine and boiler around 1886 or 1887. A cumbersome vehicle of crude design, it weighed 1200 pounds, and its front wheel was mounted in a fork, like a bicycle wheel, and steered by a tiller. The wheels, fitted with steel rims, measured about four feet in diameter each. The vehicle's steam engine and boiler were completely encased within a large box, the front part of which formed a platform for the driver's seat. A two horsepower steam engine heated by several gasoline burners could produce a speed for the vehicle of from four to ten miles an hour. At first the transmission consisted of a variable lever and ratchet drive, but this arrangement proved unsatisfactory, and gears and chains were fitted later.

It would be satisfying to be able to date the various phases of the Olds experiments with some degree of accuracy. Unfortunately, the same problems of contradiction inherent in the dating of so many inventions recur in the case of this Olds vehicle. At one time Olds claimed that he made his first test ride in a steam carriage of his own invention in 1886. Later, in 1904, he testified that he had not even finished the vehicle until 1887. On another occasion he stated that the vehicle ". . . was operated on the streets of Lansing (Michigan) in the latter part of 1887 . . ." In weighing all of this evidence Olds' biographer Glenn A. Niemeyer concludes that: "It seems likely that the first morning ride took place sometime in the summer of 1887 . . ." This seems a reasonable solution to the problem of dating the car.

Olds was not pleased with the results of his three-wheeled steamer. He dismantled it and turned his attention to other matters until 1890 or 1891 when he attempted a second steamer, a four-wheeler which utilized some of the parts from the first vehicle including the rear wheels and the axle. Like its predecessor, it was powered by steam, using gasoline for fuel. The regulation of its fire burners was automatic and its engine was attached directly to the driving wheels, eliminating the need for transmission and gearing. An article in the May 21, 1892, edition of *Scientific American* included this arch summary of the vehicle:

> "The vehicle as a whole includes many new merits. Mr. Olds states that its great advantages are that it never kicks or bites, never tires out on long runs, and during hot weather he can ride fast enough to make a breeze without sweating the horse. It does not require care in the stable, and only eats while it is on the road, which is no more than at a rate of 1 cent per mile."

The article would lead one to believe that Olds envisioned manufacture of this second vehicle, but in 1893 he received an offer from the Francis Times Co., a London-based patent medicine enterprise, to buy the car. Olds' asking price was $400; he got it and shipped the steamer to

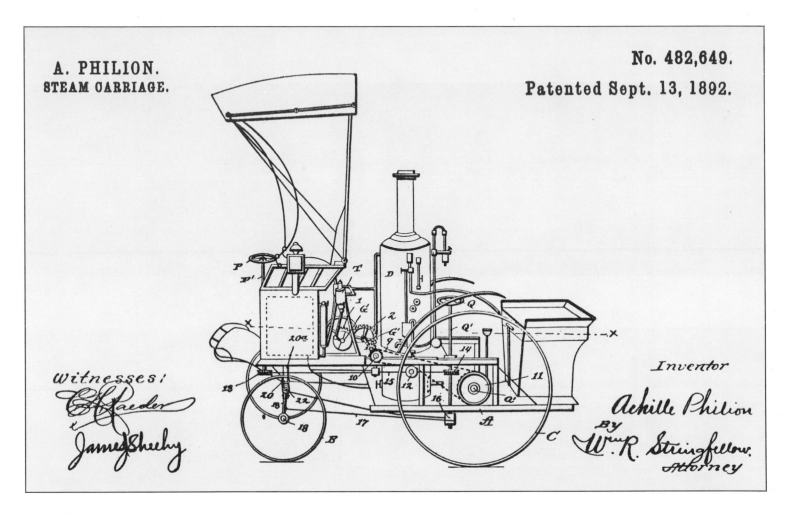

A. PHILION.
STEAM CARRIAGE.

No. 482,649.
Patented Sept. 13, 1892.

Witnesses:
C. F. Raeder
James Sheehy

Inventor
Achille Philion
By
Wm. R. Stringfellow.
Attorney

the Times' branch house in Bombay, India. It is not known whether the car actually reached its destination or not.

If the Olds vehicle was lost, there were more than enough being built during the last few years of the Nineteenth Century to take its place. One of them was Achille Philion's steam car, patented on September 13, 1892. At that time Mr. Philion claimed that he had been working on his car since 1890; and it is believed that he built it to appear in the World's Columbian Exposition of 1893 and later planned to run it in the *Times-Herald* contest of 1895, neither of which did it do. The Achille-Philion still survives; some years ago it appeared in the movie *Excuse My Dust*. In 1893 C. L. Simmonds of Lynn, Massachusetts, built a steamer which carried its passengers mounted high over a frame that was undercut so that the front wheels could turn on a continuous axle as in a horse-drawn vehicle. At the rear was mounted a vertical boiler

controlled by a hand-wheel at the side of the car, just back of the seat, where the driver could reach it. Simmond's vehicle ran on wire wheels, but was characterized by no engineering novelty; it saw little service and was later abandoned.

THE ELECTRIC VEHICLE: 1890-1895

But as the horseless carriage steamed toward the Twentieth Century, another idea, neglected for a few decades, returned to challenge inventors of the self-propelled vehicle — electric power. We have already noted the pioneering work of Thomas Davenport, Moses G. Farmer and Professor Charles G. Page in the 1830's and 1840's. As admirable as were their efforts, they had not resulted in a flurry of electric car activity. Both Farmer's and Page's vehicles had utilized Grove cells, each

C. L. Simmonds, an
engineer with the
Lynn Gas & Electric
Co., built a
steam car in 1893,
in Massachusetts.

As reported later,
it was then sold
"at a round sum to
parties who have
since used it for
exhibition purposes."

containing lead plates one foot square, and the resulting gigantic, heavy and expensive batteries were neither practical nor economical enough for widespread transport application. For this reason — and a variety of others — the electric car idea lay dormant in America until the late 1880's.

The first electric vehicle that can be counted as a resounding success was built by William Morrison of Des Moines, Iowa. Morrison has claimed 1888 for its building, but historians have since concluded that it was probably built in 1890. The discrepancy is really insignificant,

however; what cannot be denied is the ingenuity of the vehicle itself. It ran, and it ran well — its inventor demonstrating that it could be operated for thirteen consecutive hours at 14 mph. Among the vehicle's more significant features was its unique steering device, a pivot on each of the front wheels. The wheels were then linked with a yoke bar which turned by means of an ingenious rack and pinion device actuated from the driver's seat by a two-handed steering bar. Morrison patented his steering device, as he did some eighty-seven other inventions — most of them batteries and processes for the manufacture of batteries — but the most important of his patents pertained to powering vehicles by electricity. His vehicle reached a wider audience than any other electric carriage in America at that time, this through the efforts of Harold Sturges, secretary of the American Battery Company of Chicago, who made Morrison's acquaintance. In New York City, Atlantic City, across thousands of miles in America, Sturges demonstrated, paraded and exhibited the Morrison electric. It would travel the fairgrounds of the 1893 World's Columbian Exposition in Chicago and the snowbound streets from Jackson Park in the 1895 *Chicago Times-Herald* contest.

The effect of all this — in addition to enormous publicity for Sturges' company — was an outpouring of similar vehicles from electrical and battery manufacturers determined to emulate Morrison's success. Only the inventor himself remained unimpressed; as late as 1907 Morrison would declare that he "would not give ten cents" for an automobile for his own use — electrical or otherwise.

Morrison's pique was certainly not shared by many farsighted individuals after the turn of the century, and not by many before it. Contemporaneously with him, there were a number of others actively pursuing the electric vehicle idea. In 1888 Philip W. Pratt of Boston built an electric carriage, demonstrating it on July 27th, an event described in *Modern Light and Heat* magazine the following August 2nd:

> ". . . The tricycle, which is of a rather heavy and substantial build, carries a wrought iron platform under the driver's seat and close to the ground; on this are six cells of the Electrical Accumulator Company's storage batteries, weighing, all told, ninety pounds and a specially constructed electric motor which is connected to the driving apparatus of the tricycle by a chain gearing."

This vehicle was not nearly so successful nor did it even approximate the sophistication of the Morrison car. The same might be said for the vehicle or vehicles built by John A. Barrett, chief engineer of the Western Electric Company, who had been a telephone patentee and who was involved in the founding of the Philadelphia Storage and Battery Company. Reportedly he built a battery-operated horseless carriage in 1884, engaging Brewster of New York City to build the body, but no documentation exists to support this, save for the fact that when, in 1888 and 1889, he was again reported to be at work on an electric vehicle it was described as his second such effort. Substantiation of Barrett's work is, at best, inconclusive.

But well documented are the contributions of Clyde J. Coleman. Around 1890 he began his career by inventing a new dry battery, the first to use blotting paper liners. These batteries were manufactured on an extensive scale until he sold the rights to Knapp Electrical Works and Central Electric Companies and the National Carbon Company. Coleman also manufactured small motors — and one of these powered a two-seated electric surrey with side entrance, canopied top and wire wheels which he built in 1892 and operated successfully around the Chicago area. Not long afterward, he teamed up with one Fred Dagenhardt and E. E. Keller, (who later became president of Westinghouse Machine Company), to produce electrically-driven chair cars to transport visitors at the World's Columbian Exposition, a project which was ultimately abandoned because of financial difficulties. Thereafter Coleman would work with the Electric Vehicle Company, the Rockaway Automobile Company and the American Eveready Com-

The electric car built by William Morrison in 1890 was subsequently promoted for a number of years by Harold Sturges of the American Battery Company in Chicago. Touring the country, the car performed successfully at numerous fairs and exhibitions and impressed just about everyone who saw it, save for its inventor. The car was modified somewhat and then entered in the 1895 Chicago Times-Herald contest.

pany. His experimentation with the application of electric power included development of medical therapeutic apparatus, electrical protection systems for banks, electric furnaces and the electrical signal system for railroads. Apparently there was very little in which Coleman was not interested. Judging from his patents, his interests ranged from color motion picture cameras and projectors to one-man submarines, synthetic production of nitric acid and nitrates and welding processes for building seamless steel ships. Of the 165 patents issued to Coleman during his lifetime, fifteen of them covered such automotive innovations as automobile starters, electric springs and air carbon acid, to name but a few. Had Coleman wished to devote his genius solely to the development of the electric automobile conceivably we might all be driving such cars today.

Increasingly in the 1890's inventors turned to electric power, concluding perhaps that its simplicity would prove superior over its rival steam car. A steam car might be easy to build, so some said, but one had to be a locomotive fireman to run it. In Canada in 1893 an electric car was built for F. B. Featherstonhaugh at the Dickson Carriage Works in Toronto, its motor being designed by W. J. Still, who would later build his own electric car. The following year in the United States — on January 19, 1894 — Henry G. Morris and Pedro G. Salom applied for a patent on their electric vehicle. It was granted the following year. The patent car was the first of a series of electrics built by Morris and Salom which would pave the way for the electric car as we know it today. They called it the Electrobat.

The Electrobat was not the only electric vehicle of that era to carry a reference to its power source within its name. In response to a contest promoted by the *Electrical Review*, a variety of terms arose for what was assumed would be the horseless carriage of the future. Suggestions were thoughtful, clever — and occasionally whimsical: "Electromobile," "Electricmobile," "Bacrotom" ("motorcab" spelled backwards), "Autopropelectic," "Electragon," "Electropropel," "Autovolv," "Elecar," "Franklin" (in memory of Benjamin Franklin's electrical experiments with kites), "Electrola" and "Accelawatt" were but some of the names proposed to carry the vehicle triumphantly toward the Twentieth Century. To the proponents of electric power, no other means of propelling a land carriage seemed more effective. Steam was curtly dismissed; of the gasoline automobile Colonel A. A. Pope would say, "You'll never get people to sit over an explosion."

THE INTERNAL COMBUSTION ENGINE: FROM THE 1870's

Perhaps the internal combustion engine did appear unpromising as motive force for a self-propelled vehicle, if only because it was so long in arriving. Internal combustion principles had been through a number of decades of development in America, beginning with Samuel Morey's efforts, earlier related, in 1826. The explosive property of petroleum vapor being the driving force of all internal combustion engines, inventors early identified its explosive element as a hydrocarbon, although gases derived from petroleum for use in combustion engines varied through the years from pure petroleum to naptha, benzine and eventually gasoline. Experimentation was wide-reaching. The basic hurdle faced by all who dealt with non-compression engines was the loss of power caused through igniting gases by flame on the outside of the cylinder wall; when a hole in the cylinder enlarged as the piston moved in the direction of the partial charge, the gas would explode, resulting in a loss of power through leakage from the ignition hole. This problem was approached, as we've seen, by Dr. Alfred Drake of Philadelphia, whose persistent efforts in internal combustion development began in 1835, and by Stuart Perry whose engines were patented in 1844 and 1846. In the years from 1850 many, many more patents were awarded to inventors in this area. And in 1872 one was granted to George Bailey Brayton of Boston.

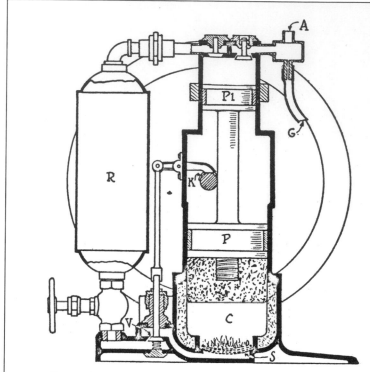

George Brayton's 1872 patented internal combustion engine. (D)

Even the United States Congress sat up and took note. Special hearings on the self-propelled vehicle were held in 1875, and "A Report of a Joint Congressional Committee on the Horseless Carriage of 1875" enthusiastically proclaimed

"... a new source of power, which burned a distillate of kerosense called gasoline and it has been produced by a Boston engineer [Brayton]. ... Instead of burning the fuel under a boiler it is exploded inside the cylinder of the engine. ... This discovery begins a new era in the history of civilization; it may someday prove to be more revolutionary in the development of human society than the invention of the wheel, the use of metals or the steam engine. Never in history has society been confronted with a power so full of potential danger and at the same time so full of promise for the future of man and for the peace of the world."

With regard to the use of this power in self-propelled vehicles, Congress tempered its praise somewhat by detailing the dangers of gas carriages moving at high speeds: Its warning against vehicles "hurtling through our streets and along our roads and poisoning the atmosphere" sounds jarringly contemporary. Yet because of the many contributions that gasoline-propelled vehicles might be expected to make, the report concluded:

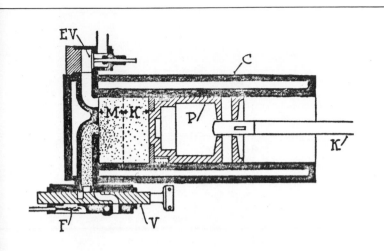

Brayton's advertising in the trade and technical press brought his engine to the attention of self-propelled vehicle exponents.

". . . we therefore earnestly recommend that Congress set up the Horseless Carriage Commission which will have a complete control over all sources of gasoline and similar explosive elements in all activities connected with their development and use in the United States. These measures may seem drastic and far-reaching, but the discovery in which we are dealing involves forces of nature too dangerous to fit into any of our usual concepts."

Brayton had built his engine in 1864, steadily improving it until 1872 when he applied for a patent. It was not an explosion engine as the term is understood today. It was ignited by a mixture of air and combustual gas in the ratio of 12:1, but his patent makes it clear that the expansion of his cylinder was less an explosive force on the piston than "a true pressure due to expansion on account of the fact that the piston is at the very commencement of its stroke when the expanding gasses begin to act upon it." Nor did Brayton employ a carburetor; the charge of air and gas was carried in a separate reservoir to be drawn upon when necessary, rather as a steam engine carries its steam in a boiler. But Brayton did depart from steam principles in one significant regard; his piston was single acting, that is, the explosive mixture was admitted at one end of the piston only. Steam engines, of course, are double acting, steam entering at each end of the piston, and until

Brayton all inventors of explosion or gas engines used a double acting system. Brayton's engine was thus a radical step in departure from the double-acting to the single-acting engine which would eventually be universally incorporated into internal combustion engine design.

The Brayton engine itself had been enthusiastically regarded by the United States Congress, but its application to land vehicles was viewed with some apprehension. Local governments shared this concern. In 1873 Brayton had arranged with a streetcar company of Providence, Rhode Island, to apply his engine to one of their cars, but city authorities refused to allow the car to run the streets without a team of horses attached to it. Consequently the car was tested on a small private track near a fair ground, but still Brayton encountered opposition from the city, and the experiment was abandoned. Later, at the 1876 Exposition in Philadelphia, Brayton's engine was put to use pumping air for an aquarium, which brought it to the attention of James A. Fawcett, who operated a bus and hack lines in Pittsburgh. Fawcett spoke with Brayton about the possibility of equipping an omnibus with the new engine — and Brayton agreed. Two years later the bus was completed. Its first transmission was hydraulic, but when that proved unsatisfactory the engine was remounted with a shaft projecting toward the rear and with bevel gear to drive a cross-shaft. The bus also featured a friction clutch and reversing arrangement. But it was all for naught. Like the first Brayton-engined land vehicle, this bus, too, was refused sanction to run on the city streets.

On August 14, 1877, in Deutz, Germany, Nicolaus August Otto was granted a patent for an internal combustion engine which was to render the Brayton engine obsolete for automotive purposes. Otto's engine operated on the four-cycle principle with compression of the mixture before exploding — a theory which had been advanced in 1862 by the Frenchman Alphonse Beau de Rochas, and had been considered thereafter by others as well. But Otto was the man who combined these ideas into a practical engine, and gasoline engine patents since his have dealt with improvements on his original.

But it was the Brayton engine — quiet, smooth-running if ponderous — which attracted the attention of a Rochester, New York, patent attorney named George B. Selden. Aware though he would be of Otto's efforts and other experimentation in Europe, Selden concluded that Brayton's was the powerplant of the future for the horseless carriage, that the ear-splitting qualities of other gasoline engines would render them unsuccessful and probably illegal in the United States. His decision was to have far-reaching consequences for the history of the American automobile. In 1879 he applied for a patent on an automobile including his vastly improved Brayton-type engine; with amendations and delays it was finally granted in November of 1895. Assigned four years later to the Electric Vehicle Company, the Selden patent was the tool by which that company hoped to extract royalties from every gasoline car manufacturer in the United States. But one such manufacturer — Henry Ford — had other ideas. He, together with a few other similarly-minded producers, fought the Selden licensers — and after a long and complicated court case, the Selden patent was held to be valid, but only as applied to the Brayton-engined structure specified. Had Selden, back in 1876 when he was introduced to the Brayton engine at the Philadelphia Exposition, tempered his enthusiasm for that configuration and had instead followed the principles soon to be laid down

by Otto, the history of the automobile industry in America would have taken a turn altogether difficult to imagine today.

But the engine, of course — be it steam, electric or gasoline — was but one of the factors to be considered in the development of the automobile. Many other hurdles remained to be solved — transmission of power to the wheels, gearing, speed control, braking and numerous other mechanical details necessary for a successful, safe, easily controlled and inexpensive self-propelled vehicle. Inventors had to equally devote their attention to these matters.

THE GASOLINE CAR: 1891-1895

Awarding credit for the first gasoline automobile in America presents a number of problems. The Duryea car, the planning of which had begun in 1891 with its first successful run two years later, was long considered to be America's first. Years ago this writer — to the considerable resentment of some living automotive pioneers — was able to document that the Lambert car, built in 1891, pre-dated the Duryea vehicle and thus could better lay claim to being America's first. Actually the controversy had begun decades before — around 1920 — when Charles E. Duryea discovered Elwood Haynes' 1894 car in the Smithsonian Institution bearing a sign reading "America's first gasoline powered vehicle." He quite rightly objected to Smithsonian officials that his car pre-dated the Haynes and brought out of storage the 1893 Duryea to prove it. The Duryea wagon was subsequently presented to the Smithsonian, and the "first gasoline car" myth thereafter grew up around it, abetted, it must be admitted, by frequent statements to that effect by the Duryea brothers themselves.

Continuing research can be expected to unearth more pioneer gasoline vehicles in America than have to date been accounted for. In an 1895 issue *The Horseless Age* reported that more than 300 companies or individuals were or had been engaged in making motorcars. A fair number of these were no doubt gasoline cars long since lost to history, some of which conceivably may have predated those cars already known to exist. What we shall explore here are those for which documentation does exist.

One such vehicle is the Nadig. The remnants of this car, built in Allentown, Pennsylvania, were recently unearthed, and it has been restored in modified form. The Nadig story is perhaps best told by its inventor, Henry Nadig, as related in transcript of the Selden patent trial. On October 5, 1905, he testified:

> "In 1888 or 1889, we began to build gasoline engines, with my brother, Phillip, then a partner. The business is now being conducted by my two sons, Charles Henry Nadig and Lawrence F. Nadig. . . . We commenced to build automobiles in 1891 and completed the first one that year. That automobile is still in existence and first it had a one-cylinder engine and two flywheels."

Nadig went on to note that the engines they built and sold were 8 hp, weighing approximately 1800 pounds apiece and averaging five feet in length. For his horseless carriage, however, he said he reduced the engine weight to 300 pounds, claiming that he ran the vehicle "under its own power when it was first finished on Fourth Street probably a dozen times in 1891." Under questioning, he admitted that he never patented his vehicle nor did he have records to verify his claim; expenses for material and so forth were not entered in the company's books, he said, because "it was built between times and was for myself, so it was not necessary." Nadig described his car to the court:

". . . Wooden wheels with iron tires were used . . . with power from the engine to a countershaft by belts, and from there to the rear wheels. One belt ran the machine at six to eight miles an hour and the other at fifteen miles an hour, at which we usually ran it. Speed was changed by a lever running up to the seat, and said lever was connected to a parallel rod which operated two clutches on the countershaft."

Nadig also testified that the one-cylinder engine's revolutions were twice that of the countershaft in low gear, the same as the countershaft in high gear, providing a 14:1 ratio in high gear. This engine normally ran at 600 to 800 rpm, a two-cylinder engine developed later reached an estimated 12 to 14 hp at 800 rpm. Testimony was also heard from

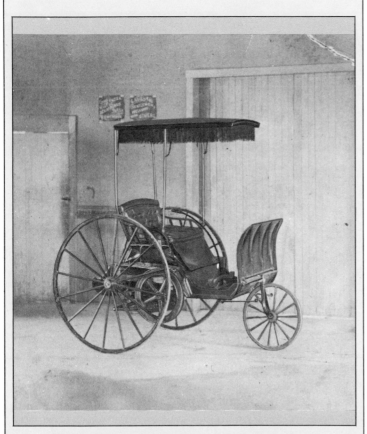

The Lambert, as photographed in 1891 by Walter Lewis.

Van Wert. O. 3-25-'27
My books show that I made 6 photographs of Mr. Lamberts buggy for which I charged $1.25 Said photographs were made in August 1891.

Walter Lewis.
742 South Walnut St
Van Wert Ohio

P.S. I made the trip in this buggy with Mr. Lambert out to the O. Koogle farm in order to get a photo, but failed to get a satisfactory negative, but later in the same month made the negative in Mr. Lamberts Hall.

W.L.

Sworn to and Subscribed to this 5th day of April 1927

Justice of Peace

The sworn testimony given by Walter Lewis regarding Lambert photography.

Charles H. Black's car, completed in 1893, now on exhibit at the Children's Museum in Indianapolis, Indiana. (D)

Nadig's son Charles who noted that they had previously built an engine of ½ hp in 1889 for use in a boat, and subsequently an entirely new car during the winter of 1895-96, although the inventors could find no trace of this second car at the time of the Selden trial. Later, in 1901, the Nadigs would build a gasoline truck.

In 1893 in Indianapolis, Indiana, Charles H. Black completed his gasoline car. The owner of a wagon works and blacksmith's shop, Black had been toying with the idea since he test-drove a friend's imported Benz in 1891. He began work a year later, constructing his vehicle along Benz-like lines. His engine was fitted into an ordinary buggy. It started by a push or turn of the flywheel, ignition was by kerosene torch, with drive via two different-sized pulleys on a crankshaft providing for high and low. Today this vehicle can be seen at the Indianapolis Children's Museum.

A year earlier in Milwaukee, Wisconsin, Gottfried Schloemer, the owner of a cooperage shop, and his locksmith friend Frank Toepfer began thinking about an automobile. According to an employee of Toepfer's, the two men "would get a bucket of beer and talk and sketch." The result was a gasoline carriage powered by a single-cylinder two-cycle engine built according to designs furnished by the Sintz Machinery Co. of Grand Rapids. Two points of steel striking together ignited the gas, while current was supplied from wet batteries. His vehicle operated with a differential and a driving engine, and this driving mechanism, as late as 1920, was considered by many to be superior to any other such device developed. The vehicle made its maiden journey in 1892, the same year Schloemer applied for and received a patent on his carburetor, which was filled with wicks extending into the gasoline tank and constructed in such a manner that it was impossible to flood. During its development, the vehicle utilized a number of different-sized wheels, all built by the Shadbolt and Boyd Iron Company of Milwaukee. The Schloemer-Toepfer car has survived and may be seen today in the Milwaukee Public Museum.

The Sintz engine, utilized by Schloemer and Toepfer, was one of the most popular gasoline engines in America during the 1890's. Widely used for marine projects, in machine shops and for pumping wells, it was the popular choice of many automobile builders of the day as well. Its make and break ignition was considered desirable, as was the fact that current was supplied through wet batteries to a spark coil. Among the many pioneer automobile builders employing the Sintz engine during these years was Elwood P. Haynes of Kokomo, Indiana. Haynes had first begun thinking about building a horseless carriage in 1891; he was at the time employed as a field superintendent for the Indiana Natural Gas Company. His thoughts weren't put into action, however, until November 3rd of 1893 when he purchased a Sintz marine engine and asked fellow townsmen Elmer and Edgar Apperson of the Riverside Machine Works to help him put it on wheels. From drawings and plans Haynes had already prepared, the vehicle took shape and saw its first run along Pumpkinvine Pike on July 4, 1894. Haynes quickly decided that here was a vehicle worthy of manufacture, and having heard of the gasoline car built earlier by John Lambert in Ohio City, just over the Indiana border, he paid Lambert a visit. The enormous publicity value of claiming his car as the "first" was not lost to Haynes, and Haynes persuaded Lambert not to publicly object when he did just that.

The Black, tilted up to show similarity to and differences from the Benz, which had served as inspiration. (D)

The car built by Henry Nadig in 1891, according to the inventor's testimony during the Selden Patent trial. (N)

The problem with John William Lambert was that he didn't have the ego sufficient to earn him his rightful place in the history of the American automobile. Although later he would be accorded honor as one of the originators of the gearless friction-drive engine for automobiles, and his patent credits would be numerous for automobiles and other machinery, his first automobile was to go unrecognized for decades. Lambert was sixteen years old when, in 1876, he saw his first gasoline engine. As the years rolled by he studied the Otto principles and became aware of the Benz automobile. He grew critical of the latter because he believed "its system of belts and pullies" resulted in an unnecessary loss of power. He thought he might try to do better. In 1890 an opportunity presented itself, when he learned that a John B. Hicks of Cleveland was working on a stationary gasoline engine. Lambert agreed to help finance this engine, planning only to invest $200. Subsequently Hicks applied for a patent on his three-cylinder stationary engine in December of 1890, but meanwhile Lambert had commissioned one of Hicks' employees to modify the engine, with component parts designed by Lambert, in order that it would be suitable for a three-wheeled vehicle he had designed. By January of 1891, and

after spending $3300, the engine was still not running. The money probably didn't bother Lambert so much — his holdings in Ohio City included a grain elevator, an implement store, the opera house, the town hall and jail, as well as a lumber yard — but he was annoyed by the lack of progress with the engine. Consequently he ordered it shipped to Ohio City, where he undertook its completion himself. The three-cylinder engine suffered repeated crankshaft failures; Lambert solved that by doing away with two of the cylinders, reducing the stress. He also devised a new carburetor and system of drives. The initial road test of the completed vehicle took place in the eighty-foot showroom of Lambert's implement store and, after a modification to its steering system, it took to the streets of Ohio City. Convinced that he had a workable self-propelled vehicle, Lambert set forth its specifications in a sales brochure, mailed to prospective buyers sometime during the first part of February, 1891. The going price for the first Lambert was $550, and there is irrefutable documentation that it did, in fact, run. Perhaps the most interesting piece of evidence is a photograph taken in 1891 by Walter Lewis, town photographer, who was commissioned by Lambert to take pictures of the car for $1.50 per shot. The first sets of negatives

Above: Elwood Haynes' first car, built at the Apperson Brothers' machine shop in 1893-94 and on display today at the Smithsonian. (P)

Left: The Schloemer wagon, built by Gottfried Schloemer and Frank Toepfer in 1892, currently on display at the Milwaukee Public Museum.

The first Duryea motor wagon.

were taken in August of that year, but they were failures and had to be reshot several days later. The results of that session are reprinted in these pages.

The Lambert vehicle, unfortunately, was destroyed in a fire later in 1891, and Lambert's plans for manufacture went up in smoke too soon after. While there can be no doubting the success of the vehicle mechanically, there can be no doubting too that, financially, its marketing at that time would probably have ended in disaster. Lambert's sales brochure had brought many inquiries, but not one sales contract. In 1892 Lambert made a number of improvements to his engine, anticipating the building of a new vehicle, but ultimately he decided to abandon the project. Two years later when Haynes approached him with a request that Lambert allow him to advertise his [Haynes] car as "America's first," Lambert agreed, reasoning that it would be several years before he might again consider automobile building. Eventually Lambert would become a manufacturer, marketing his car under the name "Union" from 1902, followed several years later by a car marketed under his own name which would be produced until World War I. In later years, when historians began to raise questions about who was first with what, Lambert refused to participate in the controversy.

THE DURYEA CONTROVERSY

Of all the controversies raging around the history of the American automobile during this period, the most heated — and confused — revolves around the Duryea. The car was certainly America's most successful pioneer gasoline automobile, and the organization in 1895 of the Duryea Motor Wagon Company, devoted exclusively to the manufacture of gasoline automobiles, was a genuine first in America. But what remains contested is which brother is responsible for what. The brothers themselves disagreed rather vigorously about that, although J. Frank was more quick to use "we," while Charles, particularly in later years, became enamoured of "I" — a practice carried forward by Charles' son who, after his father's death in 1938, pressed relentlessly to claim his father as sole inventor of the Duryea automobile. Certainly it was Charles who fell in love with the limelight; J. Frank was rather more content with personal satisfaction. In any case, a discussion of the Duryeas and their car is best founded upon an examination of the correspondence exchanged between the brothers during this period.

During the latter part of 1891 the Duryeas began planning their motor vehicle in Chicopee, Massachusetts. Charles had located there after contracting with the Ames Manufacturing Company of that city to produce bicycles for him, and his younger brother had followed him to take a position as toolmaker with the Ames company. J. Frank credits Charles with the design of their first vehicle, as initially planned; it included a type of friction transmission and a "free piston" hot-tube-ignition engine devised by Charles after discussions with C. E. Hawley of the Pope Manufacturing Company on the advantages and disadvantages of the Atkinson-type engine. It was Charles who, on March 26th, purchased for $70 a used carriage from the Smith Carriage Company of Chicopee and who, two days later, found a willing investor, Erwin F. Markham of Springfield, who advanced the brothers $1000. Space and machinery were rented at John W. Russell & Sons Company in Spring-

Construction began on the first Duryea in 1892, with the first outdoor test run in September of 1893.

Running gear of the first Duryea car, with the second engine and other components as used in January, 1894.

The Duryea, as revised in January, 1894, is on display at the Smithsonian Institution, Washington, D.C.

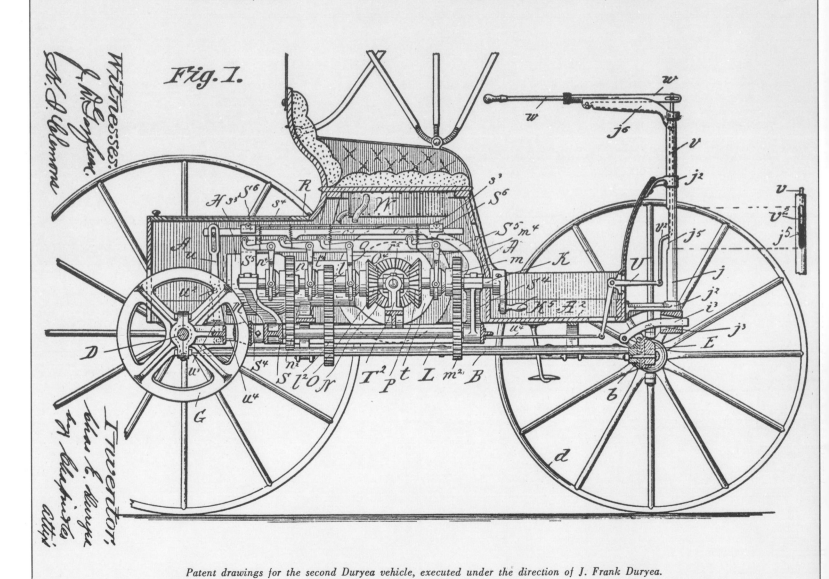

Fig. 1.

Patent drawings for the second Duryea vehicle, executed under the direction of J. Frank Duryea.

field, and young Frank was contracted to build the vehicle, receiving a ten percent pay increase over what he had been earning at Ames.

By September substantial progress had been made on construction of the carriage's running gear, and the engine was completed, save for the lamentable fact that it simply wouldn't run. Charles' bicycle enterprise, however, was faring far better and on September 22nd, after contracting with a Peoria, Illinois, firm to have bicycle parts manufactured, he moved to that city. Completion of the motor carriage was now Frank's responsibility solely. During the next two years the brothers would meet only once, in Chicago at the World's Columbian Exposition. During the intervening months they exchanged ideas through a series of affectionate letters.

Charles' move to Peoria was followed a month later by Frank's contracting of typhoid fever, which delayed further work on the motor vehicle until January, 1893. Frank returned to the non-starting engine, modifying it substantially. The result was a makeshift, but it was running in February and was tested indoors in the incomplete carriage — a short trial, long enough only to demonstrate some of the weaknesses in the friction transmission. By this time Frank was convinced the engine required a massive redesign, and this was begun in March. The new

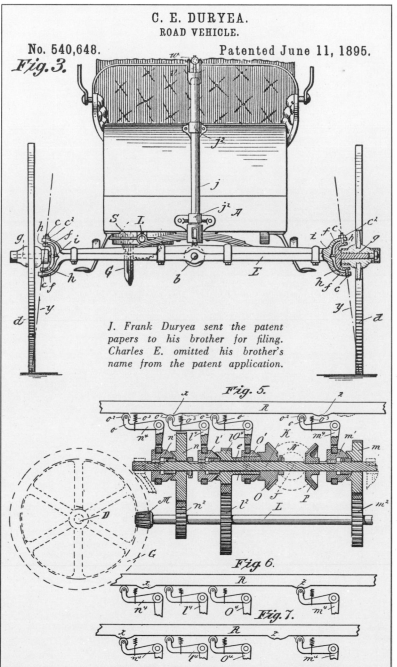

C. E. DURYEA.
ROAD VEHICLE.

No. 540,648.

Patented June 11, 1895.

J. Frank Duryea sent the patent papers to his brother for filing. Charles E. omitted his brother's name from the patent application.

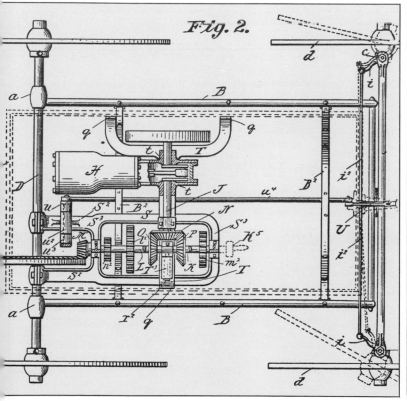

design of Frank's incorporated a cast water jacket, hand starting device, timer gears to operate the exhaust valve, electric ignition, a spray carburetor, a muffler and a governor to avoid the necessity of remote control of the engine. Charles Duryea had been in correspondence with his brother about their first engine's technical problems and had contributed some ideas. Frank in a letter to his brother (August 28, 1893) commented: "I have tho't over yr engine and am still trying to find out if it will run — there is a chance that it would — and it looks some as tho it might give trouble, — is certainly simple." Charles' engine ideas, it would appear, had already been superceded, for earlier in that same letter, Frank commented, ". . . I have got the carriage almost ready for the road — want to get it out Sat. if possible; will take it off somewhere so that no one will see us have the fun. Do not anticipate a kickup [arrest] but of course may have one." But more work remained on the carriage itself than anticipated and it wasn't until September 22nd that Frank could write his brother: ". . . have tried it finally and thoroughly and quit trying till some changes are made." Among the changes he envisioned, the most important revolved around the transmission, as he noted in that same letter, "Now if you have anything good in the line of positive gearing, Chas., send it on — as I want to be full of ideas. My intention is to adapt a system of gears and friction clutches so as to obtain at least three speeds." But evidently after their visit together in Chicago in October, the brothers decided to give the old transmission another chance. Back in Springfield by November Frank took the carriage out a number of times, but remained unsatisfied and believing that success was very near, quickly drew up new plans for his geared transmission. By January 18, 1894, he was able to report: "Dear Bro. — Have had the carriage out at last. . . . The mechanism works precisely as designed. Does not require the friction clutches that the belt required. The only question is power sufficient and I think we have enough from what I saw last night." But already Frank Duryea was anxious to begin on a second improved vehicle, as indicated in this same letter: "it will be good. Shall use a piano body buggy side spring. . . The chains I am confident are a mistake. . . Besides the sprockets on wheels look more like a machine than it would if we drove the axle. Our gears are practically noiseless — can scarcely hear them — whereas the chains rattle worse than all the rest. . . . I never had more ideas on the subject than at present nor more confidence in our ability to carry out this scheme. I certainly wish you could get east to help us on the question of money."

By March Frank Duryea was able to secure new financing himself, Markham having contributed as much to the project as he cared to. A Mr. H. W. Clapp thereafter put up the money for the patent application and the second vehicle, and it was in his name that the Duryea car would be entered in the *Chicago Times-Herald* contest. On April 7th Frank wrote his brother, "the patent papers will be forwarded to you at once — started today." (The patent would subsequently be taken in Charles Duryea's name.) And that month Frank began work on the second vehicle. The first car would be stored until 1920 — when it was acquired by Inglis M. Uppercu and presented to the United States National Museum.

Frank Duryea's letters to his brother in 1894 regarding the second

Duryea car clearly indicate that he was its designer. Its engine was entirely new, initially built along Sintz principles, but when that proved unsatisfactory, he turned to his own two-cylinder four-cycle design. The transmission shafts were mounted on ball bearings, and the free gears ran on graphite oilless bearings requiring little lubrication. It was an altogether remarkable car, and Frank Duryea was obviously pleased with it. In February of 1895 he reported to his brother: "Motor all right — can run right up to 700 — looks elegant, am casing gears." In March the new car was painted, and in April Charles was advised: "Everybody pleased with wagon. She takes Pearl Street and Maple Street in second speed six or seven miles an hour anyway. . . . She will run anything that can be found in the road."

It was an ecstatic Frank Duryea who wrote his brother on June 10th:

> "Everybody pleased with it and Clapp is getting actual orders every day. An order received this A.M. says book me for two carriages to be delivered at earliest possible date—kindly inform me what number my orders are and when you think that you will be able to deliver—etc. Some of the orders state that they do not care how much the wagon costs—send it and draw on our bank. There is no doubt but that the orders are genuine."

The Duryea motor wagon was everything a car should be. It could be built economically, it was safe, tractable and easily maintained. Only one question remained: Was America ready for the automobile?

THE AUTOMOBILE IN AMERICA: 1893

Since its beginnings in the fertile mind of Oliver Evans, no other invention save the flying machine remained so long unfulfilled in America as did the self-propelled road vehicle. It was a concept invented, only to be mislaid, and reinvented again and again. It was a device of incredible potential, a machine that would launch a new era for mankind, an idea whose sole competition was the horse. A decade or so later, when the automobile had become a practical reality, David Beecroft, editor of the magazine *The Automobile*, looked back and theorized that the creation of a marketable self-propelled vehicle in America could have been accomplished many years earlier than it had been, using material at hand and "no new devices whatever." What was lacking, he felt, were "persistent individuals . . . who, having taken up the work . . . continued until the industry became influenced by their work." While that may have been true, one should not treat too lightly the formidable competition of the horse. The animal had more than tradition on his side; he was cheap, maintenance was minimal, and if he was a she, self-perpetuating as well. In rural areas only the poorest of the poor were without one. The horse was a companion (almost a member of the family) and a chauffeur (the average farmer trusted his horse more than himself to do his driving). Indeed the earliest automobile pioneers recognized that the horse in rural areas was almost invincible. Their attention was directed instead to the towns and particularly the cities where the animal enjoyed neither the companionable nor economical advantages of farm-based horses. It was a sophisticated city dweller who wrote: "The people who tell us a motor wagon will never displace a horse because the one is 'soulless machine' while the other is a spirited animal, have been reading romances of the days of chivalry or attending Horse Shows, and never opened their eyes on the work-a-day world. Hard work is the lot of most horses and any spirit they naturally possess is soon subdued. As for pet horses, they are a special and not numerous class, and will not be disturbed." Others were even more blunt in their assessment of the situation; to those who claimed that the automobile would scare horses came the reply: "Suppose it does. So do locomotives, bicycles, street cars, Fourth of July celebrations, and a dozen other things. Horses must get used to it."

There was no dearth of men who believed in the horseless vehicle. Throughout the land in the early 1890's, in the byways of prairie towns, the back alleys of villages and the sophisticated machine shops of large cities, there were farsighted individuals tinkering, dreaming, experimenting — building and driving horseless vehicles. What was needed was something to bring them together, an attraction of capital to further their developmental work, and a public approval to ultimately see its reality. What was needed, in short, was a catalyst.

One might have thought such a catalyst would have been provided by the World's Columbian Exposition in Chicago which opened May 1st, 1893, and commemorated the 400th anniversary of the discovery of America. Costing a lofty $33,000,000 and surprisingly paying back a small dividend to its stockholders, it was an artistic and educational triumph enjoyed by a total of 27,539,521 visitors. Some of its features are fondly recalled to this day. For the first time Mr. Ferris spun the wheel he had invented high in the sky to the pleasure of young and old alike; and in the Midway a hootchy-kootchy dancer named Little Egypt displayed her many charms. But most impressive of all was Machinery Hall where a great Corliss steam engine supplied power for most of the mechanical devices on display. America had fallen in love with the machine. One awestruck reporter commented: "As one leans over the railing around the visitor's platform and looks down into the area below, it seems difficult to imagine that the quiet attendants, who so leisurely piled the coal into the furnaces and tried the various gauge cocks, are the active agents in whose control is the generation of that mighty power, steam . . . And yet so it is. Neglect on their part and all

The 1892 bus built by W. T. Harris and William Hollingsworth for transporting spectators at the Columbian Exposition.

The Keller-Dagenhardt, one of two built in 1892 for the Exposition, pictured here three years later at the Times-Herald *trials.*

the world would stop and the great wheels would remain silent and the busy hum would cease and the machinery would lose its life." Among the various exhibits was the Mohawk Dutchman, a bandsaw capable of cutting intricate wood patterns which would give rise to the "American Carpenter Renaissance," an epoch in American architecture remembered for its fabulous gingerbread tracery. There was the Ingersoll Pneumatic Rock Drill as well, and Krupp had shipped a sampling of its great weapons of war to impress the world with Germany's military might. After a thirty-year search for a high-speed cylindrical press, the answer had been found, and it was on exhibit, the "Web Printing Machine," capable of printing 25,000 sheets an hour. And there was a model of the great English Steam-Hammer, capable of dealing a blow to hundreds of tons, yet flexible enough to be brought down so gently that it would rest on a delicate pocketwatch without cracking the glass crystal. There was more mechanical power on display in this one place than had ever been assembled anywhere else in the world.

But where was the automobile? There were a few there, though they were paid scant attention either by the exposition's patrons or the press. Daimler Motoren Gesellschaft of Cannstatt, Germany, displayed a vehicle, brought to this country by William Steinway, an American piano manufacturer who had acquired the rights for the Daimler gasoline engine and who throughout the early 1890's would attempt to market this vehicle in America. A Benz was on display as well, and the directory for the exposition also listed the Ward Electrical Car Company Limited of London among the exhibitors.

Interestingly, although the exposition had obviously made no vigorous attempt to include the automobile among its prized exhibits, it had tried to attract some form of personal horseless transportation to convey visitors around the 686 acres comprising the fair grounds. At least one company and four individuals were involved. After consulting with a William Hollingsworth, a Baltimore machinist, W. T. Harris of Louisville, Kentucky, abandoned his plans for a steam-driven sightseeing bus for transporting spectators, and the two men proceeded to install a gasoline engine in the vehicle instead. It was completed and running — and a patent had been filed on its specifications — when the warehouse in which it was stored was destroyed by fire. There wasn't time to build another. Similar bad luck dogged another inventor, M. Parry of Indianapolis who had developed an improved electric storage battery to power a small vehicle. After demonstrating it before the exposition's Board of Officials, Parry received an order for 1000 electric-going chairs, but unfortunately "death of the principal figure [of the company] automatically canceled the transaction." As for Parry, his work with the self-propelled vehicle would eventually result in the famous Overland and Pathfinder automobiles. Only one three-wheeled electric roller chair actually materialized at the exposition. It was the Keller-Dagenhart. Only two were produced, and they were exhibited — in the Electrical Building, not the Hall of Machinery — rather than used as visitor conveyances. Save for a lone Sturges electric which carried passengers over the fair grounds for two years, exposition patrons had to content themselves with manually-operated wheelchairs for transport.

What is interesting, of course, is that for many years prior to the 1890's there had been hundreds of sporadic — and sometimes initially suc-

cessful — attempts to invent a self-propelled vehicle in America. Only a scattered few of these have been detailed in this work. Almost two hundred patents had been granted to inventors of road vehicles, land carriages, velocipedes, road wagons, engine-driven vehicles and self-propelled vehicles powered by electricity, steam or some form of explosive gas vapor. And there were many more built but never submitted for patent. As year passes year, they rise to the surface, records of their existence discovered among old letters, diaries, brittle and yellowed newsprint. Rarely exists a community historical file that is bereft of an account of some local mechanic's attempt to prove that he could make a machine to replace the horse. While there can be no doubting the widespread extent of this activity, there can be no doubting, too, that it most often led to ridicule, and legal ostracism, results which would certainly tend to discourage potential inventors. Without public acceptance in some measure, the American automobile simply had no place to go. The Columbian Exposition had not provided it a public forum in any sense, nor did press accounts of the event — and they were voluminous — accord it more than passing mention. Somehow the automobile was lost amid the fantastic display of machinery, the Ferris Wheel and Little Egypt.

H. H. Kohlsaat
Sponsor of the Chicago Times-Herald *contest.*

BEGINNING ANEW: 1895
THE CHICAGO TIMES-HERALD CONTEST

Fortunately at least one official of the Exposition was conscious of the omission — and disappointed by it. From even its limited exhibit and utilization at the exposition, H. H. Kohlsaat became convinced that here was a machine to replace the horse. Why, he wondered, had not the exposition promoted more vigorously by means of tempting prize money a greater exhibit of horseless vehicles. Soon he was going to remedy that oversight. And the steps he took would inalterably change the course of American automobile history.

As publisher of the *Chicago Times-Herald* newspaper, Kohlsaat was familiar with the leading publications and technical journals of this country, and a subscriber to the major newspapers of Europe. Having read in *Le Petit Journal* an account of the race they sponsored from Paris to Rouen in 1894, and aware of the Paris-Bordeaux-Paris trek to be run in mid-June of 1895, Kohlsaat became convinced that an automobile contest of some sort was just what America needed to arouse interest in the horseless carriage, and as a good businessman he decided to combine such a venture with a circulation promotion project for his own paper. To Frederick V. Adams, author of a recent book on locomotives, he assigned the task of publicity and promotion, keeping for himself the responsibility of establishing the guidelines for the contest. It was, he said, to be held "with the desire to promote, encourage, stimulate invention, development and perfection and the general adoption of the motor vehicle in the United States." His would not be a race, like the Paris-Bordeaux-Paris wherein contestants lined up in the manner of thoroughbred horses and were off at the signal, bent only on arriving first at the finish line. It was not, he added, to be supposed "that in this [Chicago] contest the question of speed is the only requisite to be considered. It would be possible for an ingenious mechanic to construct a machine with which he could easily outstrip all others in this contest and yet that device would be of no utility, the outcome of no value to the world from a practical point of view. . . . It is the earnest desire of this paper, that this contest shall add to the sum of our mechanical knowledge in this, the new branch of science of transportation."

The project was announced in the *Times-Herald* on July 9, 1895, and from that day forward the automobile began to weave itself inextricably into the American social fabric. More than a hundred inventors, Kohlsaat believed were "waiting for such an opportunity" — the clarion call of cash prizes would attract them, and a new American industry would be the result. By the end of July, fifty-two entries had been approved, and Kohlsaat predicted at least that many more by the deadline date of September 13th.

The *Times-Herald* contest has since become the most misunderstood and inaccurately reported event in the history of the American automobile, akin possibly only to the misinterpretation befalling Oliver Evans' achievement with the Amphibious Digger. It was not a race per se, and it was far more than a contest. It was a testing, an analysis and a judgment on how to produce a substitute for the horse — and an invitation to anyone who wanted to do it.

Great care was taken in the selection of the judges who were to be,

Times-Herald *entry: Kane-Pennington entered four vehicles; the two bicycles were disqualified; the Victorias ran but did not compete in the November 2nd run. These Victorias pioneered pneumatic tires in the U.S.*

Times-Herald *entry: The little Columbia perambulator was withdrawn by its sponsors after they took a look at their more powerful competition.*

Times-Herald *entry: Morrison-Sturges electric, built in 1890 and modified for the contest.*

above all, "men of great character and vision." They were: Major General Wesley Merritt, U.S. Army, Commander of the Department of Missouri, with Colonel Marshall I. Ludington as co-adjutor; Professor John P. Barrett, official city electrician of Chicago, chief of electricity at the Columbian Exposition and developer of an electric fire alarm system, among other inventions, with Leland L. Summers, editor of *Electrical Engineering*, as co-adjutor; Henry Timken, president of the National Carriage Builders' Association, a successful carriage builder and inventor of the Timken spring, with fellow carriage manufacturer C. F. Kimball as co-adjutor. J. Allan Hornsby, editor of an electric journal and one of the original founders of the soon-to-be formed American Motor League, served as secretary of the board of judges.

Since the very purpose of the event was to prove the superiority of a machine over the horse, that animal's attributes were given much attention: its responsiveness and tractability, its economy of maintenance, the unimportance of its speed in contrast to its power and docility. Again and again, these points were driven home to the judges, in Kohlsaat's words: "Consideration such as economy as to the purchase, maintenance as well as economy of operation, simplicity of control were of greater factor than speed. It was impressed upon the judges that a vehicle to attain great speed and yet be practically worthless for ordinary purposes of everyday use would not be the purpose of this paper giving away $10,000 in prizes and expenses."

Publicist Adams began a barrage of news stories announcing the contest, the number of entries, the rules, the appointment of judges, the building of special apparatus for preliminary testing and the photographing of contestants for a hoped-for widespread publication.

The rules of the contest were thirty-two in number, introduced by six paragraphs of general purposes and conditions of the preliminary trials and contest run. The judges were to carefully consider the various points of excellence and to select as prize winners those constructions which achieved the highest degree of value with regard to:

> "a) General utility, ease of control and adaptability to the various forms of work which may be demanded of a vehicle motor. In other words the construction which is in every way the most practical. b) Speed. c) Cost, which includes the original expense of the motor, and its connecting mechanisms and the probable annual item of repairs. d) The economy of operation in which shall be taken into consideration the average cost per mile of the power required at the various speeds which may be developed. e) General appearance and excellence of design. While it is desired that competing vehicles present as neat and elegant appearance as possible, it should be assumed that any skilled carriage-maker can surround a practical motor with a beautiful and even luxurious frame."

Briefly, the rules covered the following points. The contest was to be international in character. Vehicles were required to have three or more running wheels, and had to be capable of carrying at least two persons, one of whom would be an umpire selected by the judges. No vehicle would be admitted which depended in any way upon muscular exertion except for the purpose of guidance. Relay stations would be established at various points along the contest route, but contestants were to make their own arrangements for replenishing motive power. Each vehicle had to provide a trumpet, fog horn or other warning signal, as well as three lights which had to be lighted no later that 5 p.m. the day of the

contest run. Any vehicle attempting to prevent the passage of another vehicle would be disqualified, and in no case could two vehicles move along abreast of each other in a trial of speed. Further, the judges reserved the right to debar any vehicle which might "contain elements either of danger or from its construction an evidence of weakness or general impracticability."

For the purpose of possible disqualification and to inform entries of the contest rules, all contestants were required to present their vehicles for examination at a series of preliminary trials which would be held the last three days of October. Kohlsaat envisioned this preliminary testing as a reference, a basis for future estimates on performance and economy of operation of the American manufactured self-propelled vehicle which, he believed, would within a short time be marketed in large numbers for an eager public. As part of the preliminary trials, a test machine was built by the Chicago City Railway Company at the

Times-Herald *entry: The snowstorm prevented the Benton Harbor car of A. Baushke from returning to Chicago for the contest.*

direction of L. L. Summers and John Lundie. The Studebaker Carriage Company provided the warehouse for this machine. Its purpose was to measure the motor vehicle against the horse and wagon in all circumstances. It consisted of a raised platform, inclined at the rear, with a shaft containing two revolving drums and a friction brake with dynamometer for registering power consumed by the drums and the shaft. This machine measured the car as if it were on an ordinary road, calculating the load the vehicle could carry, how steep a grade it could climb, the amount of fuel it would consume and its overall power efficiency. Contestants were to be measured, weighed, examined and photographed — and therefore certified for the competition run.

Following this testing, the judges, if they so desired, were empowered to ask that a car be driven over the course — and the entrants were in any case, to be advised to familiarize themselves with the route. A time limit of thirteen hours was set to cover the course, allowing for com-

Times-Herald *entries: The Haynes-Apperson (top) and the John W. Hall & Sons car, both completed by the contest, but neither reached the starting line.*

puting corrected time taken by "prescribed and legitimate delays and unavoidable obstacles encountered en route." Any repairs had to be executed by the occupants, although umpires, along with their duties of timekeeping and rule enforcing, would be allowed to assist.

During those last three days of October allotted for it, only eight vehicles were presented to undergo the testing apparatus and the preliminary trials, at Washington Driving Park. They were: the H. Mueller-Benz/wagon, the Duryea wagon, two of the three electric vehicles produced by Morris and Salom, two Kane-Pennington Victorias and a motor tandem bicycle, and an unfinished electric wagon by the Columbia Perambulator Company.

Obviously a problem had also been presented at Washington Driving Park, and it was one with which Kohlsaat had become increasingly familiar since he established the contest. Since that first July announcement of the event, the publisher had been met daily by a line of inventors, sincere and otherwise, outside his door. Each in turn was confident that he had everything necessary to build a successful vehicle, except the money. Almost to a man they sought — some more insistently than others — his financial assistance, a loan which they would promptly repay upon winning the prize money. Still others took pen in hand for their plaints: wrote one, "If a newspaper publisher thinks it easy to build a motor vehicle in four months, then let him provide the means." That inventor's point was certainly well taken, for more than thirty of the total eighty-nine entrants also entreated Kohlsaat and the judges that they were simply not quite ready for the test. Unanimously the judges, as well as the contestants already there, recommended that the contest be postponed. This presented yet another problem for Kohlsaat. Competing papers had vigorously labelled his efforts as merely promotional, and a postponement would thus be embarrassing. Moreover, aware as he was that the Paris-Rouen race had been postponed for exactly the same reason as had presented itself in Chicago, he was nonetheless reluctant to postpone his contest for a less obvious reason. Traditionally, the Windy City would, in a few weeks, be snowbound. But finally he decided that the very reason for the contest made necessary its postponement. His decision was lambasted by some as indicative of the utter futility of the horseless-vehicle idea, but others, praised it, as, for example, a wagon builder by the name of P. E. Studebaker: ". . . None of the 75 to 100 manufacturers who sent their names in early for the race have lost heart or given up the manufacture, but they have all found that there were so many new conditions that more time is required than they expected. I congratulate the Times-Herald most heartily on the great success already achieved in attracting attention to the possibilities of the motocycle, thus concentrating the inventive faculties of the nation on this new departure."

Still Chicago had quickly become filled with spectators anxious to see these new machines in action. Adams had done his job well in promoting the "Race of the Century" — and already he had sent last-minute news stories of the event to papers throughout the country. Consequently, while Kohlsaat officially postponed the event to Thanksgiving Day, with preliminary trials set for November 25, 26 and 27, he arranged also for a consolation event to be held on November 2nd among the contestants already on hand. A prize of $500 was put

Times-Herald *entry: The Hartley Trap steamer, built by the Hartley Power Supply Company of Chicago, was one of two built in 1895 for the contest.*

Times-Herald *entry: George W. Lewis entered the second car he built* (pictured), *distinguished by the water and fuel tanks mounted as a dashboard.*

up, to be divided equally among all competitors who completed a run from Chicago to Waukegan and back within the thirteen-hour time limit. That morning thousands of spectators lined the main fifteen-mile stretch of the route between those two cities.

Competing in this consolation event was certainly not to the entrants' best interests — an accident might put them out of the running for the main event — but out of deference to Kohlsaat and the judges, those ready to run indicated their willingness to do just that. The conductors of the two Kane-Pennington Victorias agreed to demonstrate their vehicles in an exhibition over part of the course, and two of the Morris and Salom electrics would be demonstrated similarly. Electing to run the entire course were J. Frank Duryea with his brother Charles E. as passenger aboard the Duryea motor wagon; and Oscar B. Mueller, (son of Hieronymous Mueller of the H. Mueller company from Decatur, Illinois) who would be driving the Mueller-Benz carrying as passengers

Charles G. Reid and S. F. Gilmore.

The Mueller wagon was first off, followed after a brief interval by the Duryea. The latter quickly took the lead but lost it when a light chain broke, resulting in a forty-eight minute repair. On the road again and about to overtake the Mueller for a second time, Duryea happened upon a farmer and his wagon, attempted to pass but in response to the car's whistle the farmer turned suddenly to the left. Grasping the situation, Frank Duryea took to a nearby ditch to avoid a collision. It was his intention to climb out the farther side, but the deep grass was deceiving, and the car suffered a tremendous shock, damaging the steering gear and breaking the differential housing on the rear axle. Ultimately the car had to be shipped home by train. The Mueller-Benz completed the ninety-two-mile run in the corrected time of 8 hours and 40 minutes, an average of 10 miles per hour. The machine was thereafter examined by L. L. Summers and John Lundie, and a report filed.

Times-Herald entries: Max Hertel, an engineer with the American Biscuit Company, had the smallest gasoline car in the trial (above), powered by a two-cylinder engine. He would later build almost 100 cars, one of them surviving today, owned by John R. Lyman of Greenfield, Massachusetts. A. C. Ames, a South Chicago railroad man, began work on his vehicle (right), powered by two steam engines mounted on a two-bicycle chassis, on October 2, 1895, thereafter organizing the Ames Motorcycle Company with a capital of $100,000 to build cars and engines.

THE CARS OF MORRIS AND SALOM

Times-Herald entries: Henry G. Morris and Pedro G. Salom brought three electric vehicles to Chicago to demonstrate and enter in the contest trials. The partners are pictured below in their Skeleton Bat. At below right the moustachioed Morris and the bearded Salom were photographed in the second of their cars, the Crawford Wagon. Evidently this was one of the locations chosen by the official Times-Herald photographers for publicity portraits of contest entries. The car above, the Electrobat II, was ultimately chosen by the partners as their official entry in the Chicago Times-Herald contest. It was undoubtedly the most sophisticated electric car in America at the time. It weighed 1650 pounds complete, was powered by two Lundell motors and steered by two small wheels at the rear. Times-Herald testing revealed that the vehicle would have been ideal for the commuter of the day. The Electrobat was able to travel ten miles a day, twice, for one work week without a charge. If a mid-week charge was needed for extra travel, its cost was just ninety cents. The car was awarded the Times-Herald Gold Medal.

Initially, after his fateful encounter with the ditch, Charles Duryea said he didn't think the three weeks remaining were sufficient to build a new wagon. Later that evening, however, he had second thoughts; the run that day and the forthcoming Thanksgiving Day event "would be of greater influence than the awarding of any prizes and will prove the great stimulus to a new industry which will grow to enormous proportions. What we are striving for is a practical wagon, one which will go over the American roads as horses do now." Rather elated by his own prophecy, Duryea added, "we expect to have such a machine in the contest on Thanksgiving Day."

For those interested in charting dates for history-making coincidences, one might note here that George B. Selden, who in 1879 filed a patent for his horseless vehicle was finally awarded the patent on the day of the *Chicago Times-Herald* consolation race — November 2, 1895. Three days later he received official notice granting him full rights as the inventor of a gasoline automobile. But the repercussions of one seemingly innocent patent could scarcely have been imagined that November. What was being imagined was the promise of a great new industry. Interviewed by a *New York World* reporter following the *Times-Herald* consolation run, Thomas Edison was most enthusiastic. He did not see this new industry being dominated by steam power — steam vehicles, being conspicuous by their absence in Chicago. Might they not be run by electricity? "I don't think so," replied Edison, "As it looks at present it seems more likely that they will be run by a gasoline or naphtha of some kind. . . . It is only a question of a short time when the carriages and trucks of every large city will be run with motors. The expense of keeping and feeding horses in a great city like New York is very great and all this will be done away with just as the cable and trolley cars have dispersed the horses. . . . You must remember that every invention of this kind which is made adds to the general wealth by introducing a system of greater economy of force. A great invention which facilitates commerce enriches a country just as much as the discovery of vast hordes of gold."

What to call this splendid discovery was as yet unsolved. Philologists, editors and enthusiastic supporters of the cause were coming up with more than a few ideas. From England came such suggestions as autocar, automotor and petrocar. And America offered its fair share. In conjunction with the *Times-Herald* trial and contest, that paper had announced yet another contest with a prize of $500 to "some learned and ingenious person who would coin a new name" to, as they later reported, "take the place of that awkward phrase, horseless carriage." On July 25th the winner had been announced, one G. F. Shaver, the general manager of The Public Telephone Company of New York. The prize-winning entry: "motocycle." One wonders, however, how enamoured of the name was the paper's publisher Kohlsaat. There is some evidence to indicate that he was behind the launching of America's first magazine devoted exclusively to the automobile: *The Motocycle*, whose inaugural issue was published in October of 1895. Interestingly, it may have been Kohlsaat who parenthetically added another word to the full title of that magazine: Its first issue carried the legend, *The Motocycle (Automobile) Maker and Dealer*. A month later, in November, a second publication was launched also devoted exclusively to the automobile, this one in New York by E. P. Ingersoll. Its title was prophetic: It was called *The Horseless Age*.

Times-Herald entries: The M. H. Daley car (top) from Charles City, Iowa, was completed just before the contest. It weighed a mere 195 pounds. Dr. Carlos C. Booth (below) of Youngstown, Ohio, used a 3 hp W. Lee Crouch-built engine, but his car wasn't ready in time for the contest.

Times-Herald entries: De La Vergne's original entry in the contest (left) was one of four motor wagons produced by the firm in 1895. It is believed to have been at the trials, but was withdrawn as an entry at the last moment, and the company Benz (above), modified by Haas, was used instead.

*America's first magazine
devoted solely to the automobile . . .*

VOL. 1.

No. 1.

THE

Motocycle

(AUTOMOBILE)

MAKER & DEALER

CONTENTS

PUBLISHED AT CHICAGO ILL U S A

BY MOTOCYCLE PUBLISHING CO.

*Although the masthead lists only Edward E. Goff
as manager, it is believed that
H. H. Kohlsaat was involved with the magazine.*

*. . . followed one month later
by a second publication in New York.*

A MONTHLY JOURNAL

DEVOTED TO

THE INTERESTS OF THE MOTOR VEHICLE INDUSTRY.

THE

HORSELESS

AGE

VOLUME ONE.   NOVEMBER, 1895.   NUMBER ONE.

PUBLISHED BY

E. P. INGERSOLL,

157-159 WILLIAM ST., NEW YORK.

Within four months The Horseless Age *could boast
six hundred paid subscribers and
a total circulation of two thousand copies.*

AMERICAN MOTOR LEAGUE

335 DEARBORN STREET, CHICAGO.

I hereby make application for membership in **THE AMERICAN MOTOR LEAGUE**, and I agree to comply with the Constitution, By-Laws an Rules.

I enclose Two Dollars for initiation fee and one Dollar for annual dues.

Name ....

Street ....

Town .... *State* ....

EXTRACTS FROM THE CONSTITUTION.

ART. I. SEC. 2. The purposes of this Association shall be the advancement of the interests and the use of motor vehicles. This shall be done by reports and discussions of the mechanical features, by education and agitation, by directing and correcting legislation, by mutual defense of the rights of said vehicles when threatened by adverse judicial decisions, by assisting in the work of constructing better roads, better sanitary and humane conditions, and in any other proper way which will assist to hasten the use and add to the value of motor vehicles as a means of transit.

ART. 2. SEC. I. Any man or woman, eighteen years of age or over, of good moral character and respectable standing, friendly to the motor vehicle and its interests, shall be eligible to membership. and may become a member by application to the Secretary of the League.

ART. 2. SEC. I. Active members shall pay an initiation fee of $2.00 and an annual fee of $1.00, payable in advance.

Among the immediate results of the Times-Herald *contest was the formation of this organization, the first of its kind in the world.*

The Times-Herald *contest entries, as of November 2, 1895, reported as follows in* The Horseless Age:

ENTRIES.

Arnold, B. J., Chicago; Andrews, A. B., Center Point, Iowa.; Ames, D. J., Owatonna, Minn; Ames A. C., South Chicago; Bradley, Wheeler & Co, Kansas City. Mo; Bowman, E. West, Evanston, Ill.; Barrows, C. H., Willimantic. Conn.; Barcus, N., Columbus, Ohio; Brown. W. H., Cleveland, Ohio; Beck, C. W., Chicago; Chicago Fireproof Covering Co., H. C. Todd, Chicago; Chicago Carriage Motor Co, C. O. Hansen. Chicago; Cook & Gowdey, Chicago; Conklin, Oliver F., Dayton, Ohio; Carpenter, H. H., Chicago; Cross, E. D. (M. D.), Chicago; Cronholm & Stenwall, Chicago; Clapp. Henry W., Springfield, Mass; Davis Gasolene Engine Co, Waterloo, Iowa; Daley, M. H., Charles City, Iowa; De Freet. Thomas M., Indianapolis; Duryea Motor Wagon Co., Springfield, Mass.; De La Vergne Refrigerating Machine Co, New York; Flrick, George, Joliet, Ill; Elston, R. W., Charlevoix, Mich.; Feerrar. J. C. W., Lock Haven, Pa.; Gawley, T. R., Aurora, Neb; Gulford. R. W, Auburn, Ind.; Hildebrand, J. A, Chicago; Hartley Power Supply Co., Chicago; Hertel, Max, Chicago; Hill & Cummins, Chicago; Hall, John W., & Sons, Jacksonville, Ill.; Haynes & Apperson, Indiana Natural Gas Co., Kokomo, Ind.; Hagaman, J. D., Adrian, Mich.; Holmes, Lyman S., Gloversville, N. Y.; Haviland. Frank W., N. Y.; Holton, Milton E., Chicago; Flachs, W. J. H., Quincy, Ill.; Lewis, George W., Chicago; Lasher, R. E., St. Louis, Mo.; Leppo Brothers, Belleville. Ohio; Laporte Carriage Co, Laporte. Ind; Lowery, V. L. D., Eaton, Ill.; M'Donald, P. E, & Brennan, W. F., Chicago; Alliance Carriage Co, Cincinnati, Ohio; Moehn, J. N., Milwaukee; Meredith, Edwin. Batavia, Ill.; Mills, M. B, Chicago; Morris & Salom, Philadelphia; M'Arthur, A. W., Rockford, Ill.; Mueller, H., Decatur, Ill; Mills & Searls, Chicago; Maguire Power Generating Co., Chicago; Norton, Fred. G., Waukegan, Ill.; Praul, John E., Philadelphia; Pierce Engine Co., Racine, Wis.; Parks, W. J., (Ellinger & Parks), La Salle, Ill.; Patterson, William, Chicago; Pierce-Crouch Engine Co., New Brighton, Pa.; Pierce, W. A., Sistersville, W. Va.; Roberts, S. W., Chicago; Riel Import Co. (Benz motor), Chicago; Columbia Perambulator Co., Chicago; Robertson, G. W., Mount Vernon, Ind.; Radford, W. J., Oshkosh, Wis.; Strong & Gibbons, Chicago; Smith, Ira D., Pittsburg. Pa.; Stone & Maynard, Avonia, Pa.; Smith, Otis E., Hartford, Conn.; Shaver, Joseph, Milwaukee; Sturges Electric Motocycle, Co, Chicago; Schoening, C. J., Oak Park, Ill.; Sintz Gas Engine Co., Grand Rapids, Mich.; Schindler, A. J., Chicago; Templeton, John, Chicago; Thomas Kane & Co., Chicago; Taylor, Flwood E., Fitchburg, Mass.; Vanall, Frank, Vincennes, Ind.; Verret, N. J., Pine Bluff, Ark.; Woolverton, G. C., Buffalo, N. Y.; Wayne Sulkyette & Road Cart Co., Decatur, Ill.; Wilkins, Vernon H., Evanston, Ill; Booth, Carlos C., Youngstown, Ohio; Okey, Perry, Columbus, Ohio; Simons, W. A. Chicago; Tinkham Cycle Co., N. Y.; Wilson, David H. Chicago.

The Times-Herald *testing apparatus built by the Chicago City Railway Company and housed in the warehouse of the Studebaker Carriage Company. This specially-designed rig was prepared to measure the motorized vehicle against the horse-drawn wagon, as if on an ordinary road.*

The postponement of the *Chicago Times-Herald* contest did not result, as was predicted, in an additional thirty or so entries. For this reason, and, more importantly, because twelve inches of snow had fallen the previous day, there again rose a cry for a postponement. Quite rightly those entrants with heavy electric vehicles feared they could not gain traction on the frozen surface. And still others longed for an additional week or two to complete their entries. Nonetheless Kohlsaat decided, wisely, that the very purpose of the contest would suffer considerable damage — ridicule too — were the event postponed again. And so on that snowy Thanksgiving eve eleven competitors declared that they would start the race the following day. In the chill morning light of

Thanksgiving, however, only six of them were at the starting line. The Haynes and Apperson vehicle had sealed its fate earlier on the corner of Cottage Grove and 22nd Street, swerving sharply to avoid a street-car. Its forward wheel had been smashed. Another entrant. A. Baushke of Benton Harbor, and his brother, simply didn't get their vehicle to Chicago on time. Max Hertel suffered a broken steering gear, and A. C. Ames and George W. Lewis could not get their vehicles running.

And so the thousands lining the boulevards along the fifty-four mile route from Chicago to Evanston and back awaited the start. The U.S. Weather Bureau reports for this period indicate that Chicago had en-

J. Frank Duryea on the testing rack on the day after the contest run. The preliminary trials and machine tests were considered by the Times-Herald *sponsors as more important than the actual contest run. The vehicles were measured both before and after the Thanksgiving Day event.*

dured fierce winds (at 60 mph velocity) the day previous, resulting in enormous snow drifts and the extensive pulling down of telephone wires on the outskirts of Chicago. The cold had rendered inoperable numerous police alarm boxes. Race day itself (November 28th) was a bit better; temperature range was 30-39°. Six cars with drivers, passengers and umpires stood poised at Jackson Park and Midway Plaisance — two years earlier the scene of the World's Columbian Exposition — ready to brave the slippery, rutted and incredibly snowy streets of Chicago. They were: the Duryea motor wagon, Springfield, Massachusetts; the De La Vergne Benz of the De La Vergne Refrigerating Machine Company, New York City; the Electrobat II of

Morris and Salom, Philadelphia; the Mueller-Benz of H. Mueller & Co., Decatur, Illinois; a Roger-Benz of the R. H. Macy Company, New York; the Morrison-Sturges of the Sturges Electric Motor Company, Chicago.

Interestingly, there is no record as to why the Pennington Victorias did not show. Notwithstanding the controversy that has grown up around Pennington and his first American cars, there is sufficient documentation made by impartial observers that his victorias and bicycles ran and ran well. Of the consolation run entrants, obviously the Duryeas had found sufficient time to rebuild their damaged car. And the

The Duryea (above) was a participant in the November 2nd consolation run, during which it was damaged and returned to Springfield for repairs. Seated in the vehicle are Duryea investors H. W. Clapp and Erwin F. Markham. The Mueller (right), winner of the consolation run, is pictured with—from left to right—judges Colonel Marshall I. Ludington, Henry Timken and C. P. Kimball and driver Oscar B. Mueller.

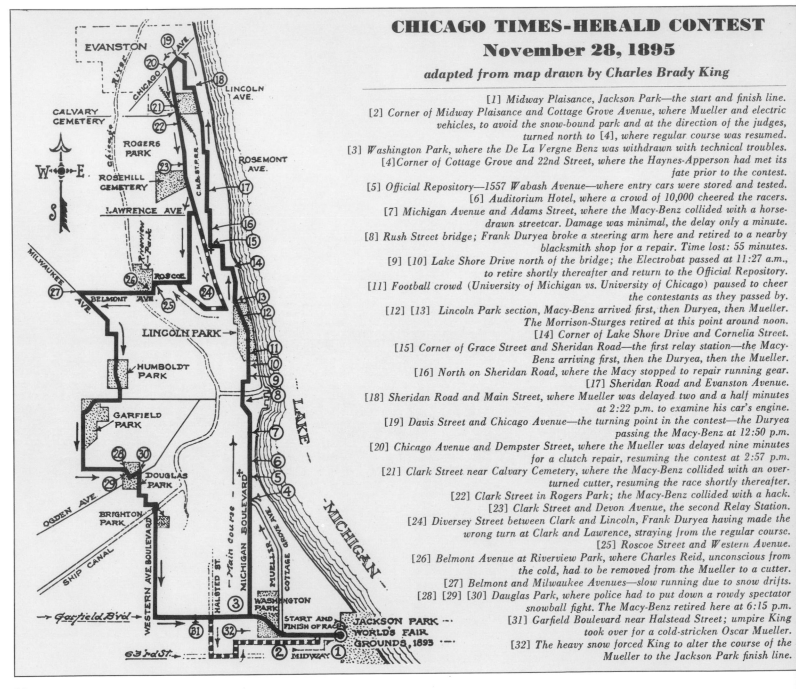

CHICAGO TIMES-HERALD CONTEST
November 28, 1895
adapted from map drawn by Charles Brady King

[1] *Midway Plaisance, Jackson Park—the start and finish line.*
[2] *Corner of Midway Plaisance and Cottage Grove Avenue, where Mueller and electric vehicles, to avoid the snow-bound park and at the direction of the judges, turned north to [4], where regular course was resumed.*
[3] *Washington Park, where the De La Vergne Benz was withdrawn with technical troubles.*
[4] *Corner of Cottage Grove and 22nd Street, where the Haynes-Apperson had met its fate prior to the contest.*
[5] *Official Repository—1557 Wabash Avenue—where entry cars were stored and tested.*
[6] *Auditorium Hotel, where a crowd of 10,000 cheered the racers.*
[7] *Michigan Avenue and Adams Street, where the Macy-Benz collided with a horse-drawn streetcar. Damage was minimal, the delay only a minute.*
[8] *Rush Street bridge; Frank Duryea broke a steering arm here and retired to a nearby blacksmith shop for a repair. Time lost: 55 minutes.*
[9] [10] *Lake Shore Drive north of the bridge; the Electrobat passed at 11:27 a.m., to retire shortly thereafter and return to the Official Repository.*
[11] *Football crowd (University of Michigan vs. University of Chicago) paused to cheer the contestants as they passed by.*
[12] [13] *Lincoln Park section, Macy-Benz arrived first, then Duryea, then Mueller. The Morrison-Sturges retired at this point around noon.*
[14] *Corner of Lake Shore Drive and Cornelia Street.*
[15] *Corner of Grace Street and Sheridan Road—the first relay station—the Macy-Benz arriving first, then the Duryea, then the Mueller.*
[16] *North on Sheridan Road, where the Macy stopped to repair running gear.*
[17] *Sheridan Road and Evanston Avenue.*
[18] *Sheridan Road and Main Street, where Mueller was delayed two and a half minutes at 2:22 p.m. to examine his car's engine.*
[19] *Davis Street and Chicago Avenue—the turning point in the contest—the Duryea passing the Macy-Benz at 12:50 p.m.*
[20] *Chicago Avenue and Dempster Street, where the Mueller was delayed nine minutes for a clutch repair, resuming the contest at 2:57 p.m.*
[21] *Clark Street near Calvary Cemetery, where the Macy-Benz collided with an overturned cutter, resuming the race shortly thereafter.*
[22] *Clark Street in Rogers Park; the Macy-Benz collided with a hack.*
[23] *Clark Street and Devon Avenue, the second Relay Station.*
[24] *Diversey Street between Clark and Lincoln, Frank Duryea having made the wrong turn at Clark and Lawrence, straying from the regular course.*
[25] *Roscoe Street and Western Avenue.*
[26] *Belmont Avenue at Riverview Park, where Charles Reid, unconscious from the cold, had to be removed from the Mueller to a cutter.*
[27] *Belmont and Milwaukee Avenues—slow running due to snow drifts.*
[28] [29] [30] *Dauglas Park, where police had to put down a rowdy spectator snowball fight. The Macy-Benz retired here at 6:15 p.m.*
[31] *Garfield Boulevard near Halstead Street; umpire King took over for a cold-stricken Oscar Mueller.*
[32] *The heavy snow forced King to alter the course of the Mueller to the Jackson Park finish line.*

Muellers rebuilt theirs in large measure as well. F. B. and Oscar Mueller had imported a Benz in April of 1895, but were not completely satisfied with its performance. For the consolation race it did run with the Benz engine, but in the weeks intervening the powerplant had been completely reconstructed along Otto principles — "a far better fashion in order to prepare it for the Times-Herald race" — with the exception of the cylinder wall. Oscar Mueller later said that had they had sufficient time they would have made a new body as well, "in order to have a completely original American invention." The following year they did just that, patented the design, and the year following they were building and selling a vehicle known as the "Mercury."

The Electrobat II was one of three electric vehicles brought to Chicago by Henry G. Morris, a mechanical engineer, and Pedro G. Salom, an

Thanksgiving Day, the Macy-Benz awaiting the start of the contest.

electrician. At the starting line the car weighed 1650 pounds complete and was powered by two Lundell Motors of 1½ hp each, attached to the front axle and pinions on the armature shaft and geared directly into the driving gears affixed to the front wheels. Steering was via two smaller wheels at the rear, Morris and Salom apparently not agreeing with the general adverse consensus with regard to rear-steered vehicles. The Electrobat could turn in a circle of twenty feet. Its tires were pneumatic cushioned, driving wheels being forty inches in diameter, steering twenty-eight inches. Batteries were furnished by the Electric Storage Battery Company of Philadelphia and gave a range of twenty-five miles at 20 mph on level ground. Unfortunately, however, the snowfall had played havoc with their plans, preventing the partners from transporting their heavy batteries, loaded the night before, on a horse-drawn wagon to the relay station. Subsequently they announced

that the Electrobat II would make only a short run to demonstrate that the electric could make sufficient headway through the six-to-eight-inch rutted snow trails that lay along the boulevard. The Electrobat ran to Lincoln Park and half way back, when its batteries expired.

As for the Macy entry, that vehicle had left New York City on November 15th, the intention being to have it driven to Chicago as part of the department store's publicity program. But the car bogged down in the bad roads and snow at Schenectady, New York, and it was shipped by rail from there to Chicago. The car had an interesting history. It was one of three Roger-Benzes brought to the United States by Emile Roger, who held the Benz license for France and who had won prizes in both the Paris-Rouen and Paris-Bordeaux-Paris races. It was Roger's intention to set up a Benz distributorship or factory in the United States. He was somewhat preempted in this regard by William Steinway who was attempting the very same thing with Daimler interests. Roger sold the three cars to Macy's, Wanamaker's and Gimbel's of New York City — those stores being interested in finding a substitute for their horse-drawn delivery wagons. Subsequently Frank A. McPherson, manager of Macy's bicycle department, had convinced the store of the publicity value of a Macy entrant in the Chicago contest — hence the R. H. Macy and Company brief fling into automobile competition.

The Sturges Electric remained basically the same vehicle as purchased from its constructor William Morrison, save for the removal of its third seat for increased battery space and the substitution of a new motor of Lundell type. The vehicle now weighed 3535 pounds loaded. Harold Sturges reported that he had been unable to complete his new electric car for the race — and hence the older vehicle was entered.

The Benz from De La Vergne was another example of a substituted entry. For some time the De La Vergne Refrigerating Machine Company had been searching for a reliable motor for securing power both for their ice-making plant and for propelling their delivery vehicles. Prior to the race they had selected the English Hornsby-Akroyd oil engine, and they had prepared four wagons using these horizontal gasoline engines built by Valentine, Lynn and Son, Carriage Builders, of Brooklyn. At least one of the vehicles was shipped to Chicago along with what is presumed to have been the personal Benz of one of the company directors. For an unexplained reason, the De La Vergne vehicle was withdrawn before the preliminary trials and the Benz substituted, although it incorporated a steering gear invented by driver Frederick C. Haas.

And so the contest began. The entrants suffered early from the cold and the deplorable condition of the roads. Driving through the deep snow severely overworked the battery of the Sturges Electric, and it was compelled to make frequent and long stops to keep its motor from burning out, as the cold air filled with the smell of ozone. By noon the vehicle was pulled off the course and the contest abandoned. The Duryea, on the other hand, made consistently good progress through the snow, a remarkable showing considering that the wagon had just a few weeks previous been severely damaged. J. Frank Duryea himself had been fearful that his car would not stand the test of snow-rutted roads for that very reason; a new vehicle already under construction had not been completed on time, and this rebuilt version of the damaged car carried an engine now over two years and a thousand miles old. Like Mueller, Duryea had wound cord around the tires of his car to increase traction through the snow. His success was underscored by Frederick Adams who had attempted to follow Duryea with a two-horse light wagon. The horses were unequal to the task. "No horse on earth could have made those fifty-four miles through the slush and mud," Adams said later, "To me this fact alone demonstrates more than anything else the great value of the horseless carriage."

The contest had begun at 8:55 in the morning, with the Duryea off first, soon to be passed by the Macy wagon which remained ahead of the Duryea by about twenty minutes. The Duryea had broken down less than ten miles from the start and forging the repair to a steering arm at a nearby blacksmith shop required about fifty-five minutes. But once back on the road, the Duryea found the going easy. Around noon the car pressed the Macy Roger-Benz for the lead. In accordance with the rules, Jerry O'Connor, the Macy driver, with Lt. Samuel Rodman as umpire, had to draw to the side at Evanston to let the faster competitor past. The Duryea was now in the lead. A few minutes later the Macy vehicle's gearing gave trouble, and the car began to drastically lose speed. Meanwhile Frederick Haas, driver of the De La Vergne Benz, with umpire James F. Bate, had had technical problems, abandoning their car at Michigan and Garfield, thereafter following the race in a horse-drawn cutter. While crossing a railroad track near Calvary Cemetery just ahead of the O'Connor car, the cutter's runner caught in a frog and the occupants were thrown upon the tracks. The Macy car smashed into the cutter, but O'Connor pressed on, only to subsequently collide with the rear wheel of a hack, chipping four spokes and bending

The lineup before the start: No. 7 is the De La Vergne Benz, No. 25 the Morrison-Sturges, No. 5 the Duryea.

The Morris and Salom Electrobat II underway to Lincoln Park.

the steering gear beyond utility. Fortunately the gauge of the vehicle was a match to the width of the streetcar tracks, and the car was steered in those tracks until it reached a relay station. An hour and twenty minutes were required for repairs.

Earlier enroute J. Frank Duryea, with umpire Arthur White, missed a turn and travelled two miles out of their way. But the Duryea still managed to keep ahead of its rivals, and when dusk had well settled, — at 7:18 p.m. — Duryea, who had been driving for eleven hours wearily drew himself out of his seat at the finish line, heartily congratulated as winner. Mumbling a few words, he exhaustedly wheeled the Duryea about and started for a garage on 16th Street.

At 8:53 p.m. the Mueller crossed the finish line second. Earlier its passenger Charles G. Reid had been overcome by the piercing cold and the fatigue of having spent most of the night previous working on the car and had to be lifted from the machine to a sleigh. Oscar Mueller and umpire Charles Brady King, an aspirant entrant-turned-umpire, continued until about an hour before the finish when Oscar collapsed over the wheel. King grasped control of the car, stopped it, wedged Mueller's limp form into the umpire's seat (in order to comply with the rule that a driver had to accompany the car until the finish), and securely gripping him with one arm, steered with the other. By the time he crossed the finish line, King, too, was almost faint from exposure.

In actual time on the road, the Mueller car was twenty-four or twenty-five minutes behind the Duryea. The Macy wagon had quit the race at 6:15 p.m. An especially excited Frederick Adams — gruffly dismissing the "scientific" value of a race like Paris-Bordeaux-Paris — summed

Above: The Duryea, after passing the Macy-Benz in Evanston, at Davis Street and Chicago Avenue. The Duryea was now leading in the contest. | *Right: The trials and contest run winner, with J. Frank Duryea at the tiller and George B. Hewitt, Duryea Motor Wagon Company president.*

The Times-Herald *Gold Medal, originally to have been awarded the trials and contest winner, was presented instead to the Electrobat for its best showing overall in the official tests.*

up the *Times-Herald* event thusly: "The progress of the preliminary trials have been watched by thousands of potential manufacturers in every part of the world and there is no doubt that there will be a great interest in the manufacture of these horseless carriages now that it has been demonstrated what can be done with them." One must excuse the overstatement. Charles Duryea's point of view regarding the effect of the *Chicago Times-Herald* event — as noted earlier — was, however, far closer to the mark. If one car could be proclaimed winner of the event, that car was, of course, the Duryea. The results brought the brother-inventors early fame, but unfortunately it would carry them as a team for only the next few years. The Duryeas won several races subsequently, and J. Frank Duryea was the first to arrive at Brighton in the famous London to Brighton run of 1896.

The awards for the *Chicago Times-Herald* event were made several days after its running, and only after re-examination of the vehicles by the judges. A full report on the preliminary tests and the run was completed the following February. It is important to note that there was no traditional scoring of prizes, no first place or second place as such. Instead the prizes were awarded in strict compliance with the rules. To the Duryea, was awarded $2000, for best performance in the road race contest, for range of speed and pull in the preliminary trials and for compactness of design. The H. Mueller and Company — the judges now omitting any Benz reference — was awarded $1500 for performance in the road race contest and overall economy of operation. Five hundred dollars was given to R. H. Macy & Company for the showing made in the road race contest, the same amount also being awarded the Sturges.

The *Times-Herald* Gold Medal — originally intended to go to the trials and contest winner — was instead presented to Morris and Salom for the best showing made in the official tests, for safety, ease of control, absence of noise, vibration, heat or odor, cleanliness and general excellence of design and workmanship. (Salom would later contend that this award was, in reality, the "first place," but this, of course, was untrue.) The committee of preliminary tests made the following awards for meritorious points of mechanical and engineering design: $200 to G. W. Lewis for a friction-driving device and brake and reduction gear for increasing speed; $150 to Haynes and Apperson for their plan to prevent vibration by balance of their two-cylinder driving engines; $100 to Max Hertel for a starting device operated from the seat of the vehicle. Evidently, the De La Vergne vehicle had been altered somewhat from the original Benz design or conceivably may have been run fitted with the Hornsby-Akroyd engine. In either case, De La Vergne received a $50 prize for a counter balance on the engine.

EPILOGUE

And so the *Chicago Times-Herald* contest passed into history. Its story has since been told and retold, but so often missing from the accounts is an analysis of its significance. The less than impressive number of starters in the contest, as compared to the number beginning the Paris-Rouen race (twenty-one) and the Paris-Bordeaux-Paris (twenty-two), has been critically regarded, but not always fairly so. One should remember that the time allowed between the announcement date of the Paris-Rouen race and—with the two postponements to encourage more entries—the race itself, was a full seven months. Seven months, too, were provided between announcement and race for the Paris-Bordeaux-Paris. But in the Chicago contest, even with the postponement, entrants had less than five months to prepare their cars. Obviously Kohlsaat would have had a more impressive starting line had he allowed more time, for it can be documented that better than one-third of the eighty-nine *Chicago Times-Herald* entrants had their cars built and running soon after the contest was held. And doubtlessly continued research will prove that many more of the *Times-Herald* entries were ultimately road-going.

But Kohlsaat, of course, had the Chicago winter to consider—and his enthusiasm for the project was such that a postponement to the spring of '96 was probably not even considered. In any case, he didn't beat the weather anyway. And that very fact should be given due consideration in any analysis of the *Times-Herald*. The Duryea's average speed (7.5 mph) was half that of the Paris-Bordeaux-Paris winner, but the latter had the amiable benefit of June weather, while the fact that the former was able to finish the course at all under those most atrocious of conditions was an achievement that, for America, promised more for the future of the horseless carriage than if the Duryea had enjoyed a fast run—it was capable of 16 mph—under ideal conditions. The purpose of the contest, after all, was to prove the automobile's superiority over the horse for transport—that it was able to demonstrate that despite the conditions carried considerable significance.

Moreover, one should not disregard the fact that the contest itself was but one part of the *Times-Herald* event. The preliminary trial and evaluation of each vehicle on the apparatus constructed for that purpose was certainly the most practical scientific testing to which the automobile had thus far been put. And if one must excuse the exuberance with which publicist Adams, with considerable nationalistic fervor, viewed the results of those tests, one must agree too with that eminent historian Gerald Rose who in 1909, regretting the absence of such tests in the earliest Paris races, commented, "The *Times-Herald* results constitute by far the most valuable record of the old cars which we now have."

But most important to America—quite beyond the testing and the contest—was what the *Times-Herald* accomplished in bringing together for the first time in one place this country's early automobile pioneers, many of whom attended the event even though they had not at that time built their first car. The event prompted Charles Brady King, in a letter to the *Times-Herald* in October, to propose the formation of the American Motor League, the first such organization of its kind in the world. The League held its first meeting in Chicago on November 1, 1895, and adopted its constitution. Section two of that constitution bears repeating:

"Sec. 2.—The purpose of this association shall be advancement of the interests and the use of motor vehicles. This shall be done by reports and discussions of the mechanical features, by education and agitation, by directing and correcting legislation, by mutual defense of the rights of said vehicles when threatened by adverse judicial decisions, by assisting in the work of constructing better roads, better sanitary and humane conditions, and in any other proper way which will assist to hasten the use and add to the value of motor vehicles as a means of transit."

Here at last was an organization dedicated to overcoming all the varied reasons which had delayed the automobile's acceptance in America: the incredible lack of good roads which had for so long made railroad travel seem the most practical mode of land transport in this country, the legislative and judicial strictures which had hampered inventors from the time of Oliver Evans, and finally the education of the public to accept the motor vehicle as a viable form of transportation.

The motor vehicle would soon be reaching a wider audience than ever before. The *Times-Herald* contest was unquestionably the stimulus. Soon after its running a widespread demand arose for special automobile shows, and a promotion began for a series of Motor Vehicle Days at county fairs throughout the country. The Barnum & Bailey circus bought a Duryea; not to be outdone the Franklin Brothers circus later bought a car built by Charles Brady King. Of more practical value certainly was the travelling exhibit sponsored by the mail order house of Montgomery Ward, who in 1896 purchased a phaeton from the American Electric Vehicle Company of Chicago and demonstrated it in small towns throughout America. And in 1896, too, William Jennings Bryan conducted his presidential campaign throughout southern Illinois aboard the Mueller wagon. Meanwhile in Washington Postmaster General Neilson let out competitive bids for "horseless carriage postal delivery wagons."

The *Chicago Times-Herald* event had not been universally applauded, of course. Competing papers in Chicago were offhandedly critical, press jealousy in those days being quite blatant. But elsewhere the contest was viewed as an enormous success. The *New York World* proclaimed that even "cautious and conservative journals for the general reader" were now convinced of the impending doom of the horse. From the Philadelphia press came word that the automobile would "drive down the price of horseflesh." And generally it was believed that the Chicago contest had advanced the automotive art in this country by no less than five years—and also saved America untold millions of dollars in royalties which would have been paid to foreign inventors and builders had not the race spurred American pioneers to redouble their automotive efforts. And there can be no doubt that the contest did inspire a good many soon-to-be manufacturers. In later years Alexander Winton, Henry Ford and R. E. Olds among others alluded to the stimulating effect the *Times-Herald* results had on their work.

There were still problems to be resolved—for one, the automobile's motive force, a question not to be answered until after the turn of the century in this country. (In 1900 gasoline cars were but twenty-two percent of the market, steam and electrics sharing the remaining preponderance.) But an industry was beginning. A scant three years after the contest more than 200 companies, capitalized at a total of $500,000,000, had been organized for the manufacture of motorcars—and quickly thereafter grew an almost equal number of suppliers and a system of ancillary support manufacturers. One might logically ask if all this would have happened so quickly without that snowy November in Chicago. And the question, perhaps, answers itself. If any single event can be pointed to as the catalyst leading to the ultimate acceptance of the automobile in America and the impetus for the beginning of a new industry, that event would have to be the *Chicago Times-Herald* contest. Mr. Kohlsaat really started something.

II

THE NEIGHBORING INDUSTRY

Growth of the Motorcar in Canada

BY HERMAN L. SMITH

The automobile in Canada really grew up with the country itself. After the colorful three and a half centuries that succeeded John Cabot's reaching its shores in 1497, followed by Jacques Cartier in 1534, and the ensuing French and English quarrels over what belonged to whom and who should rule and why — the matter was ultimately settled. In July of 1867 the provinces of Upper and Lower Canada, Nova Scotia and New Brunswick were united for administration as the Dominion of Canada. Two months later a jeweler in Stanstead, Quebec, demonstrated a steam buggy he designed and built at the local Stanstead Fair. One need scarcely mention which was the bigger news story of the year.

Actually even Stanstead was relatively unimpressed with Henry Seth Taylor's efforts, for although his steam buggy had been seven years in the making, its debut was rather inauspicious — it broke down mid-demonstration, "contretemps detracting somewhat from the interest of the occasion," so the local paper said. Yet the vehicle's flawless performance at the following year's fair drew only faint praise — and about as much newspaper space as the performance of a four-legged trotter named Canwell. Undaunted, Taylor continued to test his machine, until a hill just outside Stanstead brought that to an end. Taylor had never considered brakes for his vehicle, and after a disastrous down-hill dash, he picked up the pieces and put them in the loft of his barn. So much for Canada's first horseless carriage.

There is, of course, always some danger in attributing any "first"— history very frequently comes up with another earlier one. Indeed the year before Taylor's first demonstration, Father Georges Belcourt, a parish priest on Prince Edward Island, demonstrated a single-seater steam wagon in Rustico, although indications are that it was a complete vehicle brought in from the United States. It might thus qualify as Canada's first imported car, but it cannot be called a Canadian automobile. There is, however, always the problem of definition in Canadian car history. Just what is a Canadian car? — a question not easily answered in light of the U.S. proximity and influence in Canadian design, of which more anon. In any case, Henry Seth Taylor's marvelous little machine is the oldest known surviving Canadian automobile, owned now by Richard M. Stewart and beautifully restored. This historic Canadian vehicle is currently on display at the Ontario Science Centre in Toronto.

Scores of other Canadians would follow Henry Seth Taylor's lead. And it should be noted here that mention of them all — every Canadian who took tools in hand to create an automobile or who gathered sufficient capital to have a go at automotive production — would not be possible, even practical, within the limitations of this history. What follows is an overview — a look at the Canadian automobile through the years, with as many specific examples provided as possible to indicate the scope of and the trends in Canadian automobile history.

Henry Seth Taylor Steam Buggy, September, 1867.

Dickson Carriage Works electric, 1893. (o)

George F. Foss one-cylinder gasoline car, 1897.

The fever of indifference to which Henry Seth Taylor's invention had aroused Canadians was followed by several decades of apathy and outright hostility toward the horseless carriage. Such an attitude was scarcely confined to Canada, of course; there were few people anywhere anxious to accept the coming reality of the automobile. Yet the indomitable spirit of the inventor survived — and Canada produced its fair share of those farsighted enough to try the untried, though no doubt more than a few were dissuaded, as was John Basil Kelly of Blyth, Ontario. The steam buggy he built in 1884 was soon dismantled, probably with the encouragement of the good people of Blyth who had tired rather quickly of having their horses jump fences at the sight and sound of it.

But the automotive idea wasn't to be dashed — and as the years moved toward and into the new century, the rolls of Canadian inventors and tinkerers toiling away in sheds and stables throughout the Dominion grew. And new ideas about the automobile's motive force were being tested on what passed for roads in those pioneering days of Canadian motor history. All this was largely individual effort. Though many were probably aware of such technological progress as had been and was being made in the industrial world, the lack of rapid communication hampered an effective exchange of ideas — and the result was largely a host of one-of-a-kind cars. As for the possibility of manufacture, this was often a dream from which the inventor quickly awakened, once he

set out to find a likely investor. There weren't many around willing to gamble on as unlikely a commodity as an automobile — and a lot of them were quite right. Many of those early cars were simply not very well built. But the fact that they were being built at all remains important in the context of Canadian automotive history. Moreover a few are deserving of more than a little admiration by hindsight.

So successful, for example, was the 1893 electric car built in Ontario by Dickson's Carriage Works that it faithfully served its owner Frederick Barnard Featherstonhaugh for a meritorious fifteen years before it was honorably retired. In Sherbrooke, Quebec, George F. Foss drove the one-cylinder gasoline car he built in 1897 for four years despite threats of arrest from city officials. As legend has it, he decided finally to sell it in 1902, but the potential customer was one-legged, and when the car backfired, knocked him down and took a gouge out of his artificial limb, he changed his mind about the whole thing. The car eventually found another customer. Sadly, neither this car nor Featherstonhaugh's faithful electric survive; conceivably they both might have worn themselves out. The same might have been the case with the two vehicles produced in Sarnia, Ontario, by stove manufacturer Thomas Doherty. The first, built in 1895, was powered by a coil spring on the rear axle, the second (1901) by a conventional two-cylinder gasoline engine — which was no doubt the more successful is obvious, but neither survive.

Foss driving through streets of Sherbrooke, Quebec, despite official protest, 1897.

Gasoline motor by Doherty Co. of Sarnia, Ontario, 1903. (1)

Still, circa 1900.

Another unusual little car, the Redpath Messenger built by Alfred Robinson in Toronto, sported a wooden body and a one-cylinder engine which was partly air cooled and partly water-cooled. Conceivably several of these may have been built, although this cannot be verified; one does survive in the Chamber of Commerce Museum in Oshawa, Ontario. Certain, however, is the fact that only one steam buggy was built by Benton Neff in 1899. In what is now Port Colborne, Ontario, the former steamboat engine builder constructed the Neff Steam Buggy which rests today in Laguna Beach, California, owned and restored by Nelson Holmwood. One of the two Victorian gasoline buggies — named after the good English Queen — built in Nova Scotia around 1896 survives as well, displayed in the antique car museum in Niagara Falls.

Fittingly, the turn of the century saw a concomitant turn in Canadian automotive history as well. No longer was the idea of actual manufacture of automobiles in Canada wishful thinking. Though there were still the one-of-a-kind enthusiasts, such as D. A. Maxwell of Watford, Ontario, who built a gasoline buggy in 1900 for his own use — and obviously did rather well at it, since the car, appropriately named the Maxmobile, ran for twenty-four years — there now appeared on the scene the budding entrepreneurs. Such were the Good brothers (Nelson and Milton) of Kitchener, Ontario, who had come up with a runabout called the LeRoy around 1899 and later a little helpful advice from Detroit's Ransom E. Olds, a budding manufacturer himself, and the result was about thirty LeRoy automobiles (one of which may be seen at the Doon Pioneer Village, Ontario, just outside the Kitchener city limits where it all began.) The fact that the manufacturing phase of this enterprise lasted just two years (1901-1902) is indicative of two realities that were even then making themselves felt in the Canadian motor industry: the limited scope of the Canadian home market and the press of U.S. competition.

But such realities were, happily, ignored by a host of eager would-be manufacturers, and the result was a colorful era in Canadian motor history in which many tried, few succeeded, but all added to the exuberance of those borning years of the automobile industry. This same drama was, of course, being performed in all countries ready to accept the reality of the automobile. In Canada it produced such enterprises as Canadian Motors Limited who in 1900 apparently took over the premises of the Still Motor Company Ltd. in Toronto for the manufacture of electric vehicles to order, including a three-wheeled Motette and a bus charmingly called the Tallyho. They lasted about three years.

A. M. Thompson, later of Dominion Automobile Company, and his niece aboard a 1900 Motette. (o)

The 1905 Gray. (x)   The 1907 Chatham. (1)

Others were equally short-lived. The Queen City Cycle and Motor Works of Toronto, for example, builders of the Queen gasoline buggy, could boast of an annual production in no better than the two-figure range in 1901. They didn't try anymore after 1903. Still initial efforts, though failures, could be instructive in later years. Surely the Canada Cycle and Motor Company benefited from the experience of having produced their electric Ivanhoe in 1903, when later they became the builders of the Russell motorcar.

More significant, however, as far as history is concerned, was the decision made in 1904 by Gordon M. McGregor, president of the Walkerville (Ontario) Wagon Company. That he concluded his future lay with the nascent automobile industry rather than with his successful wagon business was not all that extraordinary. But how he decided to go about changing over proved certainly propitious. He looked across the river to Detroit and decided to associate himself with a maverick manufacturer named Henry Ford. McGregor, recognizing a comer when he saw one, secured a franchise to build Ford products in Canada and for Canada and the British Commonwealth of Nations. (Originally Great Britain and Ireland were included as well, but in 1907 McGregor relinquished these.) Under the terms of his agreement with Ford, McGregor was to form a company, finance it, operate it and give, in exchange for the franchise and design and engineering assistance — fifty-one percent of the Canadian company stock to the U.S. company, which in turn apportioned the stock to its existing stockholders. This agreement resulted in the incorporation of the Ford Motor Company of Canada Ltd. on August 17, 1904, with production commencing in the Walkerville Wagon Company factory on October 10th that same year.

The 1903 Ivanhoe roadster. (1)

100

The 1915 Gray Dort touring. (x)

The 1917 Gray Dort Cloverleaf roadster. (x)

The 1920 Gray Dort touring. (x)

The 1917 Gray Dort touring. (x)

The 1921 Gray Dort sedan. (x)

By the end of 1904 approximately twenty-five Model C Fords had been completed by the new company, one of which (considered to be the twenty-first of that series) is now in the collection of the author. Production moved slowly, the Model B was added to the line. The end of the company's first fiscal year (August 31, 1905) found production totalling 117 units. By 1908 the company still hadn't broken the 500 unit mark. Then came the Model T. And, if it be a rather heretical paraphrase, what was good for Ford was good for Canada. The Model T was as significant a factor in the social history of the Dominion as it was in the United States.

In those early days much of what went into the Canadian Fords was built in the U.S., the chassis (less wheels) being shipped across the river from Detroit and fitted with Canadian-made wheels and bodies by William Gray & Sons of Chatham, future builders of the Gray-Dort. As time progressed, more and more parts were built in Canada, until today, under the terms of the Canada-U.S. automotive trade pact, completed cars are built in Canada and shipped to the U.S.A.

Obviously back in 1904 Gordon McGregor knew exactly what he was doing, and those years produced yet another gentleman who seemed to do everything right: Robert Samuel McLaughlin — the grand old man of the Canadian motor industry. His father had started the McLaughlins down the prosperous road in the Nineteenth Century when he built himself a sleigh which so impressed a neighbor that he was asked for a duplicate, which good fortune ultimately led to the establishment of the McLaughlin Carriage Company — and con-

The 1908 McLaughlin-Buick
'five-passenger touring. (D)

McLaughlin-Buick advertisement
appearing in 1908. (I)

The 1908 Glover with unsuccessful fifth wheel traction-assist.

siderable financial success by the 1880's. As the century turned, two of McLaughlin's sons, George and Robert Samuel, were taken into partnership in the firm. And soon thereafter the younger, Robert Samuel, latched on to the automotive idea. By 1906 he had made various trips to the United States, looked at and tested a number of American cars, including a two-cylinder Buick which was being manufactured by a friend of his named William C. Durant. Ultimately, however, he decided that an all-Canadian car was for him, and he hired an engineer from Milwaukee to design it. Had not that engineer suddenly been taken ill, the McLaughlin story might have ended quite differently. But when pneumonia threatened to dash all the McLaughlin hopes for automotive manufacture, Durant came to the rescue, and he brought with him a fifteen-year contract for the McLaughlins to buy Buick engines and other parts. Shortly thereafter Durant himself went on a buying spree — of companies (Oakland, Cadillac, Oldsmobile) and brought them all together with Buick under one name: General Motors. Robert Samuel McLaughlin was made a director of this new company.

With the Buick motor and their own coachwork, McLaughlin Carriage Company embarked upon the production of automobiles in 1908, producing two hundred that year, one of which is on display at the Chamber of Commerce Museum in Oshawa. (Through the years the cars would be variously known as McLaughlin, McLaughlin-Buick and Buick.) By 1914 production had neared the two thousand mark. Meanwhile Durant, having troubles with his General Motors, was forced to relinquish his management of that corporation, which he did, only to start up another enterprise with a fellow named Louis Chevrolet. McLaughlin got in on that one too, selling their carriage business — which McLaughlin wisely felt was dying anyway — to J. B. Tudhope and taking on Canadian production of the Chevrolet motorcar. In 1918, by which time Chevrolet had joined the General Motors family with William C. Durant tentatively and rather tenuously back at the helm,

The 1909 Tudhope-McIntyre Model 109 autowagon. (U)

General Motors made McLaughlin an offer to sell. It was accepted. The company was now part of the vast General Motors organization. The terms of the sale, however, stipulated that the McLaughlins remain to operate the company. George McLaughlin retired in 1924, but his brother stayed as president of the company, and until 1967 was a director of General Motors Corporation. In that year, at the age of ninety-six, Robert Samuel McLaughlin decided to retire.

The McGregor and McLaughlin approach to Canadian manufacturing — a cooperative effort with the U.S. industry — was but one avenue explored in those days prior to World War I. That it would ultimately be the most successfully traveled road was perhaps even then somewhat evident — but that didn't curtail efforts in other directions. Between 1906 and 1908 the Comet Motor Company of Montreal came up with a car that was part Italian (engine), part French (rear axle), part German (front axle), part U.S. (radiator) — and clothed the result with Quebec-ian canvas-covered wooden coachwork.

But the honors for the most unusual Canadian car of this period must be laid elsewhere. Consider, instead, the Galt. That name was first applied to a conventional automobile built by Canadian Motors Ltd. This Galt, Ontario, company had begun in business in 1911, and was out of it by 1912. Then their remaining parts were sold to the Galt Motor Company in the same city. Aware of the failure attending the production of a conventional car by their predecessors, this new company decided that the unconventional might just be the answer. Accordingly, they obtained a patent for a gas-electric car and, literally, charged forward. The result was an automobile whose two-cylinder gasoline engine charged batteries which in turn operated an electric motor. The advantage of this was that should a Galt driver find himself out of gasoline, the batteries would provide him enough charge to run the car another ten or fifteen miles by which time he would hopefully have arrived at a gas station! This did not prove to be the overwhelming sales

point the company had anticipated, however — indeed perhaps only two of these cars were ever built. In any case, after 1915 Galts — whatever their motive persuasion — were no more.

This period spawned many more native Canadian efforts — the Tate Electric in Windsor, Ontario, the Peck Electric in Toronto, the Oxford in Montreal, the Bartlett in Toronto, among many others. Several companies tried cycle cars as well, but this type of automobile proved as unsuitable to Canadian road and climatic conditions as it did to those of its neighbor to the south.

The 1912 Oxford Wagon.

More noteworthy of the Canadian automotive efforts of these years were those embarked upon by the Canada Cycle and Motor Company Ltd. In 1905 they began Russell motorcar production. The earliest Russells sported a good many interesting features: throttle, spark and gearshift being steering-column-operated, the inclusion of two kerosene lights and an adjustable water-carbide driving light, for example. The handbrake was a novelty too; when pulled on, it automatically disengaged the transmission. A very interesting car, all considered. But it was the later Russell that was really the standout. In 1909 the company was granted exclusive Canadian rights to the U.S. Knight sleeve valve engine design, and thereafter they set about producing four- and later six-cylinder Russell-Knights of extremely high quality. Their slogan —"Made Up to a Standard — Not Down to a Price"— was the same as that used by the Chadwick, a preeminent marque in U.S. history. The company was enormously successful in the ensuing years, and enjoyed expansive and modern manufacturing facilities. The outbreak of World War I, however, found their fortunes waning. Military production gave them a reprieve. Their truck designs would serve as a basis for early armoured vehicles used in the war, and Russell cars themselves would be used by Canadian troops overseas as would other Canadian vehicles, particularly Ford Model T ambulances with special bodies assembled in France. Known as the "galloping" or "jumping" bedsteads, these ambulances became a lucrative offshoot of the Ford T passenger-car line. Canada Cycle and Motor Company Ltd., on the other hand, was so heavily into military production after 1915 that they ostensibly closed down the passenger-car side of their business. It would never be reopened. The Russell plant was soon thereafter purchased by Willys-Overland who began producing their own cars there.

Whether World War I played any part in the decision of the Tudhope Motor Car Company to forego automotive manufacture is not known. The Tudhope story is an especially interesting one in Canadian history. Builders of horse-drawn carriages in Orillia, Ontario, since the 1860's, the company decided to motorize some of their products in 1906 — and like many wagon and carriage builders they concluded initially to do it as inconspicuously as possible. Thus they travelled the high wheeler road — a high wheeler, after all, would not be viewed with undue alarm by their horse-enamoured clientele. Consequently the first Tudhope automobiles looked rather like the Tudhope carriages of old, save for their carefully hidden U.S.-built McIntyre engines. These high wheelers were called Tudhope-McIntyres, incidentally, and they did enjoy a modicum of success. In 1909 when fire destroyed their plant, however, the Tudhope company had second thoughts. They rebuilt quickly and just as quickly made plans for an altogether different automobile. This one was based on the U.S. Everitt, a medium-priced four-cylinder car, and it was quite successful. Indeed the Tudhope company was so sure of their product that they affixed a two-year guarantee to every one of their cars sold! After the Everitt company went out of business in Detroit, Tudhope continued producing cars based on the U.S. design, although considerably refined and updated. They also upgraded the four-cylinder engine, and came up with a new forty-eight horsepower six. Tudhope automotive history becomes a bit obscure around 1913. Late in that year, for some reason, there was a name change to Fisher Motor Company, and by year's end it would appear that Tudhope, who advertised their product as "The Car Ahead," found their motorcar experience now behind them. The war years put the Tudhope Carriage Company completely into military production, but upon emerging from that they entertained no further thoughts about automobile manufacture.

The Tudhope and Russell experiences were, no doubt, among the more well-grounded and potentially enduring Canadian automotive efforts of those years. But we should not pass over this pre-World War I era without mention of some of the others who found less good fortune. A rather fast entry and exit from the automotive industry was experienced by the Chatham Motor Car Company (Chatham, Ontario) who produced a number of cars with bodies by William Gray & Sons and air cooled motors built by Milton O. Reeves of Columbus, Ohio. They lasted from 1907 to 1908. Others shared similar experiences, and not a few of these were Americans who decided to seek their fortunes across the border. In 1910 Frederick Sager of Detroit traveled to Welland, Ontario, with a bit of gall, an impressive-sounding company name of United Motors Ltd., and plans for the manufacture of cars (bearing either his name or that of his newly-adopted town) with a projected production of 300 cars for 1911 — all of which, he said, had already been sold! How many cars, if any, were actually produced is not known. Suffice to say that anyone owning a Sager or a Welland today indeed has a rare car.

More substantial were the efforts of Henry Nyberg, who had built the Nyberg car in Indiana from 1912 to 1914 and who moved to Kitchener, Ontario, in that latter year to manufacture the Regal (resembling the Detroit car of that name) for a few years thereafter, until production was turned over to Dominion truck manufacture in 1917. There had

The Car You See Running

THE
RUSSELL

The Russell as it appeared in Canadian Magazine Advertiser, *July 1906.* (1)

Russell cars at Ontario City Hall, with T. A. Russell on first car at left. (0)

*The 1912 McKay roadster
built by Jack and Don McKay of the
Nova Scotia Carriage and Motor Car Company. (I)*

The 1914 Canadian Standard touring. (I)

previously been another Regal car in Canada, built in Walkerville about 1910 and billed as the "Car That Satisfied," though apparently it didn't, because it survived but one year.

The Windsor-Walkerville area, incidentally, seemed to be becoming the Detroit of Canada in those days — logically, because of its just-across-the-river proximity. In Walkerville in 1910 Dominion Motors was incorporated to manufacture a car based on the U.S. Windsor. Meanwhile in Windsor the U.S. Hupp Motor Car Company started production of their own car.

In 1911 the Harding Machine Company of London, Ontario, set up business to produce a small car resembling the Hupmobile. That same year in Kentville, Nova Scotia, two brothers — Jack and Don McKay — established the Nova Scotia Carriage Company (later moved to Amherst under the name Nova Scotia Carriage and Motor Car Company) and brought out the McKay, their version of the Pittsburgh, Pennsylvania-built Penn motorcar. Ironically, the adaptation enjoyed a year's more success than the original. The Penn quit the scene in 1913, the McKay in 1914. Between 1911 and 1913 the Brockville Atlas, initially inspired by the Tudhope and utilizing predominantly U.S.-built components, was produced in Brockville, Ontario, production totalling about 125 cars. One of the last of the series, a 1913 tourer, is currently on display at the Antique Auto Museum in Oshawa. And, too, a McKay is now undergoing restoration by an enthusiastic group of Halifax Antique Car Club members.

Canada was no different than any other automotive nation in those years, at least in so far as rapid attrition was concerned. Companies throughout the world frequently opened and closed in not much more time than it took to design the office stationery. The First World War played its part, of course, in cutting off supplies to Canadian automotive manufacturers. But there was another factor as well. The fortunes of a Canadian company often rose and fell with the fortunes of the U.S.-based company that backed or nurtured or merely supplied it.

The saddest example of this, of course, was the Gray-Dort, built by Gray-Dort Motors Ltd., Chatham, Ontario. It was one of the most popular automobiles ever built in Canada and is one of the most fondly remembered today. The enterprise grew out of the fine carriage and coachbuilding house of William Gray & Sons, whose history dated back to the 1850's. In 1905 William Gray, grandson and namesake of the company's founder, had built his own car, and soon thereafter had convinced his father Robert of the advantages of this new mode of transport. The company proceeded slowly at first into this new field, slowly but most successfully. Prior to the First World War they had become dealers for several American makes in Chatham, had made automobile bodies — as we've seen — for a number of other Canadian manufacturers and also held the distinction of operating the first curbside gasoline pump in their native city! Both father and son had for some time been exploring the ultimate plunge into the automobile field when in 1915 they found a kindred spirit in Josiah Dallas Dort of Flint, Michigan, himself a carriage builder of many years and now a budding automobile manufacturer. A deal was done, and in late 1915 the first Gray-Dorts were put onto Canadian roads. These first cars were almost entirely American-built, but by 1916 the changeover had been made to Canadian components. And it wasn't long thereafter that the Canadian offspring overtook its American parent. The U.S. Dort never approached the success the Gray-Dort enjoyed in Canada. And that success was due in no small measure to the quality and distinctive coachwork the Grays put into their cars. Most Gray-Dorts were, of course, similar to the American versions. But a special de luxe sports version put into production in Canada at the close of World War I is worthy of special note. So successful was it that no fewer than 200 of them were imported into the United States! In 1921 Gray-Dort enjoyed their best year ever, selling 8000 cars. "That year," William Gray was to later remember, "there wasn't a cloud in the sky." One appeared three years later, and it was forbidding. Josiah Dort in Flint had decided to give up automobile manufacture. Soon thereafter, following a try at affiliation with some other U.S. companies, Gray-Dort went under as well. Between 1915 and 1924 some 26,000 Gray-Dorts had been built. Nine years was certainly too short a life for this fine Canadian car.

The war years had seen a number of other firms rise, only to go under before the first roar of the Twenties. The Saskatchewan-built Moose Jaw Standard, certainly an interesting car to have if only for its marvelous name, is an example. So, too, the Crow, built by the Canadian Crow Motor Company in Mount Brydges, Ontario, under license from the Indiana Crow-Elkhart organization. Ontario's Barrie Carriage Company, an established carriage builder since 1903, tried to make it with Lycoming-engined touring cars and roadsters under the trade name of Bell, but they, too, lasted less than half a decade.

Yet, for every automobile manufacturer that went down during the Teens, another one popped up in the Twenties — only to suffer a fate similar to their precursors. In Montreal, the Forster Motor Manufacturing Company tried with the English-styled Forster, the Parker Motor Company Ltd. with a car using a Red Seal Continental engine, the

The Canadian is a Distinctive and "Smart" Car in Appearance and Performance.

The Canadian—a Distinctive Six
Has Flexible Front Axle and Good Units Throughout.

The Canadian of 1922
was designed by Earl G. Gunn
and built in Walkerville by Colonial Motors Limited.
This illustration accompanied a "rave review"
of the car in the Canadian Motorist, *February, 1922.* (o)

134-INCH WHEELBASE

The 1914 Maritime Singer five-passenger touring, from Canadian Motorist. (1)

107

Brooks steam cars rolling off the production line at Stratford, Ontario, 1926. (1)

United Iron Works Company with a car using a Hudson chassis. Lavoie Automotive Devices Ltd. came up with a most interesting car in 1923 — only to go down with it in the same year. H. E. Bourassa, a talented mechanic who had built his first car in 1899, followed by other one-of-a-kinds built to order, had plans for the marketing of an automobile using a Rickenbacker chassis. A prototype Bourassa Six was built in 1926, but lack of capital to finance it stopped the project right there. And whether the interesting Wright Flexible Axle touring car ever passed beyond its 1929 prototype stage is not known. More than likely it did not.

Meanwhile, in Ontario, the situation was much the same. The London Six, produced of U.S. components by London Motors Ltd., survived but a half decade. Windsor's Colonial Motors, incorporated in 1921 to produce an all-Canadian car called, logically, the Canadian did not survive the prototype. In 1921, too, the Anglo American Motors Ltd. of Toronto exhibited an interesting proposition at the Canadian National Exhibition: the La Marne, designed and engineered in France and sporting an eight-cylinder Hispano-Suiza engine, but here again the project died aborning.

In Lachine, Quebec, the Canadian Automobile Corporation organized in 1921 named their car the Mercury, aptly too, since it was the fleet-wheeled bearer of bad news. The company didn't survive into 1922. Lasting a bit longer, in Manitoba, was Winnipeg Motor Cars Ltd. who produced the Winnipeg ("As Good as the Wheat") from 1920 to 1923. It sported a Herschell-Spillman engine. In 1924 in Kingston, Ontario, Davis Dry Dock Ltd. put together a Locomobile-lookalike they called the Davis. (Only one was built.) That same year in Saskatchewan, Derby Motor Cars Ltd. built a car resembling the Indiana-built Davis that they called a Derby. In retrospect it all becomes a bit confusing.

Interestingly, though the Twenties generally saw the demise of the steam car on both sides of the border, Canada produced quite a nice one from 1924 to 1927: the Brooks in Stratford, Ontario. Owing some of its design concepts to the famous Stanley, it was an attractive, well-built car, with a price tag of almost $4000. A limited number were built, and when financial difficulties weighed too heavy to continue, the cars remaining were sold for as little as $250 each at the time of liquidation. A few of these cars remain extant.

If the history of the Canadian automobile industry is largely dominated by tales of those who tried and failed, it is likewise overwhelmed by the admittedly rare success stories. The McGregor and McLaughlin experiences were obviously telling. Of all those who tried to make it in the Canadian industry those to survive for any sustained length of time were either directly owned by U.S. companies or operated under franchise of U.S. manufacturers. And their longevity was dictated for the most part by the fortunes of the parent company. William C. Durant's efforts to build cars in Canada — outside, of course, the General Motors companies — proved fruitless. On the other hand, Dodge had begun manufacture in Walkerville in 1924 — and out of this, and related parent companies, was born today's Chrysler of Canada. Nash and Hudson, assembled in Canada since the Thirties, have since become American Motors. Canada's Studebaker survived a while after the death of its U.S. parent, but it now is no longer.

The McLaughlin-Buick convertible limousine, custom built in Oshawa for the Royal Visit of 1939. Two identical models were built by hand, with convertible tops replacing the standard metal roofs of two Series 90 "Limited" limousines. Both cars were finished in Royal Maroon. This example, the only known survivor, is owned by Mr. Lawrence Norton of Oshawa, Ontario. (x)

The 1947 Pontiac Fleetleader Special. (z)

TOP:
1946 Monarch. (z)

LEFT ABOVE:
1950 Meteor Custom. (z)

LEFT BELOW:
1960 Frontenac. (z)

RIGHT ABOVE:
1956 Meteor Rideau Crown Victoria. (z)

RIGHT BELOW:
1959 Monarch Lucerne. (z)

This alliance with the U.S. industry was but a natural result of a number of factors, to which we have already alluded. Canada's population being about one-tenth that of the United States, its potential automobile market was proportional. Design, engineering and tooling costs became progressively prohibitive for the relatively small producer. By using facilities from the U.S. where costs could be amortized over larger production, Canadian manufacturing costs could be kept on a reasonable, profit-making level. It was all quite simple. What stood in the way of a wholly native Canadian automobile industry was reality.

But Canada's industry, as it has evolved, is most prosperous. There can be no doubt about that at all. And recent years have seen it branch out too, into a new market with Canadian assembly of the European Renault and Volvo and the Japanese Isuzu and Toyota. Success is, after all, the name of the game — and the Canadian industry has played it well. To those scores who tried and failed, one can but offer a salute — without their efforts the successful might not have been tempted to try at all. They've provided a rich chapter in Canadian industrial history.

LEFT ABOVE:
1959 Dodge Viscount. (z)

RIGHT ABOVE:
1966 Beaumont Custom. (z)

BELOW:
1971 Manic GT, Manic Motors, Granby, Quebec. (w)

III

THE RACE TO PRODUCE

BY JAN P. NORBYE

The race to produce — to build the most cars within a twelve-month period — has always been an American phenomenon. This contest has no starting grid, no pits, no finishing line, no displacement limit, and no written rules. There are no drivers in the production race, just engineers, machinists, toolmakers, mechanics and assembly workers, and its sponsors — the men who built the companies that built the cars — comprise a veritable Automotive Hall of Fame.

The race did not start when William S. Knudsen (1879-1948) left Ford in 1921, became general manager at Chevrolet in 1922 and told his executives that he wanted "one for one" — meaning one new Chevrolet for every car that Ford produced. It started some twenty-one years earlier, before there even was a Chevrolet car, at a time when Henry Ford (1863-1947) built cars one by one — no two alike — in his small garage.

These early American cars were not factory-built, of course; they were put together by the traditional methods of the artisan. By 1896 not only Henry Ford but also Charles B. King (1868-1957) and Alexander Winton (1860-1932) — among many others — had their gasoline-driven cars on the road. King was a Cornell-educated engineer who started to design a four-cylinder, four-stroke engine in 1894. The engine was built and installed in an Emerson & Fisher wagon in less than two years, and King gave a public demonstration of this horseless carriage on the streets of Detroit on March 6, 1896.

Meanwhile Winton designed and built a motorcycle in Cleveland, Ohio, in 1895 and produced his first car in 1896. By 1898 he had built and sold twenty-odd automobiles. As for Henry Ford, he began the construction of his first car at home, on his own time, while working for the Detroit Edison Company. He received valuable advice from Charles B. King, and the car (really a quadricycle) was ready for the road on the morning of June 4, 1896.

By this time it was obvious that America had the technical know-how, material and tools to manufacture cars in great number. By the turn of the century, such makes as Knox, White, Stanley, Stearns, Locomobile, Columbia and Packard had joined the fray. Series of cars were built to the same design, side by side in these plants, but there was not yet any interchangeability of parts. Parts had to be fitted rather than assembled. Total production of automobiles (driven by gasoline, steam and electricity) nevertheless amounted to an impressive 4192 units in the calendar year 1900.

Hiram Percy Maxim (1869-1936) designed the first Columbia electric for Colonel Albert A. Pope (1843-1909) in 1895, by mounting a motor and batteries in a Crawford runabout, and Columbia gasoline-drive cars soon followed. In 1899 the Columbia car and Electric Vehicle Company of Hartford, Connecticut, led the production race. Other branches of Colonel Pope's industries later built the medium-priced Pope-Hartford and Pope-Toledo, the low-priced Pope-Tribune, and the electric Pope-

Automobile Manufacturing
in the United States

Waverley, all of which were factors in the production race until the demise of the Pope Manufacturing Company in 1907.

The pacemakers in the steam car production race were Stanley and White. The Stanley brothers, Freelan O. Stanley (1849-1940) and Francis E. Stanley (1849-1918), were twins who turned from manufacturing photographic equipment to building steam cars in 1896. During 1898 they built 100 Stanley Steamers in their Newton, Massachusetts, plant. In 1900, Windsor T. White (1860-1958) and his brother Rollin H. White (1872-1962) started to make steam cars as a sideline for their White Sewing Machine Company in Cleveland, Ohio. The first year's production totalled 193 vehicles.

The Locomobile Company was founded in June, 1899, by Amzi L. Barber who, in partnership with John Brisben Walker, purchased manufacturing rights to certain steam car patents from the Stanley brothers. Barber and Walker could not agree on where to build cars, so they amicably decided that each of them should build Stanley-type steamers where he thought best. Walker built the Locomobile at Tarrytown, New York, and was out of business within two years. Barber took over the Stanley plant at Newton and started to build Locomobile steamers. The company switched from steam to gasoline in 1902, and the business moved to Bridgeport, Connecticut. The Locomobile then became an expensive, high-quality car, and turned its back on the production race. Meanwhile the Stanley brothers had carefully observed a

contract that called for them to refrain from building steam cars for one full year; then they resumed operations and very soon recaptured their position as the number one maker of steam cars.

One of the almost-forgotten pioneers of the light gasoline-driven car was Harry A. Knox (1875-1957). He had studied mechanics at Springfield Technical Institute and started to design engines while still a student. Backed by Elihu H. Cutler (1855-1936), owner of the Elektron Manufacturing Company, he formed the Knox Automobile Company in 1900 and opened one of America's largest automobile factories at Springfield, Massachusetts.

Frank B. Stearns (1879-1955) began experiments with a steam car in 1893 while attending the Case School of Applied Science. He tested the first Stearns steamer in 1896. The F. B. Stearns Co. built a score of steam cars before 1900, but then adopted the gasoline engine.

James Ward Packard (1863-1928) ran an electrical shop in Warren, Ohio, together with his brother William Dowd Packard (1861-1923). Packard owned a Winton, and as a result of an argument with Alexander Winton about the quality of the vehicle, he resolved to build his own car in 1899. He started the Ohio Automobile Company. The firm moved to Detroit in 1902 and played an important part in the production race until 1913, when president Henry B. Joy (1864-1936) decided that Packard's place was in the high-priced market.

113

In 1903 Olds emerged as the uncontested leader of the production race, building 4000 cars. Ransom Eli Olds (1864-1950) had joined his father's mechanical workshop in Lansing, Michigan, and the business developed into the Olds Gasoline Engine Works. In 1897 he decided to build cars and obtained backing from Edward W. Sparrow, a mining and lumbering magnate. This company failed, but 1899 saw Olds in Detroit, forming the Olds Motor Works, with backing from Samuel L. Smith, a Michigan copper and lumber tycoon. Olds built a three-story plant expressly designed for manufacturing automobiles, located on the Detroit river front, and hired Charles B. King to run it. The factory burned to the ground on March 9, 1901, and Olds moved to Lansing, where operations continued with just one model — the only car that had been saved from the fire — the now-famous "curved dash" Oldsmobile. Catastrophe became success as the Olds Motor Works led the race from 1903 through 1905.

In 1903 a new company in Kenosha, Wisconsin, turned out over 1300 Rambler cars. It had started in 1878 when Thomas B. Jeffery (1845-1910) associated himself with R. Phillip Gormully to manufacture the Rambler bicycle in Chicago. Around 1900 he decided to branch out into automobiles and bought the Kenosha plant of the Sterling Bicycle Company in 1901.

In addition to Rambler, 1903 stands as a birth year for some of the greatest contenders in the race to produce: Buick, Maxwell, Cadillac,

and Ford, all of which were destined to contest the race for decades. Cadillac produced about 1700, Ford 1708, Pope-Hartford about 1500, and Rambler 1350. Respectable numbers were also turned out by Knox, Winton, White, Baker, Stevens-Duryea and Stanley.

The origin of the Cadillac car involves the unlikely combination of Henry Ford, Alanson P. Brush (who later designed the first Oakland and built the Brush Runabout) and Henry M. Leland, who built the Lincoln many years afterward. Leland (1843-1932) was head of the Leland & Faulconer Manufacturing Company in Detroit, makers of machine tools and marine engines at the time of the Olds Motor Works fire in 1901. Leland helped assure his own and Oldsmobile's future by signing a contract for making single-cylinder engines for Olds.

In 1902 Henry Ford was struggling with the management of the Henry Ford Automobile Company. Ford was not the engineer his backers wanted, and they were not the passive financiers *he* preferred. Leland was called in as a consultant, Ford resigned, and the business was reorganized as the Cadillac Automobile Company, with Brush as chief engineer and Leland as consulting engineer. In 1905 the Leland & Faulconer Manufacturing Company completed a merger with Cadillac, and Leland was made president.

Henry Ford, in the meantime, found himself another set of backers and started the Ford Motor Company on June 15, 1903, with a capital stock of $28,000. His factory occupied the corner site of Mack Avenue and

1895 Duryea. (L)
1897 Stanley Steamer. (L)

1899 Packard Model A.
1899 Locomobile steam car.

1901 Knox.
1903 Cadillac.

1903 Franklin.
1911 Brush.

Belt Line in Detroit. Ford's first Model A was powered with a twin-cylinder engine — at a time when Cadillac and Oldsmobile still used single-cylinders exclusively.

David Dunbar Buick (1855-1929) was a plumbing supplies manufacturer in Detroit who started to build marine engines and gradually got interested in cars. In 1902 Buick united with Walter L. Marr, a qualified engineer, to build a car. They secured financial backing from Benjamin Briscoe (1868-1945), one of America's foremost manufacturers of radiators and sheet metal parts for the auto industry. Buick built only sixteen cars in 1903, however. Operations almost came to a halt when Briscoe suddenly sold his stock to James H. Whiting (1842-1919), president of the Flint Wagon Works. Whiting settled Buick's debts in Detroit and moved the business to Flint, Michigan, but failed to make a success of Buick. On November 1, 1904, the Buick Motor Company was taken over by the legendary William C. Durant (1866-1946), president of the Durant-Dort Carriage Company. Buick had produced only a handful of cars that year.

Jonathan Dixon Maxwell (1864-1928) first entered the automobile industry by working as a mechanic with the Apperson brothers at Kokomo, Indiana, on the construction of Elwood Haynes' first car in 1894. For some time he was associated with Olds Motor Works, but left in 1902 to start the Northern Automobile Company in Detroit. Maxwell left Northern to organize the Maxwell-Briscoe Motor Company in 1903.

His partner was the same Benjamin B. Briscoe who that year had put up $3500 in cash and materials to get the Buick Motor Company going. Benjamin and his brother Frank sold their Buick interests, and started to build the Maxwell car. They leased a factory at Tarrytown, New York, where John Brisben Walker had built Mobile steam cars for a few years, and before long the Maxwell had become a formidable production race contender.

Another entry, the Franklin, came into existence because of an experimental vehicle built in 1900 by John N. Wilkinson (1868-1951) a Cornell-educated engineer. He demonstrated it to Herbert Henry Franklin (1867-1956), maker of die castings in Syracuse, New York, in 1901, and the two men agreed to start a car factory. In 1902, thirteen Franklin cars were built. The Thomas car, too, was a product of New York State, being manufactured by Edwin Ross Thomas (1850-1936) in Buffalo. He started his business in 1900 to make motorcycles, but was constructing cars from 1902.

While George N. Pierce (1846-1910) was making the Pierce Motorette in Buffalo, New York, Andrew James Pierce started to manufacture automobiles called Pierce in Racine, Wisconsin. To distinguish one from the other, the latter became known as the Pierce-Racine (until it became the Case in 1911). The Buffalo-built Pierce evolved into the Pierce-Arrow and became a luxury car whose manufacturer took no interest in the production car race.

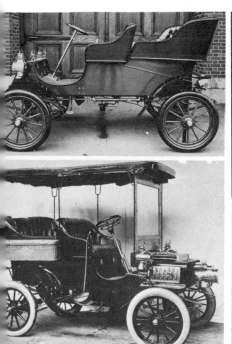

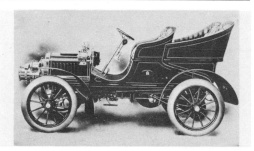

1903 Ford Model A. (F)
1903-04 Rambler. (A)

1904 curved dash Oldsmobile. (P)
1904 Locomobile gasoline car. (L)

1905 Maxwell.
1905 Oldsmobile Light Tonneau.

1908 Buick Model 5, 1908 Thomas
Flyer (L), and 1908 Packard.

1910 Brush (D), 1909 Ford Model T.
(F), and 1911 Hupmobile 20 (W).

1909 Hudson Model 20. (A)
1910 E. M. F.

The front row of the 1904 production race was occupied by Oldsmobile (over 5500 cars), Rambler and Cadillac (2400 each), and Ford (1700). Franklin astonished the experts by turning out 712 cars in their third year of operation, and White was still doing well with its steam cars, producing 710 units.

Things changed a great deal in 1905. R.E. Olds left the Olds Motor Works over a policy disagreement and formed the Reo Motor Car Company, also in Lansing, Michigan. Oldsmobile's big lead declined while Cadillac took second place with 3900 against Rambler's 3800. Maxwell built 823 and Ford 1600. White surpassed 1000 and Buick began to profit from Durant's management and salesmanship, turning out 750 cars.

Though their Model T was still to come, Ford took the lead in 1906, outproducing the Cadillac by two-to-one, with 8729 Fords against 4059 Cadillacs. Behind them came Maxwell, Reo, Rambler and Olds.

Cadillac switched to four-cylinder engines and entered the luxury car field. Production fell by nearly 1200 cars in 1907, while R. E. Olds' new venture prospered and about 4000 Reos were built as well. But by now Ford had an unchallenged lead with nearly 15,000 cars to runner-up Buick's 4600, while Maxwell and Rambler remained in the running but Olds failed to make the top fifteen.

The gap between Ford and Buick closed in 1908, with Buick producing 8800 cars against Ford's 10,200. Other principal producers were Maxwell, Franklin, Packard, Reo, Rambler, Cadillac, and a new volume car from Studebaker, the E.M.F.

The E.M.F. car was marketed as the Studebaker-E.M.F. by Studebaker wagon dealers throughout the country, and was highly successful in the production race. The initials E.M.F. represented a great triumvirate: Byron F. Everitt (1872-1940), former president of the Wayne Automobile Company; William E. Metzger (1868-1933), former sales

1910 Oakland. (L)
1910 Overland. (L)

1910 Stoddard-Dayton, 1910 Ford
Model T (F), and 1913 Studebaker (s).

1914 Chevrolet (F), 1916 Jeffery
(M), and 1915 Dodge (c).

manager of Cadillac; and Walter E. Flanders (1871-1923), former works manager of the Ford Motor Company. These three automotive giants joined forces in May, 1908, with a capital stock of $1,000,000, and took over the Wayne and Northern factories in Detroit. Studebaker agreed to sell the total output of E.M.F. cars.

Studebaker had been America's number one wagon builder since 1852, and had begun experimenting with a horseless carriage in 1897. By 1899 Studebaker was making bodies for electric runabouts built by another company. In 1902 their South Bend plants had started production of electric cars and trucks, building a total of twenty vehicles that year. In 1904 Studebaker completed their first gasoline-driven automobile and entered an agreement with the Garford Manufacturing Company of Elyria, Ohio, to supply complete chassis while Studebaker continued to build the bodies in South Bend. This gamble was not entirely successful, and Studebaker was in dire need of a new product when the E.M.F. came along. Instant success ensued that seemed like

mass production to Studebaker, but even these figures were soon to be dwarfed. The mass production idea could not be implemented as soon as Frederick William Taylor had formulated his theories. It took Henry M. Leland to perfect machine tools and Carl Edvard Johansson to provide improved means of measurement. Even then the way was not clear to men like Durant and Ford. The automobile industry lagged in *production methods*.

International Harvester Company was among the first to utilize the idea of an assembly line in their Akron, Ohio, plant in 1907. This was the factory that built the International highwheeler motor wagons. A total of 100 wagons were turned out that year, and by March, 1910, approximately 3750 International highwheelers were in use.

Somewhat misleading, as an indication of productivity, is that Ford built more cars with fewer workers than his competitors. Ford had only 2595 men in 1907, but it must be remembered that Ford did little ac-

117

1916 Saxon.
1915 Maxwell. (L)

1918 Nash Model 68L. (A)
1919 Essex. (A)

1922 Durant Model A. (L)
1922 Oakland Model 6-44. (G)

tual manufacture and was mainly an assembly plant at this time. Packard was nearly self-contained and had a labor force of 4640, while Buick and Cadillac occupied the middle ground with 4000 and 3500 workers, respectively.

With Buick as the nucleus, W. C. Durant formed the General Motors Company on September 16, 1908. Two months later the stockholders of the Olds Motor Works sold out to Durant, and General Motors bought Cadillac in July, 1909. In a short period General Motors acquired control of a number of smaller companies: Cartercar Company, Oakland Motor Car Company, Elmore Motor Car Company, Ewing Automobile Company, Welch Motor Car Company, The Marquette Company, Northway Motor & Manufacturing Company, Rapid Motor Vehicle Company, Randolph Motor Truck Company, and Reliance Motor Truck Company. The Marquette, Ewing and Welch cars were soon discontinued, Elmore and Cartercar were moderately successful, and Oakland prospered.

Alanson P. Brush designed the first Oakland in 1907 but left to start his own business, with financial backing by Frank Briscoe (1875-1954). The Brush was priced below the Buick, Reo and Maxwell, and gave Ford some real competition. Brush turned out about 2000 cars in 1909, coming in ahead of Rambler in their first full year of operations. Other runners-up in the 1909 production race were Buick (14,000), Maxwell (9500), E.M.F. (8000), Cadillac (7900), Reo (6600), and

Willys-Overland (4900). New to the top seller list was Hupmobile (1600), while Olds rallied to eleventh place with 1690 units.

The first Overland car had been built in 1902 by the Standard Wheel Company of Terre Haute, Indiana. The experimental period was not encouraging; the Overland car program was taken over by the parent firm, Parry Manufacturing Company, and production transferred to Indianapolis, Indiana. Overland met with no success until a bicycle salesman named John North Willys (1873-1935) took on an $80,000 debt accumulated by the firm by 1907 and moved operations to Toledo, Ohio, moving into the factory where Pope Manufacturing Company had built the Pope-Toledo. Willys-Overland built over 15,000 cars in 1910, against Ford's 32,000, Buick's 30,500 and E.M.F.'s 15,000.

The Stoddard-Dayton stemmed from Henry Stoddard's successful paint and varnish business in Dayton, Ohio. The company went into farming implements and later also built bicycles. The Stoddard-Dayton car was born in 1904 when John W. Stoddard (1837-1917), the founder's son, decided to build a high-powered car on European lines, using a Rutenbar engine. Production increased gradually from 125 in 1905 to 385 in 1906 and 1600 in 1909. In 1910 Stoddard-Dayton became part of Benjamin Briscoe's great combine, the United States Motor Company, along with Alden-Sampson, Brush, Columbia, and Maxwell.

The Thomas-Detroit was not the progeny of the Thomas Flyer, although

1922 Buick Model 34. (G)

1922 Studebaker Special Six.
1924 Chrysler Six. (C)

1925 Ajax Six (A), 1925 Cadillac
(G), and 1925 Dodge (C).

the company had been founded by the same Edwin Ross Thomas in 1906. During 1907 the Thomas-Detroit Company built 506 cars. They were medium-priced, like the Hupmobile and the E.M.F., and enjoyed considerable success until 1908, when Hugh Chalmers (1873-1932) took control of the company and changed the name to Chalmers-Detroit.

Robert Craig Hupp — and his brother Louis G. Hupp — had started to build Hupmobiles in Detroit during 1908. The car was of sound design and by 1910 it had established a nationwide reputation for good value and reliability.

Hudson started with money provided by Joseph Lowthian Hudson, of Hudson's department store in Detroit. The men behind the car were Roy Dikeman Chapin (1880-1936) and Howard Earl Coffin (1873-1937), who had both worked for Olds in the pioneering days. They were prime movers in the Thomas-Detroit company but left when Chalmers took over. In 1909 they built the first Hudson car in a factory that formerly belonged to the Northern Motor Car Company in Detroit, but in April of that year, Hudson moved into a newer plant formerly occupied by the Aerocar Company. By 1910, Hudson was among the top fifteen in the production race.

Durant had borrowed heavily to expand General Motors the way he did, and the bubble burst in 1910. He was forced to resign and the organization was placed in the hands of a voting trust made up of Wall Street bankers.

For 1910 the top seven—Ford, Buick, Willys-Overland, E.M.F., Cadillac, Maxwell and Brush—all produced over 10,000 cars. Behind these came Reo (6600), Chalmers (6400), and Hupmobile (5300). Charles W. Nash (1864-1948) became president of Buick in 1910, but 1911 production fell to about 13,000 cars from more than 30,000 the previous year, from whence they began a slow climb back to 30,000 by 1914.

In 1911 Studebaker acquired control of E.M.F. and the 26,000-odd cars built that year were known simply as Studebakers. The year 1911 was to be the last successful one for Maxwell and Brush as products of the U.S. Motor Company, which went bankrupt in 1912. About 16,000 Maxwells were built in 1911. Maxwell survived the fall of Briscoe's automotive empire, but considerably weakened, was soon to merge with Chalmers-Detroit.

The production race leaders in 1912 were Ford (170,000), Willys-Overland (28,500), Studebaker (28,000), Buick (20,000) and Cadillac (13,000). Reo, Hudson, Rambler, Packard, Oakland, Hupmobile and Brush also did well, but could not approach the volume of the industry leaders. In recognition of his achievements with Buick, Charles W. Nash was named president of General Motors in 1912, and his successor at Buick was Walter P. Chrysler (1876-1940).

Meanwhile, W. C. Durant had returned to Flint, Michigan, where he formed the Little Motor Car Company with William H. Little, and the Mason Motor Company with A. C. Mason. He also sponsored a six-

119

cylinder car built by a racing driver named Louis Chevrolet (1871-1914) in Detroit. Durant took over the automobile factory of the Flint Wagon Works and the former Republic truck factory in Tarrytown, New York, organizing production of Little, Mason and Chevrolet cars. A total of 2999 Chevrolet cars were built in 1912. By 1913, Little and Mason were merged into Chevrolet. The 1914 models from Chevrolet were a tremendous success, and Durant used his growing profits to buy General Motors stock. But expansion was still a synonym for Ford, who completed installation of the first automotive constant-speed assembly line in 1913. The number of Ford workers increased from 3488 in 1911 to 5710 in 1912, and paradoxically, when the labor-saving assembly line was introduced, several thousand more men were needed. In 1913 Ford employed 13,198 workers, and production rose to 202,667 cars.

Oldsmobile made only twelve hundred cars in 1912, and the factory stayed in business only because other GM divisions were doing well. Then Edward Ver Linden became production manager, moving over from Buick's plant No. I in Flint. By 1914 Olds production was over 2000 cars again, for the first time since 1904. This increased to over 7500 cars for 1915. Ver Linden was named president, and scheduled 20,000 units for 1917. He exceeded this goal by about 2000 and brought Olds back into the top ten.

Rambler sales had been slipping since the death of Thomas B. Jeffrey in 1910. The car was renamed Jeffery in 1913 but failed to finish higher than fourteenth.

In 1914 two important new names appeared: Dodge and Saxon. John F. Dodge (1864-1920) and his brother Horace E. Dodge (1868-1920) got into the auto industry by building 3000 transmissions for Oldsmobile in 1902. Later they became principal suppliers to Ford. In 1913 Dodge built engines, transmissions, and axles for the Model T, and Ford was their only important customer. John F. Dodge was a vice-president of the Ford Motor Company, and the Dodge brothers held $25 million of Ford Motor Company stock. In 1913 the Dodge brothers decided to become auto makers in their own right and bought a tract of land adjacent to their Hamtramck, Detroit, factory to erect a new plant. Prototype Dodge cars were built and tested in 1914, and production began to get under way. In 1915, Dodge built 45,000 units, and were thus far ahead of many production race veterans.

The Saxon too was a hit with the public, being a small six-cylinder car when most light automobiles had four-cylinder engines. The Saxon Motor Company was formed in Detroit in 1913 by Harry W. Ford, a former director of Chalmers, and 7000 cars were turned out in 1914. In 1915 Saxon built 19,000 units, putting them ahead of Hudson and Oakland in the production race. However, by June of 1917 the company could not meet its financial obligations; production was discontinued, and the factory was taken over by the Industrial Terminal Corporation which completed the plant and sold it to GM.

While W. C. Durant steadily increased his holdings of General Motors stock, the du Pont family of Wilmington, Delaware, also started to buy

120   1925 Hupmobile Model R. (w)
1926 Chevrolet. (G)

1926 Chrysler Imperial 80. (C)
1926 Pontiac. (G)

1927 Erskine. (s)
1926 Flint Model 55. (L)

heavily into the growing corporation. At the annual meeting on November 16, 1915, Pierre S. du Pont was elected GM chairman, with C. W. Nash retaining the president's title. But W. C. Durant — through Chevrolet — really controlled the company. In 1918 Durant incorporated Chevrolet as a division of General Motors (by letting GM buy the operating assets of Chevrolet and paying for them in GM stock). However, Durant continued to bring non-profitable companies like Scripps-Booth, Saxon and Sheridan under GM control. By 1920 Durant had lost the firm forever, and the du Pont family bought his holdings in the big corporation.

By the time Durant took charge of General Motors in 1916, Charles W. Nash had amassed enough capital to break out and start his own company. He took over the Jeffery (ex-Rambler) Company and its Wisconsin factories, and produced the first Nash car in 1917.

Walter P. Chrysler stayed on for three years of Durant management and resigned in 1919 with a small personal fortune. In 1920 he was commissioned by a group of bankers to head the reorganization of Willys-Overland, which had come close to liquidation. Chrysler never restored the company to its previous position, but it only took him a year to put operations on a profitable basis.

Walter Flanders (of E.M.F. fame) had signed a contract to head the Maxwell Motor Company for five years from January 1st, 1913, and in 1917 concluded a deal for a five-year lease of the Chalmers plant, where 21,000 cars were built in 1916. Both Maxwell and Chalmers cars

were to continue in production. When Flanders' contract ran out, W. Ledyard Mitchell became president of Maxwell-Chalmers.

Strangely, Maxwell had made a fair recovery and stayed in the top ten. Chalmers was the weak link in the enterprise, despite the fact that Hugh Chalmers was the man who had taught the industry the real meaning of scientific business methods and intensive selling efficiency. Differences arose over accounting matters between Maxwell and Chalmers during 1921, and the lease was terminated. The Chalmers company went into receivership shortly afterwards, and Maxwell purchased all its assets for $1,987,000 in December, 1922. But Maxwell was itself saddled with a debt of $26 million by that time.

The bankers who carried Maxwell asked Walter P. Chrysler for help, and he became chairman of the Maxwell reorganization and management committee while still straightening out affairs at Willys-Overland. When Chrysler was through at Willys, he asked the bankers for another $15,000,000 and together with Harry Bronner bought all assets of Maxwell and Chalmers. The Chalmers car was discontinued, but a new Maxwell was produced until 1924 when it had to make way for the Chrysler.

The 1924 Chrysler Six was something new in medium-priced cars. It looked expensive, and bristled with engineering refinements. A total of 32,000 Chrysler cars were built in the first year of operations. The Maxwell Corporation became the Chrysler Corporation, and the range expanded in 1926, when Chrysler offered four new models; a

1927 Nash Advanced Six. (A)

1927 La Salle, 1927 Whippet,
and 1927 Packard (D).

1929 Plymouth (C), 1929 Ford
Model A (F), and 1929 De Soto (C).   121

1930 Reo Flying Cloud. (J)

1930 Hudson Greater 8. (P)

1931 Plymouth. (C)

1931 Oldsmobile.

1932 Chevrolet. (G)

four-cylinder "58," a six-cylinder "60," a revised 1925 model known as the "70," and the Imperial "80." In two years Chrysler climbed from twenty-seventh to seventh place in the production race. And they were holding firm in 1927, with a daily output of 1250 cars.

After the second loss of his own creation, General Motors, W. C. Durant in 1921 also lost a $90-million fortune. But the same year saw him organize Durant Motors and prepare to challenge du Pont and GM again. He purchased the old Sheridan plant at Muncie, Indiana, and began to build Durant cars. The president of Durant Motors was a successful veteran, Edward Ver Linden, formerly with Oldsmobile. Durant soon added plants in Lansing, Michigan; Elizabeth, New Jersey; Oakland, California; and Toronto, Ontario, Canada. In these he produced a variety of automobiles: Star, Flint, Rugby and Princeton, as well as the Durant. Durant Motors never became the giant industrial combine Durant had intended, but did well in the production race, with 55,000 cars in 1922 and 172,000 cars in 1923.

Ford's pinnacle of Model T production was 1923's 1,817,891 passenger cars. The Ford production system was admired by all — but the Model T was not. An austerity-marked model, it was aging fast, and the rising standard of living increased the demand for solid, middle-class cars like Buick and Dodge.

Still it was apparent to all industry leaders that only a low-priced car could truly challenge Ford. Chevrolet's cheapest model could not undersell the T and neither could Hudson's low-priced Essex or Willys-Overland's Whippet. Studebaker's small Erskine was not a success; neither was Nash's short-lived Ajax. But all these cars resembled more

expensive models, while the Model T Ford stood out for its rustic lack of elegance and uncompromising simplicity.

The ultimate challenge was to emerge when William S. Knudsen became a general manager of Chevrolet in 1922. Knudsen had been regarded as second-in-command to Henry Ford, and his loss was felt throughout the Ford organization, although he did not bring any Ford men with him to Chevrolet. Knudsen reorganized production at Chevrolet and revitalized the dealer organization, giving the dealers a new range of cars with which to attack Ford on all fronts.

From 1924 to 1925, Chevrolet's production rose by fifty-eight percent. This tremendous upswing followed Richard H. Grant's leaving Delco to take over as Chevrolet sales vice-president. Grant's first step was to dress up the car — one of the first instances where a manufacturer consciously pursued beauty of line, harmony of color, and interior decoration as a sales tool. For 1927, Chevrolet appropriated $10 million to advertise the car purely as a thing of beauty, on the theory that the husband may buy the car, but it's often the wife who picks it. The tactic paid off — in 1927 Chevrolet outsold Ford for the first time. Ford's production ran to about 350,000 cars, while Chevrolet built over 1.7 million. For the first time, one new car in every four was a Chevrolet.

Ford's only defense against the relentless onslaught from Chevrolet was the price cut; indeed it was its low price alone kept the Model T saleable for so long in its final years of production. But one day in the spring of 1927, Henry Ford saw that the game was up and closed the entire plant. Ford had built 15,007,033 Model T's since production

1932 Auburn.

1932 Rockne Six. (P)
1933 Essex-Terraplane. (A)

1934 Lafayette. (A)
1935 Ford V-8. (F)

started in 1908. But the Model T was dead, and Ford had no replacement ready to go into production. A totally conventional four-cylinder passenger car was unhurriedly designed, tested and developed, and appeared as the Model A in the autumn of 1927. Such was the public's confidence in Ford that several month's production had been ordered before the public had any idea what the car would look like. And by all standards, the Model A was a roaring success. In 1929, Ford built 1.5 million of them to recapture first place, and over 3.5 million were made in four years.

But Ford's return to leadership was only momentary. In 1929, General Motors built 1.5 million cars out of an industry total of 4.5 million. Corporate policy was laid down by Alfred P. Sloan (1875-1966), president of GM from 1923 to 1946. One of his principles was to allocate specific price brackets to each car division. They would compete with each other only where they overlapped — and each model would be designed for a specific place in the full spectrum of GM models. In 1921 the range was fairly simple, starting with a low-priced Chevrolet, moving up through Oakland, Buick 4, Buick 6 and Oldsmobile, and ending with the high-priced Cadillac. As we now know, only Chevrolet and Cadillac had at this time found their ultimate places in the overall price structure, as Oldsmobile, Buick and Oakland experimented considerably with prices throughout the 1920's.

Harry Bassett had become president of Buick when Walter P. Chrysler "retired" in 1919. He secured third place in the production race for Buick in that year, and came in second in 1921, against keen competition from Dodge and Willys-Overland. In 1924 Buick dropped the

four-cylinder engine to build sixes only, and finished fifth. Bassett was succeeded by Edward T. Strong in 1926, and Buick continued an impressive showing in the production race despite having lost its lowest-priced models. Buick now assumed the position next to Cadillac in GM's lineup, with Oldsmobile in the middle and reaching down.

Olds president A.B.C. Hardy introduced the six-cylinder "30" in 1923, a car that undersold most Oaklands, and returned Oldsmobile to eleventh in 1924 from a weak thirteenth the previous year. But while Olds' output continued to climb, they were to remain hovering around twelfth position for much of the next ten years.

Oakland built 52,000 cars in 1919 and ranked sixth in the production race, but ran into engineering problems which often held up production in the early 1920's. Production sank to less than 35,000 cars in 1920 and again to 12,000 in 1921. The Oakland remained in production until 1931, and 60,000 were built in 1927, but they never finally recovered. The factory was saved by the Pontiac, introduced in 1926 to take the place immediately above Chevrolet in the General Motors lineup. In its first year, well over 76,000 Pontiacs were built, against 20,000 fewer Oaklands. In 1927 Pontiac built nearly 128,000 cars and took eighth place in the production race. The following year, after spending $5 million on a new foundry, production manager P. H. MacGregor turned out well over 200,000 units.

Cadillac, although not a factor in the production race, was a profitable operation, and General Motors devoted a great deal of attention to their senior division. Production rose from 11,000 cars in 1921, when the new plant on Clark Avenue first opened, to nearly 35,000 cars in 1927.

1935 Chevrolet. (G)
1935 Plymouth Six. (C)

1936 Lincoln Zephyr.
1936 Buick Model 46. (G)

1937 Willys Four. (D)

The La Salle was Alfred P. Sloan's idea for giving Cadillac Motor Car Division a higher-volume model, using available components from other divisions without detracting from the prestige of the Cadillac name. Introduced in 1927, the La Salle caught on well, but after a few years market conditions changed, and its place in the lineup was jeopardized. By 1935 it was hardly more than a disguised Oldsmobile, and Cadillac discontinued this junior line in 1941.

Before the stock market crash of October 29, 1929, a third giant was rivalling GM and Ford: the Chrysler Corporation. Walter P. Chrysler had taken over Dodge in 1928 and developed the Plymouth and De Soto, enabling Chrysler Corporation to compete in every price field. At Dodge, Chrysler enlarged the physical plant about five times, acquired a needed foundry and an established, well-oiled sales organization.

Dodge was fifth in the production race in 1917, fourth by 1919, and second in 1920. Frederick J. Haynes (1875-1925) longtime associate of the Dodge Brothers, became president when both John and Horace Dodge died during 1920. The company continued to prosper, and Dodge ran a strong third in 1921. In 1924, Dodge built 194,000 cars to place third, but the rise of Buick, Chrysler and Willys-Overland prevented them from finishing higher than seventh from 1927 to 1932.

The Plymouth was named by sales manager Joseph W. Frazer (1893-1971), destined to build 100,000 cars himself two decades later. It was the lowest-priced model, but not quite cheap enough to compete directly with Chevrolet and Ford. In its first year, 1928, only 52,000 Plymouths were built. It was not until March, 1930, that Chrysler matched Plymouth prices with those of Chevrolet and Ford, and the anticipated

breakthrough came in 1931, when Plymouth had their first 100,000-car year and displaced Buick from third place in the production battle. The corporation spent $9 million to retool the factory for a production capacity of 2000 cars per day, and Plymouth broke its previous production record every year from 1932 through 1936, achieving half a million units in the latter year.

Studebaker and Willys-Overland should be considered industrial giants even if they were not in the league of the Big Three. After John North Willys completed the move of the ailing Overland enterprise to Toledo, Ohio, in 1911, Willys-Overland enjoyed an extended period of prosperity and expansion. Willys organized the Kinsey Manufacturing Company to supply sheet metal parts and in 1912 brought the Warner Gear Company to Toledo to make gears and other machined parts. At the same time, Willys-Overland absorbed Gramm trucks, and later Tillotson carburetors, Morrow transmissions and Electric Auto-Lite. By 1912 Willys-Overland was second only to Ford, producing 28,500 cars. In 1916 output climbed to 140,000 cars, almost exceeding the aggregate production of all General Motors divisions at the time. Still Willys-Overland continued to expand, adding Wilson Foundry and Machine Company, the Fisk and Federal Rubber Companies, Curtiss Aeroplane Company, New Process Gear Company, USL Battery, Moline Plow Company, and Duesenberg Motors.

Sooner or later the bubble had to burst, and not surprisingly, disaster struck during World War I, while John N. Willys was fully occupied on defense programs for the U.S. Government. By 1919 Willys-Overland had accumulated a debt of $50 million, following a seven-month strike by 24,000 men in their Toledo, Elmira and Elyria plants. The company

124

1937 Nash Model 3722. (A)
1938 Packard Eight. (W)

1939 Mercury. (F)

1939 Studebaker Champion. (S)

wavered, falling from second to fifth in the production race. Under Walter Chrysler, financial order was restored after a period of receivership but production revived slowly. In 1921 and 1922 Willys-Overland ran a poor sixth, with only 48,016 and 95,410 cars built respectively. But by 1923 the corporation was making big money again, turning out 196,000 cars. By 1925 the Willys-Overland payroll amounted to more than $27,000,000.

In 1926 Willys introduced the four-cylinder Whippet to compete in the low-priced market, and followed up in 1927 with the Whippet Six — the lowest-priced six since the Saxon. In 1928 the revived company reached a new peak output of 315,000 cars, with a labor force of 23,000 men. Willys-Overland ran third in the production race in 1928.

After the formation of the Studebaker Corporation in 1911, the wagon plant in South Bend, Indiana, was retooled to make car bodies, springs, forgings and stampings, and new plants were added for automobile assembly. A foundry was completed in 1916. The Detroit factory taken over from E.M.F. was kept in operation until 1926. Studebaker production rose from 26,000 cars in 1911 to 28,000 in 1912 and 32,000 in 1913. Studebaker continued to build wagons until 1919, and produced great numbers of gun carriages, escort wagons and artillery wheels for the armed forces during World War I. Nevertheless, passenger car production was near 66,000 in 1916 and 40,000 in the war year of 1917. Trucks had been added in 1913 and buses in 1915. A range of new models sent production soaring to 105,000 in 1922 and 146,000 in 1923. The Light Six was the lowest priced car in the line, and president Albert Russel Erskine (1871-1933) decided it was necessary to compete in the still lower Chevrolet price range to continue the growth of the

corporation. His low-priced Erskine first appeared in 1926 — and it failed miserably.

Studebaker Corporation's total 1927 production was less than 121,000 cars, and the 1923 record was to stand for over twenty years. Studebaker was hard hit by the Wall Street crash; production dwindled year by year until only 43,000 cars were turned out in 1933 and the corporation went into receivership. The crisis was precipitated by Erskine's optimistic purchase of Pierce-Arrow in 1928 — a deal that cost the Studebaker Corporation dearly before the receivers unloaded Pierce-Arrow five years later. But Studebaker's assets were so great that there was really no danger at that time of the corporation's failure. Production revived under the management of Harold S. Vance and Paul G. Hoffman management in the aftermath of the Depression and rose to 85,000 cars in 1936.

Other independents that contested the production race throughout the 1920's were Hudson, Nash, Hupmobile, Durant (with Star and Flint), and Auburn. From 1927 onwards Graham-Paige was a factor, and in some years Packard reached impressive production figures.

Hudson won a reputation for outstanding engineering in their early years, discontinuing four-cylinder engines in 1913 to concentrate on sixes of considerable power and smoothness. Production rose from about 10,000 cars in 1914 to 13,000 in 1915 and 26,000 in 1916, although Hudsons were not cheap cars. President Roy D. Chapin recognized the need for a price-leader, and started the Essex Motor Car Company in 1919 as a wholly-owned Hudson subsidiary. He installed William J. McAneeny (1872-1935) as head of the firm. The 1919 Essex was a light, four-cylinder car and immediately sold well. Hudson and Essex combined to sell 40,000 cars that year. In 1922, the company built over 64,000 Hudson and Essex cars, and by 1924 the combined production figure exceeded 100,000. A year later, Hudson and Essex each turned out over 100,000, and by 1928 Essex alone built 230,000 units.

With the Depression Hudson sales fell sharply, at a time when the marque was at its peak popularity. Though Hudson-Essex production combined to hold fourth place, only 100,000 cars came off the Detroit production lines in 1930. By 1931 output was a mere 58,000 and Hudson-Essex slipped to seventh. Hudson fought the Depression by introducing an eight-cylinder model in 1930, but the company lost $2,000,000 in 1931 and $5,500,000 in 1932. The Essex was renamed Essex-Terraplane in 1933 and gave some promise of recovery, but it took over two years to raise the six million dollars that Hudson needed to continue operations.

The word "independent" well describes most of Charles W. Nash's activities, for Nash cars always showed independence and individuality in both styling and engineering. Nash production rose from 6500 in 1917 to 21,000 in 1921 and 57,000 in 1923. As closed cars were coming into fashion, Nash bought a half interest in the Seaman Body Corporation of Milwaukee, Wisconsin. He also purchased the LaFayette Motor Car Company, who had been building an expensive, high-speed V-8-powered luxury car for the past two years. To compete with Essex and Whippet, Nash brought out the Ajax in 1925, which failed. It was replaced by the

Nash Advanced Six in 1926, a handsome, low-to-medium priced car which sold well. In 1927 Nash built 122,000 cars; the following year, 138,000. The eight-cylinder Nash was added in 1930 (along with Buick's and Hupmobile's), but economic conditions kept sales low. Total Nash production fell short of 55,000 in 1930, 39,000 in 1931 and 18,000 in 1932. However, Nash still operated at a profit, and with the beginnings of economic recovery, prepared to launch a new low-priced car reviving the honored name of LaFayette. This appeared in 1934, and was a modest success; sales climbed up to 28,000 and Nash had won over the Depression.

Hupmobile had jumped into public favor with a light four-cylinder Model "20" in 1910 and averaged about 10,000 cars per year through 1921. During this period Hupmobile built four-cylinder cars exclusively, and then added a line of straight-eights in 1922, skipping over the six. Production rose to 34,000 cars in 1922 but Hupp could not achieve the top ten, due to the large corporations' expansionary moves at this time. They finally added a six-cylinder model for 1926 and phased out the fours, departing the low-priced field where they had won their first success. Output in 1928 was 66,000 cars. In 1929 Hupmobile took over the Chandler Motor Car Company and its subsidiary, the Cleveland Motor Car Company, and further expanded the range of Hupmobiles. However, the firm did not fare well during the Depression and production figures were disastrously low in 1933 and 1934. The Hupp

1943 Willys army jeep. (D)
1943 Ford army jeep. (F)

1950 Willys Jeep station wagon. (R)

1946 Ford Super Deluxe. (F)
1946 Plymouth Special Deluxe. (C)

Motor Car Company had a $9 million plant in Detroit and was debt-free but lacked operating capital. Production was suspended in 1936. Hupp tried to make a comeback in 1938 but finally discontinued all automotive operations in 1941.

William C. Durant's operations had five good years from 1921 to 1926. When the formation of Durant Motors, Inc. was announced, customers came forth with $31 million in firm orders before a car had been shown — such was the public's confidence in William Crapo Durant. But the Star and Flint cars failed to do the job the Chevrolet had done for Durant ten years earlier. The irrepressible tycoon was never able to work to capacity after that, and sold his Flint, Michigan, factory to General Motors in 1926. The Flint car was built in Elizabeth, New Jersey, until 1928. The Durant car (built in the Lansing plant) made a respectable showing in the production race with a 1928 output of 49,000 cars, backed by the Star (also Lansing-built) with 42,000 cars, but Durant Motors collapsed following the stock market crash and was liquidated in 1931. Wall Street took the third personal fortune that William C. Durant had made, and he gave up the auto industry for good.

The Auburn Automobile Company of Auburn, Indiana, had maintained a steady but small production from its inception in 1900 until 1923, when Roy Faulkner, who had earned a reputation as a modern super-salesman with Nash, was brought in as sales manager to enter Auburn

in the production race. But the real upswing began in 1924 when Errett L. Cord took control. Auburn sales climbed from 2500 in that year to 14,000 in 1927. As Auburn began to make a profit, Cord expanded his automotive empire by acquiring control of Duesenberg in Indianapolis, the Lycoming Manufacturing Company of Williamsport, Pennsylvania, the Limousine Body Company of Kalamazoo, Michigan, and the Central Manufacturing Company of Connersville, Indiana. Then he moved Auburn production to Connersville, into a plant with a production capacity of 200 cars a day. Auburn's assets were estimated at $10 million in 1928, and the company made a profit of $1,500,000.

Auburn sales changed remarkably little during the first Depression years, and their profit picture even improved. Output was 21,000 cars in 1929, 13,700 in 1930 and 32,000 in 1931. Cord reacted by introducing a V-12 Auburn and buying control of a few more companies, such as Columbia Axle Company and Checker Cab Corporation. Suddenly the game was over. Auburn sold only 6000 cars in 1933 and fell to twenty-first place in the production race. The V-12 was discontinued, the eight-cylinder range curtailed, and production dwindled. From January to October, 1936, Auburn built only 4830 cars, the last of the breed. The Duesenberg was discontinued at the same time, and Cord manufacturing closed a year later.

Packard was the most prosperous of the independent luxury car companies during the 1920's and far overshadowed competitors like

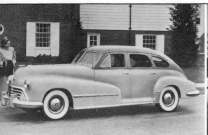

1947 Kaiser Special. (R)
1946 Oldsmobile 76. (G)

1948 Chevrolet Fleetmaster (G), 1948 Cadillac Model 62, and 1949 Oldsmobile 88 (G).

1949 Frazer Manhattan. (R)
1949 Packard Super Eight. (R)

Locomobile, Marmon, Peerless and Pierce-Arrow. Packard's reputation for advanced engineering and high quality was rivalled only by Cadillac, and their commercial success was assured by Alvan Macauley (1872-1952) who came to Packard as general manager in 1910, was named vice-president in 1913 and president in 1916. The company enjoyed steady growth regardless of wars or business slumps, and reached a production of 50,000 in 1928, at a time when Cadillac only built 21,000 V-8's (plus an almost equal number of La Salles). The Depression years affected Packard gradually but severely. The company was debt-free but demand for Packards was low. Production fell from 28,000 in 1930 to 13,000 in 1931 and 8000 in 1932. To save themselves, Packard decided to bring out a low-priced model, — the "120" — which appeared in 1935. Production climbed to 52,000 and the company was rescued.

The Graham-Paige sprang from the Paige-Detroit Motor Company, which had been organized in 1909 by Fred O. Paige (1864-1935) to build light cars with two-stroke engines. Harry Jewett (1870-1933) took control in 1910 and switched to conventional four-stroke engines. The first six-cylinder Paige-Detroit appeared in 1917. In 1927 Jewett sold out to the Graham Brothers, who had made a fortune building truck bodies, and later Dodge trucks with Graham nameplates. They sold their Dodge interests in 1927 and introduced the Graham-Paige car, building 73,000 six- and eight-cylinder cars in 1928. The company suffered a heavy blow in the middle of the Depression when Ray A. Graham (1887-1932) was drowned, but the company's solid structure and sound engineering insured its survival.

Chevrolet's answer to the Model A Ford was standardization of a six-cylinder engine across the board. Ford built 630,000 passenger cars in 1928 and 1.5 million in 1929. Chevrolet announced the six on the last Saturday in December, 1928, and by the end of August, 1929, had built a million of them. Ford then started to prepare a V-8. The initial design was completed in May, 1930, and revised the following November. Ford Motor Company had considerable experience with V-8 engines, having produced many Lincoln V-8's since 1921, but had not built a six since the Model K of 1906. The Ford V-8 was introduced on March 31, 1932, at a remarkably low price. Two years later Ford discontinued four-cylinder passenger cars, and by 1938 had built four million V-8's. In 1935 Ford recaptured the lead in the production race with a total output of over 942,000 cars against Chevrolet's less than 794,000. As usual, Plymouth was third, with 442,000 cars. The following year, however, Chevrolet's production soared to 975,000 cars, while Ford's output failed to surpass 800,000.

Henry and Edsel Ford had watched the Terraplane save Hudson, saw the LaFayette carry Nash through the Depression, and observed the "120" breathing life into Packard. They realized that the Ford Motor Company was missing a great opportunity by not closing the Ford-Lincoln price gap in a similar manner. Edsel Ford (1898-1943) had the solution: a V-12-engined, streamlined glamour car called Lincoln-Zephyr, selling at La Salle prices. Lincoln production had run at the 1000 to 1500 level for some years, but in 1936 Ford built nearly 18,000

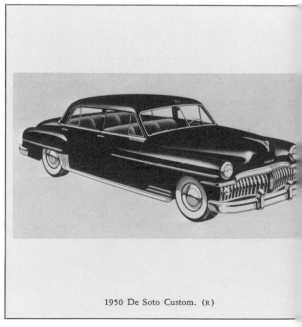

1950 De Soto Custom. (R)

128   1950 Buick Special Deluxe. (G)
      1950 Pontiac Streamliner Eight. (G)

1950 Ford Custom V-8.
1950 Nash Rambler. (A)

Lincoln-Zephyrs as well.

Ransom E. Olds named R. H. Scott to replace him as president of Reo in 1923, when Reo built 32,000 cars and gave work to 4687 workers and employees. Reo's Flying Cloud, introduced in 1926, was a successful entry in the middle-class Buick-Dodge market, while the cheaper Wolverine suffered the same fate as Studebaker's Erskine and Nash's Ajax. Total Reo production in 1928 did not exceed 25,000 cars, and output dwindled year by year until Reo finally gave up passenger car production to concentrate on trucks in 1936.

Buick was in trouble during the Depression, after having placed fourth in the production race in 1927 with an output of more than 255,000 cars. Buick sales fell to just over 40,000 in 1933 — the lowest in twenty years. General Motors sent Harlow H. Curtice (1893-1963) from AC Spark Plug Division to the rescue in Flint. Curtice revamped the plant as well as the products and the 1934 Buicks were successful. Production reached almost 80,000 cars, but even that was not enough to get Buick higher than eighth in the production race. It was not until 1938 that Buick was back in fourth place, which it was to hold for several years to come. Buick's production peak was 1941, with an output of 316,000 cars.

Willys-Knight and Whippet had disappeared early in the Depression when Willys-Overland fell into receivership, but a Willys was reborn at the end of 1932. The "77" was a small, narrow-track car by American standards, but Willys built about 55,000 of them in two years. The stormy career of John North Willys came to an end when he died in August, 1935, with his company still under reorganization. Ward M. Canaday became chairman and David R. Wilson president of Willys-Overland Motors, Inc. when production was started on a new and radically styled Willys of almost standard dimensions in 1936. It was a success. In 1937, Willys built 76,000 cars, exceeding their target by 16,000 vehicles.

General Motors' Oakland did not survive the Depression. Its last year was 1931, when Oakland became Pontiac Motor Division and Harry J. Klingeer was appointed general manager. By 1935 production was up to 1929 levels. In 1937, Pontiac set a new record at 235,000 cars, and broke it again in 1940, with an output of 249,000, which moved Pontiac ahead of Dodge into fifth place in the production race. Pontiac sales increased to 282,000 in 1941, and further gains were prevented only by the advent of World War II.

Charles W. Nash resigned the presidency of Nash to Edward H. McCarty in 1930 but continued to take an active interest in the business until 1937, when Nash merged with Kelvinator into the Nash-Kelvinator Corporation, and George W. Mason (1891-1954) took over as chief executive. Mason decided to discontinue the LaFayette after 1939 and put his engineering staff to work on a new low-priced car, which appeared in 1940 as the Nash 600. It was America's first true unit-construction car, and tooling for its production cost $7,500,000. It gave Nash a healthy sales increase to over 80,000 cars in 1941 — just short of bringing Nash into the top ten.

1951 Kaiser Deluxe. (R)
1951 Henry J Deluxe Six. (R)

1952 Nash Statesman Super. (A)

1953 Studebaker Champion Starliner. (M)
1954 Hudson Hornet. (A)

1954 Hudson Jet Liner. (A)
1954 Chevrolet Bel Air. (G)

1954 Kaiser Manhattan. (R)
1954 Willys Aero-Ace Deluxe. (R)

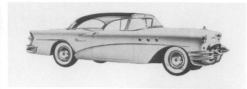
1955 Buick Special. (G)
1955 Chrysler New Yorker. (C)

Studebaker's situation had improved steadily since 1934, when nearly 50,000 cars were built. Both 1936 and 1937 were good years in South Bend, with output exceeding 80,000 cars. Studebaker had not strayed from the middle-class field since the unsuccessful Rockne was discontinued in 1933, but felt the need for a cheaper car which could bring them back into contention. Preparation for their aptly-named Champion began in 1936, when Raymond Loewy was engaged to take care of the styling. The tooling cost $3,500,000. Bigger than the Willys, smaller than the Chevrolet, the Champion was an instant success when it appeared as a 1939 model, and Studebaker production rose to 106,000 cars. A year later, nearly 120,000 were built. The last two pre-war production years almost equalled South Bend's 1928-29 record.

Though their Lincoln-Zephyr was a modest success, hindsight reveals the error Ford made when they created a car to battle the moribund La Salle — while overlooking the Pontiac market. Ford remedied this in 1939 with the introduction of the Mercury, a Ford-based luxury model selling at a Pontiac price. In 1939, Ford built over 76,000 Mercury cars, which immediately placed the new name ninth in the production race. Mercury production rose to 83,000 in 1940 but was curtailed to 80,000 in 1941 because of war production programs.

Passenger car production came to a complete halt during World War II, but several wartime industrial developments were to affect the postwar production race. First, Ford and Willys delivered more then 634,000 Jeeps to the U.S. armed forces, and second, Ford built a giant factory at Willow Run, Michigan, to produce Liberator bomber planes. More significantly, auto industry employment doubled from 1941 to 1943 in the rush to produce war matériel.

Well before the end of the war, Henry J. Kaiser (1882-1967), builder of Liberty and Victory ships, head of Kaiser Steel and Kaiser Aluminum, announced plans to build passenger cars. A little later,

Joseph Washington Frazer, chairman of Graham-Paige, determined to manufacture automobiles after the war. The two joined forces, and the Kaiser-Frazer Corporation was formed on July 25, 1945, with Frazer as president and Kaiser as chairman of the board. Ford closed operations at Willow Run on June 23, 1945, and the plant was sold to Kaiser-Frazer by the War Assets Corporation. Kaiser and Frazer cars began production in June of 1946. In 1947 Kaiser-Frazer Corporation bought out Graham-Paige Motors Corp. and by October of that year had built 100,000 cars and were beginning to make money. In 1950 the company introduced a new and smartly restyled Kaiser and a small car named Henry J, while the Frazer car was discontinued. The future looked promising, but Kaiser-Frazer's sales penetration never met expectations or returned profits after 1948. Quality control was a problem and thefts from the factory increased with a growing labor force. In addition, the dealer organization was inadequate and marketing practices questionable. By the spring of 1951, the factory had some 8000 unsold cars in storage.

Willys-Overland, meanwhile, announced a range of Jeep-based civilian vehicles, and the Toledo factories continued to hum. In 1948, Willys brought out six-cylinder Jeep models, including station wagons and a sports model called the Jeepster. Willys was operating at a profit, and was now getting ready to rejoin the true passenger car field with a small model called the Aero-Willys, introduced in January, 1952. It was a pretty car with clean lines and a willing engine, but it did not sell well. In April, 1953, Henry J. Kaiser interests purchased control of Willys-Overland Motors in Toledo, and sold the Willow Run plant to General Motors, who needed it for making automatic transmissions. All Kaiser automotive operations were transferred to Toledo. In short order, the Kaiser, Henry J and Aero-Willys were discontinued, and production centered on the Jeep-type vehicles. K-F's peak had occurred in 1948, when they produced 181,000 units and the combined Kaiser and Frazer production held eighth place in the production race.

1956 Clipper Deluxe. (R)
1957 Oldsmobile Super 88. (G)

1957 Ford Fairlane Sunliner. (F)
1957 Plymouth Fury. (R)

1957 Hudson Hornet Hollywood. (A)

While the newcomers had been defeated, the established pattern continued at the top, without major disturbance until Buick snatched third place from Plymouth in 1950, only to lose it again in 1951. Production methods had developed considerably since 1941 and productivity increased. The industry invested heavily in production equipment, and a new word appeared: "automation." It was coined by Del S. Harder, vice-president in charge of production at Ford Motor Company. He defined it as "automatical transportation and control of parts through a series of manufacturing operations." Various forms of automation were incorporated into new plants. Ford's engine plant at Cleveland, Ohio, was a pioneering effort, but GM and Chrysler as well as Ford have since added more advanced factories. Expansion was another key word. Ford Motor Company, led by Henry Ford II after the death of Henry Ford in 1947, spent $1,400,000 on plant expansions from 1946 to 1955.

Chevrolet resumed passenger car production on October 3, 1945, and in June, 1946, Nicholas Dreystadt moved from Cadillac to take charge of Chevrolet. A new and ultramodern assembly plant was opened in Flint, Michigan, in 1947, as the number one car in the production race prepared to hold on to its position. Dreystadt died in 1948 and was quickly replaced by W. F. Armstrong, who held the general manager's post for a year before giving way to T. H. Keating. In 1950 Chevrolet became the first firm to produce more than two million passenger cars and trucks in one year. Chevrolet also built its twenty-five millionth car in December, 1950. Chevrolet's success was a portent of increased General Motors domination of the production race in years to come. In 1955 GM built 3,639,120 passenger cars in the U.S. — more than half the nation's entire automobile production.

The rise of Pontiac continued after the war and production exceeded 330,000 in 1949. A new record was set in 1950, with over 460,000 Pontiacs turned out in one year. Pontiac had regained the fifth place it used to occupy during most of the Thirties, displacing Dodge.

Buick was remarkably consistent in the production race and occupied fourth place, behind Plymouth, until 1954, when both Buick and Oldsmobile jumped ahead of Chrysler's breadwinner. In 1955 Buick again captured third place, next to Chevrolet and Ford, with an output of nearly 800,000 cars. But Buick quality control was not up to the buyer's expectations, and the 1957 and 1958 Buicks had weaknesses in the brake system that called for an all-out reengineering effort. Buick's sales fell to 246,000 in 1959, and general manager Edward T. Ragsdale was hurriedly replaced by Ed Rollert, who began a hard uphill fight. Within a year, he had a car with a new brake system, and quality control was stricter than ever. Still, Buick built only 308,000 cars in 1960, and customer loyalty was shaken. In 1961, production continued at a low rate, with an output of 292,000 cars. Buick had fallen from third to eighth place in the production race.

Oldsmobile resumed production in April, 1946, and delivered 115,000 cars that year. Production almost doubled in 1947, then stabilized in 1948. Oldsmobile introduced a high-compression V-8 in its 1949 models and sales soared to almost 283,000 cars. In 1950 the division discontinued all six-cylinder engines, and raised output to a new record of 396,757, moving into sixth position in the production race. Oldsmobile broke the record in 1954 with well over 400,000 cars, and again in 1955, turning out 643,000, attaining fifth place ahead of Pontiac. In 1958 Olds ran fourth, although output was in the 300,000 range because sales were generally down throughout the industry.

The 1949 Ford was a car with an unmistakable postwar look, while the 1949 Chevrolet was restyled but mechanically not different from the 1948 model. Neither had new engines — Ford was building an enlarged version of the 1932 side-valve V-8, and Chevrolet had basically a 1929 overhead-valve six, with some modifications dating back to 1937. Ford went to the overhead-valve V-8 in 1954 and Chevrolet in the following year. Chevrolet led Ford through 1958, but the impossible happened in

1958 Dodge Custom Royal Lancer (c), 1958
Chevrolet Bel Air (g), and 1958 Buick Special (g).

1958 Packard Hawk (r), 1958 Rambler Cross
Country (a), and 1958 Edsel Citation (f).

1959 Studebaker Lark.

1959 when Ford went ahead of Chevrolet, with 1,528,592 units against 1,428,962. In 1960 Chevrolet regained the lead, only to lose it again in 1970, when their output of 1.5 million cars trailed Ford's production by 115,000.

In the mid-Fifties independent auto makers came down with an acute case of merger fever. The "small" factories felt they couldn't compete effectively and sought strength by association with others of their kind. Nash merged with Hudson to form American Motors Corporation and elected George Romney as president after Mason's death in 1954. Studebaker merged with Packard with James J. Nance as president of the resultant Studebaker-Packard Corporation. Kaiser Motors acquired Willys, and "Kaiser-Willys" dealerships sprang up where Kaiser-Frazer and Willys-Overland agencies had stood.

The Hudson plant in Detroit was sold to Cadillac and all manufacture concentrated in Nash-country (Kenosha, Milwaukee and Racine, Wisconsin). The Packard plant on Grand Boulevard in Detroit was sold as a warehouse, and Packard's modern engine-manufacturing line was moved to South Bend. No "traditional" Packards were produced after the Detroit plant was closed — only a few Studebakers with Packard nameplates. July, 1958, saw the last "Packard" leave South Bend, and in 1962, the company reverted to the old name of Studebaker Corporation.

The Kaiser-Willys combine failed to regain the old sales standings of K-F, and passenger car production was dropped in favor of Jeeps for the 1956 model year.

Nash and Hudson cars continued in production until June, 1957, when American Motors decided to drop these full-size cars to concentrate on Ramblers. The "Nash Rambler" had begun in 1950 as a small, low-priced car and had become the top money maker for Nash-Kelvinator. Beginning in 1958, Romney called the Rambler a "compact" car and dropped any pretense of making full-size passenger vehicles. The Rambler became one of the most successful cars in the production race during the late Fifties with an output of 91,000 cars in 1957, 217,000 cars in 1958 and 400,000 cars in 1959. In 1960 Rambler was third in total units with 486,000.

Studebaker's advanced Starlight/Starliner coupés had sparked sales temporarily in 1953, but after Nance arrived with the Packard merger, the South Bend firm found itself unable to tool up for production of a totally new car. After Nance had brought the company to the brink of ruin its replacement, a veteran engineer named Harold Churchill, saved the corporation by simply shortening the front and rear overhang on the standard Studebaker and calling it the Lark. It was introduced as a 1959 model, and 133,382 Larks were sold that year. Studebaker's loss of $13 million in 1958 was countered by a $25 million profit in 1959. But Churchill could not get the money he needed to develop future models — and the corporation staked everything on the Lark's initial success. It did not last, and no replacement was forthcoming. Studebaker's breakeven point was 120,000 cars, but 1962 production was only 86,974.

1960 Valiant V-200 (C), 1960 Corvair 500 (R), and 1960 Ford Falcon (F).

1961 De Soto (R), 1961 Pontiac Tempest (G), and 1961 Oldsmobile F-85 (G).

1961 Dodge Lancer 770 (R), 1962 Buick Special (G), and 1962 Rambler Ambassador (A)

The end came in December, 1963, when Studebaker transferred all its automotive operations to Hamilton, Ontario. Studebaker's foundry in South Bend was sold to the Cummins Engine Company. The ex-Packard engine plant and Studebaker's machine shop and equipment were acquired by Chrysler, the main body plant was sold to Essex Wire Corporation; the South Bend proving grounds went to Bendix Corporation; and the truck plant was bought by Kaiser Jeep. Despite a lower break-even point of only 40,000 cars, Studebaker's Canadian effort did not last long either. Production slipped below 30,000 in 1964 and below 13,000 in 1965. The last Studebaker was assembled on March 4, 1966.

There were other tragedies. One of the biggest was that of the Edsel. Henry Ford II and Ernest R. Breech, president of Ford Motor Company, decided after careful and costly market research that the Mercury should be augmented by a slightly lower-priced car. Ford spent about $250 million on design, development and tooling of the Edsel, but by the time Edsels appeared Ford's research had grown obsolete. With the ultimate production goal at 300,000 cars per year, the market had turned sharply toward the "compact" car. The result was inevitable — during 1957 production was less than 55,000 cars; for 1958, it was a poor 27,000. After fewer than 30,000 cars were unloaded in 1959, Ford discontinued Edsel production on November 19th of that year. Only a handful of 1960 models had been built.

Chrysler Corporation had their troubles too. Designing and tooling the new line of Chrysler, De Soto, Dodge and Plymouth cars for 1949 cost

about $90 million, and the corporation was rewarded with the best year in its history after producing 1,267,470 cars and trucks. Early in 1950 Chrysler had a one-hundred day strike, but by the end of the year they had set another production record. Preparing for a great future, new president Tex Colbert poured almost a billion dollars into plant expansion and modernization. But in 1954 the sales picture changed, and Chrysler Corporation's share of the total auto market fell from over 20 percent to 12.9. With pleasing facelifts, both 1955 and 1956 were exceptional years for Chrysler, and the 1957 models with long profiles and high tailfins gave the corporation nearly $120,000,000 in profits and an 18.3 percent cut of the American passenger car market. But the quality of Chrysler's 1957 cars was poor, and the penalty came in 1958 when the automotive operations returned a loss of $34 million while Chrysler's market share fell again to 13.7 percent. Plymouth held third place with a 1958 output of 367,000 cars while Dodge was tenth with about 114,000—but fewer than 50,000 Chryslers and 37,000 De Sotos were built. The whole De Soto line was discontinued in late 1960, shortly after introduction of the 1961 models.

At this time, Chrysler put the squeeze on their engineering staff and reduced it to about half. The corporation was not up to date in product planning, and this made matters worse. Financial control at Chrysler was not on par with Ford's and General Motors' methods, and productivity lagged behind the industry norm. The dealer organization had shrunk from 10,000 outlets in 1953 to 5500 by 1962. William C. Newberg became president when Tex Colbert retired in April, 1960.

133

Within two months, Newberg was involved in a conflict-of-interest case for holding stock in various supplier firms with large Chrysler contracts, and Colbert was called back. The search for a new president lasted a full year, but Lynn Townsend, an accountant and auditor, finally took over in July, 1961.

At the end of the Fifties the American automobile market changed drastically. Customers demanded smaller cars, showed their preference for more sensible size and lower price by purchasing imported cars or compact domestics like as the Nash Rambler. Small cars such as Kaiser-Frazer's Henry J, Hudson's Jet and the Aero-Willys had not succeeded earlier in the Fifties, but American Motors made a firm commitment to volume production of compact cars, and Rambler sales rose in spectacular fashion from 1957 through 1961. Ford, Chrysler and General Motors saw in these trends a definite confirmation that the public wanted smaller cars, and in 1957 each of the Big Three started to prepare accordingly. Ford and Plymouth introduced conventional, scaled-down cars named Falcon and Valiant, while Chevrolet produced the Corvair, a rear-engined vehicle with all-independent suspension and an air cooled flat-six aluminum powerplant. These three cars appeared in late 1959 as 1960 models and were quite successful, putting a temporary stop to import penetration of the market. Ford sold 507,000 Falcons against 230,000 Corvairs, while the Valiant ran third. Imported cars held 20.4 percent of the compact car market in 1960, while Ford's Falcon took 29.9 percent, Rambler 20.7 percent, Corvair 13.5 percent, Valiant 10.3 percent and the Studebaker Lark 5.2 percent.

Even if more Corvairs (319,000) were built the following year at the Falcon's (483,000) expense, it was clear to General Motors that the Corvair was too radical and unusual to secure its intended share of the compact market for Chevrolet. GM decided, therefore, to apply the Corvair concept to the burgeoning sporty-car market, and to introduce a compact Pontiac (Tempest), Oldsmobile (F-85) and Buick (Special), while Chevrolet was told to develop a car that would be better suited for the Falcon market than the Corvair. The Pontiac, Oldsmobile and Buick compacts were introduced as 1961 models; Pontiac built 116,000 Tempests, while Buick made 101,000 Specials and Oldsmobile produced 68,000 F-85's. Nevertheless, Ford took 30.6 percent of the compact market, with 27.6 percent going to General Motors.

At the same time, Mercury introduced its version of the Falcon — a compact car called Comet, and built 186,000 in 1961. Plymouth's Valiant did better in its second year, with 122,000 cars, and Dodge introduced a sister model called Lancer, selling 54,000 units. As the 1962 production race shaped up, it became clear that compact cars would account for about one-third of total production, and could, in fact, determine the results of the race.

Chevrolet's answer to the Falcon, called Chevy II, was ready for 1962. Chevrolet built 368,000 of them, close to Ford's output of 381,000 Falcons. But Ford had another better idea — something for Falcon owners to move up to — something, that is, other than a full-sized Ford. The result was the Fairlane, first of the "intermediates," which appeared as a 1962 model, and 386,000 were built. But though Chevrolet had no counterpart, they still outproduced Ford overall, for in full-size cars Chevrolet built 1.4 million against only 723,000 Fords.

Chevrolet set new production records in 1962, but the year was even more significant for Pontiac. Pete Estes took over as general manager in 1961 (he was formerly Pontiac's chief engineer), and had the satisfaction of producing 402,000 Pontiacs and 145,000 Tempests in 1962. Pontiac moved into third place in the production race, displacing Rambler, whose total output reached 454,000 cars that year, and remained firmly in third for the rest of the decade. John Zachary De Lorean, who had been chief engineer, replaced Estes as general manager in 1965, built a new engine plant and raised production capacity. In 1968 Pontiac built a record 943,000 automobiles.

1962 Chevy II 300. (G)
1963 Dodge Dart. (C)

1963 Mercury Comet Sportster. (F)
1963 Ford Fairlane 500. (F)

1964 Studebaker Gran Turismo Hawk. (R)
1964 Chevelle Malibu Super Sports. (G)

Rambler fell rapidly after the departure of George Romney, who left early in 1962 to run for Governor of Michigan. Roy Abernethy, the former sales manager, became president and Rambler began a period of neglected product evolution. Production fell with alarming rapidity: Rambler was sixth in 1963, eighth in 1964, and American Motors overall were ninth in 1965. Production fell from 346,000 cars in 1965 to less than 280,000 in 1966, with American Motors ninth among the top ten. Abernethy was replaced in January, 1967, after major stockholder Robert B. Evans resigned as chairman in favor of Roy D. Chapin, Jr., who named William Luneburg president. American Motors had heavy debts, but immediately lowered prices on the bottom-line cars to increase sales volume, and prepared new and advanced models.

It was 1964 model time before General Motors was able to react to the Fairlane from Ford. As demand for the Buick-Olds-Pontiac compacts diminished, they were redesigned as middle-size cars, sharing many body parts and using the same frame but individual engines. To allow Chevrolet to compete in the medium-size market, it got its own version of the same car, named Chevelle. Chevrolet built 321,000 Chevelles against 234,000 Fairlanes while Ford made 280,000 Falcons against 158,000 Chevy II's and 196,000 Corvairs. As for the full-size cars, Chevrolet won easily with 1.4 million cars against Ford's 881,000.

The Townsend administration at Chrysler was dominated by bookkeepers, not auto men. Serious errors were made in product planning and the corporation suffered the inevitable result. Sales in 1961 and 1962 were so poor that rumors of imminent bankruptcy began to circulate.

For 1963 Chrysler reduced Plymouth's largest models (Savoy, Belvedere, Fury) to a 116-inch wheelbase, which put the make out of competition with the full-size Ford and Chevrolet, but directly up against Ford's Fairlane. Launching of the sub-standard-size Plymouths coincided with the arrival of the five-year-or-50,000-mile warranty on

Chrysler engine and drive train parts. Plymouth sales gained forty-one percent in 1963, and another sixteen percent in 1964. For 1965 the Fury returned to full size, while the Belvedere was officially assigned intermediate status.

Dodge had maintained a line of full-sized cars throughout, added the compact Lancer in 1960 (which was renamed Dart in 1963), and also produced the intermediate 330 and 440 models from 1962 through 1964. The Coronet name had been dormant for some years when it was renewed for 1965, revived for Dodge's version of the Belvedere.

Townsend trimmed the payroll and lowered the break-even point to about 800,000 cars for the entire corporation. In 1963 Chrysler Corporation made a small profit. Plymouth and Dodge accounted for the bulk of the total with 496,000 and 421,000 cars respectively, with Chrysler at 112,000. The following year the company again prospered, with a total for all makes of 1.2 million cars. In 1965 the results were even better: 1.47 million. New records were set in 1966, with nearly 641,000 Plymouths, 532,000 Dodges, better than 255,000 Chryslers and about 18,000 Imperials. Plymouth continued to hold firm in 1967, despite general shrinkage of the domestic market.

At American Motors it became clear in early 1966 that faulty management was driving the corporation straight toward financial failure. A Wisconsin industrialist, Robert B. Evans, succeeded in buying a large block of AMC shares, and got elected to the board of directors. Within a few months, Evans became chairman and Victor Raviolo was brought in as engineering director. Early in 1967 Evans turned the chairmanship over to Roy D. Chapin Jr., who had been in charge of AMC's overseas operations, while Bill Luneberg, as was mentioned previously, was named president. The new team immediately made some difficult but wise decisions. To obtain adequate operating capital, AMC sold off Kelvinator, disposed of its Redisco financing branch, and obtained favorable credit sources from several banks. On the product end, they

1965 Chrysler Newport. (c)
1965 Ford Mustang. (F)

1965 Plymouth Barracuda. (c)

1966 Studebaker Daytona. (Q)

135

1966 Ambassador 990 DPL. (A)
1967 Chevrolet Camaro. (G)

1967 Pontiac Firebird. (G)
1968 Mercury Cougar. (F)

1969 Plymouth Barracuda. (C)
1969 Chrysler Newport Custom. (C)

began to gradually phase out the Rambler name. The "Classic" model series was replaced by "Rebel" for 1967, but this new line never caught on. Sales went down in steady regression, from 100,000 in 1967, to 67,000 in 1968, to a mere 51,000 in 1969. The Rebel was finally replaced by a completely new car called Matador for 1971.

In the course of the Sixties, the production race change was less contingent on full-size car sales. Though the two best-sellers remained Chevrolet's Impala and Ford's Galaxie, the market share of the big cars began shrinking steadily, and continues to do so as new classes of smaller cars are added. In April, 1964, Ford announced a new car that was to affect its position in the production race more than any other: the Mustang. Market research had discovered a demand for sporty looks, so product planning devised a new sporty car, using existing components except for the body shell. Mustang was a runaway success, with an output of more than 303,000 in its first ten months. Chevrolet had nothing like it, and was not to get it for two and one half years.

Bunkie Knudsen, general manager of Chevrolet when the Mustang appeared, may not have realized that the multi-carburetor, supercharged versions of the Corvair were not equal to the task of tackling the Mustang in a V-8 oriented market. But Pete Estes, the former general manager of Pontiac who succeeded Knudsen at Chevrolet in 1965, certainly did, and took every step he could to hurry the preparation of a new project known as the "F-body" car. It was introduced as a 1967 model called the Chevrolet Camaro.

Chrysler replied to the Mustang earlier, in 1965, with Plymouth's Barracuda. Basically a Valiant with a hurriedly-contrived fastback body, it failed to catch public favor until a ground-up redesign made it a good-looking car, and by that time, Ford's Lincoln-Mercury Division had a companion to the Mustang, the Mercury Cougar, sharing the same mechanical elements, but with its own distinctive body. The Cougar, Camaro and new Barracuda appeared in late 1966. In March, 1967,

Pontiac introduced its own sporty car, the Firebird, using a Camaro body with Pontiac drive train and special chassis modifications. The Firebird and Cougar enjoyed considerable success, but the Barracuda continued to lag behind. By mid-1967, the Mustang held about half of the sporty-car market, with twenty-five percent going to the Camaro and the balance divided among Cougar, Firebird and Barracuda.

For 1970, Chrysler came up with a third generation Barracuda, using the running gear from the intermediate Satellite instead of the compact Valiant. Dodge was given a companion model known as the Challenger. Neither made the expected hit with the public. Six months later, in February, 1970, General Motors revamped the Camaro and the Firebird, and the results — the prettiest shapes in some time — were instant successes. Very soon, Camaro was outselling Mustang three to two.

Ford suffered a sixty-day strike at the start of the 1968 model year, which noticeably affected the outcome of the production race. At this time, General Motors made some significant management changes. President James Roche retired, retaining only the board chairmanship, and operations vice-president Edward N. Cole became GM's chief executive. One week after the announcement, Bunkie Knudsen resigned from General Motors, and shortly later was appointed president of the Ford Motor Company — an historic switch which reversed the move his father had made in 1921. Knudsen had grown up as the son of Pontiac's general manager and joined Pontiac in 1939. He served as head of GM's Detroit Diesel Engine Division for 1955-56, whence he was named general manager of Pontiac. There he made a reputation as a dynamic businessman and fearless decision-maker. He spearheaded Pontiac's rise to third place and was promoted to general manager of Chevrolet in 1961, and to corporate office in 1965. Ford made progress in the production race under Knudsen, but the honeymoon was soon over. Henry Ford II fired him on September 11, 1969, and revamped the top echelons of the company, making Lee A. Iacocca, who started with

'70 Ford Maverick.

1970 American Motors Gremlin.

1971 Chevrolet Vega 2300 Kammback.
1971 Ford Pinto Runabout.

Ford as a truck salesman, executive vice-president of Ford Company. He was given the title of president at the end of 1970.

As the small car trend continued, Ford nearly doubled Falcon production in 1968, and introduced the sub-compact Maverick in April, 1969. By the end of the calendar year, 130,000 Mavericks had been built. The Falcon was gradually phased out early in 1970, in the face of declining demand. Shedding the Falcon line was probably premature, as it left a bad gap between Maverick and Fairlane, while the Falcon-sized Chevy Nova, Plymouth Valiant and Dodge Dart were selling rapidly. But a new section in the production race was in preparation. Truly small cars, or mini-compacts, were on the way.

American Motors was first with a mini, announcing the Gremlin in March, 1970. Ford's Pinto and Chevrolet's Vega followed in September.

General Motors took a sixty-five day strike shortly after '71 model production had started; this was throwing the 1970 production race out of its accustomed orbit. Ford built 89,000 Pintos, against Chevrolet's output of 48,000 Vegas in the same period, and due to the strike, became number one in 1970. Division to division, Ford beat Chevy by 117,000 units. The model-by-model 1970 new car registrations are interesting:

Full size	Galaxie 812,618	Impala 550,571
Intermediate	Torino 327,293	Chevelle 354,855
Compact	Falcon 26,057	Nova 254,242
Personal	Thunderbird 40,512	Monte Carlo 130,657
Sporty car	Mustang 165,415	Camaro 143,664
Subcompact	Maverick 187,087	
Sports car		Corvette 22, 585

For the whole industry, standard-sized vehicles still make up the largest single category, but taken together, compacts and intermediates outrank

the regular cars. The figures for 1970 calendar year were:

Standards	1,972,598	30.1%
Intermediates	1,643,816	25.2%
Compacts	963,021	14.7%
Medium standards	750,990	11.4%
Sporty cars	544,964	8.3%
Specialty cars	277,457	4.3%
Minicompacts	186,463	2.9%
Luxury cars	181,979	2.8%
Performance cars	22,585	0.3%
	6,546,983	100.0%

The breakdown among the corporations showed an unusually small share for General Motors, due to the long strike:

General Motors	2,979,261	45.6%
Ford Motor Co.	2,017,153	30.8%
Chrysler Corp.	1,273,459	19.4%
American Motors	276,110	4.2%
	6,546,983	100.0%

As we push further into the Seventies production race watchers are keeping an eye on several developments, including Pontiac's struggle to get in front of Buick and Oldsmobile, Dodge's fight to keep ahead of Lincoln-Mercury, Chrysler's losing battle with Cadillac, Vega's combat with the Pinto and Valiant's duel with the Chevy Nova. In the American free-market economy, the outcome lies in the hands of the consumer. His preferences will dictate demand, and demand determines supply. Competition is keener than ever, and nothing is ever to be taken for granted. Forecasts for total production are favorable, however, and a domestic production of 8.5 million cars seemed a realistic estimate at the outset of the 1971 calendar year. But the final ranking, this year and every year, is anyone's guess.

CALENDAR YEAR PRODUCTION: *1896 TO DATE*
BY JAMES J. BRADLEY AND RICHARD M. LANGWORTH

1896		1897		1898		1899		1900	
1. Duryea	13	1. Winton	4	1. Stanley	100	1. Columbia	500*	1. Columbia	1500*
2. Ford	1	2. Duryea	3*	2. Winton	22	2. Locomobile	400*	2. Locomobile	750*
3. Winton	1	3. Olds	1	3. Stearns	1	3. Winton	100	3. Knox	15
				4. Duryea	—	4. Stanley	30	4. White	1
						5. Stearns	20*	5. Winton	—
						6. Duryea	—	6. Duryea	—

*Production estimate.

1905		1906		1907		1908	
1. Oldsmobile	6,500	1. Ford	8,729	1. Ford	14,887	1. Ford	10,202
2. Cadillac	3,942	2. Cadillac	4,059	2. Buick	4,641	2. Buick	8,820
3. Rambler	3,807	3. Rambler	2,765	3. Reo	3,967	3. Studebaker	8,132
4. Ford	1,599	4. Reo	2,458	4. Maxwell	3,785	4. Maxwell	4,455
5. Franklin	1,098	5. Maxwell	2,161*	5. Rambler	3,201	5. Reo	4,105
6. White	1,015	6. Oldsmobile	1,600	6. Cadillac	2,884	6. Rambler	3,597
7. Reo	864	7. White	1,534	7. Franklin	1,509	7. Cadillac	2,377
8. Maxwell	823	8. Buick	1,400	8. Packard	1,403	8. Franklin	1,895
9. Buick	750	9. Franklin	1,283	9. Stoddard-Dayton	1,200	9. Packard	1,803
10. Stanley	610	10. Packard	959	10. White	1,130	10. Hupmobile	1,618
11. Packard	481	11. Stanley	640	11. Stanley	775	11. Stoddard-Dayton	1,400
12. Stoddard-Dayton	125	12. Stoddard-Dayton	385	12. Thomas-Detroit	506	12. White	1,024
13. Knox	—	13. Pope-Hartford	—	13. Brush	500	13. Stanley	734
14. Columbia	—	14. Knox	—	14. Overland	47	14. Brush	700

1913		1914		1915		1916	
1. Ford	202,667	1. Ford	308,162	1. Ford	501,462	1. Ford	734,811
2. Willys-Overland	37,422	2. Willys-Overland	48,461	2. Willys-Overland	91,904	2. Willys-Overland	140,111
3. Studebaker	31,994	3. Studebaker	35,374	3. Dodge	45,000	3. Buick	124,834
4. Buick	26,666	4. Buick	32,889	4. Maxwell	44,000	4. Dodge	71,400
5. Cadillac	17,284	5. Maxwell	18,000	5. Buick	43,946	5. Maxwell	69,000
6. Maxwell	17,000	6. Reo	13,516	6. Studebaker	41,243	6. Studebaker	65,536
7. Hupmobile	12,543	7. Jeffery	10,417	7. Cadillac	20,404	7. Chevrolet	62,898
8. Reo	7,647	8. Hupmobile	10,318	8. Saxon	19,000	8. Saxon	27,800
9. Oakland	7,030	9. Hudson	10,261	9. Reo	14,693	9. Hudson	25,772
10. Hudson	6,401	10. Cadillac	7,818	10. Chevrolet	13,292	10. Oakland	25,675
11. Chalmers	6,000	11. Saxon	7,100	11. Hudson	12,864	11. Reo	23,753
12. Chevrolet-Little	5,987	12. Metz	6,300	12. Oakland	11,952	12. Chalmers	21,000
13. Paige	5,000	13. Chalmers	6,200	13. Hupmobile	10,403	13. Chandler	20,000*
14. Rambler	4,435	14. Oakland	6,105	14. Chalmers	9,800	14. Cadillac	16,323
15. Packard	2,984	15. Paige	4,631	15. Oldsmobile	7,696	15. Paige	12,456

Notes: For certain early years research disclosed divergent calendar year production totals from equally reliable sources; in these cases the figure has been replaced by a dash (—). Throughout the pre-1920 period there is considerable room for expansion of the lists, but in the interests of accuracy entries have been limited to those manufacturers who were significant pioneering members of the production race. There were hundreds of others, as earlier indicated in Section I of this book, who were building cars during the early years of the automobile industry in this country. Although most did not, a number did proceed into automobile manufacture but, as is thus far known, did not sustain manufacture for any extended period—or, in some cases, their production figures cannot be verified. Finally, where a company (such as Kaiser-Frazer) built more than one make of car, the figure given applies to the company as a whole rather than any single marque, this being done to place the producer in better perspective to the industry giants, and indeed, occasionally, to include the company on the list at all. Such companies are rarely broken down by make in most sources. Additions to this production race list from readers, using the form appended in the back of this book, will be welcomed.

1901

1. Locomobile	1,500*
2. Oldsmobile	425
3. White	193
4. Autocar	140
5. Knox	100
6. Stanley	80
7. Packard	5
8. Columbia	—
9. Duryea	—

1902

1. Locomobile	2,750
2. Oldsmobile	2,500
3. Rambler	1,500
4. White	385
5. Knox	250
6. Stanley	170
7. Union	60*
8. Stevens-Duryea	50
9. Franklin	13
10. Packard	1
11. Columbia	—

1903

1. Oldsmobile	4,000
2. Ford	1,708
3. Cadillac	1,698
4. Pope Hartford	1,500*
5. Rambler	1,350
6. Winton	850
7. White	502
8. Knox	500
9. Stevens-Duryea	500*
10. Baker	400
11. Stanley	300

1904

1. Oldsmobile	5,508
2. Cadillac	2,457
3. Rambler	2,342
4. Ford	1,695
5. Franklin	712
6. White	710
7. Stanley	550
8. Packard	250
9. Overland	25
10. Maxwell	10
11. Pope-Hartford	—

1909

1. Ford	17,771
2. Buick	14,606
3. Maxwell	9,460
4. Studebaker-EMF	7,960
5. Cadillac	7,868
6. Reo	6,592
7. Willys-Overland	4,860
8. Packard	3,106
9. Brush	2,000
10. Rambler	1,692
11. Oldsmobile	1,690
12. Hupmobile	1,600
13. Stoddard-Dayton	1,600
14. White	1,377

1910

1. Ford	32,053
2. Buick	30,525
3. Willys-Overland	15,598
4. Studebaker-EMF	15,020
5. Cadillac	10,039
6. Maxwell	10,000
7. Brush	10,000*
8. Reo	6,588
9. Chalmers	6,350
10. Hupmobile	5,340
11. Hudson	4,556
12. Oakland	4,049
13. Packard	3,084
14. Lambert	3,000*

1911

1. Ford	69,762
2. Studebaker-EMF	26,827
3. Willys-Overland	18,745
4. Maxwell	16,000
5. Buick	13,389
6. Cadillac	10,071
7. Hudson	6,486
8. Chalmers	6,250
9. Hupmobile	6,079
10. Reo	5,278
11. Oakland	3,386
12. Rambler	3,000
13. Packard	2,521
14. Franklin	1,654

1912

1. Ford	170,211
2. Willys-Overland	28,572
3. Studebaker-EMF	28,032
4. Buick	19,812
5. Cadillac	12,708
6. Hupmobile	7,640
7. Reo	6,342
8. Oakland	5,838
9. Brush	5,750
10. Hudson	5,708
11. Rambler	3,550
12. Chevrolet	2,999
13. Packard	2,320
14. Franklin	1,214

1917

1. Ford	622,351
2. Willys-Overland	130,988
3. Buick	115,267
4. Chevrolet	110,839
5. Dodge	90,000
6. Maxwell	75,000
7. Studebaker	39,686
8. Oakland	33,171
9. Reo	25,000
10. Oldsmobile	22,042
11. Hudson	20,976
12. Cadillac	19,759
13. Chandler	15,000
14. Nash	12,027
15. Hupmobile	11,293

1918

1. Ford	435,898
2. Willys-Overland	88,753
3. Chevrolet	80,434
4. Buick	77,691
5. Dodge	62,000
6. Maxwell	34,000
7. Oakland	27,757
8. Oldsmobile	18,871
9. Studebaker	16,111
10. Hudson	12,526
11. Cadillac	12,329
12. Nash	10,283
13. Hupmobile	9,544
14. Reo	—
15. Chandler	—

1919

1. Ford	820,445
2. Chevrolet	123,371
3. Buick	119,310
4. Dodge	106,000
5. Willys-Overland	80,853
6. Oakland	52,124
7. Maxwell	50,000
8. Oldsmobile	41,127
9. Hudson-Essex	40,054
10. Studebaker	33,538
11. Nash	27,018
12. Cadillac	19,851
13. Chandler	18,476
14. Hupmobile	17,442
15. Reo	—

1920

1. Ford	419,517
2. Dodge	141,000
3. Chevrolet	121,908
4. Buick	115,176
5. Willys-Overland	105,025
6. Studebaker	48,831
7. Hudson-Essex	45,937
8. Chandler	45,000
9. Nash	35,084
10. Oakland	34,839
11. Maxwell	34,168
12. Oldsmobile	33,949
13. Dort	23,853
14. Cadillac	19,790
15. Hupmobile	19,225

1921		
1.	Ford	903,814
2.	Buick	82,930
3.	Dodge	81,000
4.	Studebaker	65,023
5.	Chevrolet	61,717
6.	Willys-Overland	48,016
7.	Hudson-Essex	27,143
8.	Nash	20,850
9.	Oldsmobile	18,978
10.	Maxwell	16,000
11.	Hupmobile	13,626
12.	Oakland	11,852
13.	Cadillac	11,130
14.	Reo	—
15.	Star	—

1922		
1.	Ford	1,173,745
2.	Chevrolet	208,848
3.	Dodge	142,000
4.	Buick	123,152
5.	Studebaker	105,005
6.	Willys-Overland	95,410
7.	Hudson-Essex	64,464
8.	Durant lines	55,300
9.	Maxwell-Chalmers	44,811
10.	Nash	41,652
11.	Hupmobile	34,168
12.	Cadillac	22,021
13.	Oldsmobile	21,505
14.	Oakland	19,636
15.	Reo	—

1923		
1.	Ford	1,817,891
2.	Chevrolet	415,814
3.	Buick	201,572
4.	Willys-Overland	196,038
5.	Durant lines	172,000
6.	Dodge	151,000
7.	Studebaker	146,238
8.	Hudson-Essex	88,914
9.	Maxwell-Chalmers	67,000
10.	Nash-LaFayette	56,677
11.	Hupmobile	38,279
12.	Oakland	35,847
13.	Oldsmobile	34,721
14.	Reo	31,880
15.	Cadillac	22,009

1924		
1.	Ford	1,749,827
2.	Chevrolet	262,100
3.	Dodge	193,861
4.	Willys-Overland	163,000
5.	Buick	160,411
6.	Hudson-Essex	133,950
7.	Durant lines	111,000
8.	Studebaker	105,387
9.	Chrysler-Maxwell	79,144
10.	Nash	53,626
11.	Oldsmobile	44,309
12.	Oakland	35,792
13.	Hupmobile	31,004
14.	Cadillac	17,748

1929		
1.	Ford	1,507,132
2.	Chevrolet	950,150
3.	Hudson-Essex	300,962
4.	W-O/Whippet	242,000
5.	Pontiac-Oakland	211,054
6.	Buick	196,104
7.	Dodge	124,557
8.	Nash	116,622
9.	Oldsmobile-Viking	101,579
10.	Plymouth	93,592
11.	Chrysler	92,034
12.	Studebaker-Erskine	90,473
13.	Graham-Paige	77,077
14.	DeSoto	64,911
15.	Hupmobile	50,579
16.	Packard	43,318
17.	Durant lines	47,716
18.	Cadillac-LaSalle	36,698

1930		
1.	Ford	1,155,162
2.	Chevrolet	683,419
3.	Buick	119,265
4.	Hudson-Essex	113,898
5.	Pontiac-Oakland	86,225
6.	W-O/Whippet	69,000
7.	Dodge	68,158
8.	Plymouth	67,658
9.	Chrysler	60,199
10.	Nash	54,605
11.	Studebaker	51,640
12.	Oldsmobile	49,886
13.	DeSoto	34,889
14.	Graham-Paige	33,560
15.	Packard	28,177
16.	Cadillac-LaSalle	22,559
17.	Hupmobile	22,183
18.	Durant lines	20,900

1931		
1.	Chevrolet	627,104
2.	Ford	541,615
3.	Plymouth	106,259
4.	Buick	88,417
5.	Pontiac-Oakland	86,307
6.	W-O/Whippet	74,750
7.	Hudson-Essex	57,825
8.	Dodge	56,003
9.	Chrysler	52,819
10.	Studebaker-Rockne	48,921
11.	Oldsmobile	48,000
12.	Nash	39,616
13.	Auburn	32,301
14.	DeSoto	29,835
15.	Hupmobile	17,456
16.	Cadillac-LaSalle	15,012
17.	Packard	13,123
18.	Durant lines	7,000

1932		
1.	Chevrolet	306,716
2.	Ford	232,125
3.	Plymouth	121,468
4.	Hudson Essex	57,550
5.	Pontiac	46,594
6.	Studebaker-Rockne	44,235
7.	Buick	41,522
8.	Dodge	30,216
9.	DeSoto	27,441
10.	Willys-Overland	26,710
11.	Chrysler	25,291
12.	Oldsmobile	21,933
13.	Nash	17,696
14.	Hupmobile	10,076
15.	Cadillac-LaSalle	9,153
16.	Packard	8,018

1937		
1.	Chevrolet	868,250
2.	Ford	848,608
3.	Plymouth	514,061
4.	Dodge	288,841
5.	Pontiac	235,322
6.	Buick	227,038
7.	Oldsmobile	212,767
8.	Hudson-Terraplane	111,342
9.	Packard	109,518
10.	Chrysler	107,872
11.	DeSoto	86,541
12.	Nash-LaFayette	85,949
13.	Studebaker	80,993
14.	Willys-Overland	76,803
15.	Cadillac-LaSalle	45,223

1938		
1.	Chevrolet	490,447
2.	Ford	410,048
3.	Plymouth	297,572
4.	Buick	173,905
5.	Dodge	106,370
6.	Pontiac	95,128
7.	Oldsmobile	93,705
8.	Hudson	51,078
9.	Packard	50,260
10.	Studebaker	46,207
11.	Chrysler	41,496
12.	DeSoto	32,688
13.	Nash-LaFayette	32,017
14.	Cadillac-LaSalle	27,613
15.	Willys-Overland	16,173

1939		
1.	Chevrolet	648,471
2.	Ford	532,152
3.	Plymouth	350,046
4.	Buick	231,219
5.	Dodge	186,474
6.	Pontiac	170,698
7.	Oldsmobile	158,560
8.	Studebaker	106,470
9.	Hudson	82,161
10.	Packard	76,573
11.	Mercury	76,198
12.	Chrysler	67,749
13.	Nash-LaFayette	65,662
14.	DeSoto	53,269
15.	Cadillac-LaSalle	38,520
16.	Willys-Overland	25,383

1940		
1.	Chevrolet	895,734
2.	Ford	599,175
3.	Plymouth	509,735
4.	Buick	310,995
5.	Pontiac	249,303
6.	Oldsmobile	215,028
7.	Dodge	225,595
8.	Studebaker	117,091
9.	Chrysler	115,824
10.	DeSoto	83,805
11.	Mercury	82,770
12.	Hudson	79,979
13.	Packard	66,906
14.	Nash	63,617
15.	Cadillac-LaSalle	40,245
16.	Willys-Overland	26,698

1925

1.	Ford	1,643,295
2.	Chevrolet	444,671
3.	Hudson-Essex	269,474
4.	Willys-Overland	215,000
5.	Dodge	201,000
6.	Buick	192,100
7.	Studebaker	133,104
8.	Chrysler-Maxwell	132,343
9.	Hupmobile	129,020
10.	Durant lines	127,000
11.	Nash-Ajax	96,121
12.	Oakland	44,642
13.	Oldsmobile	42,701
14.	Paige-Jewett	39,380
15.	Packard	32,125
16.	Cadillac	22,542

1926

1.	Ford	1,368,383
2.	Chevrolet	588,962
3.	Buick	266,753
4.	Dodge	265,000
5.	Hudson-Essex	227,508
6.	W-O/Whippet	182,000
7.	Chrysler	162,242
8.	Nash	135,520
9.	Pontiac-Oakland	133,604
10.	Durant lines	125,000
11.	Studebaker	103,189
12.	Oldsmobile	57,862
13.	Hupmobile	45,426
14.	Paige-Jewett	37,222
15.	Packard	34,907
16.	Cadillac	27,340
17.	Chandler	20,971

1927

1.	Chevrolet	1,749,998
2.	Ford	356,188
3.	Hudson-Essex	276,414
4.	Buick	255,160
5.	Pontiac-Oakland	188,168
6.	W-O/Whippet	188,000
7.	Chrysler	182,195
8.	Dodge	146,000
9.	Nash	122,606
10.	Studebaker-Erskine	120,542
11.	Durant lines	30,843
12.	Oldsmobile	54,888
13.	Hupmobile	41,161
14.	Packard	36,480
15.	Cadillac-LaSalle	34,811
16.	Reo	28,750
17.	Paige	21,881
18.	Chandler	20,359

1928

1.	Chevrolet	888,050
2.	Ford	633,594
3.	W-O/Whippet	315,000
4.	Hudson-Essex	282,203
5.	Pontiac-Oakland	244,584
6.	Buick	221,758
7.	Chrysler	160,670
8.	Nash	138,137
9.	Studebaker-Erskine	123,258
10.	Durant lines	115,243
11.	Oldsmobile-Viking	86,235
12.	Graham-Paige	73,195
13.	Dodge	67,327
14.	Hupmobile	65,857
15.	Plymouth	52,427
16.	Packard	50,054
17.	Cadillac-LaSalle	41,172
18.	DeSoto	33,345

1933

1.	Chevrolet	481,134
2.	Ford	334,969
3.	Plymouth	255,564
4.	Dodge	91,403
5.	Pontiac	85,772
6.	Studebaker-Rockne	43,024
7.	Hudson-Terraplane	40,982
8.	Buick	40,620
9.	Oldsmobile	36,357
10.	Chrysler	30,220
11.	Willys-Overland	29,918
12.	DeSoto	20,186
13.	Nash	14,973
14.	Packard	9,670
15.	Hupmobile	7,316
16.	Cadillac-LaSalle	6,736

1934

1.	Chevrolet	620,726
2.	Ford	563,921
3.	Plymouth	351,113
4.	Dodge	108,687
5.	Hudson-Terraplane	85,835
6.	Oldsmobile	80,911
7.	Pontiac	79,803
8.	Buick	78,757
9.	Studebaker	46,103
10.	Chrysler	36,929
11.	Nash-LaFayette	28,664
12.	DeSoto	15,825
13.	Cadillac-LaSalle	11,468
14.	Hupmobile	9,420
15.	Willys-Overland	7,916
16.	Packard	6,071

1935

1.	Ford	942,439
2.	Chevrolet	793,437
3.	Plymouth	442,281
4.	Dodge	211,752
5.	Oldsmobile	183,153
6.	Pontiac	175,268
7.	Buick	107,611
8.	Hudson-Terraplane	101,080
9.	Packard	52,256
10.	Chrysler	50,010
11.	Studebaker	49,062
12.	Nash-LaFayette	44,637
13.	DeSoto	34,276
14.	Cadillac-LaSalle	23,559
15.	Willys-Overland	20,428
16.	Hupmobile	9,346

1936

1.	Chevrolet	975,238
2.	Ford	791,812
3.	Plymouth	527,177
4.	Dodge	274,904
5.	Oldsmobile	187,638
6.	Buick	179,533
7.	Pontiac	178,496
8.	Hudson-Terraplane	123,266
9.	Studebaker	85,026
10.	Packard	80,699
11.	Chrysler	71,295
12.	Nash-LaFayette	53,038
13.	DeSoto	52,789
14.	Cadillac-LaSalle	28,479
15.	Willys-Overland	18,824

1941

1.	Chevrolet	930,293
2.	Ford	600,814
3.	Plymouth	429,869
4.	Buick	316,251
5.	Pontiac	282,087
6.	Oldsmobile	230,701
7.	Dodge	215,575
8.	Chrysler	141,522
9.	Studebaker	119,325
10.	DeSoto	85,980
11.	Nash	80,408
12.	Mercury	80,085
13.	Hudson	79,529
14.	Packard	66,906
15.	Cadillac-LaSalle	59,572
16.	Willys-Overland	28,935

1942

1.	Chevrolet	45,472
2.	Ford	43,407
3.	Plymouth	25,113
4.	Buick	16,601
5.	Pontiac	15,404
6.	Oldsmobile	12,230
7.	Dodge	11,675
8.	Studebaker	9,285
9.	Packard	6,085
10.	Nash	5,428
11.	Hudson	5,396
12.	Chrysler	5,292
13.	Mercury	4,430
14.	DeSoto	4,186
15.	Cadillac	2,873

1945

1.	Ford	34,439
2.	Chevrolet	12,776
3.	Nash	6,148
4.	Pontiac	5,606
5.	Hudson	4,735
6.	Oldsmobile	3,498
7.	Mercury	2,848
8.	Packard	2,722
9.	Buick	2,482
10.	Cadillac	1,142
11.	DeSoto	947
12.	Plymouth	770
13.	Studebaker	651
14.	Lincoln	500
15.	Dodge	420
16.	Chrysler	322

1946

1.	Chevrolet	397,104
2.	Ford	372,917
3.	Plymouth	242,534
4.	Dodge	156,128
5.	Buick	156,080
6.	Pontiac	131,538
7.	Oldsmobile	114,674
8.	Nash	98,769
9.	Hudson	90,766
10.	Studebaker	77,567
11.	Chrysler	76,753
12.	Mercury	70,955
13.	DeSoto	62,860
14.	Packard	42,102
15.	Cadillac	28,144
16.	Lincoln	13,487

1947		1948		1949		1950	
1. Chevrolet	695,986	1. Chevrolet	775,982	1. Chevrolet	1,109,958	1. Chevrolet	1,520,577
2. Ford	601,665	2. Ford	549,077	2. Ford	841,170	2. Ford	1,187,122
3. Plymouth	350,327	3. Plymouth	378,048	3. Plymouth	574,734	3. Plymouth	573,116
4. Buick	267,830	4. Buick	275,504	4. Buick	398,482	4. Buick	552,827
5. Dodge	232,216	5. Pontiac	253,469	5. Pontiac	333,954	5. Pontiac	467,655
6. Pontiac	223,015	6. Dodge	232,390	6. Dodge	298,399	6. Oldsmobile	396,757
7. Oldsmobile	191,454	7. Oldsmobile	194,755	7. Oldsmobile	282,887	7. Mercury	334,081
8. Kaiser-Frazer	144,490	8. Kaiser-Frazer	181,316	8. Studebaker	228,402	8. Dodge	332,782
9. Mercury	124,612	9. Studebaker	164,753	9. Mercury	203,339	9. Studebaker	268,099
10. Studebaker	123,642	10. Mercury	154,702	10. Nash	142,592	10. Nash	189,543
11. Nash	113,315	11. Hudson	143,697	11. Hudson	142,462	11. Chrysler	167,316
12. Chrysler	109,195	12. Chrysler	119,137	12. Chrysler	141,122	12. Kaiser-Frazer	146,911
13. Hudson	100,393	13. Nash	118,621	13. DeSoto	108,440	13. Hudson	143,006
14. DeSoto	81,752	14. Packard	98,898	14. Packard	104,593	14. DeSoto	127,557
15. Cadillac	59,436	15. DeSoto	92,920	15. Cadillac	81,545	15. Cadillac	110,535
16. Packard	55,477	16. Cadillac	66,209	16. Kaiser-Frazer	57,995	16. Packard	72,138
17. Willys	33,214	17. Lincoln	43,938	17. Lincoln	33,132	17. Willys	38,052
18. Lincoln	29,097	18. Willys	32,635	18. Willys	32,928	18. Lincoln	35,485
19. Crosley	16,162	19. Crosley	24,871	19. Crosley	8,549	19. Crosley	7,043

1955		1956		1957		1958	
1. Chevrolet	1,830,029	1. Chevrolet	1,621,005	1. Chevrolet	1,522,536	1. Chevrolet	1,255,935
2. Ford	1,764,524	2. Ford	1,373,542	2. Ford	1,522,406	2. Ford	1,038,560
3. Buick	781,296	3. Buick	535,364	3. Plymouth	655,526	3. Plymouth	367,296
4. Plymouth	742,991	4. Plymouth	452,958	4. Buick	407,271	4. Oldsmobile	310,795
5. Oldsmobile	643,460	5. Oldsmobile	432,904	5. Oldsmobile	390,091	5. Buick	257,124
6. Pontiac	581,860	6. Pontiac	332,268	6. Pontiac	343,298	6. Pontiac	219,823
7. Mercury	434,911	7. Mercury	246,629	7. Dodge	292,386	7. Rambler	217,332
8. Dodge	313,038	8. Dodge	205,727	8. Mercury	274,820	8. Mercury	128,428
9. Chrysler	176,039	9. Cadillac	140,873	9. Cadillac	153,236	9. Cadillac	125,501
10. Am. Motors	161,790	10. Am. Motors	104,190	10. Chrysler	118,733	10. Dodge	114,206
11. Cadillac	153,334	11. DeSoto	104,090	11. DeSoto	117,747	11. Stude-Packard	56,869
12. DeSoto	129,767	12. Chrysler	95,356	12. Am. Motors	114,084	12. Chrysler	49,513
13. Studebaker	112,392	13. Studebaker	82,402	13. Stude-Packard	72,889	13. DeSoto	36,556
14. Packard	69,667	14. Lincoln-Contl.	48,995	14. Edsel	54,607	14. Edsel	26,563
15. Lincoln-Contl.	41,226	15. Packard	13,432	15. Imperial	37,946	15. Lincoln	25,871
16. Imperial	13,727	16. Imperial	12,130	16. Lincoln-Contl.	37,870	16. Imperial	13,673

1963		1964		1965		1966	
1. Chevrolet	2,303,296	1. Chevrolet	2,114,691	1. Chevrolet	2,587,490	1. Chevrolet	2,202,806
2. Ford	1,638,066	2. Ford	1,787,535	2. Ford	2,164,902	2. Ford	2,038,415
3. Pontiac	625,268	3. Pontiac	693,634	3. Pontiac	860,687	3. Pontiac	866,385
4. Oldsmobile	504,556	4. Plymouth	571,339	4. Plymouth	679,539	4. Plymouth	640,450
5. Plymouth	496,412	5. Oldsmobile	510,931	5. Buick	653,838	5. Oldsmobile	594,069
6. Rambler	480,365	6. Dodge	505,094	6. Oldsmobile	650,801	6. Buick	580,421
7. Buick	479,399	7. Buick	482,685	7. Dodge	547,531	7. Dodge	532,026
8. Dodge	421,301	8. Rambler	393,863	8. Mercury	355,404	8. Mercury	334,858
9. Mercury	292,086	9. Mercury	320,660	9. Rambler	346,367	9. Rambler	279,225
10. Cadillac	164,735	10. Cadillac	154,603	10. Chrysler	224,061	10. Chrysler	255,487
11. Chrysler	111,958	11. Chrysler	145,338	11. Cadillac	196,595	11. Cadillac	205,001
12. Studebaker	67,918	12. Lincoln	37,750	12. Lincoln	45,470	12. Lincoln	52,169
13. Lincoln	33,717	13. Imperial	20,391	13. Imperial	16,422	13. Imperial	17,653
14. Imperial	18,051	14. Checker	6,310	14. Checker	6,136	14. Checker	5,761

1951		1952		1953		1954	
1. Chevrolet	1,118,096	1. Chevrolet	877,947	1. Chevrolet	1,477,287	1. Chevrolet	1,414,352
2. Ford	900,770	2. Ford	777,531	2. Ford	1,184,187	2. Ford	1,394,762
3. Plymouth	621,013	3. Plymouth	474,836	3. Plymouth	662,515	3. Buick	531,463
4. Buick	404,657	4. Buick	321,048	4. Buick	485,353	4. Oldsmobile	433,810
5. Pontiac	343,795	5. Pontiac	277,156	5. Pontiac	414,011	5. Plymouth	399,900
6. Dodge	325,694	6. Dodge	259,519	6. Mercury	320,369	6. Pontiac	370,887
7. Oldsmobile	285,634	7. Oldsmobile	228,452	7. Oldsmobile	319,414	7. Mercury	256,730
8. Mercury	238,854	8. Mercury	195,261	8. Dodge	293,714	8. Dodge	151,766
9. Studebaker	222,000	9. Studebaker	161,520	9. Studebaker	186,484	9. Cadillac	123,746
10. Chrysler	162,916	10. Nash-Rambler	152,141	10. Chrysler	160,410	10. Chrysler	101,745
11. Nash-Rambler	161,140	11. Chrysler	120,678	11. Nash-Rambler	135,394	11. Studebaker	85,252
12. DeSoto	121,794	12. DeSoto	97,558	12. DeSoto	129,963	12. DeSoto	69,844
13. Cadillac	103,266	13. Cadillac	96,850	13. Cadillac	103,538	13. Nash-Rambler	62,911
14. Kaiser-Frazer	99,343	14. Hudson	76,348	14. Packard	81,341	14. Lincoln	35,733
15. Hudson	93,327	15. Kaiser	71,306	15. Hudson	76,348	15. Hudson	32,287
16. Packard	76,075	16. Packard	62,988	16. Lincoln	41,962	16. Packard	27,593
17. Willys	28,226	17. Willys	48,845	17. Willys	40,563	17. Kaiser-Willys	16,759
18. Lincoln	25,386	18. Lincoln	31,992	18. Kaiser	21,686		
19. Crosley	4,839	19. Crosley	1,522				

1959		1960		1961		1962	
1. Ford	1,528,592	1. Chevrolet	1,873,598	1. Chevrolet	1,604,805	1. Chevrolet	2,161,398
2. Chevrolet	1,428,962	2. Ford	1,511,504	2. Ford	1,345,121	2. Ford	1,565,928
3. Plymouth	413,204	3. Rambler	485,745	3. Rambler	372,485	3. Pontiac	547,350
4. Rambler	401,446	4. Plymouth	483,969	4. Pontiac	360,336	4. Oldsmobile	458,359
5. Pontiac	388,856	5. Pontiac	450,206	5. Oldsmobile	321,838	5. Rambler	454,784
6. Oldsmobile	366,305	6. Dodge	411,666	6. Mercury	311,635	6. Buick	415,892
7. Buick	232,579	7. Oldsmobile	402,612	7. Plymouth	310,445	7. Mercury	335,446
8. Dodge	192,798	8. Mercury	359,818	8. Buick	291,895	8. Plymouth	331,079
9. Mercury	156,765	9. Buick	307,804	9. Dodge	220,779	9. Dodge	251,772
10. Studebaker	153,823	10. Cadillac	158,941	10. Cadillac	148,298	10. Cadillac	158,528
11. Cadillac	138,527	11. Studebaker	105,902	11. Chrysler	107,747	11. Chrysler	119,221
12. Chrysler	69,411	12. Chrysler	87,420	12. Studebaker	78,664	12. Studebaker	86,974
13. DeSoto	41,423	13. Lincoln	20,683	13. Lincoln	33,180	13. Lincoln	33,829
14. Lincoln	30,375	14. DeSoto	19,411	14. Imperial	12,699	14. Imperial	14,787
15. Edsel	29,667	15. Imperial	16,829	15. Checker	5,683	15. Checker	8,173
16. Imperial	20,963	16. Checker	6,980				

1967		1968		1969		1970	
1. Chevrolet	1,920,615	1. Chevrolet	2,148,091	1. Chevrolet	1,999,256	1. Ford	1,621,846
2. Ford	1,377,388	2. Ford	1,911,434	2. Ford	1,743,462	2. Chevrolet	1,504,522
3. Pontiac	857,171	3. Pontiac	943,253	3. Pontiac	772,104	3. Plymouth	699,031
4. Plymouth	610,098	4. Plymouth	683,678	4. Buick	713,832	4. Buick	459,931
5. Buick	573,866	5. Buick	652,049	5. Oldsmobile	668,399	5. Oldsmobile	439,632
6. Oldsmobile	552,997	6. Oldsmobile	637,779	6. Plymouth	651,124	6. Pontiac	422,213
7. Dodge	497,380	7. Dodge	621,136	7. Dodge	496,113	7. Dodge	405,703
8. Mercury	284,503	8. Mercury	421,252	8. Mercury	354,444	8. Mercury	310,463
9. Chrysler	240,712	9. Am. Motors	268,439	9. Cadillac	266,798	9. Am. Motors	276,110
10. Rambler	229,058	10. Chrysler	263,266	10. Am. Motors	242,898	10. Chrysler	158,614
11. Cadillac	213,161	11. Cadillac	210,904	11. Chrysler	226,590	11. Cadillac	152,859
12. Lincoln	34,333	12. Lincoln-Contl.	64,236	12. Lincoln-Contl.	65,223	12. Lincoln-Contl.	58,771
13. Imperial	15,506	13. Imperial	17,551	13. Imperial	18,627	13. Imperial	10,111
14. Checker	5,822	14. Checker	5,477	14. Checker	5,417	14. Checker	4,169

143

IV

THE MASTER CRAFTSMEN

BY HUGO PFAU

Inevitably, perhaps, when man first dreamed of a self-propelled vehicle he thought in terms of a substitute for the horse. Consequently, the earliest automobiles were wagons or coaches with a difference: steam or gasoline engines and electric motors propelled these first, crude vehicles, and a technological revolution was underway. But it was to be a revolution tempered by the best of traditional esthetics, for the automobile bore the imprint of the coachbuilders' art from the very beginning.

Unsurprisingly, the coachbuilders' transition from the equine to the motor age was a gradual one because their work so often adorned the elegant carriages of the wealthy. When motor-powered vehicles began to replace the horse-drawn variety, the same clientele demanded the services of these artisans to provide fittings for their automobiles to equal or excel those of their glamorous carriages.

In the 1890's automobiles closely resembled the buggies, phaetons and victorias being produced in the same carriage shops. Even the few closed cars produced during this era looked like horse-drawn broughams and landaus, with their passenger compartments enclosed and chauffeurs alert behind the wheel.

As the mechanics of the automobile were gradually being mastered, the coachbuilders felt free to experiment with streamlining techniques for bodies built in their shops, and the resultant designs are still envied for their grace and daring today: Copper-riveted mahogany panelling fashioned after pre-World War I speedboats lent a rakish aura to many a custom-built car, and V-windshields and convertible bodies began to appear with some frequency. Nor were these mere styling experiments,

for a real demand for unusual and innovative vehicles was already in existence by this time.

As the production of automobiles increased during the first twenty years of this century, open touring cars or roadsters of relatively simple construction were the rule, with some manufacturers making their own bodies and many others purchasing them from wagon-makers turned body builders. Expensive cars, on the other hand, were often built as chassis only, leaving the purchaser free to select a coachbuilder to supply the body. This interesting custom was not at all uncommon, for small carriage shops flourished in all parts of the country and a would-be automobile owner had only to take his new chassis to his local coachbuilder for a motorcar finished to his taste and exact specifications.

Elaborate bodies, often incorporating the latest ideas in construction and styling, came from the specialists — Brewster, Derham, Healy, Judkins — who had years of fine carriage building behind them. A few of them — Cunningham and McFarlan, for example — began by building automobile bodies and went on to build complete and very high quality cars. Brewster serves as another example of a carriage firm which made a car for a time, and Studebaker entered the field by building automobile bodies as an extension of their wagon-building trade until this sideline grew into a complete auto manufacturing enterprise.

New companies were formed by those who had learned their trade in carriage shops, drawing their staffs, in most cases, from former associates. Brunn, Holbrook, Locke and Willoughby were among this

The Golden Age
of the Coachbuilder in America

new breed, coupling experience from the past with the promise of what appeared to be a limitless future.

History teaches us that large-scale automobile production was unknown before the advent of the Model T Ford, and in this quiet before the storm coachbuilders screnely plied their trade. The Model T concept changed all that. Whereas initially the coachbuilder's art had been largely confined to individual (i.e. custom) bodies on varied chassis for specific clients, it would now also branch into design of bodies for series production by large-scale manufacturers.

Perhaps it was this pragmatism which intensified the body builders' efforts to develop cheaper and safer closed bodies after the First World War. Briggs introduced the first really inexpensive one — the Coach — for Essex and Hudson, while Budd worked at the same time to adapt their methods for building all-steel railroad cars to the automobile body . . . with complete success, one might add, as the 1921 Dodge all-steel body can attest.

Although a few automobile manufacturers retained staff designers, much of the styling came from the body builders, who often supplied several different makes. Some automobiles were assembled from stock components and fitted with bodies styled, and sometimes made, by their own firms. A few of these — Auburn, Elcar and Jordan, for example — built some of the best-looking production models of their day.

In its most advanced form, automotive styling was practiced by those who were, like Fleetwood and LeBaron, specifically set up to build custom bodies for automobiles. Thus, by the mid-Twenties, Lincoln could claim that all of their body styles were the creations of master designers. In truth, however, while some of their small-volume bodies were produced by custom builders, many more were copied in a Detroit body shop from the original coachbuilders' plans.

Many new styling ideas of the era such as convertible bodies first appeared on individual custom bodies, and were reproduced for a few years by small specialist firms before reaching mass production; a number of engineering developments — improved visibility, for instance — reached the market the same way. I spent much of my time during this period working out ways to make windshield pillars narrower and convertible tops more easily folded and flattened. Intricate moldings, raised panels and smooth-flowing fenders were also the objects of design research, and these too were destined to find their way from the bodybuilders' shops to mass-assembly lines. An interesting example of how a design could pass from obscurity to fame in those days is that of Tom Hibbard's and Ray Dietrich's pennant-shaped raised panel, developed very early in their careers with LeBaron. It was very narrow at the radiator, then broadened to the full width of the body at the windshield, continuing on to form the belt-line of the body. I later modified this to sweep down behind the spare wheels (usually side-mounted on custom bodies), and still later we carried this back into the front doors to create what is generally known as a "LeBaron sweep panel" among classic car fanciers today.

This kind of attention to detail caused both the public and Detroit to become acutely style-conscious in the mid-Twenties. To protect what they rightfully considered to be their styling lead, bodybuilders began to follow the example of Murray, who hired Amos Northup, the Wills

Sainte Claire designer, to head a new styling studio. Soon after, Ray Dietrich was lured away from LeBaron, and Dietrich, Inc. began to function both as a builder of custom bodies and as a design consultant.

The Fisher brothers acquired Harley Earl from the Don Lee Studios in Los Angeles to head their design staff, which became the Art & Colour Section of the Fisher Body Company and, later, of General Motors. A year or so later, the brothers expanded further by purchasing the Fleetwood Metal Body Company as a custom body subsidiary and source of ideas. My most personal memory of this significant era is concerned with the purchase of LeBaron in 1926 by the Briggs Manufacturing Company. While Briggs retained the firm as a separate custom body subsidiary, the prime reason for the purchase was to acquire the services of LeBaron's design staff, of which this writer was a member. Finally, in 1929, the Hayes Body Company obtained the services of Alex de Sakhnoffsky as their chief stylist. He had already made somewhat of a reputation in Europe, rising from a junior draftsman's position in the shop of Belgian coachbuilder Vanden Plas to the top echelon of that company, fitting his elegant and occasionally flamboyantly-designed bodies to such chassis as Minerva, Excelsior, Hispano-Suiza, Mercedes-Benz, Isotta-Fraschini, Packard, Voisin and Cadillac along the way.

Just as the number of automobile manufacturers declined during this period, so too would body builders discover the greater volume of business becoming concentrated in fewer hands. The four firms mentioned above — Murray, Fisher, Briggs and Hayes — were by far the largest, and they were able to absorb various and smaller competitors during the Twenties. A few other fair-sized body builders, such as Baker, Rauch & Lang in Cleveland, continued to supply bodies for several good medium-priced cars; Walker in Amesbury, Massachusetts, worked closely with Franklin; Biddle & Smart, also in Amesbury concentrated on Hudson, and Seaman in Milwaukee were so closely affiliated with Nash that they eventually became a part of that company.

The prosperous Twenties allowed quite a few custom body builders to flourish in various parts of the country, especially in the East, and to continue to develop design innovations so valuable that mass car producers would later incorporate them into their stock model designs. The times did not favor all, however; many body builders found the design competition so severe that they turned to bus, hearse, ambulance, taxicab and deluxe delivery vehicle production. Those who elected to remain with passenger car bodies sold them to automobile manufacturers, most of whom were still buying their bodies from outside sources. Even Fisher, a division of General Motors, supplied bodies to a few firms outside of that giant combine as late as the latter Twenties.

But in the wake of the stock market crash of 1929 came a further concentration of production. Many of the smaller coachbuilders closed their doors in the years that followed, as did some of the medium-sized production body builders. Walker, for instance, closed when Franklin went out of business in 1933, and Biddle & Smart did not even last that long, going out of business in 1930 when Hudson transferred their body purchases to lower-priced Detroit firms.

A few custom body firms managed to keep going by soliciting repair and repainting work plus an occasional — and heavensent — order for a complete body or alteration. One or two of the stronger firms, in-

cluding those who were subsidiaries of larger companies, struggled to turn out new ideas. Even this work stopped with the advent of World War II when their facilities were turned over to military production.

Of necessity, the entire industry underwent a drastic change after the war. Fisher Body had already been a part of General Motors for some years, but now supplied no one else. Ford followed this conservative trend by resuming the building of their own bodies, as they had done before Walter Briggs resigned as superintendent of their body shop to set up his own business some thirty years before. Ironically, his firm was absorbed by Chrysler after Mr. Briggs' death. To complete the tightening process, Baker-Raulang, Budd and Murray discontinued their business of building complete bodies to supply mere parts or subassemblies to others.

The coachbuilding art was dying. Inflation and the shortage of skilled craftsmen, many of whom had originally learned their trade in carriage shops, appeared as a terminal symptom. Minor alterations and restorations was the only type of work attempted, and even this was often done by firms whose principal business lay in other fields than passenger car bodies. The widespread adoption of the all-steel body in the Thirties was another development which hastened the demise of coachbuilding in the U.S., because its welded construction guarded against deterioration and squeaks as effectively as the most expensive custom body.

But it was the Depression that had truly delivered the *coup de grâce* to the coachbuilding industry. As the times no longer favored ostentation, the prestigious marques began to disappear. The imports were the first to go, with domestic luxury cars collapsing not long after. Cunningham, duPont, Duesenberg, Marmon, Stutz, Pierce-Arrow — all of these great names had ceased to exist by the mid-Thirties. Lincoln had already opted out of the luxury class by concentrating upon Zephyr production, and the last Packard V-12 rolled off the assembly line in 1939. Only the Cadillac V-16 and Chrysler Imperial managed to survive the years preceding World War II. And while it is true that Lincoln made a bid for the luxury field by introducing the Continental just before the war, it was a limited-production car, minus the semi-custom bodywork that had distinguished so many of the marques from the classic era.

The Depression also left its mark on workmen as well as upon the shops that had employed them; skilled craftsmen began to seek work in other areas as the great bodybuilding firms folded, and the prospect of a long and ill-paid apprenticeship drove away those who might have replaced them. The few craftsmen who remain today are mostly in their seventies, and it certainly does not appear that many younger ones are anxious to take their places, or to undertake the most strenuous aspects of coachbuilding. Even if they were, current salary scales and the many hours of hand work needed to create a custom coachbuilt car would escalate prices beyond all reason. My own estimate, after talking to the few surviving coachbuilders, is that the cost of a true custom body today would run in excess of $30,000. Few are willing to pay such a price.

Today the style center of the automobile industry has shifted to Italy, where conditions permit some custom body building to continue because of lower labor costs. There the experimental designs, sometimes to sketches drawn in Detroit, can be produced at more reasonable prices. Coachbuilding in the United States, as it existed in earlier years, is moribund.

Having completed this brief history of coachbuilding in America, I shall try to answer an often-asked question: how the work of various body builders can be identified. Most coachbuilders used a plate of distinctive design, generally applied to the lower front corner of the cowl, one exception being Brewster, who did not deign to use such an outside nameplate. Even a few production builders of the late Twenties adopted this practice.

In some cases, an identifying plate, often including the body number, may appear on the firewall under the hood. Some of these can be misleading: A few bodies built in 1931 while I was at the LeBaron-Detroit plant carry Briggs plates on the firewall, for the simple reason that we had temporarily run out of our own. Another source of bewilderment stems from the practice of some coachbuilders who added their own plates when they repaired or repainted a body. Sometimes, in fact, they substituted their own for the original nameplate. Ethics aside, such shenanigans only compound the confusion.

Almost every designer, it is true, had some unique touches of his own, but these are usually apparent only to another designer. No coachbuilder produced only one style of body, and the variety among the designs of each was often considerable; the New York office of LeBaron came up with some 1800 separate designs during the ten years of its existence, and I was responsible for perhaps a quarter of those. To add to the confusion, we all borrowed good ideas from one another, and an innovation by one designer soon found its way into the work of others.

Brewster, for example, developed an unusual windshield shape around 1915, largely to reduce glare. By the mid-Twenties, this had been copied not only by almost every other custom builder, but it was included on many production models as well. Recently, I was asked to help identify a body whose current owner was convinced it was built by Holbrook because its front doors were hinged at the rear. Because he had noticed this feature on other Holbrook bodies, he was convinced that his car was built by the master — and was considerably surprised to learn that many custom bodies from other shops had been built in the same manner.

Sometimes, though, an identifying feature does exist, as with the interior hardware which Brewster had specially made in a very slim design. The LeBaron-Detroit Company also had special hardware made. Most coachbuilders, however, purchased theirs from the same source. The results were predictable: Most of the hardware looks alike.

Often custom builders produced their most successful designs in small series, anywhere from five to perhaps fifty or one hundred of identical design. Sometimes they built almost the same body on various chassis. In such cases, it should not be impossible to find another body of the same style for comparison, or at least a photograph of one. Bear in mind that this refers to the basic design of the vehicle; details, especially those of the interior, might vary from one body to the next, and color schemes were usually individually selected.

Perhaps the best procedure for anyone seriously interested in identifying a coachbuilder's work is to check back on such lists as do exist, and then to cross-check with any other information available.

Trade magazines from the era of the car in question are apt to be more accurate than those for general consumption, for they often contain pictures of especially outstanding cars with complete identification of the body builder. Sometimes even the people for whom these cars were built are named.

Unfortunately, even these are not foolproof, for some specification tables in magazines of the period tend to mislead. Some errors have crept in because of the sheer magnitude of the list compiler's job, while others are due to the pride of many manufacturers who claimed to have built every inch of their cars, even when some of their cars' parts were purchased from outside sources. Dubious as it seems, this claim was occasionally justified — as far as they were concerned anyway — by the fact that the part, whether a simple component or an entire body, was made to their specifications.

Most true coachbuilders mounted their bodies on nearly every expensive domestic and foreign chassis available. Production body builders, on the other hand, were often identified with a smaller range of makes. In the list which follows, I have included all of the principal American body builders, and where feasible, the makes of cars with which they were especially identified.

While other listings in this book include street addresses, they are omitted from this section simply because nearly all of the firms listed have long since ceased to exist. Fisher, Fleetwood and LeBaron are names still current, but they exist as trademarks rather than as separate businesses. A very few other firms continue in business, but no longer as body builders. Rather they have become repair shops or engaged in some other business. With one or two exceptions, even these occupy premises other than those they used as body builders, and the shops they formerly used have been torn down or converted to other, more mundane, uses.

For instance, the author spent some years with LeBaron, starting in their original office at 2 Columbus Circle. This building was torn down a few years ago to make room for Huntington Hartford's museum. From there we moved to 724 Fifth Avenue, and while this building is still standing, the partitions separating the LeBaron office from the rest of the 11th floor have long since disappeared.

At the time of the merger with Bridgeport Body, the latter's factory was on Barnum Avenue in Bridgeport. The building no longer stands. Another building off Stratford Avenue was purchased after the firm passed into Briggs' ownership. A few years ago I checked it, and found it had become a rather seedy warehouse.

The LeBaron-Detroit Company was set up in a building at 3100 Meldrum Avenue, formerly an independent body trim shop taken over by Briggs. Several years ago the main factory building was still standing as a warehouse, but the office and studio building on the Meldrum Avenue side had been torn down.

The LeBaron Studios, handling the designing for LeBaron-Detroit and for Briggs, was originally housed at the Meldrum Avenue address but later moved to a building in the main Briggs plant on Mack Avenue. This is now owned by Chrysler, but it is used for different purposes.

In the list that follows, then, available information on American coachbuilders' shops has been arranged as logically as possible despite the problem outlined above.

THE HALL OF FAME

V

BY HUGO PFAU

AMERICAN BODY CO.—1919-25
  Buffalo, New York
Principally open bodies for such medium and high-priced cars as the Leland Lincoln.

AMESBURY METAL BODY CO.—1907-21
  Amesbury, Massachusetts
One of several small body builders in this old carriage-building town.

AMESBURY SPECIALTY CO.—1915-23
  Amesbury, Massachusetts
Similar firm which also built semi-custom bodies including several series for the Model T Ford.

AUTO BODY COMPANY—1908-26
  Lansing, Michigan
An early production body builder which later concentrated on bodies for Durant and was eventually absorbed by them.

AUTO BODY & FINISHING CO.—1906-22
  Amesbury, Massachusetts
Another firm on "Carriage Hill" later absorbed by Biddle & Smart.

AUTO TOP & BODY CO.—1906-15
  Philadelphia, Pennsylvania
An early body builder switching to buses after 1909.

H. H. BABCOCK CO.—1890's-1926
  Watertown, Massachusetts
Started as wagon builders, switched to automobile and light delivery truck bodies. Built some town cars on long-wheelbase Dodge chassis, also some Franklin bodies and a few for the Duesenberg Model A. Passenger car bodies 1902-25.

BAKER, RAUCH & LANG—1916 to date
  Cleveland, Ohio
Formed by merger of Baker Vehicle Co., which built electric cars before 1900, and the Rauch & Lang Carriage Co., which built electrics from 1904. Not only bodies, but two fine cars were built: the Baker Raulang Electric and the Owen-Magnetic. A few custom bodies, but primarily production bodies for such good quality cars as Stearns-Knight and Peerless. Showed a Ruxton town car at 1929 Salons. Now producing body parts and electronic equipment. Including predecessors, they made automobile bodies from 1899-1933.

BANKER BROS. & CO.—1906-16
  Pittsburgh, Pennsylvania
Custom body firm which built limousines for Pierce-Arrow, Stevens-Duryea and similar cars.

BENDER BODY CO.—1910's-1930's
  Cleveland, Ohio

Some custom bodies up to 1922, primarily bus bodies thereafter.

BIDDLE & SMART CO.—1870-1930
  Amesbury, Massachusetts
An old carriage firm which switched to automobile bodies early in the century, and subsequently became Hudson's chief source of bodies. Many custom bodies before 1920, and a few, mainly Hudsons, thereafter. Absorbed several smaller Amesbury firms during the 1920's as their business expanded, but came to an abrupt end in 1930 when Hudson switched their business to cheaper sources in Detroit. Passenger car bodies 1902-30.

BLAKESLEE VEHICLE BODY & SEAT CO.—1905-15
  Kansas City, Missouri
Built production bodies for various cars "in the white" — meaning that bodies were delivered to the customer minus paint, trim and hardware.

BLUE RIBBON BODY CO.—1890's-1925
  Bridgeport, Connecticut
Formerly the Blue Ribbon Horse & Carriage Co. Custom bodies and small series for Locomobile and other high-priced cars. Plant used briefly by Holbrook-Brewster, 1927-28.

BOHMAN & SCHWARTZ—1931-38
  Pasadena, California
Principals had been the key employees of

148

A Listing of American Coachbuilders •

Walter M. Murphy Co., and when that firm closed in 1931 they continued on their own. Best known for several Duesenbergs.

OSGOOD BRADLEY CO.—1920-27
Worcester, Massachusetts
Some bodies built for Standard 8 and other medium-priced cars. Later concentrated on trolley buses. Passenger car bodies 1920-25.

BREWSTER & CO.—1810-1938
Long Island City, New York
One of our most prestigious carriage builders, who went on to occupy a similar niche among custom body firms. Built their own car for a while before and during World War I, then acted as agents for Rolls-Royce, Lanchester, Marmon and Packard, all of which they sold with Brewster bodies only. Merged with Rolls-Royce Co. of America in 1926, but continued to build bodies on other fine chassis as well. When Rolls-Royce discontinued production in Springfield in 1932, the Brewster family resumed business under their own name, with town cars on modified Ford chassis as well as a few Packards and Buicks. Best known for high quality and conservative styling in early dates, but with more daring designs in the Thirties. Brewster windshield, developed in 1915, was widely copied. Automobile bodies, 1900-38.

BRIDGEPORT BODY CO.—1910-24; 1934-38
Bridgeport, Connecticut
Started building custom bodies for Locomobile

and similar cars until they merged with LeBaron in 1924. Principals of old company resumed business about 1934, building wood station wagon bodies on Packard and other chassis for a few years.

BRIGGS CARRIAGE CO.—1876-1923
Amesbury, Massachusetts
Built bodies for early Locomobiles, including their first steam cars. No relation to Briggs Mfg. Co. Passenger car bodies 1898-1920.

BRIGGS MFG. CO.—1909 to date
Detroit, Michigan
Founded by Walter Briggs, former manager of Ford's body plant. Developed first cheap closed bodies and became the world's largest body-builder for a time. Purchased LeBaron in 1926 and continued it as a custom body subsidiary and source of designs. Built bodies for Ford, Chrysler, Hudson, Essex, Paige, Graham-Paige, Packard, Overland and Willys-Knight, among others. After World War II their principal customer was Chrysler, who purchased all their body-building facilities in 1948 after Mr. Briggs' death. Company is still in business making plumbing fixtures, an activity started during the Depression to keep the plants busy. Passenger car bodies 1915-48.

BROOKS-OSTRUK CO.—1910-32
New York, New York
An early custom body builder. The affiliated Consolidated Motor Car Co. became agents for

Minerva automobiles. Gave up building bodies in 1924, but continued with repainting and repair work. Passenger car bodies 1910-24.

BRUNN & CO.—1908-41
Buffalo, New York
Herman Brunn formed this company to build custom bodies. After a career with other coachbuilders and an apprenticeship in his uncle's carriage shop, he built many of Henry Ford's personal cars and bodies for nearly every other fine car including Pierce-Arrow and Stearns-Knight. Especially known for town cars, but also built smart phaetons and convertibles.

BRYANT BODY CO.—1922-25
Amesbury, Massachusetts
Bodies for Jordan and others. Controlled by the Walker family and eventually absorbed into Walker Body Co.

EDWARD G. BUDD MFG. CO.—1890's to date
Philadelphia, Pennsylvania
Primarily makers of railroad cars, they pioneered the all-steel body, introduced on the Dodge in 1921. European rights to their patents were sold to Citroën, but Budd continued to build bodies for Dodge and others through the early Thirties. The first Ruxton was built in their plant. Although they gave up making complete bodies in the 1930's, they continue to supply various components and still make railroad cars. Passenger car bodies 1921-31.

BUFFALO AUTO BODY & TRIMMING CO.—1897-1915
Buffalo, New York
An early carriage firm which turned to automobile bodies.

J. T. CANTRELL & SONS—1880's-1957
Carriage and wagon builders who became custom body builders, then turned to making wood station wagon and light delivery bodies. Passenger car bodies 1910-30.

CARRIAGE FACTORIES LTD.—1920's
Orillia, Ontario

CENTRAL MFG. CO.—1908-48
Connersville, Indiana
Initially known for well-built bodies for medium to higher-priced cars, including some early Lincolns, this company was absorbed by Auburn-Cord complex as Auburn became their prime customer. Following dissolution of the A-C-D complex, they continued as independent body builders, using part of the former McFarlan plant. Early Packard-Darrins built here, before plant converted to Jeep bodies.

CHUPURDY & CO.—1912-26
New York, New York
Small custom body shop; later repairs.

THE CLAYTON CO.—1915-25
New York, New York
Another small custom body shop, which built some early LeBaron-designed bodies before that firm had its own manufacturing facilities.

COACHCRAFT, LTD.—1946-66
Los Angeles, California
Primarily modifications or customizing of standard bodies.

R. N. COLLINS VEHICLE WOODWORK CO.—1890's-1923
St. Louis, Missouri
A carriage builder who turned to good quality automobile bodies, including many for Dorris.

CONBOY CARRIAGE CO. LTD.
Toronto, Ontario
One-off automobile bodies to special order prior to and during World War I.

THOMAS CONNOLLY CARRIAGE WORKS—1890's-1910
Dubuque, Iowa
Another carriage firm which turned to automobile bodies for a time.

JAMES CUNNINGHAM SONS & CO.—1890's to date
Rochester, New York
Coachbuilders who became custom body builders, then started building complete cars in 1910. Built a very fine V-8 from 1916 through 1934, all with their own bodies. In mid-Thirties, they built a few special bodies on Ford chassis. Still in business, producing electronic components. Body builders 1900-36.

CURRIER & CAMERON—1870's-1920
Amesbury, Massachusetts
Started as coachbuilders, then built bodies for early Stanley Steamers and a few others. Passenger car bodies 1895-1920.

HOWARD A. DARRIN—1938-58; 1968 to date
Los Angeles, California
After the successive dissolutions of the partnerships of Hibbard & Darrin and Fernandez & Darrin in Paris, Mr. Darrin returned to the United States to build prototypes of his designs in a small shop on the Sunset Strip. After the war, Darrin built the prototype Kaiser-Darrin in the Los Angeles area. Production models of his designs were built elsewhere. In the last few years, Darrin has also built a limited number of special bodies for local Rolls-Royce dealers.

DAYTON FOLDING TONNEAU CO.—1907-27
Dayton, Ohio
Founder J. D. Artz later invented Artz press for forming intricate cowl and body panels.

DEMAREST & CO.
New Haven, Connecticut, 1880's-1916
New York, New York, 1908-30
Formerly A. T. Demarest & Co., coachbuilders in New Haven who turned to building custom bodies for automobiles, then moved to New York City. They built several LeBaron-designed bodies in 1921-24, including the first Locomobile Sportif. Mostly repair work and remounting of bodies on new chassis thereafter.

DERHAM BODY CO.—1884 to date
Rosemont, Pennsylvania
Coachbuilders who continued with custom bodies after 1900. Best known in 1920's for town cars and limousines on Packard, Pierce-Arrow, Lincoln and similar chassis, and for smart convertibles on these and Chrysler chassis in the 1930's. Since World War II they have done many conversions of expensive sedans to limousines.

DETROIT CARRIAGE CO.—1898-1910
Detroit, Michigan
A coachbuilding firm which supplied bodies for Ransom E. Olds' first cars.

DIETRICH, INC.—1925-33
Detroit, Michigan
Set up as a custom body subsidiary by Murray Corp., which hired Raymond H. Dietrich away from LeBaron to head the firm. Especially known for convertibles built in small series for Packard, Lincoln, Chrysler, Franklin and others. Many Dietrich designs were adapted for production models.

D. B. DUNHAM & SONS—1863-1923
Rahway, New Jersey
A coachbuilding firm which later made limited production bodies for Richelieu and similar firms. Passenger car bodies 1910-23.

ERDMAN-GUIDER CO.—1913-26
Detroit, Michigan
Succeeded Sievers & Erdman, Coachbuilders. Some low-volume production bodies.

FARNHAM & NELSON—1905-30
Roslindale, Massachusetts
An early custom body firm which turned to building bus bodies only after 1924. Some good double-cowl phaetons in the early Twenties.

FISHER BODY CO.—1908 to date
Detroit, Michigan
Started as an independent body building firm, which was merged into General Motors Corp., of which the several Fisher brothers became large stockholders. They had earlier built

bodies for Chandler and other independent firms, as well as some General Motors cars, and continued to do so for a time after the merger. Eventually became the world's largest body builders. The company was one of the last to continue wood-frame construction among the major production body builders.

FITZGIBBON & CRISP CARRIAGE & AUTO BODY CO.—1890's-1915
Trenton, New Jersey
Coachbuilders turned body builders, who turned out some Crane-Simplexes and Mercers.

J. A. FITZSIMMONS—1913-1920's
Lindsay, Ontario

FLANDREAU & CO.—1895-1912
New York, New York
One of New York's earliest automobile dealers, they operated their own body shop for a time.

FLEETWOOD METAL BODY CO.—1912 to date
Detroit, Michigan
Started by the officers of the Reading Metal Body Co., and initially located in Fleetwood, Pennsylvania where they built on nearly all fine chassis, including Daniels, Lincoln, Packard and many imports. Purchased by Fisher in 1925, and became Fleetwood Division of General Motors after a new plant was set up in Detroit in 1929. The original Fleetwood plant built some Stutz bodies and bodies on such imported chassis as Isotta-Fraschini and Maybach, even after it was owned by General Motors. Cadillacs only since 1933.

FLOYD-DERHAM CO.—1928-29
Philadelphia, Pennsylvania
Short-lived custom body firm set up by an imported car dealer and one of the Derham family. Bodies were built in the Wolfington shop.

FRANTZ BODY MFG. CO.—1898-1930
Akron, Ohio
An early production body builder which later turned to commercial bodies. Passenger car bodies 1898-1915.

R. W. GRAFF & CO.—1907-35
Chicago, Illinois

Operated in a variety of fields including custom bodies as well as truck and bus bodies. Showed a Rolls-Royce at the Chicago Salon as late as 1924, but concentrated on bus bodies thereafter with the name changed to Graff Motor Coach Co. Passenger car bodies 1907-24.

WILLIAM GRAY & SONS
THE WM. GRAY-SONS-CAMPBELL LIMITED—1855-1924
Chatham, Ontario
Successful carriage builders who produced bodies for several Canadian automotive companies after the turn of the century. Produced Gray-Dort from 1915-24.

HALE, KILBURN & CO.
Philadelphia, Pennsylvania, 1915-25
Indianapolis, Indiana, 1925-33
Originally a small body shop, taken over by Charles M. Schwab after he took control of Stutz. They merged with several similar shops and moved to Indianapolis. Built some Stutz bodies, but mainly painted and upholstered Stutz bodies built by others "in the white."

HAYES BODY CO.—1890's-1935
Grand Rapids, Michigan
A name earlier associated with wagons, then with several body manufacturers including Hayes Mfg. Co. in Detroit, Hayes-Hunt, Hayes-Ionia, Hayes-Ohio, etc. Existed as Hayes Body Co. from 1925-35. Built bodies for Marmon, Peerless, and similar cars. Styling in charge of Alexis de Sakhnoffsky from 1929 on, who also produced a few custom or experimental bodies with his typical flowing lines.

HEALY & CO.—1890's-1926
New York, New York
Coachbuilders who turned to automobile bodies. Especially known for striking interiors on sedans and town cars for Cadillac, Packard, Stevens-Duryea and other fine chassis. Built first airport bus bodies for Uppercu-Cadillac, and later merged into the latter's Aeromarine Bus Co.

HENNEY MOTOR CAR CO.—1915 to date
Moline, Illinois
Primarily hearse and ambulance builders, who made limousines for a time. Built some post-

World War II experimental and special bodies for various manufacturers, while continuing their primary business.

HESS & EISENHART—1930's to date
Cincinnati, Ohio
Successors to Sayers & Scovill, wagon manufacturers, which had been founded in 1876 and continued as special-purpose body builders. The "S & S" brand is still used for their hearse and ambulance bodies. Built last Darrin-Packard bodies in 1940-41, also many prototype and special custom bodies including some Presidential limousines.

HOLBROOK CO.
New York, New York, 1908-21
Hudson, New York, 1921-31
An early custom body firm which moved its factory to Hudson in 1921. Many bodies for Packard, but also built on such fine chassis as Lincoln, Crane-Simplex, and several of the first Duesenberg Model J's. Best known for limousines and town cars, but produced some sporty phaetons.

H. F. HOLBROOK-HENRY BREWSTER CO.—1927-28
Bridgeport, Connecticut
Founded by Henry Holbrook, who had left the firm bearing his name, and Henry Brewster, whose family had sold out to Rolls-Royce. Bodies built in the former Blue Ribbon Body plant. Showed a Mercedes-Benz at 1927 New York Salon. Also built some hearse bodies.

HOLLANDER & MORRILL—1908-25
Amesbury, Massachusetts
An early custom body firm in this coachbuilding town. Built a number of bodies for Uppercu-Cadillac, New York Cadillac distributor. Later absorbed by Biddle & Smart.

HUME & CO.
Amesbury, Massachusetts, 1850's-1909
Boston, Massachusetts, 1909-25
Another old carriage firm which moved to Boston when custom automobile bodies became their chief business. Very distinctive round-back sedan on various chassis was especially liked by Marmon, who absorbed the firm to secure its president, W. E. Pierce, as stylist. They discontinued body building operations soon after the merger. Passenger car bodies 1905-25.

HUMER-BINDER CO.—1918 to date
New York, New York
A few custom bodies early in career, but mostly repairs and repainting, with a few alterations. New York repair depot for LeBaron, 1924-31. Still in repair business and as agents for Golde Sliding Sun Roofs. Body building 1918-22.

JOHN R. INSKIP INC.—1932 to date
New York, New York
Distributor for Rolls-Royce after dissolution of the American company which built some bodies in Brewster plant under the Inskip name. Later first importer of MG and other English cars after World War II. Body building 1933-39.

JACQUES MFG. CO.—1920-25
Philadelphia, Pennsylvania
Bodies for Lexington and other medium-volume cars.

JOHN B. JUDKINS CO.—1857-1938
Merrimac, Massachusetts
An old coachbuilding firm which turned to custom bodies. Many fine town cars on various chassis, but best known for coupé and berline bodies built in series for Lincoln, Packard, Pierce-Arrow, and other fine cars. Passenger car bodies 1895-1938.

C. P. KIMBALL & CO.—1877-1929
Chicago, Illinois
Coachbuilders turned custom body builders. Liquidated their factory at the end of World War I, but continued in repair business for a time. Body builders 1900-18.

LANG BODY CO.—1920-24
Cleveland, Ohio
Started by the Lang family after they sold their

interest in Rauch & Lang Carriage Co. Semi-custom bodies for Dodge and similar cars.

LARKINS & CO.—1880's-1930
San Francisco, California
Another old coachbuilder who turned to custom bodies, but later concentrated mostly on repair work. Body builders 1900-21.

LeBARON, INC.—1920-30
New York, New York
Bridgeport, Connecticut
Started by Thomas L. Hibbard and Raymond H. Dietrich as LeBaron, Carrossiers, Inc., designers and engineers of custom bodies. Merged with Bridgeport Body Co. in 1924, shortening the name to LeBaron, Inc. Sold to Briggs Mfg. Co. in 1926. Noted for such design innovations as swept panels, all-weather fronts on town cars, and improvements on convertible bodies. Built on nearly every high-grade imported and domestic chassis, with bodies in series for Lincoln, Packard, Pierce-Arrow, Stutz and Chrysler, among others. Many Minervas designed and built by LeBaron were sold as "Body by Ostruk."

LeBARON-DETROIT COMPANY—1927-41
Detroit, Michigan
Set up as a separate company by Briggs after purchase of LeBaron as a custom body plant, with associated LeBaron Studios. The latter designed many Briggs production bodies for Ford, Graham-Paige, Chrysler and others. Especially known for Lincoln Convertible Roadsters and various other types built in series for expensive cars, as well as several Duesenbergs. Production bodies "in the white" built in the same plant for Stutz, Pierce-Arrow and Marmon 16. Some postwar bodies under LeBaron name built in Briggs plant, now part of the Chrysler Corporation which absorbed the name along with other Briggs body building activities.

DON LEE STUDIOS—1907-25
Los Angeles, California
Custom body shop operated by Cadillac distributor, but known for bodies on various expensive chassis for movie stars. Harley Earl was their designer; when he was hired away by General Motors, the body shop was closed.

LEGRAND (See UNION CITY BODY CO.).

LEHMAN-PETERSON CO.—1925 to date
Indianapolis, Indiana

Primarily builders of such special-purpose vehicles as ambulances, but have done many alterations of passenger car bodies. Built several Lincoln limousines for the White House in recent years. Predecessor Lehman Mfg. Co. was established in 1876 to build wagons and later turned out replacement bodies for Model T Fords.

LIMOUSINE & CARRIAGE MFG. CO.—1905-15
Chicago, Illinois
An early custom body firm.

LIMOUSINE BODY CO.—1915-36
Kalamazoo, Michigan
Production body builders for such medium-priced cars as Auburn, Gardner and Moon, also some early Packard Sixes. Purchased by Auburn in 1927 and continued as part of that combine.

LOCKE & CO.
New York, New York, 1902-32
Rochester, New York, 1926-32
Began as high-grade custom body builders, especially known for distinctive town cars of exquisite finish. Later series orders for Chrysler, Franklin and Lincoln led to purchase of a larger plant in Rochester. Built many Lincoln and Chrysler phaetons there, as well as other types.

McFARLAN AUTOMOBILE CO.—1886-1928
Connersville, Indiana
Coachbuilders who turned to custom automobile bodies, then began producing complete cars. Early bodies for Locomobile, Auburn, H.C.S., Lexington and others. Built custom bodies for others 1902-25, later built only on their own chassis.

GEORGE W. McNEAR—1920-23
Brookline, Massachusetts
A small custom body shop in the Boston area.

MERRIMAC BODY CO.—1918-33
Merrimac, Massachusetts
Started by Stanley L. Judkins as a facility to take care of business the John B. Judkins Co. could not handle. A few custom bodies, but mostly small volume production bodies for such expensive cars as Packard and duPont. In the

mid-Twenties, built some fabric-covered bodies on the Childs system.

MILBURN WAGON CO.—1890's-1920's
Toledo, Ohio
Started as wagon manufacturers, later built production bodies for several nearby manufacturers. Body builders 1909-20.

MILLSPAUGH & IRISH—1915-28
Indianapolis, Indiana
Some custom bodies and small run production bodies, including most of those for the Duesenberg Model A. Also built taxicabs.

WALTER M. MURPHY CO.—1921-32
Pasadena, California
Set up as Lincoln distributor and custom body builder, Murphy being a relative of Henry Leland. Many fine bodies, especially convertibles, on Lincoln, Packard, Rolls-Royce and other chassis. Probably built more Duesenberg J's than any other firm.

MURRAY CORP. OF AMERICA—1912 to date
Detroit, Michigan
Production body builder, merged in mid-Twenties with C. R. Wilson Co., Towson, Widman and some smaller firms to become the third largest body builder. Had one of the first design studios in Detroit, under Amos Northrup, who moved there from Wills Ste. Claire in 1924. Started Dietrich, Inc., as an affiliate the next year. Bodies for Lincoln, Packard, Hupmobile, Jordan, Reo and others. Still in business supplying some components.

NEW HAVEN CARRIAGE CO.—1880's-1924
New Haven, Connecticut
Coachbuilders who early switched to custom bodies. Some nice Rolls-Royces and a number of Locomobiles. Many of those who became prominent in the custom body industry had worked in their shop at one time or another. Body builders 1902-24.

OHIO BODY & BLOWER CO.—1902-24
Cleveland, Ohio
Earlier known as the Ohio Blower Co., they

built production bodies for medium-priced cars such as Jordan, Moon, etc.

OSTRUK—1924-30
New York, New York
Paul Ostruk was distributor for Minerva, and had many bodies built by LeBaron but sold as "Body by Ostruk."

S. C. PEASE & SONS—1861-1922
Merrimac, Massachusetts
Coachbuilders who turned to custom bodies. Body builders 1905-22.

PHILLIPS CUSTOM BODY CO.—1923-28
Warren, Ohio
Best known for convertible coupés for Pierce-Arrow, Stearns-Knight, Stutz and similar cars. Absorbed by Briggs, 1928. The same family had earlier operated the Phillips Carriage Co.

PONTIAC BODY CO.—1905-15
Pontiac, Michigan
An early production body firm.

PULLMAN CAR CO.—1870's to date
Chicago, Illinois
Builders of famous sleeping cars also turned out some automobile bodies for Moon and others. Showed an all-steel Packard sedan at 1924 Chicago Salon. Body builders 1919-25.

J. M. QUINBY & SONS—1834-1930
Newark, New Jersey
Coachbuilders who turned to custom bodies, later switching to truck and bus bodies. Passenger car bodies 1902-20. This company has frequently been misspelled "Quimby."

READING METAL BODY CO.—1905-12
Reading, Pennsylvania
Fleetwood, Pennsylvania
Custom body firm whose officers later organized the Fleetwood Metal Body Co.

ROBBINS BODY CO.—1921-28
Indianapolis, Indiana
Built many Stutz bodies, as well as some for other medium-priced cars and taxicabs. When Stutz production bodies were transferred to LeBaron-Detroit Co., Robbins began making radio cabinets for one of their directors.

ROLLSTON CO., New York, New York—1921-39
ROLLSON CO., New York, New York, Plainview, New York—1939 to date
Built fine quality custom bodies on various high-grade chassis, especially Packard. Many town cars during 1920's, some Stutz and Duesenberg Convertible Victorias in 1930's, as well as similar bodies for Packard up to 1942. Reorganized as Rollson when original owners retired in 1939. Still in business making airplane galleys. Body builders 1921-42.

LEON RUBAY & CO.—1905-22
Cleveland, Ohio
An early custom body builder, which also produced some series bodies for expensive cars. Attempt to market their own automobile 1921-22 forced bankruptcy, and their plant was sold to Baker, Rauch & Lang. Thomas L. Hibbard worked there briefly.

CHARLES G. SCHUETTE BODY COMPANY—1910-26
Lancaster, Pennsylvania
An early custom body builder which later switched to taxicabs.

SEABROOK & SMITH CARRIAGE CO.—1890's-1915
New Haven, Connecticut
Coachbuilders turned body builders, who later concentrated on special purpose vehicles.

W. S. SEAMAN CO.—1880's-1919
Milwaukee, Wisconsin

SEAMAN BODY CO.—1919-36
Milwaukee, Wisconsin
A woodworking firm which became a custom body builder. They also developed a soundproof telephone booth, building thousands of them for the Western Electric Co. After C. W. Nash took over the Thos. B. Jeffery Co., he relied more and more on Seaman as a source of

bodies and bought a half-interest in the firm, at which time the name was changed to Seaman Body Co. Telephone booth manufacture was discontinued to concentrate on Nash bodies. Prior to 1919, W. S. Seaman built custom bodies on Locomobile, Lozier, Dorris, Packard, Cadillac and other chassis, as well as some production bodies for Kissel, Moline and Velie. The firm was finally merged into Nash Motors.

SMITH BROS.—1850 to date
Motor Bodies Ltd.
740 Don Mills Road
Toronto, Ontario
Known for McLaughlin-Buicks. A Smith Bros. Buick is the only model of that marque accepted by the Classic Car Club of America. The company discontinued making car bodies in the late Thirties. Today production is concentrated on commercial vehicle bodies.

SPRINGFIELD METAL BODY CO.—1902-10
SMITH-SPRINGFIELD CORP.—1910-21
SPRINGFIELD BODY CO.—1924-27
Springfield, Massachusetts
Custom body firm which became the body plant of the Rolls-Royce Company of America. First built on various high-grade chassis. Former owners reorganized, taking over the former Stevens-Duryea plant to build bus bodies. The second name listed incorporated that of Hinsdale Smith, their designer and president.

STUDEBAKER CORPORATION—1840's-1964
South Bend, Indiana
Wagon-builders since gold-rush days. Built bodies for Detroit Electric cars, then for E.M.F. and Mr. Flanders, which evolved into the Studebaker automobile. Some of their earlier bodies were built in the plant of the Studebaker Bros. Mfg. Co. in Chicago. Passenger car bodies 1902-64.

E. J. THOMPSON CO.—1907-27
Pittsburgh, Pennsylvania
Another carriage-builder turned body builder. Custom and small-series bodies, including some for Dodge in early Twenties. A few fabric-covered bodies on Childs system in mid-Twenties, after which they specialized in bus bodies.

TOWSON BODY CO.—1922-25
Detroit, Michigan
Started as Anderson Electric Car Co., which also built bodies for Velie, Davis and other medium-priced cars. Reorganized as Towson Body Co., with most business from Packard, and then merged into Murray Corp.

TRIPPENSEE CLOSED BODY CO.—1923-25
Detroit, Michigan
Organized mainly to build bodies for Rickenbacker, which soon absorbed the firm.

UNION CITY BODY CO.—1903-37
Union City, Indiana
Small production body shop for medium-priced cars, which became part of Auburn complex. Built mostly Cord bodies, also some Duesenbergs under the name of "Legrand" which were copies of earlier custom bodies by other firms.

WALKER CARRIAGE CO.—1850's-1920
WALKER BODY CO.—1920-33
Amesbury, Massachusetts
Syracuse, New York, 1923-33
An old carriage firm which turned to producing automobile bodies, especially for Franklin. This led to adding a plant in Syracuse, part of which was used for a while to build custom bodies designed by Frank deCausse. They were sold as products of the "Franklin Custom Body Division."

WATERHOUSE & CO.—1928-33
Webster, Massachusetts
According to their original announcement, they were established in 1928 "to build bodies for duPont." Several of the Waterhouse family previously worked for Judkins, and they built custom bodies on a variety of chassis. Became famous for their convertible victorias, first on Packard, later on Chrysler and other chassis.

WEYMANN AMERICAN BODY CO.—1927-35
Indianapolis, Indiana
Subsidiary of the French firm which patented a

flexible fabric-covered body. Several models made in quantity for Stutz, who invested in the firm also. A few experimental bodies on other chassis. Some late Stutz bodies were aluminum panelled but retained the flexible frame.

J. C. WIDMAN CO.—1920-25
Built open bodies for Jewett, Chalmers and Franklin. Also built first Earl Brougham, a two-door sedan. Merged into Murray Corp.

WILLOUGHBY & CO.—1908-33
Utica, New York
Custom body builder, known for luxurious upholstery but rather conservative lines. Some small series for Cole and Wills Ste. Claire in early Twenties. Many Lincoln town cars and limousines, as well as some other fine chassis.

C. R. WILSON BODY CO.—1873-1927
Detroit, Michigan
Began as a carriage shop and became one of the better production body builders for Lincoln, Packard and other high-priced cars. Merged into Murray Corp. Body builders 1907-27.

WITHAM BODY CO.—1923-25
Amesbury, Massachusetts
Bodies for Stearns-Knight and others. Absorbed by Biddle & Smart.

ALEXANDER WOLFINGTON'S SONS & CO.—1880's-1950
Philadelphia, Pennsylvania
Carriage builders who turned to custom bodies in the early 1900's. Started building deluxe bus bodies in early Twenties. Plant space used by Floyd-Derham in 1928, and a few custom bodies built under their own name into 1930's. Later became agents for Superior School Bus bodies. Passenger car bodies 1902-35.

F. R. WOOD & SONS—1880's-1939
Brooklyn, New York
Carriage builders, then custom body builders. Built first attractive delivery vehicles for John Wanamaker around 1903. Later switched to truck and bus bodies, with only an occasional custom body or alteration. Passenger car bodies, 1902-26.

WOONSOCKET MFG. CO.—1921-29
Woonsocket, Rhode Island
Bodies for Dagmar cars, but mainly taxicab and bus bodies.

New York Salon of 1921 in the Hotel Commodore. Fleetwood exhibit at lower left with two Daniels cars in foreground. First three cars on right are a Porter, Pierce-Arrow and Winton.

Brewster: electric, possibly a Barrett, circa 1889. (K)

COACHBUILT MOTORCARS

Quinby: 1900 Riker electric victoria. (L)

Quinby: 1904 Simplex panel brougham. (L)

RUNABOUT BODY

ABOVE
Clayton: 1916 Hudson panel brougham.

Seaman: Packard Twin Six roadster, circa 1916. (L)

Cunningham: 1920 Cunningham touring. (P)

Willoughby: 1921 Cole sedan. (L)

Hume: 1921 Marmon sedan. (L)

Rubay: 1926 Rickenbacker sport sedan. (L)

Don Lee: Packard sport phaeton, circa 1919-21 (M)

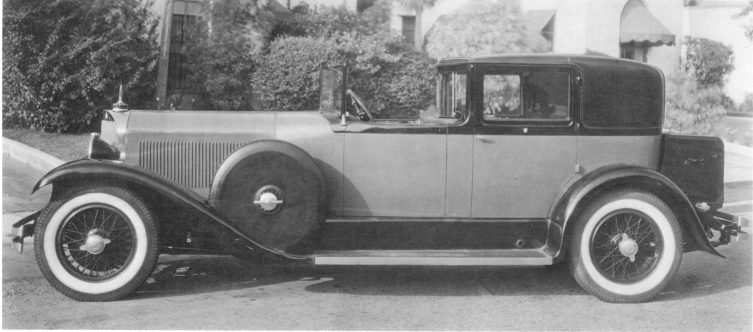

Le Baron: 1927 Stutz Prince of Wales sedan. (L)

Murphy: 1928 Mercedes Model K town car. (M)

ABOVE
Rollston: 1929 Packard Eight roadster. (L)

1929 HUDSON

ABOVE
Murphy: 1929 Hudson sport sedan. (A)

BELOW
Derham: 1929 Stutz convertible coupé. (L)

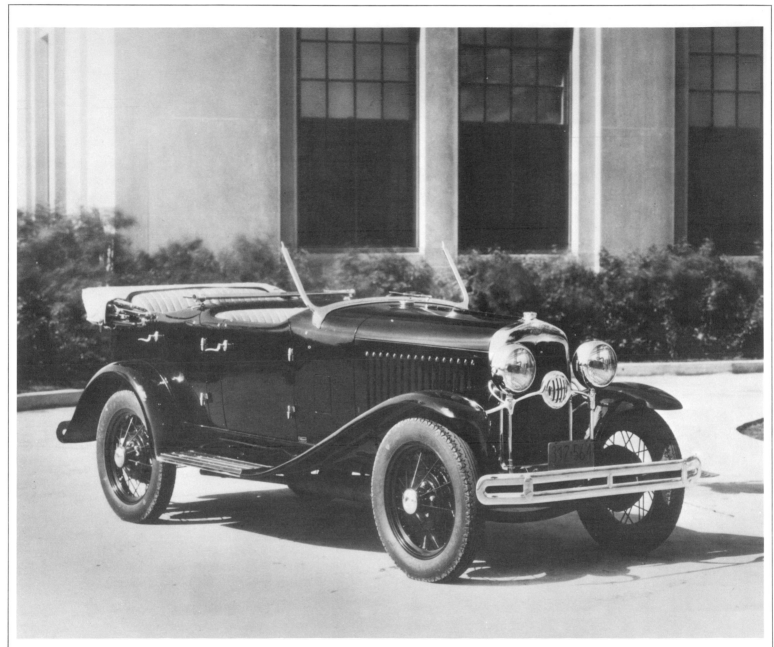

Le Baron: 1930 Ford Model A dual cowl phaeton. (F)

Brewster: 1931 Rolls-Royce Phantom II streamlined coupé. (M)

Brewster: 1930 Rolls-Royce Phantom I sport coupé. (M)

ABOVE
Baker, Rauch & Lang: 1930 Ruxton town car. (L)

BELOW
Fleetwood: 1931 Cadillac V-16 panel brougham. (L)

Hayes: 1930 Cord L-29 sport coupé.

Walker: 1931 Franklin coach. (H)

Biddle & Smart: 1931 Hudson brougham. (A)

Baker, Rauch & Lang: 1931 Jordan "Sportsman" five passenger sedan. (L)

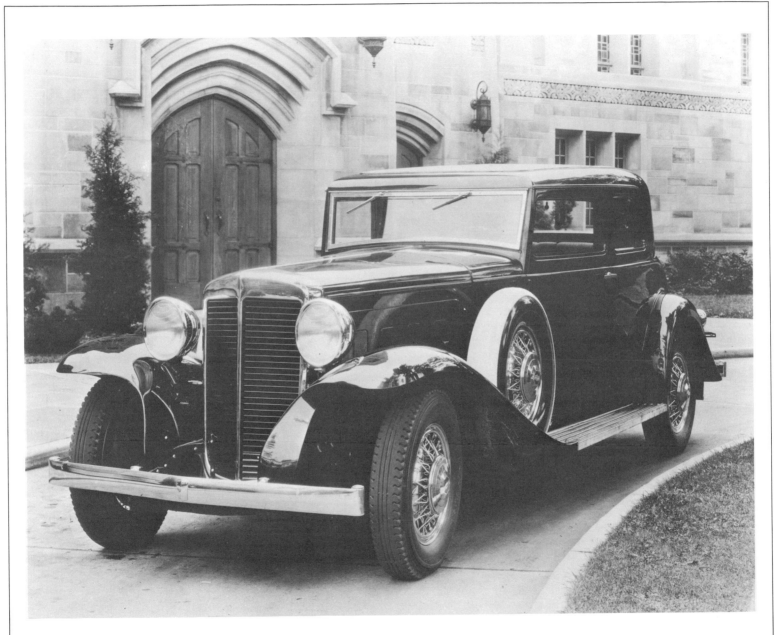

Le Baron: 1931 Marmon Sixteen victoria coupé. (M)

Le Baron: 1931 Pierce-Arrow convertible victoria. (L)

Willoughby: 1931 Pierce-Arrow town car. (L)

Hayes: 1931 Reo Royale convertible victoria. (L)

Brewster: 1931 Rolls-Royce dual cowl phaeton. (M)

Le Baron: 1932 Lincoln convertible coupé.

Brunn: 1932 Lincoln "double entry" sport sedan.

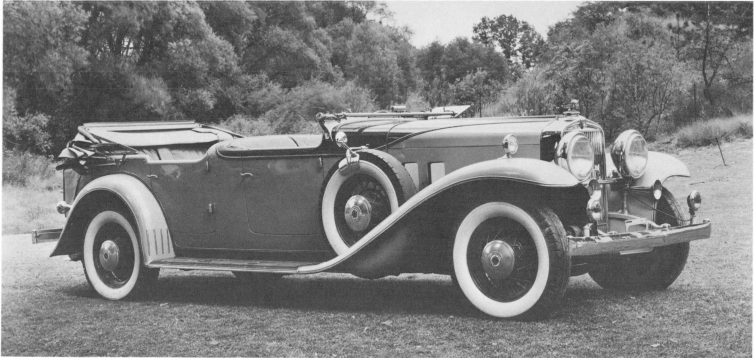

Waterhouse: 1932 Lincoln Model KB convertible victoria.

Rollston: 1932 Stutz phaeton.

Rollston: 1934 Ford V-8 town car. (F)

Le Baron: 1935 Lincoln convertible coupé. (P)

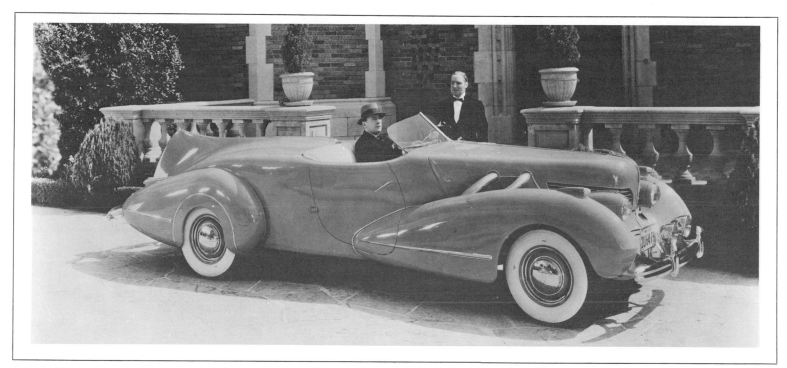

ABOVE
Bohman & Schwartz: 1936 Buick roadster built for the movie Topper. (M)

BELOW
Brunn: 1936 Lincoln town car limousine. (P)

191

Bohman & Schwartz: 1942 Packard convertible victoria. (T)

CARS OF BOTH WORLDS

The American Influence in Foreign Automobiles

• •

BY MICHAEL SEDGWICK

THE ANGLO-AMERICANS

It doesn't matter where you live or who you are: The imported automobile will always have a special snob value. Thus American cars have been part of the British scene since the earliest days.

Despite its dipsomaniac thirst for water, the Locomobile Steamer was well established by 1902, and within a year the single-cylinder runabouts of Oldsmobile and Cadillac had followed suit, aided and abetted by that great race of publicists who were Britain's most significant contribution to automobilism in the first decade of the Twentieth Century. If S. F. Edge broke lance after lance for Napier and Charlie Rolls sang the praises of Rolls-Royce, there were others who waved the Stars and Stripes. Charles Jarrott, Edge's great rival, represented Olds along with Crossley and de Dietrich, his partner, Billy Letts, headed Willys-Overland's British branch until it expired in 1933 and Frederick Coleman stayed with the White through its metamorphosis from steam to gasoline. In 1903 Percival Lea Dewhurst Perry was an unknown young man whose sole claim to fame was the promotion of a dust-sealing solution used on the Irish Gordon Bennett course, but he guided the destinies of Ford in Britain from a modest agency to the role of the nation's Number Two automobile manufacturer.

By 1910 quite a few U.S. makes were available in Britain, notably Buick, Maxwell and Overland, and more were to follow. Britons appreciated their simplicity, low price, and ease of operation, though they disliked the general coarseness of their appointments. Thus by 1914 the market could sustain things like the Bedford-Buick with British bodywork, not to mention custom versions of Hupmobile, K.R.I.T., Regal (sold in England as the R.M.C.-Seabrook) and Oakland. This last could easily be mistaken for the illustrious Belgian Métallurgique on the strength of its elegantly vee'd German silver radiator. By contrast, America's greatest makes — Packard, Peerless, Pierce-Arrow, Simplex, and the gasoline Locomobile — were unknown. Europe not only covered the market to repletion (there were sixty-six models of over six liters' capacity listed in the 1913 British Buyers' Guide), but also supplied the carriage trade in America. From 1911, of course, Ford had their own assembly plant at Manchester, and in the next sixteen years this churned out a quarter of a million vehicles. The impact of the Model T in Britain was such that in 1919 *forty-one* percent of all motor vehicles registered in the country — passenger and commercial — were Fords.

A few American designs had been made under license in Britain, but these were of little significance. America was the spiritual home of the

The 1969 Mangusta, by de Tomaso of Italy.

electric, hence both the Columbia and the Detroit were tried, the latter by the Scottish firm of Arrol-Johnston in 1913. A few Duryeas were also built at Coventry, but neither these nor the single-cylinder Adams (alias Hewitt) succeeded in challenging the little de Dion-Bouton as doctors' runabouts. The Hewitt planetary transmission, however, had quite a vogue on the bigger and otherwise conventional automobiles made by A. H. Adams at Bedford.

World War I was destined to bring Britons into far closer contact with the American automobile. Already imports were rising — 5152 cars were shipped in 1913, but an impressive 6799 the following year when the United Kingdom was Detroit's biggest individual customer. Now war meant that domestic and European supplies dried up at the same time. Across the Atlantic, everyone joined in. There were new models from established firms, like the V-8 Cadillac, and such unknowns as Crow-Elkhart, King and Scripps-Booth put in an appearance, along with a handful of Chevrolets, which passed almost unnoticed. British editors wrote angrily of this "American Invasion," as well they might; in one month of 1915 alone no fewer than 4036 American cars were shipped in. But there was nothing to be done. These inexpensive flat-headed fours might be crude and ill-trimmed, but most of them boasted electric starters, a refinement not as yet to be found on such middle-

class British makes as the best-selling Wolseley. The fixed wood wheels and demountable rims, an infuriating American fad which was later to force concessionaires to standardize wire-wheel equipment on their wares, as yet passed without comment: Britons did not demand these until 1919.

Things were even better for America after the war, when the U-Boat blockade ceased, and restrictions were lifted. Native manufacturers were slow to reconvert, and when they did their ideas were often unrealistic. Such grandiose assembled-car schemes as the Angus-Sanderson produced singularly poor results, and the same went for such oddities as the radial-engined Enfield-Allday and the huge overhead-cam Ensign Six, destined to end its days as an anglicized Owen Magnetic. In 1920 and 1921, a wave of strikes swept industry on both sides of the English channel: Fiat suffered a Red Occupation, so that there could be no anticipation of 1969-70, when the Continental imports had a field-day while Coventry, Cowley and Birmingham reeled under a series of labor disputes. America stepped into the breach quite happily, and Britons had their first sight of the Haynes, the Cole and the Apperson Eight, none of which even came with right-hand steering.

Not that a Cole Aero-Eight touring at $6000 f.o.b. London was the

FACING PAGE: *The Columbia Electric (left above) was sold under the "City and Suburban" name. This particular model was delivered to Her Majesty, Queen Alexandra of England, sometime during the year 1901.* (Y)
The 1904 British Duryea phaeton (right above) was produced under license in Coventry by Henry Sturmey. (Y)
Fords, circa 1912, rolled off the assembly line (below) in Trafford Park, Manchester, England. (AA)
THIS PAGE: *The Hewitt of New York City was the basis for the 1908 Adams shown above.* (Y)
The 1916 Morris-Cowley (below) was Continental-engined. (BB)

answer. What was demanded was a cheap medium-sized automobile to cater to the new, war-bred generation of drivers, and Detroit made hay in the two years before Treasury Rating (a formula identical to the N.A.C.C.'s system) was made to bite to the tune of a $5 levy per unit of horsepower. This iniquity rendered the owner of a Model T liable to an impost of $115 per annum, and accounts for the present-day scarcity of this breed in our islands — a good sixty percent of the survivors are trucks. The most viable solution for an aspiring "manufacturer" was to buy either a set of components or a complete chassis from the U.S.A., and dress it up in a guise that Britons would accept, with well-finished bodywork, detachable wheels, and an elongated hood crowned with a distinguished radiator.

Nor was this formula new. William Richard Morris had discovered it in 1914, and while the ambitious Oxonian was already taking the first steps which were to lead him to full manufacture and control of "Britain's Greatest Motor Business" by 1939, others were jumping aboard the bandwagon. Some, like Maiflower, were content merely to camouflage and customize the Ford, a pursuit spurred by the incredibly snobbish attitudes of the era. As late as 1924, a segregationist policy banished any classified ads for Ford to the very back of the English *Motor* magazine, and many of Lizzie's owners were determined that she should look like anything but herself. The convertible sedans of Gordon and Co. bore more than a passing resemblance to the respected if moribund Scottish Argyll, and others reverted to the mock-Métallurgique theme. My own parents commenced their motoring career on a Ford, but inflicted upon it a touring body off a Studebaker, which must have taxed both Henry's twenty horses and his bouncy suspension to the limit.

Alas!, this first generation of Anglo-Americans got precisely nowhere. Of the six makes quoted in 1920-21, two only survived until 1924, and then it was a case of selling dead stock for what it would fetch. Three (London-Pullman, Morriss-London and Perfex) started life as the transmogrified wares of American makers who were nearly dead themselves. They cost more than "real" American automobiles, and most customers preferred to buy their service through a proper dealer-network rather than from some small garage in a London suburb. Further, the regular concessionaires were learning the art of customization. From 1919 Buicks (no longer bearing the Bedford prefix) could be had with a full range of English coachwork, by such firms as Grosvenor, Carlton and Page and Hunt, not to mention a smart landaulette by Vanden Plas of Belgium. The London-bodied Dodge Four landaulette had an untidy overhang at the rear, but it had more appeal than the boxy Business Sedan. A neat Essex Four roadster with wire wheels sold on the strength of the marque's successes in local sprints and hill-climbs. The Anglo-Americans faded away. A few British makers sought to build American-type automobiles for the Colonial market, but these did not utilize American components. The sole exception was the Continental-engined Bond of 1922, but this was seldom encountered anywhere.

More successful were the attempts of American firms to assemble or manufacture in Britain. Ford never looked back. Even with the full impact of horsepower tax, Lizzie could match any of William Morris' cost-cutting expedients. A touring sold for $550 in 1924, as against $990 for the cheapest Morris-Cowley, a car half her size. When passenger-car sales slumped in the face of the Ford's archaic specification, the one-ton trucks took over, Model TT having no serious rivals until 1924 when British-assembled Chevrolets and Morris' own one-tonner reached the market. Willys-Overland were assembling in England by 1921, and went further than Ford in that already they offered specifically British variants with a high native content. But though John N. Willys, like Henry Ford, sited his plant near Manchester (within easy striking distance of the port of Liverpool), his U.K. products never quite made the grade. There wasn't, after all, any special attraction in a crossbreed made up of a Morris motor and transmission in an Overland Four chassis. In 1925 GM consolidated their foothold with the acquisition of Vauxhall. This was a sad day for connoisseurs, even if General Motors continued to market the splendid "30-98" sports car until 1928. Thereafter the Vauxhall became a car of American type, if not a true Anglo-American. Some of the effects of this marriage were beneficial, notably syncromesh (1932) and Fisher No-Draft Ventilation (1933). The less said of Knee Action as applied to the 1935 Vauxhall Light Six the better: The deferential and slightly inebriated curtsy when the brakes were applied hard at a traffic intersection remains the least affectionate memory of these hard-wearing automobiles.

Other transatlantic products were imported "in the white," which gave importers a chance to include some of the refinement sought by Perfex and Morriss-London in 1920. Equipment was comprehensive (Britons had yet to be educated to the "stripped price," a commonplace of today). The more expensive six-cylinder Plymouths came with overdrive, and Hudsons of the appropriate period with the unloved Electric Hand. Leather upholstery and "sliding roofs" (as offered in America on 1940 Buicks) were recognized *deluxe* perquisites, and from 1934 every Chrysler Corporation car delivered from the Kew assembly plant had 12-volt electrics. As sales rose from the all-time low of 1931-32 American firms dodged the horsepower tax with small-bore motors not to be found in the pages of domestic directories. The Model AF Ford of 14.9 N.A.C.C. rating is well known. Less familiar, however, are the 19.8 hp (2⅞-inch bore) sixes fitted to sundry Chryslers, Dodges and Plymouths between 1932 and 1939, and the even smaller 16.9 motor fitted to the Terraplane family. There was also a whole generation of semi-custom body styles of the type dear to the Briton. The favorite was the "foursome drophead coupé" (convertible victoria with blind rear quarters), a less discriminatory affair than the rumble-seated convertibles offered by Detroit as late as 1937. British coachbuilders proved themselves adept in blending the traditional native line with the excesses of front-end treatment that manifested themselves from 1935 on. In 1936, one could buy a Buick, Chevrolet, Chrysler, Ford V-8, Hudson-Terraplane, Packard 120, Pontiac or Studebaker in this form for a modest outlay, and Buick's "Albemarle" (by the Carlton Carriage Company) was made in respectable numbers, even if by 1939 it looked uncomfortably archaic when wedded to the fleur-de-lys grille and massive sidemounts of the RO-series. The sport-tourings were killed off by the advent of the Railton and its imitators, but another flourishing line of business was the "sports saloon," or four-door sport sedan with integral trunk. Hudson were the chief protagonists of this style, which died around 1937, partly because of the rise of the Anglo-Americans, and partly because the new razor-edge styling of the period sorted ill with

Overland fours, circa 1923, in England. (Y)

A Continental-engined Bucciali of 1930.

The 1929 Audi Zwickau five-passenger sedan. (Y)

A 1930's coupé model of the Railton.

The 1932 Lycoming-engined Burney Streamline sedan. (Y)

prevailing Detroit fashion. (I once saw a '38 Chrysler Imperial on which the two were blended catastrophically.) In any case, 1938 was the year of Cadillac's Sixty Special, which offered the best of both worlds, even if Britons considered it unattractive, quite apart from a list price of $4250 and an annual tax of another $250.

In this period, of course, most of the cheaper American cars were nominally Canadian, Buick ads urging the customer to "buy a car made in the British Empire," a ploy which had a greater effect than the House of Windsor's brief affection for the cars from Oshawa. Curiously enough, though, Britons were never given a chance of buying the curious cross-bred Chevrolet-Pontiacs current in 1938 and 1939. Chrysler, however, made life most confusing for latter-day historians. In the 1920's their smart and powerful roadsters were recognized as "the poor man's Bentley," and they preferred to cash in on this image, with amusing consequences. In 1939, there were probably as many as ten thousand satisfied Plymouth owners in the British Isles, but it is doubtful whether any of them were aware of the fact. They had bought Chrysler Kew or Wimbledon Sixes, and Chryslers they remained. After 1931, the same treatment was applied to the De Soto, only this time the type-names were Mortlake and Richmond. Other curiosities were a six-cylinder Airflow "Chrysler" (De Soto SEX and SGX, for the record), and a mysterious straight-eight Dodge shown at Earls Court in 1938 which was probably a C23 Chrysler.

The Great Depression, of course, played havoc with imports. Twenty-nine makes from America were represented in the United Kingdom in 1929, but only fifteen in 1933, while a mere four (Buick, Chrysler, Hudson and Packard) enjoyed an unbroken record of sale in the 1930's. On the credit side, the legendary "Anglo-American sports bastards" were a direct by-product of the lean years. Their creators, L. A. Cushman, Reid Railton and Noel Macklin, had a clear objective. At its best, the mass-produced American automobile possessed virtues beyond mere cheapness. There was plenty of torque in the right place, power-to-weight ratios were excellent, and for all Detroit's carefully fostered credo of planned obsolescence, the big motors didn't work hard enough to wear themselves out. Sophisticated engineers might poke fun at the Hudson's "barbarous" splash lubrication, but these units would run up to 5000 rpm without embarrassment. The fundamental weaknesses were styling (past its zenith in 1933), trim, roadholding and brakes, and in all fairness the new Lockheed hydraulics were already more generally applied in America than in Britain. If one took an American chassis, stiffened up the suspension, scrapped the 6-volt electrics in favor of a proper 12-volt system, and cloaked it with British coachbuilt bodywork, trimmed in real leather and crowned with an instrument panel made up of man-sized circular dials, it should surely find a place in the market.

What is more, the place was already there. The carriage trade had suffered worst of all from the Depression: Bentley had gone under in 1931, and Invicta, whose six-cylinder 4½-liter had to a certain extent assumed the Bentley's mantle, were on the rocks. Lagonda's promising 4½-liter had yet to be announced, and in any case nobody had considered offering anything in this class for less than $4000. A suitable American chassis could be bought and reworked for around $1200, which left its sponsors plenty of room for maneuver. Thus the original 93-horsepower Terraplane Eight (the 4.2-liter Hudson did not appear

on the scene until 1934) as delivered to Railton in the old Invicta shops at Cobham received little major attention beyond what was immediately visible. Yet one had to lift the hood to realize that this was basically an American automobile. Even the wheels were not usually changed, but the Railton looked every inch the part, with its angular rivet-studded hood, a vee radiator obviously inspired by the Rolls-Royce shape of the old Invicta, and typical British sport sedan or sport touring bodies. It would top 85 miles an hour, could out-accelerate its aristocratic rivals right up to the 60 mark, and cost $2495 all on. It also endeared itself to lazy drivers, for shifting was virtually eliminated. The three-speed transmission had quite useful ratios — a good Railton will see 65 in intermediate gear — but the lever itself was not the car's strong suit. Early ones had the usual long and willowy prong with an excess of travel, and later cars were afflicted with an indeterminate remote control with an action like stirring stew in a pot.

None the less, this masterpiece of improvisation was an excellent automobile. *The Autocar* insisted that it was "Ten Years Ahead of Its Time," on the strength of its high-gear performance: a slight overstatement, since the bigger six-cylinder touring Invictas could match this, and hadn't a Rolls-Royce been driven from London to Edinburgh and back without a downward shift as long ago as 1911? But the Railton's foot-frying propensities have also been exaggerated. The closed Anglo-Americans may have been bad offenders under this head: "double bulkheads" (firewalls) were always a strong selling point with sponsors of such cars, but the disease was endemic to this era of low lines and hoods packed to the brim with machinery. The Railton sedan was far cooler than the big M.G., which verged on the uninhabitable in hot weather.

By 1937, the Railton was only one of six Anglo-American makes on the market, but it outsold all its imitators, and total deliveries of over 1400 units probably make it Britain's best-selling straight-eight of all time: not a bad performance when one considers that such volume producers as Hillman and Wolseley tried their luck with this configuration. Of the opposition, George Brough's Brough Superior was also Hudson-based, and looked its best as a convertible victoria by Atcherley of Birmingham. Equipment included a combined rear-view mirror and clock, and the car's slogan ("Ninety In Silence") was upheld by the original eights, if not by the 3½-liter sixes which supplanted them. The Lammas, by contrast, made use of a Graham Supercharger Six chassis, while Jensen's Anglo-American was largely their own work. They had already done quite well with tuned and custom-bodied Ford V-8's, not to mention one or two similarly doctored Master Chevrolets, and their new effort used a Ford motor tuned to give 120 horsepower in a chassis with independent front suspension and Dewandre servo brakes. Options included magneto ignition, McCullough superchargers and two-speed rear axles. Especially attractive were the dual-cowl phaetons, though the sedans in their show finish of black and white ran them close. Of the others, the Atalanta of 1938 comprised a Lincoln-Zephyr motor in an advanced all-independently-sprung chassis: Speedster versions would top the 100 mark. This engine also went into a couple of Jensens (one was sold to Clark Gable), a prototype by George Brough, and one or two early Allards. This last-mentioned make, along with the seldom-encountered Batten and Leidart, were machines of an altogether starker type, aimed at competition motoring. Sydney Allard specialized in the "reliability trial," a mud-plugging event involving assaults on the unsurfaced and vertical. Total production of these three breeds can hardly have exceeded twenty-five units between 1935 and 1939, though the 1940 Allard would have been a more sophisticated roadster with better weather protection.

By this time the Anglo-Americans were on their way out. The luxurious ones had succumbed to the English disease — too much weight. The 1933 Railtons turned the scales at under 2500 pounds: A 1937 sport sedan weighed 3024 pounds and its acceleration was actually inferior to that of the regular Country Club Hudson, compound curves and all. The Ford-engined Jensen weighed in at a ponderous 3444 pounds. A native manufacturer could add some more horses or enlarge his motor, as did Alvis, Daimler and Rolls-Royce during this period. The purveyors of hybrids had to fall into line with what Detroit was doing — and Detroit didn't do enough to keep pace. Worse still, in 1938 there was an all-British automobile which, like Annie Oakley, could do everything the Railton did, only better, more cheaply and for a lighter gas consumption, provided one was prepared for rather more shifting.

William Lyons's 3½-liter SS Jaguar offered 95 miles an hour, sixteen miles to the gallon and an unburstable seven-bearing six-cylinder motor for $2325.

The Railton and Brough just couldn't compete, especially after Britain started to rearm, and the basic rate of tax was hiked to $6.20 per unit of horsepower, which meant an annual bill of $231.20 for anything with a 36.4 hp Lincoln-Zephyr under the hood. The Railton, as a Twenty-Nine, came off more lightly, but the giant-killing Jaguar was a mere baby of 25 horsepower. Some of the specialists tried to move up a class, but it didn't work. Cars like the H-series Jensen with valve-in-head Nash Eight engine and George Brough's Lincoln-powered Series XII at $6250 were up against Alvis and Lagonda, both turning out some admirable classics in the immediate prewar years. SS shipped a record five thousand units in the incomplete 1939 season; by contrast Railton sales were down to a trickle despite the introduction of a brace of companion sixes and even a batch of fifty customized Standard Tens which owed nothing to Detroit. Jensen, building up a truck business, flourished, but the Lammas had vanished during 1938, and for practical purposes Brough were back with their first love, the motorcycle.

The 1933 Railton, with Terraplane engine.

THIS PAGE: *The Brough Superior   above left, a 1936 3½-liter sport sedan; above right, the 1935 4-liter straight eight convertible coupé by Atcherley.* (CC)
Center left and right—a 1938 German Ford V-8 convertible cabriolet (EE)*; a 1938 French-built Matford.* (Y)
Below left, the 1938-39 Opel Admiral four-door sedan.
FACING PAGE: *A 1939 Atalanta speedster (left above), powered by the Lincoln Zephyr V-12 engine.* (CC)
The 1949 J.P.W. (right above), a prototype coupé. (Y)
A 1948 3.6-liter Allard (below), with one-of-a-kind two-door sport sedan body by Lea-Francis. (Y)

Nor was there any prospect of a postwar revival. The dollar crisis put a stop to American car imports, and none of the surviving hybrids were well enough known in the U.S.A. to sell there. Hudson Motors made another sixteen Railtons, and Jensen's first few postwar sedans went out with leftover Nash motors under their hoods after a short-stroke eight from Meadows of Wolverhampton had failed to materialize. An oddball was the J.B.M., a stark speedster in the old Allard idiom which escaped British Purchase Tax because it was built up from reconditioned prewar components. Only Allard throve, and he did so by continuing to draw on the only legitimate source of new material — the Ford V-8, still being made at Dagenham and therefore not subject to import restrictions. Further, his new K, L and M-types were far removed from the trials irons of 1939, being handsome aerodynamic creations designed for street use. The old V-8's gas-gobbling propensities sorted ill with rationing (not abolished in Britain until 1950), but individual appearance, cheap servicing and the traditional neck-snapping getaway made many friends for the cars from South London until the XK Jaguar began to appear in numbers — and this, remember, was not until mid-1950. Once again, however, William Lyons was to make a killing, though Allard kept his company's head above water for several years by shipping motorless chassis to the U.S.A. Here they could be fitted with engines that were off limits for Britons — the 160-horsepower Cadillac, the hemi-head Chrysler and the Oldsmobile. Home market customers continued with the Ford, but not even Zora Arkus-Duntov could make it competitive with the twin-cam Jaguar, which was good for over 200 horsepower by the mid-Fifties.

Two other firms tried to make automobiles exclusively for dollar export, both at the behest of Nash-Kelvinator. The Nash-Healey of 1951 was a rather untidy roadster with a six-cylinder valve-in-head Nash motor: It looked better after receiving the Pininfarina treatment, but Healey's operations were on a scale even more modest than Allard's, and it was all over by 1954. More significant was the Metropolitan, by Austin of Birmingham out of Nash's 1950 NXI baby-car prototype. Take a 1953 Nash Airflyte, scale it down to a coupé only 149 inches long, and install a motor already familiar to Americans, the 1.2-liter A40. Seen through British eyes, the result was unspeakably vulgar in its wonted Neapolitan ice-cream finish, while a brisk performance was matched by non-handling of the worst possible kind. (When I lived near a U.S. base in 1956, Met-baiting was a recognized sport. One let one of the little coupés creep up on one's tail, and then charged flat out into a downhill left-hander. Watching the Met's gyrations in the mirror was always good for a laugh.) Joke or not, the car went down big in the U.S.A., and also in Britain when right-hand-drive versions with the later 1½-liter unit became available in 1957. This was probably movie-influence, but it is noticeable that many of the Metropolitans one sees on the road today are in first-class condition.

The 1953 Nash-Healey LeMans hardtop sports car, designed by Pininfarina.

By 1958, be it said, the Metropolitan was the only Anglo-American automobile in series production. The Railton had faded quietly away in 1950, and Jensen had reverted to British power units. Allards were made only to special order, with Jaguar motors: The fact that these were released to the firm was a sure indication that they no longer represented a serious challenge to anyone. Nineteen-sixty, however, saw the emergence of a new star at the Geneva Show, and this was no Jaguar, but an elegant Bertone-styled GT from a new firm at Slough. This automobile, the Gordon, used a V-8 Chevrolet Corvette motor and would exceed 140 mph. There was no promise of immediate production — four years were to elapse before it reached the public as the 5350 cc Gordon-Keeble GKI — but when it did go on sale it was but one of four representatives of a new generation of Anglo-Americans.

This time it was not a case of making a cheap sports car, nor even of modifying an American chassis and clothing it in a manner calculated to appeal to British tastes. The traditional chassis frame was on its way out, and even a firm as small as Gordon-Keeble made almost everything themselves save the motor and transmission. And these came from America because America was now the only viable source of the sort of horsepower demanded by the growing GT market. Possible British alternatives were either unavailable, wouldn't fit, or weighed too much. Certainly none of them could have been bought for the $1500 inclusive of duty charged for a Corvette unit complete with ancillaries. Further, on top of proven reliability, buying American meant world-wide servicing facilities, and an assured continuity of production, which saved the small manufacturer from a frantic scramble for replacements when a favored motor was dropped. And by this time the specialist makers were already dependent on veteran designs that had reached the point of no return. Jensen's long-stroke six-cylinder Austin truck unit dated back to 1947, the Bristol six (also used by A.C.) was a direct descendant of the 1937 German 2-liter B.M.W., and A.C.'s own overhead-cam motor ("The First Light Six and Still The Finest") had taken its bow, incredibly, at the 1919 London Show. When these firms turned Detroitwards, they would be offered a package that included the cheapest and best automatic transmissions in the world, though not everyone wanted them. Gordon-Keeble preferred four-on-the-floor, and automatic would have been out of place on A.C.'s hairy Cobra, more a motorcycle on four wheels than a GT with its stark open body. Buyers of the Chrysler-engined Jensen had the choice of manual or automatic, but only the latter was available on the gentlemanly Bristol.

Import restrictions had been lifted — the horsepower tax had already gone for good in 1947. Thus the new generation started with fewer handicaps, and were able to keep going on the smaller outputs dictated by prices in the region of $12,000-14,000. (Initially the Gordon-Keeble tried to be too inexpensive, and it never recovered.) Other small makers joined in — T.V.R. of Blackpool in 1964, Ginetta of Witham in 1965 and the Trident (a new marque based on a T.V.R. prototype) in 1966. Even the big battalions had a go, for in 1964 the weakest of Britain's mass producers, Rootes, came up with the Sunbeam Tiger, a two-passenger sports car which wore a Ford V-8 where once the faithful old Hillman Minx-based 1.7-liter four had reposed. The result was something of a bomb, which the Alpine hadn't been, but it was doomed from the start. The Tiger was an anomaly not to be tolerated by American Big Business: It came from a Chrysler-owned plant, yet was powered by Ford. Such a thing had not happened since the U.A.W. strikes of '36, when not a few Chevies appeared with Warner transmissions intended for Fords. After 1967, it ceased to happen once more.

No such restrictions, however, stopped Rover from going American in 1968, for instead of buying motors from across the Atlantic, they invested in the rights of a discontinued GM design — the 3½-liter aluminum Buick V-8. This had already made an abortive appearance in a prototype GT made by Warwick of Wraysbury in 1961, and initially Rover applied it to their prestige line as replacement for an elderly in-line six. Within three years it had also been employed to put the beef back into their best-selling 2000 sedan, and to furnish them with a cross-country vehicle capable of challenging the efforts of Kaiser-Jeep and Toyota. The Rover-Buick was also smartly snapped up by the old-line Morgan sports car company, who were facing the problem of replacing another seasoned veteran, Triumph's four-cylinder TR, supplanted by a more modern six.

These cars seldom made much impression in the U.S.A. unless they were U.S.-inspired in the first instance, like T.V.R.'s Tuscan and the A.C. Cobra, brain-child of Carroll Shelby. Americans resemble Britons in demanding either a native product or something "fully imported," as the Australians say. The Chevrolet-engined de Bruyne, last of the Gordon-Keeble family, got no further than the 1968 New York Show. The hybrids sold in Britain in 1933 and 1964 alike because there was a gap, albeit a limited one, in the market. No such gap existed in the America of the 1960's, when the Corvette was an institution selling 25,000 a year, and all of it (not just the mechanical elements) could be serviced by any small-town dealer. Mustang and Camaro variants cater to those whose tastes are sporty rather than sporting, and such customers aren't really interested in paying $14,000 for individual coachwork and a built-in record player when under the hood there is the same old motor that powers $4000 worth of hardtop with the optional Performance Pack.

The future of the Anglo-American automobile is limited. We shall not, thank goodness, see the Metropolitan's like again. If Detroit really thinks the public wants this type of car, Detroit will make it themselves, and make it better and more cheaply. One also wonders if the breed can survive much longer in Britain, now that we are landed with a 70 mph speed limit and ever-growing congestion. It is a sobering reflection that on a cross-country journey of seventy-five miles I make the same time on the latest in Continental front-wheel-drive sedans, and on an eleven-year-old Hillman Minx nearing the end of its useful life. Nonetheless, there is something about the combination of a big, lazy eight-cylinder motor and a light chassis. One moment you are burbling along at twenty-five, and the next instant you step on the loud pedal, the power comes in, and you have left a whole pack of jostling Minis behind you. I remember my first ride in a Railton as a kid of ten, and my first ride in a Gordon-Keeble nearly thirty-five years later. The sensation was the same, even to bumping my head on the top as we surged forward in second gear. If I owned such an automobile in Britain today, there'd be a $250 insurance bill for two drivers, I'd need a gallon of gas every eighteen miles, and it's doubtful if a small-town

The 1958 Chrysler-engined Facel Vega FVS. (v)

FACING PAGE: *Left above, the fearsome Allard J2X sports-racer of 1952. The Batten (right above), built up from a 1932 Ford V-8 engine and chassis, pictured at England's 1955 Exeter Trial.* (Y)

THIS PAGE: *The Buick-engined Warwick (top left), built in England during the early Sixties, shown at Silverstone.* (Y)

A Parisian-built 1962 Facel II (top right), with Chrysler engine. (V)

An A.C. Cobra (above), circa 1965, racing at Norfolk, England. (Y)

Above right, the 1964 Chevrolet-engined 220 hp Opel Diplomat V-8.

Below right, the 1965 Sunbeam Tiger, with a 164 hp Ford V-8 engine.

garage could cope with the maintenance. Even a good used example would set us back $3000. But ownership of an Anglo-American GT would awaken that "Somewhere West of Laramie" spirit which has survived my first and only encounter with a Jordan Playboy.

THE FRANCO-AMERICANS

The American automobile made less headway in France than it did across the Channel in Britain. France was on a total-war footing from 1914 through 1918, and consequently there was little demand for civilian automobiles. After the war the country still boasted any number of factories capable of turning out middle-class touring cars of surpassing dullness; though a few of these attempted to follow Andre Citroën's lead with American methods, they did not import American components in any quantity, and the Briscoe-engined Bellanger of 1920 was probably the only French equivalent of things like the Morriss-London and Perfex. Five of the firms responsible for Franco-American machinery had recourse to this for experimental purposes. All (Citroën, Dubonnet, Harris, Hispano-Suiza and J.P.W.) used the Ford V-8 unit.

Nor were there many attempts to manufacture American automobiles in France, because the government insisted upon a high French content in the end-product, and only Ford could fulfill this condition. Here he took a leaf out of GM's book by taking over a large concern in the last stages of decay — Mathis of Strasbourg. The agreement allowed for the continuation of the Mathis automobile alongside the Ford V-8's, but the public preferred the latter, and after 1935 their wishes were respected, to the tune of some thirty thousand Matfords delivered up to the time of the German Occupation. Of postwar contributions, Hotchkiss' Jeeps barely count as passenger cars, while Renault's brief link with American Motors Corporation involved assembly in the organization's Belgian plant, and not on French soil. The Ford revival in 1948 is of interest if only because *la voiture du nouveau riche* (as Frenchmen christened the ungainly little Vedette) suffered an interesting series of vicissitudes, being acquired by Simca in 1954. It had gone before Chrysler gained full control at Poissy, otherwise the result would have been an intriguing reversal of the situation in their English domains, with a Chrysler factory making Fords instead of a Chrysler product using a Ford motor!

There was, however, a whole rash of Franco-Americans — thirteen makes all told — which coincided with trends in Germany, for all these were made between 1928 and 1932. Despite the presence of some sports-car-minded firms (B.N.C., Bucciali, Tracta) in this list, the Franco-Americans were far more closely related to their contemporaries across the Rhine than they were to the Railton.

Almost everyone had a straight-eight in 1929. Renault replaced their magnificent 40CV with a more American-slanted seven-liter machine, the Reinastella. Bugatti had a first-rate fast touring model (Type 44) to match his out-and-out sports cars. Léon Bollée, now under Morris management, tried to make a French-speaking Wolseley which Monsieur Dupont did not appreciate. Small and creaky firms of the stamp of Turcat-Méry were able to add eights to their range by courtesy of the proprietary-motor industry, who offered small units of this type. Unfortunately, these folk didn't venture over two-and-a-half

liters, which left the big-car specialists out in the cold. These could afford neither to tool up for a new motor, nor to lag behind. Lycoming and Continental furnished an easy answer.

Not all this crop were born of desperation. Sheer eccentricity accounts for the elongated, low-slung sport cars of Bucciali Frères, their exaggerated-Cord lines accentuated by the huge plated storks on the side of the hood. The brothers' swan song, an H-16 fabricated out of two eight-cylinder Continental blocks, could have happened only in France. The Tracta-Continental was a short-lived *mariage de convenance* which disappeared from the market when M. Grégoire adopted the native 3-liter Hotchkiss. The Lycoming-engined Messier belongs more truly to the experimentals, since it was but a vehicle for his ingenious suspension system.

The others, however, were hopeful shortcuts to the carriage trade calculated not to frighten the stockholders. All their sponsors were in trouble of one kind or another. Mathis had fought a losing battle against Citroën at the bargain counter. Sizaire wanted a six to back their overhead-cam four. B.N.C.'s staple, a natty little sports car in the Salmson/Amilcar idiom, was no longer viable. Rolland-Pilain and Georges Irat had run out of money and ideas at the same time. Delaunay-Belleville, perhaps, typify the whole situation. They had never been assemblers: far from it. Before 1914 their slogan had been "The Car Magnificent" and their hallmark a round radiator. Their list of illustrious clients was headed by Tsar Nicholas II of All the Russias. Unfortunately, they had failed to keep pace with the times, and the best they could offer in 1930 was a 3.6-liter valve-in-head six — beautifully made, but expensive, and without any real *cachet*.

So they took the short cut to survival, and by 1932 their range contained not only the usual assortment of authentic Delaunays, but a six and a brace of eights with power by Continental. The difference was not apparent until one lifted the hood; the big eight was faster than the all-French big six, and it could be sold for 22,500 fewer francs. Delaunay-Belleville didn't sell many, but this strain outlived both the Rolland-Pilain and the costly Georges Irat, on which for 120,000 francs one got a spark-plug cover intended to suggest that Lycoming had gone over to overhead valves.

The only one of this crop which may have sold in quantity was the Mathis, and this presents somewhat of a mystery. It is almost certain that their vast 5.3-liter Super-Mathis straight-eight of 1932 was Continental-powered; a total production of six units would hardly warrant the design of a special motor. Some French writers also insist that the Muskegon firm was also responsible for Mathis' smaller eights, yet Continental themselves say that the only unit they built for Emile Mathis was the little 1.2-liter PY-type four of 1931. This was, of course, the car that William C. Durant hoped to make at Lansing, and to export to New Zealand. Strasbourg certainly made quite a few PY's, but the American Mathis was stillborn.

This first generation of Franco-Americans was finished by 1932, although the Delaunay-Belleville was still available three years later. French industry was, however, thoroughly run down, and desperation breeds some curious hodgepodges when it comes to conjuring next year's models out of a bank overdraft and an outmoded factory. The less-well-heeled manufacturer was forced to shop among his more fortunate *confrères*, and some masterpieces of scissors-and-paste ensued. Certain Chenard-Walckers and Licornes were at least eighty per cent Citroën, Rosengart and Georges Irat bought motors and transmissions from the same source, and the cheaper Delages came with Citroën bodies. Berliet's last sedans wore the same coachwork as Peugeot's 402. Citroën, however, offered nothing bigger than a 2-liter until 1939, so Chenard-Walcker had to fall back on Ford for the top end of their range, their own V-8 having been discontinued in 1937. The 21CV Chenard, in fact, was hard to distinguish from a Matford, since it used identical Chausson bodies. Voisin had been going creakily downhill to the point at which their traditional Knight sleeve-valve six had given way to a supercharged L-head Graham unit. Ironically, the model's code name in the catalog was "Brick," while students of Gabriel Voisin's sometimes vituperative praise must have noted that the Graham-Voisin had both chromium plating and hydraulic brakes, features that *le patron* had vowed never to adopt. He regained control of his company in 1939, in time to discard this hybrid after only a dozen had been made, and revert to the manufacture of aero-motors. The last of the Talbots, the 13CV of 1958, really comes under the same head, though the presence of the small Ford V-8 unit under so distinguished a hood was only to be expected after Antonio Lago sold out to Simca.

The Railton and its fellows had no Gallic parallels in the 1930's, if only because France was well supplied with excellent *grand'routiers*. If the Type 57 Bugatti and the later Hispano-Suizas were too expensive, the same could not be said of the simpler 20CV Hotchkiss, 23CV Talbot, D-6-75 Delage and Type 135 Delahaye. The "Paris-Nice" Hotchkiss, indeed, was actually cheaper in Britain than a comparable Railton by 1939, thanks to devaluation of the franc. After the war there was even less potential for such automobiles, for the French government proceeded to drive the luxury car industry out of business by fiscal torture. The legislators decided that anything rated at more than 15CV — which meant the six-cylinder Citroën *traction* — was the preserve of millionaires, and taxed it accordingly. Of the *grandes marques*, only Talbot was still active after 1954, and the only Franco-American to get as far as the salon, Rosengart's front-wheel-drive sports sedan with Mercury V-8 motor, never saw series production. For the same reason Ford of France adhered to derivatives of the small and gutless V-8-60 unit, which was rated at 13 horsepower and therefore on the right side of the fiscal abyss.

Curiously, though, this state of affairs was to spawn the greatest of the Franco-Americans. As Britain's automobile industry has discovered, a healthy export trade depends upon a healthy home market, and one of the consequences of sadistic taxation in France was that it deprived Talbot, Delahaye and the others of any incentive to develop new designs. Thus the successful lineup of 1946 — which represented the best of the 1939 holdovers — could no longer challenge Jaguar, Mercedes-Benz and Ferrari. The 210 horsepower GS version of Antonio Lago's 4½-liter Talbot was the world's most powerful stock automobile in 1948: By 1955 it was a museum piece. Thus if the *grand'routier* tradition of France was to continue, it must follow the same path as Britain was later to pursue. But with one significant difference: John Gordon and the Jensen brothers turned their eyes westward because Detroit was the only source of suitable power. Pierre Daninos and

Lance Macklin of Facel S.A. bought Chrysler motors because France was no longer building anything bigger than a 3-liter, and even this was on its way out.

Their Facel Vega was a beauty, as well as being the spiritual ancestor of the more successful British and Italian cars of a decade later. She used a hemi-head Chrysler V-8 motor in a modern boxed frame. Only the power came from across the Atlantic; the regular transmission was a four-speed all-syncromesh affair by Pont-à-Mousson. The sport coupé bodies were welded to the chassis, and by 1959 the range embraced a convertible and a four-door Excellence sedan with Powerflite mounted on a lengthened 125-inch wheelbase. Thanks to the later 6.3-liter motor, the Facel would now top 130 miles an hour, despite a weight of 4032 pounds, and power steering was a factory option. Early cars had been let down by their brakes: Now Dunlop discs were standardized. Maybe it was all a little overblown, especially the aircraft-type instrument console, a trifle avant-garde for those days. Facel claimed that exports accounted for three-quarters of their production: Certainly the cars did quite well in Britain, for all the punishing price of $13,870. The Vega had performance, good workmanship, and adequate handling. What killed it was not taxation, but an attempt to back the Chrysler-powered model with a small car. This used their own twin-cam four-cylinder motor; it was fast enough (112 mph) but it proved both noisy and unreliable. Attempts to save the situation with proprietary units by Volvo and Austin came too late.

On paper the Franco-Americans should have a better future than their British counterparts. France's attitude toward speed limits is more liberal, and there has been more than one rumor of a Talbot revival under the Pentastar of Chrysler. Matra's racing successes have reawakened interest in cars more exciting than the Big Four currently produce. Such vehicles, however, may prove unnecessary. The first tangible result of the Citroën-Maserati liaison has been a front-wheel-drive GT coupé, and now that Fiat capital is also involved, there should be no embarrassing shortage of funds. One wonders. . . .

But at their best, the French *grand'routiers* were a race apart, no matter what lived under the hood, and it would be fun to see them back on the Routes Nationales.

THE GERMAN-AMERICANS

American influence in Germany was brief, and centers almost exclusively round the years 1927-1932 — or, historically, from the relaxation of tariff barriers to the advent of Adolf Hitler.

For all the pre-1914 influence of the Prince Henry Trials, German design atrophied in the lean years after the 1918 Armistice. Too many firms, even in 1924, were still turning out slightly updated 1912 models. Fixed-head side-valve motors, separate gearboxes and foot transmission brakes were the order of the day, and though such automobiles were solidly made they lacked either speed or looks. Exports were largely confined to countries where roads were poor — Scandinavia, Australia and the U.S.S.R. But once American automobiles became readily available after 1924, there was little future for things like the 2.6-liter C4-type N.A.G., much less the 17/50 PS Dux, also a four, but with 4.6 liters, no fewer, under its hood.

The 1964 Buick-engined Apollo from Italy.

Built in Milan, Italy, the Iso Grifo was advertised for the "200 km/hour 'Gentleman'." Corvette-powered, with coachwork by Bertone, a 1965 model is shown at top left.

The 1965 Iso Rivolta (top right) also carried the Corvette engine, with sports coupé body by Bertone.

Mechanically resembling the Iso Grifo was the 1966 Bizzarini GT 5300 coupé (center left). Also Chevrolet-powered, it was built in Livorno, Italy.

From England's Ginetta Cars Ltd. came the 1966 Ginetta G10 (center right), powered by a Ford Mustang V-8. (HH)

The Swiss-built 1968-69 Monteverdi 375 S High-Speed (right) sported a Chrysler V-8 engine.

Thus the bigger German models became carbon copies of American designs, albeit some of them featured four-speed transmissions. Only Hansa imported power units (by Continental) from the U.S.A., but J. S. Rasmussen, who controlled D.K.W. and Audi, purchased the rights of the defunct Rickenbacker concern, and it was said (erroneously) that 1929-32 Audis used German-built Rickenbacker motors. Even if this were not strictly true, there was nothing to distinguish the Audi Zwickau from a superior assembled American automobile of the period. The Fiedler-designed Stoewer 8's of the period were allegedly modeled on the Gardner, and there were affinities between the big Adlers and the Chrysler, if the Frankfurt firm confused the issue by furnishing Hudson-like triangular radiator emblems. Almost all the nine breeds of Teutonic eight-in-line offered in 1929 followed Detroit practice slavishly, even Mercedes-Benz, whose big "Nurburg" has prompted the comment that "only Packard can make a Packard."

And therein lay the rub. The impoverished German manufacturers could not build automobiles in quantities commensurate with competitive prices, and the equally impoverished *Herrenvolk* of Weimar days could not afford to buy them. The small 2-liter Stoewer, a very moderate performer, cost RM 8500, the eight-cylinder Audi retailed at RM 12,950, and the Continental-engined 16/70 PS Hansa for RM 14,800. A Chrysler Six could be bought for a mere RM 7330. Thus this generation could not long survive. By 1932 more progressive thinking prevailed. Already the Hansa's Continental Six lived in a forked backbone frame with swing-axle rear suspension, Stoewer and Adler were offering some advanced front-wheel-drive cars, Audi was soon to follow suit, and Mercedes-Benz' latest medium-sized sedans featured all-independent springing. By the outbreak of war, only one of the old flathead eights was left — the indestructible Mercedes "Nurburg," a favorite with Nazi ambassadors and also with the deposed Kaiser at Doorn.

A nation which passed abruptly from indifferent imitations of Detroit to the most advanced techniques in one fell swoop would have little room for license-produced American automobiles. In the first decade of the century, two firms took up the manufacture of single-cylinder Oldsmobiles, Polyphon of Leipzig condensing the familiar slogan ("Nothing to Watch But The Road") into a terse *Denkbar*. Ford's Cologne plant, like Dagenham, started with A's and V-8's, but soon concentrated on the smaller, European type of car, and in any case the *Kölnische* Ford did not become a best-seller until the 1950's. General Motors also pursued their English policy of buying a complete firm, acquiring Opel in 1929. As in the case of Vauxhall, they devoted their energies to American-inspired designs noted for low prices and peculiar handling. With very few exceptions, the Opel's content was entirely German, though when they wanted a big and prestigious V-8 to challenge Mercedes-Benz in 1964, they wisely relied on imported Chevrolet motors.

THE ITALO-AMERICANS

Before World War II, hybrids of Italo-American parentage were not even a remote possibility. The nation's automobile industry had ridden to success on the strength of its exports; the average Italian could not afford a car. As late as 1939 only one in 112 was an owner. There were few tax concessions before 1933, and these applied only to the smallest models, while the impost levied on the heavy metal was formidable. Isotta-Fraschini's 7.4-liter eight lingered on into 1935, but most of these went to America, and at one stage the 8A was actually cheaper to buy in London than in Rome. Fiat maintained a successful plant at Poughkeepsie, New York, from 1909 through 1918, and in the 1930's Pope Pius XII's stable of cars included a Graham-Paige, but American cars were a rarity in Italy. Gasoline was always expensive — double the English price in 1935, before the full effects of Mussolini's Ethiopian adventure had been felt.

As for foreign investment, this was strongly discouraged by *Il Duce*. A British sales representative who had the bright idea of selling buses to Milan was almost summarily ejected, and even Henry Ford failed to gain a foothold. He tried hard, with an assembly plant in Trieste, but the "European" Model Y was inadequately sprung and the V-8 too thirsty. There was also a protracted battle to gain control of Isotta-Fraschini, defeated by filibustering officialdom. Thus all the Italo-Americans were post-1945 creations: either attempts to cash in on the early days of the U.S. sports car boom, or developments which paralleled the later generation of large specialist GT's in Britain.

Of the first wave, the Italmeccanica of 1950 never progressed beyond the prototype stage, the Chrysler- and Crosley-powered Siatas were made in very small numbers, and the Dodge-based Dual-Ghia of 1955 was little more than a marriage of a Detroit-built chassis with Turinese bodywork. That someone would do this was inevitable, for the early postwar years had seen Italy take preeminence in the field of custom coachbuilding — largely because ninety percent of the nation's automobiles were Fiats anyway, and there were plenty of folk who wanted their Millecento to look different. Italian stylists were hired by foreign firms; Pininfarina did his best with the 1952 Nash line. Most of the big Italian houses also tried their hand at dream cars based on American chassis, and one of these was lost in the wreck of the *Andrea Doria*. Such one-of-a-kind customs ranged from an elegant simplicity, as typified by AUTOMOBILE *Quarterly*'s own Bertone-bodied Mustang, to lamentable errors of the stamp of Ghia's aptly-named *asimmetrica*, which was a Valiant under the skin.

Rather better were the GT's of the 1960's. These may seem an anomaly, for Italy is the spiritual home of all things *granturismo*, and boasts three purveyors of the exotic (Ferrari, Lamborghini and Maserati) who between them can muster an inline six, a V-6, a V-8, and five different V-12's. Such power units are not, however, for sale to rival aspirants (that would never do), and in any case U.S. prices for this brand of automotive jewelry start at around the $14,000 mark. Docile they may be, but they need expert service such as won't be found off the beaten track. Ergo, the new boys, like their British counterparts, had to shop in Detroit. Currently there are three firms offering GT automobiles with American power units — Iso and Bizzarini, who favor Chevrolet, and de Tomaso, who prefers a V-8 Ford. It could so easily be a case of Coals to Newcastle, as we say in Britain, but the stock Iso Rivolta four-passenger coupé costs under $9000; even the advanced de Tomaso Mangusta could be bought for $10,950 in the U.S.A., and the newer Pantera for even less. As a portent of things to come, one must, of course, take particular note of the agreement for "exchange of technical services" reached in 1969 between Ford Motor Company and Alejandro de Tomaso, who now heads Ghia. How far-reaching its effects will be on the Italo-American car only the future can tell.

A MISCELLANY OF HYBRIDS

Until the meteoric rise of Volkswagen in the 1950's, "Universal Cars" were invariably of American origin. Chevrolet's Stove Bolt Six replaced the Model T, which is why GM alone accounted for thirty-five percent of the world's passenger-car production in 1938. Though the current American automobile is a trifle bulky for the roads of many a nation, all the Big Three of Detroit (represented by Chevrolet, Ford and Plymouth) turned out well over a million international units in 1967. At the present time Detroit Fords are being manufactured or assembled in thirteen countries, from Belgium to Venezuela, and not a few of these plants have offered models that might puzzle a U.S. citizen. Chrysler's worst stylistic blunder since the Airflow was safely rectified by 1955, but six years later a Royal sedan delivered from the Corporation's factory at Keswick, South Australia, still wore the authentic 1954 bulboid.

Almost all the variations already observed in Britain, France, Germany and Italy can be found elsewhere. If cars like the Dutch Gatso, Denmark's Dansk, and Sweden's Thulin had U.S.-made motors under their hoods simply because these were available, (and the same applies to Minerva of Antwerp's transverse-engined f.w.d. prototype with torque converter transmission unveiled to an incredulous public at the 1937 Brussels Salon), there are echoes of Germany's Detroit phase in other breeds of the 1920's, such as the Norsk Geijer from Oslo and the Abadal from Barcelona. That Norwegians and Spaniards opted for Lycoming and Continental rather than locally-built imitations is inevitable in countries without large automobile industries. The desperation that led Chenard-Walcker to turn Ford-wards also bred a brief line of Austrian Fords from the illustrious house of Gräf und Stift, once there were no more affluent opera singers with a taste for vast overhead-cam straight-eights. The kindest thing one can say of this particular affair was that it was preferable to the Viennese firm's other second string, a license-produced six-cylinder Citroën on which the marque's silver lion mascot perched most infelicitously. Even the GT craze has been widespread. In Brazil there is a Chevrolet-based coupé variously known as the Brasinca or the Uirapuru, some of the Argentinian-built Ramblers are quite sporting and 1967 saw the advent of a super-car from Switzerland that out-Jensens Jensen: Peter Monteverdi's Chrysler-engined creation. The English price ($5725 more than was asked for a regular Rolls-Royce) was whispered with bated breath at its first Earls Court appearance in the fall of 1969, but Monsieur Monteverdi's affairs prosper.

Outside the traditional homes of the automobile we encounter a new phenomenon: the "instant industry." This has lately become a specialty of Britain's largest independent, Reliant of Tamworth, who have launched new marques in Israel (Sabra) and Turkey (Anadol). Hitherto it was, of course, an American preserve, though sometimes it wasn't all that instant. For all the hard work put in by Ford engineers, the U.S.S.R.'s vast Gorki complex made precious few automobiles before 1933. The end product, in any case, was a Model A whichever way one looked at it, and since then the larger Soviet models have reflected U.S. influence. The pre-War Z.I.S. had a lot of Buick in it, its immediate postwar successor was a Packard in all but name, and the V-8's of more recent years (Chaika, Z.I.L.) could well have emanated from Detroit. Much the same might have happened in Japan, but for a complex series of Automobile Control Laws which kept cylinder capacities down; hence America's best customer was the government, which bought either assembled U.S. makes or close imitations of them. The first Nissan Six was a '35 Graham with a Japanese accent, and the original AA-series Toyota was evolved by adapting the mechanical elements of a Chevrolet to the styling of a 1935 De Soto Airflow. In open touring form it looked most peculiar.

There remains Australia, where the low prices of assembled American automobiles rendered a native industry superfluous until the days of the dollar crisis. A few hybrids were offered, of which the least unsuccessful was the Australian Six with Rutenber motor and a Rolls-Royce-type radiator. Others were the Continental-engined Lincoln and the Lycoming-powered Summit, while as late as 1936 a Mr. Egan of Geelong exhibited a sedan with a Lycoming Six under the hood. Alas! the provisional price was $2300, at a time when a comparable Chevrolet could be bought for $1590. Understandably, no more was heard of Mr. Egan.

Instant industry, however, came to Australia in 1948, when General Motors-Holdens Ltd. branched out from assembly of GM products into actual manufacture. GMH were a forward-thinking concern, who had anticipated the "new" fastbacks offered by the parent company in 1941: I have seen similar styles in Australia on 1938 Vauxhall and Oldsmobile chassis. The new FX-type Holden was in fact a project for a "compact" Buick which had been shelved; its styling followed 1941 GM lines, though it incorporated the unitary construction of the corporation's European products. It was light and compact; the motor was a small 60 horsepower valve-in-head six, wheelbase was 103 inches, and a sedan weighed only 2228 pounds. It was fast, and it could be lethal — the unkind New South Welshman who described it as "the result of an unsanctified union between a Chevy and a Vauxhall" wasn't far wrong.

But the slogan "Australia's Own Car" was justified. Ninety-two percent of the content was of Commonwealth origin, and poor handling (improved down the years) was matched by an astonishing ride on the rough stuff. The car was backed by a first-rate service network. The story of the sales representative who broke a rear spring in the Queensland Outback and was able to buy a replacement over the bar of a remote pub is probably apocryphal, but it explains why sales have boomed: only 7725 in 1949, but 54,726 in 1954, and 190,375 in 1964. Currently Holdens are being assembled in New Zealand and South Africa, and the present-day range embraces such variations as a GT coupé with 327-cubic-inch V-8 motor — its name (Monaro) suggests its inspiration. One of these days we might see Holdens in Great Britain, as Ford have for some time been shipping in right hand drive Falcons from Geelong, and when Chrysler killed off Rootes' traditional big Humbers their immediate replacement was a Valiant all the way from Adelaide. They even corralled a live kangaroo on the Chrysler stand at Earls Court to drive the lesson home.

215

FACING PAGE: *The 1970 de Tomaso Pantera (above) sports a Ford V-8 351 "Cleveland" engine, mounted amidships, and sells in the $10,000 range.*
Also from Italy is the 1970 Iso Lele sport sedan (below left) powered by a Chevrolet engine. (FF)
The British-built 1970 T.V.R. Tuscan (below right), a product of T.V.R. Engineering Ltd. of Blackpool, Lancashire, has a 289 Ford V-8 engine. (GG)
THIS PAGE: *Originally a T.V.R. design, the 1971 Trident Clipper V-8 coupé (right) is powered by a 4.7-liter 271 hp Ford engine. (DD)*
Also from England is the Jensen, originally powered by Ford engines, later all-British built, but since 1963 Chrysler-powered. The 1969-70 model is shown below.

VIII

THE HYBRIDS
BY MICHAEL SEDGWICK

A

ABADAL—1930
F. S. Abadal y Cia
343 Consejo de Ciento
Barcelona, Spain
Early Abadals (1913-22) based on the Spanish Hispano-Suiza, though Abadal also sold a series of customized Buicks. The attempted 1930 revival involved a conventional American-type sedan powered by a 3½-liter six-cylinder Continental engine.

A.C.—1908 to date
A. C. Cars Ltd.
Ferry Works, Thames Ditton
Surrey, England
Originally makers of commercial and passenger tricars, and famous for their 2-liter overhead cam six, which had one of the longest runs in history — 1919 through 1961. The last chassis designed for this engine, the all-independently-sprung Ace speedster with multi-tubular frame, was adapted in 1963 to take the 300 hp 4.7-liter Ford V-8 unit, the result being the Cobra sponsored and marketed in the U.S. by Shelby American. All subsequent A.C.'s have had American Ford engines: 1970's offering is a 7-liter luxury convertible or coupé, the 428, with body by Frua.

ADAMS—1905-14
Adams Manufacturing Co. Ltd.
Bedford, England
The first cars were basically American Hewitts with underfloor-mounted single-cylinder engines and pedal-controlled epicyclic transmissions with two (later three) forward speeds: hence the slogan "Pedals to Push — That's All." These were made to 1910. Bigger Adams cars retained the transmission but had front vertical engines.

AEROFORD—1920-25
Aeroford Cars
Caroline Place
London, W.2, England
Customized Model T Fords with different hoods and radiators.

ALLARD—1937-60
Adlards Motors Ltd.
3 Keswick Road
London, S.W. 15, England (1937-45)
Allard Motor Co. Ltd.
24/28 Clapham High Street
London, S.W. 4, England (1946-60)
Originally a mud-plugging trials "special" built by Ford dealer Sydney Allard using Ford V-8 components, divided-axle independent front suspension and stark speedster bodywork. Later

made in small numbers, some with Lincoln-Zephyr units. Postwar Allards had more civilized sport-touring, convertible and sedan bodywork as well as coil i.f.s. and hydraulic brakes. Nineteen-fifty saw the J2 with de Dion back axle, a sports-racer sold in motorless form in the U.S.A. where it did well in competitions with V-8 engines by Cadillac, Oldsmobile and Chrysler. Home-market cars used L-head Fords and Mercurys, some with o.h.v. conversions by Zora Arkus-Duntov. Made on a special-order basis only from 1956, with British Ford or Jaguar engines.

ALPHI—1929-31
Société Alphi
5 Rue de l'Université
Paris, France
Only four sports cars made, two of them with Continental engines. A cabriolet used the 2.6-liter six, and a 2/4 passenger speedster the straight-eight.

APOLLO—1962-66
Automobili Intermeccanica
Cas. Post. 153
Turin, Italy
Buick-engined GT which generated some interest in the U.S. in the early Sixties. About ninety cars built; succeeded by the Torino. See "Torino."

A Listing of Foreign Cars
Using American Components

ARDEN—1912-16
    Arden Motor Co. Ltd.
    Balsall Common, Berkswell
    Coventry, England
Assembled light cars. The last twenty had 11.5 hp four-cylinder engines built in America.

ARROL-JOHNSTON—1897-1928
    Arrol-Johnston Ltd.
    Heathhall, Dumfries, Scotland
One of the famous "Three A's of Scotland," Arrol-Johnston built Detroit Electric automobiles under license, 1913-14. These had Renault-type dummy hoods like those of the company's gasoline cars, and wheel steering.

ATALANTA—1937-39
    Atalanta Motors Ltd.
    London Road, Staines
    Middlesex, England
Limited production of a version of their all-independently-sprung sports car powered by the Lincoln-Zephyr V-12 engine.

AUDI—1910-39
    Audi Automobilwerke A.G.
    Lessingstrasse, Zwickau
    Germany
Company founded by Dr. August Horch after his resignation from Horchwerke. Acquired by J. S. Rasmussen of D.K.W. in 1928, and merged into Auto Union group, 1932. From 1929 to 1932 the firm marketed conventional 3.8-liter sixes and eights of 4.4 liters and 5.3 liters, supposedly based on the Rickenbacker for which Rasmussen held manufacturing rights, though this connection is doubtful. Later Audis were entirely German in design and content.

AUSTIN—1906 to date
    Austin Motor Co. Ltd.
    Longbridge, Birmingham, England
This firm built (1954-62) the Metropolitan hardtop and convertible for Nash-Kelvinator (A.M.C.). Based on the Nash NX1 small-car prototype of 1950, originally with 1.2-liter Austin A40 engine, but from the end of 1955 with the bigger 47 hp A50 unit. Cars sold with both Nash and Hudson nameplates. Available with right hand drive in Commonwealth countries from 1957. Nearly 95,000 sold.

BARNARD—1919-22
    A. Ward
    St. Mark's Engineering Co. Ltd.
    104 Whitechapel Road
    London, E.1, England
A chain-drive cyclecar with aluminum sport bodywork, powered by a Henderson Four air cooled motorcycle engine. Reverse gear and electric lighting were extras.

BATTEN—1935-38
    Beckenham Motor Co. Ltd.
    High Street, Beckenham
    Kent, England
Ten sports cars using lowered and modified 1932 Model 18 Ford V-8 chassis and reconditioned and tuned engines. Standard body was a four-passenger speedster priced at $1875.

BELLANGER—1912-25
    Société des Automobiles Bellanger Frères
    1/35 Route de la Révolte, Neuilly
    Seine, France
Originally Daimler-powered, but by 1919 using a 3.2-liter four-cylinder Briscoe engine. Distinctive bullnose radiator and left-hand steering. A 6.4-liter V-8 with four-wheel brakes almost certainly used two Briscoe blocks.

BIZZARINI—1965 to date
    Prototipi Bizzarini srl
    Via della Padula 251
    Livorno, Italy
A small plant (it delivered only thirty cars in 1966) set up by the Iso designer. The GT5300 closely resembles the Iso Grifo with its de Dion back axle, servo-assisted disc brakes and 350 hp Chevrolet 327 V-8 engine. See also "Iso."

B.N.C.—1923-31
Bollack, Netter et Cie.
90 Rue des Frères Hebert
Levallois-Perret, Seine, France.
Well-known makers of 1100 cc sports cars, who tried a Franco-American sport sedan in 1930. Motor was an eight-cylinder Continental, chassis were made by Delaunay-Belleville, and styling aped the Hispano-Suiza. Only six units delivered.
See also "Lucien Bollack" and "Delaunay-Belleville."

BOND—1922-28
F. W. Bond and Co. Ltd.
Thorncliffe, Brighouse
Yorkshire, England
An American-type assembled car (1922-26) with six-cylinder Continental engine, four-wheel brakes and three-speed unit gearbox. Later sport-model Bonds were all-British.

BRISTOL—1947 to date
Bristol Cars
The Airport, Filton
Bristol, England
Originally a 2-liter B.M.W.-inspired sport sedan produced by one of Britain's oldest aircraft manufacturers. Since 1962 a very expensive bespoke two-door closed car with Chrysler V-8 engine and automatic transmission. The first of this series, the 407, used a Canadian-built unit made specially for Bristol, but later cars have had the regular 6.3-liter type. Price in 1970: $14,350. Firm is now independent of airplane interests.

BRITISH ENSIGN—1913-23
Ensign Motors Ltd.
Hawthorn Road, Willesden
London, N.W. 10, England
An insignificant firm which, under J. L. Crown's direction, tried to build a British version of the Owen Magnetic using the Entz electro-magnetic transmission in the chassis of Ensign's own 6.7-liter overhead-cam six. It was shown at the 1922 Olympia Exhibition, but never made in series.

BROUGH SUPERIOR—1935-39
Brough Superior Cars Ltd.
Haydn Road, Nottingham, England
An offshoot of the famous motorcycle firm. Anglo-American sporting automobiles based on

modified and rebodied Hudson chassis, initially 4.2-liter eights, but then (from mid-1936) the 21.6 hp six-cylinder. Apart from a few sedans and four-passenger speedsters, most were convertible victorias. A prototype sedan with Lincoln-Zephyr engine in a British-built chassis bodied by Charlesworth (1938) was too expensive at $6,250.

BUCCIALI—1923-33
Bucciali Frères
8 Avenue Gambetta, Courbevoie
Seine, France
The original Buc two-cycle and four-cycle-engined sports cars were 100 percent French, but 1928 saw the first of a series of advanced, low-built automobiles with front wheel drive and long hoods, powered by six- and eight-cylinder Continental units. Last Bucciali was a 155-hp parallel-sixteen on similar lines, the engine being built up from two four-liter Continental blocks. It never ran under its own power. Only thirty-eight f.w.d. Buccialis were made.

BURNEY—1930-33
Streamline Cars Ltd.
Cordwallis Works, Cookham Road
Maidenhead, Berkshire, England
An advanced rear-engined all-independently-sprung streamline sedan on airplane-fuselage lines, the work of airship designer Sir Dennistoun Burney. British power units usually fitted, but at least two of the thirteen cars delivered had Lycomings. Six- and eight-cylinder variants were listed.

C

CHENARD-WALCKER—1901-46
S.A. des Anciens Etablissements Chenard et Walcker
40 Rue Henri Barbusse, Gennevilliers
Seine, France
Old, established French firm renowned in the 1920's for its Touté-designed overhead-cam sports cars. Ford 221 c.i.d. V-8 engines used in larger models from 1937, these having Chausson bodies identical to those of the Matford, and Citroën chassis frames.
See also "Matford."

CHRYSLER—1970 to date
Chrysler France S.A.
Poissy, Seine-et-Oise, France
American in name only, this is the biggest model produced by the Chrysler-owned Simca plant. Motors are 5-bearing overhead-camshaft four-cylinder units in 1.6-liter and 1.8-liter sizes, and the models were unveiled at the 1970 Paris and London Shows.
See also "Simca."

CITROËN—1919 to date
S. A. André Citroën
116 Quai de Javel
Paris XVe, France
Citroën introduced American production methods to France, but in 1935 there was a Franco-American *traction avant*, the 22CV, intended to use a V-8 engine built up from two 11CV four-cylinder blocks. As this was not ready, all the twenty-odd cars built had the 221 c.i.d. Ford V-8. No series production was undertaken.

CITY AND SUBURBAN—1901-05
City and Suburban Electric Carriage Co. Ltd.
6 Denman Street
London, W1, England
Mainly Columbia Electrics with British bodywork. A phaeton supplied to Queen Alexandra in 1901.

CROSSLEY—1903-37
Crossley Motors Ltd.
Gorton, Manchester, England
Old-line upper-middle-class manufacturer who sponsored Willys-Overland assembly in Britain. One of the last passenger car prototypes (1936-37) was fitted with a six-cylinder Studebaker engine.
See also "Willys-Overland" (Great Britain).

DANSK—1901-08
Dansk Automobilfabrik, Storakongensgade
Copenhagen, Denmark
A few cars, taxis and buses made, 1903-04, with single-cylinder Oldsmobile engines. Other products had no known American content.

DE BRUYNE—1968
De Bruyne Motor Car Co. Ltd.
Heath Works, Newmarket
Suffolk, England
An attempted revival of the Gordon-Keeble in "horse country." Two prototypes only, one of which appeared at the 1968 New York Show, along with an experimental mid-engined sports coupé with five-speed trans-axle and fiberglass bodywork, also Chevrolet-powered.
See also "Gordon" and "Gordon-Keeble."

DELAUNAY-BELLEVILLE—1903-50
S.A. des Automobiles Delaunay-Belleville
Chantiers de l'Ermitage, Saint-Denis
Seine, France
A great French firm, whose round-radiatored luxury cars, usually with six-cylinder engines, were patronized by Tsar Nicholas II and other heads of State before World War I. In decline (1931-35) they padded their range with some Continental-powered sedans: a 3-liter six and eights of 4 liters' and 4.5 liters' capacity. Few were sold. In 1938-39 their T.16 had a Continental Six motor in an all-independently-sprung frame of Mercedes-Benz design.
See also "B.N.C."

DE TOMASO—1965 to date
de Tomaso Automobili SpA
Via Peri 68, Modena, Italy
The Argentinian Alejandro de Tomaso has built specialist race cars since 1959, adding GT automobiles with British Ford motors in 1965. From 1967, when he acquired the Ghia custom body firm, he has built the rear-engined Mangusta GT coupé with 289 c.i.d. (later 302 c.i.d.) Ford V-8 unit. The V-6 introduced in 1969 uses his own make of motor. Introduced Ford-engined Pantèra in 1970, following agreement for exchange of technical services with Ford Motor Company, Detroit.
See also "Dual-Ghia" (Ghia).

DUAL-GHIA; GHIA—1955-67
Carrozzeria Ghia
Via A. da Montefeltro 5
Turin, Italy
Dual Motors Corporation
9760 Van Dyke Avenue
Detroit 13, Michigan (U.S.A.)
The original Dual-Ghia (1955-57) was a $5000 sports convertible with Ghia body on a 315 c.i.d., 225 hp V-8 Dodge chassis. Later cars

were customs using, at various times, Imperial, Chrysler and Valiant mechanical elements, the L6.4 coupé with 335 hp Chrysler engine being produced in limited series, 1961 through 1964. The 450SS (1965) used a Plymouth Barracuda engine and transmission in a Ghia-built tubular frame. Company acquired by de Tomaso, 1967.

DUBONNET—1933-36
André Dubonnet
24 Rue de Belfort
Courbevoie, Seine, France
The designer of General Motors' "knee-action" suspension made several interesting prototype automobiles, last of which (1936) was an aerodynamic sedan with 221 c.i.d. Ford V-8 engine at the rear of a backbone frame. All-coil springing and a swing-up front door were other features. Demonstrated in the U.S.A. but never made in series anywhere.

DURYEA—1903-06
British Duryea Co. Ltd.
185/210 Widdrington Road
Coventry, Warwickshire, England
Three-cylinder Duryeas made in Britain, with engines by Willans and Robinson. Prices ran from $1750-$2375, and a model with conventional dummy hood was offered in 1906. The plant was later used for another of Henry Sturmey's ventures, the Lotis automobile.

FACEL VEGA—1954-64
Facel S.A.
19 Avenue Georges V
Paris VIIIe, France
A costly prestige automobile featuring a boxed frame, Chrysler-built V-8 engine, four-speed all syncromesh transmission (automatic was optional) and aircraft-type instrument panel. Standard bodywork was a four-passenger coupé, but convertible and four-door sedan versions were later added. Nineteen-sixty models had disc brakes and 6.3-liter motors; top speed was 140 mph. Production was seventy-five percent exported. Smaller Facels with French, Swedish and British motors were made from 1960. An attempt to build their own power units killed the company.

FORD (France)—1947-54
Ford S.A.F.
Poissy, Seine-et-Oise
France
Successor to the prewar Matford, which was brought up to date with hydraulic brakes, independent front suspension, and a 2158 cc development of the small V-8 later enlarged (1953) to 2351 cc. Some big 3.9-liter Vendome models were also built. Sales for 1951 were 21,078 units. Simca acquired the company in 1954.
See also "Ford" (Great Britain), "Ford" (Germany), "Matford," "Mathis" and "Simca."

FORD (Germany)—1930 to date
Fordwerke A.G.
Henry Fordstrasse 1
Köln-Niehl, Germany
Ford's German plant which, like Britain's Dagenham, produces European-type automobiles. Their front-wheel-drive 12M of 1962 (which sold half a million in its first three years) was the production version of Dearborn's Cardinal small-car project. In the 1930's Cologne also built Models A and B, and V-8's in both sizes, the latter being produced under license in Budapest as "Mavags."
See also "Ford" (Great Britain), "Ford" (France) and "Stoewer."

FORD (Great Britain)—1911 to date
Ford Motor Co. Ltd. (1911-32)
Trafford Park, Manchester
England
Ford Motor Co. Ltd. (1932 to date)
Dagenham, Essex
England
Until 1932 Ford of Great Britain made American designs (Models T and A), a quarter of a million of the former being delivered. Most A's and B's used the small-bore 14.9 hp motor. After the move to Dagenham, there was a concentration on smaller, European types of car, but from 1932 through 1939 V-8's were also assembled for the British market; the 2230 cc models of 1936-39 were entirely British, the 1937 model on a 108¼-inch wheelbase retailing for $1050. Its styling was revived in the 221 c.i.d. Pilot (1947-50), last of Dagenham's V-8's. In the middle 1960's Ford's Advanced Vehicles Division at Slough was responsible for street versions of the GT 40 competition car.
See also "Ford" (France) and (Germany)

G

GATSO—1948-50
M. Gatsonides
131 Zandvoortschelaan
Heemstede, The Netherlands
Aircraft-type tubular body structure and bubble cockpit hood on this sport coupé designed by a famous rally driver. Mercury engine with or without valve-in-head conversion, and three-speed transmission with overdrive on all gears. Very few were made. The cars were also sometimes referred to as Gatfords.

G.A.Z.—1932 to date
Zavod Imieni Molotova
Gorki, U.S.S.R.
The Soviet Union's first successful passenger-car venture, evolved with the aid of Ford engineers. The original GAZ-A was a direct copy of the Model A Ford, and subsequent designs showed strong American influence.

GEORGES IRAT—1921-46
Automobiles Georges Irat S.A.
67-9 Boulevard de Levallois
Neuilly, Seine
France
Builders of a respected fast touring car of the 1920's, and of small f.w.d. sport machines in the later 1930's. In the 1931-33 period M. Irat made some big luxury models with 4-liter and 4.9-liter Lycoming Eight motors and hydraulic brakes. They did not sell — the big ones cost 120,000 francs.

GINETTA—1957 to date
Ginetta Cars Ltd.
West End Works
Witham, Essex
England
Originally a kit-car using Ford (G.B.) components. From 1966-68 the range included the G10 with front-mounted 4.2-liter Ford Mustang V-8 engine, all-round independent suspension and disc brakes, and limited-slip differential. Competition versions were quite successful in class events.

GLOVER—1920
Glover Motors Ltd.
52/58 Woodhouse Lane, Leeds
Yorkshire, England

An American chassis restyled to British tastes, with Rolls-Royce shaped radiator. Engine was a four-cylinder Le Roi, and there are mechanical similarities with the contemporary Seneca. See also "Thor."

G.N.L.—1916
Gordon Newey Ltd.
Bristol Street
Birmingham, England
Newey offered assembled automobiles with French-built motors intermittently from 1907 to 1921. The wartime G.N.L. combined a straightforward American specification with British bodywork, and the four-cylinder motor was probably a Monroe.

GOODYEAR—1924
American Auto Agency Ltd.
Cornbrook Lane
Stretford Road
Manchester, England
Long chassis sports version of Model T Ford with tuned engine, rear gas tank, and comprehensive instrumentation. A guaranteed 50 mph for $1075.

GORDON: GORDON-KEEBLE—1960-66
Gordon Automobile Co. Ltd.
228 Bath Road, Slough
Buckinghamshire, England (1960-63)
Gordon Automobile Co. Ltd.
Southampton Airport, Eastleigh
Hampshire, England (1963-64)
Gordon-Keeble Ltd.
Southampton Airport, Eastleigh
Hampshire, England (1964-65)
Keeble Cars Ltd.
Portsmouth Road, Sholing
Southampton, Hampshire, England (1965-66)
Originally conceived by J. D. Keeble as a development of the Peerless G.T. using the 4.6-liter 290 hp Chevrolet Corvette engine. Production started 1964 under Gordon-Keeble name with later 5.4-liter unit. All-disc brakes and de Dion back axle together with coil and wishbone independent front suspension and a space-frame were featured. Top speed was around 140 mph, but during a checkered financial career only ninety-nine cars were delivered. Original list price ($7835) was unrealistic, and price increases led to canceled orders. See also "De Bruyne," "Peerless" and "Warwick."

GRÄF UND STIFT—1907-38
Gräf und Stift Automobilfabrik A.G.
Weinberggasse 58-76
Vienna 19, Austria
A celebrated maker of luxury automobiles (and now heavy trucks) who turned to license production in the 1930's. About 320 Gräffords, basically 221 c.i.d. Ford V-8's, were delivered between 1935 and 1938, alongside the company's own magnificent overhead-cam 5.9-liter straight-eights.

GUYOT SPECIALE—1926-31
Etablissements Albert Guyot et Cie.
31 Rue Petit, Clichy
Seine, France
Unlike the racing Guyots, the big sedans of 1928-31 looked like overgrown 1750 *turismo* Alfa Romeos and used L-head Continental engines with spark plug covers to give the illusion of o.h.v. There were a 3½-liter six and a 5.2-liter eight, the latter available on a chassis of 142-inch wheelbase. Very few cars were sold.

H

HANSA—1905-39
Hansa Automobilewerke A.G.
Varel-in-Oldenburg and Bremen 11, Germany
From 1928 to 1932, when Carl Borgward obtained full control, this firm was in decline, and made cars in small numbers with six- and eight-cylinder Continental engines of capacities up to 5.3 liters. Most interesting was the Matador with the 9R Six, a backbone frame, and independent rear suspension. Later Hansas used their own engines.

HARPER—1905
Harper Motor Co.
Holburn Junction
Aberdeen, Scotland
A custom landaulette based on the single-cylinder Cadillac.

HARRIS-LEON LAISNE—1920-37
Léon Laisne et Cie.
9 Rue Inkerman, Lille
Nord, France (1920-27)
Automobiles Harris-Léon Laisne
Côte St. Sebastien, Nantes

Loire-Inférieure, France (1931-37)
An ingenious design made in very small numbers under three names (Léon Laisne and Harris were the others). Peculiar suspension made up of coil springs and hydraulic stabilizers mounted on the tubular side-members of the frame. Numerous engines used, America's contributions being various types of Continental, the Ford V-8 and the Continental-designed PY-type four-cylinder Mathis. This last used in a 1932 f.w.d. version.
See also "Mathis"

HEALEY—1946-54
Donald Healey Motor Co. Ltd.
The Cape, Warwick, England
Later a British Leyland product (Austin-Healey), but originally a small-production sports car of advanced design using a 2.4-liter Riley four-cylinder engine. American units became available in 1950 with the 3.8-liter Nash-Healey roadster, for export to the U.S.A. only. In 1950-51 bodies were British; later ones by Pininfarina. Total of 506 units delivered, 1950-54.

HERBERT—1916-17
Herbert Light Car Co.
108 Cricklewood Lane
London, N.W. 2, England
A conventional assembled 1½-liter light car intended to use the French S.U.P. engine. Owing to wartime difficulties, at least some had the American Sterling unit.

HISPANO-SUIZA (France)—1919-38
Société Française Hispano-Suiza
Rue du Capitaine Guynemer
Bois-Colombes, Seine, France
This hallowed marque deserves mention only because the front-wheel drive sedan prototype of 1946 (not a Marc Birkigt design), though intended to use a valve-in-head Hispano engine, did its road trials with a Ford V-8 unit. It was never marketed.

HISPANO-SUIZA (Spain)—1904-44
S.A. Hispano-Suiza
Carretera de Ribas
Barcelona, Spain
One model of the Spanish Hispano-Suiza, the 3-liter six-cylinder T60 of 1931, was intended for license-production by Hudson in America. The Depression frustrated these plans.
See also "Hispano-Suiza" (France).

HOTCHKISS—1903-55
Automobiles Hotchkiss
Boulevard Ornano, Saint-Denis
Seine, France
Though the firm's founder, Benjamin Berkeley Hotchkiss, hailed from Watertown, Connecticut, all the cars were strictly French. In 1953, just before the end of the passenger-car production, Hotchkiss took out a manufacturing license for the Willys Jeep, and these vehicles were still being produced in 1970.

HURLINCAR—1914-15
Hurlin and Co. Ltd.
295 Mare Street
Hackney, London E.8, England
A short-lived light car and cyclecar maker who also offered a conventional 2.2-liter four-cylinder automobile said to be of American origin.

I

ISO—1962 to date
Iso SpA Automotoveicoli
Via Vittorio Veneto 16
Bresso, Milan, Italy
Made by a motorcycle and scooter firm (formerly responsible for the Isetta minicar), the Iso is a high-performance luxury automobile using the 327 or 427 V-8 Chevrolet engine, all-round disc brakes, four-speed all-syncromesh transmission, and limited-slip differential. The Rivolta is the regular four-passenger sports coupé, the Fidia a four-door sedan, and the 427-engined Grifo a super-sports coupé capable of 170 mph. U.S. prices in 1969 ranged from $8539 to $13,800.
See also "Bizzarini"

ITALIA
See "Torino"

ITALMECCANICA—1950-51
Italmeccanica
Via Gibrario 77
Turin, Italy
Sports car intended for export to America, with all-round independent transverse springing and supercharged Ford or Mercury V-8 engine. No series production.

JACKSON—1899-1915
Reynold-Jackson and Co. Ltd.
11/13 High Street, Notting Hill Gate
London, W. 11, England
Most Jacksons were light cars assembled from French components. In the 1900-03 period, however, Century, Buckmobile and Covert automobiles were imported from the U.S.A. and sold as Jacksons.

J.A.G.—1950-52
J.A.G. Cars
124 Manor Road
Thames Ditton, Surrey, England
A few sports cars using reconditioned Ford V-8 mechanical components in a tubular frame with independent coil front suspension. The aerodynamic roadster weighed 1792 pounds.

J.B.M.—1947-50
James Boothby Motors Ltd.
Mary Farm Works, Lowfield Heath
Crawley, Sussex, England
A lightweight speedster built up of Ford V-8 components, including an engine tuned to give 120 hp. Top speed, 150 mph. First cars used reconditioned parts to avoid British Purchase Tax, but Series II's with hydraulic brakes were all-new. A competition model using a Gray marine motor was planned.

JENSEN—1937 to date
Jensen Motors Ltd.
Carters Green, West Bromwich
Staffordshire, England
The Jensen brothers were custom coachbuilders who produced sport-type bodies for British (Morris, Wolseley) and later American (Ford, Chevrolet) chassis. Jensen Ford V-8's of the 1934-36 period also incorporated mechanical modifications. First true Jensen was the 3½-liter of 1937, still Ford-based, but with independent front springing and the option of a Columbia two-speed back axle. Alternative power units were the small V-8 Ford (1938) and the valve-in-head Nash Eight (1939), which later was also fitted to a few of the first postwar sedans. Jensens, from 1949-62, were all-British, but 1963 saw a reversion to an American motor, the 5.9-liter V-8 Chrysler. Subsequent products were expensive sport sedans, usually with automatic transmission:

Current production embraces Interceptor and FF series, the latter with Ferguson four-wheel-drive. Chrysler 6.3-liter motors are fitted, and prices start at $14,595.

J.P.W.—1946-49
Ford S.A.E.
Poissy, Seine-et-Oise, France
Lightweight egg-shaped rear-engined aerodynamic coupé conceived by racing driver Jean-Pierre Wimille. Tubular frame and all-round torsion-bar suspension. Taken up and dropped by Ford of France, whose small V-8 powered four of the five prototypes. Abandoned when its creator was killed.
See also "Ford" (France).

𝒦

KIEFT—1950-61
Kieft Cars Ltd.
Derry Street, Wolverhampton
Staffordshire, England
Primarily builders of racing cars, but a few road-going sport machines were made. One of these (1954) had a 4.5-liter De Soto V-8 engine in an all-independently-sprung space-frame.

𝒮

LAMMAS—1937-38
Lammas Ltd.
Green Lane, Sunbury-on-Thames
Middlesex, England
Sponsored by Lord Avebury. Sport-touring car produced in small numbers using modified 3½-liter Graham Supercharger Six chassis in 128 hp form. Sedans resembled contemporary 2½-liter SS Jaguar. Prices started at $3500.

LEIDART—1936-38
Leidart Cars Ltd.
Pontefract, Yorkshire, England
A sports car with 221 c.i.d. Ford V-8 engine, magneto ignition and their own chassis featuring Bugatti-type rear springing by reversed quarter-elliptics. Prices started at $2000, but few were made.

LONDON-PULLMAN—1923-25
Arcade Motor Co. Ltd.
90 Adelaide Road
London, N.W. 3, England
Described as "American-British assembled," and sold by Buchet's London concessionaires. It was a 1917-type Pullman Four with G.B. and S engine which sold with touring bodywork at $1975.

LUCIEN BOLLACK—1929-30
Lucien Bollack
43 Rue Copernic
Paris, XVIIe, France
The former "B" of B.N.C. who launched a Franco-American with Lycoming 8 engine, Warner transmission, Gemmer steering gear and Columbia back axle. Bodywork was a two-door sport sedan with huge rear trunk, but series production was frustrated by the Depression.
See also "B.N.C."

ℳ

MAIFLOWER—1919-21
Maiflower Motor Co.
Commercial Road, Gloucester, England
Customized Model T Ford: lowered chassis with revised rear section, central brake lever and sporting bodywork.

MATFORD—1935-46
S.A. Française Matford
200 Route de Colmar, Strasbourg
225 Quai de Aulagnier, Asnières
Seine, France
A French-built Ford V-8, the result of a deal between Henry Ford and Emile Mathis. Cars eventually had a very high French content, 136 c.i.d. versions joining the original 221 c.i.d. model in 1936. Mathis sold out in 1938. Production to 1942 was 29,018 units, best year being 1938, with 8898 Matfords delivered.
See also "Chenard-Walcker," "Ford" (France) and "Mathis."

MATHIS—1919-50
S.A. Mathis
200 Route de Colmar
Strasbourg, France

Mathis had been a German firm before World War I, and in the 1920's their mass-produced light cars ranked fourth in French sales behind Citroën, Renault and Peugeot. The series of L-head straight-eights made from 1931 onwards are believed to have used Continental motors, but Continental have no record of supplying them. The Muskegon firm did, however, design the 1.2-liter PY-type four introduced for 1931, which William C. Durant hoped to make in the U.S.A. and sell for $475. Following the Mathis-Ford agreement of 1934, Matfords gradually replaced Mathis cars on the firm's assembly lines.
See also "Matford."

MESSIER—1926-31
G. Messier
29 Avenue Gambetta
Montrouge, Seine, France
The famous specialist in airplane landing gear also built some automobiles with compressed-air pneumatic suspension, popular as ambulances. The biggest models (1929-31) used 4.9-liter eight-cylinder Lycoming engines. About fifty of these were made.

MINERVA—1900-39
Société Nouvelle Minerva-Imperia
40 Rue Karel Ooms
Antwerp, Belgium
Belgium's *marque doyenne*, which progressed from motorcycles to fast touring cars before standardizing the Knight double-sleeve-valve motor in 1909. Thirty years later the last of the Minerva-Knights had been delivered, and the 1937 Minerva featured all-round independent springing, a transversely-mounted engine driving the front wheels, and a hydraulic torque converter. The three prototypes were made in the associated Imperia plant at Nessonvaux; they were powered by 221 c.i.d. Ford V-8 engines. Series production was not, apparently, contemplated.

MONTEVERDI—1967 to date
Automobiles Monteverdi
Oberwilerstrasse 14-16
Basle-Binnigen, Switzerland
Handmade G.T. coupés with steel-tube frames and Fissore bodywork. The High-Speed uses a Chrysler V-8, offered as a two-passenger with manual transmission or a four-passenger with Torqueflite automatic. A price of $25,625 was quoted in London in October, 1960. The

hai: uses a 426 cu. in. Chrysler Hemi mid-engine developing 450 hp at 5000 rpm and ZF five-speed transaxle transmission. Price: $27,000.

MORRIS—1913 to date
W.R.M. Motors Ltd.
Cowley, Oxford, England (1913-19)
Morris Motors Ltd.
Cowley, Oxford, England (1919 to date)
A total of 1450 1½-liter Morris-Cowleys made, 1915-20, using Model-U Continental engines, three-speed Detroit Gear transmissions, and American-built back axles. From the end of 1919, Continental motors replaced with an exact copy built by Hotchkiss of Coventry, which firm Morris absorbed in 1923.

MORRISS-LONDON—1919-25
F. E. Morriss
64 Piccadilly
London W.1, England (1919-21)
Saunders Motors Ltd.
31 The Parade
London, N.W. 11, England (1922-25)
Four-cylinder Crow-Elkhart chassis with English bodywork. When the original sponsors went bankrupt, a North London garage took over the chassis still in bond at the docks and fitted them with landaulette bodies. Price of a complete car in 1924 was only $1625.

NORSK GEIJER—1926-30
A/S C. Geijer and Co.
St. Halvardsgt 35
Oslo, Norway
Twenty Lycoming-engined automobiles produced by a coachbuilder. They had hydraulic brakes and included a 65 hp straight-eight.

OPEL—1893 to date
Adam Opel A.G.
Rüsselsheim-am-Main, Germany
General Motors acquired Opel in 1929; since then American influence has predominated. Their biggest model of the immediate prewar period, the Admiral (1937-39), used a Chevrolet engine, and since 1964 Chevrolet V-8 units have powered the largest and costliest types in the Opel range.

PEERLESS—1957-60
Peerless Cars Ltd.
Farnham Road, Slough
Buckinghamshire, England
This firm's G.T. was entirely British, and based on the Triumph TR3. The company itself, however, had American connections, growing out of a business which had sold reconditioned World War I trucks by Peerless of Cleveland. The Warwick, Gordon and Gordon-Keeble are connections.
See also "De Bruyne," "Gordon" (Gordon-Keeble) and "Warwick."

PENNINGTON—1896-99
Great Horseless Carriage Co. Ltd.
The Motor Mills, Coventry
Warwickshire, England (1896-97)
Pennington and Baines
44 Berners Street
London, W.1, England (1898-99)
Pennington Motor Co. Ltd.
40 Holborn Viaduct
London E.C. 1, England (1899)
The physical results of E. J. Pennington's U.K. operations probably amounted to five Torpedo Tricars (for which Humber made the frames) and a handful of the front-wheel-drive, rear-wheel-steering Raft-Victorias which he hoped to sell for $575 complete. The usual trail of unfulfilled orders resulted in a retreat to Philadelphia before the end of 1899.

PERFEX—1920-21
Olympia Aeros and Autos Ltd.
130/132 Christchurch Road
Boscombe, Bournemouth
Hampshire, England
Closely related to the American Perfex, with 3.1-liter four-cylinder G.B. and S engine, three-speed transmission and 114-inch wheelbase. Very few sold.

POLYMOBIL—1904-08
Polyphon-Werke A.G.
Wahren, Leipzig, Germany
License-production of the Oldsmobile Curved Dash Runabout by a musical instrument and phonograph maker. "Sporty" models had dummy hoods and wheel steering, Conventional German designs also from 1907. After 1908 only the latter were marketed under the name of Dux.
See also "Ultramobil."

RAILTON—1933-50
Railton Cars
The Fairmile, Cobham
Surrey, England (1933-39)
Hudson Motors Ltd.
Great West Road, Chiswick
London W.4, England (1940-50)
First and most successful of the "Anglo-American sports bastards," assembled on Hudson-built chassis in the former Invicta plant. First cars had the 93 hp Terraplane Eight as a basis, but from 1934 the 4.2-liter Hudson was used, and in the 1937-39 period there were Railton Sixes, some of them derived from the small-bore 2.7-liter export version of the Hudson Terraplane. All Railtons were Hudson-based with the exception of fifty small cars using Standard chassis. Postwar models (only sixteen made) assembled by Hudson's U.K. branch. Best year was 1935 (337 cars delivered) and total production of 1460 units may well make the Railton Britain's top-selling in-line eight.

RALEIGH—1915-16
Raleigh Cycle Co. Ltd.
Lenton Boulevard
Nottingham, England
Famous cycle firm who also built three-wheelers, 1933 through 1936. Some of their limited-production 1915 four-cylinder cars had Continental engines.

RENAULT—1898 to date
Regie Nationale des Usines Renault
8/10 Avenue Emile Zola, Billancourt
Seine, France
France's leading automobile manufacturer,

under State control since 1945. From 1962 through 1967, their plant at Haren (Belgium) assembled Rambler Classics. Cab versions used the British Perkins diesel motor.

ROLLAND-PILAIN—1906-31
S.A. des Etablissements Rolland-Pilain
44 Place Rabelais
Tours, France
A pioneer of hydraulic brakes (in 1921) Rolland-Pilain expired in 1931 with a brace of models using 3-liter six-cylinder and 4-liter straight-eight Continental engines and cloaked in quite elegant coachwork. These wore, surprisingly, steel artillery wheels.

ROSENGART—1928-55
Société Industrielle de l'Ouest Parisienne
2/36 Boulevard de Dixmude
Paris XVIIe, France
Builders of the French Austin Seven, Rosengart (who had already marketed a Citröen-based front-wheel-drive car in 1939) offered a bigger *traction* with 3.9-liter Mercury V-8 engine and two-door sedan bodywork in 1947. Prevailing taxation ruled out such a big engine, and after 1949 the firm reverted to smaller cars along the Austin Seven line.

ROVER—1903 to date
Rover Co. Ltd.
Lode Lane, Solihull
Warwickshire, England
Rover have never used foreign-made components, but for 1968 they introduced a luxury sedan using their own version of Buick's discarded 215 c.i.d. alloy V-8 and Borg-Warner automatic transmission in the hull of their former 3-liter motor. This has been followed by the Three Thousand Five, a mating of this unit with the 2000 structure, and, in 1970, by the Range Rover 4 x 4 station wagon. Rover-built motors of Buick type are also used by Morgan in their Plus-8.

𝒮

SIATA—1949 to date
Societa Italiana Applicazione Trasformazioni Automobilistici SpA

Via Leonardo da Vinci 25
Turin, Italy
Principal business of this company (founded in 1926) has been the tuning and modification of Fiat automobiles for enthusiasts, but in 1952-55 some sports cars were made with American engines — the 721 cc overhead-cam Crosley Hotshot and the hemi-head V-8 Chrysler. The latter was used in conjunction with a separate gearbox and de Dion back axle. Crosley motors were also fitted to competition cars by Bandini and Nardi.

SIMCA—1935 to date
Société Industrielle de Mécanique et de Carrosserie Automobile
163/185 Rue Georges Clemenceau
Nanterre, Seine, France
Poissy, Seine-et-Oise, France (1935-60)
Société des Automobiles Simca S.A.
Poissy, Seine-et-Oise, France (1960 to date)
Simcas were originally Fiats made by H. T. Pigozzi in the former Donnet plant. The acquisition of Ford S.A.F. in November of 1954 added that company's 2351 cc L-head Ariane, using the Ford-type hull adapted to the mechanical elements of Simca's four-cylinder Aronde. Simca's Brazilian branch was still making a valve-in-head development of the Vedette in 1961. Since 1963 Chrysler have had a controlling interest in the parent company.
See also "Ford" (France) and "Talbot."

SIZAIRE-BERWICK—1927-28
Société Nouvelle des Autos Sizaire
52 Rue Victor Hugo
Courbevoie, Seine, France
The V-radiator was the only real connection with the British Sizaire-Berwick of 1919-25. Made in very small numbers using a Lycoming Straight Eight engine.

SIZAIRE FRERES—1923-31
Société Nouvelle des Autos Sizaire
52 Rue Victor Hugo
Courbevoie, Seine, France
Georges Sizaire's advanced fast touring car with all-round transverse independent suspension, originally with 2-liter four-cylinder motor of own manufacture. In 1928 one model used a six-cylinder Willys-Knight unit. The last cars were built in Belgium under the name Belga Rise.
See also "Sizaire-Berwick."

STOEWER—1898-1939
Gebrüder Stoewer Motorenwerke
Falkenwalderchaussee
Stettin-Neutorney, Germany
A German firm which "went American" in the 1928-32 period with a series of Fiedler-designed straight-eights inspired by the Gardner. Abortive negotiations with Ford for the acquisition of Stoewer in 1936 led to Stoewer's building some bodies for the *Kolnische* Fords of that year.
See also "Ford" (Germany).

STRALE—1967
Strale
Corso Francia 50
Collegno
Turin, Italy
Short-lived G.T. coupé with 6.3-liter V-8 Chrysler motor, composite plastic and light alloy structure, and de Dion back axle.

SUNBEAM—1953 to date
Sunbeam-Talbot Ltd.
Ryton-on-Dunsmore
Warwickshire, England
The Rootes strain of Sunbeam (formerly known as Sunbeam-Talbot). The only Anglo-American model was the Tiger two-passenger sports car (1964-67) using the 164 hp 260 c.i.d. and 200 hp 289 c.i.d. Ford V-8 units in the structure of the Hillman Minx-based Alpine.

𝒯

TALBOT—1920-59
Automobiles Talbot
33 Quai du Général Gallieni
Suresnes, Seine, France
A very famous firm, known 1896-1920 as Darracq. Under Simca control their last model (1958/59) was a G.T. coupé with the 2351 cc Simca (formerly Ford) Vedette V-8 engine.
See also "Simca."

THOR—1919-21
Simpson Taylor Ltd.
Palace Street
London S.W. 1, England
Like the Glover, probably Seneca-based, though

226

frame and running gear were allegedly British-made. It was intended to market this 2¼-liter four at $1175, but the few sold had a price tag in the $2000-$2500 bracket.
See also "Glover."

THULIN—1920-28
AB Thulinverken
Landskrona, Sweden
An aircraft plant which built cars based on the German Aga. Their last (1928) series was Swedish-designed, and one car was fitted with a Hupmobile Six engine.

TORINO—1967 to date
Automobili Intermeccanica
Cas. Post. 153
Turin, Italy
Frank Reisner's successor to the Apollo, using Ford components. Convertible & GT models. Cars have carried successively the Ford 289 Hi Performance, the 302 and the 351 Cleveland engine. The GT model was later called Italia. Production to the end of 1970 totalled more than 500 cars.

TRACTA—1926-34
Automobiles Tracta S.A.
102 Rue de Colombes
Asnières, Seine, France
J. A. Grégoire's first production front-wheel-drive automobile; inboard front brakes and independent transverse front suspension. Some bigger models (1930-32) used 2.7-liter six-cylinder Continental engines.

TRIDENT—1966 to date
Trident Cars Ltd.
Grove Road, Woodbridge
Suffolk, England (1966-68)
Trident Cars Ltd.
Turret Lane, Ipswich
Suffolk, England (1969 to date)
Originally a T.V.R. design. A G.T. coupé on a box-section frame of 90-inch wheelbase, powered by a 4.7-liter, 271 hp Ford V-8 unit. Speeds of over 140 mph are quoted.
See also "T.V.R."

T.V.R.—1954 to date
T.V.R. Engineering Ltd.
Fielding's Industrial Estate
Bispham Road, Layton
Blackpool, Lancashire, England

Initially a kit-built small sports coupé with fiberglass bodywork and tubular frame, generally with B.M.C.-built motor. During its checkered financial career it has been sold in America as the Jomar (1959) and Griffith (1964). The coupé on the 84-inch wheelbase has been available since 1964 with the American Ford 289 V-8 in various stages of tune, 1970 models being known as T.V.R. Tuscans. The Trident (1966) became a separate make.
See also "Trident."

𝒰

ULTRAMOBIL—1904-08
Ultramobil GmbH
Berlin-Halensee, Germany
Like the Polymobil, a Curved Dash Olds made under license.
See also "Polymobil."

𝒱

VANDY—1920-21
Vandys Ltd.
27a Pembridge Villas
London W.11, England
Sponsored by the Vandervell family (bearings, C.A.V. electrical equipment). American-type automobile with 3.8-liter six-cylinder Rutenber motor, but with such English features as four-speed transmission and demountable disc wheels. A touring sold for $4875.

VAUXHALL—1903 to date
Vauxhall Motors Ltd.
Grosvenor Road, Luton
Bedfordshire, England
Once a famous sports car manufacturer, Vauxhall has been owned by General Motors since 1925. Their six-cylinder automobiles, especially, have much in common with Chevrolets.

VOISIN—1919-39
S.A. des Aéroplanes G. Voisin
36 Boulevard Gambetta, Issy-les-Moulineaux
Seine, France

Builders of Knight-engined luxury automobiles in various sizes, 1919 through 1938. The last series (1938-39) made use of six-cylinder supercharged L-head Graham Six engines in regular Voisin chassis with semi-elliptic suspension. Only twelve such cars delivered before the firm turned to aero-engined manufacture.

𝒲

WARWICK—1960-62
Bernard Rodger Developments Ltd.
Horton, Wraysbury
Buckinghamshire, England
Continuation of the Peerless G.T. under its designer's sponsorship. Some prototypes also tried with the 3½-liter aluminum Buick V-8 engine, but company failed before this went into production.
See also "Peerless."

WILLYS-OVERLAND (BRITAIN)—1920-33
Willys-Overland-Crossley Ltd.
Heaton Chapel, Stockport
Cheshire, England
An associate of Crossley Motors which assembled Willys-Overland products for the British market, often with British-made bodies. Nineteen-twenty-four saw an "all-British" type using a 1.8-liter Morris-Oxford motor in an Overland Four chassis, and the 2.4-liter Willys Palatine Six of 1930 was a Whippet Six with small-bore 2.4-liter engine, In 1932-33 the factory was also building the A.J.S. automobile, taken over from the Wolverhampton motorcycle firm after this was acquired by Matchless of London.

𝒵

Z.I.S.—1936-56
Zavod Imieni Stalina
Moscow, U.S.S.R.
Soviet Russia's prestige car was American-inspired, the prewar model's 5½-liter straight-eight engine following Buick lines. Postwar Z.I.S. automobiles were closely based on the 1941 Model 180 Packard.

IX

5000 MARQUES

•

A Listing of Automobiles
Produced in
the United States and Canada

•

COMPILED BY THE EDITORS
AND RESEARCH ASSOCIATES
OF AUTOMOBILE QUARTERLY

In introducing their list of automobiles produced in America, *MoToR* magazine commented on "the immense amount of labor involved in its compilation and its great and increasing value to all who are in any way interested in the American Motor Car." "And who, today," they concluded, "is not?" That was in 1909 — and the list was, to our knowledge, the first such compilation in this country. *MoToR* clearly did not underestimate the importance of their listing, nor can one doubt the arduous task of the project itself, though it is interesting that even in those days when everything about the industry was still fresh in mind the task remained a monumental one. Charles E. Duryea, a pioneer whose efforts were dedicated to both the automobile and its history, was in large measure responsible for the data in that first list. He gave several months to the work. Herman Cuntz of the Association of Licensed Automobile Manufacturers subsequently added his records, and as *MoToR* stated, his "personal recollections and a goodly amount of time as well" — and for their March, 1909, issue the magazine's editor gathered all the information together into "*MoToR's* Historical Table of the Motor Car Industry." It covered the years 1895 to 1909 in America and included 639 entries.

One good list deserves another, and the years since publication of *MoToR's* compilation have seen a good many other — more than thirty by count. Automobile show programs of four and five decades ago frequently included rosters of cars built in the United States — and as the years passed others joined the ranks of roster-makers as well.

Credit for the first international list must go to George Ralph Doyle, who privately published *The World's Automobiles* in 1932. This list was supplemented in 1944, and went through several reprintings beginning in 1957, the fourth edition of which, published in 1963 after Mr. Doyle's death with revisions by G. N. Georgano, included some 5000 automobiles, of which 2113 were American-built.

In the United States in 1946 — to celebrate the automobile industry's Golden Jubilee — the Eaton Manufacturing Company published *A Chronicle of the Automotive Industry in America*, including in it a "Roll Call of 1876 American-made Automobiles and Trucks." Other lists often incorporated trucks as well. The Automobile Manufacturers Association has through the years published a compilation of vehicles built in the United States, commenting in their *Automobiles of America* (1962) that "more than 3000 makes of cars and trucks have been produced by some 1500 manufacturers in the United States since the dawn of the auto age."

Among the lists devoted exclusively to passenger cars, the Antique Automobile Club of America published a roster in 1949 comprising about 1525 entries. During the Fifties the best-known of all such compilations was the *Saturday Evening Post's* lists edited by Hamilton Cochran. The second edition, published in 1955, was titled "Roll Call of 2726 Automobiles Sold in America During the Past Fifty Years or More." Among the most amusing of the lists of the late Fifties was the one appended to *How to Buy and Restore an Antique Car*. AUTOMOBILE *Quarterly's* president L. Scott Bailey, together with his wife, had submitted a rough outline of the subject matter to publisher Floyd Clymer, who was then completing his own list of American cars and who decided this would be a logical addendum to the proposed book. Mr. Clymer submitted the material on hand to a printer for an estimate, left for an extended trip to Europe and on his return discovered that the book had already been printed! The text remained in its outline form, and the American car list ended somewhere in the middle of the letter "S." The result was some rather lively correspondence from collectors of Templars, Terraplanes, Velies, Wills Sainte Claires, Wintons and Zimmermans.

The Sixties found still more lists being published, frequently as appendices to automobile books. *Esquire's American Autos and Their Makers* published in 1963, for example, concluded with a "Roster of Every U.S. Passenger Car." There were 1690 entries. A more recent publication, *The Complete Encyclopedia of Motorcars* published in 1968 and edited by the G. N. Georgano, includes some 4000 marques worldwide with 1450-odd American car entries.

Nor has this been all. Tire and accessory companies have on occasion come up with their own compilations. And one enterprising entrepreneur got together his list of every car ever built in America and managed to fit it all onto a paper placemat, for restaurant-goers to peruse as they munched on their french fries.

A list of any kind, perhaps less by definition than by natural inference, has an aura of completeness about it. Unless it carries a qualifying word like "partial" or "incomplete," it is looked upon as rather absolute. Yet when the subject of the compilation is one for which continuing research is requisite, such an inference might tend to mislead. Obviously, because of the great variety of figures arrived at in the various compilations of American cars, none of the foregoing lists could be — or should have been — called complete. Nor do we make that claim for the list that follows. But with its 5000 entries, we can say that ours is the most comprehensive compilation of American automobiles ever published. The AUTOMOBILE *Quarterly* list comprises passenger cars only, and includes some fifty-four Canadian marques. "Marque," incidentally, is the word we use, as Webster's defines it, to mean "brand" or "make."

A few words are in order regarding how this list came about. It all really started with the founding of AUTOMOBILE *Quarterly* about ten years ago. As devotees of automobile history, we were particularly anxious to document the many, many cars which contributed to the early development of the industry in America, and consequently began an extensive indexing project of early automotive publications and books. The more deeply we got into this project, the more cars we discovered which had never appeared on any list and still other cars previously listed for which we could find no documentation, the more anxious we became to publish a listing of our own. Several years ago we decided to do it.

We started, of course, with the lists that had already been published. These were gathered together. As our research continued, we began enlisting the help of others. In addition to the published lists and our own growing list, we drew upon compilations undertaken by various collections, museums and libraries. For their invaluable help in this regard, we are indebted to James J. Bradley, head of the Automotive History Section of the Detroit Public Library; Mary M. Cattie, librarian-in-charge, Automobile Reference Collection, Free Library of Philadelphia; Henry Austin Clark, Jr. of the Long Island Automotive Museum. Most helpful, too, have been Leslie R. Henry, curator at the Henry Ford Museum and Don Berkebile, curator of the automotive section of the Smithsonian Institution.

Automobile history has always been fortunate to have a cadre of dedicated scholars, and their assistance has been immeasurable. Stanley K. Yost of the Society of Automotive Historians has been working for years on a list of his own, and he kindly contributed the results of his research. Walter McIlvain, editor for the Veteran Car Club of America, began filling scrapbooks with automobilia as a youngster, and his treasured collection was most helpful. Henry H. Blommel, whose favored specialty is automobiles built in Indiana; Dr. Alfred Lewerenz, research historian for the Horseless Carriage Club of America, and historian Ralph Dunwoodie of Reno were among the many others who contributed advice and listings of their own.

With all this material in hand — our own list, the various published lists, the contributions of the libraries and our fellow historians — we were ready for the next step. The material was given to Frank T. Snyder, whose assignment it was to delete the duplications, cross reference the entries, check them against original source material and contemporary motoring periodicals, correct them where necessary and add the many, many new finds he discovered as well. A tentative list was then drawn up and submitted to Henry Austin Clark, Jr., Ralph Dunwoodie, Stanley Yost and James J. Bradley. Their reading of the compilation resulted in further additions and corrections. Final editing of the list was assigned to AUTOMOBILE *Quarterly* staff member Sue Ellen Johnson.

The AUTOMOBILE *Quarterly* list, as we said, is the most comprehensive ever to be published on the American automobile. However, we consider it by no means definitive. We look at it as a growing list, one to be revised and augmented as further historical information becomes available. Our list is the groundwork upon which we plan to continue building. For that reason we have included at the end of this book a tear-out form so that readers might amend and add information about cars built in this country. The automobile has provided one of the most colorful chapters in the industrial and social history of America. It is deserving of the most ardent efforts to insure that its history is recorded as comprehensively as possible.

This list is arranged alphabetically by marque name. Entries in ROMAN LETTERS are complete entries. A sample is given below:

AMERICAN SIMPLEX—1905-10
Simplex Motor Car Co.
Mishawaka, Indiana
Company organized 1904. First car put on
the road July, 1905. Name changed to
"Amplex" 1910.

Complete entries include manufacturer's name and address and dates for the marque listed. The dates refer not to the year of incorporation of the company but to the model or actual year(s) of the car's production. Occasionally further information about the car itself is provided as well, particularly when this information may clear up previous misconceptions regarding the vehicle or may indicate the limited scope of models available or the extent of production. When a particular car was built with a specific and limited purpose in mind, note is made of this too. Mention is made also, either within the text or in a SMALL CAPS explanation following the car name, that a car is of a particular type (highwheeler, cyclecar), or that its powerplant is other than an internal combustion engine (steam, electric), or that it possesses some other feature of technical interest (rotary, air cooled). Since this compilation is a listing and not a history, such information, where included, is provided as an "accessory" for the reader's interest.

Frequently a car was built by a succession of different manufacturers or, as was more often the case, by the same company who saw fit to change their name with what can only be regarded as distressing regularity. The various company names under which a car was produced are listed chronologically in each entry, with the text delineating the different phases (with documented dates) of the car's corporate life from conception to receivership. Frequently, too, a car began its life in one place and ended it in another — and note is made of these various locations. Also mentioned are related activities (i.e., trucks, engine building) for companies whose involvement with the automobile was subsidiary to or gave way to allied areas of manufacture.

All cars mentioned within the text of an entry are set off by quotation marks. It will be noted that entries frequently refer the reader to another car carrying a different name, indicating that it either preceded or succeeded or was built simultaneously by the same company as the reference car. Automobile companies, particularly in the early years of the industry, obviously didn't keep history in mind when naming either their cars or their firms, for the succession of names for both often seem designed solely to confuse. An effort has been made to sort out the confusion. Previous lists, for example, have frequently listed as two separate cars what in reality was but one car produced under two different names. In such cases this list indicates both names with a note that they apply to the same vehicle. Likewise models of a specific vehicle have frequently found their way into American car rosters as separate marques (as, for example, the "Buggyabout" which was a model of the "Hatfield") — consequently these cars are listed and identified as models, with a cross reference to the actual marque.

NOTES ON READING THE "5000 MARQUES" LIST

Entries listed in (PARENTHESES) indicate a car which never saw production. A sample is given below:

(AMERICAN)—1896-98
American Motor Co.
New York, New York

A car listed thusly is one for which production was planned and announced, prototype(s) presumably built, but which, research indicates, probably did not proceed beyond that point into actual manufacture. In some cases this experimental stage continued for as many as four years; some cars, sadly, took a long time to die aborning. Incidentally, AUTOMOBILE *Quarterly*'s list of 5000 Marques is followed by a listing of 165 cars whose fate was even more disheartening than our parenthetical entries — being, as they were, cars proposed to be built and reported as such, but never heard of again, cars which, no doubt, never turned a wheel.

Entries listed in *ITALICS* are unsubstantiated entries. A sample is given below:

AUTO-MOTOR—1912
Bryn Mawr, Pennsylvania

A car listed thusly is one for which complete information — dates, company name and location — has not been found. The available information has been given in each case, although it may be only a name and date, or a name alone. Previous rosters and historic motoring periodicals have listed these cars as having been produced, but to date further substantiation has not been discovered. Consequently their existence can be neither denied nor verified. It is hoped, of course, that readers of this list may be able to provide us with leads by adding their amendations and additions to the special form provided for that purpose in the back of this book. In that way further research might clarify the shadowy status of these cars in American automobile history.

• • •

Entries preceded by an *ASTERISK indicate specific errors which have been made in previous lists and which are herein corrected. A sample is given below:

*AUSTIN-WESTERN—1906
Austin-Western Engine Works
Chicago, Illinois
Not a car: first motor-driven street sweeper.

Lists of any kind are inherently prone to perpetuation of error. An error on one list echoed on others is an unfortunate compounding, because repeated often enough the fallacy takes on the air of truth. For that reason cars which have been previously incorrectly listed are entered on this list as well — with an explanation. Frequently the error has been a misspelling. In other cases a company name has been erroneously carried forward as the name of a vehicle. (The Easton Machine Company, for example, did not produce a car called the "Easton," their car instead was called the "Morse.") Similarly trucks have occasionally found their way into passenger car lists, as have engines, or, as in the sample entry, a street sweeper. Wherever research has indicated such errors — or the reasonable possibility of them — note of that fact has been made. As gratifying as it is to be able to authenticate a heretofore unknown American car (and this list includes a goodly number of those), it is equally the historian's responsibility to retire those American cars whose existence has been incorrectly reported through the years.

A

ABBORN
ABBOTT—1917-18
　The Abbott Corp.
　Cleveland, Ohio
　Succeeded Consolidated Car Co. Detroit,
　Michigan. Formerly "Abbott-Detroit."
ABBOTT-CLEVELAND—1917-18
　See "Abbott"
　The Abbott Corp.
　Cleveland, Ohio
　Both names apply to same vehicle.
ABBOTT-DETROIT—1909-16
　Abbott Motor Co. (1909-14)
　Abbott Motor Car Co. (1914-15)
　Consolidated Car Corp. (1915-16)
　Detroit, Michigan
　Four and six-cylinder models used Con-
　tinental motors, eight-cylinder used Her-
　schell-Spillman motors. Became "Abbott,"
　Abbott Corp., Cleveland, Ohio.
*A.B.C. ELECTRIC—1900
　Initials stand for American Bicycle Co.
*A.B.C. STEAM—1900
　Initials stand for American Bicycle Co.
A.B.C. HIGHWHEELER—1905-11
　A.B. Cole (1905)
　1512 Locust Street
　A.B.C. Motor Vehicle Mfg. Co.
　St. Louis, Missouri
A.B.C.—1922
　Arthur Boynton Corp.
　Albany, New York
　Built for export.
A.B.C.—1939
ABEL—1901
　Abel Bros. Machine Shop
　Fond-du-Lac, Wisconsin
　One car produced May, 1901.
(ABENAQUE)—1900
　Abenaque Machine Works
　Westminster Station, Vermont
　Main products were traction engines.

ABERCROMBIE—1969 See "Glassic"
　Glassic Industries Inc.
　Palm Beach, Florida
　Both names apply to same vehicle.
ABLE EIGHT—1915-20
　See "Vernon"
　Vernon Automobile Co.
　Mt. Vernon, New York
　Both names apply to same vehicle.
ABRESCH—1899-1909
　Chas. Abresch Co.
　Abresch Carriage Co. (1900)
　Milwaukee, Wisconsin
ACADIA—1903
　Ernest R. Kelly
　Wilmington, Delaware
ACADIAN—1961-71
　General Motors Corp. of Canada
　Oshawa, Ontario, Canada
　Variation of "Chevy II" and "Nova." In
　1964-65 a variation of "Chevelle."
A CAR WITHOUT A NAME—1909
　Department C
　19 North May Street
　Chicago, Illinois
　Buyer supplied his own name.
ACCESSIBLE—1908-10
　See "Hobbie Accessible"
　Both names apply to same vehicle.
ACE—1919-22
　Apex Motor Corp.
　Ypsilanti, Michigan
　Rotary disc valve motor by Fred Gay and
　O. W. Heine.
ACER RACER—1960
　The Acer Co.
　Cockeysville, Maryland
　Juvenile racing car.
ACE SIX (model)—1933
　See "Continental"
　Continental Automobile Co.
　Grand Rapids, Michigan
ACETYLENE—1899
　See "Auto-Acetylene."
　Both names apply to same vehicle.

ACHILLE PHILION STEAM—1892
　Achille Philion
　Akron, Ohio
ACKERMAN—1897-99
　W. K. Ackerman
　Detroit, Michigan
　Became "Reliance."
ACM—1913
　Arthur C. Mason
　Mason Motor Co.
　Flint, Michigan
*ACME—1902-03
　See "Reber"
　Reber Mfg. Co.
　Reading, Pennsylvania
　This car known as "Reber" during these
　years. Became "Acme" 1904.
ACME—1904-10
　Acme Motor Car Co.
　Reading, Pennsylvania
　Succeeded Reber Mfg. Co. 1902-03.
　Became S.G.V. Co. See "Reber" and
　"S.G.V."
ACME HIGHWHEELER—1908-09
　Acme Motor Buggy Mfg. Co.
　Motor Buggy Mfg. Co.
　Minneapolis, Minnesota
　Sometimes advertised as "Roadster."
　Became "M.B."1910.
ACME—1910-11
　Acme Motor Carriage & Machine Co.
　Goderich, Ontario, Canada
　Canadian bodies with U.S. mechanical
　components.
ACME—1912
　Acme Motor Car Co.
　Worcester, Massachusetts
ACME CYCLECAR—1914
　Xenia, Ohio
　Acme Cyclecar Co.
　Became Hawkins Cyclecar Co. 1914.
　See "Xenia."
ACME ROADSTER
　See "Acme' '1908-09.
ACORN HIGHWHEELER—1911

Acorn Motor Car Co.
Cincinnati, Ohio
ADAMS—1906-07
See "Average Man's Runabout"
Adams Automobile Co.
Hiawatha, Kansas
Both names apply to same vehicle.
ADAMS—1911-12
Adams Bros. Co.
Findlay, Ohio
Trucks and some passenger cars.
ADAMS—1924
ADAMS-FARWELL—1898-1913
Adams Co.
Dubuque, Iowa
Experimental 1898-1904
First shown at Chicago Automobile Show,
1905. Revolving rotary engine of three or
five cylinders. One known car in Harrah
Collection.
ADELPHIA—1921
Winfield-Barnes Co.
20th & Erie St.
Philadelphia, Pennsylvania
Built for export only. Plant sold by
receivers June, 1922. Built by Piedmont Co.
ADETTE—1947
ADRIA—1921-22
Adria Motor Car Co.
Batavia, New York
ADRIAN—1902-03
Adrian Motor Works
Adrian, Michigan
ADVANCE—1899
Advance Mfg. Co.
Hamilton, Ohio
One experimental car built.
*ADVANCE—1909-11
"Advance" is company name of Advance
Motor Vehicle Co. Miamisburg, Ohio, not
name of vehicle. Company built "Kauff-
man."
*ADVIS CYCLECAR—1913-14
Davis Cyclecar Co.
Detroit, Michigan

Believed to be "Davis" misspelled.
A.E.C.—1915-16
Anger Engineering Co.
Milwaukee, Wisconsin
Custom-built cars only.
See "Anger."
(AERO)—1921-24
"Aero" and "Pagé" are the same car. No
production is known for either car, but at
least three prototypes were built.
See "Pagé"
Victor W. Pagé Motors Co.
Stamford, Connecticut
AERO AUTO-BOB—1914
Jack Hickman
421 Cottage Ave. East
East Pittsburgh, Pennsylvania
See "Auto Bob"
Both names apply to the same vehicle.
AEROCAR—1905-08
The Aerocar Co.
Aerocar Motor Co.
Detroit, Michigan
Some motors built by Reeves Pulley Co.,
Columbus, Ohio. First "Hudson" cars built
in this factory.
AEROCAR—1948 to date
Aerocar Inc.
Longview, Washington
Detachable wings. Production references in
1948, 1954, 1970.
AEROMOBILE—1959-61
Bertelsen Mfg. Co.
Neponset, Peoria, Illinois
AERO TYPE (model)—1921-1924
Victor W. Pagé Motors Co.
Stamford, Connecticut
See "Pagé" and "Aero."
AERO WILLYS (model)—1952-54
Willys Overland Motors, Inc.
Toledo, Ohio (1951-53)
Willys Motors, Inc.
Toledo, Ohio (1954-55)
1955 model was basically the same car as
previous models, but not designated "Aero."

See "Willys."
AGONTZ—1916
See "Ogontz"
Agontz Motor Car Co.
Sandusky, Ohio
Both names apply to same vehicle.
AIKEN—circa 1850
University of Maryland
Baltimore, Maryland
One built by Dr. William A. E. Aiken
(professor of chemistry) 1838-88.
AIRMOBILE—1916-19
Rotary Products Co.
Los Angeles, California
AIROMOBILE—1937
Lewis American Airways, Inc.
1702 W. Grand
Rochester, New York, also
Denver, Colorado
AIRPHIBIAN—1946-52
Continental Incorporated
Danbury, Connecticut
Prototypes only. First Civil Aeronautic
Authority licensed flying automobile.
AIR SCOON—1947
AIRSCOOT—1947
Aircraft Products Co.
Wichita, Kansas
AIR SCOTT—1947
AIR SCOUT—1947
AIRWAY—1948-49
T. P. Hall Engineering Co.
Airway Motors, Inc.
San Diego, California
Rear engine.
AJAX ELECTRIC—1901-03
Ajax Motor Vehicle Co.
New York, New York
AJAX CYCLECAR—1914
Brisco Motor Co.
New York, New York
AJAX—1914-15
Ajax Motors Co.
Seattle, Washington
Used sleeve or piston valve engine.

AJAX—1920-21
  Ajax Motors Corp.
  Hyde Park, Massachusetts
AJAX—1925-26
  Ajax Motors Corp.
  Racine, Wisconsin
A.J.T. (ATWOOD)—1912
  Weston, (Boston) Massachusetts
A-K—1907-09
  "A-K" name used at start of production.
  See "Allen-Kingston"
  New York Car and Truck Co.
  Allen-Kingston Motor Car Co.
  Kingston, New York
(AKRON)—1899-1900
  Akron Machine Co.
  Akron, Ohio
AKRON—1900-01
  Akron Motor Carriage Co.
  Lincoln and Forge Sts.
  Akron, Ohio
AKRON—1905
  Akron Two Cycle Automobile Co.
  Akron, Ohio
  Four touring cars built.
AKRON—1912-13
(ALAMOBILE)—1902
  Alamo Mfg. Co.
  Hillsdale, Michigan
  Stationary engine manufacturer.
ALAND—1916-17
  R. Aland
  Aland Motor Car Co.
  Detroit, Michigan
  A 16-valve four-cylinder motor designed by
  R. C. Aland, "Pilgrim" designer.
ALBANUS—1899-1900
  See "Roach & Albanus"
  Roach & Albanus
  Ft. Wayne, Indiana
  Both names apply to same vehicle
ALBANY HIGHWHEELER—1906-08
  Albany Automobile Co.
  Albany, Indiana
  Announced assets would be sold Sep-

tember, 1908. 850 cars built.
*ALBAUGH—1910
  Company name, not name of vehicle. Com-
  pany built "Aldo."
  Albaugh-Dover Co.
  Chicago, Illinois
*ALBION—1910
  Scottish car. Not built in U.S.A.
(ALBRECHT)—1900
  Charles Albrecht & Co.
  Milwaukee, Wisconsin
  Advance announcement of car production
  February, 1900.
ALCO—1909-13
  American Locomotive Automobile Com-
  pany
  Providence, Rhode Island
  Succeeded "American Berliet" 1905-08.
  Also called "Locomotive Car," 1909.
*ALDEN SAMPSON
  Company name of Alden Sampson Mfg.
  Co., Pittsfield, Massachusetts, not name of
  vehicle.
ALDO—1910
  Albaugh-Dover Co.
  Chicago, Illinois
  Buggy-type.
ALDRICH—1897-98
  Robert Aldrich
  Millville, Massachusetts
  C. H. Thurston, Worcester, Massachusetts,
  announced plans to produce the car 1898.
ALENA STEAM—1922
  Alena Steam Prod. Co.
  Indianapolis, Indiana
(ALGER)—1902
  R. A. and F. M. Alger, Jr.
  Detroit, Michigan
  Joined "Packard" 1902.
ALGONQUIN—1913
ALKEN—1958
  Alken Corporation
  Venice, California
  Kit car for VW chassis.
ALLEGHENY—1905

Allegheny Automobile Co.
  Allegheny, Pennsylvania
  Both steam and gasoline cars.
ALLEN—1896
  C. F. Allen
  Hueneme, California
ALLEN—1897-1900
  G. Edgar Allen
  302 W. 53rd Street
  New York, New York
  Two cars built.
ALLEN—1913-22
  Allen Motor Car Co.
  Fostoria, Ohio (1913-20)
  Columbus, Ohio (1920-22)
  Became part of Willys-Overland Corp.
  1921.
ALLEN CYCLECAR—1913-14
  Allen Iron & Steel Co.
  Third and Venango Sts.
  Philadelphia, Pennsylvania
ALLEN & CLARK—1908-09
  Allen & Clark Co.
  Toledo, Ohio
ALLEN-KINGSTON—1907-10
  New York Car & Truck Co. (1907-08)
  Allen-Kingston Motor Car Co. (March,
  1908)
  Kingston Motor Car Co. (1910)
  Kingston, New York
  First production cars called "A-K." Built
  by Bristol Engineering Corp., Bristol, Con-
  necticut.
ALLEN-KINGSTON JR. (model)—1910
  G.J.G. Motor Car Co.
  White Plains, New York
  See "Allen-Kingston."
ALLEN STEAM CAR
  Allen Steamer Co.
  Indianapolis, Indiana
ALLIED FALCON—1956
(ALLITH)—1908
  Allen & Clark Co.
  Toledo, Ohio
ALLSTATE—1952-53

Sears-Roebuck & Co.
Chicago, Illinois
Built by Kaiser-Frazer on "Henry J" chassis, with engine and major body stampings identical to those of "Henry J." 2,363 built.

ALL STEEL—1915-17
All Steel Motor Car Co.
St. Louis, Missouri
Macon, Missouri (1916)
Became "Macon."
See "Alstel."

ALMA STEAM—1938
Alma Steam Motors
Newton, Massachusetts

ALPENA—1910-14
Alpena Motor Car Co.
Alpena, Michigan
Absorbed Wolverine Motor Car Co., Mt. Clemens, Michigan 1910.

ALPHA—1903
R. E. Jarrige
New York, New York

*ALSACA—1920-21
Believed to be "Alsace" misspelled.

ALSACE—1919-21
Automotive Products Corp.
New York, New York and
    Philadelphia, Pennsylvania
Built by Piedmont Motor Co., Lynchburg, Virginia and Simms Motor Car Co., Atlanta, Georgia for export only.

ALSTEL—1915-16
See "All Steel"
All Steel Motor Car Co.
St. Louis, Missouri
Both names apply to same vehicle.

(ALTENBERG)—1906
George P. Altenberg
Cincinnati, Ohio

ALTER—1914-16
Alter Motor Car Co.
Plymouth, Michigan
Became Hamilton Motors Corp. Jan. 1917.

(ALTHA) ELECTRIC—1901-05

Altha Auto. and Power Co.
Dover, Delaware

ALTHAM STEAM—1896-1901
George J. Altham
Fall River, Massachusetts (1896)
Altham International Motor Co.
Boston, Massachusetts (1897-99)
Altham Auto & Motor Co.
Fall River, Massachusetts (1900-01)

ALTMAN—1898
Henry J. Altman
Mesopotamia (Cleveland) Ohio
One car produced.

ALUMINUM ELECTRIC—1897
Aluminum Motor Vehicle Co.
Chicago, Illinois
Forerunner of "Woods" electric.

ALUMINUM—1922
Aluminum Manufacturers Inc.
Cleveland, Ohio
About six built.

*ALXO—1905
New York, New York
Believed to be misspelling of "Alco."

*A&M—1901
Believed to be initials of Automobile & Machine Power Co., Camden, New Jersey. Builder of "New Era" cars, not make of vehicle.

AMALGAMATED—1905; 1917-19
Amalgamated Machinery Co.
Chicago, Illinois
Machine builders who built "Doble" steam.

AMANTE GT—1969 to date
Voegele Industries Inc.
Santa Clara, California
Kit Car. Began March, 1969 using fiberglass body and "Corvair" or "Volkswagen" chassis.

AMBASSADOR—1921-25
Yellow Cab Mfg. Co.
Chicago, Illinois
Company also built some "Hertz" cars.

AMBASSADOR—1966 to date
American Motors Corp.

Detroit, Michigan
Succeeded "Rambler" Ambassador.

AMBLER CYCLECAR—1914
King Cyclecar Co.
Cleveland, Ohio

AMCO—1920-22
American Motors, Inc.
100 Broad St.
New York, New York
A specially built car designed by D. M. Eller for export only.

AMERICA—1911
Motor Car Co. of America
New York, New York
Absorbed by W. H. McIntyre Co.
Became "McIntyre Special."

AMERICAN ELECTRIC—1896-1902
American Electric Vehicle Co.
Chicago, Illinois (1896-1900)
Hoboken, New Jersey (1900-02)

(AMERICAN) ELECTRIC—1897
American Motor Wagon Co.
Boston, Massachusetts

(AMERICAN)—1896-98
American Motor Co.
New York, New York

AMERICAN—1898-1900
Automobile Company of America
East Orange, New Jersey
Marion, New Jersey

AMERICAN—1899
American Automobile Co.
20 Broad St.
New York, New York
Car designed by J. Frank Duryea.
Three-cylinder hydro-carbon engine.

AMERICAN—1902-05
American Motor Carriage Co.
514 East Prospect St.
Cleveland, Ohio
Became American Automobile Co.

AMERICAN—1903
American Motor Car Co.
St. Louis, Missouri

AMERICAN—1903-04

---

*ASTERISK: Error corrected from previous list. See introduction to this section for complete code.

American Touring Car Co.
Brooklyn, New York
AMERICAN—1904
American Mfg. Co.
Alexandria, Virginia
AMERICAN—1904
American Automobile Co.
Huron, South Dakota
(AMERICAN)—1905-06
American Motor Co.
Brockton, Massachusetts
Also called "Marsh."
AMERICAN—1906-11
American Motor Car Co.
Indianapolis, Indiana
Became American Motors Co.
See "American Underslung."
AMERICAN—1907
American Metal Wheel & Auto Co.
Toledo, Ohio
AMERICAN—1907
American Automobile Vehicle Co.
Detroit, Michigan
*AMERICAN—1911-12
Believed to be company name of American Automobile Mfg. Co., Kansas City, Missouri, not name of car. Company affiliated with "Jonz" of Beatrice, Nebraska, and continued production of "Jonz" at New Albany, Indiana.
Re-organized as Ohio Falls Motor Co. to manufacture light commercial cars.
AMERICAN CYCLECAR—1913-14
American Cyclecar Co.
Seattle, Washington
AMERICAN CYCLECAR—1914
American Mfg. Co.
Chicago, Illinois
AMERICAN—1916-20
American Motor Vehicle Co.
16th and Union Sts.
Lafayette, Indiana
AMERICAN—1916-24
American Motors Corp.
Plainfield, New Jersey

Designed by Louis Chevrolet. 1923 became Bessemer-American Motors Corp. 1924 joined "Winther" and "Northway" truck in Amalgamated Motors Corp.
AMERICAN AUSTIN—1930-36
American Austin Car Co. Inc. (1929-34)
American Bantam Car Co. (1935-41)
See "American Bantam," "Bantam" (1938-41) and "Austin Bantam."
AMERICAN AUTOMOBILE—1899
See "American"
American Automobile Co.
35-37 Nassau Street
New York, New York
Both names apply to the same vehicle.
AMERICAN BALANCED SIX—1916-24
See "American"
American Motors Corp.
Plainfield, New Jersey
Both names apply to the same vehicle.
AMERICAN BANTAM—1937-41
American Bantam Car Co.
Butler, Pennsylvania
Succeeded "American Austin." See "Bantam." Became first Army "Jeep."
*AMERICAN BEAUTY—1916
American Motors Corp.
Plainfield, New Jersey
This is the Plainfield, New Jersey "American." See "American."
AMERICAN BEAUTY ELECTRIC—1915-16
American Beauty Car Co.
Adrian, Michigan
Colonial Car Co.
Jonesville, Michigan
AMERICAN BEAUTY—1920
Pan American Motors Corp.
Decatur, Illinois
Automobile Trade Journal for February, 1920 lists car as a make.
AMERICAN BENHAM—1914
About 19 cars built.
See "Benham"
Benham Mfg. Co.
Detroit, Michigan

Both names apply to same vehicle.
AMERICAN BERLIET—1905-08
See "Berliet"
American Locomotive Automobile Co.
Providence, Rhode Island
Both names apply to the same vehicle.
AMERICAN-BORLAND ELECTRIC—1914
American Electric Car Co.
Saginaw, Michigan
Succeeded "Borland" electric.
AMERICAN BRASS—1907-08
American Brass Co.
Waterbury, Connecticut
AMERICAN BROC ELECTRIC—1914-16
American Electric Car Co.
Saginaw, Michigan
Succeeded "Broc" electric.
(AMERICAN CARBONIC ACID)—1900
American Automobile Motor & Power Co.
Brooklyn, New York
(AMERICAN CARRIAGE) ELECTRIC—1896-97
American Carriage Motor Co.
New York, New York
AMERICAN C.G.V.—1903
Seven built.
See "C.G.V."
Smith & Mabley
New York, New York
Built at Rome Locomotive Works, Rome, New York.
Both names apply to the same vehicle.
AMERICAN CHOCOLATE—1903-06
American Chocolate Machinery Co.
New York, New York
AMERICAN EAGLE—1909
See "Eagle"
Eagle Automobile Co.
St. Louis, Missouri
Both names apply to same vehicle.
AMERICAN EAGLE—1911-12
American Eagle Motor Car Co.
AMERICAN ELECTRIC—1899-1902
See "American" electric

American Electric Vehicle Co.
Chicago, Illinois
Both names apply to same vehicle.
*AMERICAN ELECTRIC—1902-03
American Motor Car Co.
Cleveland, Ohio
Believed to be "American" gasoline, American Motor Carriage Co., Cleveland, Ohio.
AMERICAN ELECTROMOBILE—1906-08
American Electromobile Co.
1571 River Street
Detroit, Michigan
Built by Massick Mfg. Co., Detroit.
AMERICAN FIAT—1910-18
See "Fiat"
Fiat Company
Poughkeepsie, New York
Both names apply to same vehicle.
*AMERICAN-GAS—1895
American Motor Carriage Co.
Cleveland, Ohio
Company is only listed as in business 1902-05.
AMERICAN JUNIOR (model)—1916-20
See "American"
American Motor Vehicle Co.
16th & Union Streets
Lafayette, Indiana
AMERICAN JUVENILE ELECTRIC—1907
See "American"
American Metal Wheel Co.
Toledo, Ohio
Both names apply to same vehicle.
AMERICAN LIQUID AIR—circa 1900
American Liquid Air Co.
1 Broadway
New York, New York
AMERICAN LOCOMOTIVE—1907
American Locomotive Automobile Co.
Providence, Rhode Island
From 1905 to 1906 vehicle was known as "Berliet" or "American Berliet." In 1908 they returned to the Berliet name and then to "Alco" in 1909.

*AMERICAN LOCOMOTOR steam—1901
Company name, not name of vehicle. Company changed name to American Locomotor Mfg. Co. January, 1901.
See "Baldwin"
Baldwin Automobile Co.
Connellsville, Pennsylvania
AMERICAN MATHIS—1930
American Mathis, Inc.
Dover, Delaware
Lansing, Michigan
AMERICAN MERCEDES—1904-07
Daimler Mfg. Co.
939 Steinway Ave.
Long Island City, New York
Exact copy of German "Mercedes." Plant destroyed by fire December 13, 1907.
AMERICAN MORS—1906-09
St. Louis Car Co.
St. Louis, Missouri
Absorbed "Kobusch." Successor to Kobusch Automobile Co. Became Standard Automobile Co. of America.
See "Standard Six"
AMERICAN MOTOR—1900
American Motor & Vehicle Co.
New York, New York
AMERICAN MOTORETTE cyclecar—1913
American Motorette Co.
Detroit, Michigan
Name changed to Lincoln Motor Car Co. December, 1913.
AMERICAN NAPIER—1906-09
Napier Motor Co. of America
Boston, Massachusetts (office)
Jamaica Plains, New York (plant)
AMERICAN PEUGEOT—1906
(AMERICAN PNEUMATIC)—1900
American Vehicle Co.
West Virginia
AMERICAN POPULAIRE—1904
American Automobile & Power Co.
Lawrence, Massachusetts and
Sandford, Maine
AMERICAN POWER CARRIAGE—1899-

1900
American Power Carriage Co.
Boston, Massachusetts
AMERICAN ROTARY—1900
American Rotary Engine Co.
Boston, Massachusetts
AMERICAN SCOUT (model)—1913
American Motor Car Co.
Indianapolis, Indiana
A model of "American Underslung."
AMERICAN SIMPLEX—1905-10
Simplex Motor Car Co.
Mishawaka, Indiana
Company organized 1904. First car put on the road July, 1905. Name changed to "Amplex" 1910.
AMERICAN SIX—1921
Name used in advertising "American."
See "American" 1916-24
American Motors Corp.
Plainfield, New Jersey
AMERICAN SOUTHERN (model)—1920-21
American Southern Motors Corp.
Greensboro, North Carolina
Company formed to build version of "American Balanced Six" for southern market.
See "American" 1916-24
American Motors Corp.
Plainfield, New Jersey
AMERICAN STANDARD—1914
American Standard Automobile Co.
Edwardsville, Missouri
AMERICAN STANDARD—1914
American Standard Motor Co.
Indianapolis, Indiana
AMERICAN STEAM—1903-04
American Steam Motor Co.
Milwaukee, Wisconsin
AMERICAN STEAM BUGGY—1898-99
American Waltham Mfg. Co.
Waltham, Massachusetts
See "American Waltham" steam
Both names apply to the same vehicle.
AMERICAN STEAM CAR—1929-31

American Steam Automobile Co.
West Newton, Massachusetts
Built with "Hudson" components.
AMERICAN STEAMER—1860
American Steam Carriage Co.
(J. K. Fisher)
New York, New York
AMERICAN STEAMER—1903
AMERICAN STEAMER—1922-24
American Steam Truck Co.
20 E. Jackson Blvd.
Elgin (Chicago), Illinois
Very limited production of passenger cars.
AMERICAN TOURIST (model)—1907-11
See "American"
American Motor Car Co.
Indianapolis, Indiana
AMERICAN TRAVELER (model)—1909-11
See "American"
American Motor Car Co.
Indianapolis, Indiana
AMERICAN TRICAR—1912
Tricar Company of America
Denver, Colorado
AMERICAN UNDERSLUNG—1911-14
American Motors Company
American Underslung Company
Indianapolis, Indiana
Previously called "American" (1906-11)
AMERICAN VOITURETTE—1899-1900
Automobile Co. of America
Marion, New Jersey
AMERICAN WALTHAM STEAM—1898-99
American Waltham Mfg. Co.
Waltham, Massachusetts
AMERICAR (model)—1941-42
See "Willys"
Willys-Overland Inc.
Toledo, Ohio
AMES—1895-1898
Owatonna Mfg. Co.
Owatonna, Wisconsin
*AMES—1895
A. C. Ames
Chicago, Illinois

Believed to be same as "Ames Steamer," A. C. Ames, Chicago, Illinois.
AMES STEAMER—1896
A. C. Ames
Chicago, Illinois
AMES—1910-17
Carriage Woodstock Co.
Owensboro, Kentucky
Became Ames Motor Car Co.
(AMESBURY) ELECTRIC—1899
Amesbury Automobile Co.
Amesbury, Massachusetts
AMESBURY—1902
See "Boston-Amesbury"
Boston-Amesbury Mfg. Co.
Amesbury, Massachusetts
Both names apply to same vehicle.
AMESBURY—1915
Amesbury Auto Co.
Amesbury, Massachusetts
AMES DEAN—1909-10
Ames-Dean Carriage Co.
Jackson, Michigan
AMEX—1895
AMHURST—1912
Two in One Co.
Amhurstburg, Ontario, Canada
Seven-passenger touring car that converted to a pickup truck.
No more than six made.
AMOX—1913
AMPHIBIAN
AMPHI CAT AMPHIBIAN—1967 to date
Mobility Unlimited Inc.
Auburn Heights, Michigan
All-terrain vehicle.
AMPLEX—1910-15
American Simplex Co. (1910-12)
Amplex Motor Co. (1912-13)
Amplex Mfg. Co. (1914-15)
Mishawaka, Indiana
Succeeded "American Simplex" 1905-10.
Bought by Gillette Motors Co. 1916 (King C. Gillette).
AMS-STERLING—1917-18

Sterling Motor Co.
Amston Motor Car Corp.
Bridgeport, Connecticut (office)
Amston, Connecticut (factory)
See "Sterling," Paterson, New Jersey.
(AMSTUTZ-OSBORN)—1900-02
Amstutz-Osborn Co.
Cleveland, Ohio
AMX—1969-70
American Motors Corp.
Detroit, Michigan
ANCHOR—1910-11
Anchor Buggy Co. (1910)
Anchor Motor Car Co. (1911)
Cincinnati, Ohio
(ANDERSON) STEAM CARRIAGE—1899
Albert and J. M. Anderson
289 A Street
South Boston, Massachusetts
To have been built under Whitney patents.
*ANDERSON ELECTRIC—1907-19
Company name, not name of vehicle. Company built "Detroit Electric."
Anderson Electric Car Co.
Detroit, Michigan
ANDERSON HIGHWHEELER—1906
Anderson Machine Co.
Bedford, Indiana
Succeeded by "Postal" 1907.
ANDERSON—1908
N.N. & F. Anderson
Los Angeles, California
ANDERSON—1909-10
Anderson Carriage Mfg. Co.
Anderson, Indiana
Also called "Anderson Motor Carriage."
ANDERSON—1916-26
Anderson Motor Co.
Rock Hill, South Carolina
Subsidiary of Rock Hill Buggy Co.
See "Rock Hill" (1910-15).
ANDERSON STEAM—1902
Anderson Steam Carriage Co.
Anderson, Indiana
ANDERSON STEAMER—1873

CODE = ROMAN LETTERS: Complete entry. *ITALICS:* Unsubstantiated entry. (PARENTHESES): Production planned, but not realized.

Leonard Anderson
Painesville, Ohio
One car produced.
(ANDERSON-WHITNEY) STEAM—1899-
1900
See "Anderson" steam carriage
Albert and J. M. Anderson (1899)
Anderson Mfg. Co. (1900)
South Boston, Massachusetts
Both names apply to same vehicle. No
known production of either car.
ANDOVER ELECTRIC 1914-16
Andover Motor Vehicle Co.
Andover Electric Truck Co. (1915)
Joly & Lambert Electric Co. (1916)
Andover, Massachusetts
Also built commercial cars.
ANDREWS—1895
A. B. Andrews
Center Point, Iowa
Listed entry for Chicago Times-Herald
Race.
ANGELES CYCLECAR—1913
Los Angeles Cyclecar Co.
Los Angeles, California
Pacific Model for 1913
See "Los Angeles"
ANGER—1914-17
See "A.E.C."
Anger Engineering Co.
Milwaukee, Wisconsin
Both names apply to same vehicle.
*ANGLADA CYCLECAR—1914
See "Liberty"
Joseph Anglada
New York, New York
Anglada was name of "Liberty" designer.
(ANGLIN)—1899
M. I. Anglin
La Porte, Indiana
ANGLO-AMERICAN—1900
Anglo-American Rapid Vehicle Co.
New York, New York
*ANGUS—1908-09
Company name, not name of vehicle. Com-

pany built "Fuller."
Angus Automobile Co.
Angus, Nebraska
ANHEUSER EXPERIMENTAL—1905
Mathias Anheuser
Green Bay, Wisconsin
ANHUT—1910-11
Anhut Motor Car Co.
Detroit, Michigan
Became Barnes Motor Car Co.
ANNA—1912
Anna Motor Car Co.
Anna, Illinois
Had kerosene engine.
ANN ARBOR—1903-04
Ann Arbor Automobile Co.
Ann Arbor, Michigan
ANN ARBOR—1911-12
Huron River Mfg. Co.
Ann Arbor, Michigan
(ANNESLEY)—1899
C. G. Annesley
Detroit, Michigan
ANNESLEY LIGHT CAR—1914-15
ANSTED—1921-22
Lexington Motor Car Co.
Connersville, Indiana
ANSTED (model)—1926-27
Ansted Motors
Connersville, Indiana
See "Lexington." Model of "Lexington"
using Ansted engine.
ANTHONY ELECTRIC—1897
Earl C. Anthony
Los Angeles, California
One car produced.
ANTHONY—1900-02
W. O. Anthony
Anthony Motor & Mfg. Co.
Colorado Springs, Colorado
Three or four built.
APELL—1911
APEX—1901
Apex Wheel Co.
Rochester, New York

APOLLO—1905-08
Chicago Recording Scale Co.
Waukegan, Illinois
Announced entry into automobile manu-
facturing May, 1904. No known production
until 1906.
APOLLO—1962-64
International Motor Cars Inc.
Oakland, California (1962)
Apollo International Corp.
Pasadena, California (1963-64)
See "Vetta Ventura"
APOLLO MOPS—1962-64
See "Apollo"
International Motor Cars Inc.
Oakland, California
Both names apply to the same vehicle.
*APPEL—1916
Believed to be "Apple" misspelled.
APPERSON—1902-26
Apperson Bros. Automobile Co.
Kokomo, Indiana (1902-24)
Apperson Automobile Co
Kokomo, Indiana (1924-26)
Reincorporated 1924. Also petitioned to
change name to "Pioneer Automobile Co."
(APPERSON-TOLEDO)—1909
Toledo Motor Co.
Toledo, Ohio
APPLE—1915-16
W. A. Motor Car Co.
Apple Automobile Co.
Dayton, Ohio
Incorporation announced September, 1915.
APPLETON—1921-22
Appleton Mfg. Co.
Batavia, New York
ARABIAN—1917-19
The William Galloway Co.
Waterloo, Iowa
ARBENZ—1911-18
Scioto Auto Car Co.
Arbenz Car Co.
Arbenz Motor Car Co.
Chillicothe, Ohio

*ASTERISK: Error corrected from previous list. See introduction to this section for complete code.

Formerly "Scioto" 1910-11.
Taken over by National United Service Co.
of New York March 18, 1916.

*ARCADIA—1903
Believed to be "Acadia" misspelled.

ARDSLEY—1905-06
Ardsley Motor Car Co.
Yonkers, New York
Designed by W. S. Howard. See "Howard,"
1903.

ARGO ELECTRIC—1910-16
Argo Electric Vehicle Co.
Saginaw, Michigan
Became American Electric Car Co. with
"Borland" and "Broc."

ARGO—1914-16
Argo Motor Co.
602 Main St.
Jackson, Michigan
Called "Ajax" in France. Name changed to
"Hackett" 1916.

ARGO-CASE—1905

ARGONAUT STEAM—1877
J. W. Wilkins
San Francisco, California

ARGONAUT—1959-63
Argonaut Motor Machine Co.
Cleveland, Ohio

*ARGONE FOUR—1920
Believed to be error for "Argonne."

ARGONNE—1919-20
Argonne Motor Car Co. (1919)
Jersey City, New Jersey
Custom-built roadster only.

ARIEL—1905-07
Ariel Motor Car Co.
Boston, Massachusetts (1905-06)
The Ariel Co.
Sinclair-Scott Co. (1907)
Bridgeport, Connecticut (April, 1906)
Baltimore, Maryland (October, 1906)
Named changed to "Maryland" 1907.

(ARISTON)—1906
L. D. Sheppard
52 South Morgan

Chicago, Illinois

*ARISTOS—1912-13
Aristos Company
New York, New York
Company built Mondex-Magic engines, but
may have built a car as well in 1914.

ARKANSAS—1912
W. L. Fodrea Co.
Arkadelphia, Arkansas
No information has been found on this car.
One car was offered for sale used in
September 1913.

ARMAC—1905
Armac Motor Co.
472 Carroll St.
Chicago, Illinois

ARMSTRONG—1896-97
Armstrong Mfg. Co.
Bridgeport, Connecticut

ARMSTRONG ELECTRIC—1903-04
M. Armstrong & Co.
New Haven, Connecticut

(ARNOLD) ELECTRIC—1895
B. J. Arnold
Chicago, Illinois

ARNOLT-BRISTOL—1953-64
S. H. Arnolt, Inc.
415 E. Erie St.
Chicago, Illinois
Also called "Arnolt," 1953.

ARROW—1903
George N. Pierce Co.
Buffalo, New York

ARROW—1912-13
Arrow Motor Car Co.
Long Island City, New York

ARROW CYCLECAR—1914
M. C. Whitmore Co.
Whitmore Motor Co.
Dayton, Ohio

ARROW CYCLECAR—1914
Arrow Cyclecar Co.
Minneapolis, Minnesota

(ARROW)—1922
Arrow Motors

Sandusky, Ohio
Company formed to take over assets of
"Maibohm." Car sold as "Courier" (1923-
24) not "Arrow."

ARROWHEAD THREE-WHEELER—1936
Advance Auto Body Works, Inc.
Los Angeles, California

ARROW LOCOMOTOR—1896
Adolph Moesch & Co.
Buffalo, New York

ARROW MOTOR BUGGY—1907
Arrow Motor Buggy Co.
St. Louis, Missouri

ARTZBERGER—1904
Artzberger Automobile Co.
712 Cedar Ave.
Allegheny, Pennsylvania
Built both steam and gasoline cars.
See "Foster" steam.

ASARDO—1959
American Special Automotive
Research & Design Org.
(Asardo Company)
North Bergen, New Jersey

ASCOT—1955

ASHEVILLE—CYCLECAR—1914-15
E. C. Merrill
Asheville Light Car Co.
Asheville, North Carolina

ASPINWALL EXPERIMENTAL THREE-WHEEL
ELECTRIC—1892
L. M. Aspinwall
Washington, D.C.

ASPROOTH-LEONI GAS-ELECTRIC—1926-27
A. M. Leoni
Philadelphia, Pennsylvania

ASQUITH—1910
S. A. Asquith Runabout Co.
Waterloo, Iowa

ASTER—1906
Aster & Co.
New York, New York
Also built "Aster Tricar" 1906-07.

ASTON—1908-09
Aston Motor Car Co.

Bridgeport, Connecticut
ASTRA—1920
Astra Motors Corp.
St. Louis, Missouri
Built by Dorris. Astra existed November, 1919-June, 1920.
ASTRA—1962
Fiberglass Products
Sacramento, California
Fiberglass kit bodies—various chassis.
ASTRA-GNOME—1956
Richard Arbib Co., Inc.
New York, New York
ATCO—1927-30
ATKINS—1899-1900
See "Hughes" steam
Hughes & Atkin
Providence, Rhode Island
Both names apply to the same vehicle.
See also "Rhode Island" (1899-1900).
Eighty cars built.
ATLANTA—1910-11
Atlanta Motor Car Co.
Atlanta, Georgia
*ATLANTIC steam—1899-1900
Company name for Atlantic Automobile Manufacturing Company which succeeded Marsh Motor Carriage Company, Brockton, Massachusetts.
See "Marsh" steam
ATLANTIC electric—1912-14
Atlantic Vehicle Co.
Newark, New Jersey
ATLAS—1902
Atlas Automobile Co.
Newark, New Jersey
(ATLAS)—1907
Atlas Automobile Co.
Pittsburgh, Pennsylvania
ATLAS—1907-12
Atlas Motor Car Co.
Springfield, Massachusetts
ATLAS-DETROIT—1916
Atlas-Detroit Motor Co.
Detroit, Michigan

ATLAS-KNIGHT—1912-13
Atlas Motor Car Co.
Springfield, Massachusetts
Became Lyons-Atlas Co., Indianapolis, Indiana, along with Atlas Engine Works.
ATLAS MOTOR BUGGY—1909
Atlas Engine Works
Indianapolis, Indiana
Built two-cylinder Auto Buggy. Became part of Lyons-Atlas Co.
(ATTERBURY)—1911
Atterbury Motor Car Co.
Buffalo, New York
AUBREY—1900
L. J. Aubrey Carriage Co.
New Haven, Connecticut
AUBURN—1900-36
Auburn Automobile Co.
Auburn, Indiana
Formerly Eckhart Carriage Works. Became part of Cord Corp. with "Duesenberg" 1929.
AUBURN—1911-15
Auburn Motor Chassis Co.
Auburn, Indiana
Handy Wagon, some trucks.
AUBURN—1967 to date
Auburn-Cord-Duesenberg Co.
Tulsa, Oklahoma
Produced replica of 1935 "Auburn" Speedster.
AUBURN-CUMMINS experimental—1935
Auburn Automobile Co.
Cummins Diesel Co.
Columbus, Indiana
Four-cylinder diesel engine in Auburn car.
AUBURN MOORE—1906
H. S. Moore
160-162 Crawford St.
Cleveland, Ohio
One car produced.
See "Moore" (1902-03).
*AUBURN MOTOR BUGGY highwheeler —1911-14
Built by Auburn Motor Chassis Company

at Auburn, Indiana.
See "Auburn" (1911-15).
AULTMAN steam—1898; 1901-02
Henry J. Aultman
Cleveland, Ohio (1898)
The Aultman Company
Canton, Ohio (1901-02)
AURORA—1905-09
Aurora Automobile Co. (1905)
Aurora Motor Works
Emancipator Automobile Co. (1909)
Aurora, Illinois
AURORA experimental—1958
Fr. Alfred Juliano
Bradford, Connecticut
Safety car.
*AUSTEN steam—1863
William Austen
Lowell, Massachusetts
This car is a "Roper." W. Austen was S. Roper's agent. Car is now in the Ford Museum. See "Roper"
*AUSTENIUS steam—1864
Possibly an error for "Roper."
AUSTIN—1901-21
Austin Automobile Co.
Grand Rapids, Michigan
AUSTIN-BANTAM—1930-37
American Austin Car Co.
Butler, Pennsylvania
Became American Bantam Car Co.
See "American Bantam."
AUSTIN-LYMAN—1909
Austin-Lyman Co.
Buffalo, New York
*AUSTIN-WESTERN—1906
Austin-Western Engine Works
Chicago, Illinois
Not a car: first motor-driven street sweeper.
AUTO-ACETYLENE—1899-1900
Auto-Acetylene Co.
New York, New York
Three models described and illustrated 1899.
AUTO-BOB—1914-15

Jack Hickman
421 Cottage Ave. East
East Pittsburgh, Pennsylvania
Juvenile car listed in Chilton's, October, 1914.

AUTO-BUG HIGHWHEELER—1909-10
Auto-Bug Co.
Norwalk, Ohio
Became "Norwalk."

AUTO BUGGY HIGHWHEELER—1906-08
Auto Buggy Manufacturing Co.
4395 Olive Street
St. Louis, Missouri
No relation to the "A.B.C."

AUTO BUGGY—1906-07
Success Auto Buggy Co.
St. Louis, Missouri
Became "Success."

AUTOCAR—1897-1911
The Autocar Co.
Pittsburgh, Pennsylvania
Ardmore, Pennsylvania
Succeeded Pittsburgh Motor Vehicle Co.

(AUTOCAR)—1900
Autocar Company
Hartford, Connecticut
Compressed air car.

AUTO-CAR—1904-10
Auto-Car Equipment Co. (1904-09)
Auto-Car Mfg. Co. (1909-10)
1453 Niagara St.
Buffalo, New York
Trucks and 8-12 passenger limousines.
Became "Atterbury."

AUTOCARETTE—1900-01
American Autocarette Co.
Washington, D.C.
Automobile Mfg. Co.
Baltimore, Maryland

AUTO-CARRIAGE—1905
See "Johnson"
Johnson Service Co.
Milwaukee, Wisconsin
Both names apply to the same vehicle.

(AUTOCRAT)—1899

The Autocrat Manufacturing Co.
Hartford, Connecticut
Compressed air carriage was announced but actual production is unknown.

AUTO CUB—1956

AUTOCYCLE—1900
Keystone Motor Co.
Philadelphia, Pennsylvania
Became "Keystone."

AUTOCYCLE—1907
See "Vandegrift"
Vandegrift Automobile Co.
13th and Cumberland Sts.
Philadelphia, Pennsylvania
Both names apply to same vehicle.

AUTOCYCLE CYCLECAR—1913
Toledo Autocycle Car Co.
Toledo, Ohio

AUTO-CYCLECAR—1913
Automobile Cyclecar Co.
Detroit, Michigan

AUTO-DYNAMIC ELECTRIC—1900-05
Auto-Dynamic Co.
New York, New York

AUTOETTE CYCLECAR—1912-14
Manistee Motor Car Co.
Manistee, Michigan (1912-13)
Autoette Co.
Christman, Illinois (1914)

AUTOETTE ELECTRIC—1952-57
Autoette Electric Car Co.
(Triangle Boat Co.)
Long Beach, California
Three-wheel electric golf cart.

*AUTO FORCAR—1900
Believed to be error for "Automobile Fore Carriage."

AUTO FORE CARRIAGE—1900-01
See "Automobile Fore Carriage"
Automobile Fore Carriage Co.
New York, New York
Both names apply to the same vehicle.

AUTOGO (model)—1900-01
See "Orient"
Waltham Mfg. Co.

Waltham, Massachusetts

AUTO KING—1900
New England Auto King Co.
Portland, Maine

AUTOLET ELECTRIC—1904
Holson Motor Patents Co. Inc.
Grand Rapids, Michigan

AUTO-LOCO-STEAM

AUTOMATIC ELECTRIC—1921-22
Automatic Electric Transmission Co.
Buffalo, New York
Small two-seater.

AUTOMATIC STURTEVANT—1904-07
See "Sturtevant"
Sturtevant Mill Co.
Boston, Massachusetts
Both names apply to the same vehicle.

(AUTOMOBILE AIR CARRIAGE)—1898-1900
Automobile Air Carriage Co.
Albany, New York

AUTOMOBILE FORE CARRIAGE—1900-01
Automobile Fore Carriage Co.
New York, New York
Converted carriages to motor-powered vehicles.

AUTOMOBILE VOITURETTE—1899-1900
See "American Voiturette"
Automobile Company of America
Marion, New Jersey
Both names apply to the same vehicle.
Became "Gasmobile," 1900.

AUTOMOTE—1900
Schaap Cycle Co.
Brooklyn, New York

AUTOMOTOR—1900-05
Automotor Co.
Springfield, Massachusetts
Body and sheet metal by Springfield Body Co. Formerly Springfield Cornice Works, 1900-01.

AUTOMOTOR—1902
Lowell Model Co.
Lowell, Massachusetts

AUTO-MOTOR—1912

CODE = ROMAN LETTERS: Complete entry. *ITALICS:* Unsubstantiated entry. (PARENTHESES): Production planned, but not realized.

Bryn Mawr, Pennsylvania
AUTOMOTORETTE—1900-02
  A. L. Dyke
  St. Louis, Missouri
  See "Dyke."
  Both names apply to same vehicle.
AUTO PARTS—1909-11
  Auto Parts Company
  52 and 54 Jackson Boulevard
  Chicago, Illinois
  A $600 air or water-cooled car sold in kit
  form.
AUTO PLANE—1947
AUTO-QUAD—1901
  E. R. Thomas Motor Co.
  Buffalo, New York
AUTO-QUADRICYCLE—1903
  Auto-Cycle Carriage Co.
  Chicago, Illinois
AUTO RED BUG—1916-23
  American Motor Vehicle Co.
  Lafayette, Indiana (1916-20)
  Automotive Electric Service Corp., North
  Bergen, New Jersey bought rights to
  Briggs & Stratton (Smith) Flyer electric
  and gasoline buckboards.
AUTO-TRI (model)—1899
  See "Kelsey & Tilney"
  C. W. Kelsey & I. S. Tilney
  Chestnut Hill
  Philadelphia, Pennsylvania
  Both names apply to same vehicle.
AUTOTRI—1900-01
  E. R. Thomas Motor Co.
  Buffalo, New York
AUTO TRICAR THREE-WHEELER—1914
  A. E. Osborn
  New York, New York
AUTO-TWO—1900
  Buffalo Auto and Auto-Bi Co.
  Buffalo, New York
AUTO-VEHICLE—1902-05
  The Auto-Vehicle Co.
  Los Angeles, California
  See "Tourist"

AUTO WAGON—1909
  See "International"
  International Harvester Co. of America
  Chicago, Illinois
  Both names apply to the same vehicle.
AVANTI (model)—1963
  Studebaker Corp.
  South Bend, Indiana
AVANTI II—1965 to date
  Avanti Motor Corporation
  South Bend, Indiana
AVERAGE MAN'S RUNABOUT AIR-COOLED
  —1906-07
  Adams Automobile Co.
  Hiawatha, Kansas
  See "Adams."
AVERY CYCLECAR—1914
  Avery Stalnaker
  Chicago, Illinois
AYERS—1900-02
  Ayers Gasoline Engine & Automobile Co.
  Saginaw, Michigan
AZTEC—1965
  FiberFab
  Sunnyvale, California
  Kit car for "Corvair" or "Volkswagen"
  chassis.

ℬ

BABCOCK ELECTRIC—1906-12
  Babcock Electric Carriage Co.
  Buffalo, New York
  Merged into Buffalo Electric Vehicle Co.
  1912.
BABCOCK HIGHWHEELER—1909-13
  H. H. Babcock Co.
  Watertown, New York
BABY (model)—1902-03
  See "Fournier-Searchmont"
  Fournier-Searchmont Co.
  Philadelphia, Pennsylvania
BABY (model)—1924
  See "Dagmar"
  M. P. Moller Car Co.
  Hagerstown, Maryland

BABY LA SABRE—1952
  Los Angeles, California
BABY MOOSE CYCLECAR—1914
  Bull Moose-Cutting Automobile Co.
  St. Paul, Minnesota
  Formerly "Continental" cyclecar.
BACHELLE ELECTRIC—1901-02
  Bachelle Automobile Co.
  Chicago, Illinois
BACKBAY—(model)—circa 1899
  See "McCullough"
  Back Bay Motor & Cycle Co.
  Boston, Massachusetts
BACKUS—1903
  Backus Water Motor Co.
  Newark, New Jersey
BACON—1901
  Frank W. Bacon
  Omaha, Nebraska
  Seven cars built.
(BACON)—1920-21
  Bacon Motors Corp.
  Newcastle, Pennsylvania
  Philadelphia, Pennsylvania
BADGER (F.W.D.)—1909-11
  The Four Wheel Drive Auto Co.
  Clintonville, Wisconsin
BADGER—1910-11
  Badger Motor Car Co.
  Columbus, Wisconsin
BAILEY AIR-COOLED—1907-10
  Bailey-Perkins Auto Co. (1906-08)
  Bailey Automobile Co. (1908-10)
  Springfield, Massachusetts
  Four-cylinder two-cycle revolving engine.
BAILEY ELECTRIC—1907-15
  S. R. Bailey & Co.
  Amesbury, Massachusetts
  Service parts only after December, 1915.
BAILEY—1912
  G. D. Bailey Mfg. Co.
  Detroit, Michigan
BAILEY-CLAPP—1915
  Elwood Iron Works Co.
  Elwood, Indiana

See "Elco."

BAILEY ELECTRIC—1902
F. G. Bailey & Co.
Manheim, Pennsylvania

BAINES

(BAKER) ELECTRIC—1896-97
Herbert C. Baker
Manchester, Connecticut
To have been built in plant of Mather Electric Company.

(BAKER)—1899
Baker Mfg. Co.
Tarentum, Pennsylvania

BAKER—1899
National Machine Co.
Hartford, Connecticut
Founder and inventor, Herbert C. Baker, Manchester, Connecticut.

BAKER ELECTRIC—1899-1916
Baker Motor Vehicle Co.
Cleveland, Ohio (1899-1914)
Merged with Rauch & Lang 1914 into Baker, Rauch & Lang Co. Merged with Owen-Magnetic 1915 (Baker-Raulang Co.) Industrial Truck Division started 1922, continued as Division of Otis-Elevator 1968.

BAKER STEAM—1917-24
Baker Steam Motor Car & Mfg. Co.
    (1917-19)
Steam Automotive Works (1920)
Baker Motors Inc. (1921)
Denver and Pueblo, Colorado

BAKER-BELL—1913
Baker-Bell Motor Co.
Philadelphia, Pennsylvania
Also built "Princess" commercial cars for "Metz."
See "Humming-Bird"

BAKER-ELBERG ELECTRIC—1894-95
Dr. H. C. Baker & J. R. Elberg
Kansas City, Missouri

BAKER-RAUCH & LANG (model)
ELECTRIC—1915-20
See "Baker" electric
Baker Motor Vehicle Co.
Cleveland, Ohio

BAKER-RAULANG ELECTRIC—1915-16
See "Baker" electric
Baker Motor Vehicle Co.
Cleveland, Ohio
The 1915-16 name for the Baker car.

BALBOA—1924-25
Balboa Motor Corp.
Fullerton, California

BALDNER—1901-04; 1906
Baldner Motor Vehicle Co.
Xenia, Ohio

BALDWIN STEAM—1899-1901
Baldwin Automobile Co. (1899-1900)
Baldwin Motor Wagon Co. (1901)
Providence, Rhode Island

BALDWIN—1900-02
Baldwin Automobile Mfg. Co.
Connellsville, Pennsylvania
Sold to J. C. Kurtz at Trustees' sale April 19, 1902 and moved to Morgantown, West Virginia.

BALL STEAM EXPERIMENTAL—1868
Charles A. Ball
Paterson, New Jersey
One car built.

BALL STEAM—1901-02
See "Ramapaugh" steam
Charles A. Ball
Middletown, Ohio
Paterson, New Jersey
Both names apply to same vehicle.

BALL—1902
New York Gear Works
New York, New York
Designed by Frederick W. Ball

BALLARD—1894-95
H. C. Ballard and Son Co.
Oshkosh, Wisconsin

(BALTIMORE)—1900
Baltimore Automobile and Mfg. Co.
Baltimore, Maryland

BALZER—1894-99
Stephen M. Balzer
370 Gerard Avenue

New York, New York (1894-98)
Became Balzer Motor Carriage Co. 1898-1900.
Three-cylinder revolving gasoline engine. Balzer's first car, only one known to exist, is in Smithsonian collection.

BALZER—1917
Gus Balzer Co.
1777-79 Broadway
New York, New York
Juvenile car

BANGERT—1956
Bangert Enterprises
Hollywood, California

BANKER—1905
A. C. Banker
Chicago, Illinois

(BANKER BROTHERS) ELECTRIC—1896
Banker Brothers Co.
Pittsburgh, Pennsylvania

BANKER ELECTRIC—1905
Banker Bros.
Pittsburgh, Pennsylvania

(BANKS) STEAM—1900
Robert Banks
Stanton, Delaware

BANNER—1910-11
Banner Automobile Co.
St. Louis, Missouri
Division of Banner Buggy Co.

BANNER—1915

BANNER BOY BUCKBOARD—1958-59
Banner Welder Inc.
Milwaukee, Wisconsin

BANTAM CYCLECAR—1914
Bantam Motor Co.
Boston, Massachusetts
Announced in Automobile Trade Journal April, 1914.

BANTAM (model)—1938-41
American Bantam Car Co.
Butler, Pennsylvania
See "American Bantam"
"American Austin" and "Austin."

BARAUF—1920

Barauf Motor Co.
Port Jefferson, New York
For export.

BARBARINO—1924-25
Barbarino Motors Co.
Advance Motors Corp.
21-23 Lenox Rd.
New York, New York (office)
Stamford, Connecticut (factory)

(BARBER)—1899
George Barber
Danbury, Connecticut

BARBOUR—1916
Barbour Buggy Co.
South Boston, Virginia

BARCUS—1895
Nemo Barbus
Columbus, Ohio

BARDWELL ELECTRIC—1901
H. H. Bardwell
Flint, Michigan

BAR HARBOR STEAM—1901
Boston Automobile Co.
Boston, Massachusetts

BARHOFF ELECTRIC—1900
Hartford Accumulator Co.
Hartford, Connecticut
Electric car built to test batteries.

BARLEY—1922-24
Barley Motor Car Co.
Roamer Motor Car Co.
Kalamazoo, Michigan
Also made taxicabs (Pennant).

(BARLOW) STEAM—1917-22
Barlow Steam Car Co.
Detroit, Michigan

BARLOW—1924
Barlow Motors Corp.
Philadelphia, Pennsylvania

(BARNARD-BRIGGS)—1907
Barnard-Briggs Motor Car Mfg. Co.
Boston, Massachusetts
Company offered prize for best name.

BARNES ELECTRIC—1899
Barnes Cycle Co.

Syracuse, New York
See "Van Wagoner" (Century Vehicle Co.
in 1900).

BARNES—1908-12
Formerly "Servitor"
Barnes Mfg. Co.
Sandusky, Ohio

BARNES—1910
Barnes Motor Co.
Detroit, Michigan
Purchased "Anhut" assets summer, 1910.
Company reported sold to Frank Howard
January, 1911.

BARNHART & BETTS—1899
H. E. Barnhart & C. E. Betts
Warren, Pennsylvania

BARNHART—1905
Warren Automobile Co.
Warren, Pennsylvania
Experimental cars built from 1895-1905.
Publicly shown 1905.

BARRACUDA (model)—1964 to date
See "Plymouth"
Chrysler Corporation
Plymouth Motor Division
Detroit, Michigan

BARRETT STEAM—1900
S. H. Barrett
M. J. Dunn & Co.
Springfield Motor Vehicle Co.
Springfield, Massachusetts

BARRETT & PERRÉT ELECTRIC—1895
J. A. Barrett & F. Perrét
New York, New York

BARRIE—1919-20
Barrie Carriage Co. Ltd.
Barrie, Ontario, Canada

BARROWS ELECTRIC—1895-99
Charles H. Barrows
Willimantic, Connecticut (1896)
New York, New York (1897-99)
Built a tri-cycle and one wheel
"Mechanical Horse."

BARSALEAUX—1897
Joseph Barsaleaux

Sandy Hill, New York
Built in shape of a horse. Known also as
"Motor Horse."

BARTHEL—1903
Barthel Motor Co.
Detroit, Michigan
One car built.

BARTHOLOMEW—1901-03
The Bartholomew Co.
Peoria, Illinois
Became "Glide"

BARTLETT—1914-17
Toronto, Ontario, Canada

BARTLETT ELECTRIC—1915
J. C. Bartlett Co.
Philadelphia, Pennsylvania

BARTLETT—1921
National Brick Co.
Chicago, Illinois

BARTON STEAM—1903
Barton Boiler Co.
Chicago, Illinois
Two "special steam tonneau cars" built to
order.

BARVER—1925

BARY—1878
James B. Bary
Waverly, New York
One car produced.

BASSON'S STAR THREE-WHEELER—1956
Minicar with two-cycle, single-cylinder
engine. Sold for $999.00.

*BATEMAN—1917
Bateman Mfg. Co.
Greenlock, New Jersey
Car actually called "Frontmobile."

BATES—1903-05
Bates & Edmunds Motor Co.
Bates Automobile Co.
Lansing, Michigan

BATTEN ELECTRIC—1911
Batten-Dayton Motor Co.
Chicago, Illinois

BATTIN STEAM—1856
Joseph Battin

BATTEY & CRICKLER—1900
Battey & Crickler
Springfield, Massachusetts
BATTLE STEAM CARRIAGE—1812
Mellen Battle
Herkimer, New York
BATTLESHIP—1909
Zachow & Besserdich Automobile Co.
Clintonville, Wisconsin
Became "FWD"
BAUER CYCLECAR—1914
Bauer Machine Works
Kansas City, Missouri
Succeeded "Gleason"
Built standard car 1915-16.
BAUER STEAM—1901
E. H. Bauer
Beaver Falls, Pennsylvania
Built car with one lever control 1901.
*BAUROTH—1899
Believed to be misspelling of "Blaurock."
BAYER—1920
Bayer Bros.
Leavenworth, Kansas
BAYERSDORFER—1899
See "Ottomobile"
Otto Bayersdorfer
Omaha, Nebraska
Both names apply to same vehicle.
BAYMONT—1955
*BAY STATE—1896
Believed to be company name of Bay State
Motive Power Co., Springfield, Massachu-
setts, not name of vehicle.
See "Walkins"
BAY STATE—1900
Bay State Automobile & Engine Co.
Boston, Massachusetts
BAY STATE—1906-08
Bay State Automobile Co.
112 Norway St.
Boston, Massachusetts
First car put on road January, 1906. First
car shown March, 1907.
BAY STATE—1922-26

R. H. Long Motors Corp.
Framingham, Massachusetts
Became Bay State Cars Inc. Creditors peti-
tioned bankruptcy December, 1923.
B&B THREE WHEEL—1947
B&B Specialty Co.
Rossmoyne, Ohio
Thirty units built.
B.C.K.—1910-11
B.C.K. Motor Co.
Bath, New York and York, Pennsylvania
See "Kline Kar"
*B.D.A.C.—1904
Company name (Black Diamond
Automobile Co.), not name of vehicle. Cars
were produced under "Buckmobile" name.
See "Buckmobile"
Buckmobile Co.
Utica, New York
BEACH—1900
Beach Motor Vehicle Co.
Everett, Massachusetts
BEACH—1962 to date
Competition Components Inc.
Clearwater, Florida
Kit car
BEACH CAR—1947
BEACON—1917
Morgan Potter Motor Co.
Beacon, New York
Two built.
BEACON (model)—1933-34
See "Continental"
Continental Automobile Co.
Grand Rapids, Michigan
BEACON FLYER—1908
BEAN—1901
A. E. Bean Automobile Co.
Boston, Massachusetts
BEARCAT—1956
*BEARDSLEY—1901-02
Company name, not name of vehicle. Com-
pany produced "Darling."
See "Darling"
Beardsley & Hubbs Mfg. Co.

Shelby, Ohio
BEARDSLEY ELECTRIC—1914-17
Beardsley Electric Co.
Los Angeles, California (1914-15)
Culver City, California (1915-17)
Absorbed by Moreland Truck Co.
BEAU BRUMMEL—1917
Universal Car Equipment Co.
Detroit, Michigan
BEAU-CHAMBERLAIN (model)—1901
See "Hudson Steamer"
Beau-Chamberlain Mfg. Co.
Hudson, Michigan
Both names apply to same vehicle.
*BEAVER—1905
Company name of Beaver Mfg. Co. engine
builders, not vehicles.
BEAVER—1912-20
Beaver State Motor Co.
Portland, Oregon (1912-15)
Gresham, Oregon (1916-20)
BECK—1895
C. W. Beck
Chicago, Illinois
(BECK & CLAUSEL)—1908
Beck & Clausel
Memphis, Tennessee
Advance announcement February, 1908.
BEE
BEEBE—1906-07
Western Motor Truck & Vehicle Works
Chicago, Illinois
Offered both a highwheel runabout and a
conventional touring car.
(BEECH PLAINSMAN)—1948
Beech Aircraft Co.
Wichita, Kansas
Promotional car
BEETLE FLYER—1909
Fodrea-Malott Mfg. Co.
Noblesville, Indiana
Buggy-type built to order.
BEETLE DUNE BUGGY—1968 to date
Beetle Auto Haus
Vancouver, Washington

CODE = ROMAN LETTERS: Complete entry. *ITALICS*: Unsubstantiated entry. (PARENTHESES): Production planned, but not realized.

Kit car
BEGGS—1918-23
    Beggs Motor Car Co.
    Kansas City, Missouri
BEISEL CYCLECAR—1914
    Beisel Motorette Co.
    Monroe, Michigan
B.E.L.—1921-22
    Consolidated Motor Car Co. Inc.
    Middlefield, Connecticut
    New London, Connecticut (1922)
    See "Sterling" (1922-23)
BELDEN—1907-11
    Belden Automobile Co. (1907)
    Belden Motor Car Co. (1908-11)
    Pittsburgh, Pennsylvania
Company started in 1907. No production to 1909.
(BELGER & BOWKER) STEAM—1900
    James E. Belger & Samuel Bowker
    Natick, Massachusetts
To have been built in Francis Bigelow Factory.
*BELKNAP ELECTRIC—1899
Believed to be company name of Belknap Motor Company, Portland, Maine, not name of car. See "Chapman" electric.
BELKNAP STEAM—1907-08
    Belknap Motor Co.
    Detroit, Michigan
Changed to Michigan Steam Motor Co. Pontiac, Michigan 1907.
*BELL—1907
Believed to be company name of W. L. Bell, Kansas City, Missouri. Not name of car. See "Croesus Jr."
BELL—1915-23
    Bell Motor Car Co. Inc.
    York, Pennsylvania
    Formerly "Sphinx"
BELL—1917-18
    Barrie Carriage Co. Ltd.
    Barrie, Ontario, Canada
    Assembled from U.S. parts.
BELLEFONTAINE—1900

Bellefontaine Carriage Body Co.
    Columbus, Ohio
BELLEFONTAINE—1908-17
    Bellefontaine Automobile Co.
    Bellefontaine, Ohio
*BELLEFONTAINE-TIFFIN—1916
    Bellefontaine, Ohio
    Believed to be "Bellefontaine."
BELLEFONTE—1913
    Bellefonte Automobile Mfg. Co.
    Bellefonte, Pennsylvania
*BELLMAY—1904
Believed to be the one of a kind French "Bellamy."
BELMOBILE—1912
    Bell Motor Car Co.
    Detroit, Michigan
20 hp two-passenger roadster shown at 1912 Detroit Auto Show.
BELMONT—1909-13
    Belmont Automobile Co.
    New Rochelle, New York (May, 1909)
    Castleton, New York (June, 1909)
    Belmont Automobile Mfg. Co.
    New Haven, Connecticut (1910-12)
Company organized May 6, 1909. No records have been found after May, 1910.
(BELMONT) ELECTRIC—1916
    Belmont Electric Automobile Co.
    Wyandotte, Michigan
Announcement March, 1916 of gas-electric car.
(BELMONT)—1917
    Belmont Motor Car Co.
    Toledo, Ohio
Advertised March, 1917.
BELMONT—1919-22
    Belmont Motor Co.
    Lewiston, Pennsylvania
BELVIDERE—1903-06
    National Sewing Machine Co.
    Belvidere, Illinois
BEMMEL & BARNHAM—1898
BENDIX AIR-COOLED HIGHWHEELER 1908-09
    Bendix Company

Chicago, Illinois
Company succeeded Triumph Motor Car Co. and built a line of four-cylinder long wheelbase highwheelers.
BENDIX-AMES—1911
BENHAM—1914
    Benham Mfg. Co.
    Detroit, Michigan
Announced April, 1914. Goodrich & Ditzler petitioned bankruptcy Fall, 1914. Company dissolved March, 1915. Formerly "S&M."
BEN-HUR—1916-17
    Ben-Hur Motor Co.
    Cleveland, Ohio
    Willoughby, Ohio (factory)
35-40 cars produced, all 1917 models.
BENNER—1908-09
    Benner Motor Car Co.
    New York, New York
Company incorporated May, 1908. First cars finished October 1908. 150-200 units built.
BENNETT-BIRD—1905
    Bennett-Bird Co.
    Chicago, Illinois
BENSON—1901
    Andrew & John B. Benson
    Chicago, Illinois
BENSON STEAM—1901
    Benson Automobile Co.
    Cleveland, Ohio
    Formerly Eastman Auto Co.
BENTEL—1901
    Theo. F. Bentel Co.
    Pittsburgh, Pennsylvania
BENTEL—1919
    Geo. R. Bentel Co.
    Los Angeles, California
BENTON—1913
    Benton Motor Car Co.
    Benton, Illinois
BENTON HARBOR—1895-96
    A. Baushke & Bros. (1895)
    Benton Harbor Motor Carriage Co. (1896)

Benton Harbor, Michigan
Experimented with gasoline and electric vehicles.

BENTON-WINTON—1920
The Benton Co.
Los Angeles, California

BENZ SPIRIT MOTOR VEHICLES—1900
The Columbus Automobile Co.
32 South Front St.
Columbus, Ohio

BERG—1902-06
Berg Automobile Co.
Cleveland, Ohio (1902-04)
Became Worthington Automobile Co. New York, New York. Was an exact copy of "Panhard." First car built for Berg by Cleveland Machine Screw Co.

BERGDOLL—1908-14
Bergdoll Motor Car Co. (1908-10)
Louis J. Bergdoll Motor Co.
16th & Callowhill Streets
Philadelphia, Pennsylvania (1911-14)
Bergdoll Automobile Co.
Trenton, New Jersey (September, 1914)

(BERGER)—1909
Berger Mfg. Co.
Canton, Ohio

BERKELEY—1903-04
J. H. Neustadt Co.
St. Louis, Missouri

BERKSHIRE—1904-07; 1909-13
Berkshire Motor Co. (1904)
Berkshire Automobile Co. (1905-07)
Berkshire Motor Car Co. (1907)
Berkshire Auto Car Co. (1909-12)
Berkshire Motors Co. (1912)
Pittsfield, Massachusetts
Berkshire Motors Co. (1912)
Belcher Engineering Co. (1912-13)
Cambridge, Massachusetts
Effects reported sold at auction May, 1908.
Reorganized early 1910. In financial trouble again November, 1911.

*BERLIET—1906-08
American Locomotive Automobile Co.

Providence, Rhode Island
Known only as "American Berliet."
Succeeded 1909 by "Alco."

(BERLO)—1900
Peter Berlo
Boston, Massachusetts

BERRENBERG—1897
Motor mounted on wheel.

BERTELSEN AEROMOBILE   1959-61
William R. Bertelsen Mfg. Co.
Neponset, Illinois

BERTOLET—1908-12
Dr. J. M. Bertolet (1908)
Bertolet Motor Car Co. (1909-10)
Reading, Pennsylvania
Model "X" sold with interchangeable 2 or 5-passenger convertible body.

BERTRAND—1902

BERWICK ELECTRIC—1904
Berwick Auto Car Co.
Grand Rapids, Michigan

BERWICK—1917
Berwick Car Works
Mahanoy City, Pennsylvania

*BESSERDICH & ZACHOW—1910
See "Zachow & Besserdich" 1908
Clintonville, Wisconsin
Both names apply to same company which built "Battleship."

BEST HIGHWHEELER   1898-1900
Daniel Best Mfg. Co.
San Leandro, California
Only one built.

BEST—1910
Best Motor Car Co.
Indianapolis, Indiana

BETHLEHEM—1907-08
Bethlehem Automobile Co.
South Bethlehem, Pennsylvania
First car announced November, 1907.

BETHLEHEM—1920
Bethlehem Motor Truck Corp.
Allentown, Pennsylvania
Built for export.

BETTERIDGE—1933

Billy Betteridge
Los Angeles, California

BEVERLY—1904-05
Upton Machine Co.
New York, New York (1904)
The Motor & Mfg. Works Co.
Ithaca, New York (1905)

*BEWIS—1915
Believed to be "Lewis" misspelled

BEWMAN—1912

BEYSTER-DETROIT—1910-11
Beyster-Detroit Motor Car Co.
Detroit, Michigan
Formerly Beyster-Thorpe Motor Co.

B.F.G.—1946
B. F. Goodrich Co.
Akron, Ohio
Composite test vehicle.

B.F.S.—1908

*B.G.S.—1900
Believed to be name of French racer not a United States car.

B&H—1904-05
See "Brew-Hatcher"
Brew & Hatcher Co.
34-38 Columbus St.
Cleveland, Ohio
Both names apply to the same vehicle.

*BIANCHI
Percy Owen, Inc.
New York, New York
Believed to be Italian "Bianchi" 1898-1937.

BI-AUTO-GO TWO-WHEEL EXPERIMENTAL
—1908-12
James Scripps Booth
Detroit, Michigan
V-8 engine. Took four years to build.

BIBBS—1904
Bibbs Engineering Co.
New York, New York

(BI-CAR)—1912
Detroit Bi-Car Co.
Detroit, Michigan

BI-CAR CYCLECAR—1914
See "Fauber Bi-Car"

W. H. Fauber
Elgin, Illinois
Both names apply to same vehicle.
BIDDLE—1902
Biddle Mfg. Co.
Knoxville, Tennessee
BIDDLE—1915-21
Biddle Motor Car Co.
Philadelphia, Pennsylvania
Moved to New York 1919. Became Biddle-Crane Motor Co. 1921.
BIDDLE—1921-23
Biddle-Crane Motor Car Co.
New York, New York
Limited production by November, 1921. Chassis built in New York, then shipped to Baker-Rauch and Lang, Cleveland, Ohio for bodies.
BIG BROWN LUVERNE—1909
See "Luverne"
Luverne Automobile Co.
Luverne, Minnesota
Local nickname for "Luverne"
BINGMAN—1912
P. Bingman & Son
Detroit, Michigan
*BILLIE FOUR—1910
Believed to be "Billy Four" misspelled.
BILLIKEN CYCLECAR—1914
Billiken Cyclecar Co.
Green Bay, Wisconsin
BILLINGS—EXPERIMENTAL STEAMER—1902
Billings & Spencer Co.
Hartford, Connecticut
Patents sold to American Bicycle Co. Toledo, Ohio. Believed to be the basis of "Toledo Steamer."
BILLY—1910
See "Billy Four"
McNabb Iron Works
Atlanta, Georgia
Both names apply to same vehicle.
BILLY FOUR—1909-10
McNabb Iron Works
Atlanta, Georgia

BIMEL—1916-17
Bimel Buggy Co.
Sydney, Ohio
Formerly "Elco"
*BINATE—1902
Engines built by Coffee & Sons and sold by C. E. Miller, New York, New York. Did not build vehicles.
See "Coffee"
BINFORD—1905
BINGHAM—1916
BINGHAMTON—circa 1900
Binghamton Gas Engine Co.
Binghamton, New York
BINNEY & BURNHAM STEAM—1902-03
Binney & Burnham
54 Devonshire St.
Boston, Massachusetts
Cars built to customers special order.
BIRCH—1917-22
Birch Motor Corp.
Birch Motor Cars Inc. (1921-22)
Birch Motor Cars
Chicago, Illinois
Mail order car.
BIRD—1895-97
Henry R. Bird
Buffalo, New York
A friction drive, kerosene-fueled Chicago Times-Herald race entry, 1895. Four built.
BIRD—1911
Bird Automobile Co.
New York, New York
BIRD
Theo. Bird Automobile Co.
BIRDSALL—1909
BIRMINGHAM ELECTRIC—1903
Birmingham Electric & Mfg. Co.
Birmingham, Alabama
BIRMINGHAM—1921-22
Birmingham No-Axle Motor Co.
Jamestown, New York
Affiliated with Parker Motor Car Mfg. Co. Montreal, Quebec, Canada.
Fraud charged 1922.

BIRNEL—1911
BISON—1904
Bison Motor Co.
Buffalo, New York
(BISSELL) ELECTRIC—1909
Bissell Electric Co.
Toledo, Ohio
BJELLA—1905-06
McIntosh Iron & Wood Works
McIntosh, Minnesota
One car produced.
BLACK—1897-1900
C. H. Black Mfg. Co.
Indianapolis, Indiana
Some references claim one car built 1891.
BLACK—1904
Seth C. Black
W. Chester, Pennsylvania
BLACK HIGHWHEELER—1906-09
Black Manufacturing Co.
Chicago, Illinois
Two models (10 and 14 hp) succeeded by "Black Crow."
BLACK CROW—1910-11
Black Manufacturing Co.
Chicago, Illinois (1910)
Crow Motor Car Co.
Elkhart, Indiana (1911)
Built five models of conventional cars and two highwheel models. Succeeded by "Crow."
BLACK CROW MOTOR BUGGY (model)
HIGHWHEELER—1910
See "Black Crow"
Black Mfg. Co.
Chicago, Illinois
A model of "Black Crow."
*BLACK DIAMOND—1904-05
Company name of Black Diamond Automobile Co., Utica, New York, not name of automobile.
See "Buckmobile"
BLACK HAWK—1903
Clark Mfg. Co.
Moline, Illinois

BLACKHAWK—1929-30
  Stutz Motor Car Co. of America
  Blackhawk Division
  Indianapolis, Indiana
  See "Stutz"
  A lower-priced companion to "Stutz."
BLACKMORE
BLACK MOTOR BUGGY
  HIGHWHEELER—1909
  See "Black" highwheeler
  Black Mfg. Co.
  Chicago, Illinois
  Both names apply to same vehicle.
BLACKSTONE—1916
  Blackstone Motor Co.
  Momence, Illinois
(BLAIR)—1911
  Blair Motor Co.
  Cincinnati, Ohio
BLAIR STEAM—1906-09
  Blair Light Co.
  Northboro, Massachusetts
  Claimed to be entirely automatic in opera-
  tion, no fuel or air pumps needed.
*BLAIR LIGHT—1906-09
  Company name, not name of vehicle. Com-
  pany built "Blair" steam.
  Blair Light Co.
  Northboro, Massachusetts
BLAISDELL STEAM—1903
  J. P. Blaisdell
  Blaisdell & Co.
  Brooklyn, New York
BLAKE—1901
  James E. Blake
  Attleboro, Massachusetts
BLAKELY ELECTRIC—1902
  Edward B. Blakely
  Newport, Rhode Island
  Race car
BLAKESLEE—1906-07
  Blakeslee Electric Vehicle Co.
  Cleveland, Ohio
BLAKESLEE (model) STEAM—1967
  See "Williams" steam

Williams Engine Co. Inc.
  Ambler, Pennsylvania
  Both names apply to the same vehicle.
BLANCHARD STEAM—1825
  Thomas Blanchard
  Springfield, Massachusetts
*BLANCHE—1906
  Believed to be misspelling of Italian
  "Bianchi."
BLAUROCK—1899-1900
  E. & F. W. Blaurock
  Blaurock Carriage Co.
  New York, New York
BLEVNEY STEAM—1901
  John C. Blevney
  Newark, New Jersey
  One vehicle built.
BLIMLINE—1898-99
  Sebastian Blimline
  Sinking Springs, Pennsylvania
BLISS STEAM—1901-02
  A. H. Bliss & Son
  Bliss Chainless Automobile Co.
  North Attleboro, Massachusetts
BLISS—1906
  E. W. Bliss & Co.
  Bliss Engineering Co.
  Brooklyn, New York
B.L.M.—1906-07
  B.L.M. Motor Car & Equipment Co.
  B.L.M. Motor Car Co.
  Brooklyn, New York
  (Breese, Lawrence & Moulton)
  "Some assets to be sold" announced April,
  1908.
B.L.M.C.—1907-09
*BLOCK BROS.—1905
  Believed to be misspelling of "Blood Bros."
BLODGETT—1921
  Blodgett Engineering & Tool Co.
  Detroit, Michigan
BLOMSTROM—1897; 1899; 1902-03
  C. H. Blomstrom
  Detroit, Michigan
  One car in '97, one in '99. 25 cars 1902-03.

Became "Queen."
BLOMSTROM—1907-09
  Charles Blomstrom Co.
  Detroit, Michigan (office)
  Adrian, Michigan (factory)
  Later C. H. Blomstrom joined "Front-
  mobile."
  See "Gyroscope"
*BLOMSTROM QUEEN—1902-07
  Known only as "Queen."
  C. H. Blomstrom Motor Co.
  Detroit, Michigan
BLOOD—1900
  Blood & Co.
  Minneapolis, Minnesota
BLOOD—1901-05
  Kalamazoo Cycle Co.
  Kalamazoo, Michigan (1901-02)
  Blood Brothers
  Kalamazoo, Michigan (1902-05)
  Blood Brothers Auto & Machine Co.
  Kalamazoo, Michigan (1905)
  Also known as "Kalamazoo" 1901-02.
BLOOD CYCLECAR—1913
  Blood Bros. Machine Co.
  Kalamazoo, Michigan
  Also built "Cornelian."
BLOOM CYCLECAR—1914
  A. J. Bloom
  Detroit, Michigan
(BLUE)—1910
  See "True Blue"
  True Blue Motor Co.
  Detroit, Michigan
BLUEBIRD (model)—1903
  See "Loomis"
  Loomis Automobile Co.
  Westfield, Connecticut
BLUE BIRD—1910
(BLUE & GOLD)—1910-13
  A Automobile Co.
  Sacramento, California
BLUE STREAK (model) SEMI RACER—1906
  See "Logan"
  Logan Construction Co.

Chillicothe, Ohio
A runabout "Logan."
BLUFFCLIMBER steam—1901
Neustadt-Perry Co.
St. Louis, Missouri
BLUMBERG—1915-22
Blumberg Motor Mfg. Co.
San Antonio and Orange, Texas
B.M.C. SPORTS—1952
British Motor Car Co.
San Francisco, California
English "Singer" chassis with U.S.-built body.
BOBBICAR—1945-47
Bobbi Motor Car Co.
San Diego, California
Purchased 1946 by Dixie Motor Car Co. Birmingham, Alabama. Became Keller Motors Corp. 1947.
*BOB CAT steam—1922-25
See "MacDonald" steam
MacDonald Steam Automotive Corp.
Garfield, Ohio
Name for "MacDonald" roadster.
BOBSY—1962 to date
C. W. Smith Engineering Co.
Medina, Ohio
Small sports and racing cars.
BOCAR—1957-61
Bocar Mfg. Co.
Denver, Colorado
BOGGS—1903
BOHNET steam—1901
George J. Bohnet
Bohnet Motor Car Co.
Lansing, Michigan
Two cars produced.
BOISSELOT—1901
Boisselot Automobile & Special
Gasoline Motor Co.
Jersey City, New Jersey
Built motors to attach to bicycles.
Built one prototype three-wheeler for show purposes.
BOLIDE—1970

Bolide Motor Car Corp.
7 High Street
Huntington, New York
Two prototype cars: A Can-Am type street car with "Ford" power and a two-passenger electric shopper.
*BOLLEE—1904
Bollee is the wrong name for the "Worthington" Bollee by Worthington Automobile Company, New York, New York.
See "Berg" and "Meteor"
BOLTE—1900
Thomas H. Bolte
Kearney, Nebraska
BONNER—1910-11
C. E. Bonner Mfg. Co.
Christman, Illinois
BOON DOCKER dune buggy—1968 to date
Boon Docker Buggies
Bellflower, California
BOOTH—1896
See "Booth-Crouch"
Pierce & Crouch Engine Co.
New Brighton, Pennsylvania
Both names apply to same vehicle built for Dr. Carlos C. Booth, 230 North Phelps Street, Youngstown, Ohio.
BOOTH-CROUCH—1896
Pierce & Crouch Engine Co.
New Brighton, Pennsylvania
One one-cylinder vehicle was built for Dr. Carlos C. Booth.
BORBEIN—1904-10
H. F. Borbein Co. (1904-07)
Borbein Automobile Co. (1907-10)
2108-2110 North 9th St.
St. Louis, Missouri
Complete cars were offered less engine.
Borbein succeeded "Brecht."
BORLAND electric—1910-14
Ideal Electric Vehicle Co.
Borland-Grannis Co. (1912-13)
Chicago, Illinois
American Electric Car Co. (1914)

Saginaw, Michigan
BORNTRAEGER—1932-33
Edward A. Borntraeger
Chicago, Illinois
BORTZ—1904
BOSS steam—1898-1909
Boss Knitting Machine Works
Reading, Pennsylvania
BOSS—1905
Long-Crawford Automobile Co.
Massilon, Ohio
BOSTON electric—1899
Boston Automobile Mfg. Co.
Boston, Massachusetts
BOSTON steam—1900
Boston Automobile Co.
Bar Harbor, Maine
BOSTON—1903
BOSTON-AMESBURY—1902-03
Boston-Amesbury Mfg. Co.
Amesbury, Massachusetts
BOSTON ELECTRIC—1907
Concord Motor Car Co.
Concord, Massachusetts
BOSTON HAYNES-APPERSON—1898
Boston Haynes-Apperson Co.
Boston, Massachusetts
BOSTON HIGHWHEEL—1908
Boston Highwheel Auto Mfg. Co.
179 Claredon St.
Boston, Massachusetts
BOURASSA "6"—1926
Montreal, Quebec, Canada
BOUR-DAVIS—1915-22
Bour-Davis Motor Car Co., 1916-17
Detroit, Michigan
Absorbed with "Frankfort" into Shadbourne Bros., Frankfort, Indiana, 1918. Bour-Davis reorganized as Louisiana Motor Car Co., Shreveport, Louisiana, 1918. 1923 became "Ponder."
BOURNONVILLE—1914
Bournonville Motors Co.
Hoboken, New Jersey
BOURNONVILLE—1922-23

See "Rotary" 1922-23
  The Bournonville Rotary Valve Motor
    Co.
  130 Harrison St.
  Hoboken, New Jersey
Both names apply to same vehicle.
BOWEN—1901
  George B. Bowen
  Buffalo, New York
BOWKER—1900
  Bowker Automobile & Machine Co.
  Portland, Maine
BOWLING GREEN—1911-15
  Bowling Green Motor Car Co.
  Bowling Green, Ohio
BOWMAN—1895
  E. W. Bowman
  Evanston, Illinois
(BOWMAN)—1900
  John & Paul Bowman
  Bellefontaine, Ohio
Advance announcement
BOWMAN—1902
  Bowman Automobile Co.
  New York, New York
BOWMAN—1921-22
  Bowman Motor Car Co.
  Covington, Kentucky
BOYD—1910
  Boyd Steel Spring Co.
  Brooklyn, New York
BOYD FWD—1915
  Neustadt Auto & Supply Co.
  St. Louis, Missouri
Three built for H. M. Boyd.
BOYER—1905
*BOYERSDOFER
  Believed to be "Bayersdofer" misspelled.
  Otto Bayersdofer, Omaha, Nebraska.
BOYNTON—1922
  See "A.B.C."
  Arthur Boynton Corp.
  Albany, New York
Both names apply to same vehicle.
(BRADDON)—1919-?

Braddon Motors Co.
Downers Grove, Illinois
Listed in 1919 Standard Automobile Electric Manual.
BRADFORD—1901
  William H. Bradford
  Lenox, Massachusetts
BRADFORD—1904-05
  Bradford Motor Works
  Bradford, Pennsylvania
An unassembled car for $277.50. Used left-over "Holley" parts.
BRADFORD—1919-20
  Consolidated Motor Car Co.
  Bradford, Connecticut
  Bradford Motor Car Co.
  Haverhill, Massachusetts
BRADFORD CYCLECAR—1914
  Cyclecar Co. of Delaware
  Wilmington, Delaware
BRADLEY—1895
  Wheeler & Co.
  Kansas City, Missouri
BRADLEY—1900
  Hiram T. Bradley
  Oakland, California
BRADLEY—1920-24
  Bradley Motor Car Co.
  Cicero, Illinois
BRAMWELL—1900-02
  Bramwell Motor Co.
  Boston, Massachusetts
One carriage built 1900 to test engine. Succeeded 1904 by Springfield Automobile Co., Springfield, Massachusetts.
BRAMWELL—1904-05
  Springfield Automobile Co.
  Springfield, Massachusetts
Formerly "Springfield"
BRAMWELL-ROBINSON—1898-99
  Bramwell-Robinson Co.
  Hyde Park, Massachusetts
(BRANDON)—1911
  Commercial Motor Car Co.
  Houston, Texas

Report made September, 1911 of a front wheel drive car being manufactured.
BRASIE CYCLECAR—1914-16
  Brasie Motor Truck Co.
  Brasie Motor Car Co.
  2743 Lyndale Ave. South
  Minneapolis, Minnesota
Became Packett Motor Truck Co.
(Reported March, 1916).
BRAUCKS—1898-1927
  George S. Braucks
  St. Louis, Missouri
Seven cars built 1898-1927.
BRAY—1897
  James B. Bray
  Waverly, New York
One unit built for builder's own use.
BRAZIER—1902-04
  H. Bartol Brazier
  Philadelphia, Pennsylvania
Cars built to special order only. Company retired from business 1904. Production in 1904 is questionable.
BRECHT—1901-02
  Brecht Automobile Co.
  1201-1211 Cass Ave.
  St. Louis, Missouri
Retired from automobile business. Business taken over by H. F. Borbein & Co.
BREER—1902
  Carl Breer
  Los Angeles, California
BREESE & LAWRENCE—1905
  Breese & Lawrence
  5 West 16th St.
  New York, New York
  Southhampton, Long Island, New York
  (factory)
Became B.L.M., 1906.
BREEZE—1910
  Jewel Carriage Co.
  Cincinnati, Ohio
  (Carthage, Ohio)
BREMAC EXPERIMENTAL—1932
  Bremac Motor Corp.

Sidney, Ohio
Detroit, Michigan (factory)
To have been shown at N.Y. Auto Show
1933.
BREMAN—1908
BRENENSTUL & CARPENTER—1900
Brenenstul & Carpenter
Wakeman, Ohio
BRENNAN—1905-08
Brennan Motor Co.
Syracuse, New York
BRENNER
(BRENNING)—1900-01
Brenning Brothers
Springfield, Ohio
Designed by C. W. Russell.
BREW-HATCHER—1904-05
The Brew & Hatcher Co.
Cleveland, Ohio
BREWSTER—1915-25
See "Brewster-Knight"
Brewster & Co.
Long Island City, New York
Both names apply to the same vehicle.
BREWSTER—1934-36
Springfield Mfg. Co.
(Brewster & Co.)
Springfield, Massachusetts
Used "Ford" and other chassis. Formerly
body building division of "Rolls-Royce."
BREWSTER-KNIGHT—1915-25
Brewster & Co.
Long Island City, New York
Carriage building firm 1819, importer of
Delaunay-Belleville 1909. Used 4-cylinder
Knight engine. Taken over by Rolls-
Royce 1922. Also called "Brewster."
BRICE—1912
Brice Motor Car Co.
Warrensville, Ohio
(BRIDGEPORT) STEAM—1901
Bridgeport Boiler Works
Bridgeport, Connecticut
BRIDGES—1900
J. Miller Bridges

Carlisle, Pennsylvania
BRIDGES—1918
Bridges Motor Car & Rubber Co.
Fort Worth, Texas
BRIDGES THREE-WHEELER—1936
Dr. Calvin B. Bridges
Pasadena, California
Prototype built only.
BRIGGS—1912
BRIGGS—1933-34
Briggs Manufacturing Co.
Detroit, Michigan
Custom cars
BRIGGS-DETROITER—1911-16
See "Detroiter"
Briggs-Detroiter Co.
Detroit, Michigan
Both names apply to same vehicle.
BRIGGS & STRATTON FLYER—1919-23
Briggs & Stratton Mfg. Co.
Milwaukee, Wisconsin
Formerly "Smith Flyer"
(BRIGHTON)—1896
Pierce-Crouch Engine Co.
New Brighton, Pennsylvania
BRIGHTON "6" (model)—1913-14
See "Palmer-Singer"
Palmer & Singer Mfg. Co.
Long Island City, New York
(BRIGHTWOOD)—1912-14
Brightwood Motor Mfg. Co.
Springfield, Massachusetts
Company built "Orson."
BRILL—1909
Edward Brill
Appleton, Wisconsin
BRINTNELL—1912
Brintnell Motor Car Co. Ltd.
Toronto, Canada
Company also built "Guy" and "Gray-
Dort."
BRISCOE—1914-22
Briscoe Motor Corp.
Jackson, Michigan
See "Earl"

BRISCO FRERES CYCLECAR—1914-15
Argo Motor Co. Inc.
Jackson, Michigan
See "Argo"
BRISTOL—1896
H. S. Bristol
Chicago, Illinois
BRISTOL—1902-03
Bristol Motor Car Co.
Bristol, Connecticut
Absorbed by Corbin Motor Vehicle Co.
BROC ELECTRIC—1909-17
Broc Carriage & Wagon Co.
(Broc Carriage Co.)
The Broc Electric Co.
Cleveland, Ohio
Became American Electric Car Co.,
Saginaw, Michigan, 1914.
(BROCK SIX)—1921
Brock Motors Ltd.
Amhurstburg, Ontario, Canada
BROCKVILLE—1911-15
Brockville Atlas Auto Co. Ltd.
Brockville, Ontario, Canada
BRODHEAD—1910
Brodhead Motor Car Co.
Brodhead, Wisconsin
BROGAN THREE-WHEELER—1946-48
B. & B. Specialty Co.
Rossmoyne, Ohio
BROGANETTE—1946-51
BROOK—1909
Brook Motor Car Co.
Brook, Indiana
BROOK—1920-22
Spacke Machine & Tool Co.
Indianapolis, Indiana
See "Spacke" cyclecar
BROOK-LATTA—1911
Brook-Latta Co.
St. Louis, Missouri
BROOKS—1905-08
Brooks Automobile Co.
Detroit, Michigan
BROOKS—1913

Brooks Motor Wagon Co.
Brooks Mfg. Co.
Saginaw, Michigan
BROOKS STEAM—1923-26
Brooks Steam Motors Inc.
Buffalo, New York
Factory at Stratford, Ontario, Canada.
*BROOMELL SIX-WHEELER—1903
Designed by A. P. Broomell, York,
Pennsylvania. Correct name for vehicle is
"Pullman."
BROTHERTON—1909-10
N. T. Brotherton
Detroit, Michigan
BROWER—1884
Fred G. Brower
610 So. Crouse Ave.
Syracuse, New York
Built one car for his daughter.
(BROWN) STEAM—1884-91
Edwin F. Brown
Chicago, Illinois
Evanston, Illinois
See "Brown's Touring Cart"
(BROWN)—1899
George D. Brown
Fargo, North Dakota
BROWN—1909-10
Brown Cotton Gin Co.
New London, Connecticut
BROWN—1914
Great Western Automobile Co.
Kalamazoo, Michigan
BROWN AIR-COOLED CYCLECAR—1914
Brown Cyclecar Co.
Asbury Park, New Jersey
Announced November, 1913.
BROWN—1913-16
Brown Carriage Co.
Cincinnati, Ohio
Assembled car, used Le Roi engine.
BROWN—1922
*BROWN-BURTT—1904
Company name, not name of vehicle. 1904
company built "Cannon."

Burtt Mfg. Co.
Kalamazoo, Michigan
BROWN STEAM—1905
Brown Brothers
Hutchinson, Kansas
BROWNE—1903
F. O. Browne
Denver, Colorado
BROWNELL—1910
F. A. Brownell Motor Co.
Rochester, New York
Marine engines. Three cars built.
BROWNIE—1915-16
J. O. Carter
Carter Mfg. Co.
Hannibal, Missouri
BROWNIEKAR—1909-11
Omar Motor Co.
Newark, New York
Juvenile car designed by W. H. Birdsall,
chief engineer of the Mora Motor Car Co.
See "Mora"
BROWN'S TOURING CART—1898
Edwin F. Brown
Evanston, Illinois
Built by George W. Lewis.
BRUCE—1956
Don Bruce
BRUNN ELECTRIC—1906-11
Brunn's Carriage Mfg. Co.
Brunn Automobile Co.
Buffalo, New York
BRUNNER—1909-10
Brunner Motor Car Co.
Buffalo, New York
(BRUNSWICK)—1917
Brunswick Motor Car Co.
Newark, New Jersey
Formation of company announced January,
1917.
BRUSH—1907-11
Brush Runabout Co.
Detroit, Michigan
Absorbed by U.S. Motor Co. 1910.
*BRUSS—1907

Believed to be misspelling of "Brush."
BRYAN STEAM—1918-23
Bryan Automobile Mfg. Co.
Bryan Steam Corp.
Bryan Boiler Co.
(Bryan Harvester Co.)
Peru, Indiana
Six cars built.
1913 car built by George A. Bryan while
he was Atcheson Topeka & Santa Fe R.R.
engineer.
BUCKAROO—1957
Cleveland, Ohio
BUCKBOARD—1904
H. S. Moore
Cleveland, Ohio
BUCKBOARD—1960
McDonough Power Equipment Inc.
McDonough, Georgia
Juvenile car. Replica of "Red Bug."
BUCKEYE—1901
Peoples Automobile Mfg. Co.
Cleveland, Ohio
BUCKEYE—1902
Motor Storage & Mfg. Co.
Chillicothe, Ohio
*BUCKEYE—1905-09
Company name, not name of vehicle. Com-
pany produced "Lambert."
See "Lambert"
Buckeye Mfg. Co.
Anderson, Indiana
BUCKEYE—1909-10
Buckeye National Motor Car Co.
Columbus, Ohio
BUCKEYE CYCLECAR—1914
Buckeye Cyclecar Co.
Columbus, Ohio
BUCKEYE GAS BUGGY—1895-1904
J. W. Lambert
Buckeye Mfg. Co.
Anderson, Indiana
BUCKEYE MOTOR WAGON—1911
Buckeye Wagon & Motor Car Co.
Dayton, Ohio

CODE = ROMAN LETTERS: Complete entry. *ITALICS*: Unsubstantiated entry. (PARENTHESES): Production planned, but not realized.

BUCKLES CYCLECAR—1914
T. E. Buckles
Manchester, Oklahoma
BUCKLEY-RIDER—1914-16
Buckley-Rider Tractor Co.
Los Angeles, California
BUCKMOBILE—1903-05
Buckmobile Co. (1903-04)
Utica, New York
Black Diamond Automobile Co., Utica,
New York (1904-05).
BUFFALO—1899
Buffalo Cycle Supply Co.
Buffalo, New York
BUFFALO—1899-1910
Auto-Car & Equipment Co.
Buffalo, New York
Became "Atterbury" (truck).
BUFFALO—1900-03
Buffalo Gasoline Motor Works
Buffalo Auto & Auto-Bi Co.
Buffalo, New York
Became E. R. Thomas Motor Co.
BUFFALO—1900
Buffalo Gasoline Engine Co.
Dewitt & Bradley Streets
Buffalo, New York
Complete except for body, gasoline and
water tanks.
BUFFALO ELECTRIC—1912-15
Buffalo Electric Vehicle Co.
Buffalo, New York
Succeeded Babcock & Van Wagoner.
See "Babcock" electric
BUFFALO—1913-14
Buffalo Co-operative Motor Car Co.
Buffalo, New York
BUFFALO ELECTRIC—1900-06
Buffalo Electric Carriage Co.
Buffalo, New York
Became Babcock Electric Car Co.
BUFFALOMOBILE—1902
Auto-Bi Co.
Buffalo, New York
BUFFALO-ROCHESTER—1900

Buffalo-Rochester Electric Power
and Automobile Co.
Buffalo, New York
BUFFINGTON—1900
*BUFFMAN—1900
Believed to be misspelling of "Buffum."
BUFFUM—1900-07
H. H. Buffum Co.
Abington, Massachusetts
Experiments in 1895. First company to of-
fer 8-cylinder car for sale 1904.
BUFFUM—1914
See "Laconia" cyclecar
H. H. Buffum
Laconia, New Hampshire
Both names apply to the same vehicle.
BUG—1914
BUG—1959-60
See "Crofton Bug"
Crofton Marine Engine Co.
San Diego, California
Both names apply to the same vehicle.
BUGGETTA DUNE BUGGY—1968 to date
Jerry Eisert Enterprises
1245 Logan Ave.
Costa Mesa, California
BUGGYABOUT HIGHWHEELER—1906-08
See "Hatfield"
Hatfield Motor Vehicle Co.
Cortland, New York
Miamisburg, Ohio
BUGGYAUT (model)—1908-10
Charles S. Duryea
Reading, Pennsylvania
BUGGYCAR AIR-COOLED HIGHWHEELER—
1908-09
Buggycar Company
Cincinnati, Ohio
Succeeded Postal Automobile & Engine
Co., Bedford, Indiana.
BUGGYMOBILE (model) HIGHWHEELER—
1907-09
See "Firestone Columbus"
Columbus Buggy Co.
Columbus, Ohio

BUGMOBILE HIGHWHEELER—1907-09
Bugmobile Co. of America
Chicago, Illinois
BUICK—1904 to date
Buick Motor Co.
Flint, Michigan
Buick Motor Co. succeeded Buick Auto
Vim and Power Co. Absorbed Pope-
Robinson 1904 and was the first division of
General Motors Corp. First Buick started
May 20, 1904 and was put on road July 1,
1904. Car was sold to Dr. Hills of Flint,
Michigan July 27, 1904.
BULLARD STEAM—1885-86
James H. Bullard
Springfield, Massachusetts
BULLARD—1904
G. A. Bullard
Marshall, Michigan
BULL MOOSE CYCLECAR—1914
Bull Moose Cutting Automobile Co.
St. Paul, Minnesota
BUNDY STEAMER—1895
W. L. Bundy Co.
Binghamton, New York
One car produced.
BURCH AUTOSLEIGH—1906
Theodore A. Cook
Calicoon, New York
Three built for use by Burch Brothers for
proposed trip to South Pole.
BURDICK—1909-11
Burdick Motor Car Co.
Eau Claire, Wisconsin
BURG—1910-13
L. Burg Carriage Co.
Dallas City, Illinois
BURG WAGON—1901
Burg Wagon Co.
Burlington, Illinois
BURLINGAME—1896
A. Burlingame & Co.
Worcester, Massachusetts
BURMAN—1912
L. C. Erbes Co.

St. Paul, Minnesota
BURNS—1901
BURNS highweeler—1908-11
　　Burns Bros.
　　Havre de Grace, Maryland
*BURR—1897
　　Burr & Co.
　　New York, New York
　　Believed to be body builders only.
BURR—1906
　　E. M. Burr Co.
　　Champaign, Illinois
BURRINGTON—1902- ?
　　B. G. Burrington
　　Holyoke, Massachusetts
BURRO dune buggy—1968 to date
　　Burro Co.
　　1353 Santiego Ave.
　　Santa Ana, California
BURROWS—1908- ?
　　Burrows Motor Car Co.
　　Portland, Maine
　　One car in existence 1969.
BURROWS cyclecar—1914-15
　　Burrows Cyclecar Co.
　　Ripley, New York
*BURTT—1904
　　Burtt Mfg. Co.
　　Kalamazoo, Michigan
　　Believed to be company name, not name of
　　vehicle. See "Cannon"
(BURWELL)—1899
　　George A. Burwell
　　Toledo, Ohio
BUSH—1916-24
　　Bush Motor Co.
　　Chicago, Illinois
　　Mail order sales.
　　Built by Piedmont, Crow-Elkhart and
　　possibly others.
BUSHBURY—1897
BUSHMASTER—1968 to date
　　Bushmaster Co.
　　6615 North Lamar
　　Austin, Texas

BUSHWHACKER dune buggy—1968 to date
　　Fiber-Motive
　　11412 Collins St.
　　North Hollywood, California
BUSSE—1903
　　H. F. Busse
　　St. Louis, Missouri
BUSSER—1915
BUTCHER & GAGE—1903
　　Butcher & Gage
　　Jackson, Michigan
　　Two cars produced.
BUTLER experimental—1901
　　Butler Co.
　　Butler, Pennsylvania
BUTLER HIGH WHEEL—1908
　　Butler Co.
　　Butler, Indiana
BUZMOBILE—1917
BYRIDER electric—1907-09
　　Byrider Electric Co.
　　Cleveland, Ohio
B.Z.T. cyclecar—1914-15
　　B.Z.T. Cyclecar Co.
　　Oswego, New York

C

C.A.C. (model) cyclecar—1914-15
　　See "Coey"
　　Coey Motor Co.
　　2010-12 Wabash Ave.
　　Chicago, Illinois
CADILLAC—1903 to date
　　Cadillac Automobile Co.
　　Detroit, Michigan
　　Formerly Detroit Automobile Co. and
　　Henry Ford Co.
　　Became Cadillac Motor Car Co.
　　Purchased 1909 by General Motors.
　　Became General Motors Division 1917.
(CADY)—1899
　　Frank E. Cady
　　Auburn, New York
CAESAR cyclecar—1914
　　A. R. Marsh

Anderson, Indiana
*CAILLE—1904
　　See "Dubrie-Caille"
　　Caille Bros. Co.
　　Detroit, Michigan
　　Motor company, not name of car.
CALIFORNIA—1900-01
　　California Automobile Co.
　　San Francisco, California
　　Steam and gasoline
　　See "Calimobile" gasoline
CALIFORNIA—1910
　　Auto Vehicle Co.
　　Los Angeles, California
　　Succeeded "Tourist"
CALIFORNIA cyclecar—1914
　　California Cyclecar Co.
　　Los Angeles, California
　　Two-cylinder designed by L. E. French,
　　later "Los Angeles" designer.
CALIFORNIA—1920-21
　　California Motor Car Corp.
　　Los Angeles, California
CALIFORNIA MIDGET—1908
　　See "Cowan"
　　Brice Cowan
　　Los Angeles, California
　　Both names apply to same vehicle.
CALIFORNIAN—1912
　　Californian Motor Car Co.
　　San Francisco, California
CALIFORNIAN—1916
CALIFORNIAN—1945-46
　　Warner Mfg. Co.
　　Glendale, California
CALIFORNIAN—1946
　　Californian Motor Car Co.
　　Los Angeles, California
CALIMOBILE—1902
　　California Automobile Co.
　　San Francisco, California
　　See "California"
CALL—1911
　　Call Motor Car Co.
　　New York, New York

CODE = ROMAN LETTERS: Complete entry. *ITALICS:* Unsubstantiated entry. (PARENTHESES): Production planned, but not realized.

CALORIC—1901-03
    Chicago Moto-Cycle Co.
    Chicago Caloric Engine Co.
    Chicago, Illinois
    Three-cylinder hydro-carbon car. Could be run as hot-air engine or with gasoline or kerosene as fuel.
CALVERT—1927
    Calvert Motor Associates
    Baltimore, Maryland
CAMARO (model)—1966 to date
    See "Chevrolet"
    General Motors Corp.
    Chevrolet Division
    Detroit, Michigan
CAMERON—1902-19
    United Motors Corp.
    Pawtucket, Rhode Island (1902-04)
    James Brown Mach. Co.
    Pawtucket, Rhode Island (1904-05)
    Cameron Car Co.
    Brockton, Massachusetts (1907-08)
    Cameron Car Co.
    Beverly, Massachusetts (1908-12)
    Six-cylinder models at New London, Connecticut from 1909.
    Cameron Motor Co.
    West Haven, Connecticut (1912-13)
    Cameron Motor Co.
    New Haven, Connecticut (1914-16)
    Cameron Motors Co.
    Norwalk, Connecticut (1917-18)
    Cameron Motors Co.
    Stamford, Connecticut (1919)
CAMERON AIR-COOLED EXPERIMENTAL—1922
    F. F. Cameron in plant of
        F. H. Bultman Co.
    Cleveland, Ohio
CAMERON STEAMER EXPERIMENTAL—1899
    E. S. Cameron
    Brockton, Massachusetts
    Three-cylinder radial engine 1899-1900.
CAMPBELL—1917-20
    Campbell Motor Car Co.
    Kingston, New York

Formerly "Emerson" (1916-17).
CANADA (model)—1911-12
    See "Galt"
    Canadian Motors Ltd.
    Galt, Ontario, Canada
CANADIAN—1921
    Colonial Motors Ltd.
    Windsor, Ontario, Canada
CANADIAN BABY CAR CYCLECAR—1914
    Montreal, Canada
CANADIAN BRISCOE—1916
    Canadian Briscoe Co.
    Montreal, Canada
CANADIAN MOTORS—1900
    Canadian Motors Ltd.
    Toronto, Ontario, Canada
CANADIAN QUEEN—1909
    Canadian Queen Cycle & Motor Works
    Toronto, Canada
CANDA—1900-02
    Canda Mfg. Co.
    11 Pine St.
    New York, New York
    Carteret, New Jersey
    Remaining cars sold August 1902 by George W. Condon, Newark, New Jersey.
CANNON STEAM RACER—1901-04
    George C. Cannon
    Cambridge, Massachusetts
CANNON—1902-06
    Burtt Mfg. Co.
    Burtt Manufacturing Co.
    Kalamazoo, Michigan
CANNON—1912
    Cannon Motor Car Co.
    Des Moines, Iowa
CANNON—1955
    Cannon Engineering Co.
    North Hollywood, California
CANNONBALL—1921
    Cannonball Motor Car Co.
    Texico, New Mexico
CANTON—1906
CANTONO ELECTRIC—1903-07
    Cantono Electric Tractor Co.

    Marion, New Jersey
    New York, New York
CAPITOL STEAM—1902
    Capitol Automobile Co.
    Washington, D.C.
CAPITOL ELECTRIC—1912-14
    Washington Motor Vehicle Co.
    Washington, D.C.
    Also built "Washington" truck.
CAPITOL—1914
    Denver, Colorado
CAPITOL—1919-20
    Capitol Motors Corp.
    Fall River, Massachusetts
CAPS—1902-05
    Caps Brothers Manufacturing Co.
    Kansas City, Missouri
    See "Kansas City"
CARBON—1902
CARCOVAN—1948
CAR DELUXE—1906-09
    See "Deluxe"
    Deluxe Motor Car Co.
    Detroit, Michigan (1906)
    Toledo, Ohio (1906-09)
    Both names apply to same vehicle.
CARDWAY—1923-25
    Fred Cardway
    New York, New York
    Six built.
CARETTE—1913
    Carette Mfg. Co.
    Chicago, Illinois
CAREY—1906
    Carey Motor Co.
    208-214 W. 124th St.
    New York, New York
    Five-cylinder Balzer rotary engine.
CARGY—1904-05
    Cargy Mfg. Co. (1904)
    Cargy Motor Car Co. (1905)
    Fairmount, Indiana
CARHART STEAM—1871
    Dr. J. W. Carhart and H. S. Carhart
    Racine, Wisconsin

CARHARTT—1910-12
Carhartt Automobile Corp.
Detroit, Michigan
(CARL ELECTRIC)—1913-14
Carl Electric Vehicle Co.
Toledo, Ohio
Formerly Chicago Electric Car Co.
CARLEY—1900-02
Carley Iron Works
Colfax, Washington
CARLISLE ELECTRIC—1899
Carlisle Mfg. Co.
Chicago, Illinois
CARLISLE—1900
CAR-NATION CYCLECAR—1913-15
American Voiturette Co.
Detroit, Michigan
Succeeded Keeton Motor Co.
Became Car-Nation Motor Car Co. 1914.
CARNEGIE—1915-16
Carnegie Engineering Corp.
New York, New York
Kalamazoo, Michigan (factory)
CARPENTER ELECTRIC—1895
H. H. Carpenter
Denver, Colorado
CARPENTER—1910
Carpenter Motor Vehicle Co.
Brooklyn, New York
CARQUEVILLE-McDONALD STEAM—1930
CARR CYCLECAR—1914
W. G. Carr
Tacoma, Washington
CARRIAGE MOBILE—1907
Summit Carriage Mobile Co.
Waterloo, Iowa
See "Summit" and "Farmer-Mobile."
CARRICO—1909
Carrico Motor Car Co.
214 Elm St.
Cincinnati, Ohio
A few buggy-type chassis utilizing a two-cylinder air-cooled engine were built. Company did not build bodies.
CARRICO-DE TAMBLE—1896

Speed Changing Pulley Co.
Indianapolis, Indiana
CARRISON—1908
*CARRM—1921-23
Carrm Convertible Body Co.
New York, New York
Company name, not name of vehicle. Company built bodies.
CARROL—1909
Compressed Air Power Co.
East Boston, Massachusetts
CARROLL—1908-13
John Carroll
Philadelphia, Pennsylvania
CARROLL—1920-22
Carroll Automobile Co.
Lorraine, Ohio
(CARSON)—1920
Carson Motor Co.
Detroit, Michigan
CARTER—1899-1904
Byron J. Carter Motor Car Co.
Jackson, Michigan
CARTER STEAM—1901
Michigan Automobile Co.
Grand Rapids, Michigan
CARTER—1907-09
Carter Motor Car Corp.
Washington, D.C.
CARTER—1916
(CARTER) STEAM—1919-20
Richard Carter Co.
Gulfport, Mississippi
CARTERCAR—1906-16
Motorcar Company (1906-08)
Detroit, Michigan
Cartercar Company (1908-16)
Pontiac, Michigan
Absorbed by General Motors.
(CARTERMOBILE)—1921-22
Carter Motor Car Co.
Hyattsville, Maryland
CARTHAGE—1914-15
Carthage Motor Car Co.
Carthage, Ohio

CARTONE—1905
CASADAY—1904-05
W. L. Casaday Mfg. Co.
South Bend, Indiana
CASE—1907-09
Howard Case & Co.
Lethbridge, Alberta, Canada
CASE—1911-27
J. I. Case Threshing Machine Co.
Racine, Wisconsin
Formerly "Pierce-Racine."
See "Jay Eye See"
CASELER ELECTRIC—1901
CASEY—1914
F. A. Casey Co.
Billerica, Massachusetts
CASWELL STEAM—1901
M. J. Caswell
Sandusky, Ohio
CATARACT—1904
Cataract Machine & Automobile Co.
Niagara Falls, New York
CATO—1907-?
J. L. Cato
San Francisco, California
Six-cylinder air-cooled model built 1910 and four-cylinder water-cooled car reportedly built in 1912. Production data on these cars is uncertain.
CATROW—1900
Herbert Catrow
Miamisburg, Ohio
CAVAC—1910-11
Small Motor Car Co.
Plymouth, Michigan
CAVALIER—circa 1911
CAVALIER—1926
Cavalier Motor Associates
Mt. Vernon, New York
(Baltimore, Maryland)
CAWARD-DART—1924
(CAWLEY)—1917
C. A. Cawley
Salt Lake, Utah
C.B.—1917

CODE = ROMAN LETTERS: Complete entry. *ITALICS:* Unsubstantiated entry. (PARENTHESES): Production planned, but not realized.

Carter Bros. Motor Co.
Hyattsville, Maryland
C. de L—1913
C. de L Engineering Works
Nutley, New Jersey
Passenger car and truck chassis.
CECO CYCLECAR—1914-15
Continental Engineering Co.
Minneapolis, Minnesota
Chicago, Illinois
CELFOR—1916
Buchanan, Michigan
CELT—1927
CENTAUR—1902-03
Centaur Motor Vehicle Co. (1902)
Centaur Motor Co. (1903)
Buffalo, New York
Became Towanda Motor Vehicle Co.
Gasoline and electric vehicles.
CENTRAL—1903
Central Motor Car Co.
Indianapolis, Indiana
CENTRAL—1904
Central Machine & Engineering Co.
Detroit, Michigan
CENTRAL STEAM—1905
Connersville, Indiana
CENTRAL STEAM—1905
Central Automobile Co.
Pittsfield, Massachusetts
Rotary steam engine.
CENTRAL—1953
St. Louis, Missouri
CENTRAL GRAYHOUND (model)—1905
Eight-cylinder race car built for Central
Automobile Co., New York, New York. On-
ly one built.
See "Buffum"
H. H. Buffum Co.
Abington, Massachusetts
CENTURY—1901
Century Mfg. Co.
St. Louis, Missouri
CENTURY ELECTRIC—1900-04
Century Motor Vehicle Co.
Syracuse, New York

Formerly "Barnes" electric (1899).
Also built gasoline and steam cars.
Bankrupt June, 1904 and sold out.
CENTURY ELECTRIC—1911-15
Century Electric Vehicle Co.
Detroit, Michigan (1913-15)
Also known as Century Electric Motor Car
Co. (1911-13).
Reported bankrupt June, 1915.
CENTURY—1927
CENTURY STEAM (model)—1901-02
See "Century" electric
Century Motor Vehicle Co.
Syracuse, New York
CENTURY STEAMER—1906
Century Auto Power Co.
East Orange, New Jersey
Built to order.
CENTURY TOURIST—1901
Ward-Leonard Electric Co.
Bronxville, New York
Also built "Knickerbocker" 1901-03.
CENTURY TOURIST (model)—1902-03
Century Motor Vehicle Co.
Syracuse, New York
See "Century" electric
C.F.—1907-09
Cornish-Friedberg Motor Car Co.
Chicago, Illinois
Sometimes listed as "Cornish-Friedberg."
C.G.P.—1915
Dr. Chas. G. Percival
New York, New York
One car produced.
C.G.V. (AMERICAN)—1902-03
Charron, Girardot & Voigt
Rome, New York
French car built by Rome Locomotive
Works in Rome, New York. Sold by Smith
& Mabley, New York, New York. Seven
cars built.
CHADWICK—1904-16
Fairmount Engineering Co. (1904-05)
Fairmount Engineering Works (1905-07)
Chadwick Engineering Works (1907-08)

Philadelphia, Pennsylvania
Chadwick Engineering Works (1908-16)
Pottstown, Pennsylvania
CHADWICK—1960
CHALFANT—1906-12
Chalfant Gasoline Motor Car Co.
(Chalfant Motor Car Co.)
Chalfant, Pennsylvania
CHALMERS—1910-23
Chalmers-Detroit Motor Co.
Chalmers Motor Co.
Detroit, Michigan
Formerly "Chalmers-Detroit"
Merged with Maxwell Motor Co. 1919.
Became "Chrysler"
CHALMERS-DETROIT—1908-10
E. R. Thomas-Detroit Co.
Detroit, Michigan
Became Chalmers-Detroit Motor Co. July,
1908.
Became "Chalmers" 1910.
CHAMPION ELECTRIC—1899
CHAMPION AIR-COOLED—1909-10
Famous Mfg. Co.
East Chicago, Indiana
CHAMPION—1909-11
Champion Motor Car Co.
Milwaukee, Wisconsin (1909-10)
CHAMPION ELECTRIC—1912-13
Champion Electric Vehicle Co.
New York, New York
CHAMPION—1913
Champion Motor Car Co.
Minneapolis, Minnesota
CHAMPION—1916-17
Champion Auto Equipment Co.
Wabash, Indiana (factory)
Chicago, Illinois (office)
Small 4-cylinder car. Tires inflatable while
in motion.
CHAMPION—1919-25
Direct Drive Motor Co.
Champion Motors Corp.
Philadelphia, Pennsylvania
Factory at Gloucester, New Jersey.

*ASTERISK: Error corrected from previous list. See introduction to this section for complete code.

CHANDLER—1913-29
 Chandler Motor Car Co.
 Cleveland, Ohio
1919 Cleveland Automobile Co. was subsidiary. Company name changed to Chandler-Cleveland Motors Corp. 1925. Sale of plant to "Hupmobile" announced November 30, 1928.
CHAPMAN ELECTRIC—1891-1905
 Edward D. Chapman
 (Chapman & Sons Mfg. Co.)
 Stoughton, Massachusetts
CHAPMAN ELECTRIC—1899-1901
 William H. Chapman
 163 Kennebec St.
 Portland, Maine
Main production was electric car chassis components.
Became Belknap Motor Co., 1900
CHAPMAN STEAMER—1905
 Odell M. Chapman
 Stonington, Connecticut
CHARGER (model)—1965 to date
 See "Dodge"
 Chrysler Corp.
 Detroit, Michigan
CHARLES TOWN-ABOUT ELECTRIC—1958-59
 Stinson Aircraft Tool & Engineering Corp.
 San Diego, California
CHARRON, GIRARDOT & VOIGT—1902
 American-built with "Quinby" body.
 Seven cars built.
 See "C.G.V."
 Charron, Girardot & Voigt
 (Rome Locomotive Works)
 Rome, New York
Both names apply to same vehicle.
CHARTER—1903-04
 James A. Charter
 Chicago, Illinois
Gas & water vapor engine.
CHARTER OAK—1916-17
 Eastern Motors Inc.

 (New Britain, Connecticut)
 Hartford, Connecticut
One car built with $30,000 authorized by Allen Shelden. Fred A. Law, chief engineer. Company in receivership August 1917.
CHASE—1907-12
 Chase Motor Truck Co.
 Syracuse, New York
Passenger cars 1907-12, trucks to 1917.
CHATHAM—1907-08
 Chatham Motor Car Co. Ltd.
 Chatham, Ontario, Canada
CHAUTAUQUA CYCLECAR—1913-14
 Chautauqua Cyclecar Co.
 Jamestown, New York
CHAUTAUQUA ELECTRIC—1919-20
 Chautauqua Electric Mfg. Co.
 Falconer, New York
CHAUTAUQUA STEAMER—1911
 Chautauqua Motor Co.
 Dunkirk, New York
CHECKER—1922 to date
 Checker Motors Corp.
 Kalamazoo, Michigan
Produced taxicabs only before 1959.
*CHELSEA—1901-04
 Chelsea Mfg. Co.
 Chelsea, Michigan
Company name of "Welch Tourist" manufacturer, not name of vehicle.
CHELSEA CYCLECAR—1914
 Chelsea Mfg. Co.
 Chelsea, Michigan
Standard tread.
CHEVELLE (model)—1963 to date
 See "Chevrolet"
 General Motors Corp.
 Chevrolet Division
 Detroit, Michigan
CHEVROLET—circa 1909
CHEVROLET—1913 to date
 Chevrolet Motor Co.
 Detroit, Michigan
First car introduced 1913 at New York

Auto Show. Absorbed Little Motor Car Co. 1913. Also Republic Motor Car Co. Detroit, Michigan. Absorbed into General Motors 1918.
CHEVY II (model)—1961 to date
 See "Chevrolet"
 General Motors Corp.
 Chevrolet Division
 Detroit, Michigan
(CHICAGO) ELECTRIC—1899
 Chicago Electric Vehicle
 and Transportation Co.
 Chicago, Illinois
CHICAGO ELECTRIC—1899-1901
 Chicago Electric Vehicle Co.
 Faribault, Minnesota
 Chicago, Illinois
CHICAGO STEAM—1905-06
 Chicago Automobile Mfg. Co.
 4212 State St.
 Chicago, Illinois
Company was in business from 1904 to 1907 but only built a 1906 model.
CHICAGO—1906
 Chicago Pneumatic Tool Co.
 Chicago, Illinois
Built 50 highwheelers. See "C.P.T." Both names apply to same vehicle.
*CHICAGO—1905-07
Company name of Chicago Recording Scale Co. Chicago, Illinois not name of vehicle.
 See "Apollo"
*CHICAGO—1907
 Chicago Coach & Carriage Co.
 Chicago, Illinois
Company name of "Duer" manufacturer.
CHICAGO ELECTRIC—1912-16
 Chicago Electric Motor Car Co.
 Walker Electric Vehicle Co. (1915-16)
 35th & Morgan Sts.
 Chicago, Illinois
Frederick J. Newman, designer. Bought by Anderson Electric Car Co. 1916.
CHICAGO CYCLECAR—1914

Chicago Cyclecar Co.
Chicago, Illinois
CHICAGOAN—1952-54
Triplex Industries Inc.
Blue Island, Illinois
Used "Willys" engine.
CHICAGO LIGHT 6—1917
Pan American Motors Corp.
Chicago, Illinois
Became "Pan American"
CHICAGO MOTOR BUGGY
HIGHWHEELER—1908
Chicago Motor Buggy Co.
171 La Salle St.
Chicago, Illinois
(CHIEF)—1908
Chief Mfg. Co.
624 Ellicott Square
Buffalo, New York
CHIEF—1947
CHIVILLE CYCLECAR—1914
Gerald D. Chiville
Chicago, Illinois
CHOATE—1896
P. C. Choate
Portland, Maine
CHRISTIE—1904-16
Christie Iron Works
New York, New York (1904-05)
1906 became Christie Direct Action Motor
Car Co., New York, New York.
Became Front Drive Motor Co., Hoboken,
New Jersey 1907.
CHRISTMAN—1901-02
Chas. G. Christman
Los Gatos, California
Christman Automobile Co.
(Christman Motor Carriage Co.)
San Jose, California
Became Golden State Automobile Co. 1902.
Christman continued with mufflers.
*CHRISTOPHER—1908-10
Christopher Bros.
Chicago, Illinois
Company name, not name of vehicle. Com-

pany built "Triumph."
CHRYSLER—1924 to date
Chrysler Motor Corp.
Detroit, Michigan
Absorbed Maxwell Motor Corp. 1925,
Dodge Bros. Motor Car Co. 1928.
See "DeSoto," "Dodge" and "Plymouth."
CHRYSLER 6—1921
Chrysler Motor Division
Willys Corp.
Elizabeth, New Jersey
(CHURCH)—1901
Church Automobile Co.
Pittsburgh, Pennsylvania
CHURCH PNEUMATIC—1913-14
Church Motor Car Co.
Chicago, Illinois
A simple car without clutch or valves.
CHURCH-FIELD ELECTRIC—1911-15
Church-Field Motor Co.
Sibley, Michigan
CINCINNATI STEAM—1901-03
Cincinnati Automobile Co.
Cincinnati, Ohio
*CINCO—1911
Believed to be "Cino" misspelled.
CINO—1900-13
Haberer & Co.
Gest & Summer Sts.
Cincinnati, Ohio
CIRA-HERMANN—1914
CLA-HOLME—1922
Cla-Holme Motor Car Sales Co.
15th E. Larimer Sts.
Denver, Colorado
One car produced.
CLAPP—1898-1900
Henry W. Clapp
New Haven, Connecticut (1898-99)
Clapp Motor Vehicle Co.
Jersey City, New Jersey (1900)
CLARK STEAM—1899-1911
Edward S. Clark
242 Freeport St.
Boston, Massachusetts

Steam Boiler Company founded 1895.
Gasoline commercial vehicles 1911.
CLARK ELECTRIC—1903
A. F. Clark & Company
Philadelphia, Pennsylvania
Became Electric Vehicle Equipment Co.
(CLARK)—1901-03
Clark Manufacturing Co.
Moline, Illinois
CLARK—1905-06
Clark Motor Car Co.
E. C. Clark Motor Co.
Jackson, Michigan
CLARK ELECTRIC—1908
Allen & Clark Co.
Toledo, Ohio
CLARK—1910-12
Clark Motor Car Co.
Shelbyville, Indiana
Anderson, Indiana
Absorbed by "Meteor."
CLARK HIGHWHEELER—1910-12
Clark & Co.
Lansing, Michigan
CLARK—1911-12
Clark Motor Car Co.
Louisville, Kentucky
*CLARK-CARTER—1909-11
Clark-Carter Automobile Co.
Jackson, Michigan
Believed to be company name, not name of
vehicle. Company built "Cutting."
CLARK HATFIELD HIGHWHEELER 1908-09
Clark-Hatfield Automobile Co.
Oshkosh, Wisconsin
CLARK STEAM—1900-01
Clark & Co.
Cleveland, Ohio
CLARK STEAM—1901-05
William G. Clark
Cambridge, Massachusetts
CLARKE—1907
Clarke Automobile & Launch Co.
Jacksonville, Florida
CLARKMOBILE—1903-06

Clarkmobile Company
Lansing, Michigan
Succeeded by Deere-Clark Automobile Co. January, 1906. No known production in 1905.
CLASSIC—1916-17
Classic Motor Car Corp.
Chicago, Illinois
CLASSIC—1920-21
Classic Motor Car Co.
Lake Geneva, Wisconsin
Reincorporation of 1916-17 "Classic."
(CLEAR & DUNHAM)—1900
Clear & Dunham
Cleveland, Ohio
CLEARMONT—1903
CLEARMONT STEAMER—1922
Clearmont Steamer Inc.
New York, New York
Allen-Powers Co. Inc.
New York City distributor
Same as "Coats Steamer."
CLEAVER—1903
Cleaver Motor Vehicle Co.
Fond-du-Lac, Wisconsin
CLEBURNE—1913
Cleburne Motor Car Mfg. Co.
Austin, Texas (office)
Cleburne, Texas (factory)
CLEGG STEAMER—1885
John and Thomas Clegg
Memphis, Michigan
CLEMENT—1903
A. Clement Cycle Motor & Light
    Carriage Co.
Hartford, Connecticut
Builder's father was the famous French automotive pioneer.
CLENDON—1908
CLEVELAND THREE-WHEELER—1900
American Bicycle Co.
Westfield, Massachusetts
CLEVELAND ELECTRIC—1900
Cleveland Machine Screw Co.
Cleveland, Ohio

(CLEVELAND)—1902
Hansen Automobile Co.
Cleveland, Ohio
Became General Automobile & Manufacturing Co. 1902.
CLEVELAND—1903-04
Cleveland Automobile Co.
Cleveland, Ohio
CLEVELAND—1905-09
Cleveland Motor Car Co.
Cleveland, Ohio (1905-08)
New York, New York (1908-09)
Not connected with "Cleveland" 1903-04.
CLEVELAND—1904-09
Cleveland Motor Carriage Co.
Clcvcland, Ohio
Merchant & Evans Co.
Philadelphia, Pennsylvania
Used "Garford" chassis.
CLEVELAND ELECTRIC—1909
Cleveland Electric Vehicle Co.
Cleveland, Ohio
Former Cuyahoga Motor Car Co.
CLEVELAND CYCLECAR—1914
Cleveland Cyclecar Co.
Cleveland, Ohio
Discontinued January, 1915.
CLEVELAND—1919-26
Cleveland Automobile Co.
Cleveland, Ohio
Subsidiary of Chandler Motor Car Co.
Succeeded by Chandler-Cleveland Motor Corp., December, 1925.
CLIMAX AIR-COOLED—1908-09
Climax Electric Works
New Salem, Massachusetts
Became T.&F. Cyclecar Co.
CLIMBER—1918-24
Climber Motor Corp.
Detroit, Michigan
Little Rock, Arkansas
Company started at Poteau, Oklahoma. 1924 became New Climber Co.
CLINTON CYCLECAR—1914
Clinton Motor Car Co.

Clinton, Ontario, Canada
Later advertised as "American" cyclecar.
CLINTON STEAM—1902
Clinton Machine & Dusting Works
Clinton, Massachusetts
CLINTON E. WOODS ELECTRIC—1899-1902
Clinton E. Woods & Co.
Chicago, Illinois
Became Woods-Waring & Co. 1901 and Woods Motor Vehicle Co. 1902.
(CLIPPER)—1902
Clipper Autocar Co.
Grand Rapids, Michigan
CLIPPER (model)—1941-47; 1953-57
Packard Motor Car Co.
Studebaker-Packard Corp.
Detroit, Michigan
CLODHOPPER DUNE BUGGY—1968 to date
Fiber Fab
2365 Lafayette St.
Santa Clara, California
CLOSE—1902
Close Cycle Co.
Olean, New York
CLOUGH—1869
Enos M. Clough
Lakeport, New Hampshire
One car produced. Also called "Fairy Queen."
CLOUGHLEY—1895-1903
Robt. H. Cloughley
Cloughley Motor Vehicle Co. (1901)
Parsons, Kansas
Early steam and gasoline cars. First patents, 1891. Production began 1902, ended 1903. Plans announced to resume 1904.
CLOYD—1911
Cloyd Auto Co.
Nashville, Tennessee
CLUB CAR—1910-11
Club Car Co. of America
New York, New York
Merchant & Evans Co.
Philadelphia, Pennsylvania
Shareholders got 25% discount toward

purchase of the car.

CLYMER—1908
    Durable Motor Car Co.
    St. Louis, Missouri

COATES TRI-CAR—1913
    Coates Commercial Car Co.
    Goshen, New York

COATES-GOSHEN—1909-10
    Coates-Goshen Automobile Co.
    Goshen, New York
    Joseph S. Coates built experimental four-cylinder car 1903.
    Showed "Mercedes" type car at 1909 New York Auto Show. Reported bankrupt October, 1911. Less than 20 cars built.

COATS STEAMER—1921-23
    Coats Machine Co.
    Indianapolis, Indiana
    Coats Steam Car Co.
    1675 South High St.
    Columbus, Ohio

COBRA—1962-69
    Based on "Ford," "A.C."
    See "Shelby"
    Shelby-American Inc.
    Venice, California

COBRA (model)—1969 to date
    See "Ford"
    Ford Motor Co.
    Dearborn, Michigan

(COBURN)—1911
    Coburn Motor Car Co.
    Norfolk, Virginia

COEY ELECTRIC—1900-02
    C. A. Coey & Co.
    177 La Salle St.
    Chicago, Illinois

COEY BEAR CYCLECAR—1914
    Coey Motor Co.
    Chicago, Illinois
    Stripped racing cyclecar offered in quantity sale.

COEY FLYER—1912-16
    Coey-Mitchell Automobile Co.
    Coey Motor Co.
    Chicago, Illinois

COEY JR. (model) CYCLECAR—1914
    See "Coey"
    Coey Motor & Co.
    Chicago, Illinois

COFFEE—1902
    R. W. Coffee & Sons
    Richmond, Virginia
    Built gas car for Charles E. Miller.
    Transmission gear builders 1903.

COFFIN STEAMER—1898-99
    Howard E. Coffin
    Ann Arbor, Michigan
    One car built.

(COGSWELL)—1911
    Cogswell Motor Car Co.
    Grand Rapids, Michigan

COLBURN—1907-11
    Colburn Automobile Co.
    15th & Colfax Ave.
    Denver, Colorado

COLBY—1910-14
    Colby Motor Co.
    Mason City, Iowa
    Absorbed by Standard Motor Co., Minneapolis, Minnesota with Nevada Mfg. Co.
    Formerly "Midland."

COLE—1903-04
    Cole & Son
    Rockford, Illinois

COLE—1909-25
    Cole Motor Car Co.
    Indianapolis, Indiana
    Succeeded Cole Carriage Co.

COLE MOTOR BUGGY HIGHWHEELER—1909
    Cole Carriage Co.
    Indianapolis, Indiana
    Became Cole Motor Car Co. Formerly Gates-Osborne Carriage Co.

COLEMAN—1933-35
    Coleman Motors Corp.
    Littleton, Colorado
    Front wheel drive

COLE-PACKARD—1920

COLE & WOOP ELECTRIC—1902

Cole & Woop
    New York, New York
    One miniature electric car built for Jay Gould, Jr.

COLLIER—1916-20
    Paynesville, Ohio

(COLLINET)—1922
    Collinet Motor Co.
    Garden City, New York

COLLINGS—1913-15
    Collings Carriage Co.
    Camden, New Jersey

COLLINS ELECTRIC—1900
    P. J. Collins
    Collins Electric Vehicle Co.
    Scranton, Pennsylvania

COLLINS STEAM—1902
    Hartford Motor Machine Co.
    Hartford, Connecticut

COLLINS—1920
    Collins Motors Inc.
    Huntington, Long Island, New York

COLLINS 8—1921-23
    Collins Motor Car Co.
    Detroit, Michigan

*COLLMAN—1928
    Denver, Colorado
    Believed to be misspelling of "Coleman,"
    Littleton, Colorado 1933.

COLLY—1901

COLONIAL STEAM—1899-1900
    See "Kent's Pacemaker"
    Colonial Automobile Co.
    Boston, Massachusetts
    Both names apply to same vehicle.

COLONIAL ELECTRIC—1911-12
    Colonial Electric Car Co.
    Detroit, Michigan

COLONIAL—1916-18
    Colonial Car Co.
    Detroit, Michigan
    Colonial Automobile Co.
    Indianapolis, Indiana

COLONIAL—1921
    Mechanical Development Corp.

San Francisco, California
Straight 8 engine. One car produced.
COLONIAL—1920-21
Walden W. Shaw Livery Co.
Chicago, Illinois
Became "Shaw," "Ambassador," later "Hertz."
COLONIAL—1921-23
Colonial Motors Corp.
Woburn and Boston, Massachusetts
COLONIAL 6—1922
Colonial Motors
Detroit, Michigan
Windsor, Ontario, Canada
COLONIAL ELECTRIC—1902
Colonial Carriage Co.
Cleveland, Ohio
COLT—1907
Colt Runabout Co.
Yonkers, New York
Incorporated June 3, 1907.
Bankrupt December, 1907.
COLT AIR-COOLED—1958
Colt Mfg. Co.
Milwaukee, Wisconsin
COLUMBIA ELECTRIC—1892-95
Columbia Perambulator Co.
Chicago, Illinois
COLUMBIA—1897-1913
Pope Manufacturing Co.
Hartford, Connecticut (1897-99)
Columbia Automobile Co.
Hartford, Connecticut (1899)
Columbia & Electric Vehicle Co.
Hartford, Connecticut (1899)
Electric Vehicle Co.
Hartford, Connecticut and
    New York City (1899-1902)
Electric Vehicle Co.
Hartford, Connecticut (1899-1909)
Columbia Motor Car Co.
Hartford, Connecticut (1909-13)
Gasoline and electric vehicles to 1910.
COLUMBIA STEAM—1900
Columbia Motor & Mfg. Co.

Washington, D.C.
Baltimore, Maryland
*COLUMBIA—1900-07
Believed to be company name of Columbia Electric Co. Not name of vehicle.
See "Leader"
COLUMBIA ELECTRIC—1906
Columbia Electric Co.
Indianapolis, Indiana
COLUMBIA CYCLECAR—1914
American Cyclecar Co.
Seattle, Washington
COLUMBIA—1916-24
Columbia Motor Car Co.
Detroit, Michigan
COLUMBIA ELECTRIC—1914
Columbia Electric Vehicle Co.
Detroit, Michigan
COLUMBIA HIWHEEL—1909
Columbia Carriage Co.
Hamilton, Ohio
COLUMBIA-KNIGHT—1911-12
Columbia Motor Car Co.
Hartford, Connecticut
COLUMBIA-MAGNETIC—1907-08
Electric Vehicle Co.
Hartford, Connecticut
COLUMBIA WAGONETTE (model)—1901
Electric Vehicle Co.
Hartford, Connecticut
An eleven-passenger station-wagon-type "Columbia."
COLUMBIAN ELECTRIC—1914-15
Columbian Electric Vehicle Co.
Detroit, Michigan
(COLUMBUS)—1903-04
Columbus Carriage & Harness Co.
Columbus, Ohio
COLUMBUS ELECTRIC—1903-07
Columbus Buggy Co.
Columbus, Ohio
See "Firestone-Columbus"
Also built gasoline car.
COMET RACER—1904
Marion Motor Car Co.

Indianapolis, Indiana
COMET—1906-09
Hall Auto Repair Co.
San Francisco, California
COMET—1907-09
Comet Motor Co. Ltd.
Montreal, Quebec, Canada
COMET CYCLECAR—1913-14
Comet Cyclecar Co.
Indianapolis, Indiana
COMET—1916-23
Comet Automobile Co.
Rockford, Illinois
Racine, Wisconsin
Decatur, Illinois
Shown at Chicago, Illinois January, 1917.
Received large foreign order June, 1920.
COMET ELECTRIC—1921
COMET THREE-WHEELER—1948
General Developing Co.
Ridgewood, Long Island,
    New York
Car weighed 175 pounds.
COMET—1951
Comet Mfg. Co.
Sacramento, California
COMET (model)—1960 to date
See "Mercury"
Ford Motor Co.
Lincoln-Mercury Division
Dearborn, Michigan
COMMANDER—1921-22
Commander Motors Corp.
Milwaukee, Wisconsin
Designed by Otto Ogren.
Successor to Hugo W. Ogren Motors Corp.
Chicago, Illinois
COMMERCE HIGHWHEELER—1906-09
American Machine Mfg. Co.
Detroit, Michigan
COMMERCE—1922
Commerce Motor Car Co.
Detroit, Michigan
Model 20 Deluxe Sedan with four-cylinder engine offered by this truck company.

COMMERCIAL ELECTRIC—1903-05
    Commercial Motor Vehicle Co.
    108 St. Antoine Street
    Detroit, Michigan
    Company also built the "Quadray" truck.
COMMERCIAL STEAM—1904-09
    Commercial Motor Vehicle Co.
    Jersey City, New Jersey
COMMODORE—1921
    Commodore Motors Corp.
    New York, New York
COMMONWEALTH—1903
    Coburn & Company
    Boston, Massachusetts
COMMONWEALTH—1917-22
    Commonwealth Motors Co.
    Joliet, Illinois
    Succeeded "Partin-Palmer"
COMPOUND—1904-06
    Eisenhuth Horseless Vehicle Co.
    Middletown, Connecticut
COMPTON STEAM
*CONCORD—1907
    Believed to be company name of Concord
    Motor Car Co. Boston, Massachusetts. Not
    name of car.
    See "Boston Electric"
CONCORD—1914
    Connersville, Indiana
*CONDA
    Believed to be "Canda" misspelled.
CON-FERR COUGAR DUNE BUGGY—1964 to
    date
        Con-Ferr Mfg. Co.
        Burbank, California
CONGER—1902
    Conger Mfg. Co.
    Groton, New York
CONKLIN ELECTRIC TRICYCLE—1895
    Oliver F. Conklin
    Dayton, Ohio
CONLEY CYCLECAR—1914
    G. F. Conley
    Chicago, Illinois
*CONNECTICUT—1908

Believed to be company name of Con-
necticut Automobile Works New Haven,
Connecticut. Not name of car.
See "Fulton"
CONNOLLY STEAM—1901
    C. J. Connolly
    Rochester, New York
CONOVER—1907-10
    Conover Motor Car Co.
    Paterson, New Jersey
    Built by Watson Machine Co., Paterson.
CONRAD—1900-03
    Conrad Motor Carriage Co.
    Buffalo, New York
    Gasoline and steam cars.
CONSOLIDATED—1904-06
    Consolidated Motor Co.
    New York, New York
    See "Moyea"
CONSOLIDATED—1934
    Consolidated Motors
    Los Angeles, California
CONSTANTI ELECTRIC—1906
CONTINENTAL—1906-09
    University Automobile Co.
    Continental Automobile Mfg. Co.
    New Haven, Connecticut
CONTINENTAL—1909-16
    Indiana Motor & Mfg. Co.
    Martindale & Millikin Co.
    Franklin, Indiana
    Continental Automobile Co.
    Knightstown, Indiana
CONTINENTAL—1911-13
    Continental Motor Co.
    Buffalo, New York
CONTINENTAL CYCLECAR—1913-14
    Continental Engine Mfg. Co.
    Minneapolis, Minnesota
    Chicago, Illinois
CONTINENTAL—1933-34
    Continental Automobile Co.
    Grand Rapids, Michigan
    See "De Vaux"
CONTINENTAL (model)—1940-48; 1958 to

date
See "Lincoln"
    Lincoln Motor Division
    Continental Motor Division (1955-57)
    Ford Motor Co.
    Dearborn and Detroit, Michigan
A make for 1956-57 model years.
CONTINENTAL ROADSTER—1908
    Continental Motor Car Co.
    Chicago, Illinois
CON VAIRCAR—1947
    Consolidated Aviation Co.
    San Diego, California
    Flying auto. Prototype only built.
COOK—1896
    James M. Cook
    Mt. Gilead, Michigan
    Built by Thurman & Silvius, Indianapolis,
    Indiana.
COOK—1900
    C. E. Cook
    Delaware, Ohio
*COOK—1906
    Three vehicles were built by Theodore A.
    Cook, Calicoon, New York. These are
    believed to be the same as "Burch" auto-
    sleigh.
*COOK—1908-09
    Cook Motor Vehicle Co.
    St. Louis, Missouri
    Company name, not name of vehicle. Com-
    pany built "Simplo" highwheeler.
COOK & GOWDY—1895
    Cook & Gowdy Co.
    Chicago, Illinois
*COOK-SIMPLE—1908
    Error in spelling.
    See "Cook" (1908-09).
    See "Simplo" highwheeler.
COOLEY—1900
    R. L. Cooley
    Batavia, New York
COOLEY—1902
    Cooley Cycloidal Engine Co.
    Allston, Massachusetts

Built to demonstrate Cooley Instantaneously Reversible Rotary Steam Engine.

COOPER—1901

COOT—1964 to date
 Carl Enos, Jr. & Robert Mauser
 San Francisco, California
 Became Rand Tron, San Francisco, California December, 1968.
 Jeep-type all-terrain vehicle.

COPELAND STEAM THREE-WHEELER—
 1884; 1887
 Northrup Manufacturing Company
 Camden, New Jersey
 Designed by Lucius D. Copeland who built Steam Bicycle about 1884.

COPELAND & BROWN—1887
 Philadelphia, Pennsylvania
 See "Copeland" Camden, New Jersey

COPELAND & BROW—1887
 See "Copeland," Camden, New Jersey.

COPLEY MINOR—1907

COPPAGE—1920

(COPPOCK)—1906-10
 Coppock Motor Car Co.
 Marion, Indiana
 Decatur, Indiana

CORBIN—1903-12
 Corbin Motor Vehicle Co.
 New Britain, Connecticut
 Division of American Hardware Co.
 Retired from business early 1912.

CORBITT—1907-15
 J. W. Corbitt
 Corbitt Automobile Co.
 Henderson, North Carolina

CORD—1929-32; 1935-37
 Auburn Automobile Co.
 Auburn, Indiana
 Front wheel drive.
 Division of Cord Corp.

CORD—1964-70
 Cord Automobile Co.
 Tulsa, Oklahoma (1964-67)
 Elfman Motors Inc.

Philadelphia, Pennsylvania (1968)
S.A.M. Co. Inc.
Manford, Oklahoma (1969-70)

CORINTHIAN—1921-22
 Corinthian Motors Inc.
 Philadelphia, Pennsylvania
 Company formed by Charles B. Lewis, formerly with Lewis Motor Truck Co. San Francisco, California.

CORLISS—1909-10
 Corliss Motor Co.
 (Corliss Steel Co.)
 Corliss, Wisconsin

CORNELIAN CYCLECAR—1914-15
 Cornelian Co.
 Kalamazoo, Michigan
 Blood Bros. Machine Co.
 Kalamazoo, Michigan
 Allegan, Michigan
 Discontinued after building 100 cars.

CORNISH-FRIEDBERG—1907-09
 See "C.F."
 Cornish-Friedberg Motor Car Co.
 Chicago, Illinois
 Both names apply to the same vehicle.

CORONA CAR—1922

CORREJA—1908-14
 Vandewater & Co.
 Ilion, New Jersey
 Correja Automobile Co.
 Elizabeth, New Jersey
 Correja Motor Car Co.
 New York, New York

CORT—1914

CORTEZ—1947-49
 North American Motors Inc.

CORVAIR (model)—1960-69
 Rear engine model of "Chevrolet."
 Last car built May 14, 1969.
 See "Chevrolet"
 Chevrolet Motor Co.
 Detroit, Michigan

CORVETTE (model)—1953 to date
 See "Chevrolet"
 General Motors Corp.

Chevrolet Division
Detroit, Michigan

(CORWEG)—1905
 Corweg Shuttle Valve Motor Co.
 Atlantic City, New Jersey

CORWEG—1921
 Corweg Shuttle Valve Motors Co.
 Atlantic City, New Jersey
 Engine builder only at this time.

CORWIN—1905-07
 Believed to be company name of Corwin Manufacturing Co., Peabody, Massachusetts, not name of vehicle.
 See "Gas-Au-Lec"

CORY—1907
 Albany-Cory Automobile Co.
 Albany, Indiana

COSCOB—1900

COSHOCTON—1913
 Coshocton Motor Car Co.
 Coshocton, Ohio

COSMOPOLITAN HIGHWHEELER—1907-10
 D. W. Haydock Auto Mfg. Co.
 St. Louis, Missouri
 See "Haydock"

COTAY—1920-21
 Coffyn-Taylor Motors Co.
 New York, New York

COTTA STEAM—1901-03
 Cotta Automobile Co.
 Lanark, Illinois (1901-02)
 Rockford, Illinois (1902-03)
 Four-wheel drive vehicle. Later transmissions were manufactured under this name.

(COTTON)—1901
 I. F. Cotton
 Topeka, Kansas

COUGAR (model)—1966 to date
 See "Mercury"
 Lincoln-Mercury Division
 Ford Motor Co.
 Dearborn, Michigan

COUNTRY CLUB—1903-04
 Country Club Car Co.
 Boston, Massachusetts

CODE = ROMAN LETTERS: Complete entry. *ITALICS*: Unsubstantiated entry. (PARENTHESES): Production planned, but not realized.

COURIER—1903-04
Sandusky Automobile Co.
1122 Camp St.
Sandusky, Ohio
COURIER—1909-12
Courier Car Co.
Dayton, Ohio
Taken with "Stoddard-Dayton" into U.S.
Motors Co. 1910.
COURIER—1923-24
Courier Motors Co.
Sandusky, Ohio
Formerly named "Maibohm" taken over by
Arrow Motors.
COVEL—1916
Benton Harbor, Michigan
COVEL ELECTRIC—1912
COVERT—1901-07
B. V. Covert & Co.
(Covert Motor Vehicle Co. 1904)
Lockport, New York
Later built transmissions.
Steam car also 1901.
COVERT MOTORETTE—1902
See "Covert"
B. V. Covert & Co.
Lockport, New York
Both names apply to same vehicle.
COWAN—1908
Brice Cowan
Los Angeles, California
Boy's home-built car.
*COWLES-McDOWELL—1915
Cowles-McDowell Pneumobile Co.
Chicago, Illinois
Company name, not name of vehicle. Company built "Pneumobile."
COX MOTORBUGGY
COYOTE—1909-10
Redondo Beach Car Works
Redondo Beach, California
C-P-T—1906
See "Chicago"
Chicago Pneumatic Tool Co.
Chicago, Illinois

Both names apply to same vehicle.
(CRAIG-HUNT)—1920
Craig Hunt Motor Co.
Indianapolis, Indiana
City prevented erection of plant November 1920. In receivership for $125.50 debt.
CRAIG-TOLEDO—1906-07
Craig-Toledo Motor Co.
Toledo, Ohio
CRANE—1908-15
Crane Motor Car Co.
Bayonne, New Jersey
CRANE & BREED ELECTRIC—1902
Crane & Breed Mfg. Co.
Cincinnati, Ohio
CRANE & BREED—1910-20
Crane & Breed Mfg. Co.
Cincinnati, Ohio
CRANE-SIMPLEX—1915-24
Simplex Automobile Co.
New Brunswick, New Jersey
Formerly "Simplex." Absorbed Crane Motor Car Co. Purchased 1919 by Mercer Automobile Co. Marketed with "Locomobile" and "Mercer" by Hare's Motors Inc.
CRAWFORD—1901
J. B. Crawford
Sioux City, Iowa
CRAWFORD—1905-24
Crawford Automobile Co.
Hagerstown, Maryland
Founded by Robert S. Crawford. Company bought by M. P. Moller 1922. Became M. P. Moller Motor Car Co. 1923.
See "Dagmar"
CRESCENT—1900
Crescent Automobile Mfg. Co.
Wilmington, Delaware
CRESCENT TRICYCLE—1900
Western Wheel Works
Chicago, Illinois
CRESCENT—1900-05
Crescent Automobile Co.
New York, New York
CRESCENT—1905

Crescent Automobile & Supply Co.
St. Louis, Missouri
CRESCENT—1907-08
Crescent Motor Car Co.
Meldrum & Champlain Sts.
Detroit, Michigan
Increased capital $75,000 to produce touring car "Reliance" and runabout "Marvel." Reportedly bought plant in Goshen, Indiana 1908.
CRESCENT—1914-15
Crescent Motor Co.
Cincinnati, Ohio
Formerly "Ohio" (1909-13). Liquidated 1915 by Ralph E. Northway.
CRESCENT—1923
CRESCENT ROYAL (model)—1914
See "Crescent"
Crescent Motor Co.
Cincinnati, Ohio
CRESSON—1915
Cresson-Morris Co.
Philadelphia, Pennsylvania
Former "Crowther Cyclecar"
CREST—1901
Early name for "Crestmobile."
Crest Mfg. Co.
Cambridge, Massachusetts
CREST—1907
Hub Automobile Exchange
Boston, Massachusetts
CRESTMOBILE—1902-05
Crest Mfg. Co.
Cambridge (Cambridgeport)
Massachusetts (1901-04)
Dorchester, Massachusetts (1905)
Formerly made parts. Absorbed with "Moyer" into Alden-Sampson Mfg. Co.
C.R.G.—1908
Charles R. Greuter
Wilkes-Barre, Pennsylvania
Formerly chief engineer for Matheson.
CRICKET CYCLECAR—1914
Cricket Cyclecar Co.
Detroit, Michigan

Reported absorbed by Motor Products Co., 1914.

CRITERION—1911-12
Criterion Motor Co.
Pittsburgh, Pennsylvania
Kent, Ohio

CROCK—1909

CROCK—1920
Crock Motor Car Co.
Cuyahoga Falls, Ohio

CROCKETT—1917
J. B. Crockett Co.
4244 Whitehall St.
New York, New York
For export only.

CROESUS—1906-07
Croesus Motor Car Co. (1906)
W. L. Bell (1907)
Kansas City, Missouri
Company charged with fraud after two cars built.

CROESUS JR. (model)—1906-08
See "Croesus"
Croesus Motor Car Co.
W. L. Bell
Kansas City, Missouri
The runabout model of "Croesus."

CROFTON BUG—1959-61
Crofton Marine Engineering Co.
San Diego, California
About 200 cars sold. Retained mfg. rights to "Crosley" engine.

CROMPTON STEAM—1901-03
Crompton Motor Carriage Works
Worcester, Massachusetts

CRONHOLM & STENWALL—1895
Cronholm & Stenwall Co.
Chicago, Illinois

CROSLEY—1939-52
Crosley Motors Inc.
Cincinnati, Ohio
Marion, Indiana
Affiliated with Crosley Radio Corp.

CROSMOBILE—1948-53
Crosley Motors Inc.

Marion, Indiana
For export only (export model of "Crosley.")

CROSS—1895
E. D. Cook
Chicago, Illinois

CROSS STEAM—1897
A. T. Cross
Providence, Rhode Island

CROSS EXPERIMENTAL—1924
Harry Cross
Indianapolis, Indiana
Four cars built.

CROSSLAND—1919-23
Crossland Steamotive Car Co.
Peoria, Illinois
Crossland Steam Motive Corp.
Chicago, Illinois

CROSSLEY—1913-14
Albert D. Crossley
Hartford, Connecticut
Crossley formerly with "Pope." No connection with English car of same name.

*CROTHER-DURYEA—1915
Believed to be "Crowther-Duryea" misspelled.

CROUCH STEAM—1897-1900
W. Lee Crouch
New Brighton, Pennsylvania
Crouch Automobile Mfg. and Transport Company.
Baltimore, Maryland

*CROUGH-STEAMER—1900
Believed to be "Crouch" steam misspelled.

CROW—1911
Crow Motor Car Co.
Elkhart, Indiana
Became "Crow-Elkhart"

CROW—1915-18
Canadian Crow Motor Co. Ltd.
Mt. Bridges, Ontario, Canada

CROWDUS ELECTRIC—1900-02
Crowdus Automobile Co.
Chicago, Illinois

*CROWDVS—1902

Believed to be "Crowdus" electric misspelled.

CROWE 30—1911
W. A. Crowe
Detroit, Michigan
Crowe Motor Car Co.
Grand Rapids, Michigan

CROW-ELKHART—1911-23
Crow Motor Car Co.
Crow-Elkhart Motor Co.
Elkhart, Indiana
Became Century Motors Corp. 1923.

CROWN—1905-06
Detroit Auto Vehicle Co.
Detroit & Romeo, Michigan
Organized August 1904. First car put on road April, 1905.

CROWN HIGHWHEELER—1908-10
Crown Motor Vehicle Co.
Amesbury, Massachusetts
Boston, Massachusetts
See "Graves & Congdon"

CROWN 30—1913-14
Buckeye Mfg. Co.
Anderson, Indiana
Crown Motor Car Co.
Louisville, Kentucky
New Albany, Indiana
Formerly "Jonz," became "Hercules."
See "Dixie-Flyer"

CROWN CYCLECAR—1914
Crown Cyclecar Co.
Amesbury, Massachusetts
Dates and information not clear on this make.

CROWN—1915
Crown Automobile Mfg. Co.
Kalamazoo, Michigan

CROWN—1953

CROWN-MAGNETIC—1921-22
Owen-Magnetic Motor Car Co.
Wilkes-Barre, Pennsylvania

CROWTHER CYCLECAR—1914
Cresson-Morris Co.
Philadelphia, Pennsylvania

CROWTHER—1915
  Became "Crowther-Duryea"
  Crowther Motor Car Co.
  Rochester, New York
CROWTHER-DURYEA—1916-17
  Crowther-Duryea Motor Co.
  Rochester, New York
  Greece, New York
  In hands of receiver early 1917. Plant
  reported sold July, 1918.
CROXTON—1911-15
  Croxton Motors Co.
  Cleveland, Ohio
  Washington, Pennsylvania
  Formerly Croxton-Keeton Motor Co.
  Became Universal Motor Car Co.
CROXTON-KEETON—1909-10
  Croxton-Keeton Motor Co.
  Massillon, Ohio
  Succeeded Jewel Motor Car Co. Became
  Croxton Motors Co. 1911.
  See "Keeton" and "Croxton."
CRUICKSHANK STEAM—1896-98
  Cruickshank Steam Engine Works
  Providence, Rhode Island
CRUISER—1917-19
  Cruiser Motor Co.
  Madison, Wisconsin
  Joliet, Illinois
  Convertible touring-camping car.
CRUSADER—1915-16
  Crusader Motor Car Co.
  Joliet, Illinois
CRUSADER—1923
  Crusader Motors Corp.
  York, Pennsylvania
C.R.V. EXPERIMENTAL—1964
  Centaur Research Vehicle Company
  Detroit, Michigan
CRYSTAL CITY CYCLECAR—1914
  Charles Troll and
    Charles Manning
  Corning, New York
CUB CYCLECAR—1914
  Szekely Cyclecar Co.

Richmond, Virginia
CUBSTER—1949
  Osborn Wheel Co.
  Doylestown, Pennsylvania
  Home-assembled 6.6 hp car. Available as
  chassis only.
CUCMOBILE—1907
CULL—1901
  A. B. Cull
  St. Louis, Missouri
CULLMAN STEAM—1902
  Cullman Wheel Works
  Chicago, Illinois
CULVER HIGHWHEELER—1905-09
  Culver Practical Automobile Co. (1905)
  Practical Automobile Co. (1906)
  446-447 Mercantile Block
  Aurora, Illinois
CULVER—1917
  Culver Mfg. Co.
  Culver City, California
  One-cylinder juvenile car.
*CUMMINGS-MONITOR—1916
  Company name, not name of vehicle.
  See "Monitor"
    Cummings-Monitor Co.
    Columbus, Ohio
CUNNINGHAM—1908-36
  James Cunningham Son & Co. Inc.
  15 Canal Street
  Rochester, New York
  Later turned to electronics mfg.
CUNNINGHAM—1951-55
  Cunningham Sports Cars
  B. S. Cunningham Co.
  Palm Beach, Florida
CUNNINGHAM STEAM—1900-07
  Cunningham Engineering Co.
  Massachusetts Steam Wagon Co.
  Boston, Massachusetts
CURRAN STEAM—1923
  Curran Steam Commercial Vehicle Co.
  New York, New York
(CURTIN)—1905-06
  Curtin-Williams Automobile Co.

Columbus, Ohio
CURTIS STEAM—1866
  Frank Curtis
  Newburyport, Massachusetts
  Built a steam carriage and sold it on the
  installment plan. Had to repossess it.
CURTIS—1912-13
  Pittsburgh Machine Tool Co.
  Braddock, Pennsylvania
CURTIS—1919-22
  Curtis Motor Car Co.
  Little Rock, Arkansas
  30 cars built.
CURTISS-WRIGHT—1948
  Curtiss-Wright Industries
  El Monte, California
  The Curtiss-Wright who also operated an
  aircraft school. (No connection with
  Curtiss-Wright Aviation).
CURTISS-WRIGHT AIR CAR—1959
  Curtiss-Wright
  (South Bend Division)
  South Bend, Indiana
CUSHMAN—1948 to date
  Cushman Motor Works Inc.
  Lincoln, Nebraska
  Package cars and scooters.
CUSTER—1920-46
  The Custer Specialty Company
  Dayton, Ohio
  Experimental electric 1898. Gasoline, elec-
  tric, handicapped & amusement park cars.
CUSTER-BUCKBOARD—1959-60
  Custer Specialty Co.
  Dayton, Ohio
CUTTING—1909-13
  Cutting Motor Co.
  C.V.I. Motor Car Co.
  Jackson, Michigan
  Formerly "C.V.I."
  Absorbed by Clark-Carter Automobile Co.
  1909.
  Absorbed by Cutting Motor Car Co. 1912.
  Property bought by Wm. M. Thompson
  1913.

CUYAHOGA ELECTRIC—1909
    Cuyahoga Motor Car Co.
    Cleveland, Ohio
C.V.I.—1907-08
    C.V.I. Motor Car Co.
    Jackson, Michigan
    Became "Cutting"
C.W.B.—1927-30
    C.W.B. Sports Automobiles
    New Haven, Connecticut
CYCLECAR—1914
    Cycle Car Co.
    Wilmington, Delaware
CYCLEPLANE CYCLECAR—1914-15
    Cycleplane Co.
    Westerly, Rhode Island
*CYCLEPLANT CYCLECAR—1914
    The Cycleplane Co.
    Westerly, Rhode Island
    Believed to be "Cycleplane" misspelled.
(CYCLOMOBILE)—1920-21
    Cyclomobile Mfg. Co.
    Toledo, Ohio
CYCLONE—1921
    Cyclone Motors Corp.
    Greenville, South Carolina
CYCLONE ROAD RUNNER DUNE BUGGY—
1968 to date
    Road Runner Division
    Burbank, California
CYCLOP—1910
    L. Porter Smith & Bros.
    Indianapolis, Indiana
CYCLOPS CYCLECAR—1914
    Cyclops Cyclecar Co.
    Indianapolis, Indiana
*CYCLOPLANE—1914
    Believed to be "Cycleplane" misspelled.

D

D.A.C. AIR-COOLED—1922-23
    Detroit Air-Cooled Car Co.
    Detroit, Michigan
    Designed by W. J. Doughty.
DAGMAR—1922-27

Crawford Automobile Co.
Hagerstown, Maryland
1923 M. P. Moller Motor Co.
See "Crawford"
DAIMLER—1895-1902
    Daimler Mfg. Co.
    Long Island City, New York
    Most lists carry this make to 1907. Name
changed to "Mercedes" 1902.
DALEY GASOLINE VEHICLE—1895
    M. H. Daley
    Charles City, Iowa
    Entered Chicago Times-Herald Race.
DALEY STEAM—1900
    W. A. Lang Mfg. Co.
    Barre, Vermont
DALLAS—1931
DALTON—1911-12
    Dalton Motor Car Co.
    Flint, Michigan
    Formerly "Dalton-Whiting."
    Only three made.
D'ANDREA—1956
    Gilbert D'Andrea
    New York, New York
DANDURAN & JENNINGS—1895
    J. H. Danduran and William Jennings
    (and Father)
    Montreal, Canada
    Car made 1895. Presented to Chateau De
Romera Museum.
DANIELS—1912
    Daniels Motor Car Co.
    East St. Louis, Missouri
DANIELS—1915-24
    Daniels Motor Car Co.
    Reading, Pennsylvania
    Daniels bought by Levene Motor Co.;
planned move to Philadelphia 1924.
DAN PATCH—1910-12
    M. W. Savage Co.
    Minneapolis, Minnesota
    Mail order car. Became "Savage."
DARBY—1909-10
    Darby Motor Car Co.

St. Louis, Missouri
DARCO—1918-20
DARLING—1901-02
    Beardsley & Hubbs Mfg. Co.
    Massillon, Ohio
    Shelby, Ohio
1902 became Shelby Motor Car Co. Three
cars at Chicago show 1902.
DARLING—1917
    Darling Motor Car Co.
    Dayton, Ohio
DARLING STEAM—1899
    F. A. Darling
    Franklin, Massachusetts
DARRIN—1946
    Howard A. Darrin Automotive Design
    Los Angeles, California
    Five-passenger convertible. One prototype
only.
DARRIN (model) SLIDING DOOR ROADSTER—
1953-54
    Kaiser-Frazer Corporation
    Willow Run, Michigan
    Built or commissioned building of sixty-
two 1953 prototypes.
    Kaiser-Willys Corp.
    Toledo, Ohio (1954)
    Built 435 production vehicles at Jackson,
Michigan.
    See "Kaiser"
    Several 1954 models customized by Darrin
Studios with hard tops and/or V-8 engines
up to 1958.
DARROW—1902-04
    Stuart Darrow
    Decker & Hinckley Co.
    Owego, New York
DART—1909-11
    Dart Engineering Co.
    New York, New York
DART—1914-15
    Automatic Registering Co.
    Jamestown, New York
    (Pittsfield, Massachusetts)
DART CYCLECAR—1914

Dart Cyclecar Co.
Toronto, Ontario, Canada
Basically a "Scripps-Booth."
DART (model)—1960 to date
See "Dodge"
Chrysler Corp.
Dodge Division
Detroit, Michigan
DARTMOBILE—1922
Dart Mfg. Co.
Waterloo, Iowa
Lone passenger car effort by successful truck company.
DAVENPORT—1902-03
Davenport Cycle Works
Davenport, Iowa
Plant reported closed October, 1902 under landlord's attachment.
DAVENPORT STEAM—1902-03
Davenport Mfg. Co.
Minneapolis, Minnesota
DAVIDS—1902
DA VINCI—1922-25
James Scripps Booth
Indianapolis, Indiana
DAVIS—1895
Davis Gasoline Engine Co.
Waterloo, Iowa
DAVIS—1908-31
George Davis Co.
George W. Davis Motor Car Co.
Richmond, Indiana and
    Baltimore, Maryland
Continued as maker of power lawn mowers.
DAVIS CYCLECAR—1913-15
Davis Cyclecar Co.
510 Free Press Bldg.
Detroit, Michigan
Used Spacke engine.
DAVIS (TOTEM)—1922
Davis Car Co.
Seattle, Washington
DAVIS—1924
Davis Dry Dock Co. Ltd.
Kingston, Ontario, Canada

DAVIS THREE-WHEELER—1947-49
Davis Motor Car Co.
8055 Woodley Ave.
Van Nuys, California
17 prototypes built.
DAWSON STEAM—1901
Dawson Manufacturing Co.
Basic City, Pennsylvania
DAWSON—1904
J. H. Dawson Machinery Mfg. Co.
Chicago, Illinois
DAY STEAM—1902
Day Automobile Co.
Kansas City, Missouri
DAYTON STEAM—1900-01
Dayton Motor Vehicle Co.
Dayton, Ohio
Succeeded Warner Mfg. Co.
Steam boilers, pumps, engines and running gear manufacturers.
*DAYTON—1904-09
Believed to be name of Dayton Motor Car Company, Dayton, Ohio. Not name of vehicle.
DAYTON HIGHWHEELER—1909
See "Reliable-Dayton"
W. O. Dayton Automobile Co.
Chicago, Illinois
Both names apply to same vehicle.
DAYTON ELECTRIC—1911-16
Dayton Electric Car Co.
Dayton, Ohio
In receivers' hands December, 1914.
DAYTON CYCLECAR—1913-14
William Dayton Cyclecar Co.
Joliet, Illinois
Company formed by William O. Dayton of "Reliable-Dayton."
DAYTON—1915
Dayton Motor Car Co.
Joliet, Illinois
Formerly "Dayton" cyclecar.
DAYTONA—1956
Randall Products
Hampton, New Hampshire

DAY UTILITY—1911-15
Day Automobile Co.
Detroit, Michigan
DEACO
DEAL—1908-11
Deal Buggy Co.
Deal Motor Vehicle Co.
Jonesville, Michigan
Became Deal Motor Car Co. 1911.
DEARBORN—1910-11
J&M Motor Car Co.
Lawrenceburg, Indiana
DEBONNAIRE—1955
DECATUR—1896
Decatur Gasoline Engine Co.
Decatur, Illinois
DECATUR—1909-11
Decatur Motor Car Co.
Decatur, Indiana
DECKER—1902-03
Decker Automatic Telephone
    Exchange Co.
Decker Automobile Co.
Owego, New York
Three cars built.
DECROSS CYCLECAR—1914-15
Decross Cyclecar Co.
Cincinnati, Ohio
DE DION-BOUTON—1900-04
De Dion Motorette Co.
Brooklyn, New York
*DEEMASTER—1923
Believed to be "Deemster" misspelled.
DEEMSTER—1923
Deemster Corp. of America
Hazleton, Pennsylvania
DEERE—1906-07
Deere-Clark Motor Car Co.
Moline, Illinois
Started as John Deere Plow Works.
Formerly "Deere-Clark."
DEERE—1916
DEERE-CLARK—1906
Deere-Clark Motor Car Co.
Moline, Illinois

Reorganized as Midland Motor Car Co.
1908. Became "Deere."
Absorbed Clarkmobile Co.
See "Midland" and "Clarkmobile."

DEERING—1902
R. S. Deering
Chicago, Illinois

DEERING MAGNETIC—1918-19
Magnetic Motors Corp.
Chicago, Illinois

DEFIANCE—1909
Miller Machine Co.
Defiance, Ohio

DE FREET—1895
T. M. DeFreet
Indianapolis, Indiana

DE GROOT—1902
George F. De Groot
Morristown, New Jersey

DE HAVEN—1904
De Haven Brothers
Chicago. Illinois

DE KALB—1908
Auburn, Indiana

DE KALB—1915
DeKalb Motor Car Co.
St. Louis, Missouri

DEKALB—1915
DeKalb Mfg. Co.
Ft. Wayne, Indiana

DE LA BUIRE
E. Lillie
New York, New York

DE LA VERGNE—1895
De La Vergne Refrigerating
    Machine Co.
New York, New York
Hincks & Johnson Co.
Bridgeport, Connecticut

DELCAR—1947-49
American Motors Inc.
Troy, New York
Small delivery car. At least one station wagon, possibly more built.

DE LEON—1905-06
Archer & Co.

New York, New York
Exhibited at 1905 New York Auto Show.

DELLING STEAM—1923-29
Delling Steam Motor Co.
West Collingswood, New Jersey

DEL MAR—1949
Del Mar Motors Inc.
San Diego, California
Prototypes only.

DELMORE THREE-WHEELER—1923
Delmore Motors Corp.
New York, New York

DE LONG—1920
Industrial Machine Co.
New York, New York
DeLong Motor Car Co.
Pittsburgh, Pennsylvania

DE LOURA—1902-03
H. G. DeLoura
Ft. Madison, Iowa

DELTA—1923-25
Delling and Moulta
Brooklyn, New York

DELTAL—1913-14
E. H. Delling
Brooklyn, New York
Racing car.

DELUXE—1906-09
Deluxe Motor Car Co.
Detroit, Michigan (1906)

(DELUXE)—1910
Deluxe Motor Car Co.
Cleveland, Ohio
Organized to manufacture a two-wheel automobile.

DE MARS ELECTRIC—1902; 1905-06
De Mars Electric Vehicle Co.
Cleveland, Ohio

*DE MATS—1905
Believed to be a misspelling of "De Mars."

*DE MONT—1910
Believed to be "De Mot" (DeMotcar).

DE MOOY—1900-04
De Mooy Bros.
Cleveland, Ohio

DEMOT—1909-12

DEMOTCAR Company
45 State Street
Detroit, Michigan

DEMOTOR—1923

DE MOTTE—1904
De Motte Motor Car Co.
Philadelphia and
    Valley Forge, Pennsylvania

DENEGRE—1920

DENISON THREE-WHEELER—1898-1903
Denison Motor Carriage Co. (1898)
Denison Motor Wagon Co. (1899)
Denison Electrical Engineering Co.
    (1900-02)
Julian F. Denison (1903)
New York, New York (offices)
New Haven, Connecticut (factory)
Associated with Tinkham Cycle Co.
See "Tinkham"

DE PALMA—1905-11; 1916
Ralph De Palma
New York, New York
Detroit, Michigan
Special order cars only.

DEPPE—1917-20
Deppe Motors Corp.
New York, New York
New York Air Brake Co.
Watertown, New York

DE RAIN—1908-11
De Rain Motor Co. (1908)
Simplex Mfg. Co. (1909)
De Rain Motor Co. (1910-11)
Cleveland, Ohio

DERBY—1924-26
Derby Motor Cars Ltd.
Saskatoon, Saskatchewan, Canada

DERR STEAM—1926-35
American Steam Auto Co.
West Newton, Massachusetts

DESBERON—1901-04
Desberon Motor Car Co.
New Rochelle, New York

DE SCHAUM HIGHWHEELER—1908-09
De Schaum Motor Syndicates Co.
Buffalo, New York

CODE = ROMAN LETTERS: Complete entry. *ITALICS:* Unsubstantiated entry. (PARENTHESES): Production planned, but not realized.

See "Seven Little Buffalos"
(DE SCHAUM-HORNELL)—1909-10
    DeSchaum-Hornell Automobile Co.
    Hornell Motor Car Co.
    Hornell, New York
    Wyandotte, Michigan
    See "DeSchaum"
DESERTER BEACH BUGGY—1968 to date
    Dearborn Automobile Co.
    Marblehead, Massachusetts
DESERT-FLYER—1907-08
    Nevada Motor Car Co.
    Council Bluffs, Iowa
Company was never incorporated, only one car built. Promoted car was 1906 "Pope-Toledo." Also a 1906 "Stearns."
DE SHAW AIR-COOLED—1906-10
    Charles De Shaw
    Brooklyn, New York
    De Shaw Motor Co. 1907-10
    Evergreen, Long Island, New York
(DESMARIS)—1904-05
    P. Desmaris & Sons Motor Co.
    Holyoke, Massachusetts
DESMOINES—1902
    Des Moines Automobile Co.
    Des Moines, Iowa
(DESMOND)—1906
    Desmond Automobile Co.
    Chicago, Illinois
Factory to have been built at Oklahoma City, Oklahoma.
DESOTO—1913-14
    De Soto Motor Car Co.
    Auburn, Indiana
    Fort Wayne, Indiana
    Built Motorette and larger cars.
DE SOTO—1929-61
    De Soto Motor Corp. and
    De Soto Division
    Chrysler Motors Corp.
    Detroit, Michigan
DE SOTO—1931-61
    De Soto Motor Corp. of
      Canada Ltd.

    Windsor, Ontario, Canada
DE SOTO MOTORETTE—1914-15
    De Soto Motor Car Co.
    Ft. Wayne, Indiana
DE TAMBLE—1906-14
    Speed Changing Pulley Co.
    Anderson, Indiana (1908-09)
    De Tamble Motors Co.
    Anderson, Indiana (1910-14)
DETROIT—1899-1902
    Detroit Automobile Co.
    Detroit, Michigan
DETROIT—1904
    Wheeler Mfg. Co.
    Detroit, Michigan
DETROIT—1904-07
    Detroit Auto Vehicle Co.
    Detroit, Michigan
DETROIT—1905
    Detroit Automobile Mfg. Co.
    177 Larned St.
    Detroit, Michigan
    Became "La Petite"
DETROIT CYCLECAR—1914
    Detroit Cycle Car Co.
    Detroit, Michigan
Moved to Saginaw, changed name to "Saginaw."
DETROIT—1916
    Detroit Chassis Co.
    Detroit, Michigan
    After 1916 made chassis for "Gem."
DETROIT AIR COOLED—1922-23
    See "D.A.C."
    Detroit Air Cooled Car Co.
    Detroit, Michigan
    Both names apply to the same vehicle.
DETROIT-CHATHAM—1911-12
    Chatham Mfg. Co.
    Chatham, Ontario, Canada
DETROIT-DEARBORN—1909-10
    Detroit-Dearborn Motor Car Co.
    Dearborn, Michigan
DETROIT ELECTRIC—1907-39
    Anderson Carriage Co.

    Anderson Electric Car Co.
    Detroit, Michigan
    Became Detroit Electric Car Co. 1919.
    Absorbed Elwell-Parker Co.
    Purchased "Chicago Electric" (1899-1916)
    from Walker Vehicle Co.
DETROITER—1911-19
    Briggs-Detroiter Co.
    Briggs-Detroiter Motor Car Co.
      (1911-15)
    Detroiter Motor Car Co. (1915-17)
    Detroiter Motors Co. (1917-19)
    Detroit, Michigan
DETROIT-OXFORD—1906
    See "Oxford"
    Detroit-Oxford Mfg. Co.
    Oxford, Michigan
    Both names apply to same vehicle.
DETROIT SPEEDSTER—1914
    See "Detroit" cyclecar
    Detroit Cyclecar Co.
    Detroit, Michigan
    Both names apply to same vehicle.
DETROIT STEAM—1905
    Detroit Steam Engine Co.
    Detroit, Michigan
DETROIT STEAM CAR—1924
    Detroit Steam Motors Corp.
    Detroit, Michigan
    See "Trask-Detroit" steam
(DEVAC)—1907
    Devac Automobile Co.
    Newark, New Jersey
Name meant: D-double, E-explosion, V-valveless, A-air, C-cooled.
DEVAUX—1931-32
    Devaux-Hall Motors Co.
    Oakland, California
Absorbed Durant Motor Co. of California, moved to Grand Rapids, Michigan. Absorbed by Continental-Devaux Corp. 1932.
DEVIN—1958-61
DE-VO—1936
    De-Vo Motor Car Co.
    Dover, Delaware

DEWABOUT—1899-1901
  Thomas B. Dewhurst
  Blue Grass Cycle Co.
  Lexington, Kentucky
DE WEESE steam—1909
  Chauncy De Weese
(DE WITT)—1908-10
  De Witt Automobile Co.
  De Witt Motor Vehicle Co.
  North Manchester, Indiana
DEY electric experimental—1915-17;
1919-25
  Dey Electric Vehicle Syndicate
  Dey Electric Corp.
  New York, New York
  Harry E. Dey Inc.
  Jersey City, New Jersey
(DEY-GRISWOLD) electric—1895-98
  Harry E. Dey
  New York, New York
  Dey-Griswold Co.
  New York, New York
  Became U.S. Motor Vehicle Co.
DHK—1909
  DHK Motor Car Co.
  Detroit, Michigan
DIAL—1923
DIAMOND—1904-05
  Diamond Motor Co.
  New Haven, Connecticut
  Meriden, Connecticut
DIAMOND—1910
  Diamond Automobile Co.
  South Bend, Indiana
  1911-12 known as "R.A.C." Formerly
  "Ricketts."
DIAMOND cyclecar—1914
  Cyclecar Co. of Wilmington
  Wilmington, Delaware
DIAMOND ARROW—1909-12
  Diamond Arrow Motor Car Co.
  Ottawa, Ontario, Canada
DIAMOND T—1907-11
  Diamond T Motor Car Co.
  Chicago, Illinois

DIANA—1925-28
  Moon Motor Car Co.
  St. Louis, Missouri
  See "Moon"
DICTATOR—1913
DIEBEL—1900-01
  J. H. Diebel
  W. Unity, Ohio
  Diebel-Eppler Mfg. Co.
  Diebel Cox Mfg. Co.
  Philadelphia, Pennsylvania
DIEBOLD—1901
  Henry C. Diebold
  Belleville, Illinois
DIEHLMOBILE three-wheeler—1962-64
  H. L. Diehl Co.
  South Willington, Connecticut
  Folding car
*DIEXEL
  Believed to be "Drexel" misspelled.
DILE cyclecar—1915-16
  Dile Motor Car Co.
  Reading, Pennsylvania
  Introduced August, 1914.
  In receivers' hands August, 1916.
DILLON STEAM—1920
DINGFELDER—1902-03
  Dingfelder Motor Co.
  Detroit, Michigan
*DIPPARD-STEWART
  Believed to be "Lippard Stewart" (truck)
  misspelled.
DIRECT DRIVE—1917-18
  Direct Drive Motor Company
  Philadelphia, Pennsylvania
  See "Champion"
  Champion Motors Corp.
  Philadelphia, Pennsylvania
DISBROW—1917-18
  Disbrow Motor Co.
  Cleveland, Ohio
  Two racers shown in New York January,
  1917.
DISPATCH—1911-22
  Dispatch Motor Car Co.

  Minneapolis, Minnesota
DITTMAR—1937
DITWILER CYCLECAR—1914
  Ditwiler Mfg. Co.
  Galion, Ohio
*DIVOO—1927
  Believed to be "Divco" (truck) misspelled.
DIXIE—1908-10
  Southern Motor Car Factory
  Southern Motor Car Co.
  Houston, Texas
  Four-cylinder conventional roadster and
  "Dixie Jr." highwheeler.
(DIXIE)—1910-12
  Dixie Motor Co.
  Frederick, Oklahoma
  Also listed as Dixie Motor Car Co.
  Oklahoma City, Oklahoma
DIXIE—1915
  Dixie Mfg. Co.
  12 South Third St.
  Vincennes, Indiana
  Dixie Motor Car Co.
  Louisville, Kentucky
  Became "Dixie-Flyer."
DIXIE-FLYER—1916-23
  Dixie Motor Car Co.
  Louisville, Kentucky
  1919 merged with Kentucky Wagon Works
  (founded 1859). Joined "National" (1900-
  24) and "Jackson" (1903-23) in Associated
  Motors Corp. Later became National
  Motors Corp.
DIXIE JUNIOR (model)
  highwheeler—1908
  See "Dixie"
  Southern Motor Car Factory
  Houston, Texas
DIXIE TOURIST—1908-09
  See "Dixie"
  Southern Motor Car Factory
  Houston, Texas
  Both names apply to the same vehicle.
D.L.G.—1907
  D.L.G. Motor Car Co.

St. Louis, Missouri
DOBLE STEAM—1913-17; 1920-32
    Abner Doble
    Waltham, Massachusetts (1913)
    Doble Motor Vehicle Co.
    Waltham, Massachusetts (1914)
    General Engineering Co.
    Detroit, Michigan (1916)
    Doble-Detroit Steam Motors Co. (1917-18)
    Merged with Amalgamated Machinery Co.
    Chicago, Illinois 1919. Doble Motors Inc.
    San Francisco, California 1921. Reorganized as Doble Steam Motor Car Corp. 1922.
    See "Trask-Detroit."
DOBLE-DETROIT STEAM—1918-19
    Doble-Detroit Steam Motors Co.
    Detroit, Michigan
    See "Doble"
DOBLE-SIMPLEX STEAM—1923
    Doble Steam Motors Corp.
    San Francisco, California
    Built on "Jordan" Big Six chassis.
DODDSMOBILE—1947
    Canadian car. One prototype only.
*DODGE STEAM CAR—1913-24
    Believed to be "Doble" misspelled.
DODGE—1914
    Dodge Motor Car Co.
    Detroit, Michigan
    Light friction drive car by Alvan M. Dodge, formerly with Wahl Motor Car Co.
DODGE—1914 to date
    Dodge Bros. Motor Car Co. (1915-28)
    Dodge Division
    Chrysler Motors Corp. (1928 to date)
    Detroit, Michigan
    First car built May, 1914. 1915 model car announced December, 1914.
DODGE BROTHERS—1906
    Dodge Brothers Mfg. Co.
    Detroit, Michigan
DODGESON—1926
    John Duval Dodge
    Dodgeson Motors
    Detroit, Michigan

    Rotary valve straight-eight.
    Built by son of J. F. Dodge.
    Prototypes only.
DODO CYCLECAR—1909
    Auto Parts Mfg. Co.
    Detroit, Michigan
DOE-WAH-JACK—1909; 1911
    Tulsa Auto Mfg. Co.
    Dowagiac, Michigan
DOLAN ELECTRIC—1900
    Clarence W. Dolan
    Philadelphia, Pennsylvania
DOLLY MADISON (model)—1915-16
    Name of "Madison" Model 6-40 Roadster.
    See "Madison"
    Madison Motors Co.
    Anderson, Indiana
DOLPHIN—1961
DOLSON—1904-07
    John L. Dolson Co.
    J. L. Dolson Automobile Co.
    Charlotte, Michigan
    Plant closing reported November, 1907. Receiver permitted 25 more cars to be finished. Spring, 1908 plant was sold. Times Square Auto Co. bought stock.
DOMAN—1899-1900
    H. C. Doman
    Oshkosh, Wisconsin
DOMAN-MARKS—1936-37
    Engine builders who also built two three-wheel cars.
DOMINION—1911
    New Dominion Motor Co.
    Windsor, Ontario, Canada
DOMINION—1914
    Dominion Motor Car Co.
    Coldbrook, New Brunswick, Canada
DORCHESTER—1906-07
    Dorchester Motor Car Co.
    Dorchester, Massachusetts
    Hub Automobile Co.
    Boston, Massachusetts
    Succeeded "Crestmobile"

DORMANDY—1903-05
    United Shirt Collar Co.
    Troy, New York
    (Troy Carriage Co.)
    Four cars built.
*DORN—1910
    Dorn Motor Car Co.
    St. Louis, Missouri
    Believed to be error for "Dorris."
DORRIS—1895-97
    George Preston Dorris
    Nashville, Tennessee
    One car only.
DORRIS—1905-26
    St. Louis Motor Carriage Co. (1905-06)
    Dorris Motor Car Co.
    St. Louis, Missouri
    Absorbed Astra Motors Corp.
    See "Astra."
DORT—1915-24
    Dort Motor Car Co.
    Flint, Michigan
    Canadian version built by Wm. Gray. See "Gray-Dort"
DOUGHERTY—1955-56
    Frazer Dougherty
    Sierra Madre, California
DOUGLAS—1917-18
    Douglas Motor Corp.
    Omaha, Nebraska
DOW ELECTRIC ELECTRIC—1960
    Dow Testing Laboratory Inc.
    Detroit, Michigan
    Two-passenger, 47-inch wheelbase car.
DOWAGIAC—1909-11
    See "Lindsley"
    Dowagiac Motor Car Co.
    Dowagiac, Michigan
    Dowagiac Motor Car Company finished building the last 15 "Lindsley" cars. These are sometimes called "Dowagiac" as well.
DOWNING—1901
    C. J. Downing
    New York, New York
DOWNING CYCLECAR—1914

Downing Cyclecar Co.
Detroit, Michigan
DOWNING—1915
Downing Motor Car Co.
Detroit, Michigan
DOWNING-DETROIT CYCLECAR—1913-14
Downing Motor Car Co.
Detroit, Michigan
Cleveland, Ohio
DOYLE—1900
Joseph Doyle
Homestead, Pennsylvania
DOYLESTOWN
DRAGON—1906
Dragon Automobile Co.
Detroit, Michigan
DRAGON—1906-08
Dragon Automobile Co.
Philadelphia, Pennsylvania
Reorganized as Dragon Motor Co.
(DRAGON)—1908
Dragon Automobile Works
4212 State St.
Chicago, Illinois
(DRAGON)—1921
Dragon Motors Corp.
Chicago, Illinois
February, 1921 stock sale banned in Illinois. September, 1921 Blue Sky Law violation investigated.
DRAKE—1921-22
Drake Motor & Tire Mfg. Co.
Knoxville, Tennessee
DRAPER—1904
Draper Corp.
Hopedale, Massachusetts
DREADNAUGHT (model)—1911-13
See "Moline"
Moline Automobile Co.
East Moline, Illinois
DREXEL—1917
Drexel Motor Car Corp.
Chicago, Illinois
Succeeded "Farmack." Car built in "Staver" plant owned by Studebaker.

DRIGGS—1921-23
Driggs Ordnance & Mfg. Co.
New Haven, Connecticut and
New York, New York
Car advertised in 1921 and 1922.
Taxicabs built 1923-24.
DRIGGS-SEABURY—1915-16
Driggs-Seabury Ordnance
& Engineering Co.
Sharon, Pennsylvania
See "Ritz," "Sharon" and "Twombly."
DRIVER TRAINER CAR—1961
Midget Motors Corp.
Athens, Ohio
DRUBON
DRUMMOND—1915-18
Drummond Motor Car Co.
Omaha, Nebraska
DUAL-GHIA—1955-58
Dual Motors Corp.
Detroit, Michigan
Used "Chrysler" components.
DU BRIE-CAILLE—1905
Du Brie Motor Co.
Detroit, Michigan
(DUCK)—1913
Jackson Automobile Co.
Jackson, Michigan
Also known as "Jackson" Back Seat Steer.
DUDGEON STEAM—1857; 1866
Richard Dudgeon
24-26 Columbia Street
New York, New York
First car destroyed 1857 in New York Crystal Palace fire. Car No. 2 is in collection of George H. Waterman and Kirkland Gibson.
DUDLEY ELECTRIC—1915
DUDLY BUG CYCLECAR—1913-14
Dudly Tool Co.
Menominee, Michigan
Reported June, 1914 plant taken by Menominee Electric Co. to build electric pleasure car.
DUEBON

DUER HIGHWHEELER—1907-10
Chicago Coach & Carriage Co.
Chicago, Illinois
DUESENBERG—1914-15
Maytag-Mason Auto Co. (1914)
Waterloo, Iowa
Duesenberg Brothers (1915)
Minneapolis, Minnesota
DUESENBERG—1920-37
Duesenberg Automobile and
Motors Co. Inc.
Duesenberg Automobile Co.
Elizabeth, New Jersey
Duesenberg Motors Co.
Indianapolis, Indiana
First eight cars built in Elizabeth, New Jersey plant. Company bought by E. L. Cord 1926. Duesenberg Inc. became part of Cord Corp. 1929.
DUESENBERG—1966
Duesenberg Corp.
Indianapolis, Indiana
One car produced.
*DUGEON—1858
Believed to be "Dudgeon" misspelled.
DUMONT—1904
See "Santos-Dumont"
Columbus Motor Vehicle Co.
Columbus, Ohio
(DUNBAR)—1923
David Dunbar Buick Corp.
Walden, New York
DUNE BUGGY—1968 to date
Bob Irwin Mfg. Co.
1649 Weston Rd.
Weston, Ontario, Canada
DUNE MASTER DUNE BUGGY—1968 to date
Haddock Sand Buggy Const. Co.
Santa Ana, California
DUNN AIR-COOLED CYCLECAR—1915-16
Dunn Motor Works
Ogdensburg, New York
DUPLEX—1907-09
Duplex Automobile Works (1907)
Duplex Motor Car Co. (1908-09)

Chicago, Illinois
DUPLEX—1923
 United Iron Works Co.
 Montreal, Quebec, Canada
DUPONT—1915
 Dupont Motor Car Co.
 Reading, Pennsylvania
DUPONT—1919-33
 Dupont Motors Inc.
 Wilmington, Delaware
 Assembled in Moore, Pennsylvania.
 Combined with Indian Motorcycle Co.
 Springfield, Massachusetts (1930).
DUQUESNE—1903-06
 Duquesne Motor Car Co.
 Buffalo, New York
 1904 became Duquesne Construction Co.,
 Jamestown, New York.
DUQUESNE—1912-13
 Pittsburgh Garage & Supply Co.
 Duquesne Motor Car Co.
 Pittsburgh, Pennsylvania
DURABILE—1902
 Amstutz-Osborn Co.
 Cleveland, Ohio
DURANT—1921-32
 Durant Motors Inc.
 Flint, Michigan
 Lansing, Michigan
 Elizabeth, New Jersey
 Muncie, Indiana
 See "Star," "Flint" (1924-27), "Locomo-
 bile" and "Princeton."
DURANT—1922-32
 Durant Motors
 Leaside, Toronto, Canada
DURENSEN—1921
 Andrew Durensen
 Minneapolis, Minnesota
DURO-CAR—1907-11
 Duro-Car Mfg. Co.
 Los Angeles, California
 Became Amalgamated Motors Corp.
 Alhambra, California 1911.
DURYEA—1895-1913

Duryea Motor Wagon Co.
Springfield, Massachusetts (1895-98)
J. Frank Duryea (1899)
Springfield, Massachusetts
Duryea Motor Mfg. Co. (1898-1900)
Peoria, Illinois
Duryea Power Co. (1900-07)
Reading, Pennsylvania
Western Duryea Mfg. Co. (1901)
Los Angeles, California
Charles E. Duryea (1908-13)
Reading, Pennsylvania
DURYEA TRAP (model)—1898-1900
 National Motor Carriage Co.
 Continental Auto Co.
 Stamford, Connecticut
 Office in New York, New York
DURYEA CYCLECAR—1914
 Cresson-Morris Co.
 Philadelphia, Pennsylvania
 (C. E. Duryea) Became "Crowther-Dur-
 yea."
DURYEA BUGGYAUT (model)—1908
 See "Duryea"
 Charles E. Duryea
 Reading, Pennsylvania
DURYEA ELECTA (model)—1911-12
 C. E. Duryea Co.
 Duryea Auto Co.
 Saginaw, Michigan
DURYEA GEM—1916-17
 Duryea Tricycle Co.
 Reading, Pennsylvania
 Duryea Motors Inc.
 Wilkes-Barre, Pennsylvania
DUSSEAU—1910-12
 Dusseau Motor Car Co.
 Dusseau Fore & Rear Drive Auto Co.
 Toledo, Ohio
 Four wheel drive, at least one built.
DUYO—1914
D&V—1903
 De Vigne & Van Sickle
 Paterson, New Jersey
DYKE—1900-07

A. L. Dyke (1900-03)
A. L. Dyke Automobile Supply Co.
 (1903-07)
St. Louis, Missouri
Sold unassembled
DYKE-BRITTON—1902-04
 See "Dyke"
 A. L. Dyke Automobile Supply Co.
 St. Louis, Missouri
DYMAXION THREE-WHEELER—1933-34
 Buckminster Fuller
 Bridgeport, Connecticut
 Four egg-shaped cars built in old "Loco-
 mobile" factory.
DYNAMO JR.—1958-59
DYNO CAR—1962-64

E

EAGLE—1904-05
 Eagle Automobile Co.
 Buffalo, New York
EAGLE AIR COOLED—1905-08
 Eagle Automobile Co.
 Rahway, New Jersey
 Company incorporated 1906 with $60,000
 capitalization by F. C. & E. Van Dernater,
 A. G. Spencer, G. W. Loft and H. S. Griffin.
EAGLE AIR COOLED—1906-08
 Eagle Motor Car Co.
 Middletown, Connecticut
EAGLE HIGHWHEELER—1908
 Eagle Motor Carriage Co.
 Elmira, New York
EAGLE—1909
 Eagle Automobile Co.
 St. Louis, Missouri
EAGLE CYCLECAR—1914-15
 Eagle Cyclecar Co.
 Chicago, Illinois
 Became "Eagle Macomber"
EAGLE ROTARY—1917-18
 Eagle Macomber Motor Co.
 Sandusky, Ohio
EAGLE—1923-24

Durant Motors, Inc.
Flint, Michigan

EAGLE ELECTRIC—1915-16
Eagle Electric Automobile Co.
Detroit, Michigan

EAGLE MACOMBER—1915-17
Eagle Macomber Motor Car Co.
Chicago, Illinois
Sandusky, Ohio

EAGLET CYCLECAR—1914
Eagle Motors Co.
1877 W. Jefferson
Los Angeles, California
Reported building factory September, 1914.

EARL—1907-08
Earl Motor Car Co.
Kenosha, Wisconsin
Became "Petrel," Petrel Motor Car Co.,
Kenosha, Wisconsin (1908).

EARL—1922-24
Earl Motors Inc.
Earl Motors Mfg. Co.
Jackson, Michigan
Succeeded "Briscoe"
Clarence R. Earl took control of Briscoe
Motor Corp. March, 1921.

EARLY—1911
Early Motor Car Co.
Columbus, Ohio

EASTERN—1896-97
Eastern Motor Carriage Co.
New Haven, Connecticut

(EASTERN)—1910
Eastern Motor Car Co.
Brockton, Massachusetts

EASTERN—1916
Eastern Motors Inc.
Hartford, Connecticut
Eastern Motors Syndicate
New Britain, Connecticut
Became "Charter Oak"

EASTERN ELECTRIC—1921
South Boston, Massachusetts

EASTMAN ELECTRIC—1899-1901
H. F. Eastman

Eastman Automobile Co.
Cleveland, Ohio

EASTMAN STEAM—1900-02
Eastman Automobile Co.
Cleveland, Ohio

*EASTON—1907 See "Morse"
Believed to be company name of Easton
Machine Co., So. Easton, Massachusetts,
not name of automobile.

*EASTON ELECTRIC—1898
Believed to be "Eaton" electric misspelled.

EATON—1896
W. S. Eaton
S. Hampton, New Hampshire

EATON ELECTRIC—1898-1900
Eaton Electric Motor Carriage Co.
Boston, Massachusetts
First car designed and built in 6 weeks.

ECK—1899; 1902-03
Boss Knitting Machine Works
Reading, Pennsylvania
Eckhardt & Souter
Eckhardt & Souter Automobile Co.
Buffalo, New York

ECKHART—1903
Auburn, Indiana

ECLIPSE—1896; 1904
Eclipse Bicycle Co.
Eclipse Mfg. Co.
Elmira, New York

ECLIPSE STEAM—1900-03
Eclipse Automobile Co.
Boston, Massachusetts
Easton, Massachusetts

ECLIPSE—1902
Eclipse Buggy Co.
Ft. Wayne, Indiana
Buyer supplied own engine.

ECLIPSE—1903-04
Eclipse Machine Co.
Columbus, Ohio
Custom built only.

ECLIPSE—1905-08
Kreuger Mfg. Co.
Milwaukee, Wisconsin

ECO—1921-22
G. Hamilton-Grapes
Detroit, Michigan
For export to Australia.

ECONOMIC STEAM—1902
Economic Mfg. Co.
Orange, New Jersey

ECONOMY HIGHWHEELER—1908-11
Economy Motor Buggy Co.
Fort Wayne, Indiana
Kankakee, Illinois
Joliet, Illinois

ECONOMY—1917-20
Economy Motor Car Co.
Tiffin, Ohio
Consolidated with Bellefontaine Automobile Co. January, 1917 and moved to Bellefontaine, Ohio.

ECONOMYCAR—1913-14
Economycar Co.
Indianapolis, Indiana
Also listed as International Cyclecar Co.,
Providence, Rhode Island.

ECONOMY-VOGUE—1920-21
Vogue Motor Car Co.
Tiffin, Ohio

(EDDY) ELECTRIC—1898-1902
Eddy Manufacturing Co.
Windsor, Connecticut

EDDY—1914-15
Eddy Automobile Co.
Cincinnati, Ohio

EDIE MAC—1900
Edie Mac Automobile Co.
Reading, Pennsylvania

EDISON—1903-04
Thomas A. Edison
West Orange, New Jersey
Edison Automobile Co.
Camden, New Jersey
One only for testing electrical devices.

EDISON ELECTRIC—1922
Edison Electric Co.
New York, New York

EDISON-FORD ELECTRIC—1914

CODE = ROMAN LETTERS: Complete entry. *ITALICS:* Unsubstantiated entry. (PARENTHESES): Production planned, but not realized.

T. A. Edison & A. Ford
Detroit, Michigan
EDMOND TRICYCLE—1899-1901
E. J. Edmond Cycle Mfg. Co.
Matteawan, New York
EDSEL—1958-60
Ford Motor Company
Dearborn, Michigan
EDWARDS—1912
Edwards Motor Car Co.
Louisville, Kentucky
EDWARDS—1949-55
Edwards Sport Car
(Emil Diedt)
5822 West Washington Blvd.
Culver City, California
Sports, street or track car.
EDWARDS-KNIGHT—1912-13
Edwards Motor Car Co.
Long Island City, New York
Absorbed 1913 by Willys-Overland Co.
Became "Willys-Knight"
EHRENTRAUT—1911
Carl P. Ehrentraut
Pittsburgh, Pennsylvania
Custom built only.
EHRLICH ELECTRIC—1918-23
Lambert & Mann Co.
Chicago, Illinois
E.H.V. (model)—1904-06
See "Compound"
Eisenhuth Horseless Vehicle Co.
Middletown, Connecticut
EICHSTAEDT—1902
Roman Eichstaedt
Michigan City, Indiana
Built to order.
E.I.M.—1915-16
Eastern Indiana Motor Car Co.
Richmond, Indiana
EINIG STEAM—1896
John Einig
Jacksonville, Florida
EISENHUTH—1896-1903
J. W. Eisenhuth

San Francisco, California
Newark, New Jersey
Eisenhuth Horseless Vehicle Co.
Middletown, Connecticut
Called "Graham Fox" 1904.
After 1904 "Compound."
*EISENHUTH-COMPOUND—1904
Should be "Graham Fox." Later "Compound." See "Compound" and "E.H.V."
ELBERON STEAMER—1903
(ELBERT) CYCLECAR—1914-16
Elbert Motor Car Co.
Seattle, Washington
Elbert Motor Car Co. of California
San Francisco, California
Acquired plant at Sunnyvale, California.
ELCAR—1915-31
Elkhart Carriage & Motor
Car Co.
Elkhart, Indiana
Succeeded "Pratt" (1911-15).
ELCAR-LEVER—1930
An "Elcar" with Lever engine.
See "Elcar"
Elcar-Lever Motor Co.
Elkhart, Indiana
ELCO—1915-16
Elwood Iron Works
Elwood, Indiana
Bimel Buggy Co.
Sidney, Ohio
(Indianapolis, Indiana)
1916 re-named "Bimel."
1917 plant sold to American Motors Parts.
ELCURTO—1921
ELDREDGE—1903-06
National Sewing Machine Co.
Belvedere, Illinois
Succeeded Friedman Road Wagon Co.
ELECTRA ELECTRIC—1913-15
Electra Mfg. Co.
Los Angeles, California
ELECTRA KING—1961- ?
B.&Z. Electric Car Co.
Long Beach, California

ELECTRETTE (model)—1906-07
See "Lansden" electric
Lansden Co.
Newark, New Jersey
ELECTRICAR—1950
ELECTRIC CARRIAGE—1896-97
Electric Carriage & Wagon Co.
Philadelphia, Pennsylvania
ELECTRIC MOTORCYCLE—1895
Sturges Motorcycle Co.
Chicago, Illinois
Built for Times-Herald race.
ELECTRIC SHOPPER THREE WHEELER—1956-62
Electric Shopper
Long Beach, California
ELECTRIC SPORTS RACER—1964
ELECTRIC VEHICLE—1897
Electric Carriage & Wagon Co.
New York, New York and
Philadelphia, Pennsylvania
Succeeded Morris & Salom
ELECTRIC VEHICLE—1897-1901
Electric Vehicle Co.
New York, New York
ELECTRIC WAGON—1897
See "Electric Vehicle"
Electric Carriage & Wagon Co.
New York, New York and
Philadelphia,. Pennsylvania
Both names apply to the same vehicle.
ELECTRIQUETTE—1915
Osborn Electriquette Mfg. Co.
Los Angeles, California
ELECTROBAT—1895-97
Morris & Salom
Philadelphia, Pennsylvania
Original car built by Crawford Wheel & Gear Co., with body by Chas. S. Caffrey Co., for Chicago Times-Herald Race. Completed August 1894. The Times-Herald car, called Electrobat II, won the Gold Medal in that event. See also "Electric Vehicle."
ELECTROBILE—1902
National Vehicle Co.

Indianapolis, Indiana

ELECTROMASTER—1962-64
Nepa Manufacturing Co.
Div. of Parker Pattern & Foundry Co.
Distributed by Auto Electric Car Co.
Pasadena, California
Small shopping car.

ELECTROMOBILE—1899-1902
Belknap Motor Co.
Portland, Maine

ELECTROMOBILE—1905-07
American Electromobile Co.
Detroit, Michigan

(ELECTRONIC LA SAETTA)
ELECTRIC—1955
Electronic Motor Corp.
Salt Lake City, Utah
A "turbo-electric car" propelled by battery.

ELECTRONOMIC STEAM—1900-01
Simplex Motor Vehicle Co.
Danvers, Massachusetts
See "Hood" steam

ELECTROVAIR EXPERIMENTAL ELECTRIC—
1966
General Motors Corp.
Detroit, Michigan
"Corvair" body

ELGIN—1899-1901
Elgin Automobile Co.
Elgin, Illinois

ELGIN—1916-24
Elgin Motor Car Corp.
Chicago, Illinois
Elgin Motors Inc.
Indianapolis, Indiana
Absorbed "New Era"
(New Era Motor Car Co. 1916.)
Receiver discontinued production July,
1924.

ELGIN LIGHT CAR—1914
Elgin Light Car Co.
Fenton, Michigan

ELIJAH WARE STEAM—1871
Elijah Ware
San Francisco, California

ELINORE—1903

ELITE STEAM—1901-02
D. B. Smith & Co.
Utica, New York
See "Saratoga Tourist"

ELITE—1906

ELITE—1909-10
Johnson Service Co.
Milwaukee, Wisconsin

ELITE JUNIOR—1907
Hughson & Burchett Motor Co.
Newark, New Jersey
Spring-driven juvenile car.

ELKHART—1908-11
Elkhart Carriage & Mfg. Co.
(1908)
Elkhart Motor Car Co. (1908-09)
Elkhart, Indiana

ELKHART—1910-16
Elkhart Carriage & Harness Mfg. Co.
Elkhart, Indiana
See "Pratt" and "Pratt-Elkhart."

ELK-HART—1922-25
Crow-Elkhart Motor Corp.
Elkhart, Indiana

ELLICOTT—1906-07
Buffalo, New York

ELLINGEN & PARKS—1896
W. Ellingen & W. J. Parks
LaSalle, Illinois

ELLIOT—1902
Elliot Motor Carriage Co.
Oakland, California
See "Elliot" (1897-99).

ELLIOT—1925
H. F. Elliot & C. W. Lang
Dayton, Ohio

ELLIOTT—1897-99
W. L. Elliott
Elliot Motor Carriage Co.
Oakland, California

ELLIS ELECTRIC—1901
Triumph Motor Vehicle Co.
Chicago, Illinois

ELLIS & TURNER—1901

Ellis & Turner Co.
Peoria, Illinois

ELLSWORTH—1907-08
J. H. Ellsworth
New York, New York

ELMORE—1899
Becker Bros.
Elmore Bicycle Co.
Clyde, Ohio
Ten cars built.
Resumed production 1902-12.
Elmore Mfg. Co.
Clyde, Ohio

EL MOROCCO—1956-57
Almquist Engineering Co.
Milford, Pennsylvania

ELRICK—1896
George Elrick
904 Irving St.
Joliet, Illinois

ELSTON—1895
R. W. Elston
Charlevoix, Michigan
Chicago Times-Herald race entry.

ELVICK—1895

ELWOOD—1915
Elwood Iron Works
Elwood, Indiana
See "Elco"

EMANCIPATOR—1909
Emancipator Automobile Co.
Aurora, Illinois
See "Aurora" (1905-09)

EMBLEM—1910

EMBLEM—1915

EMBREE-McLEAN—1910
McLean Carriage Co.
Embree-McLean Carriage Co.
St. Louis, Missouri

EMERSON—1900-01
Emerson-Fisher Co. (1900)
V. L. Emerson (1901)
Cincinnati, Ohio

EMERSON—1916-17
Emerson Motors Co.

New York and
     Kingston, New York
See "Campbell" (1917-20)
EMERSON-FISHER—1896
     Emerson & Fisher Co.
     Cincinnati, Ohio
E.M.F.—1908-13
     Everett-Metzger-Flanders
     Detroit, Michigan
     Absorbed "Northern," "Wayne" (1904-08).
     Absorbed by Studebaker Corp. 1910.
EMPHE—1920
     Tsacomas Demos
     New York, New York
     At least two cars built for export to Greece.
EMPI-IMP—1968 to date
     Motor Products Inc.
     Box No. 1120
     Riverside, California
     Dune Buggy built on cut down
     "Volkswagen" chassis.
EMPIRE—1896
     Empire Motor Co.
     Pittsburgh, Pennsylvania
EMPIRE—1909-18
     Empire Motor Car Co.
     Indianapolis, Indiana
     Reorganized 1912 as Empire Auto. Co.
EMPIRE STATE—1898
     Empire State Motor Co.
     Catskill, New York
EMPIRE STATE steam—1900-01
     Empire State Automobile Co.
     Rochester, New York
EMPIRE STEAMER—1901-02
     Empire Mfg. Co. Inc.
     Sterling, Illinois
EMPIRE STEAMER—1904-05
     Wm. H. Terwilliger & Co.
     Amsterdam, New York
EMPRESS—1908-10
     Johnson Service Co.
     Milwaukee, Wisconsin
     Gasoline car; firm also built steam.
     See "Johnson" (1905-12)

E.M.S.—1908
(ENDURANCE) steam—1922-24
     Endurance Steam Car Co.
     Los Angeles, California
ENERGETIC—1909
ENGELHARDT—1901
     A. J. Engelhardt
     Northampton, Massachusetts
ENGER—1909-17
     Frank J. Enger
     Cincinnati, Ohio
     Enger Motor Car Co., 1910.
     Plant sold at auction, May 24-26, 1917.
*ENGER-EVERITT—1906-07
     Both names are separate makes.
ENGLER cyclecar—1914-15
     William B. Engler
     Pontiac, Michigan
ENSLOW—1910
     Frank Enslow
     Huntington, West Virginia
ENTERPRISE—1901
ENTIRO
*ENTYRE—1910-11
     Believed to be "Etnyre" misspelled.
ENTZ—1914
     Entz Motor Car Corp.
     New York, New York
EPPS—1902
     Sold by Mead Cycle Co.
     Chicago, Illinois
     One car produced.
ERIE—1897
     Eric & Sturgis
     Los Angeles, California
     J. Phillip Erie, inventor. (Sturgis Iron
     Works).
     Large rear and small front wheels. Four
     one-cylinder connected engines.
ERIE—1900-02
     Erie Cycle & Motor Carriage Co.
     Anderson, Indiana
ERIE—1916-19
     Erie Motors Co.
     Painesville, Ohio

ERIKSON—1916
     Front drive
ERNST—1895-96
     Ernst Power Vehicle Co.
     New York, New York
ERSKINE—1927-30
     Studebaker Corp.
     South Bend, Indiana
     See "Studebaker"
     Cars initially built in Detroit; relocated in
     early 1929.
ERWIN—1913-16
     Erwin Motor & Machine Co.
     Philadelphia, Pennsylvania
ESHELMAN—1955-60
     The Eshelman Co.
     Baltimore, Maryland
ESS-EFF—1912
     Ess-Eff Silent Motor Co.
     Buffalo, New York
ESSEX—1901-02
     Essex Automobile & Supply Co.
     Haverhill, Massachusetts (1901)
     Essex Automobile Co.
     Lynn, Massachusetts (1902)
ESSEX steam—1906-08
     Essex Motor Car Co.
     Boston, Massachusetts
ESSEX—1918-33
     Essex Motors
     Detroit, Michigan
     Subsidiary of Hudson Motor Car Co.
     Absorbed by "Hudson" 1922. Became
     "Essex Terraplane" 1932, and "Ter-
     raplane" 1933.
E&T cyclecar—1914
     E & T Cyclecar Co.
     Charlotte, Michigan
ETNYRE—1908-11
     E. E. Etnyre Motor Car Co.
     Oregon, Illinois
EUCLID—1904
     Berg Automobile Co.
     New York, New York
EUCLID air-cooled—1907-08

*ASTERISK: Error corrected from previous list. See introduction to this section for complete code.

Euclid Motor Car Co.
Cleveland, Ohio
Company formed May, 1907 to build a three-cylinder, two-cycle car.
EUCLID—1909-10
Euclid Motor Car Co.
Trenton, New Jersey
EUCLID CYCLECAR—1914
Euclid Motor Car Co.
New York, New York
By E. S. Cameron. Built at West Haven, Connecticut.
EUREKA—1899-1900
Eureka Automobile & Transportation Co.
San Francisco, California
EUREKA—1907-09
Eureka Motor Co.
Seattle, Washington
F. A. Mitchell, designer.
EUREKA—1907-08
Eureka Motor Buggy Co.
Beavertown, Pennsylvania
Name changed to "Kearns" 1908. Kearns Motor Buggy Co.
EUREKA HIGHWHEELER—1907-10
Eureka Motor Buggy Mfg. Co.
St. Louis, Missouri
Charles Zimmerman, designer.
EUREKA HIGHWHEELER—1909
Eureka Motor Car Manufacturing Co. Inc.
3029 Olive Street
St. Louis, Missouri
EUREKA HIGHWHEELER—1909
Eureka Co.
Rock Fall, Illinois
EVANS STEAM AMPHIBIAN—1804
Oliver Evans
Philadelphia, Pennsylvania
EVANS ELECTRIC—1903-05
F. S. Evans Co.
Detroit, Michigan
EVANS—1911
Automobile Mfg. & Engineering Co.
Detroit, Michigan

EVANS—1914
Evans Motor Car Co.
Nashville, Tennessee
EVANSVILLE HIGHWHEELER—1907-09
Evansville Automobile Co.
Evansville, Indiana
Became "Simplicity"
EVANSVILLE—1914-17
EVERITT—1909-12
Metzger Motor Car Co.
Detroit, Michigan
Absorbed Hewitt Motor Co. 1911. Absorbed with Flanders Motor Co. into Maxwell Motor Co. 1913.
EVERITT—1915
Barney Everitt
Detroit, Michigan
EVERETT STEAMER—1899
Everett Motor Carriage Co.
Everett, Massachusetts
Built under Whitney license.
EVERYBODY'S—1907-09
Everybody's Motor Car Mfg. Co.
St. Louis, Missouri (office)
Also listed at Alton, Illinois (factory).
EWBANK ELECTRIC—1916-18
Ewbank Electric Transmission Co.
Portland, Oregon
EXCALIBUR—1952-53
Beassie Engineering Company
Milwaukee, Wisconsin
Three prototypes built using re-worked "Henry J." chassis.
EXCALIBUR—1964 to date
S. S. Automobiles, Inc.
Milwaukee, Wisconsin
Replica of SSK "Mercedes-Benz."
Power and suspension same as "Chevrolet" Corvette.
EXCEL CYCLECAR—1914
Excel Distributing Co.
Detroit, Michigan
EXCELLENT SIX—1907-09
Rider-Lewis Motor Car Co.
Muncie, Indiana

Trade name for six-cylinder car by Rider-Lewis.
EXCELSION—1910
EXCELSIOR—1899
Excelsior Machine Co.
Buffalo, New York
EXCELSIOR STEAM—1904
Augusta, Maine
EYRE—1936
Los Angeles, California

F

FACTOR—1915
Bloomfield, New Jersey and
New York, New York
FADELEY-HILL—1910
Fadeley-Hill Co.
Washington, D.C.
FAGEOL—1917-18
Fageol Motors Inc.
Oakland, California
Used Hall-Scott Aviation Engines. 13.5 litre luxury car, $17,000.
FAIRBANKS-GRANT—1905
Fairbanks-Grant Mfg. Co.
Ithaca, New York
FAIRBANKS-MORSE—1908-09
Fairbanks-Morse Co.
Chicago, Illinois
FAIRBURY HIGHWHEELER—1909
Fairbury Motor Car Works
Fairbury, Illinois
FAIRFIELD—1926
Automotive Development Corp.
Stamford, Connecticut
FAIRFIELD STEAM—1895-96
C. S. Fairfield
Portland, Oregon
F.A.L.—1909-15
F.A.L. Motor Co.
Chicago, Illinois
Succeeded Reliable-Dayton Motor Car Co.
Also "F.A.L. Greyhound," 1915.

FALCAR—1909-15
  See "F.A.L."
    F.A.L. Motor Co.
    Chicago, Illinois
    Both names apply to the same vehicle.
FALCAR—1922
F.A.L. GREYHOUND (model)—1915
  See "F.A.L."
    F.A.L. Motor Co.
    Chicago, Illinois
FALCON—1905
  F. W. Flynn
  Youngstown, Ohio
  Bay City, Michigan
FALCON—1909-11
  Falcon Engineering Co.
  Chicago, Illinois
  Formerly Larsen Machine Co.
FALCON—1910
  Falcon Motor Car Mfg. Co. Inc.
  Philadelphia, Pennsylvania
FALCON CYCLECAR—1913-14
  Falcon Cyclecar Co.
  Cleveland, Ohio
FALCON—1921
  Halladay Motors Corp.
  Newark, Ohio
  Former "Halladay"
  In hands of receiver March, 1921.
FALCON—1921
  Moller Motor Car Co.
  Lewistown, Pennsylvania
FALCON—1938-43
FALCON (model)—1960-69
  See "Ford"
    Ford Motor Co.
    Dearborn, Michigan
FALCON (model)—1970
  See "Ford"
    Ford Motor Co.
    Dearborn, Michigan
  Re-introduced January, 1970 as economy
  model of Fairlane Series.
FALCON-KNIGHT—1927-28
  Falcon Motors Corp.

Detroit, Michigan
Subsidiary of "Willys-Overland."
Absorbed by "Willys-Overland" 1928
FALL
  One registered in Michigan 1916.
FALLS—1913
  Falls Garage Co.
  Chagrin Falls, Ohio
FALLS—?-1924
  Falls Motors Corp.
  Sheboygan Falls, Michigan
  Mostly engines, few complete cars. Also
  built racing models.
FAMOUS HIGHWHEELER—1906-09
  Famous Mfg. Co.
  East Chicago, Illinois
  Became "Champion."
FANNING—1901-03
  Fanning Mfg. Co.
  (F. J. Fanning Mfg. Co.)
  Chicago, Illinois
  Electric and air-cooled gasoline cars.
FANVIEN—1910
  Fanvien Motor Co.
  Detroit, Michigan
FARMACK—1915-16
  Farmack Motor Car Corp.
  332 South Michigan
  Chicago, Illinois
FARMER—1915
(FARMER'S AUTO)—1905
  Farmer's Auto Motor Car Co.
  Sheffield, Kansas
FARMER-MOBILE—1907
  Summit Carriage-Mobile Co.
  407 Sycamore St.
  Waterloo, Iowa
FARMOBILE—1907-09
  Farmobile Mfg. Co.
  Columbus, Ohio
  Offshoot of Oscar Lear Auto Co.
FARMOBILE—1914
  Farmobile Co.
  San Francisco, California
FARNER—1922-24

Farner Motor Car Co.
Streator, Illinois
FAUBER STEAM—1900-04
  Fauber & Marr
  Fauber Automobile Co.
  Elgin, Illinois
  Became "Marr."
FAUBER BI-CAR CYCLECAR—1914
  W. H. Fauber
  Elgin, Illinois
FAULKNER-BLANCHARD—1910
  Faulkner-Blanchard Motor Car Co.
  Detroit, Michigan
  E. J. Cook, designer.
FAULTLESS CYCLECAR—1914
FAWICK FLYER—1907
  Thomas L. Fawick
  Milwaukee, Wisconsin
  See "Silent Sioux"
FAY—1912
  Greenville Metal Products Co.
  Greenville, Pennsylvania
  Subsidiary of Salisbury Axle Co.
*FEDELIA CYCLECAR—1913-14
  Believed to be misspelling of "Fidelia."
FEDERAL STEAM—1900-02
  Federal Motor Vehicle Co.
  Brooklyn, New York
  Designed by C. L. King.
FEDERAL AUTO BUGGY
  HIGHWHEELER—1906-10
  Federal Automobile Co.
  Chicago, Illinois (1906-08)
  Industrial Automobile Co.
  Elkhart, Indiana (1909)
  Became Rockford Automobile & Engine
  Co., Rockford, Illinois, 1908-09-10.
FEE—1908-09
  Fee Motor Car Co.
  Detroit, Michigan
FEENY CYCLECAR—1914
  Feeny Mfg. Co.
  Muncie, Indiana
FEERRAR—1895
  J. C. W. Feerrar

Lock Haven, Pennsylvania
FENN—1904
    Fenn-Sadler Machine Co.
    Hartford, Connecticut
FENTON—1905
    Fenton Automobile Co.
    Fenton, Michigan
FENTON CYCLECAR—1914
    Fenton Engineering Co.
    Fenton Cyclecar Co.
    Fenton, Michigan
FERGUS—1907
FERGUS—1920-23
    Fergus Motors of America, Inc.
    Newark, New Jersey
    Prototype shown 1916.
    Production started 1920.
FERGUS—1949
    Fergus Motors Inc.
    New York, New York
    Prototype only.
FERGUSON—1902
    Ferguson Buggy Co.
    Ann Arbor, Michigan
FERRER G.T.—1966
    Bottier Engineering
    Camden, New Jersey
    Reworked "Volkswagen" chassis with fiberglass body.
FERRIS—1920-22
    Ohio Motor Vehicle Co.
    Cleveland, Ohio
    Succeeded Ohio Trailer Co. First shown at 1920 New York Auto Show.
FETZGER—1910
    Fetzger Automobile Mfg. Co.
    Galion, Ohio
FEWMAL CYCLECAR—1914
    Fewmal Motors Co.
    California
FEY—1896-1905
    Lincoln H. Fey
    Northfield, Minnesota
FIAT—1909-18
    Fiat Co.

Poughkeepsie, New York
    Italian origin.
    Sued "Oldsmobile," "S.G.V." and "Daniels" on radiator design 1916.
FIBERSPORT—1954
FIDELIA CYCLECAR—1914
    J. H. Sizelan Co.
    Cleveland, Ohio
FIDELITY—1909
    Fidelity Motor Car Co.
    Chicago, Illinois
FIELD—1910
    Field Automobile Mfg. Co.
    Lincoln, Nebraska
FIELD—1924
    Field Motor Co.
    Rice Lake, Wisconsin
FIELDS STEAM—1885-87
    E. F. Fields
    (Field & Crabshaw Machine Co.)
    Lewiston, Maine
    Gave the Stanleys inspiration.
FIFTY-FIFTY CYCLECAR—1914
    Sheppard Mfg. Co.
    1331 Jackson Blvd.
    Chicago, Illinois
FILBY
    Columbus, Kansas
FILLOW—1913
    Fillow Auto Co.
    Danbury, Connecticut
FINA SPORT—1953-55
    Perry Fina
    New York, New York
    "Ford" chassis with "Cadillac" power.
FINCH—1903-04
    E. B. Finch
    Michigan Yacht & Power Co.
    Detroit, Michigan
    Also called "Finch-Limited."
FINCH-LIMITED (model)—1906
    See "Pungs-Finch"
    Pungs-Finch Automobile and
      Gas Engine Co.
    Jefferson & Baldwin Avenues

Detroit, Michigan
FINDLAY—1910-12
    Findlay Motor Co.
    Findlay, Ohio
    Absorbed by General Motors, 1912.
FINDLAY 40—1909-10
    Findlay Carriage Co.
    Findlay, Ohio
FIREBOMB—1955-56
FIRESTONE HIGHWHEELER—1908
    Columbus Buggy Co.
    Columbus, Ohio
    About 25 cars built.
FIRESTONE-COLUMBUS—1906-15
    Columbus Buggy Co.
    Columbus, Ohio
    1914 became New Columbus Buggy Co.
FIRTH—1911
    Firth Motor Car Co.
    Mansfield, Ohio
FISCHER—1900-05
    S. M. Fischer
    Chicago, Illinois
    Fischer Motor Vehicle Co.
    Hoboken, New Jersey
    Mostly gas-electric trucks. Trucks only after 1904.
FISCHER—1914
    C. J. Fischer Co.
    Detroit, Michigan
    A light car, formerly known as "Fischer-Detroit" cyclecar.
FISH—1908
    Fish Automobile Co.
    Bloomington, Illinois
FISHER STEAM—1840; 1853
    J. K. Fisher
    New York, New York
    Both vehicles resembled locomotives.
FISHER—1904
    Fisher Automobile Co.
    Mooresville, Indiana
FISHER—1914-20
    Fisher Motor Corp.
    New York, New York

FISHER THREE-WHEELER—1917
    F. E. Fisher
    Baltimore, Maryland
FITCH—1909
    Fitch Gear Co.
    Rome, New York
    Formerly "Maxwell-Fitch"
FITCH—1949-51
    Sport & Utility Motors Inc.
    31 East Post Road
    White Plains, New York
    A sports, street or track car.
FITCH PHOENIX PROTOTYPE—1966
    John Fitch & Co. Inc.
    Falls Village, Connecticut
FITT—1904
    James Fitt
    Rochester, New York
FLAGLER CYCLECAR—1914
    Flagler Cyclecar Co.
    Chicago, Illinois
    Sheboygan, Wisconsin
FLAIR—1901
    Henry Flair
    St. Louis, Missouri
    Two cars built, one gasoline, one steam.
FLANDERMOBILE—1901
    Flandermobile Co.
    Anderson, Indiana
FLANDERS—1909-13
    E.M.F. Co.
    (Flanders Motor Co.)
    Detroit, Michigan
Absorbed 1912 by Maxwell and U.S. Motor
Company
FLANDERS ELECTRIC—1911-13; 1914-15
    Flanders Mfg. Co.
    Pontiac, Michigan
    Became Flanders Electric Co. (1914-15)
    From October 1913 to March 1914 the
    "Flanders" automobile carried the name of
    "Tiffany."
FLEMING—1901
    Fleming Motor Vehicle Co.
    Ossining, New York

FLEXBI—1904
FLINN STEAM—1904
    Richard J. Flinn
    W. Roxbury, Massachusetts
FLINT—1902-03
    Flint Automobile Co.
    Flint, Michigan
    Founded by A.B.C. Hardy.
    Also called "Flint Roadster.
    See also "Hardy"
FLINT—1924-27
    Flint Motor Co.
    Long Island City, New York
    Elizabeth, New Jersey and
        Flint, Michigan
Handmade prototypes shown at Hotel
Commodore January, 1923. First pro-
duction cars started October, 1923 (1924
models). Subsidiary of Durant Motors.
FLINT-LOMAX—1905
    Flint-Lomax Electric Mfg. Co.
    Denver, Colorado
    Shown at 1905 Denver Auto Show.
FLINTRIDGE—1957
FLYER CYCLECAR—1913-14
    Flyer Motor Co.
    Elizabeth, New Jersey and
        Mt. Clemens, Michigan
FLYER (model)—1933-34
    See "Continental"
    Continental Automobile Co.
    Grand Rapids, Michigan
FLYING AUTO—1947
FLYING AUTO—1950
FLYING DUTCHMAN—1908
    N. C. Gauntt
    North Yakima, Washington
FLYNN—1905
    Walter F. Flynn
    Youngstown, Ohio
FOOL-PROOF—1912
FOOS—1910
    Foos Gas Engine Co.
    Springfield, Ohio
FORBES—1899

Joseph N. Forbes
Cromanton, Florida
FORD—1901
    The Henry Ford Co.
    Detroit, Michigan
Succeeded Detroit Automobile Co. Became
Cadillac Automobile Co.
FORD—1904 to date
    The Ford Motor Co.
    Dearborn, Michigan
Absorbed Lincoln Motor Car Co. 1922.
See "Mercury," "Falcon," "Continental,"
"Lincoln," "Edsel."
FORD—1912 to date
    Ford Motor Co. of Canada, Ltd.
    Windsor, Ontario, Canada
FORD LIGHT CAR CYCLECAR—1914
    Ford Motor Co.
    Detroit, Michigan
FORD 1901 REPLICA—1968
    Horseless Carriage Corp.
    Ft. Lauderdale, Florida
    A ¾ scale replica of 1901 "Ford."
FORDMOBILE—1903
    The Fordmobile Company Ltd.
    Detroit, Michigan
FORE RIVER—1903
    Fore River Shipbuilding Co.
    Quincy, Massachusetts
FOREST—1902
FOREST—1905-06
    Forest Motor Car Co.
    Boston, Massachusetts
FOREST—1908-09
    Forest Automobile Co.
    St. Louis, Missouri
FOREST CITY—1905
    Forest City Motor Car Co.
    Massillon, Ohio
    Became "Jewell," 1906.
FORMCAR—1963
    Formcar Constructors Inc.
    Orlando, Florida
FORSTER—1920-22
    Forster Motor Mfg. Co. Ltd.

Montreal, Canada
Also called "Forster Six."
FORTH—1910
Forth Motor Car Co.
Mansfield, Ohio
FORT PITT—1908-09
Fort Pitt Motor Mfg. Co.
New Kensington, Pennsylvania
See also "Pittsburgh"
FORT WAYNE POWER WAGON—1911
Fort Wayne Auto Mfg. Co.
Ft. Wayne, Indiana
FOSS—1908
Foss-Hughes Co.
Philadelphia, Pennsylvania
FOSTER—1896
Foster & Brown Co.
Westbrook, Maine
FOSTER—1899-1903
Foster & Co.
Foster Automobile Mfg. Co.
Rochester, New York
   Gasoline and electric cars.
FOSTER—1901
Improved Gasoline Motor & Automobile
Company.
Haverhill, Massachusetts
FOSTER—1906
Foster Motor Car Co.
New Haven, Connecticut
FOSTER HIGHWHEELER—1908
W. O. Foster Co.
Newton, Iowa
FOSTER STEAM—1904
Artzberger Automobile Co.
721 Cedar Ave.
Allegheny, Pennsylvania
From Foster Automobile Mfg. Co., Rochester, New York.
FOSTLER—1904-05
Chicago Motorcycle Co.
Chicago, Illinois
FOSTORIA—1904
Fostoria Foundry Co.
Fostoria, Ohio

FOSTORIA—1906-07
Fostoria Motor Car Co.
Fostoria, Ohio
Succeeded "Detroit-Oxford."
FOSTORIA—1915-16
Fostoria Motor Co.
(Fostoria Light Car Co.)
Fostoria, Ohio
Became Seneca Motor Car Co. in December, 1916. See "Seneca"
FOUCH—1913-15
James R. Fouch
Los Angeles, California
FOURNIER-SEARCHMONT—1902-03
Fournier-Searchmont Co.
Saratoga Springs, New York
Philadelphia, Pennsylvania
Succeeded Searchmont Motor Car Co.
Became Searchmont Automobile Co.
See "Searchmont"
FOUR TRACTION—1907-09
Four Traction Automobile Co.
Mankato, Minnesota
FOUR WHEEL DRIVE—1902-07
Four Wheel Drive Wagon Co.
Milwaukee, Wisconsin
FOUR WHEEL DRIVE (model)—1909-11
Four Wheel Drive Automobile Co.
Clintonville, Wisconsin
Trucks only after 1911.
See "F.W.D."
FOX—1904
Charles A. Fox
Syracuse, New York
FOX AIR-COOLED—1921-25
Fox Motor Car Co.
Philadelphia, Pennsylvania
Introduced at Hotel Commodore, New York City, January, 1922.
FOYE STEAMER—1901
Foye Hubmotor & Automobile Co.
Jersey City, New Jersey
Carriage with hub motors. Designed by Carl Bergman.
FRANCISCO-MARTIN—1915

Francisco-Martin Motor Co.
Newport, Michigan
FRANCKE—1904
George O. Francke Auto Co.
Milwaukee, Wisconsin
FRANCO-AMERICAN—1903
Automobile Co. of America
Manion, New Jersey
Formerly "Gasmobile"
FRANCO-AMERICAN—1907
Franco-American Car Co.
1501-1523 E. 7th St.
Los Angeles, California
French motor with steel cylinders and four-wheel brakes.
FRANKFORD—1922
Frankford Motors Co.
Philadelphia, Pennsylvania
Designed by Lee Oldfield.
(FRANKFORT)—1917
Frankfort Motor Car Co.
Frankfort, Indiana
Incorporation reported February, 1917.
FRANKLIN AIR-COOLED—1902-34
H. H. Franklin Co.
Franklin Automobile Co.
Syracuse, New York
Founded 1893.
Absorbed New York Motor Car Co.
FRANTZ STEAM—1901-02
Rev. H. A. Frantz
Allentown, Pennsylvania
(Frantz Automobile Co.)
Cherryville, Pennsylvania
FRAYER-MILLER—1904-10
Oscar Lear Automobile Co.
Springfield and Columbus, Ohio
FRAZEE—1897
Osage, Iowa
FRAZER—1947-51
Graham-Paige Motors Corp.
Detroit and Willow Run,
   Michigan
Absorbed by Kaiser-Frazer Corporation Willow Run, Michigan, February, 1947.

CODE = ROMAN LETTERS: Complete entry. *ITALICS:* Unsubstantiated entry. (PARENTHESES): Production planned, but not realized.

Production began in June, 1946.
See "Kaiser"
FRAZIER CYCLECAR—1914
    W. S. Frazier & Co.
    Aurora, Illinois
    Also called "Sprite."
FRAZIER-ELKHART—1915
    O. Z. Frazier
    Elkhart, Indiana
FREDERICKSON CYCLECAR—1914
    Frederickson Patents Co.
    Chicago, Illinois
    Tandem cyclecar
FREDONIA—1895
    Fredonia Mfg. Co.
    Fredonia, New York
FREDONIA—1902-04
    Fredonia Mfg. Co.
    Fredonia Automobile Co.
    Youngstown, Ohio
    Carriages, experimental cars from 1896.
FREDRICKSON—1909
    H. E. Fredrickson Automobile Co.
    Omaha, Nebraska
FREEMAN STEAM—1901
    J. W. Freeman
    Joplin, Missouri
FREEMAN—1906
    Chicago, Illinois
(FREEMAN)—1920
    Freeman Motor Car Co.
    Omaha, Nebraska and
        Cleveland, Ohio
    Proposed production: 50 passenger cars
    and 500 trucks.
FREMONT—1920-24
    Fremont Motors Corp.
    Fremont, Ohio
FRENCH—1905
    French Automobile Co.
    Rumford Falls, Maine
    Clinton, Massachusetts
FRENCH CYCLECAR—1913
    Earl French
    914 8th St.

Washington, D.C.
FRENCH-AMERICAN—1909
    French-American Motor Car Co.
    Cleveland, Ohio
FRENCH STEAMER—1900
    Thomas French
    Andover, Maine
    Later United States Motor Carriage Co.
FRENIER—1912
    Frenier Automobile Co.
    Rutland, Vermont
FRICK—1955
FRIDDLE—1915
    Friddle Motor Car Co.
    Tacoma, Washington
FRIEDBERG—1908
FRIEDMAN—1900-03
    National Sewing Machine Co.
    Belvidere, Illinois
    Became "Ideal" 1903.
    See "Eldredge"
FRIEND—1920-21
    Friend Motors Corp.
    Pontiac, Michigan
    Succeeded "Olympian"
    Bankruptcy reported May, 1922.
FRISBEE—1921
FRISBIE—1901
    R. A. Frisbie
    Cromwell, Connecticut
    One car extant today.
FRITCHLE ELECTRIC—1904-20
    Fritchle Auto & Battery Co.
    Denver, Colorado
    Fritchle Electric Co. 1919 (gas-electric
    car).
FRONT-AWAY—1917
    Millington Motor Car Co.
    Chicago, Illinois
    Absorbed Millington Auto Engineering Co.
    (front drive conversions).
    Built a runabout, but mostly trucks.
(FRONT DRIVE)—1905
    Automobile Front Drive Mfg. Co.
    St. Louis, Missouri

FRONTENAC—1906-13
    Abendroth & Root Mfg. Co.
    Newburgh, New York
    40-50 cars built 1906, 100 in 1907.
FRONTENAC—1916
    Frontenac Motor Car Co.
    Indianapolis, Indiana
FRONTENAC—1922-24
    Frontenac Motor Corp.
    Indianapolis, Indiana
    Speed cars by Chevrolet Brothers.
FRONTENAC—1931-33
    Dominion Motors Ltd.
    Toronto, Ontario, Canada
    Discontinued mfg. December 31, 1933.
FRONTENAC—1959-60
    Based on U.S. "Falcon." Succeeded by
    "Comet," built in U.S. and Canada.
    Ford Motor Co.
    Oakville, Ontario, Canada
FRONTMOBILE—1917-18
    Bateman Mfg. Co.
    Safety Motor Co.
    Camden Motors Co.
    Grenloch (Camden) New Jersey
    Front-wheel drive
    Some lists erroneously carry this make as
    "Bateman.".
FRONT WHEEL DRIVE—1926
    Positive Traction Motors Corp.
    Brookline, Massachusetts
F.R.P.—1915-17
    Finley Robinson Porter Co.
    Port Jefferson, Long Island,
        New York
    Five to ten hand-made cars.
    Became "Porter" (1919-22)
FUJIOKA—1923
    Fujioka Motor Car Co.
    Los Angeles, California
    For export to Japan.
FULLER—1908-10
    Angus Automobile Co.
    Angus, Nebraska
FULLER—1909-11

*ASTERISK: Error corrected from previous list. See introduction to this section for complete code.

Fuller Buggy Co.
Jackson, Michigan
Became Jackson Automobile Co. 1911.
FULLER ELECTRIC—1914
Fuller Electric Car Co.
Detroit, Michigan
FULTON—1900-01
Fulton Machine Works
Chicago, Illinois
FULTON—1908-09
Fulton Motor Car Co.
New York, New York
FULTON—1908
Connecticut Motor Works
New Haven, Connecticut
Also called an Air-Cooled Cyclecar
FULTON & WALKER—1900-01
Fulton & Walker Co.
Philadelphia, Pennsylvania
FUN HUGGER DUNE BUGGY—1968 to date
Fun Hugger Co.
824 Kendall Drive
San Bernardino, California
FURGESON—1910
Furgeson Motor Car Co.
Lansing, Michigan
F.W.D.—1910-12
See "Badger" (F.W.D.)
The Four Wheel Drive Auto Co.
Clintonville, Wisconsin
Formerly "Z&B"
*FWICK—1910-12
Believed to be "Fawick" misspelled.

GABRIEL—1901-12
Gabriel Carriage Co.
Gabriel Auto Co.
Cleveland, Ohio
Cars and trucks
GADABOUT CYCLECAR—1913-16
Gadabout Motor Corp.
Newark, New Jersey
Wicker body

First announced August, 1913.
GADABOUT—1945-46
Detroit Industrial Designers
Detroit, Michigan
GAETH EXPERIMENTAL STEAM—1898; 1902-03
Paul Gaeth
Cleveland, Ohio
GAETH STEAM—1902-04
Paul Gaeth
Cleveland, Ohio
GAETH—1904-11
Gaeth Automobile Co.
Cleveland, Ohio
Became Stuyvesant Motor Car Co., 1910.
GAGE STEAM—1900
A. S. Gage
West Gardner, Massachusetts
One car produced for owner's use.
GAGE CYCLECAR—1914
Gage Mfg. Co.
Los Angeles, California
GAGEMOBILE STEAM—1902
W. M. Gage
Saratoga Springs, New York
Built-to-order cars.
GALE—1901
Gale Mfg. Co.
Albion, Michigan
GALE—1904-11
Western Tool Works
Galesburg, Illinois
Succeeded by Robson Mfg. Co., 1908.
GALE 4—1920-22
Gale Motors Co.
Indianapolis, Indiana
McCurdy-Hercules Corp.
Evansville, Indiana
GALLIA ELECTRIC—1906-08
Gallia Electric Carriage Co.
New York, New York
GALLOWAY—1908-16
William Galloway
Galloway Station
Waterloo, Iowa

Bought Mason-Maytag Motor Car Co.
See "Arabian."
GALT—1911-12
Canadian Motors Limited
Galt, Ontario, Canada
GALT GAS ELECTRIC—1913-15
Galt Motor Company
Galt, Ontario, Canada
GARBUTT—1908
GARDNER—1896
Gardner Motor Co. Ltd.
New Orleans, Louisiana
GARDNER—1919-31
Russell E. Gardner & Sons
Gardner Motor Car Co.
St. Louis, Missouri
Russell Gardner formerly made "Banner"
buggies and "Banner" highwheelers, 1910.
GAREAU 35—1909-10
Gareau Motor Car Co. Ltd.
Montreal, Quebec, Canada
GARFIELD—1904
Garfield Automobile Co.
Chicago, Illinois
GARFORD—1907-14
Garford Motor Car Co.
Cleveland, Ohio
Built chassis for "Studebaker," "Cleveland," "Rainier," "Ardsley," "Gaeth" and "Royal."
Acquired by "Studebaker" 1906. Sold to
and absorbed by Willys-Overland 1912.
(Garford Co. Division of Willys-Overland
Co. Elyria, Ohio 1913).
GARICAR—1909
W. M. Pease
Aberdeen, South Dakota
GAROSCOPE—1907
GARRETT HIGHWHEELER—1909
Garrett Machine Works
Garrett, Indiana
GARRISON CYCLECAR—1914
Garrison Machine Works
Dayton, Ohio
GARVIN—1901

Garvin Machine Co.
New York, New York
GARY SIX—1914-15
Gary Automobile & Mfg. Co.
Gary, Indiana
GAS-AU-LEC—1905-07
Vaughn Machine Co. (1905)
Corwin Mfg. Co. (1906)
Peabody, Massachusetts
Gasoline-electric car
GASLIGHT—1960-61
Gaslight Motors Corp.
Detroit, Michigan
Replica 1902 "Rambler."
GASMOBILE—1900-02
Automobile Co. of America
New York, New York (office)
Marion, New Jersey (plant)
GASOLINE MOTOR CARRIAGE—1897
Sintz Gas Engine Co.
Grand Rapids, Michigan
GATES—1928-30
A. J. Gates Co.
Detroit, Michigan
GATTS—1905
Alfred Parma Gatts
Hamersville, Ohio
GAWLEY—1895
T. R. Gawley
Aurora, Nebraska
One built for Chicago Times-Herald Race
GAYLORD—1910-13
Gaylord Motor Car Co.
Gaylord, Michigan
Passenger car that converted to a truck.
GAYLORD—1955
Gaylord Cars Ltd.
Chicago, Illinois
GEARLESS—1907-09
Gearless Transmission Co. (1907-08)
Gearless Motor Car Co. (1908-09)
Rochester, New York
Used planetary cone friction drive.
See also "Olympic"
GEARLESS STEAM—1921-23

Gearless Motor Corp.
Pittsburgh, Pennsylvania
Built by Duncan MacDonald.
GEARLESS STEAMER—1919
The Peterson-Culp Gearless
Steam Automobile Co.
Denver, Colorado
GEBER—1904
Geber Automobile Mfg. Co.
Pittsburgh, Pennsylvania
G.E.C. ELECTRIC EXPERIMENTAL—1898; 1902-05
General Electric Co.
West Lynn, Massachusetts (1898)
Schenectady, New York (1902-05)
Developed by Prof. Elihu Thompson.
GEER STEAM—1900
GEM—1917-19
Gem Motor Car Co.
Grand Rapids, Michigan
GENERAL—1902-03
General Automobile & Mfg. Co.
General Automobile Co.
Cleveland, Ohio
Succeeded Hansen Automobile Co.
"Studebaker" bid in all property,
machinery, parts and real estate. Reported
October, 1903.
(GENERAL)—1911
General Automobile & Repair Co.
Chicago, Illinois
Believed to be garage, not manufacturer.
GENERAL ELECTRIC—1898-1900
General Electric Automobile Co.
Philadelphia, Pennsylvania
Manayunk, Pennsylvania
GENERAL ELECTRIC—1902-04
General Electric Co.
Schenectady, New York
Four-cylinder gasoline-electric.
GENESEE—1904
Genesee Auto Co.
Rochester, New York
GENESEE—1911-12
Genesee Motor Co.

Batavia, New York
GENEVA—1899
Geneva Wagon Co.
Geneva, New York
GENEVA—1901-04
Geneva Automobile & Mfg. Co.
Geneva, Ohio
Built both steam and gasoline cars. Became
Cleveland Auto Cab Co. Cleveland, Ohio.
GENEVA—1916-17
Schoeneck Co.
Harvey, Illinois
GENEVIEVE—1903
Neustadt-Perry Co.
St. Louis, Missouri
GENIE—1962
British Motor Car Importers
San Francisco, California
Junior and sports racing cars.
GEORGE WHITE HIGHWHEELER—1909
The George White Buggy Co.
Rock Island, Illinois
*GEOUT
Believed to be "Grout" misspelled.
GERMAN-AMERICAN—1902-03
German-American Automobile Co.
New York, New York
Petition in bankruptcy by employees and
others reported November, 1902.
GERONIMO—1917-21
Geronimo Motor Car Co.
Enid, Oklahoma
GERSIX—1920-21
Gersix Mfg. Co.
Seattle, Washington
Gerlinger Motor Co.
Portland, Oregon
Mostly truck production.
GETABOUT—1901
George T. Turner Co.
Philadelphia, Pennsylvania
GETAWAY DUNE BUGGY—1968 to date
D.M.C.O.
East Derry, New Hampshire
GHENT—1917-18

Ghent Motor Co.
Ottawa, Illinois
Built by S. G. Gay Co.
Building sold to A. L. Richards for $5,382, January, 1919.

GIBBS STEAM—1901
American Tractor Co.
Elizabethport, New Jersey

GIBBS ELECTRIC—1903-05
Gibbs Engineering & Mfg. Co.
Glendale, New York

GIBSON STEAMER—1899
Charles D. P. Gibson
Jersey City, New Jersey

GIDDINGS & STEVENS—1900
Giddings & Stevens Motor Vehicle Co.
Rockford, Illinois

GIFFORD—1907-08
Gifford-Pettit Mfg. Co.
Chicago, Illinois

GILLETTE—1916-17
Gillette Motors Co.
Mishawaka, Indiana
1915 succeeded American Simplex Co. mfg. of "Amplex."
Company formed by King C. Gillette (Gillette Razors). Receiver appointment announced September, 1917.

GILMORE—1901-04
G. A. Gilmore
Detroit, Michigan

GILMORE ELECTRIC—1904
Gilmore Electric Co.
Boston, Massachusetts

(GILSON)—1921
Gilson Mfg. Co.
Guelf, Ontario, Canada

GITHEN—1902-03
Githen Brothers Inc.
Chicago, Illinois

*G.&J.—1900
Thomas B. and Charles T. Jeffrey
Chicago, Illinois
Wrong name for the first "Rambler."

G.J.G.—1909-15

George J. Grossman
(G.J.G. Motor Car Co.)
White Plains, New York

GLASSIC—1966 to date
Glassic Industries, Inc.
3175 Belvedere Road
West Palm Beach, Florida
Fiberglass replica of 1930 Ford roadster or phaeton on "International" Scout chassis.

GLASSPAR—1953-56
Glasspar Co.
Santa Ana, California

GLEASON—1909-13
Kansas City Vehicle Co.
Kansas City, Missouri
Former "Kansas City" car.
Became "Bauer" (1914).

GLEN CYCLECAR—1921
Scarboro Beach, Ontario, Canada

GLENWOOD—1922
Glenwood Motor Car Corp.
Findlay, Ohio

GLIDE—1903-19
Bartholomew Co.
Peoria, Illinois
First models called "Glidemobile."
See also "Bartholomew"

GLIDEABOUT (model)—1905
See "Glide"

GLOBE—1910
Globe Motor Car Co.
Detroit, Michigan

GLOBE—1915
Globe Motor Car Co.
Canton, Ohio

GLOBE—1920-22
Globe Motors Co.
Cleveland, Ohio
Announced September, 1920.

GLOVER—1902-11
George T. Glover
Chicago, Illinois

GLOVER—1921
Sold by Glovers Motors Ltd.
Leeds, York, England

American car built for export by Glover Motor Co., New York, New York. Also called "Glover-American."

GNAT—1935

GOABOUT—1901-02
Standard Mfg. Co.
Kokomo, Indiana

GOBY CYCLECAR—1914
Motor Engineering Co.
Cleveland, Ohio

GODDEN—1897-98
Louis Godden
Winchester, Massachusetts

*GOETHE—1900-02
Believed to be "Gaeth" misspelled.

GOLDEN—1915
Golden Motor Car Co.
Chicago, Illinois

GOLDEN EAGLE—1906
Atlanta, Georgia

GOLDEN GATE—1895
A. Schilling & Sons
Santa Maria, California

GOLDEN STATE—1902
Golden State Automobile Co.
San Jose, California
Succeeded Christman Motor Carriage Co.

GOODEV—1897

GOODSPEED—1922
Commonwealth Motors Co.
Joliet, Illinois

GOODWIN—1913
Goodwin Car Co.
Chicago, Illinois

GOODWIN—1923
Goodwin Car & Mfg. Co.
Poughkeepsie, New York

GORDON—1948
H. Gordon Hansen
San Lorenzo, California

GORSON—1907

GOTHAM—1911-15
Gotham Motor Car Co.
New York, New York
About 50 cars built.

GOULD STEAMER—1900
  Gould Mfg. Co.
  Seneca Falls, New York
GOVE—1921
  Gove Motor Truck Co.
  Detroit, Michigan
  Truck company which built a four-cylinder,
  air-cooled car.
G.-P.—1931
GRAHAM STEAM—1899-1900
  Graham Equipment Co.
  Boston, Massachusetts
  See "Compound" and "Graham Fox."
GRAHAM—1903-04
  Graham Bros.
  Graham Automobile & Launch Co.
  Chicago, Illinois
GRAHAM—1930-41
  Graham Paige Motors Corp.
  Detroit, Michigan
  Succeeded "Graham-Paige"
GRAHAM-FOX—1901-04
  Graham-Fox Co.
  New York, New York and
    Middletown, Connecticut
  1904 merged with Eisenhuth Horseless
  Vehicle Co.
  See "Compound"
GRAHAM MOTORETTE—1902-04
  Charles Sefrin Motor Carriage
    Co.
  Brooklyn, New York
GRAHAM-PAIGE—1928-30
  Graham-Paige Motors Corp.
  Detroit, Michigan
  Succeeded "Paige," Paige Detroit Motor
  Car Company.
(GRAMM) AIR-COOLED CYCLECAR—1913
  Gramm Motor Truck Co.
  Walkersville, Ontario, Canada
  Truck company to have built two-cylinder
  cyclecars with air-cooled engines.
GRAND—1912
  Grand Rapids Motor Truck Co.
  Detroit, Michigan

GRAND RAPIDS—1913
GRANGER—1909
  Granger Motor Works
  Chicago, Illinois
GRANITE FALLS—1912
  Granite Falls Machine Shop
  Granite Falls, Minnesota
GRANT—1896-97
  W. Wallace Grant
  Brooklyn, New York
  Long Island City, New York
GRANT—1900
  Grant Brothers
  Boston, Massachusetts
GRANT—1914-22
  Grant Bros. Automobile Co.
  Detroit, Michigan
  Grant Motor Co.
  Findlay, Ohio
  1916 became Grant Motor Car Corp.,
  Cleveland, Ohio.
GRANT CYCLECAR—1913-14
  Grant Cyclecar Co.
  Grant Motor Co.
  Detroit, Michigan
GRANTHAM—1956
GRAVES & CONGDON HIGHWHEELER—1909
  Graves & Congdon Co.
  Amesbury, Massachusetts
  Became "Crown"
GRAY CYCLECAR—1920
  Gray Light Car Corp.
  Longmont, Idaho
  Denver, Colorado
  Two cars produced. Used Harley-Davidson
  engines.
GRAY—1921-26
  Gray Motor Corp.
  Gray Mfg. Co.
  Detroit, Michigan
GRAY & COUCH
  Gray & Couch Motor Vehicle Co.
  Stoneham, Massachusetts
GRAY-DORT—1917-21
  Gray-Dort Motors Ltd.

Chatham, Ontario, Canada
  Famed coachbuilders, William Gray &
  Sons.
GREAT—1903
GREAT ARROW—1904-08
  George N. Pierce Co.
  Buffalo, New York
  Renamed "Pierce-Arrow" 1909.
GREAT EAGLE—1910-15
  U.S. Carriage Co.
  Columbus, Ohio
  Trucks only after 1915.
GREAT SIX—1907
  Gearless Transmission Co.
  Rochester, New York
GREAT SMITH—1907-11
  Smith Automobile Co.
  Topeka, Kansas
  Formerly "Smith" from 1904.
GREAT SOUTHERN—1909-16
  Great Southern Automobile Co.
  Birmingham, Alabama
  Montgomery, Alabama
GREAT WESTERN—1904-16
  Great Western Mfg. Co.
  LaPorte, Indiana
  Model Automobile Co.
  Auburn, Indiana (1908-09)
  Peru, Indiana
  Great Western Auto Co. Kalamazoo,
  Michigan and Peru, Indiana (1909-16)
  Reported March, 1916 Claude Andrews
  (receiver) to continue business.
GREELEY—1903
  E. N. Miller
  Greeley, Colorado
GREEN—1913
  Green Mfg. Co.
  Cobleskill, New York
GREEN BAY STEAM—1887
  Green Bay, Wisconsin
GREEN LEAF—1902
  Green Leaf Cycle Co.
  Green Leaf Automobile Co.
  Lansing, Michigan

*ASTERISK: Error corrected from previous list. See introduction to this section for complete code.

GREEN MINI BUG—1968
    Green Leaf Cycle Co.
    Green Motors Inc.
    Livonia, Michigan
GREENVILLE—1925
GREER—1916-17
    Greer College of Motoring
    Greer Auto Co.
    Chicago, Illinois
GREER STEAM—1901
    H. R. Greer
    St. Louis, Missouri
GREGG—1916
    Elmore E. Gregg
    Motors Co. of Philadelphia
    Pittsburgh, Pennsylvania
GREGORY EXPERIMENTAL—1920-23
    Gregory-Crann Motor Co.
    Front Drive Motor Co.
    Kansas City, Missouri
    A "Scripps-Booth" with front drive.
GREGORY 555—1948
    Ben F. Gregory
    Gregory Front Drive Motor Cars
    Kansas City, Missouri
    Prototypes only
GREMLIN—1970 to date
    American Motors Corp.
    Detroit, Michigan
    Two-door subcompact announced February
12, 1970. For sale April 1, 1970.
GRENSFELDER—1901
    J. M. Grensfelder
    St. Louis, Missouri
GREUTER—1898-99
    Charles R. Greuter
    Holyoke, Massachusetts
    Became "Holyoke"
GREYHOUND—1909
    Burdick Motor Car Co.
    Eau Claire, Wisconsin
GREYHOUND—1914-16
    Greyhound Cyclecar Co.
    Greyhound Motor Co.
    States Motor Car Co.

    Toledo, Ohio
    Kalamazoo, Michigan
    Initially a cyclecar (1914-15).
GREYHOUND—1918-19
    American Motor Vehicle Co.
    Lafayette, Indiana
    Formerly built "American Junior."
GREYHOUND—1920-21
    Greyhound Motor Car Co.
    Greyhound Motors
    New York, New York
    E. Warren, Rhode Island
GREYHOUND—1929
*GRIDE—1903
    Believed to be "Glide" misspelled.
GRIFFIN—1930-31
    Gardner Motor Co.
    St. Louis, Missouri
    Front wheel drive. See "Gardner"
GRIFFIN—1937
    R. H. Griffin
    San Diego, California
GRIFFITH—1964-66.
    Griffith Motor Car Co.
    Syosset, Long Island,
      New York (1964-65)
    Griffith Motors, Plainview, Long Island,
New York (1965-66).
GRIFFITHS STEAM—1899-1900
    W. H. Griffiths
    Boston, Massachusetts
GRINNELL ELECTRIC—1912-16
    Grinnell Electric Automobile Co.
    Detroit, Michigan
    Former "Phipps-Grinnell"
GRISWOLD—1905-06
    Griswold Mfg. Co.
    Quincy, Massachusetts
GRISWOLD—1907-09
    Griswold Motor Car Co.
    Griswold Motor & Body Co.
    Detroit, Michigan
GROFF & RUNKLE—1902
    Groff & Runkle Motor Vehicle Co.
    Columbus, Ohio

GROUT—1898-1915
    Grout Bros.
    Grout Brothers Automobile Co.
    Grout Automobile Co.
    Orange, Massachusetts
    Steam to 1905; gas vehicles from 1903.
    Became "Red-Arrow" (1915).
GRUBB—1902
    Light Cycle Co.
    Pottstown, Pennsylvania
GRUBE—1900
    Grube Carriage Works
    Rahway, New Jersey
G.T.B. DUNE BUGGY—1968 to date
    Denk Plastics Inc.
    Chester, Pennsylvania
GUARANTY—1917-21
    Guaranty Motors Co.
    Cambridge, Massachusetts
GURLEY—1900-01
    T. W. Gurley
    Meyersdale, Pennsylvania
GUY—1911
    Brintnell Motor Car Co.
    Toronto, Ontario, Canada
GUY VAUGHAN—1910-13
    W. A. Woods Co.
    W. A. Wood Automobile Mfg. Co.
    Kingston, New York
    Vaughan Motors Co. (1912-13)
    Name was to be changed to "Vaughan" for
1914. See "Vaughan"
G.V.—1907
    General Vehicle Co.
    Long Island City, New York
    Absorbed Vehicle Equipment Co. May,
1908. Wright-Martin bought plant.
GYROSCOPE THREE-WHEELER—1900
    Western Wheel Works
    Chicago, Illinois
    On display in New York City November,
1900. Also called "Tri Moto."
GYROSCOPE—1908-09
    Gyroscope Co. Inc.
    New York, New York

Rotary type engine.
Patents sold to "Page-Adrian."
GYROSCOPE—1908
    Blomstrom Mfg. Co.
    Detroit, Michigan
GYROSCOPE—1914
    Blomstrom Automobile Co.
    Detroit, Michigan
    Built by Lion Motor Car Co., Adrian.

H

HAASE—1903-04
    Northwestern Automobile Co.
    H. Brothers
    Milwaukee, Wisconsin
    See "H.B." highwheeler.
HABERER—1908
    Cincinnati, Ohio
HACKETT—1916-19
    Hackett Motor Car Co.
    Jackson, Michigan
    Grand Rapids, Michigan
    Succeeded "Argo"
    Became "Lorraine," Lorraine Motor Car Co.
HACKLEY steam—1905-06
    George T. Hackley
    Los Angeles, California
*HACKNEY
    Believed to be misspelling of "Hackley."
HAGAMAN—1895
    J. D. Hagaman
    Adrian, Michigan
HAGMANN—1904
    Hagmann & Hammerly
    Chicago, Illinois
HAHN—1902
    Pueblo, Colorado
H.A.L.—1915-18
    Harry A. Lozier
    H. A. Lozier & Co.
    Cleveland, Ohio (1915)
    Reorganized as H.A.L. Motor Car Co., 1916.
    Reported auction April, 1918.

HALF BREED—1916
    Wiley Griffin
    McCracken, Kansas
    Assembled from two production cars.
    One off.
HALL—1902-04
    Hall Motor Carriage Co.
    Dover, New Jersey
    Became Hall Motor Vehicle Co. 1903.
HALL—1905-06
    Specht & Kuntz
    St. Louis, Missouri
    Two cars built.
HALL cyclecar—1914-16
    Hall Cyclecar Mfg. Co.
    Waco, Texas
    1915 became Hall Motor Car Co.
HALL—1950
    T. P. Hall
    San Diego, California
HALLADAY—1907-22
    1907-14 Streator Motor Car Co.
    Streator, Illinois
    1914-17 A. C. Barley Mfg. Co.
    Streator, Illinois
    1917-18 Halladay Motor Car Co.
    1918-20 Halladay Motor Co.
    Attica, Ohio
    1920-22 Halladay Motors Corp.
    Newark, Ohio
    Became "Falcon"
HALL GASOLINE TRAP—1895
    John W. Hall & Sons
    Jacksonville, Illinois
(HALLOCK)—1915
    Hallock Engineering Co.
    Cleveland, Ohio
HALSEY—1901-10
    Halsey Motor Vehicle Co.
    Philadelphia, Pennsylvania
HALSEY steam—1904
    James T. Halsey
    New York, New York
*HALSMAN
    Believed to be "Holsman" misspelled.

HALTON—1901
HALVERSON juvenile—1908
    New York, New York
    A. Halverson
    New York, New York
HAMBRICK—1905-06
    J. W. Hambrick
    Huntington, West Virginia
    Hambrick Motor Car Co.
    Parkersburg, West Virginia
    Also known as "Grey Goose."
HAMBRICK—1908
    Hambrick Motor Car Co.
    Washington, Indiana
HAMELY—1903
HAMILTON—1909-10
    Columbia Carriage Co.
    Hamilton, Ohio
HAMILTON—1917
    Hamilton Motor Car Co.
    York, Pennsylvania
HAMILTON—1917-18
    Hamilton Motors Co.
    Grand Haven, Michigan
    Absorbed Alter Motor Car Co.
    Mostly trucks
HAMILTONIAN—1911
    Hamilton Motor Car Co.
    Greensburg, Indiana
    Listed in Automobile Trade Journal April, 1911, but production is questioned.
HAMLIN—1930
    Hamlin Motor Co.
    Harvey, Illinois
    Front-wheel drive prototype. Company failed before starting production.
HAMLIN-HOLMES—1919-30
    Hamlin-Holmes Motor Car Co.
    Harvey, Illinois
    Detroit, Michigan
    Front-wheel drive. 38 cars built.
HAMMER—1905-06
    Hammer Motor Co.
    313-315 Rio Pellc
    Detroit, Michigan

Succeeded Hammer-Sommer Auto Carriage
Co. Touring cars and limousines were built.

HAMMER-SOMMER—1902-04
Hammer-Sommer Automobile
Carriage Co.
Detroit, Michigan
Became Hammer Motor Co.
See "Hammer" and "Sommer."

HAMMETT STEAM CARRIAGE—1900
H. M. Hammett
Boston, Massachusetts

HAMPDEN—1899-1901
Hampden Automobile and
Launch Co.
Springfield, Massachusetts
Chicopcc Falls, Massachusetts
F. J. Duryea's interim project.

HAMROCK—1908

HANAVER—1901
Charles Hanaver Cycle Co.
Cincinnati, Ohio

HANCHETT—1900
George T. Hanchett
New York, New York

HANDLEY—1923
Handley Motors Inc.
Kalamazoo, Michigan
Purchased by "Checker Cab" 1923.

HANDLEY-KNIGHT—1920-23
The Handley-Knight Co.
Kalamazoo, Michigan
Used "Willys-Knight" engine.
Became "Handley"

HANFORD-RODGERS
George Hanford

HANOVER—1921-24
General Gas-Electric Co.
Hanover, Pennsylvania
Hanover Motor Car Co.
Hanover, Pennsylvania
Purchase of "Parenti" plant in Buffalo,
New York reported June, 1922.

HANSEN—1895
Chicago Carriage Motor Co.
Chicago, Illinois

HANSEN—1902
Hansen Automobile Co.
Cleveland, Ohio
Became General Automobile Mfg. Co.

HANSEN—1906
Four Wheel Drive Wagon Co.
Milwaukee, Wisconsin

(HANSEN-WHITMAN)—1907
Hansen Auto & Machine Works
Pasadena, California

HANSON—1917-23
George W. Hanson (1916)
Hanson Motor Co.
Atlanta, Georgia
Company incorporated 1916.
Production to have started May, 1917 with
100 per day scheduled.

HARBER—1904
Harber Bros.
Bloomington, Illinois

HARBERER—1910

HARDIE—1896
American Air Power Co.
New York, New York

HARDIE—1900
Hardie-Lynes Foundry & Machine Co.
Birmingham, Alabama

HARDING—1899
Harding Mfg. Co.
Nashville, Tennessee

HARDING—1911-12
Harding Motor Car Co.
London, Ontario, Canada

HARDING—1916-17
Harding Motor Car Co.
Cleveland, Ohio
Twelve-cylinder motor

HARDINGE SIX-WHEELER—1903-04
Hardinge Co.
York, Pennsylvania
Two built. Became "York-Pullman"

HARDY—1902-03
Flint Automobile Co.
Flint, Michigan
Former "Flint" and "Roadster."

*HARE—1918
Holding company for "Mercer,"
"Locomobile," "Simplex"; no "Hare" car.

HARKNESS—1904
Harkness Automobile Co.
Flushing, New York

HARPER—1907-08
Harper Buggy Co.
Columbia City, Indiana

HARRIE—1925

(HARRIGAN)—1922
Harrigan Motor Corp.
Jersey City, New Jersey (office)
Cleveland, Ohio (factory)

HARRIS—1891; 1896
G. T. Harris
Washington, D.C.
Philadelphia, Pennsylvania

HARRIS—1900
Peter Harris
Manchester, New Hampshire

HARRIS 6—1923
U.S. Tractor & Machinery Co.
Wisconsin Automotive Corp.
Menasha, Wisconsin

HARRIS—1935-37
Benjamin F. Harris III
Chicago, Illinois

HARRISBURG—1922

HARRISON—1905-07
Harrison Wagon Co.
Grand Rapids, Michigan

HARROLDS—1905
Harrolds Motor Car Co.
New York, New York

HARROUN—1905
R. W. Harroun
Chicago, Illinois

HARROUN—1917-22
Ray Harroun
Detroit, Michigan
Harroun Motors Corp.
Wayne, Michigan

HARRUFF—1930
J. W. Harruff

Toledo, Ohio

HART—1953-54
Los Angeles, California

HART STEAM—1904-05
Frederick Hart
Poughkeepsie, New York

HARTFORD—1914- ?
Hartford Motor Car Co.
Hartford, Connecticut
1916 one car registered in Michigan.

HARTFORD-APPERSON—1916
Hartford-Apperson Motor Co.
Hartford, Connecticut

HARTLEY STEAM—1896-98
Hartley Power & Supply Co.
Chicago, Illinois
A steam unit adaptable to horse-drawn vehicles.

HARTMAN—1898

HARTMAN—1914-20
George V. Hartman
(Maine Machine Works)
Los Angeles, California
About 20 cars built.

HARVARD—1908
Pioneer Motor Car Co.
York, Pennsylvania

HARVARD—1915-21
Pioneer Motor Car Co.
Troy, New York
1916 became Harvard-Pioneer Motor Car Co., Troy, New York, with assembly in Hudson Falls, New York.
1920 became Harvard-Pioneer Motor Car Co. Hyattsville, Maryland.

HARVEY—1914

HASBROUCK—1899-1902
Hasbrouck Motor Co.
Newark, New Jersey
Hasbrouck Motor Works
Piermont, New York

HASCHKE ELECTRIC—1904
J. E. Haschke
Chicago, Illinois

*HASELTINE—1916

Believed to be "Heseltine" misspelled.

*HASSE—1904
Northwestern Furniture Co.
Milwaukee, Wisconsin
Believed to be misspelling of "Haase."

HASSLER—1917
Hassler Motor Car Co.
Indianapolis, Indiana

HASSLER MOTOR BUGGY—1898
R. H. Hassler
Indianapolis, Indiana

HASTINGS—1910
Hastings Motor Car Co.
Detroit, Michigan

HATFIELD HIGHWHEELER—1906-08
Hatfield Motor Vehicle Co.
Cortland, New York
Advance Motor Vehicle (1908)
Miamisburg, Ohio
See "Buggyabout"

HATFIELD—1917-24
Cortland Cart & Carriage Co.
Sidney, New York
Operated in receivership July, 1924.

HAUSHALTER—1910
H. P. Haushalter
Milwaukee, Wisconsin

HAVERS—1910-14
Havers Motor Car Co.
Port Huron, Michigan

HAVILAND—1895
Dr. Frank M. Haviland
210 West 123rd St.
New York, New York

HAVOC CYCLECAR—1914
Havoc Cyclecar Mfg. Co.
Rochester, New York

HAWK CYCLECAR—1914
Hawk Motor Car Co.
Hawk Cyclecar Co.
Detroit, Michigan

HAWK (model)—1956-64
See "Studebaker"
Studebaker-Packard Corp.
South Bend, Indiana

HAWKINS—1905-06
Hawkins Automobile & Gas Engine Co.
Houston, Texas

HAWKINS CYCLECAR—1914
Hawkins Cyclecar Co.
Xenia, Ohio
January, 1915 directors sued to close company. See "Xenia"

HAWLEY—1906-08
Hawley Automobile Co.
Constantine, Michigan
Mendon, Michigan

HAY-BERG—1907-08
Hay-Berg Motor Car Co.
Milwaukee, Wisconsin

HAYDOCK—1906-08
D. W. Haydock Automobile Mfg. Co.
St. Louis, Missouri
Front-wheel drive.

HAYDOCK—1915-16
Haydock Motor Car Co.
Cincinnati, Ohio

HAY & HOTCHKISS—1898-99
Walter Hay
Hay & Hotchkiss Co.
New Haven, Connecticut
Original car extant, 1950.

HAYN—1901
Western Gas Engine Co.
Mishawaka, Indiana

HAYNES—1894; 1904-25
Haynes Automobile Co.
Kokomo, Indiana

HAYNES-APPERSON—1895-1905
Haynes-Apperson Co.
Kokomo, Indiana

HAYWARD—1913

HAZARD—1914-15
Hazard Motor Mfg. Co.
Rochester, New York

HAZELTON STEAM—1908
M. W. Hazelton
Oneonta, New York

H.B. HIGHWHEELER—1908
H. Brothers

Chicago, Illinois
See "Haase"
H-C—1916
  H-C Motor Car Co.
  Detroit, Michigan
H.C.S.—1920-25
  Harry C. Stutz
  H.C.S. Motor Car Co.
  Indianapolis, Indiana
  1919: 125 cars built
  Became H.C.S. Cab Mfg. Co.
  Taxicabs built 1925-27.
HEADLAND—1899
  Harry Headland
  Freedom, Pennsylvania
*HEALEY—1953-55
  Nash Motors
  Kenosha, Wisconsin
  See "Nash-Healey"
HEALY—1900
  Healy Bros.
  Madera, California
HEALY ELECTRIC—1910-11
  Healy & Co.
  New York, New York
  Also gasoline car in 1910.
*HEARSEY HORSELESS—1899
  Hearsey Horseless Vehicle Co.
  Indianapolis, Indiana
  Believed to be error for "Horsey Horse-less."
HEIFNER—1919-22
  L. M. Heifner Mfg. Co.
  Heifner-Douglas-Perkins Co.
  Chester Pennsylvania
  Heifner Motor Car Co.
  Geneva, Ohio
HEILMAN—1905-08
  John C. Heilman
  Cincinnati, Ohio
HEINE-VELOX—1906-08; 1921-24
  Heine Velox Motor Co.
  San Francisco, California (1906-08)
  Heine-Velox Engineering Co. (1921)
HEINZELMAN HIGH WHEEL—1908

Heinzelman Bros. Carriage Co.
Belleville, Illinois
HENDEE—1902
  Hendee Mfg. Co.
  Springfield, Massachusetts
HENDEL—1903
  William Hendel & Son
  Red Wing, Minnesota
HENDERSON—1912-14
  Henderson Motor Car Co.
  Indianapolis, Indiana
  June, 1912 introduction announcement.
  July, 1914 liquidation notice.
HENLEY STEAM—1899
  Henley-Kimball Co.
  Boston, Massachusetts
HENNEGIN HIGHWHEELER—1908
  Commercial Automobile Co.
  Chicago, Illinois
HENNEY—1931
  Henney Motor Co.
  Freeport, Illinois
  Custom convertible sedans.
  Owned by Moline Plow Co.
HENNEY-KILOWATT EXPERIMENTAL
  ELECTRIC—1960-64
  The Henney Motor Co.
  Bloomington, Illinois
  Division of Eureka Williams Corp.
  Canastota, New York
HENRIETTA STEAM—1901
  Henrietta Motor Co.
  New York, New York
HENRY—1910-12
  D. W. Henry
  Henry Motor Car Co.
  Muskegon, Michigan
  Bankrupt 1912
  1909 succeeded Gary Motor Car Co.
HENRY GRAY—1912
  Henry Gray
  Los Angeles, California
  One car produced. Now in Harrah's Collection, Reno, Nevada.
HENRY J.—1950-54

Kaiser-Frazer Corp.
Willow Run, Michigan
See "Allstate"
HERCULES ELECTRIC—1902
  Smith Stamping Factory
  Milwaukee, Wisconsin
HERCULES ELECTRIC—1906-07
  James MacNaughton Co.
  Buffalo, New York
HERCULES—1914-15
  Hercules Motor Car Co.
  Hercules Automobile Co.
  Hercules Sales Co.
  New Albany, Indiana
  Kentucky Wagon Mfg. Co.
  Louisville, Kentucky
  Former "Crown" and "Ohio Falls" cars.
HERCULES ELECTRIC—1919
  The Hercules Corp.
  Evansville, Indiana
HERFF-BROOKS—1914-16
  Herff-Brooks Corp.
  Indianapolis, Indiana
  Absorbed Marathon Motor Works.
  See "Marathon" (1908-14)
HERKIMER—1903-04
  James A. Clark Co.
  Utica, New York
HERMES—1920
  Tsacomas Desmos
  New York, New York
  Built for export to Greece only.
HERMITAGE—1912
  Hermitage Motor Co.
  Nashville, Tennessee
HERRESHOFF STEAM—1880
  Herreshoff Engine Co.
  Providence, Rhode Island
HERRESHOFF—1909-14
  Herreshoff Motor Co.
  Detroit, Michigan
  Later Herreshoff Motor Car Co.
(HERRESHOFF LIGHT CAR)—1914
  Herreshoff Light Car Co.
  97 First Street

CODE = ROMAN LETTERS: Complete entry. *ITALICS:* Unsubstantiated entry. (PARENTHESES): Production planned, but not realized.

Troy, New York
Became "Harvard."
HERRMANN—1905
    Herrmann Automobile Co.
    Tell City, Indiana
HERSCHELL-SPILLMAN—1904-07
    Herschell-Spillman Mfg. Co.
    North Tonawanda, New York
HERSCHMANN STEAM—1903-05
    Columbia Engineering Works
    Brooklyn, New York
    Commercial Automobile Co.
    New York, New York
HERTEL—1895-1900
    Max Hertel
    Chicago, Illinois
    Reorganized 1898 as Oakman Motor Vehi-
    cle Co. Greenfield, Massachusetts.
    By 1899 there was no mention of "Hertel"
    in "Oakman" publicity.
HERTZ—1925-26
    Yellow Cab Mfg. Co.
    Chicago, Illinois
    Formerly "Ambassador"
    General Motors control in 1925.
    A "Drive It Yourself" rental car.
HESELTINE—1916-17
    Heseltine Motor Corp.
    Buffalo, New York
    Succeeded "Gadabout"
(HESS) STEAM—1902
    Hess Steam Vehicle Co.
    Philadelphia, Pennsylvania
    Charcoal burner manufacturer.
HESSE—1895
    Gregory C. Hesse
    New York, New York
HEWITT—1905-11
    William Hewitt
    Hewitt Motor Co.
    New York, New York
    Formerly Standard Motor Construction Co.
    See "Standard" (1904-05) and "United
    States Long Distance."
HEWITT-LINDSTROM ELECTRIC—1900-04

Hewitt-Lindstrom Electric Co.
Chicago, Illinois
HEYMAN—1901-04; 1907
    Edward Heyman
    Boston, Massachusetts
    Five-cylinder rotary motor.
HEYMANN—1898-1904
    Heymann Motor Vehicle and
        Mfg. Co.
    Melrose, Massachusetts (1898)
H.F.—1902
    H. F. Construction Co.
    New London, Connecticut
H&F ELECTRIC—1910
    H&F Electromobile Co.
    Detroit, Michigan
HIAWATHA—1903-04
    Hiawatha Mfg. Co.
    Hiawatha, Kansas
HICKENHULL—1904
HICKEY TRAIL-BLAZER—1961- ?
    Trail-Blazer
    Downey, California
    Four-wheel drive cross country vehicle.
HICKS FIVE-WHEELER—1899-1900
    John C. Hicks
    Hicks Motorcycle Co.
    Chicago, Illinois
    Fifth wheel in center of rear axle for driv-
    ing.
*HICO—1900
    John C. Hicks
    Chicago, Illinois
    Believed to be "Hicks" (5-wheeler) mis-
    spelled.
HIDLEY STEAM CARRIAGE—1901
    Hidley Automobile Co.
    Troy, New York
HIGDON—1905-07
    John C. Higdon
    St. Louis, Missouri
    Seven cars built
    Sold 980 motor buggies.
HIGDON & HIGDON—1896
    John L. Higdon

Kansas City, Missouri
HIGHLANDER 6—1918-22
    Frankfort Motor Car Co.
    Indianapolis, Indiana
    Midwest Motor Co.
    Kansas City, Missouri
HILDEBRAND—1895; 1897
    J. A. Hildebrand
    R. F. McMullin & Co.
    Chicago, Illinois
HILL—1868-70; 1885
    James F. Hill
    Fleetwood, Pennsylvania
HILL—1900
    C. C. Hill Automobile Co.
    Chicago, Illinois
HILL—1901
    J. J. Hill Co.
    Knightsville, Rhode Island
    Became "Rhode Island"
HILL—1905-08
    Hill Automobile Co.
    Hill Motor Car Co.
    Haverhill, Massachusetts
HILL CLIMBER—1904-05
    Hill Climber Auto Mfg. Co.
    San Francisco, California
HILL LOCOMOTOR—1896
    Hill & Cummings
    Chicago, Illinois
(HILLSDALE)—1908
    Hillsdale Motor Co.
    Hillsdale, Michigan
HILTON—1908
HILTON—1921
    Motor Sales & Service Co.
    Philadelphia, Pennsylvania (office)
    Riverton, New Jersey (factory)
    Introduced August 13, 1920.
HINES—1901; 1908
    Moehlhauser Machine Co.
    National Screw & Tack Co.
    Cleveland, Ohio
HINES CAR—1908-10
    See "Hines"

*ASTERISK: Error corrected from previous list. See introduction to this section for complete code.

National Screw & Tack Co.
Cleveland, Ohio
Both names apply to the same vehicle.
HINKEL—1925
(HITCHCOCK)—1909
Hitchcock Motor Car Co.
Warren, Michigan
HOBBIE ACCESSIBLE
HIGHWHEELER—1908-09
Hobbie Automobile Co.
Hampton, Iowa
HOBBS—1903
John O. Hobbs
Self-starting
Became "Lorraine"
*HOCKENHULL—1904
Believed to be name of a driver, not a car.
HODDETTS—1916
HODGSON—1902
HOFFMAN STEAM—1900-04
Hoffman Automobile Mfg. Co.
Cleveland, Ohio
Formerly Hoffman Bicycle Co.
Became "Royal Tourist"
Name changed to Royal Motor Car Co.
Later gasoline cars
HOFFMAN—1931
Roscoe C. Hoffman
Detroit, Michigan
Front-wheel drive
HOFWEBER—1914
Hoff Motor Co.
Detroit, Michigan
HOLBROOK—1912
Holbrook-Armstrong Co.
Racine, Wisconsin
HOLCOMB—1913
American Box Ball Co.
Indianapolis, Indiana
HOLDEMAN—1895
HOLDEN CYCLECAR—1914
George B. Holden
Indian Cycle Co.
Springfield, Massachusetts
HOLDEN THREE-WHEELER—1915

C. Clarence Holden
Comanche, Texas
HOLIBIRD—1930-33
HOLIHAN—1916
HOLLAND—1901-05
Holland Automobile Co.
Jersey City, New Jersey
Also built "Boisselot"
HOLLAND—1910
Holland Automobile Mfg. Co.
Holland, Michigan
HOLLEY—1897; 1900-04
George M. Holley
Bovaird & Sefang Mfg. Co.
Holley Bros., (Holley Motor Co.)
Bradford, Pennsylvania
Became Bradford Motor Works
HOLLIER—1915-22
Lewis Spring & Axle Co.
Jackson, Michigan
Chelsea, Michigan
1922 Hollier Automobile Co.
1914 built "Briscoe" chassis.
HOLLIS ELECTRIC—1922
Hollis Tractor Co.
Tiffin, Ohio
First car built in Hollywood, California.
*HOLLY—1900
Believed to be "Holley" misspelled.
HOLLY—1913-20
Holly Motor Co.
Mt. Holly, New Jersey
See "Otto-Mobile"
HOLMES—1900
Frank C. Holmes
Binghamton, New York
HOLMES STEAM—1902
Robert Holmes & Sons
Danville, Illinois
HOLMES—1906-08
Holmes & Childs Motor Co.
Holmes Motor Vehicle Co.
East Boston, Massachusetts
HOLMES AIR-COOLED—1917-23
Holmes Automobile Mfg. Co.

Canton, Ohio
HOLMES GAS TRICYCLE—1895
Lyman S. Holmes
Gloversville, New York
HOLSMAN HIGHWHEELER—1902-12
Holsman Automobile Co.
Chicago, Illinois
Plano, Illinois
HOLSON AUTOMOBILE CART—1901
A. B. Holson
Chicago, Illinois
HOLSON ELECTRIC—1904-05
Holson Motor Patents Co.
Grand Rapids, Michigan
See "Autolet" electric
HOLT—1925
HOL-TAN—1907-08
Hollander & Tangeman
New York, New York
Built by Moon Motor Car Co.
Company formerly New York "Fiat" dealer.
HOLTON—1919
Clyde Cars Co.
Clyde, Ohio
Also built "Clydesdale" trucks.
HOLTZER-CABOT ELECTRIC—1892-95
Holtzer-Cabot Electric Co.
Brookline, Massachusetts
Built-to-order vehicles.
1892 car built for Fiske Warren.
HOLYOKE—1901-03
Holyoke Motor Works
Holyoke Automobile Co.
Holyoke, Massachusetts
Became Matheson Motor Car Co., see "Matheson."
HOMER-LAUGHLIN—1916-18
Homer-Laughlin Engineering Corp.
Los Angeles, California
Front wheel drive.
HOMESTEAD—1900
Homestead Motor Vehicle Co.
Homestead, Pennsylvania
HONEY BEE—1959

Swift Mfg. Co.
El Cajon, California
HOOD STEAM—1899-1901
R. O. Hood
Simplex Motor Vehicle Co.
Danvers, Massachusetts
HOOSIER LIMITED—1907-08
Coppock Motor Car Co.
Decatur, Indiana
HOOSIER SCOUT CYCLECAR—1914
Warren Electric & Machine Co.
Indianapolis, Indiana
HOOVER CYCLECAR—1913
H. H. Hoover
St. Louis, Missouri
HOPKINS—1902-03
Hopkins Motor Carriage Co.
Wellington, Massachusetts
E. P. Hopkins
New York, New York
HOPPENSTAND—1948-49
Hoppenstand Motors Inc.
Greenville, Pennsylvania
HORACK—1902
Kittery, Maine
HORNET—1970 to date
American Motors Corp.
Detroit, Michigan
HORSELESS CARRIAGE—1901
Horseless Carriage Co.
Barberton, Ohio
HORSEY HORSELESS—1899
Uriah Smith
Battle Creek, Michigan
"Haynes-Apperson" with horse head and rigged with reins.
HORTON—1911
Horton Autoette Mfg. Co.
Detroit, Michigan
HOSEMER—1903
HOSKINS—1920
G. J. Hoskins & Sons
Los Angeles, California
HOTSHOT (model)—1949
Roadster model of "Crosley"

See "Crosley"
Crosley Motors Inc.
Cincinnati, Ohio
HOUCK—1917
HOUGHTON STEAMER—1900-01
Houghton Automobile Co.
West Newton, Massachusetts
HOUPT—1909-10
Harry S. Houpt Mfg. Co.
New York, New York
Factory at Bristol, Connecticut. 1910 became New Departure Mfg. Co. Afterwards "Houpt-Rockwell."
HOUPT-ROCKWELL—1910-12
New Departure Mfg. Co.
Bristol, Connecticut
Succeeded "Houpt"
HOUSE STEAM—1898-99; 1901
The Steam Car Co.
Bridgeport, Connecticut
HOUSE STEAMER—1866
Henry A. & James House
Bridgeport, Connecticut
Henry A. House built also "Lifu" steam trucks in England.
HOUSE—1920
HOUSER—1906
Orville Houser
Chillicothe, Ohio
HOWARD—1895-1900
The Howard Cycle Co.
Trenton, New Jersey
Became Howard Automobile Co.
See "Howard Steamer"
HOWARD—1901
Grant-Ferris Co.
Troy, New York
HOWARD—1903-08
Howard Automobile Co.
Yonkers, New York
Succeeded Trojan Launch & Autoworks, Troy, New York.
HOWARD—1908
Howard Motor Works
Yonkers, New York

Sold assembled or unassembled cars.
HOWARD—1911
Howard Automobile Co.
Jackson, Michigan
Macon, Georgia
HOWARD—1913-14
Central Car Co.
Connersville, Indiana
Also Howard Motor Car Co. Succeeded Lexington Motor Car Co. as Lexington Howard Co.
See "Lexington" (1909-28).
HOWARD—1916-17
A. Howard Co.
Galion, Ohio
HOWARD—1928-30
Howard Motors Corp.
Detroit, Michigan
Howard Motor International Co.
New York, New York
Former Acme Brass Co.
HOWARD STEAM—1901- ?
Howard Motor Car Co.
Galion, Ohio
HOWARD STEAMER—1900-02
Howard Automobile Co.
Trenton, New Jersey
Succeeded Howard Cycle Co.
HOWELL—1900
Wisconsin Wheel Works Co.
L. A. Howell
Racine, Wisconsin
HOWEY—1903-08
Howey Motor Car Co.
Kansas City, Missouri
HOWMET T.X.—1968
Howmet Corp.
New York, New York
HOYT STEAM—1901
A. H. Hoyt
Penacook, New Hampshire
H.P. CYCLECAR—1913
For export
H.T.V. DUNE BUGGY—1968 to date
Bermoco Inc.

Berkeley, California
HUB ELECTRIC—1899-1900
Hub Motor Co.
Chicago, Illinois
HUB—1906
Hub Automobile Co.
Boston, Massachusetts
HUBER—1894
Ide-Sprung-Huber Automobile Co.
Oxford, Michigan
HUBER—1903-09
Huber Automobile Co.
Detroit, Michigan
HUDSON—1899-1900
Hudson Gas Motor & Vehicle Mfg. Co.
Saratoga, New York
HUDSON—1909-57
Hudson Motor Car Co.
Detroit, Michigan
Company founded February 24, 1909.
Started production July, 1909. First 1100
cars were 1909 models.
Merged with Nash-Kelvinator Corp. into
American Motors Corp. 1954.
HUDSON STEAM—1904
C. J. Hudson
Covington, Georgia
HUDSON STEAMER—1900-02
Beau-Chamberlain Mfg. Co.
Hudson, Michigan
Also known as "Beau-Chamberlain."
HUEBNER ELECTRIC CYCLECAR—1914
O. E. Huebner
Brooklyn, New York
HUFFMAN 6—1920-25
Huffman Bros. Motor Co.
Elkhart, Indiana
In August, 1920 stockholders asked re-
ceivership charging mismanagement and
fraud.
HUGHES STEAM—1899-1900
Hughes & Atkin Auto Carriage Co.
Providence, Rhode Island
See "Rhode Island"
One car built

HUMMING BIRD (model)—1912
See "Baker-Bell"
Baker-Bell Motor Co.
Philadelphia, Pennsylvania
HUMMING BIRD—1946
Talmadge Judd
Kingsport, Tennessee
HUMPHREY—1899
John D. Humphrey
New Britain, Connecticut
HUNT—1905
Hunt Automobile Co.
San Diego, California
HUNT SPECIAL—1910
Hunt & Hunt Automobile Specialists
San Diego, California
Built one five-passenger touring car.
HUNT STEAM—1936-40
J. Roy Hunt
Los Angeles, California
HUNTER—1900
Hunter Gun & Cycle Works
Fulton, New York
HUNTER—1920-21
Hunter Motor Car Co.
Harrisburg, Pennsylvania
At least one chassis completed November,
1920.
HUNTER ELECTRIC—1899-1904
Rudolph M. Hunter
Philadelphia, Pennsylvania
Last models built by Electric Vehicle Co.
HUNTER & STEUR—1935
E. F. Hunter and Allyn F. Steur
HUNTINGBURG—1901-03
Huntingburg Wagon Works
Huntingburg, Indiana
HUNTINGTON—1906-07
Huntington Automobile Co.
Huntington, New York
See "Merciless"
HUNTINGTON BUCKBOARD—1899
HUNT & OLSEN—1901
Hunt & Olsen Co.
San Jose, California

HUPMOBILE—1908-41
Hupp Motor Car Co.
Detroit, Michigan
Started delivering cars September, 1908.
Bought Chandler Factory and absorbed
"Chandler" 1929.
Operations suspended January, 1936 to
June, 1937. End of production mid-summer,
1940.
HUPP-YEATS ELECTRIC—1910-18
Hupp-Yeats Electric Car Co.
Hupp Corp.
Detroit, Michigan
June, 1911 five Hupp Companies con-
solidated, except Hupp Motor Car Co.
1912, R.C.H. Corp.
HURON—1915
Huron Motor Car Co.
Detroit, Michigan
HUSELTON—1914
HUSSEY—1903
Hussey Automobile & Supply Co.
Detroit, Michigan
H.W.O.—1922
HWO Motors Corp.
Chicago, Illinois
Milwaukee, Wisconsin
HYDE—1904
W. W. Hyde Co.
Milwaukee, Wisconsin
HYDRAMOTIVE—1961-62
HYDRO—1916
Hydro Motor Car Co.
Canton, Ohio
HYDROCAR—1901-02
Automobile Dept.
American Bicycle Co.
Toledo, Ohio
Sometimes misspelled "Hydra-Car."
Became "Rambler"
HYDRO-CARBON—1901-03
Friedman Automobile Co.
Chicago, Illinois
HYDRO-IMP BUCKBOARD—1948
Centerscope Products Inc.

CODE = ROMAN LETTERS: Complete entry. *ITALICS:* Unsubstantiated entry. (PARENTHESES): Production planned, but not realized.

Glendale, California
HYDROMOBILE—1902
American Hydromobile Works
Winchester, Ohio
HYDRO STEAM—1919
Hydro Engineering Co.
Cincinnati, Ohio
HYDROMOTOR—1916-17
Automobile Boat Mfg. Co.
Seattle, Washington
Became Hydromotor Car Mfg. Co.
Indian Motor & Mfg. Co.
Indianapolis, Indiana
HYLANDER—1919-22
See "Highlander"
Midwest Motor Co.
Kansas City, Missouri
Both names apply to the same vehicle.
HYSLOP CYCLECAR—1914
Hyslop & Clark
Toledo, Ohio

I

IDEAL—1902-03
B & P Co.
Milwaukee, Wisconsin
IDEAL—1903-09
Ideal Motor Vehicle Co.
Chicago, Illinois
IDEAL—1905-06
Ideal Motor Car Co.
Cleveland, Ohio
IDEAL STEAM—1906
Ideal Steam Automobile Co.
S. Berwick, Maine
IDEAL—1908-09
Ideal Mfg. Co.
Portsmouth, Ohio
IDEAL ELECTRIC—1909-11
Ideal Electric Co.
Chicago, Illinois
1910 Borland-Grannis Co.
IDEAL CYCLECAR—1914
The Ideal Cyclecar Shop
Buffalo, New York

IDEAL LIGHT CAR—1915-16
Ideal Light Car Co.
Columbus, Ohio
IDEAL RUNABOUT—1907-08
Ideal Runabout Mfg. Co.
Buffalo, New York
I & F—1910
I & F Motor Car Co.
New Britain, Connecticut
I.H.C. HIGHWHEELER—1907-11
See "International"
International Harvester Co.
Chicago, Illinois
Both names apply to the same vehicle.
I.H.C. AIR-COOLED HIGHWHEELER—1911
Independent Harvester Co.
Plano, Illinois
Similar to "Holsman" highwheeler. Four-cylinder engine. Also called "Independent Harvester."
ILLINOIS—1905
Illinois Auto-Motor Co.
Chicago, Illinois
ILLINOIS—1910-14
Overholt Co.
Illinois Automobile Co.
Galesburg, Illinois
Succeeded "Overholt" highwheeler.
ILLINOIS CYCLECAR—1914
Illinois Cyclecar Co.
Kankakee, Illinois
ILLINOIS ELECTRIC—1897-1901
Illinois Electric Vehicle &
Transportation Co.
Chicago, Illinois
IMHOF—1900
J. I. Imhof
Racine, Wisconsin
IMP CYCLECAR—1914
Imp Cyclecar Co.
(W. H. McIntyre Co.)
Auburn, Indiana
Designed by William B. Stout
Subsidiary of W. H. McIntyre Co. in hands of creditors' committee January, 1915.

IMP—1949-50
International Motor Products Co.
Glendale, California
A 7 1/2 hp plastic bodied auxiliary car.
IMPERIAL—1900
Imperial Automobile Co.
Chicago, Illinois
IMPERIAL—1900-01
Philadelphia Motor Vehicle Co.
Philadelphia, Pennsylvania
IMPERIAL—1903-05
Rodgers & Co.
Columbus, Ohio
Air-cooled cars 1904
Electrics 1905
IMPERIAL ELECTRIC—1903-05
Imperial Automobile Co.
Detroit, Michigan
IMPERIAL—1906-08
Imperial Motor Car Co.
Williamsport, Pennsylvania
Reported in hands of receivers October, 1908.
IMPERIAL—1907-15
Imperial Automobile Co.
Jackson, Michigan
Merged with "Marion" (1904-15) in Mutual Motors Corp.
IMPERIAL—1909
Imperial Motor Car Co.
Hamilton, Ohio
IMPERIAL—1955-70
Chrysler Corp.
Detroit, Michigan
Formerly "Chrysler Imperial"
Emerged as separate make 1955.
IMP-McINTYRE—1915
W. H. McIntyre
Auburn, Indiana
IMPROVED GAS—1901
Improved Gasoline Motor & Automobile Company.
Haverhill, Massachusetts
(INDEPENDENCE)—1912
Independence Motor Co.

Washington D.C. (office)
Hyattsville, Maryland
H. O. Carter organized new company to take over plant of defunct Carter Motor Car Corp.
INDEPENDENCE—1915
    Independence Motor Car Co.
    Lima, Ohio and Atlanta, Georgia
INDEPENDENT—1903
    Independent Automobile Mfg. Co.
    Sioux Falls, South Dakota
INDEPENDENT—1927
INDIAN—1909-10
    Indian Motor & Mfg. Co.
    Indianapolis, Indiana
    Indian Motor Car Co.
    Franklin, Indiana
INDIAN—1920
    Indian Motorcycle Co.
    Springfield, Massachusetts
    Prototypes only
    Plant built to build cars. Sold to Wire Wheel Company, then to "Rolls-Royce."
INDIAN—1927
    Indian Motorcycle Co.
    Springfield, Massachusetts
    Midget car prototype only.
INDIANA—1901
    Indiana Motor & Vehicle Co.
    Indianapolis, Indiana
INDIANA—1904
    Indiana Scale & Truck Co.
    Bluffton, Indiana
INDIANAPOLIS—1899
    Indianapolis Automobile and
        Vehicle Co.
    Indianapolis, Indiana
    Formerly C. H. Black Co.
INDIAN TRICAR—1905
    Hendee Mfg. Co.
    Springfield, Massachusetts
INGERSOLL-MOORE STEAMER—1888-95
    Ingersoll-Moore
    Bloomington, Illinois
    Built a 4-wheel 2-seat vehicle 1888. Three-

wheel and 6-wheel vehicles 1889. A car for the 1895 Chicago Times-Herald Race was designed but not completed by race day.
INGOT—1915
    Ingot Automobile Co.
    Calumet, Michigan
INGRAM-HATCH—1914-17
    Ingram-Hatch Co.
    Ingram-Hatch Motor Corp.
    Ingram-Hatch Motor Car Co.
    Rosebank, Staten Island, New York
    One chassis built only. Shown at 1917 New York Auto Show.
INMAN—1946
    Frank Inman
    Goose Creek, Texas
INNES—1921-22
    American Motors Export Co.
    Jacksonville, Florida
INTERNATIONAL 1899-1900
    International Auto Co.
    International Auto & Vehicle Co.
    Boston, Massachusetts
INTERNATIONAL steam—1899-1904
    International Power Co.
    Hartford, Connecticut
    Providence, Rhode Island
INTERNATIONAL—1900-01
    International Power Vehicle Co.
    (International Motor Carriage Co.)
    Stamford, Connecticut
    See "Klock"
INTERNATIONAL—1907-11
    International Harvester Co.
    Chicago, Illinois
    Experimental 1901
    Trucks after 1911
    Also known as "I.H.C." "International Auto Buggy," "Auto Wagon" and "Farmer's Auto."
INTERNATIONAL—1909
    International Automobile Co.
    Chicago, Illinois
INTERNATIONAL—1914
    International Cyclecar Co.

New York, New York
    See "Economycar"
INTERNATIONAL (SCOUT)—1961 to date
    International Harvester Co.
    Chicago, Illinois
INTERSTATE—1908-18
    Interstate Automobile Co.
    Muncie, Indiana
    1914 reorganized as Interstate Motor Co.
INTERURBAN electric—1905
    F. A. Woods Auto Co.
    Chicago, Illinois
    Front-wheel drive
INTREPID—1904-05
    Rotary Motor Vehicle Co.
    Boston, Massachusetts
    See "Rotary." The name "Intrepid" used in advertisements and catalogue.
IOWA—1908-09
    Iowa Motor Car Co.
    Kellogg, Iowa
IROQUOIS—1903-07
    John S. Leggett Mfg. Co.
    Syracuse, New York
    Became Iroquois Motor Co. February, 1905, and moved reportedly to Seneca Falls.
IROQUOIS STEAMER—1906-08
    Iroquois Iron Works
    Buffalo, New York
    One car built by W. Grant King.
IRVIN—1902
IVANHOE—1903
    Canada Cycle & Motor Co.
    Toronto, Ontario, Canada
IVERSON—1902-08
    J. E. Iverson & Co.
    Milwaukee, Wisconsin
IZZER—1910
    Irvington Izzer
    Irvington, New York
IZZER—1910
    Mier Carriage & Buggy Co.
    (and Model Engine Co.)
    Ligonier, (Peru) Indiana
    Three built

J

JACK FROST ELECTRIC—1903
  Kammann Mfg. Co.
  Chicago, Illinois
JACK RABBIT (model)—1912
  See "Apperson"
  Apperson Bros. Automobile Co.
  Kokomo, Indiana
JACKS—1899-1900
  Fred S. Jacks
  Jacks Autobain Co.
  Napa, California
JACKSON—1897
  Byron Jackson Machine Works
  San Francisco, California
JACKSON—1903-23
  Jackson Motor Carriage Co.
  Jackson Automobile Co.
  Jackson, Michigan (1903-19)
  Reorganized as Jackson Motors Corp. 1919.
  Absorbed Fuller Buggy Co. 1910.
  Absorbed with "National" and "Dixie-Flyer" into Associated Motor Industries.
  Renamed "National" (Model 651) 1923.
  See "Jaxon," "Duck" and "Orlo."
JACKS RUNABOUT—1900
  See "Jacks"
  Jacks Autobain Co.
  (F. S. Jacks)
  Napa, California
  Both names apply to the same vehicle.
JACQUET FLYER—1920
  Jacquet Motor Corp. of America
  Belding, Michigan
JAEGER—1933
  Jaeger Motor Car Co.
  Belleville, Michigan
JAMES STEAM—1829-30
  William T. James
  New York, New York
JAMES—1904
  Alfred James Foundry Co.
  La Crosse, Wisconsin
JAMES MOTOR BUGGY—1909-11

J. & M. Motor Car Co.
  Lawrenceburg, Indiana
  Succeeded "Dearborn"
JAMESON—1902
  M. W. Jameson Co.
  Warren, Pennsylvania
JAMIESON STEAM CARRIAGE—1899-1900
  Robert W. Jamieson
  Rochester, New York
JANNEY—1906-07
  Janney Motor Co.
  Flint, Michigan
  Absorbed by "Buick" 1907.
JARVIS & HUNTINGTON—1912-13
  Jarvis Machine & Supply Co.
  Jarvis-Huntington Automobile Co.
  Huntington, West Virginia
JAVELIN—1968 to date
  American Motors Corp.
  Detroit, Michigan
JAXON STEAM—1902-03
  Jackson Automobile Co.
  Jackson, Michigan
JAY—1907-08
  See "Webb-Jay" steam
  Webb-Jay Motor Co.
  Chicago, Illinois
JAY EYE SEE—1914
  J. I. Case Threshing Machine Co.
  Racine, Wisconsin
  Racing car
JAY-EYE-SEE (model)—1925
  See "Case"
  J. I. Case Threshing Machine Co.
  Racine, Wisconsin
JEANNIN—1908-09
  Jeannin Co.
  Jeannin Auto. Mfg. Co.
  St. Louis, Missouri
JEEP—1941 to date
  Willys-Overland, Inc. (1941-53)
  Willys Motors, Inc. (1953-63)
  Kaiser-Jeep Corp. (1963-70)
  Jeep Corporation (1970 to date)

Toledo, Ohio
  During the Second World War the car was an Army general purpose vehicle. Similar cars built by the Ford Motor Co. and American Bantam Car Co., 1941-45.
JEFFERY—1914-17
  Thomas B. Jeffery Co.
  Nash Motors Co.
  Kenosha, Wisconsin
  Succeeded "Rambler" (1902-13). Company bought by Charles W. Nash in July, 1916. Car renamed "Nash."
JEM—1922
  John E. Meyers
  New York, New York
  Also known as "Jem Special."
JENKINS—1900-06
  C. Francis Jenkins
  (Jenkins Auto. Co.)
  Washington, D.C.
  Steam and gasoline vehicles
JENKINS—1907-12
  J. W. Jenkins
  Jenkins Motor Car Co.
  Rochester, New York
JENNIS—1903-05
  P. Jennis
  Philadelphia, Pennsylvania
*JERSEY CITY—1919
  Wrong name for "Argonne."
JET (model)—1953-54
  See "Hudson"
  Hudson Motor Car Co.
  Detroit, Michigan
JETMOBILE THREE-WHEELER—1952
JEWEL—1906-10
  Forest City Motor Car Co.
  Massillon, Ohio
  1909 reorganized as Jewel Motor Car Co.
  1909 became Croxton-Keeton Motor Car Co. Name changed to "Croxton-Keeton."
JEWEL ELECTRIC—1911
  Jewel Electric Co.
  Chicago, Illinois
JEWELL—1905-06

---

*ASTERISK: Error corrected from previous list. See introduction to this section for complete code.

Forest City Motor Car Co.
Massillon, Ohio
Became "Jewel"

JEWETT—1901-02
Jewett Motor Carriage Co.
Jewett, Ohio

JEWETT—1922-27
Jewett Motors Inc.
Detroit, Michigan
Subsidiary of Paige-Detroit Motor Car Co.
Introduced January 12, 1922.

J.H.N. (model)—1903
Kit form or assembled.
See "Neustadt-Perry"
Neustadt-Perry Co.
St. Louis, Missouri

JOERNS—1910
Joerns Bros.
St. Paul, Minnesota

JOHNSON—1902
Johnson-Jennings Co.
Cleveland, Ohio

JOHNSON—1902-07
Johnson Gasoline Motor Co.
Manchester, New Hampshire

JOHNSON—1903

JOHNSON—1905-12
Johnson Service Co.
Milwaukee, Wisconsin
See "Elite" (1909-10) and "Empress"
Steam and gasoline vehicles.

JOHNSON steam—1911
Johnson Bros.
Philadelphia, Pennsylvania

JOHNSON—1913
Daniel E. Johnson
Hartford, Connecticut

JOHNSON MOBILE—1959
Horton Johnson Inc.
Highland Park, Illinois
One prototype (copy of a 1904 car) produced.

JOHNSON STEAMER—1896
Charles W. Johnson
Uniontown, Pennsylvania

Reportedly built one car a day until fire destroyed the company plant.

JOMAR—1956-60
Saidel Sports Racing Cars
Manchester, New Hampshire

JONAS—1904
Jonas Automobile Works
Milwaukee, Wisconsin

JONES—1905
Lewis Jones Machine Works
Philadelphia, Pennsylvania

JONES 6—1915-20
Jones Six Motor Car Co.
Jones Motor Car Co.
Wichita, Kansas
Manufacture began November, 1914.
Reported creditors asked receiver August, 1920.

JONES-CORBIN—1902-07
Jones-Corbin Co.
Jones-Corbin Automobile Co.
Philadelphia, Pennsylvania
Reported reorganized December, 1903.
Became "Sovereign," Matthews Motor Co.
Camden, New Jersey.

JONES STEAMER—1898-99
Joseph W. Jones
New York, New York

JONZ—1908-12
American Automobile Mfg. Co.
Jonz Automobile Co.
Beatrice, Nebraska
1911 absorbed American Automobile Mfg. Co. Kansas City, Missouri and moved to New Albany, Indiana.
Became Crown Motor Car Co. Louisville, Kentucky.
See "Crown"

JORDAN—1916-31
Jordan Motor Car Co.
Cleveland, Ohio
Jordan Motors Inc. in 1932 was an unsuccessful attempt at revival.

*JOY—1899
Believed to be an error for "Packard."

J.P.L. cyclecar—1914
J.P.L. Cyclecar Co.
Detroit, Michigan

JUDD-COMISKEY—1899-1900
Judd-Comiskey Motor Vehicle Co.
New York, New York

JUDSON—1915
Judson Motor Car Co.
Detroit, Michigan

JUERGENS—1908
Juergens Motor Car Co.
Chicago, Illinois

JULES 30—1911-12
Jules Motor Car Co. Ltd.
Guelph, Ontario, Canada

JULIAN—1919
Julian Motor Car Co.
Detroit, Michigan

JULIAN—1925
Julian Brown
Julian Brown Development Co.
Syracuse, New York
Radial-engined prototype. Although production was contemplated, Brown could not obtain the financing necessary, and the project died aborning. Only known "Julian" is in Harrah's Collection.

JULIAN BROWN—1925
See "Julian'
Julian Brown
Julian Brown Development Co.
Syracuse, New York
Both names apply to the same vehicle.

JUNIOR—1900

JUNIOR (model)—1925-27
A model of "Locomobile." Replaced by Model 8-70 "Locomobile."
See "Locomobile"
Locomobile Co. of America
Bridgeport, Connecticut

JUNZ—1902

JUVENILE electric—1906-07
The American Metal Wheel & Auto Co.
Toledo, Ohio
See "American Juvenile Electric"

K

KAISER—1947-55
Kaiser-Frazer Corp.
Willow Run, Michigan
First cars in late 1946.

KAISER-DARRIN—1953-54
Sport roadster
See "Darrin"
Kaiser-Frazer Corp.
Willow Run, Michigan

KALAMAZOO—1903-04
Michigan Buggy Co.
Kalamazoo, Michigan

KANE-PENNINGTON—1894-1900
Thos. Kane & Co.
Anglo-American Rapid Vehicle Co.
Racine, Wisconsin
Sold stock, little production.

KANSAS CITY—1905-09
Kansas City Motor Car Co.
Kansas City, Missouri
Former "Caps" Became "Gleason"

KANSAS CITY HUMMER—1904-05
Hummer Motor Car Co.
Kansas City, Kansas

KANSAS CITY WONDER—1909
Wonder Motor Car Co.
Kansas City, Missouri
See "Wonder"

KAPPE—1895
W. J. H. Kappe
Quincy, Illinois

KARBACH—1905-07
Karbach Automobile & Vehicle Co.
Omaha, Nebraska

KARNS KAR—1898-1905
Chester Karns
Everett, Pennsylvania

KATO—1907-09
Four Traction Automobile Co.
Mankato, Minnesota

KAUFFMAN—1909-12
Advance Motor Vehicle Co.

Miamisburg, Ohio
Reorganized as Kauffman Motor Car Co.
Formerly "Buggyabout." See "Hatfield"

KAVAN—1905
Kavan Mfg. Co.
Chicago, Illinois
A $200 vehicle

K-D—1912-14
K-D Motor Co.
Brookline, Massachusetts
(K-D is Knight-Davidson)
Crescent valve invented by Margaret
Knight.

KEARNS—1909-16
Kearns Motor Car Co. Inc.
Beavertown, Pennsylvania
Trucks and fire engines after 1911. 1912
located in Rockville Center, New York.

KEARNS MOTOR BUGGY—1908-09
Kearns Motor Buggy Co.
Beavertown, Pennsylvania
Became "Kearns"

KEARNS CYCLECAR—1914
Kearns Motor Car Co.
Beavertown, Pennsylvania

*KEASLER—1916
Believed to be misspelling of "Kessler"

KEATING—1899-1901
Keating Automobile & Wheel Co.
Middletown, Connecticut
Gas and electric cars

KEENE STEAMER—1900-01
Trinity Cycle Mfg. Co.
Keene, New Hampshire
Sold to Steamobile Co. of America.
Became "Steamobile"

KEEN STEAM—1955-61
The Keen Mfg. Co.
Madison, Wisconsin

KEETON—1913-15
Keeton Motor Co.
Chicago, Illinois
Detroit, Michigan
Became American Voiturette Co.
See "Car-Nation" cyclecar

Bankruptcy reported October, 1914.

KEETON TOWN CAR—1908
Keeton Town Car Works
Detroit, Michigan

KELLER CYCLECAR—1914
See "Keller Kar"
Keller Cyclecar Corp.
Chicago, Illinois
Both names apply to the same vehicle.

KELLER—1948-49
Keller Motors Corp.
Huntsville, Alabama
Succeeded "Bobbicar"
Two models only: station wagon and coupé
with soft or hard top.

KELLER KAR CYCLECAR—1914
Keller Cyclecar Co.
Chicago, Illinois

KELLISON—1960-63
Kellison Engineering & Mfg. Co.
Kellison Car Co.
Folsom, California

KELLOGG STEAMER—1903

KELLY—1901
William Kelly
Detroit, Michigan

KELLY—1904
Ernest R. Kelly
Wilmington, Delaware

KELLY—1905
Kelly-Bridgett Co.
Danville, Illinois

KELLY STEAM—1902
O. S. Kelly Co.
Springfield, Ohio

KELSEY—1902
C. W. Kelsey Co.
Philadelphia, Pennsylvania

KELSEY CYCLECAR—1913-14
Kelsey Car Corp.
Connersville, Indiana

KELSEY—1921-24
Kelsey Motor Co.
Newark, New Jersey
Friction-drive cars and taxi cabs.

KELSEY MOTORETTE THREE-WHEELER
—1910-12
    C. W. Kelsey Mfg. Co.
    Hartford, Connecticut
    Also called "Motorette"
KELSEY & TILNEY EXPERIMENTAL—1899
    C. W. Kelsey & I. S. Tilney
    Chestnut Hill
        (Philadelphia) Pennsylvania
    This car is now in the Smithsonian In-
    stitution, Washington D.C.
KELVIN—1906
KENDALL—1897
    Kendall Carriage Co.
    Camden, New Jersey
KENILWORTH—1923
KENMORE SEMI-HIGHWHEELER—1909-12
    Kenmore Mfg. Co.
    Chicago, Illinois
KENNEDY ELECTRIC—1898-1903
    C. W. Kennedy
    Philadelphia, Pennsylvania
KENNEDY—1905
    Kennedy Automobile Co.
    Cortland, New York
KENNEDY—1909-10
    Kennedy Mfg. Co.
    Preston, Ontario, Canada
KENNEDY—1911
KENNEDY—1915-18
    W. J. Kennedy Mfg. Co.
    Los Angeles, California
KENSINGTON—1899-1904
    Kensington Automobile Co.
    Kensington Automobile Mfg. Co.
    Buffalo, New York
    Formerly Kensington Bicycle Co.
    Electric and steam 1899-1902, gasoline
    1902-04.
KENT STEAM—1901
    A. W. Kent
    Marietta, Ohio
KENT—1916-17
    Kent Motors Corp.
    Newark (Belleville P.O.)

New Jersey
    Formerly exporters to Latin America.
    June, 1917 bankruptcy reported.
    November, 1917 officials indicted for using
    mails to defraud.
KENT'S PACEMAKER STEAM—1900
    Colonial Automobile Co.
    Boston, Massachusetts
KENTUCKY ELECTRIC—1914-15
    Kentucky Wagon Works
    Louisville, Kentucky
KENTUCKY KAR—1916
    Kentucky Wagon Works
    Louisville, Kentucky
KENTUCKY THOROUGHBRED
    (model)—1914
    See "Ames"
    Ames Motor Car Co.
    Owensboro, Kentucky
KENWORTHY—1920-22
    Kenworthy Motor Corp.
    Mishawaka, Indiana
    First shown at 1920 Chicago Auto Show.
KEPLER-BERRY—1903-04
    Kepler-Berry Motor Car Co.
    Dayton, Ohio
*KERBACH—1908-09
    Believed to be an error for "Karbach."
KERMATH—1907-08
    Kermath Motor Car Co.
    Detroit, Michigan
KERMET—1900
KERMOTOR—1900-01
    Kermotor Co.
    Newark, New Jersey
KERNS—1914
KERNMOBILE—1902
    Brooklyn, New York
KEROSENE MOTOR SURREY—1900
    Kerosene Oil Engine Co.
    New York, New York
KERSTON GAS ELECTRIC—1917
    Harry Kerston
    South Bend, Indiana
KESSLER—1912-21

Kessler-Detroit Motor Car Co.
Kessler Motor Co.
Detroit, Michigan
Also called "Kessler-Super-Charge 4"
KESS-LINE 8—1921-25
    Kess-Line Motors
    Detroit, Michigan
    Became "Balboa"
KEYSTONE—1899-1901
    Keystone Motor & Mfg.
    Keystone Wagon Co.
    Reading, Pennsylvania
    Formerly Keystone Motor Cycle Co.
    Became Searchmont Motor Co.
KEYSTONE—1914-15
    H. C. Cook & Bros.
    Pittsburgh, Pennsylvania
KEYSTONE 6—1909-10
    Munch-Allen Motor Car Co.
    Du Bois, Pennsylvania
    Formerly Munch Motor Car Co., Yonkers,
    New York.
KEYSTONE WAGONETTE—1900
    Keystone Motor Co.
    Philadelphia, Pennsylvania
KIBLINGER HIGHWHEELER—1907-08
    W. H. Kiblinger Company
    Auburn, Indiana
    See "McIntyre"
KIDDER—1899-1903
    W. P. Kidder
    Jamaica Plain, Massachusetts
    Kidder Motor Vehicle Co.
    New Haven, Connecticut
    See "Springer"
KILBOURNE
KIMBALL ELECTRIC—1898-1912
    C. P. Kimball & Co.
    Chicago, Illinois
    Custom body builder after 1912.
KIMPEL CYCLECAR—1914
    George W. Kimpel
    Cleveland, Ohio
KING EXPERIMENTAL—1896
    Charles B. King

CODE = ROMAN LETTERS: Complete entry. ITALICS: Unsubstantiated entry. (PARENTHESES): Production planned, but not realized.

Detroit, Michigan
Claimed to be Detroit's first car.
KING—1909
KING—1911-24
King Motor Car Co.
Detroit, Michigan
Buffalo, New York (1923-24)
Charles B. King incorporated company in 1911. Built "King Light Car" 1914.
KING MIDGET—1948-69
Midget Motors Corp.
Athens, Ohio
KING-REMICK—1909-10
A. O. Dunk
Auto Parts Mfg. Co.
Detroit, Michigan
KINGSBURY—1915
Kingsbury Gas-Electric Motor Car Co.
Great Falls, Montana
KING STEAM CAR—1904
Osgood, Indiana
KINGSTON—1907
Kingston Motor Car Co.
Kingston, New York
Name changed to "Allen-Kingston" 1907.
Transferred to Bristol Engineering 1908.
KINNEAR—1913
Kinnear Mfg. Co.
Columbus, Ohio
Four-wheel drive
Built F.W.D. racer 1913.
KINNEY—1922
Boston, Massachusetts
KINSLEY BENNETT—1907
Hartford, Connecticut
KIRK—1903-04
Kirk-Snell Co.
Kirk Mfg. Co.
Toledo, Ohio
KIRKHAM—1906
Kirkham Motor Car Co.
Bath, Maine
KIRK-LATTY—1902
Kirk-Latty Mfg. Co.

Cleveland, Ohio
KIRKSELL—1907
Dr. James Selkirk
Aurora, Illinois
Prototype only, built in shop of C. C. Hinckley.
KIRKWORTH
KISH ELECTRIC—1961
KISSEL—1919-31
Kissel Motor Car Co.
Hartford, Wisconsin
Formerly "Kissel Kar"
KISSEL KAR—1906-19
Kissel Motor Car Co.
Hartford, Wisconsin
Name shortened to "Kissel" starting with 1919 models.
KISSEL-SILVER—1918-19
C. T. Silver Co.
New York, New York
Special design Kissels.
Also known as "Silver-Kissel"
KITE—1903
Kite Bros.
Ft. Scott, Kansas
KLAVER—1936-37
KLEIBER—1924-29
Kleiber Motor Truck Co.
San Francisco, California
Built trucks to 1930.
KLEPFER—1903
Klepfer Bros.
Depew, New York
KLEMM—1917
E. R. Klemm
Chicago, Illinois
KLINE—1909-11
B.C.K. Motor Car Co.
York, Pennsylvania and
Bath, New York
Reorganized 1911 as Kline Motor Car Co.
Name changed to "Kline Kar."
KLINE KAR—1911-23
Kline Motor Car Corp.
York, Pennsylvania

Opened Richmond, Virginia factory late 1912. Name changed to Kline Kar Corp. 1918.
KLING—1900-01
Kling Cycle Mfg. Co.
Harrisburg, Pennsylvania
*KLING—1907
Believed to be misspelling of "Klink."
KLINK—1907-10
Klink Motor Car Mfg. Co.
Dansville, New York
KLOCK—1900
Percy L. Klock
Stamford, Connecticut
Former National Motor Carriage Co.
Absorbed by International Motor Car Co.
KLONDIKE—1914-17
W. H. Kohlmeyer
Logansville, Wisconsin
K&M HIGHWHEELER—1908
Kreider Machine Co.
Lancaster, Pennsylvania
KNICKERBOCKER—1901-03
Ward-Leonard Electric Co.
Bronxville, New York
See "Century Tourist"
KNICKERBOCKER—1905
Knickerbocker Friction Drive Automobile Co.
Worcester, Massachusetts
KNIGHT STEAM—1900-01
Frank D. Knight & Son
Hudson, Massachusetts
KNIGHT & KILBOURNE—1906-09
Knight & Kilbourne Co.
Chicago, Illinois
See also "Silent Knight"
KNIGHT-SPECIAL—1917
Watson & Stoekle
New York, New York
KNOW—1900
Know Automobile Co.
New York, New York
KNOWLES—1904
Knowles Automobile Mfg. Co.

Buffalo, New York
Former "Kensington"
KNOWLES KHAKI FLYER—1901
Kensington Automobile Mfg. Co.
Buffalo, New York
KNOX—1898-1914
Knox Automobile Co.
Springfield, Massachusetts
Re-organized 1914 as Knox Motors Corp.
Continued with trucks.
KNOXMOBILE—1902
See "Knox"
Knox Automobile Co.
Springfield, Massachusetts
KNUDSEN ELECTRIC—1899
Karsten Knudsen
Chicago, Illinois
KNUDSEN—1948
Knudsen Mfg. & Design Co. Inc.
Buffalo, New York
Prototypes only
K.O.—1921
KOBUSCH—1906
Kobusch Automobile Co.
St. Louis, Missouri
Merged with St. Louis Car Co. 1906.
See "American Mors"
KOEB-THOMPSON—1910-11
Koeb-Thompson Motors Co.
Leipsig, Ohio
KOEHLER—1910-12
H. J. Koehler Co.
Newark, New Jersey
Announced February, 1910.
Trucks only after 1912.
KOEHRING—1932-40
KOETON—1908
KOHL—1902
Edward Kohl
Cleveland, Ohio
KOHL—1903
Kohl Automobile Co.
Whitney Point, New York
KOKOMO SIX (model)—1915
See "Haynes"

Haynes Automobile Co.
Kokomo, Indiana
KOMET—1898
Keith Bros.
Elkhart, Indiana
KOMET—1911
Elkhart Motor Co.
Elkhart, Indiana
KONIGSLOW—1900-04
Otto Konigslow
45-49 Michigan St.
Cleveland, Ohio
KONOLIMAN—1900
KOPPIN CYCLECAR—1914
Koppin Motor Car Co.
Fenton, Michigan
Succeeded "Fenton" cyclecar
KORFF—1952
Walter H. Korff
Burbank, California
KOSMATH—1916
Kosmath Co.
Detroit, Michigan
KOS MOS ELECTRIC—1906
KRAFT STEAM—1896-1901
J. F. Kraft
St. Louis, Missouri
KRALL
KRAMER—1915
Kramer Auto & Carriage Co.
Lancaster, Pennsylvania
KRAMER STEAM—1920
E. M. Kramer
Peoria, Illinois
KRASTIN—1902-03
August Krastin
Krastin Automobile Mfg. Co.
Krastin Automobile Co.
Cleveland, Ohio
KRIM-GHIA—1966
Krim-Ghia Import Co.
Detroit, Michigan
KRIT—1909-16
Krit Motor Car Co.
Puritan Machine Co.

Detroit, Michigan
Organized September 3, 1909.
"Packard" bought plant April, 1916.
KRON—1915
One registered in Michigan 1916.
KROTZ ELECTRIC—1902-05
Krotz Mfg. Co.
Springfield, Ohio
KRUEGER—1904-09
Krueger Mfg. Co.
Krueger Automobile Co.
Milwaukee, Wisconsin
KRUEGER—1947
KULAGE—1896
J. J. Kulage
St. Louis, Missouri
KUNZ—1897-1905
John L. Kunz (1897)
Appleton, Wisconsin
Kunz Automobile Co. (1901)
Kunz Automobile & Motor Co. (1902)
Speedwell Automobile Co. (1902-03)
J. L. Kunz Machine Co. (1904)
Milwaukee, Wisconsin
Company built cars 1902 and changed
name to Speedwell Automobile Co. No cars
built 1903 or 1904. Cars built again under
Kunz name 1905. Engines only after 1905.
KURTIS—1949-55
Kurtis-Kraft Inc.
Glendale, California
Kurtis Corp.
Los Angeles, California
After building 34 sports cars in 1949,
Frank Kurtis sold the entire operation to
Earl Muntz, who produced the "Muntz
Jet." Kurtis later produced other models of
his "Kurtis Kraft."
KURTZ AUTOMATIC—1921-23
Kurtz Motor Car Co.
Cleveland, Ohio
Pre-selector gearshift control
KYOTE DUNE BUGGY—1968- ?
Dean Jeffries Automotive Styling
Hollywood, California

CODE = ROMAN LETTERS: Complete entry. *ITALICS:* Unsubstantiated entry. (PARENTHESES): Production planned, but not realized.

L

LACONIA—1900
    Laconia Car Co.
    Laconia, New Hampshire
LACONIA CYCLECAR—1914
    H. H. Buffum
    Laconia, New Hampshire
LA DAWRI—1962- ?
    La Dawri Coach Craft
    Long Beach, California
    Mostly special bodies.
LAD'S CAR—1912-14
    Niagara Motor Car Corp.
    Niagara Falls, New York
    Juvenile car
LAFAYETTE—1904
    Lafayette Automobile Co.
    Detroit, Michigan
LAFAYETTE—1920-24
    Lafayette Motor Co.
    Mars Hill, Indiana
    Lafayette Motors Corp.
    Indianapolis, Indiana
    1924 re-organized as part of Nash Motors,
then moved to Milwaukee, Wisconsin. Also
a "Nash" subsidiary.
LAFAYETTE—1934-39
    Nash Motors Corp.
    Kenosha, Wisconsin
LA FRANCE—1903
    International Fire Engine Co.
    Elmira, New York
    Starting date of this company is not clear.
Pleasure car shown at Madison Square
Garden 1903. Reported bankrupt January,
1904. Revived later as American La France
Fire Engine Company.
LAHER ELECTRIC—1960-63
    Laher-Spring & Electric Car Corp.
    Oakland, California
    Memphis, Tennessee
LAKEWOOD ELECTRIC—1920
    Lakewood Engineering Co.
LA MARNE—1919-20

La Marne Motor Car Co.
Cleveland, Ohio
Later moved to Ontario, Canada (1921) as
Anglo-American Motors Inc.
LA MARNE, JR. (model)—1916
    La Marne Motor Car Co.
    Cleveland, Ohio
LAMB ELECTRIC—1901-02
    Lamb & Vedder Co.
    Lamb & Co.
    Adrian, Michigan
LAMB—1905
    Lamb Automobile Co.
    Clinton, Iowa
LAMBERT THREE-WHEELER—1891
    John W. Lambert
    Ohio City, Ohio
    One-cylinder engine by John B. Hicks
modified from a three-cylinder engine.
Offered for sale at $550 February, 1891.
LAMBERT—1903
    Lambert-Marion Co.
    St. Louis, Missouri
LAMBERT—1904-17
    Union Automobile Co.
    Union City, Indiana
    1905 became Lambert Automobile Co.
    Anderson, Indiana
    See "Union"
*LAMPHEN, LAMPHER
    Believed to be "Lanpher" misspelled.
LAMPO—1915
    Adams & Montant Co.
    New York, New York
LANCAMOBILE—1900-01
    James H. Lancaster, Co.
    New York, New York
    Electric and gasoline vehicles.
LANCASTER—1900-01
    James H. Lancaster Co.
    New York, New York
    See "Lancamobile"
LANCER (model)—1961-62
    See "Dodge"
    Chrysler Corp.

Detroit, Michigan
LANDRY—1913
    J. A. Landry Motor Car Co.
    New Orleans, Louisiana
LANE STEAM—1899-1910
    Lane Bros. Co.
    Lane Motor Vehicle Co.
    Poughkeepsie, New York
    First car in summer, 1900. Five cars sold
that year.
LANE & DALEY STEAM—1902
    Lane & Daley Co.
    Barre, Vermont
LANE STEAM WAGON—1901
    Lane & Daley Co.
    Barre, Vermont
    One car produced.
LANGAN—1897-1905
    Louis Langan
    St. Louis, Missouri
LANGER—1896
LANPHER—1909-12
    Lanpher Motor Buggy Co.
    Carthage, Missouri
    Often misspelled "Lampher"
LANSDEN ELECTRIC—1905-08
    The Lansden Co.
    Newark, New Jersey
    Continued with trucks. Basis of General
Motors Corporation electric trucks.
LA PETITE—1905
    Detroit Automobile Mfg. Co.
    Detroit, Michigan
    Became Marvel Motor Car Co.
    See "Marvel" and "Paragon."
LA POINTE—1948
    Albert A. La Pointe
    W. Hartford, Connecticut
LA POINTE-SIMPLEX—1903-04
    Hodge Iron Works
    Houghton-Hancock, Michigan
LA PORTE—1895
    La Porte Carriage Co.
    La Porte, Indiana
LARCHMONT STEAM—1900

*ASTERISK: Error corrected from previous list. See introduction to this section for complete code.

(LARCHMONT)—1920
  Larchmont Motors Corp.
  Newark, Delaware
LARK (model)—1959-64
  See "Studebaker"
  Studebaker-Packard Corp.
  South Bend, Indiana
LA ROCHE—1905
  La Roche Automobile Co.
  Dover, Delaware
LARSEN—1908-09
  John M. Larsen
  Larsen Machine Co.
  Chicago, Illinois
  Became "Falcon"
LARSON—1966 to date
  Larson Boat Works
  Little Falls, Minnesota
LA SAETTA—1955
LA SALLE—1927-41
  Cadillac Division
  General Motors Corp.
  Detroit, Michigan
LA SALLE-NIAGARA—1905-07
  La Salle-Niagara Automobile Co.
  Niagara Falls, New York
LASHER—1895
  R. E. Lasher
  St. Louis, Missouri
LASKY—1916
LAUER—1894
  John Lauer
  Detroit, Michigan
LAUGHLIN—1914-18
  Homer-Laughlin Engineering Corp.
  Los Angeles, California
  Front-wheel drive
LAUREL—1916-17
  Laurel Motor Car Co.
  Richmond, Indiana
LAUREL—1917-21
  Laurel Motors Corp.
  Anderson, Indiana
LAUTH—1905
  J. Lauth & Co.

Chicago, Illinois
LAUTH-JUERGENS—1907-09
  Lauth-Juergens Motor Car Co.
  Chicago, Illinois
  Trucks only after 1909.
LA VIGNE CYCLECAR—1913-14
  La Vigne Cyclecar Co.
  Detroit, Michigan
  See "J.P.L.," "La Petite," "Marvel" and
  "Paragon."
LAVIGNE LIGHT CAR—1914
  Lavigne Motor Co.
  Detroit, Michigan
  Former cyclecar
(LA VOIE)—1923
  Lavoie Automobile Devices Ltd.
  Montreal, Quebec, Canada
LAW—1901-02; 1904
  Frederick A. Law
  Hartford, Connecticut
  Inventor constructed several successful gas
  autos which became "Pope" gasoline cars.
  Then he incorporated in 1904 with several
  cars which were already built. See below.
LAW—1905-07
  Law Automobile Corp.
  Bristol, Connecticut
  Company dissolved March, 1907.
LAWLER STEAM—1948-50
  Lawler Steamobile
  South Gate, California
LAWRENCE & HOLLISTER—1902
  Lawrence & Hollister
  New Haven, Connecticut
LAWSON—1895
  Welch & Lawson
  New York, New York
LAWSON—1900
  Western Wheel Works
  Chicago, Illinois
LAWTER—1908-10
  Safety Shredder Co.
  Newcastle, Indiana
L.C.E.—1914-16
  L. C. Erbes

Jackson, Michigan and
  Waterloo, Iowa
  Former "Cutting"
L&E—1922-36
  Lundelius & Eccleston
  Los Angeles, California
LEACH STEAM—1899-1901
  Leach Motor Vehicle Co.
  Everett, Massachusetts
LEACH BILTWELL—1918-23
  Leach Motor Car Co.
  Leach-Biltwell Motor Car Co.
  Los Angeles, California
LEADER—1905-12
  Columbia Electric Co.
  McCordsville, Indiana (1905-06)
  Leader Manufacturing Co.
  Knightstown, Indiana (1906-12)
LEAR—1900
  Oscar Lear
  Columbus, Ohio
LEAR EXPERIMENTAL STEAM—1968 to date
  Lear Motor Co.
  Reno, Nevada
LEBANON—1906-08
  Lebanon Motor Works
  Lebanon, Pennsylvania
  Absorbed "Upton" 1904-07.
*LEBGETT—1903
  Believed to be "Leggett" misspelled.
(LE COMPTE) CYCLECAR—1914-15
  George W. Le Compte Co.
  65 Murray Street
  New York, New York
LEE—1910-11
  Diamond Mfg. Co.
  Detroit, Michigan
LEE & LARNED STEAM—1863
  Lee & Larned
  New York, New York
LEE & PORTER—1905
  Lee & Porter Mfg. Co.
  Buchanan, Michigan
LEGGETT—1903-05
  J. S. Leggett Mfg. Co. (1903)

J. S. Leggett Automobile Co. (1904-05)
Syracuse, New York
LEHR—1905; 1908-09
Lehr Agricultural Co.
Fremont, Ohio
LEIGHTON—1910
Leighton Auto Co.
Brockton, Massachusetts
LE JEAL—1902
Le Jeal Cycle & Mobile Works
Erie, Pennsylvania
*LELAND—1908
Motors only, not a car.
*LE MARNE—1921
Anglo American Motors Ltd.
Believed to be misspelling of "La Marne."
LENAWEE—1903-04
Church Mfg. Co.
Adrian, Michigan
See also "Murray"
LENDE—1908-09
Lende Automobile Mfg. Co.
Minneapolis, Minnesota
LENGERT—1896
Lengert Co.
Philadelphia, Pennsylvania
LENNON—1909
LENOT—1912-22
LENOX—1911-18
Lenox Motor Car Co.
Hyde Park, Massachusetts
Lawrence, Massachusetts
Succeeded "Martell"
LENOX (model)—1916
Paige-Detroit Motor Car Co.
Detroit, Michigan
See "Paige-Detroit"
LENOX—1920
A. G. Dalamater
New York, New York
For export only.
LENOX ELECTRIC—1908-09
Maxim & Goodridge
Hartford, Connecticut
LEON MENDEL—1890

LEON RUBAY—1923-24
Rubay Co.
Cleveland, Ohio
A line of town cars by famous body builder. Also called "Rubay."
*LEPHBRIDGE—1908-09
Misspelling of "Lethbridge"
LEPPO—1895
Leppo Bros.
Belleville, Ohio
LEROUX STEAM—1918
Marquette Motor Sales Co.
Chicago, Illinois
LEROY—1901-07
Dr. Milton H. Good & Nelson Good
Kitchener, Ontario, Canada
Experimental 1899-1900
32 cars built
Patterned after "Oldsmobile"
LESCINA—1916-17
Lescina Automobile Co.
Newark, New Jersey
First cars assembled at Chicago, Illinois.
LESLIE—1916
Leslie Motor Car Co.
Detroit, Michigan
(L'ESPERANCE)—1911
L'Esperance Motor Co.
Detroit, Michigan
Incorporated early 1911 with $10,000.
LESTER
LETHBRIDGE—1908-09
Lethbridge Motor Car Co.
Lethbridge, Alberta, Canada.
LEVER—1930-33
Formerly "Elcar"
Lever Motors, Inc.
Quapaw, Oklahoma
Others proposed to have been built by Kissel Inc. in 1933.
LEWIS—1894-99
George W. Lewis
Chicago, Illinois
Won prize for friction drive device in Chicago Times-Herald Race.

LEWIS—1895; 1899-1900
Lewis Wagon Co.
Lewis Motor Vehicle Co.
Philadelphia, Pennsylvania
LEWIS—1901
Lewis Cycle Co.
Brooklyn, New York
LEWIS—1913-15
L.P.C. Motor Co.
(Lewis, Petard & Cram)
Racine, Wisconsin
Later Lewis Motor Co.
Absorbed by Mitchell-Lewis Motor Co. 1915.
LEWIS AIRMOBILE—1937
Lewis-American Airways
Rochester, New York
LEWIS ELECTRIC—1893-97
J. D. Perry Lewis
St. Louis, Missouri
LEWIS-MIGHT—1914
*LEWIS SIX—1913
Correct name for this vehicle is "Lewis."
LEXINGTON—1909-28
Lexington Motor Car Co.
Lexington, Kentucky (1910)
Moved to Connersville, Indiana. Absorbed by Howard Motor Car Co. 1913 and reorganized as Lexington-Howard Co. Reorganized as Lexington Motor Co. 1917. Properties acquired by "Auburn" 1926.
See "Howard"
LEXINGTON-HOWARD (model)—1916
"Lexington 4" and "Howard 6" were models of "Lexington." See "Lexington"
Lexington-Howard Co.
Connersville, Indiana
LIBERTY—1903
LIBERTY—1910
Belmont Automobile Mfg. Co.
New Haven, Connecticut
LIBERTY CYCLECAR—1914
Joseph A. Anglada
Liberty Motor Co.
New York, New York

*ASTERISK: Error corrected from previous list. See introduction to this section for complete code.

LIBERTY—1916-24
Liberty Motor Car Co.
Detroit, Michigan
Bought by Columbia Motors Co. 1923.

LIBERTY—1926

LIBERTY BRUSH—1911-12
Brush Runabout Co.
Detroit, Michigan
Became United States Motor Co., Brush Division.

LIBERTY LIGHT CAR—1921
Liberty Mfg. Co.
New York, New York

LIBERTY-MUTUAL experimental—1960-61
Liberty-Mutual Insurance Co.
Boston, Massachusetts
Safety car

*LIFU
English model of "House."

LIGHT—1905
Kauan Mfg. Co.
Chicago, Illinois

LIGHT—1914
Light Motor Car Co.
Detroit, Michigan

LIGHT STEAMER—1901
Light Cycle Co.
Pottstown, Pennsylvania

LILIPUTIAN—1902
Turner Automobile Co. Ltd.
Philadelphia, Pennsylvania

LIMA—1915
C. E. Miller & F. M. McGraw
Lima Light Car Co.
Lima, Ohio

LINCOLN HIGHWHEELER—1904; 1908-09
Lincoln Motor Vehicle Co.
Lincoln, Illinois

LINCOLN HIGHWHEELER—1911-14
Lincoln Motor Car Works
1348 W. Harrison
Chicago, Illinois
Company built cars for "Sears" (Sears Roebuck) late 1911 and into 1912.
Also built trucks.

LINCOLN CYCLECAR—1914
Lincoln Motor Car Co.
Detroit, Michigan
Successor to American Voiturette Co.

LINCOLN—1921 to date
Lincoln Motor Co.
Detroit, Michigan
Purchased by Ford Motor Co. 1922.

LINCOLN ELECTRIC—1900
Lincoln Electric Co.
Cleveland, Ohio

LINCOLN HIGHWAY (model)—1914
See "Lincoln" cyclecar, 1914.
Lincoln Motor Car Co.
Detroit, Michigan

LINCOLN ZEPHYR—1935-42
Ford Motor Co.
Detroit, Michigan
See "Zephyr"

LINDSAY ELECTRIC—1902-03
Lindsay Automobile Parts Co.
Lindsay-Russell Co.
Indianapolis, Indiana
Mfg. of electric running gears and parts.

LINDSAY HIGHWHEEL—1908
T. J. Lindsay Co.
Indianapolis, Indiana

LINDSLEY HIGHWHEELER—1907-08
J. V. Lindsley & Co.
Chicago, Illinois
J. V. Lindsley Auto Chassis Co.
Dowagiac, Michigan
Became Dowagiac Motor Car Co.

LINSCOTT—1916

LION—1909-12
Lion Motor Car Co.
Adrian, Michigan
Founded when Page Gas Engine Co. bought gyroscope patents owned by Blomstrom Mfg. Co. Assets sold to A. O. Dunk Auto Parts Mfg. Co. reported February, 1913.
See "Page" and "Gyroscope."

LIPMAN—1911
Lipman Mfg. Co.

Beloit, Wisconsin

LIPPINCOTT ELECTRIC—1960

(LIQUID AIR)—1900-02
Liquid Air Power and Automobile Co. Ltd.
Boston, Massachusetts

LITTLE—1911-13
Little Motor Car Co.
Flint, Michigan
1913 absorbed with "Republic" into Chevrolet Motor Co.

LITTLE DETROIT—1910
See "De Motcar"
De Mot Car Co.
Detroit, Michigan
Both names apply to same vehicle.

LITTLE DETROIT SPEEDSTER CYCLECAR—1913-14
Detroit Cyclecar Co.
Detroit, Michigan
See also "Detroit Speedster"

LITTLE FOUR—1904
McLachlen & Brown
Little Four Automobile Mfg. Co.
Detroit, Michigan

LITTLE KAR—1911
Little Motor Kar Co.
Arlington, Texas

(LITTLE KAR)—1920-22
Little Motor Kar Co.
Grand Prairie, Texas
Dallas, Texas
Reported officers arrested for fraud April, 1920.

*LITTLE-KAT—1921
Believed to be "Little-Kar" misspelled.

LITTLE-MAC—1930-31
Thompson Motor Corp.
Muscatine, Iowa

LITTLE PRINCESS CYCLECAR—1913-14
Princess Cyclecar Co.
Detroit, Michigan

LITTLE SIX—1913
Republic Motor Co. of Michigan
Detroit, Michigan

See "Little," Little Motor Car Co. Flint, Michigan. Both names apply to the same vehicle.

LITTLE WASP
Little Wasp Motor Car Co.
Molvane, Kansas

L.M.—1913
L.M. Motor Co.
Brooklyn, New York
Two built; formerly "B.L.M."

(LOCKE) STEAM—1902
Locke Regulator Co.
Salem, Massachusetts
Steam engines only.
See "Puritan"

LOCOMOBILE—1899-1929
Locomobile Co. of America
Bridgeport, Connecticut
Before 1902 at Newton, Massachusetts, Westfield, Massachusetts.
Purchased "Stanley" patents 1899.
Absorbed Overman Automobile Co. 1902.
Controlled by Hare's Motors 1920-22, Durant Motors 1922-29.
Steam 1899-1903, gasoline 1902-29.

LOCOMOTOR—1900-01
American Locomotor Mfg. Co.
Connellsville, Pennsylvania

LOCO SURRY (model)—1903
A six-passenger larger and heavier "Locomobile."
See "Locomobile"
Locomobile Co. of America
Bridgeport, Connecticut

LOGAN—1903-08
Logan Construction Co.
Chillicothe, Ohio
Formerly Motor Storage and Mfg. Co. Air and water-cooled cars to 1906, later air-cooled cars only. After 1908 trucks only.

LOGAN CYCLECAR—1914
Northwestern Motorcycle Works
Chicago, Illinois

LOHR—1910-11
Lohr Motor Co.

Elkhart, Indiana

LOMAX—1913-14
Lomax Motor Car Co.
Lomax, Illinois

LOMAX FLINT—1905
Denver, Colorado

LOMBARD—1900
A. O. Lombard
Waterville, Maine

LOMGARD—1921

LONDON—1905
London Auto & Supply Co.
Chicago, Illinois

LONDON SIX—1922-24
London Motors Ltd.
London, Ontario, Canada

LONE—1906

LONE STAR—1917-22
Lone Star Motor Truck and Tractor Association
San Antonio, Texas
Lone Star Motor Co.
El Paso, Texas

(LONG)—1922-26
R. H. Long & Co.
(Long Motor Sales)
Framingham, Massachusetts
Company built "Bay State" 1922-24.

LONG DISTANCE—1902
See "United States Long Distance"
U.S. Long Distance Automobile Co.
Marion, New Jersey
Both names apply to the same vehicle.

LONGEST—1906
Longest Bros. Co.
Louisville, Kentucky

LONG ISLAND—1901
Long Island Motor Vehicle Co.
Brooklyn, New York

LONG STEAM CAR—1875-82
George A. Long
Hinsdale, New Hampshire (1875-78)
Northfield, Massachusetts (1880-82)
Only known "Long Steam Car" is in Smithsonian collection.

LOOMIS—1896-1904
Gilbert J. Loomis (1896-97)
Loomis Automobile Co. (1898-1904)
Westfield, Massachusetts
About 50 cars built.

LORD BALTIMORE—1911-13
Lord Baltimore Automobile Co.
Baltimore, Maryland

LORRAIN—1922
Lorrain Car Co.
Richmond, Indiana

LORRAINE—1907-09
Lorraine Automobile Mfg. Co.
Chicago, Illinois

LORRAINE—1920-22
Lorraine Motors Corp.
Grand Rapids, Michigan
Formerly "Hackett"
David Buick employed by company.

LOS ANGELES CYCLECAR—1914
Los Angeles Cyclecar Co.
Los Angeles, California
Buffalo, New York
Home office and factory, Compton, California.
L. E. French, designer.

LOST CAUSE (model)—1963
Lost Cause Motors
Louisville, Kentucky
A specially-customized "Chevrolet."
Bodywork by Derham.

LOTZ—1910
Lotz Automobile Co.
Detroit, Michigan

LOUISIANA—1900

LOUISIANA—1921
Louisiana Motor Car Co.
Cedargrove, Louisiana

LOUIS J.—1911
See "Bergdoll"
Louis J. Bergdoll Motor Co.
Philadelphia, Pennsylvania
Both names apply to the same vehicle.

LOUISVILLE ELECTRIC—1911
Electric Vehicle Co.

Louisville, Kentucky

LOVEJOY—1895
Elmer F. Lovejoy
Laramie, Wyoming

(LOWELL-AMERICAN)—1908-09
Lowell-American Automobile Co.
Lowell, Massachusetts
Built motors and supplied automobile plans as early as 1902.

LOWERY—1895
V.L.D. Lowery
Eaton, Illinois

LOWY—1916
Layman-Lowy Motor Car Co.
New York, New York

LOZIER STEAM—1898; 1901
Lozier Motor Co.
Plattsburg, New York

LOZIER—1905-17
Lozier Motor Co.
Plattsburg, New York
(Detroit, Michigan 1910)
After steam experimentation, built gasoline marine engines and launches only 1901-05.
First car exhibited Madison Square Garden January, 1905.

L.P.C.—1900
L.P.C.—1913
See "Lewis"
L.P.C. Motor Co.
Racine, Wisconsin
Both names apply to same vehicle.

LUCK UTILITY—1912-13
Cleburn Motor Car Mfrs. Co.
Cleburn, Texas

LUDWIG—1914
Ludwig Motor Car Co.
Detroit, Michigan

LUETH—1903
Lueth Bros.
Kankakee, Illinois

LUGO ELECTRIC—1891
Electric Road Carriage Co.
Boston, Massachusetts

LU-LU CYCLECAR—1914-15
Kearns Motor Truck Co.
Beavertown, Pennsylvania

LUNKENHEIMER—1900-02
Lunkenheimer Brass Works
Lunkenheimer Motor Vehicle Co.
Cincinnati, Ohio

LUTWEILER—1909
Lutweiler Pumping Engine Co.
Rochester, New York

LUTZ STEAM—1898
G. H. Lutz
San Antonio, Texas

(LUTZ) STEAM—1917
Lutz Steam Car Co.
Buffalo, New York

LUVERNE—1903-18
Luverne Automobile Co.
Luverne, Minnesota

LUXOR—1900
C. R. Harris
Williamsport, Pennsylvania

LYBE—1895
D. I. Lybe
Sidney, Iowa

LYKKE—1901
A. Lykke
Grand Island, Nebraska

LYMAN—1903-04
C. F. Lyman
Boston, Massachusetts

LYMAN—1909

LYMAN & BURNHAM—1903-04
Lyman & Burnham
Boston, Massachusetts
Successor to Binney & Burnham.
Built by Fore River Ship & Engine Co.
Quincy, Massachusetts.
Concurrent with "Lyman."

LYNN—1903
Lynn Automobile Co.
Lynn, Massachusetts

LYNN HIGHWHEEL—1908
Lynn Car Co.
Everett, Massachusetts

LYON—1911
Lyon Motor Car Co.
Adrian, Michigan

LYONS-ATLAS—1912-14
Lyons-Atlas Co.
Indianapolis, Indiana
See "Lyons-Knight" 1912-15.

LYONS-KNIGHT—1914-15
Lyons-Atlas Co.
Indianapolis, Indiana
Successor to Atlas Engine Co. 1912 and Atlas Motor Car Co.
Springfield, Massachusetts

M

MacDONALD STEAM—1922-25
MacDonald Steam Automotor Car Co.
MacDonald Steam Automotive Corp.
Garfield, Ohio
About 48 cars built.

MacINNES ELECTRIC—1909-13
MacInnes Bros.
Toledo, Ohio

MacKENZIE—1914

MacKENZIE & McARTHUR—1895
MacKenzie & McArthur Co.
New Haven, Connecticut

MACKER—1902
Macker Automobile Co.
Westboro, Massachusetts

MACKEY—1902-03
J. C. Mackey
Mackey Automobile Co.
Detroit, Michigan

MacLEOD—1895
W. MacLeod
New York, New York

MACKLE-THOMPSON—1903
Mackle-Thompson Automobile Co.
Elizabeth, New Jersey

MacNAUGHTON ELECTRIC—1907-08
James MacNaughton, Co.
Buffalo, New York

MACOMBER—1917

Walter G. Macomber
(Macomber Motors Co.)
Los Angeles, California
Formerly supplied motors for "Eagle" cyclecar.
MACON—1915-17
All Steel Motor Car Co.
Macon Motor Car Co.
Macon, Missouri
MACY-ROGER—1895-96
Roger-American Mechanical Carriage Co.
New York, New York
Entered Chicago Times-Herald Race.
MADISON—1915-21
Madison Motor Co.
Madison Motors & Tractor Corp.
Madison Motors Corp.
Anderson, Indiana
Reorganized as Madison Motors Co. 1916.
Used old "Rider-Lewis" and "Nyberg" plant.
MADSEN—1901
L. P. Madsen
Council Bluffs, Iowa
(MAGIC)—1914
Fisher Motor Corp.
New York, New York
Pilots built with Mondex Magic engines.
MAGIC SIX (model)—1921
See "Premocar"
Preston Motors Corp.
Birmingham, Alabama
MAGNETIC—1921-22
A gas-electric vehicle.
See "Crown-Magnetic"
Owen Magnetic Motor Co.
Both names apply to same vehicle.
(MAGNOLIA)—1902
Magnolia Automobile Co.
Riverside, California
MAGOMOBILE—1930
MAGUIRE—1895
Maguire Power Generating Co.
Chicago, Illinois

MAHONING AIR-COOLED—1904-05
Mahoning Motor Car Co.
Youngstown, Ohio
MAHS—1903-04
W. H. Mahs
Detroit, Michigan
MAIBOHM—1916-22
Maibohm Motors Co.
Racine, Wisconsin
Sandusky, Ohio
Formerly Maibohm Wagon Co.
Became Arrow Motors. See "Courier"
MAINE—1915-18
MAJA—1908
Daimler Mfg. Co.
Long Island City, New York
MAJESTIC—1910-11
Milwaukee Auto Engine
and Supply Co.
Milwaukee, Wisconsin
MAJESTIC—1916
Majestic Motor Corp.
Chicago, Illinois
MAJESTIC— 1916-17
Majestic Motor Co.
New York, New York
MALBOMB—1900
MALCOLM—1900
C. P. Malcolm & Co.
Oxford, Michigan
MALCOLM CYCLECAR—1914
Malcolm-Jones-Detroit Co.
Malcolm-Jones Cyclecar Co.
Detroit, Michigan
Malcolm Cyclecar Co. Plymouth, Michigan, successor.
MALCOLM—1915-16
Malcolm Motor Car Co.
Detroit, Michigan
Successor to "Malcolm" cyclecar.
MALCOLMSON—1906
Alexander Malcolmson
Detroit, Michigan
MALDEN STEAM—1898
Malden Automobile Co.

Malden, Massachusetts
MALDEN—1902
Malden Automobile Co.
Malden, Massachusetts
MALTBY—1900-02
Maltby Automobile Co.
Brooklyn, New York
MALVERN—1905
MALVERUN-MANARD—1905
MANCHESTER STEAM—1901-04
Manchester Locomotive Works
Manchester, New Hampshire
MANEXALL—1921
Manufacturers & Exporters Alliance
New York, New York
MANHATTAN—1901-05
Manhattan Automobile Co.
New York, New York
Both gas and electric cars.
MANHATTAN—1921
MANIC—1969-71
Ecurie Manic Inc.
Les Automobiles Manic (Ltée)
Granby, Quebec, Canada
MANISTEE—1912
Manistee Motor Car Co.
Manistee, Michigan
MANLIUS—1910
Manlius Motor Co.
Manlius, New York
MANN—1895
Mann Press Co.
(L. C. Mann)
Gladbrook, Iowa
MANSFIELD—1919
MANX DUNE BUGGY (model)—1966 to date
B. F. Meyers Co.
Fountain Valley, California
MAPLEBAY—1908-09
Maplebay Mfg. Co.
Crookston, Minnesota
MAPLE LEAF—1905
Maple Leaf Electric Automobile
& Mfg. Co.
London, Connecticut

MARATHON—1908-14
  Marathon Motor Car Co.
  Cincinnati, Ohio
  Southern Motor Works
  Nashville, Tennessee
  Name changed to Marathon Motor Works 1912.
  Absorbed by Herff-Brooks Corp.
  Bankruptcy reported June, 1914.
MARATHON—1920
  Marathon Motor Export Co.
  Elkhart, Indiana
  For export only.
MARBLE-SWIFT—1903-05
  Marble-Swift Automobile Co.
  Chicago, Illinois
*MARELOCK
  Believed to be "Morlock" misspelled.
MARION—1901
  Marion Automobile Co.
  Marion, Ohio
MARION—1904-15
  Marion Motor Car Co.
  Indianapolis, Indiana
  Marion-Handley Mutual Motors Corp.
  Jackson, Michigan
  Marketed in 1912 with "Overland" and "American Underslung" by John N. Willys in American Motors Corp. Reorganized 1914 with "Imperial" in Mutual Motors Corp. May, 1912 assets sold to J. I. Handley. Became "Marion-Handley"
MARION FLYER—1909-11
  Hartman Motor Car Co.
  Omaha, Nebraska
MARION-HANDLEY—1916-19
  Mutual Motors Corp.
  Jackson, Michigan
  Became "Handley-Knight"
MARION-OVERLAND—1910
  Willys-Overland Co.
  Toledo, Ohio
MARITIME—1913
  Maritime Motor Car Co. Ltd.
  Goldbrook, New Brunswick, Canada

MARK ELECTRIC—1902
  Harry J. Mark
  New York, New York
MARKETEER ELECTRIC—1954
  Electric Marketeer Mfg. Co.
  Redlands, California
MARKETOUR—1964
  Marketour Electric Cars
  Long Beach, California
MARLAN—1920
MARLBORO STEAM—1899-1902
  Marlboro Automobile Co.
  Marlboro Automobile & Carriage Co.
  Marlboro, Massachusetts
  See "Walker"
MARLIN (model)—1965-67
  See "Rambler"
  American Motors Corp.
  Detroit, Michigan
MARMON—1902-33
  Nordyke & Marmon Co.
  Indianapolis, Indiana
  Reorganized 1926 as Marmon Motor Car Company. Also produced a low-priced car called the "Roosevelt."
  See "Roosevelt"
MAR-POWER—1921
MARQUETTE—1912
  Marquette Motor Co.
  Saginaw, Michigan
  Organized by General Motors in 1909 to consolidate "Rainier" and "Welch-Detroit." Built both cars into 1911.
  Company renamed Peninsular Motor Co. April, 1912.
MARQUETTE—1929-30
  Buick Motor Co.
  Flint, Michigan
MARQUIS—1954
MARR—1903-04
  Marr Auto Car Co.
  Detroit, Michigan
  Cars built by Fauber & Marr, Elgin, Illinois.

MARR CYCLECAR—1914
  Marr Automobile Co.
  Detroit, Michigan
  Walter L. Marr had been chief engineer for "Buick." One car extant in Flint, Michigan museum.
*MARREL—1906
  Believed to be misspelling of "Marvel."
*MARRON—1903
  Believed to be misspelling of "Marmon."
MARS ELECTRIC—1966 to date.
  Electric Fuel Propulsion, Inc.
  366 West Eight Mile Road
  Ferndale, Michigan
  One experimental car built and tested 1966. Nine cars ordered and tested by utility companies 1967-68. Mars II built in "Renault" R-10 body shell.
MARSH STEAM—1899
  Marsh Brothers
  Marsh Motor Carriage Company
  Brockton, Massachusetts
  One prototype after three years' work.
MARSH—1905-06
  American Motor Co.
  Brockton, Massachusetts
  Organized by Marsh Brothers. Built motor cycles 1900-05. Absorbed by Waltham Mfg. Co.
MARSHALL—1919-21
  Marshall Motor Car Co.
  Chicago, Illinois
MARSHALL—1924
  See "Norwalk"
  Norwalk Motor Car Co.
  Martinsburg, West Virginia
  "Norwalk" sold under "Marshall" name.
MARSHALL STEAM—1940-41
MARSH FOUR—1920-23
  Marsh Motors Co.
  Cleveland, Ohio
MARTELL—1908-10
  Martell Motor Car Co.
  Jamaica Plain, Massachusetts
  Became "Lenox"

M'ARTHUR—1895
   A. W. M'Arthur
   Rockford, Illinois
MARTIN—1898-99
   Martin Motor Wagon Co.
   Buffalo, New York
MARTIN—1900
   A. J. Martin
   Buffalo, New York
MARTIN—1905
   Palmer & Christie
   New York, New York
MARTIN—1910-11
   Martin Carriage Works
   York, Pennsylvania
MARTIN—1920-22
   Martin Motor Co.
   Martin Motor & Trailer Corp.
   Springfield, Massachusetts
   Also a three-wheel Scootmobile
MARTIN—1926-32
   J. V. Martin
   Martin Aeroplane Co.
   Garden City, New York
MARTIN STATIONETTE THREE-WHEELER—
1954
   Commonwealth Research Corp.
   New York, New York
   J. V. Martin designer.
MARTIN-WASP—1919-25
   Martin Wasp Co.
   Bennington, Vermont
   See "Wasp"
MARVEL—1907
   Marvel Motor Car Co.
   Detroit, Michigan
   Succeeded Detroit Auto Mfg. Co.
MARYLAND STEAM—1900
   Maryland Automobile Mfg. Co.
   Cumberland, Maryland
MARYLAND STEAM—1900-01
   Maryland Automobile & Mfg. Co.
   Maryland Automobile Co.
   Luke, Maryland
   Westernport, Maryland

MARYLAND—1907-10
   Sinclair Scott Co.
   Baltimore, Maryland
   Succeeded "Ariel" September, 1906.
   First shown New York, January, 1907.
MARYLAND ELECTRIC—1914
   Maryland Electric Automobile & Mfg.
   Baltimore, Maryland
MARYLAND 1922
   Maryland Motor Car Co.
   Frederick, Maryland
MARYSVILLE—1905
   Marysville Motor Car Co.
   Marysville, Ohio
MASCOTTE (model)—1910-12
   See "Maxwell"
   Maxwell-Briscoe Motor Co.
   Tarrytown, New York
MASON STEAM—1898-99
   William B. Mason
   (Mason Steam Regulator Co.)
   Milton, Massachusetts
   Similar to Stanley.
MASON—1906-13
   Mason Motor Car Co.
   Mason Motor Co.
   Des Moines, Iowa
   First auto venture of Fred Duesenberg.
   Became Mason Automobile Co. Reorganiz-
   ed 1910 as Maytag-Mason Motor Co.
MASON—1907
   Puritan Machine Co.
   Boston, Massachusetts
MASON—1922
MASON-MOHLER—1914
   Mason Motor Co.
   Waterloo, Iowa
   Car used Mason-Duesenberg engine.
MASSACHUSETTS STEAM—1901
   Massachusetts Steam Wagon Co.
   Pittsfield, Massachusetts
MASSIE—1903
   Massie & Sons
   Quincy, Illinois
MASSILLON—1909

W. S. Read Co.
   Massillon, Ohio
MASTER—1907-08
   Master Motor Car Co.
   Cleveland, Ohio
MASTERBILT 6—1926-27
   Govreau-Nelson Engineering Works
   Detroit, Michigan
*MATAG—1910-15
   Believed to be "Maytag" misspelled.
MATHER—1901
MATHESON—1903-13
   Matheson Motor Car Co.
   Grand Rapids, Michigan
   Holyoke, Massachusetts
   Merged with Holyoke Motor Works. Moved
   to Wilkes-Barre, Pa. 1905
   Sales Dept. reorganized as Matheson
   Automobile Co. 1909.
MATHEWS—1907-08
   Mathews Motor Co.
   Camden, New Jersey
   Succeeded "Jones-Corbin"
   See "Sovereign"
MATHIS—1931
   Durant Motors
   New York, New York
   Lansing, Michigan
   Limited production under French license.
MATILDA—1894
MAUMEE—1906-07
   Maumee Motor Car Works
   Toledo, Ohio
   Absorbed Wolverine Auto & Commercial
   Vehicle Co. and transferred to Craig-Toledo
   Motor Co. Bankrupt 1907.
   See "Wolverine" and "Craig-Toledo"
MAVERICK—1953-55
   Maverick Motors
   Mt. View, California
MAVERICK (model)—1970 to date
   See "Ford"
   Ford Motor Co.
   Dearborn, Michigan
   Introduced New York Auto Show 1969.

MAXIM ELECTRIC—1913-14
  Maxim Munitions Co.
  Cedar Rapids, Iowa
MAXIM-GOODRIDGE ELECTRIC—1908-09
  Maxim-Goodridge Co.
  Hartford, Connecticut
  See "Lenox"
MAXIM MOTOR TRICYCLE—1894-95
  American Projectile Co.
  Lynn, Massachusetts (1894)
  Maxim Mfg. Co.
  Hartford, Connecticut (1895)
  Three-cylinder tricycle
MAXIM TRICAR—1911-14
  Bushnell Press Co.
  Thompsonville, Connecticut
  Maxim Tricar Mfg. Co.
  New York, New York
*MAXON ELECTRIC—1913
  Believed to be misspelling of "Maxim"
  electric.
MAXWELL—1904-25
  Maxwell Motor Co.
  Detroit, Michigan
  Reorganized 1921 as Maxwell Motor Corp.
  Formerly Maxwell Briscoe Motor Co.
MAXWELL-BRISCOE—1904-13
  See "Maxwell"
  Maxwell Briscoe Motor Co.
  Tarrytown, New York
  Became unit of United States Motor Co.
  1910. This is the early name for "Max-
  well."
MAY—1912
MAYER—1899-1900
  Si Mayer
  Chicago, Illinois
MAYER—1913
MAYES—1948
MAYFAIR—1925
  Mayfair Mfg. Co.
  Boston, Massachusetts
  A fabric-bodied stretched out "Ford."
MAYTAG—1910-15
  Maytag-Mason Motor Co.

Waterloo, Iowa
  Successor to Mason Automobile Co.
  Became Mason Motor Car Co.
  See "Mason"
M.B.—1909-10
  Motor Buggy Mfg. Co.
  Minneapolis, Minnesota
M & C ELECTRIC—1913
  National Contracting Co.
  New York, New York
McCORD—1914
  McCord Automobile Co.
  Chicago, Illinois
McCORMACK STEAM—1921-22
  McCormack Bros. Motor Car Co.
  Birmingham, Alabama
McCORMICK AUTO WAGON—1899
McCUE—1908-11
  McCue Co.
  Hartford, Connecticut
  Automobile and carriage fittings from
  December, 1904. Very few cars built.
McCULLOUGH—1899-1900
  W. T. McCullough Automobile Co.
  Boston, Massachusetts
  Also Back Bay Cycle & Motor Co.
  Became U.S. Motor Vehicle Co.
McCURDY STEAM—1901
McCURDY—1922
  Hercules Corp.
  McCurdy-Hercules Corp.
  Evansville, Indiana
  See also "Gale 4"
McDUFFEE—1905
  McDuffee Automobile Co.
  Dayton, Ohio
McFARLAN—1902-28
  McFarlan Carriage Co.
  McFarlan Motor Corp.
  Connersville, Indiana
  Reorganized as McFarlan Motor Car Co.
McGEE STEAM—1937
McGILL—1922
  McGill Motor Car Co.
  Ft. Worth, Texas

McHARDY—1904
  McHardy-Peterson Car Works
  Detroit, Michigan
McINTYRE—1908-16
  W. H. McIntyre
  Toledo, Ohio
  W. H. McIntyre Co.
  Auburn, Indiana
  Formerly "Kiblinger"
  Absorbed Motor Car Co. of America 1912.
  Made "Imp" Cyclecar 1914.
McKAY—1900-02
  Stanley Mfg. Co.
  Boston, Massachusetts
  Succeeded "Stanley-Whitney" steam.
McKAY—1911-14
  Nova Scotia Carriage Co.
  Kentville, Nova Scotia, Canada
  Similar to "Penn"
McLAUGHLIN—1908-22
  McLaughlin Motor Car Co. Ltd.
  Oshawa, Ontario, Canada
  Based on "Buick" components.
McLAUGHLIN AMPHIMOTOR—1927
  George McLaughlin
  Bangor, Maine
McLAUGHLIN-BUICK—1923-42
  McLaughlin Motor Car Co. Ltd.
  Oshawa, Ontario, Canada
  Succeeded "McLaughlin"
McLEAN—1910
McMULLEN—1900-01
  McMullen Power & Construction Co.
  Chicago, Illinois
McMURTY STEAM—1896
  A. L. McMurty
  Chester, Pennsylvania
*McNABB—1910
  Believed to be dealer's name, not name of
  vehicle.
  See "Billy"
  McNabb Iron Works
  Atlanta, Georgia
McQUESTION STEAM—1901-02
  George McQuestion

CODE = ROMAN LETTERS: Complete entry. *ITALICS:* Unsubstantiated entry. (PARENTHESES): Production planned, but not realized.

Boston, Massachusetts
Became "Binney & Burnham"
*MEAD—1905
    Company name of Mead Cycle Co.
    Chicago, Illinois, a used car dealer, not
    name of vehicle.
MEAD—1912
    Mead Engine Co.
    Dayton, Ohio
    Rotary valves
MEARO—1909
MECCA CYCLECAR—1914
    Mecca Motor Car Co.
    Teaneck, New Jersey
MECCA—1915-16
    Times Square Automobile Co.
    New York, New York
    Built by Princess Motor Car Co., Detroit,
    Michigan
MECHALEY—1903
    Mechaley Bros.
    Stamford, Connecticut
    Steam and gasoline cars built to order.
MECHANICS—1925-28
    Los Angeles, California
MECKY—1902
    A. Mecky
    Philadelphia, Pennsylvania
(MED-BOW)—1907-08
    Med-Bow Automobile Co.
    Springfield, Massachusetts
    Possibly this car is "Springfield."
*MED-CRAFT—1907-08
    Believed to be an error for "Med-bow."
MEDIA—1899-1907
    Media Carriage Works
    (Media Automobile Works)
    Media, Pennsylvania
    Electric car in 1899.
MEECH-STODDARD—1924
MEISENHELDER—1919
    Meisenhelder Motors
    York, Pennsylvania
    Based on "Paige."
MELBOURNE—1904

MEL SPECIAL—1923
    Mel Stringer
    Pottstown, Pennsylvania
MEMPHIS STEAM—1904-05
    Memphis Motor Carriage Co.
    Memphis, Tennessee
MENARD—1908-10
    Windsor Carriage & Wagon Works
    Windsor, Ontario, Canada
MENGES—1902
    Menges Engine Co.
    Memphis, Tennessee
MENGES—1908
    Menges Motor Carriage Co.
    Grand Rapids, Michigan
    A. L. Menges ex-designer of "Harrison."
MENOMINEE ELECTRIC—1912; 1915
    Menominee Electric Mfg. Co.
    Menominee, Michigan
MENUS-VAN HORN—1902
    Menus-Van Horn Motor Co.
    Boston, Massachusetts
MERCANTILE—1905
    Mercantile Motor Co.
    Jersey City, New Jersey
    Gasoline and steam vehicles.
MERCEDES—1904-09
    See "American Mercedes"
    Daimler Mfg. Co.
    Long Island City
    Both names apply to same vehicle.
MERCER—1909-25
    Mercer Automobile Co.
    Walter Automobile Co.
    Trenton, New Jersey
    Formerly "Roebling-Planche"
    See also "Walter"
    With "Locomobile" and "Crane-Simplex"
    into Hare's Motors Inc.
MERCER—1931
    Mercer Motors Corp.
    Elkhart, Indiana
    Prototypes only
MERCER COBRA—1964
    Copper Development Asso. Inc.

Detroit, Michigan
MERCILESS—1906-07
    Huntington Automobile Co.
    Long Island, New York
MERCURY STEAM—1904
    Mercury Machine Co.
    Philadelphia, Pennsylvania
MERCURY CYCLECAR—1913-14
    Mercury Cyclecar Co.
    Michigan State Automobile School
    Detroit, Michigan
    Bankruptcy reported September, 1914.
MERCURY—1918-20
    Mercury Cars Inc.
    Hollis, New York
    Weidely engine
MERCURY—1920
    Mercury Motor Car Co.
    Cleveland, Ohio
    Duesenberg engine
MERCURY—1930
MERCURY—1939 to date
    Lincoln Mercury Division
    Ford Motor Co.
    Dearborn, Michigan
    See "Ford" and "Lincoln."
    Introduced August 26, 1938.
MERCURY SPECIAL—1946
    Paul Omohundro
    Los Angeles, California
    Prototypes only
MEREDITH—1895
    E. Meredith
    Batavia, Illinois
MERIT—1920-23
    Merit Motor Co.
    Cleveland, Ohio
MERKEL—1904-07
    Merkel Mfg. Co.
    Merkel Motor Co.
    Milwaukee, Wisconsin
MERKEL CYCLECAR—1914
    J. F. Merkel
    Milwaukee, Wisconsin
MERRILL—1905

Frank H. Merrill
Plainfield, New Jersey
MERRY OLDS—1958-62
American Air Products Corp.
Ft. Lauderdale, Florida
Replica 1904 "Oldsmobile."
MERZ CYCLECAR—1914
Merz Cyclecar Co.
Indianapolis, Indiana
Receiver reported appointed July, 1914.
January, 1915 receiver sold for $1200.
Creditors received 20%.
MESERVE STEAM—1901-04
W. F. Meserve
Canobie Lake, New Hampshire
West Derry, New Hampshire
Custom built cars only.
MESSENGER—1914
Brazie Motor Car Co.
Minneapolis, Minnnesota
MESSERER—1896-1901
Stephen Messerer
Messerer Automobile Co.
Newark, New Jersey
METCAR—1901
METEOR—1900-01
Springfield Cornice Works
Howell & Meehan Co.
Springfield, Massachusetts
Became Automotor Co.
METEOR—1902-03
Meteor Engineering Co.
Reading, Pennsylvania
Succeeded Reading Steam Vehicle Co. and
Steam Vehicle Co. of America.
See "Reading Steam Carriage"
METEOR—1904-05
Lemon Automobile & Mfg. Co.
St. Louis, Missouri
METEOR—1904-06
Worthington Automobile Co.
New York, New York
Absorbed Berg Automobile Co. 1905.
See "Berg" and "Worthington"
METEOR—1907-10

Meteor Motor Car Co.
Bettendorf, Iowa (1907-09)
Davenport, Iowa (1909-10)
METEOR—1909-27
Meteor Motor Car Co.
Indianapolis, Indiana
Shelbyville, Indiana
(Piqua, Ohio)
Cars to 1916. Special order to 1930. Then
ambulances and hearses.
Body builders to date.
METEOR—1918-21
Meteor Motors Inc.
Philadelphia, Pennsylvania
METEOR—1949-61, 1963 to date
Ford Motor Co. of Canada, Ltd.
Windsor, Ontario, Canada
METEOR SPORTS—1956
Meteor Sports Cars
Denver, Colorado
METROPOL—1913-14
Metropol Motor Co.
Port Jefferson, New York
Outgrowth of "Only."
METROPOLITAN—1922-23
Metropolitan Motors Inc.
Kansas City, Missouri
METROPOLITAN (model)—1954-62
American Motors Corp.
Kenosha, Wisconsin & Detroit, Michigan
Sold under "Hudson" and "Nash" name-
plates, 1954-57, "Rambler" from 1958.
METZ—1908-22
Metz Co.
Waltham, Massachusetts
Succeeded Waltham Mfg. Co.
See "Waltham-Orient"
Became Waltham Motor Mfrs. Inc.
See "Waltham" (1922)
METZCAR—1901-02
Detroit, Michigan
METZGER—1910
Metzger Motor Car Co.
Lansing, Michigan
Company incorporated September 20, 1909.

MEYER—1919
A. J. Meyer Corp.
Chicago, Illinois
MEYERS-MANX—1964 to date
B. F. Meyers & Co.
Newport Beach, California
M.H.C.—1916-17
Michigan Hearse & Motor Co.
Grand Rapids, Michigan
MIAMI STEAM—1901-02
Miami Cycle Co.
Middletown, Ohio
MICHAELSON CYCLECAR—1914
M. Michaelson
Michaelson Motor Co.
Brasie Motor Car Co.
Minneapolis, Minnesota
MICHELET—1921
MICHIGAN—1903-08
Michigan Automobile Co.
Kalamazoo, Michigan
Formerly Blood Bros. See "Blood"
Continued making transmissions.
MICHIGAN—1904
Michigan Motor & Machine Co.
Detroit, Michigan
MICHIGAN—1904
Michigan Automobile Co.
Grand Rapids, Michigan
MICHIGAN—1908-14
Michigan Buggy Co.
Kalamazoo, Michigan
1912 reorganized as Michigan Motor Car
Co. Also called "Mighty Michigan"
MICHIGAN SIX—1910
Michigan Motor Car Mfg. Co.
Rochester, Michigan
Concurrent with Michigan Buggy Co.
MICHIGAN STEAMER—1907-09
Michigan Steam Motor Co.
Pontiac, Michigan
Changed from Belknap Motor Co. Detroit,
Michigan. Reported May, 1907.
MIDDLEBY—1908-13
Middleby Automobile Co.

Reading, Pennsylvania
Succeeded Duryea Power Co.
Added "Reading" (1910-13) September, 1910. Property auctioned May, 1913.
MIDDLEBY—1920
MIDDLETON—1905
  Middleton Mfg. Co.
  Milwaukee, Wisconsin
MIDDLETOWN HIGHWHEELER—1909-11
  Middletown Buggy Co.
  Middletown, Ohio
  See "Ohio" and "Crescent"
  Company became Crescent Motor Co.
MIDGET—1915
  Midget Cyclecar Co.
  Springfield, Massachusetts
MIDGET—1947
  Greenfield-Lippman
  Buffalo, New York
MIDGLEY—1902-05
  Midgley Mfg. Co.
  Columbus, Ohio
MIDLAND—1908-13
  Midland Motor Car Co.
  Moline, Illinois
  Succeeded "Deere-Clark"
  See "Colby"
MIDWAY—1910
  Mountain Bros. Co.
  Los Angeles, California
MIDWEST—1918-20
  Midwest Motor Co.
  Kansas City, Missouri
MIER HIGHWHEELER—1908-09
  Mier Carriage & Buggy Co.
  Ligonier, Indiana
  See "Izzer" and "Star."
MIEUSSET—1907
  J. P. Bruyere
  New York, New York
MIGHTY-MICHIGAN—1912-13
  See "Michigan"
  Michigan Buggy Co.
  Kalamazoo, Michigan
  Both names apply to same vehicle.

MILAC—1916
  Linthwaite-Hussy Co.
  Los Angeles, California
  Race cars
MILBURN STEAM—1903
MILBURN ELECTRIC—1914-23
  Milburn Carriage & Wagon Co.
  Toledo, Ohio
MILITARY—1907
  V. L. Emerson
  Cincinnati, Ohio
MILLER ELECTRIC—1900-02
  George C. Miller Carriage Co.
  Cincinnati, Ohio
  George Miller
  Kenton, Ohio
  Miller Storage Battery Electric Co.
  Bellefont, Ohio
MILLER—1902
  Miller Bros.
  Amesbury, Massachusetts
MILLER—1902-03
  Charles E. Miller
  New York, New York
MILLER—1905-06
  Miller Carriage Co.
  Goshen, Indiana
MILLER—1911-15
  Miller Motor Car Co.
  Miller Car Co.
  Kosmath Co.
  Detroit, Michigan
MILLER—1912
  Miller Machine Co.
  Defiance, Ohio
MILLER—1915-32
  Harry A. Miller Inc.
  Los Angeles, California
MILLER CAR—1911-15
  Miller Car Co.
  Detroit, Michigan
  See "Miller" 1911-15.
MILLER SPECIAL—1917, 1923, 1930
  Harry A. Miller Inc.
  H. A. Miller Mfg. Co.

(Kirchoff Body Works)
  Pasadena, California
  Los Angeles, California
MILLER STEAMER—1902
  Charles E. Miller
  New York, New York
  Also built gasoline vehicle.
MILLERSVILLE—1910
  Millersville Machine Co.
  Millersville, Ohio
*MILLIONAIRE'S CAR
  Believed to be wrong name for "Orson" built by Orson Automobile Co. Springfield, Massachusetts.
MILLS—1895
  M. B. Mills
  Chicago, Illinois
MILLS ELECTRIC—1917
  Mills Electric Co.
  Lafayette, Indiana
*MILLS-MILWAUKEE—1900
  Believed to be error for "Mills Steamer" 1876.
MILLS & SERLS—1895
  Mills & Serls Co.
  Chicago, Illinois
MILLS STEAMER—1876
  Isaac Mills, Jr.
  Pittsburgh, Pennsylvania
MILNE STEAMER—1901
  Frank Milne
  Everett, Massachusetts
  Steam vehicles built to order.
MILWAUKEE—1901
  Milwaukee Automobile &
    Brass Specialty Co.
  Milwaukee, Wisconsin
MILWAUKEE—1904
  Milwaukee Motor Mfg. Co.
  Milwaukee, Wisconsin
(MILWAUKEE)—1906
  Eagle Automobile Co.
  Milwaukee, Wisconsin
  Two-seater, prototype only.
MILWAUKEE CYCLECAR—1914

Milwaukee Cyclecar Co.
Milwaukee, Wisconsin
MILWAUKEE STEAM—1900-02
Milwaukee Automobile Co.
Milwaukee, Wisconsin
W. H. McIntyre, later of Auburn, Indiana, connected with company.
See "McIntyre"
MINI BUG DUNE BUGGY—1968 to date
Green Motors Inc.
34501 Plymouth Road
Livonia, Michigan
MINI-T DUNE BUGGY—1968 to date
Berry Plastics
Long Beach, California
MINIVOLKS DUNE BUGGY—1968 to date
Dunbar's Inc.
171 Howard Street
Framingham, Massachusetts
MINNEAPOLIS—1914-15
Minneapolis Motor Car Co.
Minneapolis, Minnesota
MINNEAPOLIS CYCLECAR—1914
Minneapolis Motor Co.
Minneapolis, Minnesota
MINO CYCLECAR—1914
Mino Cyclecar Co.
New Orleans, Louisiana
MISSION—1914-16
Mission Motor Car Co.
Los Angeles, California
MISSION—1921
West Coast Automobile Mfg. Co.
Los Angeles, California
MISSOURI—1913
Missouri Motor Car Co.
St. Louis, Missouri
MITCHELL—1902-03
Wisconsin Wheel Co.
Racine, Wisconsin
Became "Pierce-Racine"
MITCHELL—1903-23
Wisconsin Wheel Works
Mitchell Motor Car Co.
Racine, Wisconsin

1910 merged with Mitchell & Lewis Co.
Absorbed L.P.C. Motor Co. ("Lewis") and reorganized 1916 as Mitchell Motors Inc.
"Lewis" plant purchased by "Nash" 1923.
MITCHELL CYCLECAR—1914
Mitchell Automobile Co.
Chicago, Illinois
M.J.G.—1910
Allen-Kingston Co.
New York, New York
M.M.C.—1910
Manlius Motor Co.
Manlius, New York
See "Manlius"
MOBILE STEAM—1899-1903
Automobile Co. of America
Tarrytown, New York
Started by purchasing (with "Locomobile") one-half interest in Stanley Motor Carriage Co.
MOBILETTE ELECTRIC—1965 to date
Mobilette Electric Cars
Long Beach, California
MOCK—1906
MODEL STEAM—1902
Steam Vehicle Co. of America
New York, New York
MODEL—1901-07
Model Gas & Gasoline Engine Co.
Model Gas Engine Works
Model Engine Works
Auburn, Indiana
Model Automobile Co.
Peru, Indiana
MODERN—1906-09
Modern Tool Co.
Erie, Pennsylvania
See "Payne Modern"
MODOC—1909-11; 1914
Chicago Motor Car Co.
Chicago, Illinois
Mail order car for Montgomery Ward & Co.
MOEHN—1895
J .N. Moehn
Milwaukee, Wisconsin

MOHAWK—1903-04
Mohawk Automobile & Cycle Co.
North Indianapolis, Indiana
MOHAWK CYCLECAR—1914-15
Mohawk Motor Co.
Boston, Massachusetts
MOHAWK CYCLECAR—1914-15
Mohawk Cyclecars
Mohawk Motor Corp.
New Orleans, Louisiana
MOHLER—1901
A. B. Mohler
Kokomo, Indiana
MOHLER & DE GRESS—1901-04
Mohler & De Gress
Astoria, Long Island, New York
Long Island City, New York
First built 1896 in Mexico City, Mexico, then brought to Astoria, New York.
MOHS—1948 to date
Mohs Seaplane Corp.
Madison, Wisconsin
"Vehicles of Compelling Interest."
All cars built to order.
MOLIGAN—1920
MOLINE—1904-13
Root & Vandervoort
Moline Automobile Co.
East Moline, Illinois
Became "Moline Knight"
MOLINE-KNIGHT—1914-19
Moline Automobile Co.
East Moline, Illinois
Formerly "Moline"
Became "R&V Knight"
January, 1918, Root & Vandervoort Engineering Co.
MOLLENHOUR—1908
A. T. Mollenhour
Mentone, Indiana
MOLLER—1920-21
Moller Motor Co.
Moller Motor Car Co.
Lewiston, Pennsylvania
Became "Falcon"

CODE = ROMAN LETTERS: Complete entry. *ITALICS:* Unsubstantiated entry. (PARENTHESES): Production planned, but not realized.

Also built taxi cabs.

MONARCH—1902-09
Monarch Motor Vehicle Co.
Chicago, Illinois
Monarch Automobile
Monarch Motor Car Co.
North Aurora, Illinois
Franklin Park, Illinois
Leyden, Illinois
Monarch Motor Mfg. Co.
Chicago, Illinois

MONARCH—1903
Sold by P. J. Dasey Co.
Chicago, Illinois
See "Morlock"

MONARCH—1907-09
Monarch Machine Co.
Des Moines, Iowa

MONARCH HIGHWHEELER—1908-09
Monarch Motor Car Co.
Chicago Heights, Illinois
Company formed March, 1906 to use patents of J. J. Boucher. Four models shown at 1907 Chicago Show.

MONARCH—1914-17
Monarch Motor Car Co.
Detroit, Michigan (1914-16)
Carter Bros. Co.
Hyattsville, Maryland (1916-17)
Eight and twelve-cylinder cars.
R. C. Hupp, president.

MONARCH—1946-61
Ford Motor Co. of Canada, Ltd.
Windsor, Ontario, Canada

MONCRIEFF STEAM—1901-02
J. A. Moncrieff
Pawtucket, Rhode Island

*MONDEX MAGIC—1912-14
Believed to be a side valve engine built by Aristos Company New York, New York. Not a make of car.

MONITOR—1909-11
Monitor Automobile Works
Chicago, Illinois (1909-10)
Became Monitor Auto Co. Janesville,

Wisconsin (1910-11).
Highwheel and standard vehicles.
Also dual purpose car.

MONITOR—1915-22
Cummins-Monitor Co.
(Cummins Auto Sales Co.)
Columbus, Ohio
Reorganized 1916 as Monitor Motor Car Co. Liquidation reported January, 1922.

MONROE—1914-24
Monroe Motor Co.
Monroe Automobile Co.
Stratton Motors Corp.
(Monroe Division)
Flint, Michigan
Reorganized 1918 as William Small Co., Indianapolis, Indiana. Sold 1923 to "Premier." Became "Stratton-Premier"

MONSEN—1908-09
Monsen Automobile Garage
Chicago, Illinois

MONTANA SPECIAL—1920
Luverne Automobile Co.
Luverne, Minnesota

MONTGOMERY-WARD ELECTRIC—1898
Montgomery-Ward & Co.
Chicago, Illinois
Two cars built, both used for advertising and not offered for sale. See "Wardway"

MONTPELIER—1937-39

MOODY—1900-03
Charles L. Moody

MOOERS—1900-01
Louis P. Mooers
New Haven, Connecticut
Louis P. Mooers later was designer for "Peerless," "Moon," "Geneva" and "Excelsior."

MOON—1905-29
Joseph W. Moon Buggy Co.
St. Louis, Missouri
Moon Motor Car Co. 1905. Reorganized 1928 with same name. Windsor Corp. formed to take over production of straight eight cars. Name changed to "Windsor" 1930.

Factory built "Ruxton" 1930. Last of Moon assets distributed 1966. See "Diana," "Hol-Tan" and "Windsor."

MOORE—1902-03
H. S. Moore
Moore Auto Co.
Cleveland, Ohio

MOORE—1906-08
Moore Automobile Co.
New York, New York
Factory at Bridgeport, Connecticut.

MOORE—1907
Indianapolis, Indiana

MOORE—1916-21
Moore Motor Co.
Minneapolis, Minnesota
Reorganized 1919 as Moore Motor Vehicle Co. Danville, Illinois
Used "Pontiac" chassis and Wayne Works Body.
Company sold out at auction December 22, 1920 for $54,807. 612 cars marketed.

MOORE AUTOMOBILE SLEIGH—1902
W. E. Moore
Goodwin's Mills, Maine

MOORE AUTOPLANE—1925-34
Virgil B. Moore
Los Angeles and Glendale, California

MOORESPRING VEHICLE STEAM—1888-90; 1895
Ingersoll Moore
Bloomington, Illinois

*MOORE STEAMER—1902-03
Charles J. Moore Mfg. Co.
Westfield, Massachusetts
This company did build steamers but it is believed they were sold under "Westfield" name.

MOOSEJAW STANDARD—1916-18
Moose Jaw, Saskatchewan, Canada

MORA—1906-10
Mora Motor Car Co.
Newark, New York
Bankrupt October, 1910.
Property sale November 15, 1911, 9 acres,

50 cars and parts. Plant sold for $120,000.

MORE—1902
  Rochester, New York

MORGAN CYCLECAR—1914
  W. M. Steele
  Worcester, Massachusetts

MORGAN MOTOR CARRIAGE—1897
  Morgan Construction Co.
  Worcester, Massachusetts

MORLOCK—1903
  Sold by P. J. Dasey Co.
  Chicago, Illinois
  Built by Morlock Automobile Co. Buffalo, New York.
  See "Monarch"
  Succeeded Spaulding Automobile Co.

MORRIS-LONDON—1923-25
  Century Motor Co.
  Elkhart, Indiana
  Export car for England.

MORRIS & SALOM—ELECTRIC—1894-97
  Became Electric Carriage & Wagon Co. (Hansom Cabs for New York City.)
  See "Electrobat"
  Morris & Salom
  Philadelphia, Pennsylvania
  Both names apply to same vehicle.

MORRISON ELECTRIC—1891-92
  William Morrison
  Des Moines, Iowa
  Early U.S. electric vehicle.
  1891 vehicle sold to Harold Sturges.
  See "Sturges" electric

MORRISON—1935
  Willard L. Morrison
  Buchanan, Michigan

*MORRISSEY—1923-28
  Morrissey Motor Car Co. Bridgeport, Connecticut built trucks and buses under "Bridgeport" name.

MORSE—1904
  Morse Motor Co.
  Brookline, Massachusetts

(MORSE) STEAM—1904-06
  Morse Motor Vehicle Co.

Morse Automobile Co.
  5 Elm Street
  Springfield, Massachusetts
  Incorporated late 1904

MORSE—1907-16
  Easton Machine Co.
  South Easton, Massachusetts
  Morse Motor Car Co.
  Brookline, Massachusetts

MORSE CYCLECAR—1914-16
  Frank H. Morse
  Morse Cyclecar Co.
  Pittsburgh, Pennsylvania
  Front-wheel drive

MORSE-RADIO—1909-10
  Morse-Radio Automobile Co.
  Springfield, Massachusetts

MORSE STEAMER—1901
  J. S. Morse
  Newton, Massachusetts

MORT—1917-24
  Meteor Motor Car Co.
  Piqua, Ohio
  Funeral coaches and limousines on "Meteor" chassis.

MOTO-BLOCK—1908

MOTO-KAR THREE-WHEELER—1938
  Moto-Skoot Mfg. Co.
  Chicago, Illinois

MOTOR BOB—1914
  E. N. Bowen
  Buffalo, New York
  Unassembled juvenile car

MOTOR BUGGY HIGHWHEELER—1908
  Motor Buggy Co.
  Ft. Wayne, Indiana

MOTOR BUGGY HIGHWHEELER—1908-09
  Motor Buggy Mfg. Co.
  Minneapolis, Minnesota

MOTOR CAR—1903
  See "Murray"
  Church Mfg. Co.
  Adrian, Michigan
  Both names apply to the same vehicle.

*MOTOR CAR—1906

Believed to be company name of Motor Car Co. Detroit, Michigan
  See "Cartercar"

MOTORETTE (model)—1901-03
  See "Pierce"
  George N. Pierce Co.
  Buffalo, New York

MOTORETTE THREE-WHEELER—1910-12
  See "Kelsey Motorette"
  C. W. Kelsey Mfg. Co.
  Hartford, Connecticut
  Both names apply to the same vehicle.

MOTORETTE—1946-48
  Motorette Corp.
  Buffalo, New York

MOTOR HORSE—1897
  See "Barsaleaux"
  Joseph Barsaleaux
  Sandy Hill, New York
  Both names apply to the same vehicle.

MOTORMOBILE—1901
  Carl E. Lipman
  Beloit, Wisconsin

MOTOR TRANSIT

MOTZ—1900
  Charles A. Motz
  Akron, Ohio

MOUNTAIN ROAD—1917

MOUNT PLEASANT—1914
  See "M.P.M."
  Mount Pleasant Motor Co.
  Mount Pleasant, Michigan
  Both names apply to the same vehicle.

MOVER—1902
  B & F Mover Co.
  Chicago, Illinois

MOYEA—1903-04
  Moyea Automobile Co.
  New York, New York
  Pittsfield & Springfield, Massachusetts
  1904 became Consolidated Motor Co.
  Absorbed by Alden-Sampson Mfg. Co.

MOYER—1902

MOYER—1910-15
  H. A. Moyer

Moyer Automobile Co.
Syracuse, New York
M.P.M.—1915-16
M.P.M. Motor Car Co.
Mount Pleasant, Michigan
Formerly called "M.P."
See "Mount Pleasant"
M.P.M.—1920
M. P. Moller Motor Co.
Lewiston, Pennsylvania
Separate from "M.P.M." Mount Pleasant.
MUELLER HIGHWHEELER—1909-10
Mueller Motor Car Co.
Milwaukee, Wisconsin
MUELLER-BENZ—1895
H. Mueller Mfg. Co.
(Mueller & Co.)
Decatur, Illinois
Later built "Mueller Trap"
MUIR COMPRESSED AIR—1900
John S. Muir
South Norfolk, Connecticut
MUIR STEAM—1903
MULFORD—1909
MULFORD—1922
Mulford Motors Co.
New York, New York
Cars built by racing driver Ralph Mulford.
MULTIPLEX—1912-14
Multiplex Mfg. Co.
Berwick, Pennsylvania
MULTIPLEX—1952-54
Multiplex Manufacturing Co.
Berwick, Pennsylvania
MUNCH-ALLEN—1910
Munch-Allen Motor Car Co.
DuBois, Pennsylvania
See "Keystone"
MUNCIE—1903
Muncie Wheel & Jobbing Co.
Muncie, Indiana
MUNCLE—1904
MUNSING—1908-10
Munsing Mfg. Co.
Hoboken, New Jersey

MUNSING—1913
New York, New York
MUNSON—1895-1900
The Munson Co.
La Porte, Indiana
MUNTZ—1950-55
Muntz Motor Works
Chicago, Illinois
Evansville, Indiana
MURDAUGH—1900-05
Murdaugh Automobile Co.
Oxford, Pennsylvania
MURENA—1969 to date
Murena Motors Inc.
New York, New York
Luxury station wagon with Ford V-8 engine and Italian bodywork.
MURILLO—1906-07
Murillo Motor Car Co.
Marion, Indiana
Became Coppock Motor Car Co.
MURLOCK—1903
Murlock Automobile Mfg. Co.
Buffalo, New York
MURPHY SPECIAL—1906
Murphy Auto Construction Co.
Minneapolis, Minnesota
MURRAY—1896
Oliver C. Murray
Homer, New York
MURRAY—1902-03
Church Mfg. Co.
Adrian, Michigan
Became "Lenawee"
MURRAY—1916-21
Murray Motor Co.
Murray Motor Car Co.
Pittsburgh, Pennsylvania
Newark, New Jersey
Became "Murray-Mac"
MURRAY-MAC—1921-29
Murray-Mac Motor Co.
Boston, Massachusetts
Everett, Massachusetts
Built intermittently by J. J. McCarthy.

Succeeded "Murray"
MUSCATEER AMPHIBIAN—1968 to date
Muscat Corp.
Forest Lake, Minnesota
Jeep-type off-the-road vehicle.
MUSTANG—1948
Mustang Engineering Corp.
Renton, Washington
MUSTANG (model)—1965 to date
See "Ford"
Ford Motor Company
Dearborn, Michigan
MUTUAL—1915
Mutual Motor Car Co.
Buffalo, New York
MYER—1921
B&F Myer
MYERS—1901
Thomas Myers
New York, New York
MYSTERY—1925
Chicago, Illinois

N

NADIG—1899-1900
Henry Nadig & Sons
Allentown, Pennsylvania
Built "Eureka" truck in Allentown from 1905-06.
NANCE—1910-13
Nance Motor Car Co.
Philadelphia, Pennsylvania
Became "Touraine"
NAPIER—1904-05, 1908
Napier Motor Co. of America
Roxbury, Massachusetts
Built in Jamaica Plains, Massachusetts.
NAPOLEON—1916-19
Napoleon Automobile Mfg. Co.
Napoleon, Ohio
Reorganized 1917 as Napoleon Motors Co. Traverse City, Michigan. Trucks only 1920-22.
NARRAGANSETT—1915

NASH—1917-57
Nash Motors Co.
Kenosha, Wisconsin
Succeeded Thomas B. Jeffery Co. Became
Nash-Kelvinator Corp. 1936. Merged with
Hudson Motor Car Co. to form American
Motors Corp. 1954.

NASH AUTO-CAR—1906-11
Nash Auto-Car Co.
Detroit, Michigan

NASH-HEALEY—1951-54
Nash Motors Co.
Kenosha, Wisconsin
Built in England for U.S. market.
506 cars sold.

NATIONAL—1898-1900
National Motor Carriage Co.
Stamford, Connecticut

NATIONAL—1899-1901
National Motor Co.
St. Louis, Missouri

NATIONAL—1900
National Automobile Co.
Wilmington, Delaware

NATIONAL electric—1900-05
National Automobile & Electric Co.
Indianapolis, Indiana

NATIONAL—1902-03
National Automobile & Motor Co.
Oshkosh, Wisconsin

NATIONAL—1903
National Automobile Co.
Providence, Rhode Island
Electric and steam vehicles

NATIONAL—1904-24
National Automobile & Electric Co.
Indianapolis, Indiana
Reorganized as National Motor Vehicle Co.
1902. See "National" electric.
Reorganized as National Motor Car & Vehi-
cle Co. 1916.
Merged with "Dixie Flyer" and "Jackson"
into Associated Motors Corp. 1922.

NATIONAL cyclecar—1914
National Cyclecar Co.
Detroit, Michigan

NATIONAL ROAD CAR—1903-06
National Sewing Machine Co.
Belvidere, Illinois

NATIONAL SEXTET (model)—1919-20
See "National"
National Motor Car & Vehicle Co.
Indianapolis, Indiana

NATIONAL STEAM—1899-1900
National Transportation Co.
Boston, Massachusetts

NAVAJO—1954
Navajo Motor Car Co.
New York, New York
Sports car using Mercury V-8 engine.

NAVARRE—1921
A. C. Schulz
Package Machinery Co.
Springfield, Massachusetts
Possibly only prototype built.

NEBRASKA cyclecar—1914
Nebraska Cyclecar Co.
Omaha, Nebraska

NEFTEL—1902-03
Neftel Automobile Co.
Brooklyn, New York
Gasoline-electric

NEILSON—1906-07
Neilson Motor Car Co.
Detroit, Michigan

NELSON—1905
T. K. Nelson Motor Co.
Harlan, Iowa

NELSON—1917-23
E. A. Nelson Motor Car Co.
Detroit, Michigan
Absorbed Gray Motor Co.
1919 reorganized as Nelson Motor Car Co.
1920 reorganized as E. A. Nelson Automobile Company.

NELSON-BRENNAN-PETERSON—1914-15
Detroit, Michigan

NER-A-CAR—1922-24
Ner-A-Car Corp.
Syracuse, New York

NESKOV-MUMPEROW—1921-22
Neskov-Mumperow Motor Car Co.
St. Louis, Missouri

NESTER ELECTRIC—1912

NEUMAN ELECTRIC—1922

NEUSTADT—1904-12
J. H. Neustadt Co.
Neustadt Auto & Supply Co.
St. Louis, Missouri

NEUSTADT-PERRY—1901-07
Neustadt-Perry Co.
St. Louis, Missouri
Formerly J. H. Neustadt Co. (steamers).
Running gear for other companies.
See "Neustadt"

(NEVADA)—1908
Nevada Motor Car Co.
Reno, Nevada
See "Desert Flyer" and "Reno"

NEVILLE 1910
T. Neville
Oshkosh, Wisconsin

NEVIN—1927

NEWARK—1901-03
Newark Motor Vehicle Co.
Newark, New Jersey

NEW BRISTOL—1916

NEW CASTLE—1907-08
New Castle Automobile Co.
New Castle, Pennsylvania

NEWCOMB steam—1906-08
Newcomb Motor Co.
Long Island City, New York

NEW ENGLAND steam—1898
New England Motor Carriage Co.
Waltham, Massachusetts

NEW ENGLAND—1898-1901
New England Electric Vehicle & Trans-
portation Co.
Camden, New Jersey

NEW ENGLAND MOBILE—1903-04

NEW ERA—1900
New Era Motor Co.
Boston, Massachusetts

NEW ERA—1901-02

CODE = ROMAN LETTERS: Complete entry. ITALICS: Unsubstantiated entry. (PARENTHESES): Production planned, but not realized.

Automobile & Marine Power Co.
Camden, New Jersey
NEW ERA—1912
New Era Motor & Mfg. Co.
Lansing, Michigan
NEW ERA—1915-16
New Era Engineering Co.
Joliet, Illinois
Became Elgin Motor Car Co.
See "Elgin" (1916-24)
*NEW ERA—1929-31
Name of company that built "Ruxton," not
name of car.
*NEW ERIE
Believed to be misspelling of "New Era."
NEW HAVEN—1899
New Haven Carriage Co.
Hartford, Connecticut
NEW HAVEN—1902-03
New Haven Carriage Co.
New Haven, Connecticut
Absorbed by Electric Vehicle Co.
NEW HOME STEAM—1898-1901
Grout Bros.
Orange, Massachusetts
See "Grout"
NEW LONDON—1895
New London Specialty Co.
New London, Ohio
NEW MONARCH—1903
Milwaukee Motor & Mfg. Co.
Milwaukee, Wisconsin
NEW ORLEANS—1901
NEW ORLEANS CYCLECAR—1914
New Orleans Cyclecar Co.
New Orleans, Louisiana
NEW PARRY—1911-12
The Motor Car Mfg. Co.
Indianapolis, Indiana
Former "Parry"
NEW PITTSBURGH—1915
Motors Co. of Pittsburgh
Pittsburgh, Pennsylvania
NEWPORT—1903
Newport Engineering Works

Newport, Rhode Island
NEW PORT—1916
NEWPORT—1920
Newport Motors Inc.
New York, New York
NEW POWER—1896
New Power Co.
New York, New York
NEW ROCHELLE—1909
New Rochelle Motor Car Co.
New Rochelle, New York
NEW SOUTH—1910
New South Automobile Co.
Augusta, Georgia
NEW WAY—1905-07
New Way Motor Co.
Lansing, Michigan
Seven cars built.
NEW YORK—1900-01
New York Automobile Co.
New York, New York
NEW YORK—1900-02
New York Automobile Co.
Syracuse, New York
Transferred to H. H. Franklin Co.
NEW YORK—1903
NEW YORK—1905-07
New York Car & Truck Co.
Kingston, New York
NEW YORK & OHIO—1899-1900
The New York & Ohio Co.
Warren, Ohio
See "Packard"
NEW YORK SIX—1928-29
Automotive Corp. of America
(New York Motors Corp.)
Moline, Illinois
Car built in Richmond, Indiana, by the
Automotive Corp. of America, Baltimore,
Maryland.
Parent corp. of G. W. Davis Motor Car Co.
Richmond, Indiana. New car announced
1929.
NEW YORK STEAM—1900-01
New York Motor Vehicle Co.

Middletown, Connecticut
See "Volomobile"
*NEYBERG
Believed to be "Nyberg" misspelled.
NIAGARA—1899-1901
Niagara Automobile Co.
Niagara Falls, New York
NIAGARA ELECTRIC—1902
Niagara Motor Vehicle Co.
Buffalo, New York
Asked voluntary dissolution, reported
November, 1902.
NIAGARA—1903-05
Wilson Automobile Mfg. Co.
Wilson, New York
LaSalle-Niagara Auto Co.
Niagara Falls, New York
NIAGARA—1913
Niagara Motor Car Corp.
Niagara Falls, New York
Dunkirk, New York
Juvenile car
NIAGARA—1915-16
Wilson-Niagara Co.
Wilson, New York
NIAGARA—1919
NIAGARA FOUR—1915-16
Mutual Motor Car Co.
Niagara Automobile Co.
Buffalo, New York
Former "Mutual"
NICHOLS—1908
D. P. Nichols & Co.
Boston, Massachusetts
NICHOLS-SHEPARD—1910-11
Nichols-Shepard & Co.
Battle Creek, Michigan
Built tractors after 1911.
NIC-L-SILVER PIONEER EXPERIMENTAL
ELECTRIC—1959
Nic-L-Silver Battery Co.
Santa Ana, California
NIELSON—1907-09
Nielson Motor Car Co.
Detroit, Michigan

NIKE (model)—1904-09
A 20 hp roadster model.
See "Napier"
Napier Motor Co. of America
Jamaica Plain, Massachusetts
NILES—1903
Automobile & Gas Engine Co.
Niles, Michigan
NILES—1916
NOBLE—1902
Noble Automobile Mfg. Co.
Cleveland, Ohio
NOBLE—1933
Warren Noble
Buffalo, New York
NOBLE—1960
Satellite Corp. of America
Wiscasset, Maine
NOEL DUPLEX—1923
J. C. N. Noel Motor Car Co.
Jersey City, New Jersey
NOLAN—1924
NOMA—1919-23
Noma Motor Corp.
New York, New York
(NORCROSS)—1907
United Electrical Mfg. Co.
Norcross, Georgia
*NORDYKE
Company name of Nordyke & Marmon Co.,
Indianapolis, Indiana, not name of car.
See "Marmon"
NORMAN-LIONEL SLEIGH—1904-05
Norman Motor Sleigh Co.
Boston, Massachusetts
Shown at New York City Auto Show.
NORTH AMERICAN—1948
NORTHERN—1902-09
Northern Mfg. Co.
Detroit, Michigan
Organized by J. D. Maxwell and C. B.
King. Reorganized as Northern Motor Car
Co. 1906.
Absorbed by "E.M.F." 1908.
NORTHWAY—1918-22

Northway Motors Corp.
Boston, Massachusetts
Natick, Massachusetts
NORTHWESTERN—1904
Northwestern Automobile Co.
Milwaukee, Wisconsin
NORTHWESTERN—1914
Northwestern Automobile Mfg. Co.
Seattle, Washington
NORTHWESTERN CYCLECAR—1914
Northwestern Cyclecar Co.
Chicago, Illinois
NORTON—1895
F. G. Norton
Waukegan, Illinois
NORTON STEAM—1901-02
James J. Norton
Lowell, Massachusetts
NORTON STEAM—1903
W. P. Norton
Torrington, Connecticut
NORVELL—1946
Jack Norvell
Los Angeles, California
NORWALK—1911-16 and 1920-22
Norwalk Motor Car Co.
Martinsburg, West Virginia
Norwalk, Ohio
Succeeded "Auto-Bug"
NOVARRA—1917
Herreshoff Mfg. Co.
Bristol, Rhode Island
Sports cars only.
See "Herreshoff"
NUGENT—1909-10
Nugent Automobile Works
New York, New York
NU-KLEA ELECTRIC—1959-60
Nu-Klea Automobile Corp.
Lansing, Michigan
NYBERG—1904
Nyberg-Waller Automobile Works
Chicago, Illinois
NYBERG—1911-14
Nyberg Automobile Works

Anderson, Indiana
Succeeded "Rider-Lewis" February 28,
1911.
Became "Madison."

O

OAKLAND—1907-31
Oakland Motor Car Co.
Pontiac, Michigan
Succeeded Pontiac Buggy Co.
Purchased by General Motors 1909.
Division of G.M. Corp. 1917.
Introduced "Pontiac" 1926.
Became Pontiac Motor Division 1932.
See "Pontiac"
OAKLAND—1931
General Motors Products of
Canada Ltd.
Oshawa, Ontario, Canada
OAKMAN—1899-1900
Oakman Motor Vehicle Co.
Greenfield, Massachusetts
OAKMAN-HERTEL—1898
Oakman Motor Vehicle Co.
Greenfield, Massachusetts
Became "Oakman" 1899
OAK SIX—1917
Oak Mfg. Co.
Chicago, Illinois
OBERLIN—1903
O. S. Oberlin
McKeesport, Pennsylvania
OBERTINE—1915
O'BRIEN ELECTRIC—1900
O'Brien & Sons
San Francisco, California
OCELOT DUNE BUGGY—1968 to date
Sand Chariots
Fullerton, California
O'CONNOR—1916
O'Connor Corp.
Chicago, Illinois
O.C.R. DUNE BUGGY—1968
Orange County Recreation Enterprises

CODE = ROMAN LETTERS: Complete entry. ITALICS: Unsubstantiated entry. (PARENTHESES): Production planned, but not realized.

Santa Ana, California

OCTO-AUTO (model) EXPERIMENTAL
8-WHEELER—1912
Built by Milton O. Reeves.
Used "Overland" body and chassis. Running gear by Reeves. See "Reeves"

ODD-VW-ARK—1970
Automotive Design Associates, Inc.
Monroe, Connecticut

ODELOT—1915
Lawrence Stamping Co.
Toledo, Ohio
Spells Toledo backwards.

ODENBRETT—1897
George L. Odenbrett
Milwaukee, Wisconsin

OFELT STEAM—1887-99
F. W. Ofelt & Sons
Jackson-on-the-Hudson and
Brooklyn, New York

OFELT STEAM—1900-01
Ofelt Automobile & Steam Launch Co.
Newark, N. J.

OFFENHAUSER—1934-38
Offenhauser Engineering Co.
Los Angeles, California
Racing cars

OGONTZ—1916
Ogontz Motor Car Co.
Sandusky, Ohio

OGREN—1907

OGREN—1914-23
Ogren Motor Car Co.
Chicago, Illinois
Racers only, 1914-17. Became "H.W.O."
1916 reorganized as Ogren Motor Works,
Waukegan, Illinois.
1917 reverted to Ogren Motor Car Co.
Moved to Milwaukee, Wisconsin 1919.

OHIO—1899-1902
Synonym for "Packard"
See "Packard"
Ohio Automobile Co.
Warren, Ohio

OHIO—1909-15
Jewel Carriage Co.
Ohio Motor Car Co.
Cincinnati, Ohio
Carthage, Ohio
1912 absorbed by Northway Motor & Mfg.
Co. Became Crescent Motor Co.

OHIO—1913-15
Crescent Motor Co.
Cincinnati, Ohio

OHIO—1914-15
Ohio Motor Car Co.
Carthage, Ohio

OHIO ELECTRIC—1909-18
Ohio Electric Carriage Co.
Ohio Electric Car Co.
Toledo, Ohio

OHIO FALLS—1913-14
Ohio Falls Motor Co.
New Albany, Indiana
Succeeded "Jonz."
Also built "Pilgrim."

OHMPHUNDRA—1946
Los Angeles, California

OKEY—1896
Perry Okey
Okey Automobile Co.
Okey Motor Car Co.
Columbus, Ohio

OKEY—1907-08
Okey Motor Car Co.
Columbus, Ohio

OKLAHOMA SIX—1917-18
Midland Motor Car & Truck Co.
Oklahoma City, Oklahoma

OLDFIELD—1917
Oldfield Motors Corp.
Los Angeles, California
Detroit, Michigan

OLDFIELD CYCLECAR—1914
L. W. Oldfield
Minneapolis, Minnesota

OLDS—1896-97
P. F. Olds & Son Engine Works
Lansing, Michigan

After building steam cars in late 1880's
and early '90's, turned to gasoline car.
One built 1896, four more built 1897. Only
1897 car is in Smithsonian collection.

OLDS ELECTRIC—1899-1901
Olds Motor Works
Detroit, Michigan
Lansing, Michigan
See "Oldsmobile"

OLDSMOBILE—1899 to date
Olds Motor Vehicle Co.
Lansing, Michigan
Formerly P. F. Olds & Son Engine Works.
1899 reorganized as Olds Motor Works,
Detroit, Michigan.
Moved to Lansing after 1901 fire.
Became a unit of General Motors Corp.
1908, a division 1917.
See "Viking" (1929-30)

OLDS 1901 REPLICA—1968
Horseless Carriage Corp.
Ft. Lauderdale, Florida
A ¾ scale replica of original "Oldsmobile."

OLIVE STEAM—1901
Olive Wheel Co.
Syracuse, New York

OLIVER—1905
Oliver Trackless Car Co.
South Bend, Indiana

OLIVER ELECTRIC—1906
Oliver Electric Vehicle Co.
Cleveland, Ohio

OLSSON—1900-05
Ivan W. Olsson
Chicago, Illinois
Gas, electric and steam to 1903; gas and
steam 1903-05.

OLYMPIAN—1897

OLYMPIAN—1917-20
Olympian Motors Corp.
Pontiac, Michigan
Succeeded Pontiac Chassis Co.
Became Friend Motor Corp.
See "Friend"

OLYMPIC—1909

Gearless Transmission Co.
Rochester, New York
Gear-driven companion car to "Gearless."

OMAHA—1899
Omaha Gas Engine & Motor Co.
Omaha, Nebraska

OMAHA—1912-14
Omaha Motor Co.
Omaha, Nebraska
Temporarily used plant of T. F. Stroud Co.

OMEGA—1966-67
Suspensions International Corp.
Charlotte, North Carolina
Sports car using Ford V-8 engine.

O'NEIL—1903
John O'Neil
Lawrence, Massachusetts

*ONLICAR—1910
Believed to be "Only" misspelled.

ONONDAGA—1906
Cronin Automobile Co.
Syracuse, New York

ONLY—1909-15
Only Car Co.
Echo, New York
Port Jefferson, New York

ONO—1912

OPHIR steam—1901

ORCUTT STEAM—1899
E. L. Orcutt
Somerville, Massachusetts

OREGON—1916
Beaver State Motor Car Co.
Gresham, Oregon

ORIENT—1899-1904
Waltham Manufacturing Co.
Waltham, Massachusetts
1899-1901 the company produced two-passenger runabout equipped with either a three or five hp water-cooled engine. During 1903 and 1904 air-cooled cars using 20 hp engine were built. 1905 name changed to "Waltham-Orient."

ORIENTAL-DETROIT—1910

Oriental-Detroit Co.
Birmingham, Michigan

ORIENT-AUTO-GO (model)—1900
See "Orient"
Waltham Mfg. Co.
Waltham, Massachusetts

ORIOLE—1910
Giddings & Lewis Mfg. Co.
Fond Du Lac, Wisconsin

ORION
One registered in Michigan 1916.

ORION—1921

ORLO—1904-05
Jackson Automobile Co.
Jackson, Michigan
See "Jaxon" and "Jackson."

ORMOND steam—1904-05
United Motor & Vehicle Co.
Boston, Massachusetts

ORR—1915
Orr Motor Co.
Yazoo City, Mississippi

ORSON—1910-14
Orson Automobile Co.
New York, New York
(Brightwood Motor Mfg. Co.)
(Drenco Machine Co.)
Springfield, Massachusetts
100 cars built for wealthy capitalists.
Also called "Millionaire's Car."

O-S—1914-16
Owen-Schoeneck Co.
Rock Island, Illinois

OSBORN—1899
Pioneer Iron Works
Clarksburg, West Virginia

OSCAR-LEAR—1903
Oscar Lear Automobile Co.
Columbus, Ohio
See "Frayer-Miller"

OSEN & HUNT—1900
Osen & Hunt
San Jose, California
Often misspelled "Olson & Hunt." One vehicle of five extant July, 1969.

OSHKESCH—1926
Believed to be "Oshkosh" (truck)

OSHKOSH STEAMER—1878
Oshkosh, Wisconsin

O.T. SIX AIR-COOLED—1909
Owen Thomas Motor Car Co.
Janesville, Wisconsin
Three body styles, six-cylinder rotary valve engine.

OTTO—1909-12
Otto Gas Engine Co.
Ottomobile Co.
Philadelphia, Pennsylvania
Mt. Holly, New Jersey
See "Otto-mobile"

OTTO-CROSS DUNE BUGGY—1968 to date
Auto Craft Inc.
Portland, Oregon

OTTO-KAR—1903-04
Otto Konigslow
Cleveland, Ohio

OTTOMOBILE—1899
Baysdorfer Dumbleton & Co.
Omaha, Nebraska
Prototype only

OTTO-MOBILE—1912
Holly Motor Co.
Mt. Holly, New Jersey
Succeeded bankrupt Otto Gas Engine Co.

OUTING—1910
Outing Motor Co.
Detroit, Michigan

OVENDEN STEAMER—1899
W. C. Ovenden
West Boylston, Massachusetts
One sold

OVERHOLT steam—1899

OVERHOLT HIGHWHEELER—1909
The Overholt Co.
Galesburg, Illinois
Became "Illinois"

OVERLAND—1903-26; 1939
Standard Wheel Co. (Division of
Parry Mfg. Co.)
Terre Haute, Indiana (1903-07)

CODE = ROMAN LETTERS: Complete entry. *ITALICS*: Unsubstantiated entry. (PARENTHESES): Production planned, but not realized.

Overland Automobile Co. Terre Haute and
Indianapolis, Indiana (1907-08).
Willys-Overland Co. (1908-36)
With "Marion" and "American" in
American Motor Sales Co. 1912.
Became "Whippet" 1926-30.
OVERMAN (model) STEAM—1899-1902
Absorbed by "Locomobile," 1902.
See "Victor" steam
Overman Automobile Co.
Chicopee Falls, Massachusetts
Both names apply to same vehicle.
(OWATONNA)—1903
Virtue & Pound Mfg. Co.
Owatonna, Minnesota
O-WE-GO CYCLECAR—1914
O-We-Go Car Co.
Owego, New York
Company started March, 1914. Failed and
put in receivers' hands by December, 1914.
OWEN—1898
R. M. Owen Carpet & Rug Mfg. Co.
Cleveland, Ohio
Experiments only
OWEN—1901-03
Owen Motor Carriage Co.
Owen Motor Co.
Cleveland, Ohio
OWEN—1910-12
Owen Motor Car Co.
Detroit, Michigan
OWEN—1914
Owen Motor Car Co.
Toledo, Ohio
OWEN-MAGNETIC—1914-22
R. M. Owen Co.
New York, New York
1915 Baker, Rauch & Lang Co. Cleveland,
Ohio.
International Fabricating Co. Wilkes-Barre,
Pennsylvania, 1919.
1920 Owen-Magnetic Motor Car Corp.
Wilkes-Barre, Pennsylvania
Had magnetic transmission.
OWENS STEAM—1900

H. E. Owens
Thomas Mfg. Co.
Springfield, Ohio
*OWEN-SCHOEHECK—1915-16
Believed to be company name of the Owen
Schoeheck Co. Chicago, Illinois. Not name
of car.
OWENS CORNING—1945
OWEN-THOMAS—1909
See "O.T. Six"
Owen Thomas Motor Car Co.
Janesville, Wisconsin
Both names apply to same vehicle. Com-
pany advertised car as "O.T. Six."
OWOSSO MOTOR BUGGY—1903
Owosso Buggy Co.
Owosso, Michigan
OXFORD STEAM—1900
Oxford Automobile Co.
Everett, Massachusetts
OXFORD STEAM—1900-01
Oxford Automobile Co.
Augusta, Maine
OXFORD—1905-06
Detroit-Oxford Mfg. Co.
Oxford, Michigan
Became "Fostoria"
OXFORD—1913-15
Oxford Motor Cars & Foundries Ltd.
Montreal, Quebec, Canada
OYLER—1900
Oyler Mfg. Co.
Minneapolis, Minnesota

𝒫

PACIFIC—1900-04
Pacific Motor Co.
Pacific Motor Vehicle Co.
Oakland, California
PACIFIC—1913
Seattle Car & Foundry Co.
Renton, Washington
PACIFIC CYCLECAR—1914
Pacific Cyclecar Co.

Seattle, Washington
PACIFIC CYCLECAR—1914
Portland Cyclecar Co.
Portland, Oregon
See "Portland"
PACIFIC SPECIAL—1911
Cole California Car Co.
Oakland, California
PACKARD—1895-96
Lucius B. Packard
Salem, Massachusetts
One vehicle built.
PACKARD—1899-1958
New York & Ohio Co.
Warren, Ohio
1899 two experimental cars.
1900 Ohio Automobile Co., Warren, Ohio.
1902 reorganized as Packard Motor Car Co.
and moved to Detroit, Michigan.
Merged with Studebaker Corp. 1954 as
Studebaker-Packard Corp.
See "Clipper"
PACKET CYCLECAR—1914
Pacific Cyclecar Co.
Seattle, Washington
PACKET CYCLECAR—1914
Scripps-Booth Cyclecar Co.
Detroit, Michigan
PACKETT—1914-18
See "Brasie"
Brasie Motor Car Co.
Packett Motor Car Mfg. Co.
Minneapolis, Minnesota
Name for "Brasie" roadster.
Mostly trucks after 1916.
PACO HIGHWHEELER—1908
Pietsch Auto and Marine Co.
Chicago, Illinois
PAGE AIR-COOLED—1906-07
Page Motor Vehicle Co.
Providence, Rhode Island
PAGE—1909
J. I. Page
Owosso, Michigan
(PAGE)—1921-24

Victor Pagé Motors Corp.
Stamford, Connecticut
Raymond Engineering Co.
Farmingdale, New York
Liquidation reported January, 1924. No cars sold.

PAGE-ADRIAN EXPERIMENTAL
AIR-COOLED—1907-09
Page Gas Engine Co.
Adrian, Michigan
Organized August, 1906
Built two-cycle cars
Bought Bloomstrom "Gyroscope" patents 1909.
Became "Lion" 1909.
1916 made windshields.

PAGENKOPF—1906
William Pagenkopf
Goldfield, Nevada

PAGE-TOLEDO—1910-11
Toledo Motor Co.
Toledo, Ohio
Succeeded "Pope-Toledo"

PAIGE—1901
F. E. Paige
Batavia, New York

PAIGE—1912-1927
Paige-Detroit Motor Car Co.
Detroit, Michigan
1927 purchased by Graham-Bros.
1928 became Graham-Paige Motors Corp.
Formerly called "Paige-Detroit."
See "Jewett" and "Graham-Paige."

PAIGE-DETROIT—1909-11
See "Paige"
Paige-Detroit Motor Car Co.
Detroit, Michigan
Became "Paige"

PAISANO DUNE BUGGY—1968
V. W. C. Specialty Co.
Kermit, Texas

PALM—1918-19
Distributed by
E. W. Brown Motors Ltd.
Milbourn, Victoria, Canada

Basically Canadian Model T "Ford."

PALMER HIGHWHEELER—1905-06
Palmer Automobile Mfg. Co.
Cleveland, Ohio
Ashtabula, Ohio

PALMER—1912-13
Palmer Motor Car Co.
Ecorse, Michigan
Combined with Partin Mfg. Co.
Became "Partin-Palmer"

PALMER—1914-15
Palmer Bros.
Cos Cob, Connecticut

PALMER-SINGER—1908-14
Palmer & Singer Mfg. Co.
Mt. Vernon, New York
Company former agents for Matheson and Simplex cars.
Car built by "Matheson" 1908.
New factory at Long Island City, New York 1911.
1914 became Singer Motor Co.
See "Singer"

PAN—1917-22
Pan Motors Co.
St. Cloud, Minnesota
Company promoted by Samuel Conner Pandolfo who was ultimately convicted for fraud.
Approximately 737 cars built.

PAN-AM—1901-04
Pan American Automobile Co.
Pan-American Motor Co.
Mamaroneck, New York
Also called "Pan American"
Became Commercial Motor Co., Marion, New Jersey.

PAN AMERICAN—1901-04
See "Pan-Am"
Pan American Motor Co.
Mamaroneck, New York
Both names apply to same vehicle.

PAN AMERICAN—1917-22
Pan American Motors Corp.
Decatur, Illinois

Former "Chicago Light 6"
Reported liquidated January, 1922.

PANDA—1955-56
Small Cars Inc.
Kansas City, Missouri

PANKOTAN—1940
Paul Pankotan
Miami, Florida

PANTHER—1909
Panther Car Co.
Boston, Massachusetts

PANTHER—1962
Panther Automobile Co.
Bedford Hills, New York

PARAGON—1905-07
Detroit Automobile Mfg. Co.
Detroit, Michigan
See "La Petite"
Became "Marvel"

PARAGON—1917

PARAGON—1920-22
Paragon Motor Car Co.
Connellsville, Pennsylvania
(February, 1920)
Paragon Motor Co.
Cumberland, Maryland
(May, 1921)

PARDESSUS—1900
R. Pardessus
New London, Connecticut

*PARENTH—1921
Believed to be "Parenti" misspelled.

PARENTI—1920-23
Parenti Motors Corp.
Buffalo, New York
Plywood unit built body and frame.
Plant sold 1922 to Hanover Motor Car Co.
Hanover, Pennsylvania.

PARKER (model)—1922
Formerly "Forster" 1920-22.
See "Royal Six"
Parker Motor Car Co. Ltd.
Montreal, Quebec, Canada

PARKER—1934
Harry S. Parker

Ellsworth, Maine
One car produced.
PARKER STEAMER—1825
T. W. Parker
Edgar County, Illinois
PARKET
PARKIN—1903-09
Parkin & Son
Philadelphia, Pennsylvania
PARRY—1896; 1900
Parry Bros.
Indianapolis, Indiana
PARRY—1910-12
Parry Automobile Co.
Indianapolis, Indiana
Became Motor Car Mfg. Co.
Called "New Parry" 1911
See "Pathfinder"
PARSONS STEAM—1900
J. H. Parsons
McClean & Kendall Co.
Wilmington, Delaware
PARSONS ELECTRIC—1905-08
Parsons Electric Motor Carriage Co.
Cleveland, Ohio
PARTIN—1913
Partin Mfg. Co.
Chicago, Illinois
Became "Partin-Palmer"
PARTIN-PALMER—1913-17
Partin Mfg. Co.
Chicago, Illinois
Partin-Palmer Motor Car Co., Chicago, Illinois manufacturers, 1914.
Reorganized as Commonwealth Motors Co.
April, 1915.
1917 name changed to "Commonwealth."
*PARTIN-PARLER—1915
Believed to be "Partin-Palmer" misspelled.
PARTS MAKER—1934-35
Leaf Spring Institute
PASCO—1908
PASTORA—1913
One registered in Michigan 1916.

PATERSON—1895
William Paterson
Chicago, Illinois
PATERSON—1908-24
W. A. Paterson Carriage Co.
W. A. Paterson Co.
Flint, Michigan
PATHFINDER—1899
Pathfinder Mfg. Co.
Chicago, Illinois
PATHFINDER—1911-18
Motor Car Mfg. Co.
Pathfinder Automobile Co.
Indianapolis, Indiana
Succeeded Parry Mfg. Co.
1917 reorganized as Pathfinder Motor Car Co. of America.
PATRICIAN—1917
PATRICIAN—1930
PATRICK—1916
Seattle, Washington
PATRIOT—1920
Patriot Mfg. Co.
Havelock, Nebraska
Formerly Hebb Motors Co. Lincoln, Nebraska.
Mostly trucks
PATTERSON-GREENFIELD—1916-18
C. R. Patterson & Son
Greenfield, Ohio
PATTON GAS-ELECTRIC—1890
PAUL—1900
J. E. Paul
Eureka, California
PAWTUCKET STEAM—1901-02
Pawtucket Steam Boat Co.
Pawtucket, Rhode Island
PAXTON—1951-53
Paxton Engineering Co.
Los Angeles, California
Steam and air-cooled cars.
PAYNE-MODERN—1907-09
Modern Tool Co.
Erie, Pennsylvania
See "Modern" 1906-09.

PEABODY—1907
PECK—1897-98
Barton L. Peck
Detroit Horseless Carriage Co.
Detroit, Michigan
PECK—1913
Peck Electric Ltd.
Toronto, Ontario, Canada
PECKHAM—1915
Peckham Motor Car Co.
Toledo, Ohio
PEDALMOBILE—1912
Pedalmobile Mfg. Co.
Indianapolis, Indiana
PEDERSEN CYCLECAR—1922
Some sold by mail order.
PEDRO—1902-03
Franco-American Automobile Co.
Marion, New Jersey
PEEP (model)—1942-45
Military "Jeep." See "Jeep"
American Bantam Car Co.
Butler, Pennsylvania
Willys-Overland Co.
Toledo, Ohio
PEERLESS—1899
Liquid Air Power & Automobile Co.
New York, New York
PEERLESS STEAM—1900-01
Peerless Long Distance Steam **Carriage** Company
Washington, D.C.
PEERLESS—1901-32
Peerless Mfg. Co.
Cleveland, Ohio
1902 reorganized as Peerless Motor Car Co.
1925 as Peerless Motor Car Corp.
PEET—1923-26
Peet Motor Corp.
Hollis, New York
Also made trucks.
PEET STEAMER—1900-01
Dr. A. J. Peet and
Dr. William T. Jenkins
Brooklyn, New York

PELL—1910
  David W. Pell
  Pell Motor Car Co.
  Oswego, New York
PELLITIER—1906
  Pellitier-Duquesne Motor Co.
  Jamestown, New York
  Formerly Duquesne Motor Car Co.
PENDLETON—1905
  Trumbull Mfg. Co.
  Warren, Ohio
PENDLETON CYCLECAR—1914
  Pendleton Cyclecar Mfg. Co.
  Culver City, California
PENFORD—1924
PENINSULAR—1912-13
  Peninsular Motor Co.
  Saginaw, Michigan
  Former "Marquette"
PENN—1906
PENN THREE-WHEELER—1908
  Dr. Shakespeare Penn
  Washington, D.C.
  One car produced.
PENNEY—1899
  J. W. Penney & Sons
  Mechanic Falls, Maine
PENNINGTON—1890-95; 1900
  E. J. Pennington
  Cleveland, Ohio
  Racine, Wisconsin
  Carlisle, Pennsylvania
PENNSY—1916-17
  Pennsy Motors Corp. of Pittsburgh
  Pittsburgh, Pennsylvania
  Former "Kosmath" Became "Pennsylvania"
PENNSYLVANIA STEAM—1895-1900
  Pennsylvania Steam Vehicle Co.
  Carlisle, Pennsylvania
PENNSYLVANIA—1900
  Pennsylvania Horseless Carriage Co.
  Washington, D.C.
PENNSYLVANIA—1907-11
  Pennsylvania Auto-Motor Co.
  Bryn Mawr, Pennsylvania

PENNSYLVANIA—1918-19
  Pennsylvania Electric Vehicle Co.
  Pennsylvania Motor Car Co.
  Pittsburgh, Pennsylvania
PENNSYLVANIA ELECTRIC—1905-06
  Pennsylvania Electric Vehicle Co.
  Philadelphia, Pennsylvania
PENN THIRTY—1911-13
  Penn Motor Car Co.
  East Liberty, Pennsylvania
  New Castle, Pennsylvania
PENTON—1928
  Penton Motor Co.
  Cleveland, Ohio
PEOPLES—1900-05
  Peoples Automobile Co.
  Cleveland, Ohio
  Became Troy Automobile & Bicycle Co.,
  Troy, Ohio.
PEORIA—1904
  Peoria Automobile Co.
  Peoria, Illinois
PERFECT—1906
  Saint Anna Kerosene Motor Co.
  Saint Anna, Illinois
PERFECTION—1906-08
  Perfection Automobile Works
  South Bend, Indiana
  Became "Ricketts"
PERFEX—1912-14
  Perfex Co.
  Los Angeles, California
PERKINS EXPERIMENTAL—1906
  Perkins Mfg. Co.
  Springfield, Massachusetts
  Produced as "Bailey" 1907.
PERKINS—1914-15
  Massnick-Phipps Mfg. Co.
  Detroit, Michigan
PERRY—1896
  O. H. Perry
  (Perry Mfg. Co.)
  Boston, Massachusetts
  See "Boston-Haynes-Apperson" designed
  and built by O. H. Perry 1898.

PERRY FINA SPORT—1953-55
  See "Fina Sport"
PERRY-LEWIS ELECTRIC—1895
  J. D. Perry Lewis Electric Wagon Co.
  St. Louis, Missouri
PERRYMOBILE—1942-45
  The Perrymobile Co.
  Los Angeles, California
PERRY STEAMER—1945
  Perry-Braver Motor Co.
  Los Angeles, California
PESAGUS—1902
  Pesagus Automobile Co.
  Harvey, Illinois
(P.E.T.) CYCLECAR—1914
  P. E. Teats
  P.E.T. Cyclecar Co.
  Detroit, Michigan
PETELER—1912-13
  Peteler Car Co.
  St. Paul, Minnesota
PETER PAN CYCLECAR—1914
  Randall Co.
  Norfolk Downs, Massachusetts
  Randall Motor Car Co.
  Wollaston, Massachusetts
PETERS—1915
  Walton-Ludlow Auto Engineering Co.
  Philadelphia, Pennsylvania
  Became "Peters Tricar"
PETERS—1921-22
  Peters Motor Car Co.
  Pleasantville, New York
  Trenton, New Jersey
  Peters Autocar Co.
  Bethlehem, Pennsylvania
  Became Peters Motor Car Division of
  Romer Motors Corp.
PETERS TRICAR—1916
  Peters Tricar Corp.
  Philadelphia, Pennsylvania
PETREL—1908-12
  Petrel Motor Car Co.
  Kenosha, Wisconsin
  Formerly "Earl" 1907

CODE = ROMAN LETTERS: Complete entry. *ITALICS:* Unsubstantiated entry. (PARENTHESES): Production planned, but not realized.

Combined with Beaver Mfg. Co. in Fuller & Stowell Motors Co.

PETROMOBILE—1900
  Kidder Motor Vehicle Co.
  New Haven, Connecticut

PETROMOBILE—1902
  Petromobile Co.
  Brooklyn, New York

PHANTOM CORSAIR—1939
  Rust Heinz
  Pasadena, California
  One car produced.

PHELEINE

PHELPS—1903-05
  Phelps Motor Vehicle Co.
  Stoneham, Massachusetts
  Became "Shawmut" 1905-09

PHIANNA—1917-21
  Phianna Motor Co.
  Newark, New Jersey
  Succeeded "S.G.V."
  1919 became M. H. Carpenter Co. Long Island City, New York.

PHILADELPHIA electric—1899-1900
  Philadelphia Motor Carriage Co.
  Philadelphia, Pennsylvania

PHILADELPHIA—1900-01
  Philadelphia Motor Vehicle Co.
  Philadelphia, Pennsylvania

PHILADELPHIA electric—1911
  Philadelphia Electric Co.
  Philadelphia, Pennsylvania

PHILADELPHIA—1924

PHILBRICK—1900
  H. B. Philbrick
  Middletown, Connecticut

*PHILBRIN—1909
  Believed to be ignition systems, not cars.

PHILION STEAMER—1892
  Achille Philion
  Akron, Ohio
  See "Achille Philion" steamer.

PHIPPS electric—1912
  Phipps Electric Automobile Co.
  Detroit, Michigan

PHIPPS-GRINNELL electric—1909-11
  Phipps-Grinnell Automobile Co.
  Detroit, Michigan
  See "Grinnell" electric

PHIPPS-JOHNSON—1909

PHOENIX—1899-1900
  Phoenix Motor Vehicle Co.
  Cleveland, Ohio

PHOENIX (model)—1966
  See "Fitch Phoenix"
  John Fitch & Co. Inc.
  Falls Village, Connecticut
  Both names apply to the same vehicle.

PICKARD—1908-12
  Pickard Bros.
  Brockton, Massachusetts

PIEDMONT—1912
  Piedmont Auto Mfg. Co.
  Atlanta, Georgia

PIEDMONT—1917-22
  Piedmont Motors
  Lynchburg, Virginia
  Also built cars for "Bush," "Lone Star" and "Alsace."

PIERCE—1895
  Pierce Engine Co.
  Racine, Wisconsin

PIERCE-ARROW—1909-38
  Pierce-Arrow Motor Car Co.
  Buffalo, New York
  Formerly George N. Pierce Co. Under "Studebaker" control 1928-33.
  Reorganized 1933 as Pierce-Arrow Motor Car Co.

PIERCE-CROUCH—1895
  Pierce-Crouch Engine Co.
  New Brighton, Pennsylvania

PIERCE GREAT ARROW—1904-09
  George N. Pierce Co.
  Buffalo, New York
  Formerly "Pierce Motorette" 1901-03.
  Became "Pierce-Arrow" 1909-38.

PIERCE-MOTORETTE—1901-03
  George N. Pierce Co.
  Buffalo, New York

Used De Dion engine.
  Became "Pierce Great Arrow."

PIERCE-RACINE—1903-10
  Pierce Engine Co.
  Racine, Wisconsin
  1903 merged with Wisconsin Wheel Co.
  See "Mitchell"
  1909 absorbed by Pierce Motor Co. Bought by J. I. Case Threshing Machine Co. 1910.
  Name changed to "Case," 1911.

PIERCE STEAM TRICYCLE—1895
  W. A. Pierce
  Sistersville, West Virginia

PIGGINS—1909-10
  Piggins Bros.
  (Piggins Motor Truck Co.)
  Racine, Wisconsin
  Trucks only after 1910.

PILAIN—1907-08
  De Barress Automobile Co.
  New York, New York

PILGRIM steam—1900
  Pilgrim Motor Co.
  Somerville, Massachusetts

PILGRIM—1900
  Pilgrim Motor Vehicle Co.
  Cambridge, Massachusetts

PILGRIM—1913-14
  Ohio Falls Motor Co.
  New Albany, Indiana
  Also built "Ohio Falls"

PILGRIM—1915-17
  Pilgrim Motor Car Co.
  Detroit, Michigan
  Designed by W. H. Radford formerly with "Warren," 1913-14. Later designer for "Balboa." R. C. Aland designed '16 model.

PILGRIM—1916-17
  Pilgrim Motor Co.
  Portland, Maine

(PILLIOD)—1915-16
  Pilliod Motor Car Co.
  Toledo, Ohio
  Company formed March, 1915.
  Bankrupt June, 1916.

*ASTERISK: Error corrected from previous list. See introduction to this section for complete code.

PILOT—1909-24
Pilot Motor Car Co.
Richmond, Indiana
PIONEER EXPERIMENTAL—1896
J. A. Meyer
San Francisco, California
Three cars built.
PIONEER—1898
Patrick Sullivan
Detroit, Michigan
PIONEER HIGHWHEELER—1906-11
Pioneer Car Co. Inc.
El Reno, Oklahoma
Pioneer Car Mfg. Co.
Oklahoma City, Oklahoma
PIONEER—1910
Pioneer Motor Co.
Marquette, Michigan
PIONEER—1913
Pioneer Motor Co.
Muskogee, Oklahoma
PIONEER CYCLECAR—1914
American Manufacturing Co.
Chicago, Illinois
PIONEER ELECTRIC—1959
See "Nic-L-Silver"
Nic-L-Silver Battery Co.
Santa Ana, California
Both names apply to the same vehicle.
PIPER & TINKER—1895-99
J. W. Piper & G. M. Tinker
Waltham, Massachusetts
Three cars built.
PIRANHA—1967
AMT Corporation
Phoenix, Arizona
PIRATE—1905-07
Breese & Lawrence
Brooklyn, New York
See "B.L.M.," B.L.M. Motor Car Co.
Brooklyn, New York.
Bankrupt October, 1907.
PISCORSKI—1901
Dan J. Piscorski
St. Louis, Missouri

PITCHER—1920
PITTSBURGH—1897-99
Pittsburgh Motor Vehicle Co.
Pittsburgh, Pennsylvania
Organized 1896, two cars built by 1898.
See "Autocar" (1897-1911)
PITTSBURGH—1905
Pittsburgh Automobile Co.
Pittsburgh, Pennsylvania
PITTSBURGH ELECTRIC —1905-11
Pittsburgh Motor Vehicle Co.
Pittsburgh, Pennsylvania
PITTSBURGH 6—1909-11
Ft. Pitt Motor Manufacturing Co.
General Engineering Co.
New Kensington, Pennsylvania
1911 Pittsburgh Motor Car Co.
PITTSBURGH—1912
Chester Engineering Co.
Chester, Pennsylvania
PITTSBURGH STEAMER—1905-08
Pittsburgh Machine Tool Co.
Allegheny, Pennsylvania
PITTSFIELD—1907
Pittsfield Motor Carriage Co.
Pittsfield, Massachusetts
See "Stetson" and "Stilson"
PIXLEY
PIZAZZ DUNE BUGGY—1968
Tomco Division
Milwaukee, Wisconsin
PLANCHE—1908-09
See "Roebling-Planche"
John A. Roebling & Sons Co.
Roebling-Planche Co.
Trenton, New Jersey
"Walter" and "Mercer" (1909-25)
PLANEMOBILE—1946
PLANET CYCLECAR—1914
Planet Motor Works
Minneapolis, Minnesota
PLASS—1900
Plass Motor Wagon Co.
Pierre, South Dakota
PLASS MOTOR SLEIGH—1895

Reuben H. Plass
Brooklyn, New York
PLAYBOY—1946-51
Playboy Motor Car Corp.
Buffalo, New York
PLAYBOY DUNE BUGGY—1968 to date
Playboy Mfg. Co.
San Mateo, California
PLEASANTON—1903
Pleasanton Iron Works
Pleasanton, California
PLYMOUTH EXPERIMENTAL—1910
Plymouth Motor Truck Co.
Plymouth, Ohio
One car produced.
PLYMOUTH—1928 to date
Plymouth Motor Co.
Chrysler Corp.
Detroit, Michigan
Introduced July 28, 1928 at Madison
Square Garden, New York, New York.
See "Chrysler," "De Soto," "Dodge" and
"Imperial."
PLYMOUTH—1932 to date
Chrysler Corp. of Canada
Windsor, Ontario, Canada
P.M.C. HIGHWHEELER—1908
C. S. Peets Mfg. Co.
New York, New York
PNEUMATIC—1896-99
Pneumatic Carriage Co. Inc. (1896)
New York Auto Truck Co. (1899)
New York, New York
All units built by A. H. Hoadley at
American Wheelock Engine Co. Worcester,
Massachusetts.
PNEUMOBILE—1914-15
Cowles-McDowell Pneumobile Co.
Pneumobile Motor Car Co.
Chicago, Illinois
Anderson, Indiana
POCOCK—1899
Francis A. Pocock
Philadelphia, Pennsylvania
POKORNEY—1904-06

H. Pokorney
Richards Automobile & Gas Engine Co.
Guthrie, Indiana
See "Tricolet"
POLHEMUS & THOMAS steam—1902
Polhemus & Thomas
New Brunswick, New Jersey
POLO—1927
POMEROY electric—1902
Pomeroy Motor Vehicle Co.
Brooklyn, New York
POMEROY—1922-27
Pomeroy Aluminum Manufacturers Inc.
Cleveland, Ohio
Aluminum Co. of America
Buffalo, New York
POND—1905
L. W. Pond Machine & Foundry Co.
Worcester, Massachusetts
PONDER—1923
Ponder Motor Mfg. Co.
Shreveport, Louisiana
Succeeded "Bour-Davis"
PONTIAC—1906
Pontiac Motor Vehicle Co.
Pontiac, Michigan
PONTIAC highwheeler—1907-09
Pontiac Buggy Co.
Pontiac Spring & Wagon Co.
Pontiac, Michigan
Rockford, Illinois
PONTIAC—1910
Pontiac Motor Car Co.
Pontiac, Illinois
PONTIAC—1915-16
Pontiac Chassis Co.
Pontiac, Michigan
Chassis only
Became Olympian Motors Co.
PONTIAC—1926 to date
Oakland Motor Car Co.
Pontiac Motor Car Co.
Pontiac, Michigan
Pontiac Motor Division, General Motors
Corp. succeeded "Oakland" and Oakland

Motor Car Co. 1932.
PONTIAC—1933 to date
General Motors of Canada Ltd.
Oshawa, Ontario, Canada
POPE-HARTFORD—1903-14
Pope Mfg. Co.
Hartford, Connecticut
POPE-ROBINSON—1903-04
Pope-Robinson Co.
Hyde Park, Massachusetts
Succeeded J. T. Robinson Co. ("Robinson").
Purchased by "Buick."
POPE-TOLEDO—1903-08
Pope Motor Car Co.
Toledo, Ohio
Succeeded "Toledo"
Became Toledo Motor Car Co.
POPE TRIBUNE—1904-08
Pope Manufacturing Co.
Hagerstown, Maryland
POPE WAVERLEY—1903-08
Pope Motor Car Co.
Indianapolis, Indiana
See "Waverley" electric (1908-16)
POPPY CAR—1917
Eisenhuth Motor Co.
Los Angeles, California
Five-cylinder, self starting, no transmission.
POPULAIRE—1904
American Automobile & Power Co.
Boston, Massachusetts
Also known as "American Populaire."
PORTER steam—1900-01
Porter Automobile Co.
Boston, Massachusetts
PORTER—1919-22
American & British Mfg. Co.
Bridgeport, Connecticut
Finley Robertson Porter Co.
Port Jefferson, New York
Succeeded "F.R.P."
PORTER-KNIGHT—1915
Finley Robertson Porter Co.
Port Jefferson, New York

Three race cars built for Indianapolis late 1914. Motor problems kept them out. Shortened "F.R.P." chassis with Knight engine.
PORTERMOBILE—1901
Porter Motor Co.
Allston, Massachusetts
PORTLAND cyclecar—1914-15
Lewis L. Thompson
(Portland Cyclecar Co.)
Portland, Oregon
See "Pacific" cyclecar.
PORTSMOUTH—1912
Portsmouth Automobile & Machine Co.
Portsmouth, Ohio
POSTAL—1907-08
Postal Automobile & Engineering Co.
Bedford, Indiana
Became Buggy Car Co., Cincinnati, Ohio.
POSTE—1899
Poste Bros. Buggy Co.
Columbus, Ohio
POWELL—1912
POWELL SPORTSWAGON—1955-56
Powell Sportswagon
Compton, California
POWER CAR—1909-12
Power Car Automobile Co.
Powercar Co.
Cincinnati, Ohio
POWER CAR—1959
Power Car Division
125 Main St.
Springfield, Massachusetts
Juvenile and adult fun cars.
PRACTICAL—1906-09
Practical Auto Co.
Genoa, Illinois
(Practical Automobile Co.
Aurora, Illinois)
See "Culver" (1906-09)
PRADO—1920-22
Prado Motors Corp.
New York, New York
Curtiss OX-5 engine

PRATT SIX-WHEELER—1907
    Pratt Chuck Works
    Frankfort, New York
PRATT—1911-15
    Elkhart Carriage & Harness
        Mfg. Co.
    Elkhart, Indiana
    Formerly "Pratt-Elkhart" 1909-11
    Became "Elcar" Elcar Motor Co.
PRATT-ELKHART—1909-11
    Elkhart Carriage & Harness
        Mfg. Co.
    Elkhart, Indiana
    Became "Pratt" (1911-15)
PRAUL—1895
    John E. Praul
    (Praul Motocycle Co.)
    262 North Broad St.
    Philadelphia, Pennsylvania
    Rotary gasoline engine.
*PREFEX 1912-14
    Prefex Co.
    Los Angeles, California
    Believed to be "Perfex" misspelled.
*PREFLEX—1912
    Believed to be "Perfex" misspelled.
PREMIER—1903-25
    Premier Motor Mfg. Co.
    Indianapolis, Indiana
    1915 reorganized as Premier Motor Car Co.
    1916 Premier Motor Corp.
    1921 Premier Motor Car Corp.
    1923 reorganized as Premier Motors Inc.
    Purchased "Monroe" 1923.
    Merged with "Stratton."
    See "Stratton-Premier"
PREMIER-WEIDELY—1914-15
    Premier Motor Mfg. Co.
    Indianapolis, Indiana
PREMOCAR—1919-23
    Preston Motors Corp.
    Birmingham, Alabama
    One model used four-cylinder Rochester
    Duesenberg engine.
    Six-cylinder model called "Magic Six."

Blue Sky Law indictment reported October, 1923.
PRESCOTT STEAM—1901-05
    Prescott Automobile Mfg. Co.
    Passaic, New Jersey
PRESTON—1917-20
    Preston Motors Corp.
    Birmingham, Alabama
    Became "Premocar"
PRIBEL—1936-37
    Pribel Safety Air-Car Co.
    Saginaw, Michigan
PRICE—1907-09
    W. C. Price
    Chicago, Illinois
    Shown at Chicago 1907 Auto Show.
PRIDEMORE CYCLECAR—1914-15
    Pridemore Machine Works
    Northfield, Minnesota
PRIGG CYCLECAR—1914
    H. Paul Prigg Co.
    Anderson, Indiana
PRIMO—1910-15
    Primo Motor Co.
    Atlanta, Georgia
    Reported bankrupt July, 1915.
PRINCE—1902
PRINCESS—1904-05
    Royal Automobile Co.
    Chicago, Illinois
    See "Royal Princess"
PRINCESS CYCLECAR—1914
    Princess Cyclecar Co.
    Detroit, Michigan
    Former "Little Princess"
    Notice of dissolution reported September, 1914.
PRINCESS—1914-18
    Princess Motor Car Co.
    Detroit, Michigan
    Succeeded "Princess" cyclecar
PRINCESS RUNABOUT—1904
    Neustadt-Perry Co.
    St. Louis, Missouri
PRINCETON—1923

    Durant Motors Corp.
    Muncie, Indiana
    Car resembled "Flint" (1924-27).
PRODAL—1908
    Motor Car Repair Co.
    New York, New York
*PRODO—1921
    Believed to be "Prado" misspelled.
PROSPECT—1902
    Wottring Bros.
    Prospect, Ohio
P&S—1908-14
    See "Palmer-Singer"
    Palmer & Singer Mfg. Co.
    Long Island City, New York
    Both names apply to same vehicle.
*P&S MAGIC—1913-14
    Wrong name for "Palmer-Singer" with Magic Engine.
P-T—1901-02
    P-T Motor Co.
    New York, New York
PUBLIX—1947-48
    Publix Motor Car Co.
    Fort Erie, Ontario, Canada
PUBLIX THREE-WHEELER—1947-48
    Publix Motor Car Co.
    Buffalo, New York
    Mini car
PUG—1968
    Brice Mfg. Co.
    Minneapolis, Minnesota
    Jeep-type all-terrain vehicle.
PULLMAN SIX-WHEELER—1903
    Broomell, Schmidt & Steacy Co.
    York, Pennsylvania
    Front and rear wheel steering.
PULLMAN—1904-09
    Pullman Auto Carriage Co.
    Pullman Motor Car Co.
    Chicago, Illinois
    Reorganized as Pullman Motor Vehicle Co. (in addition to the York, Pennsylvania "Pullman").
    Built by Model Automobile Company,

CODE = ROMAN LETTERS: Complete entry. *ITALICS:* Unsubstantiated entry. (PARENTHESES): Production planned, but not realized.

Peru, Indiana.
PULLMAN—1907-17
  York Motor Car Co.
  York, Pennsylvania
  Succeeded "York," York Automobile Co.
  Became Pullman Motor Car Co. 1910.
PUNGS-FINCH—1904-10
  Pungs-Finch Auto and
    Gas Engine Co.
  Detroit, Michigan
  Acquired Sintz Gas Engine Co.
  See "Finch-Limited"
PUP—1948
  Pup Motor Car Co.
  Spencer, Wisconsin
PURITAN STEAM—1902-03
  Locke Regulator Co.
  Salem, Massachusetts
  Later Puritan Motor Car Co.
PURITAN CYCLECAR—1913-14
  F. A. Choate
  Puritan Motor Co.
  Chicago, Illinois
PURITAN—1917
  Puritan Motors Co.
  Framingham, Massachusetts
PURMAX—1915
  Union Car Co.
  Los Angeles, California
PYRAMID—1902
PYRO-PNEUMATIC—1897
  P. E. McDonnell & W. A. Brennan
  Chicago, Illinois

QUAKER CITY—1904
  Quaker City Automobile Co.
  Philadelphia, Pennsylvania
QUAKERTOWN—1904-14
  Quakertown Automobile Mfg. Co.
  Quakertown, Pennsylvania
QUANTUM—1965
  Automotive Development Corp.
  Seymore, Connecticut

QUEEN—1901-03
  Queen City Cycle & Motor Works
  Toronto, Ontario, Canada
QUEEN—1904-07
  C. H. Blomstrom Motor Co.
  Detroit, Michigan
  Reported merged with DeLuxe Motor Car
  Co. October, 1906.   Became "Deluxe."
QUESA—1905
QUICK—1899-1900
  H. M. Quick Mfg. Co. (1899)
  Quick Mfg. Co. (1900)
  Paterson, New Jersey
  Absorbed by Remington Automobile and
  Motor Co., Ilion, New York.
QUINBY ELECTRIC—1899
  J. M. Quinby & Co.
  Newark, New Jersey
  Electric carriages for special order and ex-
  port.
  Built bodies for "Simplex," "S.G.V." and
  others.
QUINCY—1906
  Quincy Automobile Co.
  Quincy, Illinois
QUINLAN—1904
  M. W. Quinlan, Jr.
    (Quinlan & Co.)
  Brookline, Massachusetts
QUINSLER—1904
  Quinsler & Co.
  Boston, Massachusetts
QUINSLEY—1904

R

RABER & LANG—1909
  Raber & Lang Co.
  South Bend, Indiana
  At least two cars.
R.A.C.—1910-12
  Diamond Automobile Co.
  South Bend, Indiana
  Succeeded "Diamond" 1910
RACINE—1895

Racine Motor Vehicle Co.
Racine, Wisconsin
RACINE-SATTLEY—1910
  Racine-Sattley Co.
  Racine, Wisconsin
RACINE WAGON—1902
  Racine Wagon & Carriage Co.
  Racine, Wisconsin
RADFORD—1895
  W. J. Radford
  Oshkosh, Wisconsin
RADFORD LIGHT CAR—1914
  W. H. Radford
  Detroit, Michigan
RAE—1902
  Rae Motor Cycle Co.
  Chicago, Illinois
RAE ELECTRIC—1909
  Rae Electric Vehicle Co.
  Boston, Massachusetts
  Springfield, Vermont
RAILSBACH CYCLECAR—1914
  L. M. Railsbach
  Saginaw, Michigan
RAINIER—1905-11
  Rainier Motor Car Co.
  New York, New York (office)
  Flushing, New York (factory)
  Chassis made by "Garford" to 1907.
  Reorganized 1907; moved to Saginaw,
  Michigan 1908; bought by General Motors
  1909.
  Combined with "Welch-Detroit" into "Mar-
  quette".
RALCO—1904
RALEIGH—1920-22
  Raleigh Motors Inc.
  Bridgeton, New Jersey
  Later at Reading, Pennsylvania.
RAMAPAUGH STEAM—1901-02
  Charles A. Ball
  Paterson, New Jersey
  Three cars built for $10,000 each.
RAMBLER—1900-03
  Rockaway Bicycle Co.

Rockaway, New York
RAMBLER—1902-13
Thomas B. Jeffery Co.
Kenosha, Wisconsin
Became "Jeffery," 33,512 cars built.
RAMBLER—1950-69
Nash Motors Co. (1950-54)
Kenosha, Wisconsin
American Motors Corp. (1954-69)
Detroit, Michigan
See "Nash" and "Hudson."
Discontinued 1969.
RAMBLER 1902 REPLICA—1959-60
American Air Products Corp.
Ft. Lauderdale, Florida
Gaslight Motors Corp.
Lathrup Village, Michigan.
RANDALL STEAM—1902-03
G. N. Randall
Meadville, Pennsylvania
RANDALL THREE-WHEELER—1903-05
J. V. & C. Randall & Co.
Newtown, Pennsylvania
RANDALL—1905
Charles J. Randall
San Jose, California
RANDALL—1910
Randall Motor Car Co.
Ft. Wayne, Indiana
RAND & HARVEY STEAM—1899-1901
Rand & Harvey
Lewiston, Maine
RANDS—1906-07
Rands Mfg. Co.
Detroit, Michigan
RANGER—1909-11
Ranger Automobile Co.
Ranger Motor Works
Chicago, Illinois
Bankruptcy reported November, 1910.
RANGER—1919-22
Southern Motor Mfrs. Association
Houston, Texas
First cars distributed September, 1920.
RANLET—1900

Ranlet Automobile Co.
St. Johnsbury, Vermont
RAPID—1903
Rapid Motor Car Co.
Grand Rapids, Michigan
*RAS ELECTRIC
Believed to be "Rae" electric misspelled.
*RASSLER—1907
Believed to be "Rossler" misspelled.
RATTLER DUNE BUGGY—1968 to date
B & N Rattler Club
Springfield, Ohio
RAUCH & LANG ELECTRIC—1905-30
Rauch & Lang Carriage Co.
Cleveland, Ohio
Merged with "Baker" into Baker, Rauch
and Lang Co. 1915. Built "Owen Magnetic"
1916-19. 1920 reorganized as Rauch & Lang
Inc., at Chicopee Falls, Massachusetts.
Absorbed Rubay Co. 1924.
1930 used "Willys-Knight" chassis.
Built "Raulang" electric taxicabs.
RAUCH & LANG GAS-ELECTRIC—1929-30
Rauch & Lang Inc.
Chicopee Falls, Massachusetts
G.E. Co.
Schenectady, New York
RAULET—1900
RAYFIELD—1911-13
Rayfield Motor Car Co.
Springfield, Illinois
Chrisman, Illinois
No connection with Rayfield Motor Co.
Former "Springfield"
RAYFIELD CYCLECAR—1913-15
Rayfield Motor Co.
Springfield & Chrisman, Illinois
Sued Great Western Auto Co. of Peru, Indiana for failure to build cars.
RAYMOND—1908
Hillsdale Motor Co.
Hillsdale, Michigan
RAYMOND—1912-13
Raymond Engineering Corp.
Hudson, Massachusetts

Lincoln Park, Massachusetts
R.C.H.—1911-14
Hupp Corp.
Detroit, Michigan
Reorganized 1912 as R.C.H. Corp.
REA—1901-02
Rea Machine Co.
Rushville, Indiana
READ—1913-14
Read Motor Car Co.
Detroit, Michigan
READING—1910-13
Middleby Automobile Co.
Reading, Pennsylvania
See "Middleby" (1908-13)
(READING)—1917
Reading Chassis & Motor Co.
Reading, Pennsylvania
READING-DURYEA—1904-05
Waterloo Motor Works
Waterloo, Iowa
READING STEAM—1960
READING STEAM—1900-03
Steam Vehicle Co. of America
Reading, Pennsylvania and
New York, New York
1902 absorbed by Meteor Engineering Co.
See "Meteor" (1902-03)
REAL CYCLECAR—1914
H. Paul Prigg Co.
(Real Cyclecar Co.)
Anderson, Indiana
Five cars built.
Became "Real Light Car"
REAL LIGHT CAR—1915
Real Light Motor Car Co.
Converse, Indiana
Bankrupt December, 1915.
REBER—1901-03
Reber Mfg. Co.
Reading, Pennsylvania
Became Acme Motor Car Co.
See "Acme" and "S.G.V."
RECH—1900
Jacob Rech & Sons

Philadelphia, Pennsylvania
RECH-MARBAKER ELECTRIC—1906
   Rech-Marbaker Co.
   Philadelphia, Pennsylvania
RED—1905
   J. W. Linscott & Co.
   Boston, Massachusetts
(RED ARROW)—1915-16
   Red Arrow Automobile Co.
   Orange, Massachusetts
   Former "Crout"
RED BUD CYCLECAR—1916
   Lafayette, Indiana
RED BUG ELECTRIC—1928
   Automotive Standards Inc.
   Newark, New Jersey
   Electric slat car.
   Also built "Red Bug Jr."
RED DEVIL STEAM—1866
RED DIAMOND—1920-21
   Red Diamond Motors
   Atlanta and Athens, Georgia
RED JACKET—1904
   O.K. Machine Works
   Buffalo, New York
RED PATH—1903
   Berlin (Kitchener) Ontario, Canada
RED SHIELD—1911
   Red Shield Hustler Power Co.
   Detroit, Michigan
RED WING—1906
*REED—1909
   Believed to be company name of W. S.
   Reed Co. Massillon, Ohio
   See "Massillon"
REES—1921
   Rees Motor Corp.
   Attica, Ohio
REESE THREE-WHEELER—1887-99
   S. Reese Machine & Tool Works
   Plymouth, Pennsylvania
REESE MIDGET—1921-22
   Sheldon F. Reese Co.
   Huron, South Dakota
REEVES—1896-99; 1904-10

Reeves Pulley Co.
   Columbus, Indiana
   First cars multi-passenger "Motocycles."
   Experimental only after 1910.
   See "Octo-Auto" and "Sexto-Auto."
REGAL—1907-18
   Regal Motor Car Co.
   Detroit, Michigan
   1907 fifty cars built and sold.
   Plant reported auctioned off May, 1918.
REGAL—1914-17
   Canadian Royal Motor Car Co.
   Kitchener, Ontario, Canada
REGAS—1903-05
   Regas Automobile Co.
   Rochester, New York
   Motorcycles in 1900
REGENT—1902
   Regent Automobile & Machine Co.
   Boston, Massachusetts
REGENT—1917
REILLY STEAM—1902-03
   James Reilly Repair & Supply Co.
   New York, New York
REINERTSEN—1902
   Rex Reinertsen
   Milwaukee, Wisconsin
   See "Rex Buckboard"
*RELAX—1921
   Believed to be "Relay" misspelled.
RELAY—1904
   Relay Motor Car Co.
   Reading, Pennsylvania
   Three-cylinder, water-cooled, overhead valve
   Wyoma Engine.
RELIABLE—1906
   Dayton-Mashey Co.
   Chicago, Illinois
   Became "Reliable-Dayton"
RELIABLE-DAYTON HIGHWHEELER—
   1906-09
   Reliable-Dayton Motor Car Co.
   Chicago, Illinois
   Became F.A.L. Motor Co.
   See "F.A.L."

RELIANCE—1903-06
   Reliance Auto Mfg. Co.
   Reliance Motor Car Co.
   Detroit, Michigan
   1906 reorganized as Reliance Truck Co.
   Passenger car business carried on by Crescent Motor Car Co. See "Crescent"
   Also built "Reliance-Detroit"
RELOT—1921-22
   George Hannum
REMAL-VINCENT STEAM—1923
   Remal-Vincent Steam Car Co.
   Oakland, California
REMINGTON EXPERIMENTAL—1895
   Remington Motor Vehicle Co.
   Utica, New York
REMINGTON—1900-04
   Quick Mfg. Co.
   Newark, New Jersey
   Remington Automobile & Motor Co.
   Ilion, New York
   Utica, New York
REMINGTON—1910-13
   Remington-Standard Motor Co.
   Charleston, West Virginia
REMINGTON CYCLECAR—1914-15
   P. E. Remington
   Remington Arms Co.
   Remington Motor Co.
   Rahway, New Jersey
REMINGTON EIGHT—1915-17
   Remington Motor Car Co.
   New York, New York
   1915, Kingston, New York
   Planned by Philo E. Remington.
REMINGTON STANDARD—1900-01
   Remington Automobile & Motor Co.
   Ilion, New York
(RENO)—1908
   Nevada Motor Car Co.
   Reno, Nevada
   See "Desert Flyer," and "Nevada."
RENVILLE—1911
   Motor Buggy Mfg. Co.
   Minneapolis, Minnesota

REO—1904-36
    R. E. Olds Co.
    Lansing, Michigan
    Name changed 1904 to Reo Motor Car Co.
    R. M. Owen was selling agent.
    Trucks only after 1936.
REPUBLIC ELECTRIC—1901-02
    Republic Motor Vehicle Co.
    Minneapolis, Minnesota
REPUBLIC—1910-16
    Republic Motor Car Co.
    Hamilton, Ohio
    Tarrytown, New York
    Built "Little" in 1913.
RESERVE—1902
    Reserve Automobile Co.
    Camden, New Jersey
REUTER—1905-06
    Reuter Motor Car Co.
    Trainer, Pennsylvania
REUTER—1900-01
    Reuter Automobile Co.
    Davenport, Iowa
REVERE—1900
REVERE—1917-26
    ReVere Motor Car Co.
    Logansport, Indiana
    1923 reorganized as ReVere Motor Co.
REX—1908-09
    Rex Automobile Car Co.
    Indianapolis, Indiana
REX CYCLECAR—1914
    Rex Machine Works
    Brooklyn, New York
    Not related to "Rex" of Wyandotte, Michigan.
REX CYCLECAR—1914
    Rex Motor Co.
    Ford City (Wyandotte) Michigan
    Front-wheel drive.
REX—1919-20
    Rex Motor Car Co.
    New Orleans, Louisiana
REX BUCKBOARD—1902-04
    Pennsylvania Electrical & R.R.

Supply Co.
Pittsburgh, Pennsylvania
Designed by Rex Reinertsen.
RHODE ISLAND—1899-1900
    Hughes & Atkin
    Providence, Rhode Island
RHODE ISLAND ELECTRIC—1904
    Rhode Island Electromobile Co.
    Providence, Rhode Island
RHODE ISLAND AUTO CARRIAGE—
1900-01
    Rhode Island Auto Carriage Co.
    Olneyville, Rhode Island
    See "Hill"
RICHARD—1914-18
    M. Richard Automobile Co.
    Richard Automobile Mfg. Co.
    Cleveland, Ohio
    Also known as "Ri-Chard."
RICHARDS—1910
    Richards Iron Works
    Manitowoc, Wisconsin
RICHARDSON—circa 1899
    C. F. Richardson & Son
    Athol, Massachusetts
RICHELIEU—1922-23
    Richelieu Motor Car Co.
    United Auto Body Corp.
    Asbury Park, New Jersey
    Became "Barbarino"
RICHLAND—1899
    Richland Buggy Co.
    Mansfield, Ohio
RICHMOBILE—1912
    Richmobile Co.
    Boston, Massachusetts
RICHMOND STEAM—1902-04
    Richmond Automobile & Cycle Co.
    Richmond, Indiana
RICHMOND AMPHIBIOUS THREE-WHEELER—
1905
    T. Richmond
    Jessup, Iowa
RICHMOND—1905-16
    Wayne Works

Richmond, Indiana
RICHMOND—1916
    Richmond Motor Co.
    Custer, Michigan
RICKENBACKER—1922-27
    Rickenbacker Motor Co.
    Detroit, Michigan
    Introduced at 1922 New York Auto Show.
RICKETTS—1902
RICKETTS—1905-09
    Ricketts Automobile Works
    White Pigeon, Michigan
    South Bend, Indiana
    See "Diamond"
RICKMOBILE—1948
    Rickmobile Co.
    San Francisco, California
    Motorized rickshaw for export.
RIDDLE—1916-26
    Riddle Manufacturing Co.
    Ravenna, Ohio
RIDER-LEWIS—1908-10
    Rider-Lewis Motor Car Co.
    Muncie & Anderson, Indiana
    Property reported attached October, 1910.
    February, 1911 reported sold for $38,500.
    Plant went to Madison Motors Corp.
RIESS-ROYAL—1922
    Riess Motor Inc.
    York, Pennsylvania
*RIGS THAT RUN—1904
    Advertising slogan for "St. Louis," St.
    Louis Motor Carriage Co. St. Louis, Missouri. Not name of car.
RIKER ELECTRIC—1896-1900
    The Riker Motor Vehicle Co.
    Elizabethport, New Jersey
    1894 experimental (Riker Motor Co.
    Brooklyn, New York).
    Merged 1900 with Electric Vehicle Co.
    Hartford, Connecticut.
    Also gas autos 1901-02.
RILEY & COWLEY STEAM—1902
    Riley & Cowley
    Brooklyn, New York

*RILSBACH—1914
  Believed to be "Railsbach" misspelled.
*RINKER ELECTRIC—1898
  Believed to be "Riker" misspelled.
RIOTTE—1895
  Riotte & Hadden Mfg. Co.
  New York, New York
RIOTTE—1901
  U.S. Long Distance Automobile Co.
  Jersey City, New Jersey
RIPER—1917
RIPPER—1903
  Ripper Motor Carriage Co.
  Buffalo, New York
  October, 1903, V. E. Ripper disappeared.
RITCHIE—1899
  William Ritchie
  Hamilton, Ohio
RITTER—1896
  C. E. Ritter
  Milton, Pennsylvania
RITTER STEAM—1901
  C. E. Ritter
  Milton, Pennsylvania
RITTER—1912
RITZ CYCLECAR—1914-15
  Ritz Cyclecar Co.
  New York, New York
  Built by Driggs-Seabury Ordnance Co.
  Became "Sharon" cyclecar.
RIVAL CYCLECAR—1914
  T. F. Lang
  Wichita Motor Co.
  Wichita Falls, Texas
RIVIERA—1906-07
  Milton H. Schnader
  Reading, Pennsylvania
  Became "Schnader"
RIVIERA—1920
R.L. MORGAN'S MOTOR CARRIAGE
  See "Morgan"
  Morgan Construction Co.
  Worcester, Massachusetts
  Both names apply to same vehicle.
R.M.C. (model)—1908- ?

Export model "Seabrook-R.M.C."
See "Regal"
  Regal Motor Car Co.
  Detroit, Michigan
R-O—1911
  R. M. Owen & Co.
  Lansing, Michigan
ROACH—1899
  W. E. Roach
  Philadelphia, Pennsylvania
ROACH & ALBANUS—1899-1900
  Roach & Albanus
  Fort Wayne, Indiana
ROADABLE—1946-47
  Southern Aircraft
  Garland, Texas
  Ted Hall design.
ROADAPLANE (model)—1917
  See "Apperson"
  Apperson Automobile Co.
  Kokomo, Indiana
ROAD CART—1896
  R. S. Scott
  Flint, Michigan
ROADER—1911-12
  Roader Car Co.
  Brockton, Massachusetts
ROAD KING—1922-26
ROAD PLANE—1945
ROADRUNNER—1904
  Roadrunner Automobile & Power Co.
  Los Angeles, California
ROAD RUNNER—1963
  Cyclone Sales Co.
  Los Angeles, California
ROADSTER—1902-03
  See "Flint"
  Flint Automobile Co.
  Flint, Michigan
  Both names apply to the same vehicle.
ROADSTER—1915
ROAMER CYCLECAR—1914
  H. J. Roamer Co.
  Taunton, Massachusetts
ROAMER—1915

Adams & Montant
New York, New York
Also spelled "Romer"
ROAMER—1916-30
  RomeR Co.
  (Adams & Montant)
  New York, New York
  Barley Mfg. Co.
  Streator, Illinois
Succeeded Streator Consolidated Corp.
Renamed Barley Motor Car Co. at
Kalamazoo, Michigan 1917.
1923 reorganized as Roamer Motor Car Co.
ROBB—1901
  Dr. Malcolm Robb
  St. Louis, Missouri
ROBE CYCLECAR—1913-14
  W. B. Robe & Co.
  Portsmouth, Ohio
ROBE—1923
  W. B. Robe & J. D. Strong
  Nansemond, Virginia
  Robe Motor Corp.
  Norfolk, Virginia
ROBERTS—1904
  O. G. Roberts
  Columbus, Ohio
ROBERTS—1915
  Roberts Motor Co.
  Sandusky, Ohio
ROBERTS ELECTRIC—1895-97
  S. W. Roberts
  Chicago, Illinois
ROBERTSON—1895
  G. W. Robertson
  Mt. Vernon, Indiana
ROBERTSON—1921
  Robertson Co.
  San Antonio, Texas
ROBERTS SIX—1921
  Canadian Automobile Corp.
  Lachine, Quebec, Canada
ROBIE CYCLECAR—1914
  Robie Cyclecar Co.
  York, Pennsylvania

*ASTERISK: Error corrected from previous list. See introduction to this section for complete code.

Chicago, Illinois
Detroit, Michigan
ROBINSON—1900-02
  J. T. Robinson, Co.
  Hyde Park, Massachusetts
  Formerly "Bramwell-Robinson" 1898-99.
  1901 renamed Robinson Motor Vehicle Co.
  Became "Pope-Robinson"
ROBINSON—1910
  Robinson Motor Car Co.
  Detroit, Michigan
ROBSON—1908-09
  Robson Mfg. Co.
  Galesburg, Illinois
ROBY—1899
  George L. Roby
  Albion, Michigan
ROCHE—1920-26
  Clifton R. Roche
  Los Angeles, California
  Two-cycle engine, four-wheel drive.
ROCHESTER steam—1900-03
  Rochester Cycle Mfg. Co.
  Rochester Gasoline Carriage & Motor Co.
  Rochester, New York
ROCHESTER—1951
ROCHESTER SPECIAL—1910
  C. P. Smith & Co.
  Rochester, New York
ROCKAWAY—1902-04
  Rockaway Automobile Co.
  Rockaway, New Jersey
  Mohler & DeGress
  Long Island City, New York
*ROCKCLIFF—1905
  Believed to be "Rockliff" misspelled.
ROCK CREEK—1906
  Rock Creek Auto & Wagon Works
  Alexandria, Virginia
ROCKEFELLER YANKEE—1949-50
  Rockefeller Sports Car Corp.
  Rockville Center, Long Island,
    New York
  Sports car using Ford V-8 engine.
ROCKET cyclecar—1913-14

Rocket-Batterman & Booth
Scripps-Booth Cyclecar Co.
Detroit, Michigan
Became "Scripps-Booth"
Scripps-Booth Motor Co.
ROCKET—1948
  Hewson Pacific Corp.
  Los Angeles, California
ROCK FALLS—1917-26
  Rock Falls Mfg. Co.
  Sterling, Illinois
ROCK HILL—1910-15
  Rock Hill Buggy Co.
  Rock Hill, South Carolina
  Became "Anderson"
ROCKLIFF—1901-05
  Charles Rockliff
  Brooklyn, New York
  Also built trucks.
ROCKNE—1931-33
  Rockne Motors Corp.
  Detroit, Michigan
  South Bend, Indiana
  Subsidiary of Studebaker Corp.
ROCKNE—1933
  Studebaker Corp. of Canada Ltd.
  Walkerville, Ontario, Canada
  Started December 27, 1932
ROCK RIVER—1904
  Rock River Mfg. Co.
  Dixon, Illinois
*ROCKWELL—1909-12
  Name of taxicab marketed by the New
  Departure Mfg. Co. who built the "Houpt-
  Rockwell."
ROCOIT—1909
  Rocoit Motor Car Co.
  Beloit, Wisconsin
  Rockford, Illinois
RODABLE
RODEFELD—1920
  Richmond, Indiana
RODGERS—1903-04
  See "Imperial"
  Rodgers & Co.

Both names apply to the same vehicle.
RODGERS—1921
  Scientific Automotive Corp.
  New York, New York
ROEBLING-PLANCHE—1909
  Roebling-Planche Motor Co.
  Trenton, New Jersey
  Became "Mercer"
ROGER PETROLEUM CARRIAGE—1895
  Roger-American Mechanical Carriage Co.
  New York, New York
  Built for Chicago Times-Herald Race.
  Became "Macy-Roger."
ROGER—1903
ROGERS steam—1899
  W. S. Rogers Steamobile Co.
  Boston, Massachusetts
ROGERS—1901-04
  W. S. Rogers
  Rogers Automobile Co.
  Beloit, Wisconsin
ROGERS highwheeler—1911-13
  Ralph Rogers
  Ralston, Nebraska
  Rogers Motor Car Co.
  Omaha, Nebraska
ROGERS & HANFORD—1901-03
  The Rogers & Hanford Co.
  Cleveland, Ohio
ROGERS & THATCHER—1903
  Rogers & Thatcher
  Cleveland, Ohio
ROGUE—1954
ROLAND—1915
  Roland Gas-Electric Vehicle Corp.
  New York, New York
ROLLIN—1924-25
  Rollin Motors Co.
  Cleveland, Ohio
  Former "Zeder"
  Subsidiary of Cleveland Tractor Co.
  Reported bankrupt January, 1926.
  Rollin White (founder) son of Thomas
  White, founder of White Co.

ROLLSMOBILE—1959-60
  Starts Manufacturing Co.
  Ft. Lauderdale, Florida
  2/3 scale replica of 1901 "Oldsmobile."
ROLLS-ROYCE—1920-32
  Rolls-Royce of America Inc.
  Springfield, Massachusetts
  Bought factory of Wire Wheel Corp. of America, formerly built by Hendee Mfg. Company.
  Production announced July, 1920.
ROMAN—1909
  Rome Motor Vehicle Co.
  Rome, New York
ROMANO—1916
ROMER
  See "Roamer"
ROMER—1912-24
  Romer Motors Corp.
  Danvers, Massachusetts
  Taunton & Boston, Massachusetts
  Absorbed "Peters" cyclecar Trenton, New Jersey.
ROOSEVELT—1929-30
  Marmon Motor Car Co.
  Indianapolis, Indiana
ROPER STEAM—1860's-96
  Sylvester H. Roper
  Roxbury, Massachusetts
  Ten two-, three- and four-wheel vehicles built by Sylvester Roper and exhibited from the 1860's to the 1890's throughout New England and the Midwest.
ROSENBAUER—1900-01
  Rosenbauer Automobile & Power Co.
  Milwaukee, Wisconsin
ROSENGART—1939
ROSS—1929
ROSS EIGHT—1915-18
  Ross Automobile Co.
  Detroit, Michigan
  Formerly Ross & Young Machine Co.
ROSS & KRAMER—1904
  Ross & Kramer Automobile Co.
  Chicago, Illinois

ROSSLER—1906-07
  C. Rossler Mfg. Co.
  Buffalo, New York
  Speedwagon builders planned to build light runabout 1906.
  Production not clear.
ROSS STEAMER—1905-09
  Louis S. Ross
  Newtonville, Massachusetts
ROTARIAN—1921
  Became "Rotary Six"
  Bournonville Rotary Valve Motor Co.
  Hoboken, New Jersey
ROTARY—1904-05
  See "Intrepid"
  Rotary Motor Vehicle Co.
  Boston, Massachusetts
  Both names apply to the same vehicle.
ROTARY SIX—1921-23
  Bournonville Rotary Valve Motor Co.
  Hoboken, New Jersey
  See "Rotarian"
ROUND-THE-TOWN—1949-50
ROVENA—1926
  Rovena Motor Co.
  Kansas City, Missouri
  Front drive
ROWE—1908-11; 1920
  Rowe Motor Co.
  Pennsylvania and West Virginia
*ROWENA FRONT DRIVE—1926
  Believed to be "Rovena" misspelled.
ROYAL—1904-09
  Royal Motor Works
  Augusta, Maine
ROYAL—1904-10
  Royal Motor Car Co.
  Detroit, Michigan
ROYAL ELECTRIC—1905
  Royal Automobile Co.
  144-148 South Green Street
  Chicago, Illinois
  Also called "Royal Queen Electric."
  Also built "Princess" gasoline cars.
ROYAL—1913

Royal Motor Car Co.
  Elkhart, Indiana
ROYAL—1914
  Crescent Motor Co.
  Cincinnati, Ohio
  Companion to "Ohio" (1913-15).
ROYAL CYCLECAR—1915
  Royal Cyclecar Co.
  Bridgeport, Connecticut
ROYAL AMSTON—1915
  Charles M. Ams
  Amston, Connecticut
  Also called "Ams-Sterling."
  Pilot model only.
ROYAL PRINCESS—1904-05
  See "Princess"
  Royal Automobile Co.
  Both names apply to the same vehicle.
ROYAL SIX—1921
  Parker Motor Car Co. Ltd.
  Montreal, Quebec, Canada
ROYAL TOURIST—1904-11
  Royal Motor Car Co.
  Cleveland, Ohio
  Reorganized as Royal Tourist Car Co., 1909; Consolidated Motor Car Co. 1911
  Succeeded "Hoffman" (1900-04)
RSL—1969 to date.
  RSL Corporate
  Cleveland, Ohio
RUBAY—1922-24
  See "Leon-Rubay"
  Rubay Co.
  Both names apply to the same vehicle.
RUBEL—1911
  R. O. Rubel Jr. & Co.
  Louisville, Kentucky
RUDOLPH—1901
  William F. Rudolph
  Philadelphia, Pennsylvania
RUGBY
RUGER—1968 to date
  Sturm, Ruger & Co. Inc.
  Southport, Connecticut
  Replica of mid-Twenties tourer for $13,000.

RUGGLES—1905
F. A. Ruggles
Ware, Massachusetts
RUGGMOBILE—1922
RULER—1917
Ruler Motor Car Co.
Aurora, Illinois
Frameless
RUNNER CYCLECAR—1914
RUSHMOBILE STEAM—1901-03
Brecht Automobile Co.
St. Louis, Missouri
See "Brecht"
RUSSELL—1903-04
Russell Motor Vehicle Co.
Cleveland, Ohio
Vehicle invented by Dr. C. W. Russell,
Springfield, Ohio.
RUSSELL—1905-16
Canada Cycle & Motor Car Co.
Toronto, Ontario, Canada
Changed to Russell Motor Car Co. 1911.
RUSSELL—1946
Raymond Russell
Detroit, Michigan
Run by oil pressure.
RUSSELL-KNIGHT—1910-15
Canada Cycle & Motor Car Co.
Russell Motor Car Co.
Toronto, Ontario, Canada
Plant acquired by "Willys-Overland" re-
portedly in November, 1915.
RUSSELL-SPRINGFIELD—1902-03
C. W. Russell Co.
Springfield, Ohio
RUTH HIGHWHEELER—1909
Ruth Automobile Co.
North Webster, Indiana
RUXTON—1929-31
New Era Motors Inc.
New York, New York
Front wheel drive. New Era projected
12,000 cars to be built at unnamed plants
in '29, but only prototypes built that year.
Most cars produced at "Moon" plant in

'30. About 500 built.
R&V KNIGHT—1920-24
Root & Vandervoort
Engineering Co.
East Moline, Illinois
Succeeded Moline Automobile Co.
See "Moline" and "Moline-Knight."
RYDER—1900-01
California Automobile Co.
San Francisco, California
RYLANDER—1914

S

SAFARI DUNE BUGGY—1968 to date
Safari Enterprises Inc.
Gardena, California
SAFETY STEAM—1901-02
Safety Steam Automobile Co.
Boston, Massachusetts
Ipswich, Massachusetts
SAFETY—1909
SAFETY—1917
SAFETY FIRST—1914-16
Safety First Motor Car & Truck Co.
Kalamazoo, Michigan
Plainwell, Michigan
SAGER—1910
United Motors Ltd.
Welland, Ontario, Canada
SAGINAW—1914
Saginaw Motor Car Co.
Saginaw, Michigan
Also called "Saginaw Speedster."
SAGINAW CYCLECAR—1914-15
Valley Boat & Engine Co.
Saginaw, Michigan
(SAGINAW 8)—1916
Lehr Motor Co.
Saginaw, Michigan
Became "Yale"
ST. CLOUD—1921
ST. JOE—1908-09
St. Joe Motor Car Co.

Elkhart, Indiana
Succeeded Shoemaker Automobile Co.
Became Sellers Automobile Co.
See "Sellers" and "Shoemaker"
ST. JOHN EXPERIMENTAL—1902-03
S.H. St. John & Son
Canon City, Colorado
One car produced.
ST. LOUIS—1898-1907
St. Louis Motor Carriage Co.
St. Louis Motor Car Co.
St. Louis, Missouri
1905 moved to Peoria Heights, Illinois.
Affairs wound up and plant sold for
$10,000, reported December, 1907.
ST. LOUIS—1899-1900
St. Louis Gasoline Motor Co.
St. Louis, Missouri
ST. LOUIS ELECTRIC—1900-01
St. Louis Automobile & Supply Co.
St. Louis, Missouri
ST. LOUIS—1900
St. Louis Auto Supply Co.
St. Louis, Missouri
See "Dyke"
ST. LOUIS—1905
St. Louis Car Co.
St. Louis, Missouri
Few built. Became "American Mors."
ST. LOUIS—1921
John M. Neskou
St. Louis, Missouri
ST. LOUIS—1923
St. Louis Automotive Co.
St. Louis, Missouri
Five built.
SALISBURY THREE-WHEEL ELECTRIC—
1895-96
Horseless Carriage Co.
Chicago, Illinois
Designed by Wilber S. Salisbury.
SALSBURY—1947-48
Salsbury Motors, Inc.
Pomona, California
SALTER—1909-12

CODE = ROMAN LETTERS: Complete entry. *ITALICS:* Unsubstantiated entry. (PARENTHESES): Production planned, but not realized.

William A. Salter Motor Co.
Kansas City, Missouri
Salter Motor Car Co.
Centropolis, Kansas
1910 Salter Motor Mfg. Co.
SALVADOR CYCLECAR—1914
Salvador Motor Co.
Boston, Massachusetts
SALVADORE—1916
Salvadore Motor Co.
Boston, Massachusetts
SAMPSON—1904-11
Alden-Sampson Mfg. Co.
Pittsfield, Massachusetts
United States Motor Co.
Detroit, Michigan
Absorbed "Crestmobile" and
"Consolidated"
SAMPSON CARRYALL—1920
Sampson Tractor Co.
Janesville, Wisconsin
SAMPSON—1957
SAMUELS ELECTRIC—1899-1900
A. A. Samuels
Moline, Ohio
SAN ANTONIO—1910
Commercial Motor Car Co.
San Antonio, Texas
SANDERS STEAM—1904
SAND PIPER DUNE BUGGY—1968 to date
Kellison, Inc.
Lincoln, California
SAND ROVER DUNE BUGGY—1968 to date
Poty Enterprises
Santa Fe Springs, California
SAND SHARK DUNE BUGGY—1968 to date
Diana Imports
Royal Oak, Michigan
SANDUSKY—1899-1904
Sandusky Automobile Mfg. Co.
Sandusky Automobile Co.
Sandusky, Ohio
Succeeded Ohio Gas Engine Co.
Became "Courier"
SANTOS-DUMONT—1902-04

Columbus Motor Vehicle Co.
Columbus, Ohio
Former "Columbus" Became "Dumont"
SARATOGA TOURIST—1901
D. B. Smith Co.
Utica, New York
Also built "Elite" steam.
SAVAGE—1912
M. W. Savage Factories
Minneapolis, Minnesota
See "Dan Patch"
SAVAGE—1914
Savage Motor Car Co.
Detroit, Michigan
One built
SAVAGE—1968-69
SAWYER—1913
SAWYER—1920
SAXON—1913-23
Saxon Motor Co.
Detroit, Michigan
Reorganized 1915 as Saxon Motor Corp.
SAXON-DUPLEX (model)—1921-22
See "Saxon"
Saxon Motor Car Corp.
Ypsilanti, Michigan
SAYERS SIX—1916-24
Sayers & Scovill Co.
Cincinnati, Ohio
Became Hess & Eisenhart Co.
S.B.M. STEAM—1901
Shaeffer, Bunce & Marvin
Lockport, New York
SCARAB—1935-46
Stout Engineering Laboratories
(Stout Motor Corp.)
Detroit, Michigan
Rear-engined streamlined eight.
*SCARAD—1946
Believed to be misspelling of "Scarab."
SCAT—1960-61
Saviano Vehicles Inc.
Warren, Michigan
SCHAAP—1900

Schaap Cycle Co.
Brooklyn, New York
Also called "Automote."
SCHACHT—1904-13
G. A. Schacht Mfg. Co.
Cincinnati, Ohio
Schacht Motor Car Co. 1909-13.
Continued after 1913 with trucks.
Became Schacht Motor Truck Co.
SCHAEFER—1901
W. E. Schaefer Mfg. Co.
Ripon, Wisconsin
SCHARF GEARLESS—1913-14
Scharf Gearless Motor Car Co.
Westerville, Ohio
SCHAUM—1900- ?
Schaum Automobile Mfg. Co.
872 Park Ave.
Baltimore, Maryland
Motors and vehicles built to special order.
SCHEBLER—1908-09
Wheeler & Schebler
(George Schebler)
Indianapolis, Indiana
Reportedly built a V-12 roadster.
SCHILLING TRICYCLE—1894-95
A. Schilling & Son
San Francisco, California
SCHINDLER—1895
A. J. Schindler
Chicago, Illinois
SCHLEICHER—1895
SCHLIG—1904-05
Schlig Automobile Works
Schlig & Moore Automobile Works
Lockport, New York
SCHLOEMER—1890
Frank Toepfer Machine Shop
Milwaukee, Wisconsin
Both 1890 and 1892 dates are claimed.
SCHLOSSER—1912
W. H. Schlosser Mfg. Co.
New York, New York
SCHNADER—1907
Milton H. Schnader

Reading, Pennsylvania
See "Riviera"
SCHNADER—1914-18
SCHNEIDER—1902-04
J. P. Schneider
Detroit, Michigan
SCHNERR—1916
San Francisco, California
SCHOENECK—1914-16
Schoeneck Co.
Chicago, Illinois
SCHOENING KEROSENE CARRIAGE—
1895
J. W. & C. J. Schoening
Oak Park, Illinois
(SCHRAM)—1913-14
Schram Motor Car Co.
Seattle, Washington
SCHULER—1924
Schuler Motor Car Co.
Slinger, Wisconsin
SCHULTZ—1901-03
John L. Schultz
New York, New York
SCHUTT MOTOR BUGGY—1909
SCHUYLER—1899
Wilton S. Schuyler
Oceanside, California
SCHWARTZ—1899-1900
Schwartz Automobile & Carriage Co.
Philadelphia, Pennsylvania
SCHWINN ELECTRIC—1896
Arnold Schwinn & Co.
Chicago, Illinois
SCIMITAR—1959
Brooks Stevens Associates
Milwaukee, Wisconsin
SCIOTO—1910-11
Scioto Motor Car Co.
Chillicothe, Ohio
Became Arbenz Motor Co.
See "Arbenz"
SCOOTAMOBILE (model) THREE-WHEELER
—1920-22

See "Martin"
Martin Rocking Fifth Wheel Co.
Springfield, Massachusetts
SCOOTER CAR—1947
SCOOTMOBILE—1947
Norman Anderson
Corunna, Michigan
Prototype three-wheeler.
SCOOTMOBILE—1952
SCOTT—1900-04
Ashley Scott & Tod Cooper Co.
Scott-Cooper Mfg. Co.
J. A. Scott Motor Works
St. Louis, Missouri
Built three vehicles.
Absorbed by Scott Automobile Co.
See "Scott Electric"
SCOTT—1901-04
Scott Iron Works
Baltimore, Maryland
SCOTT & CLARK—1912-13
Scott & Clark Corp.
Norwich, Connecticut
SCOTT ELECTRIC—1898-1901
St. Louis Electric Automobile Co.
(1898-1900)
Scott Automobile Co. (1900-01)
Bought out Scott-Cooper Co. and continued
"Scott" production.
SCOTTER CAR—1949
*SCOTT-MOBILE—1946
Believed to be misspelling of "Scootmo-
bile" 1947.
SCOTT-NEWCOMB STEAM—1920-22
Standard Engineering Corp.
Scott-Newcomb Steam Motor Co.
St. Louis, Missouri
See "Standard Steam"
SCOUT CYCLECAR—1914
Scout Cyclecar Co.
Muskogee, Oklahoma
SCOUT (model)—1961 to date
See "International" (1961 to date)
International Harvester Co.
Ft. Wayne, Indiana

SCRAMBLER SIX-WHEELER—1968 to date
Action Age
Cleveland, Ohio
All-terrain vehicle.
SCRIPPS—1911
Scripps Motor Car Co.
Detroit, Michigan
SCRIPPS-BOOTH—1914-22
The Scripps-Booth Co.
Detroit, Michigan
Succeeded "Rocket" cyclecar.
Absorbed Sterling Motor Co. and reorgan-
ized as Scripps-Booth Corp.
Joined General Motors Corp. 1917.
SCRIPPS-BOOTH CYCLECAR—1914
Scripps-Booth Cyclecar Co.
Detroit, Michigan
January, 1915 Puritan Machine Co. bought
cyclecar parts business.
SEABERRY—1948
SEABROOK R.M.C.—1912
Regal Motor Car Co.
Detroit, Michigan
English export model of "Regal."
SEAGRAVE—1914; 1960-61
Seagrave Fire Apparatus Co.
Columbus, Ohio
Prototypes only
SEARCHMONT—1900-04
Searchmont Motor Co.
Philadelphia, Pennsylvania
1902 became Fournier-Searchmont Co.
1903 became Searchmont Automobile Co.
See "Keystone" and "Chadwick"
SEARS STEAM—1901
Sears Bros.
Indianapolis, Indiana
SEARS HIGHWHEELER—1908-11
Sears, Roebuck & Co.
Chicago, Illinois
Lincoln Motor Car Works of Chicago took
over production 1911.
SEBRING—1910-11
Sebring Motor Car Co. (1910)
Sebring Automobile Co. (1911)

Sebring, Ohio
SEBRING G.T.2—1967
Universal Plastics
San Carlos, California
SEDGWICK—1901
I. H. Sedgwick
Richmond, Indiana
SEELIGER—1902-04
Emil Seeliger
Lockhart, Texas
One car produced.
SEELY—1901-03
Seely Mfg. Co.
Pittsburgh, Pennsylvania
SEENEY CYCLECAR—1914
Seeney Mfg. Co.
Muncie, Indiana
SEFRIN—1904-05
Charles Sefrin Motor Carriage Co.
Brooklyn, New York
SEIG—1899
C. H. Seig Mfg. Co.
Milwaukee, Wisconsin
SEKINE—1923
I. Sekine & Co. (Japan)
Austin M. Wolf
New York, New York
One-wheel drive vehicle for export to Japan.
SELDEN "1877"—1906
Electric Vehicle Co.
Hartford, Connecticut
One car built as court exhibit for defense in Selden Patent case. Another car built by George Selden's sons in Rochester, New York, for the same purpose.
SELDEN—1907-14
Selden Motor Vehicle Co.
Rochester, New York
Absorbed Buffalo Gas Motor Car Co. Continued with trucks.
SELF-CONTAINED—1896
Self Contained Equipment Motor Vehicle Co.
Dorchester, Massachusetts

SELLERS—1909-12
Sellers Automobile Co.
Elkhart, Indiana
Succeeded St. Joe Motor Car Co. Later moved to Hutchinson, Kansas. In 1919 became Central States Engineering Co.
SELLEW-ROYCE—1911
Sellew Motors Limited
Toronto, Ontario, Canada
SELMA—1900
Selma Automobile Co.
Selma, California
S.E.M.—1914
Sharp Engineering & Mfg. Co.
Detroit, Michigan
Became "Sharp"
SEMINOLE—1928
SENATOR—1906-10
Victor Automobile Co.
Ridgeville, Indiana
SENECA—1917-24
Seneca Motor Car Co.
Fostoria, Ohio
Succeeded "Fostoria" (1915-16).
SEQUOIA ELECTRIC—1916
Sequoia Motor Car Co.
San Leandro, California
SERPENTINA EXPERIMENTAL—1915
Claudius Mezzacasa
New York, New York
1:2:1 wheel arrangement.
SERRIFILE—1921
Serrifile Motor Co.
Hollis, New York
SERVICE HIGHWHEELER—1911
Service Motor Car Co.
Chicago, Illinois
SERVICE CYCLECAR—1914
Rochester Motors Co.
Rochester, New York
Optional friction or gear drive.
SERVITOR—1907
Barnes Mfg. Co.
Sandusky, Ohio
Became "Barnes"

SESSIONS STEAM—1904
SEVEN LITTLE BUFFALOS HIGHWHEELER —1908
De Schaum Motor Syndicate
Buffalo, New York
SEVERIN—1920-22
Severin-Mokaw Motors Co.
Severin Motor Car Co.
Kansas City, Missouri
Metropolitan Motors Corp.
Oakland, California
SEXTO-AUTO 6-WHEEL EXPERIMENTAL—1912
Built by "Reeves"
Reeves Sexto-Octo Co.
Columbus, Indiana
(also Reeves Pulley Co.)
SEXTUPLET—1908
S.G.V.—1911-15
Acme Motor Car Co.
(S.G.V. Co.)
Reading, Pennsylvania
Succeeded "Acme." Sold in New York City as "American Lancia." See "Phianna" Reported sold by receiver September, 1915 for $55,000.
SHA—1920
SHADOW—1920
(SHAD-WYCK)—1917-23
Shadburne Brothers Company
Chicago, Illinois
Factory at Elkhart, Indiana.
Associated with Combined Motors Corp.
See "Bour-Davis"
SHAEFFER-BUNCE—1902
Shaeffer-Bunce & Co.
Lockport, New York
Complete vehicles, less engines.
Formerly Shaeffer-Bunce & Marvin.
See "S.B.M."
SHAFER—1915
C. B. Shafer
Detroit, Michigan
SHAFFER STEAMER—1903-04
Shaffer Boiler & Engine Mfg. Co.
Baltimore, Maryland

SHAMROCK—1917
SHANNON—1902-03
  Shannon Automobile Co.
  Owosso, Michigan
SHARON CYCLECAR—1915
  Driggs-Seabury Ordnance Corp.
  Sharon, Pennsylvania
  Illustrations of this car exist but it is ques-
  tionable if it was ever built. Introduced as
  the "Twombly" (1913-15).
SHARP STEAM—1901
  Harry Sharp
  Omaha, Nebraska
SHARP CYCLECAR—1914-15
  Sharp Engineering & Mfg. Co.
  Detroit, Michigan
  Formerly "S.E.M."
SHARP ARROW—1908-10
  The Sharp Arrow Automobile Co.
  Trenton, New Jersey
  Reorganized February, 1910 with $75,000
  new capital. Factory moved to East
  Stroudsburg, Pennsylvania as International
  Boiler Co. One car known to exist.
SHATSWELL STEAM—1901-05
  H. K. Shatswell & Co.
  (Dr. H. K. Shatswell)
  Dedham, Massachusetts
  Mostly steam components and running
  gear for home assembly.
SHAUM—1905
  Shaum Automobile Mfg. Co.
  Baltimore, Maryland
SHAVER STEAMER—1895
  Joseph Shaver Granite & Marble Co.
  Milwaukee, Wisconsin
  Built for Chicago Times-Herald Race.
SHAW—1900
  Shaw Motor Vehicle Co.
  Boston, Massachusetts
SHAW—1924-30
  Shaw Manufacturing Co.
  Galesburg, Kansas
SHAWMUT—1905-09
  Shawmut Motor Car Co.

  Stoneham, Massachusetts
  Succeeded Phelps Motor Vehicle Co.
  See "Phelps"
SHAW-WICK—1904
SHELBY—1902-03
  Shelby Motor Car Co.
  Shelby, Ohio
  Succeeded Beardsley & Hobbs Mfg. Co.
  Formerly "Darling"
SHELBY—1962-69
  Shelby-American Inc.
  Venice, California (1962-67)
  Became Shelby Automotive, Iona, Michi-
  gan. Sports cars. Same as "Cobra."
SHELDON—1905
  Robert E. Sheldon
  Fairbanks, Alaska
SHELDON—1909
  Sheldon Axle Co.
  Wilkes-Barre, Pennsylvania
SHERIDAN—1920-21
  Sheridan Motor Car Co.
  Muncie, Indiana
  General Motors subsidiary, plant and tools
  sold to Durant, announced May, 1921.
  Became "Durant 6"
SHERILL & SMITH HIGHWHEELER—1911
  Sherill & Smith
  Tullahoma, Tennessee
SHILLITO STEAM—1901
  John Shillito Co.
  Cincinnati, Ohio
SHOEMAKER—1906-08
  Shoemaker Automobile Co.
  Freeport, Illinois
  Moved to Elkhart, Indiana 1908.
  Reported bankrupt June, 1908 and absorb-
  ed by St. Joe Motor Car Co.
SIBLEY—1910-11
  Sibley Motor Car Co.
  Detroit, Michigan
  Became "Sibley-Curtis"
SIBLEY-CURTIS—1911-12
  Sibley-Curtis Motor Co.
  Simsbury, Connecticut

  Succeeded "Sibley"
SIGMA CYCLECAR—1914
  Sigma Motor Car Co.
  Boston, Massachusetts
*SIGNET CYCLECAR—1913-14
  Fenton Engineering Co.
  Fenton, Michigan
  Known as "Fenton," then "Koppin."
  Name "Signet" never used.
SILENT—1910-12
  See "Silent Sioux"
  Sioux Automobile Co.
  Milwaukee, Wisconsin
  Both names apply to same vehicle.
SILENT—1915
  Silent Engine Co.
  Los Angeles, California
SILENT-KNIGHT—1906-10
  Knight & Kilbourne Co.
  Chicago, Illinois
*SILENT NORTHERN—1902
  Correct name for this vehicle is
  "Northern."
SILENT-SIOUX—1909-13
  Sioux Automobile Mfg. Co.
  Sioux Falls, North Dakota (1909-10)
  Milwaukee, Wisconsin (1910-12)
  Fawick Motor Car Co.
  Sioux Falls, South Dakota (1913)
SILVER-APPERSON—1917-19
  C. T. Silver
  New York, New York
SILVER ARROW (model)—1933
  See "Pierce Arrow"
  Pierce Arrow Motor Car Co.
SILVER-KISSEL—1918-19
  C. T. Silver
  New York, New York
SILVER KNIGHT—1914-15
  C. T. Silver
  New York, New York
  Rebuilt "Willys-Knight"
SILVEX
  Bethlehem, Pennsylvania
SIMISOR—1899

SIMMONDS STEAM—1891-94
  Clarence L. Simmonds
  Lynn, Massachusetts
SIMMONS—1910
  Simmons Motor & Truck Co.
  Wilmington, Delaware
(SIMMS)—1920
  Simms Motor Car Co.
  Atlanta, Georgia
  Started in Wilmington, Delaware, reported
  March, 1920. Reported bankrupt October,
  1920.
SIMPLEX STEAM—1899-1901
  Simplex Motor Vehicle Co.
  Danvers, Massachusetts
  See "Hood"
SIMPLEX—1907-15
  Simplex Automobile Co. Inc.
  Simplex Motor Car Co.
  New Brunswick, New Jersey
  Succeeded S & M Simplex
  (Smith & Mabley) 1904-07.
  Merged with Crane Motor Co. 1915.
  Became "Crane-Simplex," model of "Sim-
  plex-Crane."
SIMPLEX-CRANE—1915-19
  See "Crane-Simplex"
  Simplex Automobile Co.
  New Brunswick, New Jersey
  Both names apply to same vehicle.
SIMPLICITIES—1904-10
  Simplicities Automobile Co.
  Middletown, Connecticut
SIMPLICITY—1906-11
  Evansville Automobile Co.
  Evansville, Indiana
  Former "Windsor"
SIMPLICITY SIX—1920-21
  Simplicity Motors Corp.
  Seattle, Washington
SIMPLO HIGHWHEELER—1908-09
  Cook Motor Vehicle Co.
  St. Louis, Missouri
SIMPSON STEAM CAR—1902
SINCLAIR-SCOTT—1906-07

Sinclair-Scott Co.
  Luke, Maryland
  Succeeded "Ariel"
  Became "Maryland"
SINGER—1914-21
  Singer Motor Co.
  Long Island City, New York
  Mount Vernon, New York
  Succeeded Palmer & Singer Mfg. Co.
  Formerly "Palmer-Singer"
SINGLE-CENTER—1906-10
  Single-Center Buggy Co.
  Evansville, Indiana
  Became "Traveler"
SINTZ—1898, 1902
  Sintz Gas Engine Co.
  Grand Rapids, Michigan
  Acquired by "Pungs-Finch"
SIPE & SIGLER ELECTRIC—1901-02
  Sipe & Sigler Co.
  Cleveland, Ohio
SIROCCO—1970
  Sirocco Industries
  3034 South Oak Street
  Santa Ana, California
  Kit car with gull wing door, hard top body
  on a "Volkswagen" chassis.
SIR VIVAL—1960
  Hollow Boring Co.
  Worcester, Massachusetts
  Prototype safety car.
SIZER—1911
  Sizer Co.
  Buffalo, New York
S.J.R.—1915-16
  S.J.R. Motor Co.
  Boston, Massachusetts
SK DUNE BUGGY—1968
  Stevens Boat Co.
  Gardena, California
*SKELETON
  Believed to be "Skelton" misspelled.
SKELTON—1920-22
  Skelton Motors Corp.
  Traves Motors Co.

St. Louis, Missouri
  Car introduced December, 1919.
  Built in plant of St. Louis Car Co.
SKENE STEAM—1900-01
  J. W. Skene Cycle & Automobile Co.
  Lewiston, Maine (plant)
  Offices at Springfield, Massachusetts.
  In 1901, Skene American Automobile Co.
  Two cars built.
SKIMABOUT—1908
  Palmer & Singer Mfg. Co.
  New York, New York
SKLAREK—1904-05
  Clifford Sklarek
  Canton, Illinois
  One built for inventor's use.
SKORPION—1952-54
  Wilro Company
  Pasadena, California
SKYLINE—1954
  Skyline Inc.
  Jamaica, Long Island, New York
  Sports car
*SLATER—1909
  Believed to be "Salter" misspelled.
SLOAN—1905
  Sloan & Olds
  Chicago, Illinois
S&M—1913-14
  S&M Motor Co.
  Strobel & Martin
  Detroit, Michigan
  Became "Benham"
S & M SIMPLEX—1904-07
  Smith & Mabley Mfg. Co.
  New York, New York
  Became Simplex Automobile Co.
  See "Simplex"
SMALL—1915
  Small Motor Car Co.
  Detroit, Michigan
SMALL—1919-22
SMELTZER—1904
  Smeltzer Automobile Co.
  Akron, Ohio

SMISA—1899
   Smisa Bros.
   Webster, Iowa
SMITH—1895
   O. E. Smith
   Hartford, Connecticut
SMITH—1895
   I. D. Smith
   Pittsburgh, Pennsylvania
SMITH—1896-99
   Springfield Cornice Co.
   (Hinsdale Smith)
   Springfield, Massachusetts
   See "Meteor"
   Also called "Smith Spring Motor."
SMITH—1899-1907
   Smith Automobile Co.
   Topeka, Kansas
   Also known as "Veracity" (1899-1904).
   Became "Great Smith" (1907-11).
SMITH—1900
   Smith Automobile & Machine Co.
   Los Angeles, California
   One car produced.
SMITH—1910-15
   A. O. Smith Co.
   Milwaukee, Wisconsin
SMITH—1912
SMITH FLYER—1917-19
   A. O. Smith Co.
   Milwaukee, Wisconsin
   Patents sold to Briggs & Stratton 1919.
   See "Briggs & Stratton"
SMITH F.W.D. BUGGY—1906
   D. W. G. Smith
   Lexington Junction, Missouri
SMITH & MABLEY SIMPLEX—1904-07
   Smith & Mabley Co.
   New York, New York
SMITH STEAMER—1902
   Smith Co.
   Topeka, Kansas
   Two cars produced.
SMOKE—1959
   Argonaut Motor Machine Co.

Cleveland, Ohio
   Listed at $26,000-$32,000.
   See "Argonaut"
S.N.—1921
   Standard Engineering Co.
   St. Louis, Missouri
   See "Standard Steam" (1920)
SNELL—1904-05
   Snell Motor Car & Truck Co.
   Toledo, Ohio
SNOBURNER—1914
   Pittmans & Dean
   Detroit, Michigan
SNODEAL ELECTRIC—1902
   Snodeal Mfg. Co.
   Baltimore, Maryland
SNYDER STEAM—1900
   H. P. Snyder & Co.
   Little Falls, New York
SNYDER—1908-09
   D. D. Snyder & Co.
   Danville, Illinois
SNYDER CYCLECAR—1914
   Snyder Motor & Mfg. Co.
   Cleveland, Ohio
SOLAR KING EXPERIMENTAL ELECTRIC—1965
   International Rectifier Corp.
   El Segundo, California
SOMMER—1905
   Sommer Motor Co.
   Detroit, Michigan
   "Sommer" was built late 1904 and 1905.
   Production after 1905 not documented.
   Company built engines at Bucyrus, Ohio
   into 1915. Also reportedly built "Allen"
   Cyclecar in 1916.
SORRELL—1956
   Sorrell Engineering Co.
   Inglewood, California
SOUTH BEND—1913-16
   South Bend Motor Car Works
   South Bend, Indiana
SOUTH CAROLINA—1901
   South Carolina Automobile Co.
   Columbia, South Carolina

(SOUTHERN) HIGHWHEELER—1906
   Southern Automobile Mfg. Co.
   Jacksonville, Florida
SOUTHERN—1908-10
   Southern Motor Works
   Nashville, Tennessee
   Became "Marathon" 1910
   Company renamed Marathon Motor Works
   1911.
SOUTHERN CYCLECAR—1914
   Southern Car Mfg. Co.
   Southern Automobile Co.
   New Orleans, Louisiana
SOUTHERN—1920-22
   Southern Automobile & Equipment Co.
   Atlanta, Georgia and
      Memphis, Tennessee
SOUTHERN SIX—1920-24
   Southern Motors Co.
   Houston, Texas
SOVEREIGN—1906-07
   Mathews Motor Car Co.
   Camden, New Jersey
   Also known as "Mathews."
SPACKE—1917-22
   F. W. Spacke Machine & Tool Co.
   Indianapolis, Indiana
   Reported September, 1920 receiver had
   been named. See "Brooke"
SPAHR—1900
   Otto A. Spahr
   Millersburg, Ohio
SPARKS—1899-1900
   Sparks Automobile Co.
   San Francisco, California
SPARTAN—1911
   C. W. Kelsey Mfg. Co.
   Hartford, Connecticut
   Prototype only
   Became "Kelsey Motorette"
SPAULDING—1902-03
   Spaulding Automobile & Motor Co.
   Buffalo, New York
   Became "Morlock"
SPAULDING—1909-17

Spaulding Mfg. Co.
Grinnell, Iowa
SPEAR—1902
William H. Spear
Cleveland, Ohio
SPECIAL—1904
Special Motor Vehicle Co.
Cincinnati, Ohio
SPECIAL—1909-10
Johnson Service Co.
Milwaukee, Wisconsin
SPECIALTY—1898
Specialty Carriage & Motor Vehicle Co.
Cincinnati, Ohio
SPEEDWAY—1905-06
Gas Engine & Power Co.
Morris Heights, New York
SPEEDWAY SPECIAL—1917-18
Wolverine Motors
Kalamazoo, Michigan
SPEEDWELL—1903
Speedwell Automobile Co.
Milwaukee, Wisconsin
Formerly Kunz Automobile & Motor Co.
SPEEDWELL—1907-15
Speedwell Motor Car Co.
Dayton, Ohio
Featured Mead rotary valve engine de-
signed by Cyrus E. Mead.
Reported bankrupt March, 1915. Plant sold
to W. M. Pattison Supply Co.
SPEEDWELL ROTARY SIX—1914
See "Speedwell"
Speedwell Motor Car Co.
Dayton, Ohio
Both names apply to same vehicle.
SPENCER STEAM—1862-64
C. M. Spencer
South Manchester, Connecticut
Windsor, Connecticut
SPENCER STEAM—1901-02
Spencer Automatic Screw Machine Co.
Hartford, Connecticut
Founded by C. M. Spencer.
SPENCER—1914

(SPENCER)—1921-22
Research Engineering Co.
Dayton, Ohio
*SPENCER-STEARNS
Believed to be error for "Spencer Steam."
(SPENNY)—1913-14
Spenny Motor Car Co.
Tucson, Arizona
Holland, Michigan
SPERLING—1921-23
Associated Motors Corp.
Elkhart, Indiana
Associated Motors Corp.
New York, New York
Announced December, 1921.
SPERRY ELECTRIC—1898-1902
Cleveland Machine Screw Co.
Cleveland, Ohio
National Battery Co.
Buffalo, New York
Sold to American Bicycle Co.
See "Waverley"
SPERRY—1915
SPHINX—1914-15
Sphinx Motor Car Co.
York, Pennsylvania
Became Bell Motor Car Co.
See "Bell" (1915-21).
SPICER—1902-03
Clarence W. Spicer
Plainfield, New Jersey
One car produced while inventor was stu-
dent at Cornell University.
SPIERS—1900
Spiers Mfg. Co.
Worcester, Massachusetts
SPILLER—1900
Pringst-Spiller Power & Auto Co.
Trenton, New Jersey
Spiller Motor Carriage Co.
Dorchester, Massachusetts
SPILLMAN—1900-01
Herschell-Spillman Co.
North Tonawanda, New York
SPOERER—1909-16

Carl Spoerer & Sons Co.
Baltimore, Maryland
SPOKANE STEAM—1905
Spokane Motor Co.
Spokane, Washington
SPRAGUE—1896
H. A. Sprague
Fowlerville, Michigan
SPRINGER—1902-06
Springer Motor Vehicle Co.
New York, New York
Succeeded Kidder Motor Vehicle Co.
See "Kidder"
SPRINGFIELD—1899
Springfield Automobile & Industrial Co.
Springfield, Ohio
SPRINGFIELD STEAM—1900-01
Springfield Motor Vehicle Co.
Springfield, Massachusetts
SPRINGFIELD—1900 01
Springfield Cornice Works
Springfield, Massachusetts
SPRINGFIELD—1903-04
Springfield Automobile Co.
Springfield, Ohio
See "Bramwell"
SPRINGFIELD—1907
Med-Bow Automobile Co.
Springfield, Massachusetts
SPRINGFIELD ELECTRIC—1908
R. Huss Electric & Mfg. Co.
Springfield, Ohio
SPRINGFIELD—1909-10
Springfield Motor Car Co.
Springfield, Illinois
SPRITE CYCLECAR—1914
W. S. Frazier & Co.
Aurora, Illinois
SPURR—1900-01
Spurr Automobile Co.
East Orange, New Jersey
SQUARE DEAL HIGHWHEELER—1910
Auto Parts Co.
Chicago, Illinois
SQUIRE & ROOT—1899

(E. Squire & A. J. Root)
Virginia City, Nevada

SRK—1915
S.R.K. Motor Co.
Detroit, Michigan

S.S.E.—1916-17
S.S.E. Co.
S.S.E. Automobile Co.
Kensington, Pennsylvania

STAFFORD—1908-15
Perry Stafford
Stafford Motor Car Co.
Topeka, Kansas (1908)
Kansas City, Kansas (1910-15)
Perry Stafford bought out Paul Mulvance
reported October, 1908.

STAHL—1910

STAMMOBILE STEAM—1900-05
Stammobile Mfg. Co.
Stamford, Connecticut

STANDARD—1899
Standard Motor Carriage Co.
Boston, Massachusetts

STANDARD—1899-1901
Standard Automobile Co.
Chicago, Illinois

STANDARD STEAM—1900
Boston Automobile Co.
Bar Harbor, Maine

STANDARD—1900-03
Standard Motor Vehicle Co.
Philadelphia, Pennsylvania

STANDARD STEAM—1900-01
Standard Auto-Vehicle Co.
Winchester, Massachusetts

STANDARD—1902
Standard Mfg. Co.
Kokomo, Indiana

STANDARD—1902-03
Standard Automobile Co.
Pittsburgh, Pennsylvania
Former Seely Mfg. Co.

STANDARD—1903
Standard Automobile Co.
Indianapolis, Indiana

STANDARD—1904-05
Standard Motor Construction Co.
Jersey City, New Jersey
Succeeded "United States Long Distance"
(1901-03).
Became Hewitt Motor Co.

STANDARD—1908-10
Standard Gas & Electric Power Co.
Philadelphia, Pennsylvania

STANDARD—1913-15
Standard Automobile Co.
Warren, Ohio

STANDARD—1913-23
Standard Steel Car Co.
Pittsburgh, Pennsylvania
Butler, Pennsylvania
Reorganized as Standard Motor Car Co.
1922.
1920 absorbed "Vim" truck

STANDARD CYCLECAR—1914
Standard Engineering Co.
Chicago, Illinois

STANDARD—1916
Standard Car Construction Co.
Philadelphia, Pennsylvania

STANDARD ELECTRIC—1911-15
Standard Electric Car Co.
Standard Car Mfg. Co.
Jackson, Michigan

STANDARD SIX—1909-11
St. Louis Car Co.
St. Louis, Missouri
1910 reorganized as Standard Automobile
Co. of America, Wabash, Indiana.
Formerly "American Mors" (1906-09).

STANDARD STEAM—1919-21
Standard Engineering Corp.
Standard Steam Corp.
St. Louis, Missouri
See "Scott-Newcomb"

STANDARD STEAMER—1905
Standard Automobile & Vehicle Co.
Boston, Massachusetts

STANDARD TOURIST—1905
See "Standard"

Standard Motor Construction Co.
Jersey City, New Jersey
Both names apply to same vehicle.

*STANHOPE—1904
Synnestvedt Machine Co.
Pittsburgh, Pennsylvania
Body designation, not a car.

STANHOPE—1904-06
Twyford Motor Car Co.
Brookville, Pennsylvania

STANLEY STEAMER—1896-99
Stanley Bros. Motor Carriage Co.
Newton, Massachusetts
Became Automobile Co. of America and
Locomobile Co. of America.
See "Mobile" and "Locomobile."

STANLEY STEAMER—1901-29
Stanley Motor Carriage Co.
Newton, Massachusetts
1923 reorganized as Steam Vehicle Corp. of
America.
1925 moved to Allentown, Pennsylvania.
Sold to Stanley Steam Motors Corp. Chicago, Illinois.

STANLEY—1906-08
Stanley Automobile Mfg. Co.
Mooreland, Indiana
Became Troy Automobile & Buggy Co.,
Troy, Ohio (gasoline runabouts).
Absorbed Peoples Automobile Co., Cleveland, Ohio 1908.

STANLEY—1910-12
Stanley Motor Car Co.
Detroit, Michigan
Reported two cars being built December,
1910.

STANLEY-WHITNEY STEAM—1899
Stanley Machine Co.
Lawrence, Massachusetts
See "McKay" and "Whitney."

STANTON STEAM—1901
Stanton Mfg. Co.
Waltham, Massachusetts
Absorbed New England Motor Carriage Co.
See "Waltham Steamer"

STANTON—1905
    Stanton Mfg. Co.
    Roselle, New Jersey
STANWOOD—1920-22
    Stanwood Motor Car Co.
    St. Louis, Missouri
STAPLES—1899-1900
    W. J. Staples
    Maryville, Missouri
STAR—1903-04
    Star Automobile Co. (1903)
    H. S. Moore Co. (1903-04)
    Cleveland, Ohio
STAR—1907-08
    Model Machine Co.
    Peru, Indiana
    Mier Carriage & Buggy Co.
    Ligonier, Indiana
    See "Mier" and "Izzer."
STAR—1909
    Minneapolis Motorcycle Co.
    Minneapolis, Minnesota
STAR—1910
    Star Motor Car Co.
    Indianapolis, Indiana
    One car produced.
STAR CYCLECAR—1914
    Star Cyclecar Co.
    Los Angeles, California
(STAR) STEAM—1916
    Star Motor Car Co.
    Cincinnati, Ohio
STAR—1922-28
    Durant Motors Inc.
    Elizabeth, New Jersey
    Office in New York, New York.
STAR—1949
STAR DUST—1953
    Los Angeles, California
STARIN—1903-04
    Starin Co.
    North Tonawanda, New York
STAR LIGHT ELECTRIC—1962-63
STATES CYCLECAR—1915-16
    States Cyclecar Co.

Detroit, Michigan
    First deliveries reported August, 1916.
STATES—1916-17
    States Motor Car Mfg. Co.
    Toledo, Ohio
    Kalamazoo, Michigan
STATIC SUPER AIR-COOLED—1923
    Static Motor Co.
    Philadelphia, Pennsylvania
STATIONETTE—1950-55
    Martin Development Co.
    Rochelle Park, New Jersey
STAVER—1906-10
    Staver Carriage Co.
    Chicago, Illinois
    Experimental 1906. Highwheeler 1907-08.
STAVER-CHICAGO—1911-14
    See "Staver'
    Staver Motor Co.
    Chicago, Illinois
STEALY—1899
    A. D. Stealy
    San Francisco, California
STEAMOBILE STEAM—1900-02
    Steamobile Co.
    Steamobile Co. of America
    Keene, New Hampshire
    See "Keene Steamer," "Rogers," "Transit Steamer" and "Trinity."
STEAM VEHICLE—1900-03
    Steam Vehicle Co. of America
    Reading, Pennsylvania
    See "Reading Steam Carriage"
STEARING—1898
STEARNS—1896-1911
    F. B. Stearns Co.
    Cleveland, Ohio
    Became "Stearns Knight"
STEARNS ELECTRIC—1899-1901
    E. C. Stearns Co.
    Syracuse, New York
    Became Stearns Automobile Co., 1900.
STEARNS-KNIGHT—1912-30
    F. B. Stearns Co.
    Cleveland, Ohio

Former "Stearns" car.
    Absorbed by Willys-Overland Co. 1925
STEARNS STEAM—1900-02
    Stearns Steam Carriage Co.
    Syracuse, New York
    No connection with E. C. Stearns.
STECO CYCLECAR—1914
    Stephens Engineering Co.
    Chicago, Illinois
STEEL BALL STEAM—1900-01
    Steel Ball Co.
    Chicago, Illinois
STEEL KING—1915
STEEL SWALLOW HIGHWHEELER—1906-09
    Steel Swallow Automobile Co.
    Jackson, Michigan
STEGMAIER STEAM—1906-07
    Stegmaier Bros.
    Cumberland, Maryland
STEINHART-JENSEN—1908
    Steinhart-Jensen Automobile Co.
    Joliet, Illinois
STEINMETZ—1901
    Jenny-Steinmetz & Co.
    Philadelphia, Pennsylvania
STEINMETZ ELECTRIC—1920-27
    Steinmetz Electric Motor Car Co.
    Baltimore, Maryland
    Arlington, Maryland
STEPHENS—1916-24
    Stephens Motor Branch,
        Moline Plow Co.
    Stephens Motor Car Co. Inc.
    Freeport, Illinois
    1918 Moline Plow Co. became subsidiary of Willys-Overland Co.
    1920 name changed to Stephens Motor Co.
    Moline and Freeport, Illinois.
    First car completed May 8, 1916.
STERKENBERG EXPERIMENTAL—1931
    John Tjaarda
    Detroit, Michigan
STERLING—1897-99
    Clarence Sterling
    Bridgeport, Connecticut

STERLING—1901
    Howell & Meehan Co.
    Boston, Massachusetts
STERLING—1908
    Sterling Engine Co.
    Buffalo, New York
STERLING—1908-11
    Elkhart Motor Car Co.
    Elkhart, Indiana
STERLING—1913-16
    Sterling Motor Co.
    Flint, Michigan
    Detroit, Michigan
Controlled by "Little" in 1912.
See "Little"
STERLING—1920-23
    Consolidated Motor Car Co.
    New London, Connecticut
Erroneously reported to have been manufactured at Amston, Bridgeport and New Britain, Connecticut.
STERLING-KNIGHT—1921-25
    J. G. Sterling
    Sterling-Knight Motors Co.
    Cleveland, Ohio
    Warren, Ohio
STERLING-NEW YORK—1915-16
    Sterling Automobile Mfg. Co.
    Paterson, New Jersey
    Became "AMS Sterling."
STERLING STEAMER—1900-02
    Sterling Automobile & Engine Co.
    Sterling, Illinois
STERNES steam—1923
    Sternes Steam Car Co.
STETSON 1907-11
    Stetson Motor Car Co.
    Dover, Delaware
    Pittsfield, Massachusetts
Possible misnomer for "Stilson."
STEVENS—1915
STEVENS-DURYEA—1902-27
    J. Stevens Arms & Tool Co.
    The Stevens-Duryea Co.
    Stevens-Duryea Motors Inc.

Stevens-Duryea Inc.
Final years with Rauch & Lang electric, "Rauling" electric cars and taxicabs.
STEWART—1895
    Richard F. Stewart
    Pocantico Hills, New York
STEWART—1904
    Alfred C. Stewart Co.
    Los Angeles, California
    40 hp racer for Frank A. Garbutt.
STEWART—1915-16
    Stewart Motor Corp.
    Buffalo, New York
STEWART-COATS steam—1922
    Y. F. Stewart Motor Car Mfg. Co.
    Columbus, Ohio
Succeeded Coats Steam Car Co.
See "Coats Steamer"
STICKNEY MOTORETTE cyclecar—1913-14
    Charles A. Stickney Co.
    St. Paul, Minnesota
Reported out of business June, 1914.
STILL—1899-1903
    Canadian Motor Syndicate
    Toronto, Ontario, Canada
STILSON—1907-10
    Stilson Motor Car Co.
    Pittsfield, Massachusetts
In receivers' hands January, 1911.
STIRLING—1920
    Stirling Motors Inc.
    Newark, New Jersey
STOCKWELL—1905
    M. E. Stockwell
    Grand Rapids, Michigan
STODDARD-20—1911
    Courier Car Co.
    Dayton, Ohio
STODDARD-30—1911
    Dayton Motor Car Co.
    Dayton, Ohio
STODDARD-DAYTON—1904-11
    Dayton Motor Car Co.
    Dayton, Ohio

Successor to Stoddard Mfg.
Division of U.S. Motor Corp. 1910.
Became Maxwell Motor Co. 1914.
STODDARD-DAYTON KNIGHT (model)—1911-12
See "Stoddard-Dayton"
    Dayton Motor Car Co.
    Dayton, Ohio
STOKESBURY steam—1922-23
    Steam Automotive Works
    Denver, Colorado
    Stokesbury Steam Motors Co.
    Los Angeles, California
STOLZ—1900-02
    The Stolz Cycle Co.
    Brooklyn, New York
    W. G. Stolz Automobile & Cycle Works
    Groton, New York
Gasoline cars built to order.
STOMMEL—1899
    Hugo Stommel
    Plainfield, New Jersey
STONE & MAYNARD—1895
    Stone & Maynard Co.
    Avonia, Pennsylvania
STORCK steam—1901-02
    Frank C. Storck
    Red Bank, New Jersey
STORK-KAR—1919-20
    Stork-Kar Sales Co.
    New York, New York
Four-cylinder touring car. Factory at Martinsburg, West Virginia.
STORM—1954
    Sports Car Development Corp.
    Detroit, Michigan
Two-passenger sports car using Dodge V-8 engine in Bertone body.
STORMS electric—1915-16
    Storms Electric Car Co.
    Detroit, Michigan
STORY—1950-51
STOUT—1935; 1946
    William B. Stout
    Owens-Corning Fiberglass Corp.

CODE = ROMAN LETTERS: Complete entry. *ITALICS:* Unsubstantiated entry. (PARENTHESES): Production planned, but not realized.

Newark, Ohio
STOUT CYCLECAR—1914
    Stout Engineering Co.
    Stout Cyclecar Co.
    Chicago, Illinois
STOUT SCARAB—1934-39
    See "Scarab"
    Stout Engineering Laboratories
    Both names apply to same vehicle.
STOVER—1909
    Stover Motor Car Co.
    Freeport, Illinois
STRANAHAN—1906-08
    Stranahan-Eldridge Co.
    Boston, Massachusetts
STRATHMORE STEAM—1899-1902
    Strathmore Automobile Co.
    Boston, Massachusetts
    Former International Auto Co.
STRATTON—1901
    Stratton Motor Cycle Co.
    (Stratton Motor Co.)
    New York, New York
STRATTON HIGHWHEELER—1908-09
    C. H. Stratton Carriage Co.
    Muncie, Indiana
STRATTON-BLISS—1922
    Stratton-Bliss Co.
    New York, New York
STRATTON-PREMIER—1923
    Stratton Motors Corp.
    Indianapolis, Indiana
    Absorbed "Monroe"
    Absorbed by "Premier"
STRAUSS
STREAMLINE—1913
    Streamline Motor Car Co.
    Indianapolis, Indiana
STREATOR—1903-09
    Streator Automobile Mfg. Co.
    Streator Motor Car Co.
    Streator, Illinois
    Former Erie Cycle & Motor Carriage Co.
STREIT—1907
    Cincinnati, Ohio

STRINGER STEAM—1899-1901
    J. W. Stringer
    Stringer Automobile Co.
    Marion, Ohio
STROBEL & MARTIN—1910
STRONG—1904
    Strong Automobile Mfg. Co.
    Minneapolis, Minnesota
STRONG & GIBBONS—1895
    Strong & Gibbons Co.
    Chicago, Illinois
STRONG & ROGERS ELECTRIC—1900-01
    Strong & Rogers
    Cleveland, Ohio
STROUSE—1915
    Strouse, Ranney & Knight
    Detroit, Michigan
    Name changed to S.R.K. Motor Co.
*STROUSE STEAM—1915
    Believed error for "Strouse" or "S.R.K."
*STROUSS—1897
    Believed to be "Struss" misspelled.
STRUSS—1897
    Henry Struss
    New York, New York
STUART ELECTRIC—1961
    Stuart Motors
    Kalamazoo, Michigan
    Prototypes only
STUDEBAKER—1902-66
    Studebaker Automobile Co.
    Studebaker Corp.
    South Bend, Indiana
    Electric 1902-12; gas cars 1904-66.
    Studebaker Automobile Co. absorbed "Tin-cher" 1907 and "Garford" 1908. Contracted to sell output of "E.M.F." 1909. "Flanders," 1909-10. Purchased "E.M.F." 1910. Reorganized as Studebaker Corp. 1911. Absorbed "Pierce-Arrow" 1928. Controlled White Corp. 1928 and Indiana Truck Corp. Released "Pierce-Arrow" 1933 and "White" 1934. Amalgamated with Packard Motor Car Co. into Studebaker-Packard Corp. 1954. Dropped "Packard" from name 1962.

STURGES ELECTRIC—1895
    Sturges Electric Motorcycle Co.
    Chicago, Illinois
    Chicago Times-Herald Race entry.
STURGIS ELECTRIC—1898-1904
    Sturgis & Bros.
    Los Angeles, California
STURTEVANT—1904-08
    Sturtevant Mills Co.
    Boston and Hyde Park, Massachusetts
    Automatic transmission
STUTZ—1911-35
    Stutz Auto Parts Co.
    Ideal Motor Car Co.
    Indianapolis, Indiana
    1913 name changed to Stutz Motor Car Co.
    "of America" added 1916.
    See "Blackhawk"
STUTZ—1970 to date
    Stutz Motor Car Co. of America Inc.
    52 Broadway
    New York, New York
    On "Pontiac" Grand Prix chassis.
STUYVESANT—1910-13
    Stuyvesant Motor Car Co.
    Cleveland, Ohio
    Succeeded Gaeth Motor Car Co.
    See "Gaeth"
    Bought by Grant-Lees 1911
SUBURBAN—1912-13
    Suburban Motor Car Co.
    Wyandotte, Michigan
    Became Palmer Motor Car Co.
SUBURBAN LIMITED—1911
    DeSchaum Motor Car Co.
    Detroit, Michigan
    Became "Suburban"
SUBURBAN STEAM—1904
    Edward S. Clark
    Boston, Massachusetts
SUCCESS AUTO BUGGY
    HIGHWHEELER—1906-09
    J. C. Higdon
    Success Auto Buggy Mfg. Co.
    St. Louis, Missouri

*ASTERISK: Error corrected from previous list. See introduction to this section for complete code.

SULLIVAN—1904
Roger J. Sullivan & Co.
Detroit, Michigan
SULLIVAN CYCLECAR—1914
A. H. Sullivan
St. Louis, Missouri
SULTAN—1906-12
Sultan Motor Co.
Sultan Motor Car Co.
Springfield, Massachusetts (factory)
New York, New York (office)
Not connected with "Sultan" taxicab.
SULTANIC—1913
SUMMIT HIGHWHEELER—1907-09
Summit Carriage-Mobile Co.
Waterloo, Iowa
Also called "Carriage-Mobile."
SUN—1915-18
Sun Motor Car Co.
Buffalo, New York (1915)
Elkhart, Indiana (1916-18)
Founded by R. Crawford and R. C.
Hoffman, formerly of "Haynes"
Plant reported sold to W. L. Huffman,
Omaha, Nebraska for truck mfg. Sep-
tember, 1918.
SUN AIR-COOLED—1918-23
The Automotive Corp.
Toledo, Ohio
SUNSET—1900-09
Sunset Automobile Co.
San Francisco, California
Victor Motor Car Co.
San Jose, California
1900-04 steam
1904-06 gasoline
Factory burned down during San Francisco
earthquake.
SUNSET STEAM—1901-04
Sunset Automobile Co.
San Francisco, California
SUPERBA (model)—1960 to date
Checker Motors Corp.
Kalamazoo, Michigan
See "Checker"

SUPER CHIEF (model)—1957-58
See "Pontiac"
Pontiac Motor Co.
Pontiac, Michigan
A model of "Pontiac."
SUPER COOLED—1923
SUPERHEATED STEAM CAR—1920
Gearless Steam Auto. Mfg. Co.
Denver, Colorado
One car produced.
SUPERIOR—1901
Superior Gas Engine Works
Superior, Wisconsin
SUPERIOR—1902
Superior Motor Carriage Co.
Cleveland, Ohio
SUPERIOR—1910
Superior Motor Vehicle Co.
Buffalo, New York
SUPERIOR—1910
William English
Petrolia, Ontario, Canada
SUPERIOR—1914
Crescent Motor Car Co.
St. Louis, Missouri
SUPER KAR THREE-WHEELER—1946
Louis R. Elrad
Cleveland, Ohio
Prototype only; midget car.
SUPER SPORT—1970
Automotive Design Associates, Inc.
Monroe, Connecticut
Fiberglass street buggy, kit car, with 78
1/2 inch "Volkswagen" chassis.
SUPER STEAMER
SUPREME—1922
Supreme Motors Corp.
Cleveland, Ohio
Company formed in 1918 to build engines
(Warren, Ohio).
SUPREME—1930
SURREY—1959-60
E. W. Bliss Co.
Canton, Ohio
Replica of 1903 Oldsmobile.

SUTTLE STEAM—1948
SWALLOW—1907
SWAN—1903-04
Swan Electric Co.
(W. J. Swan)
Middletown, California
SWARTZ—1920
Reading, Pennsylvania
SWEANY STEAM—1895
Charles S. Caffrey Co.
Camden, New Jersey
One car produced.
SWIFT—1899-1900
Swift & Co.
St. Joseph, Missouri
SWIFT—1959 to date
Swift Manufacturing Co.
El Cajon, California
5/8 scale copies of antique cars carrying
model names of Swift-T, Swift-Cat and
Swifter.
SWINGER DUNE BUGGY—1968
Fibercraft, Inc.
Reno, Nevada
SYNNESTVEDT ELECTRIC—1904-05
Synnestvedt Vehicle Co.
Synnestvedt Machine Co.
Pittsburgh, Pennsylvania
After 1905 built trucks only.
SYRACUSE ELECTRIC—1899-1903
Saul & Van Wagoner Co.
Syracuse, New York

TACOMA RACER—1917
Tacoma Radiator & Fender Works
Tacoma, Washington
TAFT STEAMER—1901-02
W. E. Taft
Boston, Massachusetts
TALBERT—1948
*TALLY-HO—1902
Wrong name applied to 1902 "Packard."
"Tally-Ho" was a gasoline name brand.

(TARKINGTON)—1920-23
Tarkington Motor Car Co.
Rockford, Illinois
TARRYTOWN—1914
Tarrytown, New York
TASCO—1947-48
The American Sports Car Co.
Hartford, Connecticut
One prototype built. Body by Derham, Rosemont, Pennsylvania.
TATE ELECTRIC—1912-13
Tate Electrics Ltd.
Windsor, Ontario, Canada
TAUNTON STEAM—1901-04
Taunton Automobile Co.
Taunton, Massachusetts
TAUNTON—1905
Taunton Motor Carriage Co.
Taunton, Massachusetts
One-cylinder runabout with 68-inch wheel base was the only model built.
TAYLOR STEAM—1867
Henry Seth Taylor
Stanstead, Quebec, Canada
Derby Line, Vermont
TAYLOR—1895
E. E. Taylor
Fitchburg, Massachusetts
TAYLOR THREE-WHEELER—1899
George W. Taylor
Long Beach, California
T-BUG DUNE BUGGY—1968
Lincoln Industries
Lincoln, California
TEMPEST (model)—1960 to date
See "Pontiac"
Pontiac Motor Division
Pontiac, Michigan
TEMPLAR—1917-24
S. P. Mfg. Co. (1917)
Templar Motors Corp. (1918-24)
Templar Motor Car Co. (1924)
Cleveland, Ohio
TEMPLE—1899
Robert Temple

Denver, Colorado
TEMPLETON—1895
John Templeton
Chicago, Illinois
TEMPLETON-DUBRIE—1910
Templeton-Dubrie Car Co.
Detroit, Michigan
TEMPLE WESTCOTT—1922
Bealer Body Co.
Framingham, Massachusetts
TENNANT—1915
Tennant Motors Ltd.
Chicago, Illinois
TERMAAT-MONAHAN CYCLECAR—1914
Termaat-Monahan Co.
Oshkosh, Wisconsin
TERRA BUGGY DUNE BUGGY—1968
Terra Knife Inc.
Crawfordsville, Indiana
TERRAPLANE—1933-38
Hudson Motor Car Co.
Detroit, Michigan
Formerly "Essex-Terraplane"
TERRA TIGER SIX-WHEELER—1968 to date
Feldmann Engineering & Mfg. Co.
Sheboygan Falls, Wisconsin
Jeep-type all-terrain vehicle.
TERWILLIGER STEAM—1897; 1902
Terwilliger & Co.
Amsterdam, New York
See "Empire Steamer" (1904-05)
(TEX)—1915-16
Texas Motor Car Co.
San Antonio, Texas
TEXAN—1918-22
Texas Motor Car Association
Fort Worth and Cleburne, Texas
Receiver operated from October, 1920.
TEXAS—1920
Texas Truck & Tractor Co.
Dallas, Texas
TEXMOBILE—1922
Little Motors Kar Co.
Dallas, Texas
THAYER-ISHAM—1909

Thayer Isham Automobile Co.
Marinette, Wisconsin
*THERMONT-MONOHAN CYCLECAR—1914
Believed to be "Termaat-Monahan" cyclecar misspelled.
THIBAULT—1921
THIEM—1901-05
Thiem & Co.
St. Paul, Minnesota
Virtue, Pound & Co.
Rushford, Minnesota
THOMAS—1902-15
E. R. Thomas Motor Co.
Buffalo, New York
Founded 1898. Absorbed Buffalo Auto. & Auto. Bi Co. 1902. Established Detroit Branch 1906. See "Thomas-Detroit." Merged with Columbus Buggy Co. 1914. See "Firestone-Columbus."
THOMAS-DETROIT—1907-08
E. R. Thomas-Detroit Co.
Detroit, Michigan
Became Chalmers-Detroit Co.
See "Chalmers-Detroit"
THOMPSON—1899-1900
Thompson Automobile Co.
Camden, New Jersey
THOMPSON—1900-02
Thompson Automobile Co.
Philadelphia, Pennsylvania
Steam and gas vehicles.
THOMPSON ELECTRIC—1901
Andrew C. Thompson
Plainfield, New Jersey
THOMPSON STEAM—1901-07
Zenas Thompson & Bros.
Thompson Automobile Co.
Providence, Rhode Island
THOMSON STEAM—1900
General Electric Co.
Lynn, Massachusetts
Built by Prof. Elihu Thomson.
THORNE CYCLECAR—1914
THORNE TIGER—1944-45
Thorne Engineering Co.

Los Angeles, California
Designed by Art Sparks.
Became "Californian" and "Davis."
THOROBRED—1901
THOROUGHBRED 6—1920
THRESHER ELECTRIC—1900
Thresher Electric Co.
Dayton, Ohio
T.H.T.—1910
T.H.T. Motor Co.
Detroit, Michigan
THUNDERBIRD (model)—1955 to date
See "Ford"
Ford Motor Co.
Dearborn, Michigan
THURSTON—1898
TIFFANY ELECTRIC—1913-14
Tiffany Electric Car Co.
Pontiac, Michigan
TIFFANY-BIJOU ELECTRIC—1914
E. L. Pelletier
New York, New York
TIGER CYCLECAR—1914-15
Automobile Cyclecar Co.
(W. A. DeSchaum)
Detroit, Michigan
TILEY—1904-13
Tiley-Pratt Co.
Essex, Connecticut
Experimental 1904
About 25 cars built.
TILIKUM CYCLEAR—1914-15
Yukon Auto Shop
Tilikum Cyclecar Co.
Seattle, Washington
Sometimes spelled "Tilicum."
TIME—1916
Time Mfg. Co.
Oustburg, Wisconsin
TINCHER—1903-08
Chicago Coach & Carriage Co.
Chicago, Illinois
1904 became Tincher Motor Car Co. South Bend, Indiana. Absorbed by Studebaker Automobile Co. 1907.

TINKHAM THREE-WHEELER—1895-99
Denison & Walton
Tinkham Cycle Co.
New York, New York
New Haven, Connecticut
Built by Denison Motor Carriage Co.
See "Denison"
TINKHAM STEAM—1900-01
Piper & Tinkham Co.
Waltham, Massachusetts
TIN-LIZZIE—1960 to date
McDonough Power Equipment Co.
McDonough, Georgia
1/2 scale 1910 "Ford" replica.
TISCHER THREE-WHEELER—1914
Tischer-Linton Tri-Car Co.
Peoria, Illinois
TIVY STEAM—1902-03
Tivy Cycle Mfg. Co.
Williamsport, Pennsylvania
TJAARDA EXPERIMENTAL—1935
Briggs Mfg. Co.
Detroit, Michigan
Prototype of "Lincoln Zephyr."
T.M.F. HIGHWHEELER—1909
Termott, Monahan & Farney
Oshkosh, Wisconsin
TODD—1895
Chicago Fireproof Covering Co.
Chicago, Illinois
TOLEDO—1902-03
American Bicycle Co.
Toledo Motor Carriage Co.
International Motor Car Co.
Toledo, Ohio
Became Pope Motor Car Co.
See "Pope-Toledo"
See "Hydrocar"
Steam and gasoline vehicles.
TOLEDO—1909
Apperson-Toledo Motor Co.
Toledo, Ohio
TOLEDO CYCLECAR—1914
Toledo Autocycle Co.
National United Service Co.

Detroit, Michigan
Toledo, Ohio
TONAWANDA ELECTRIC—1900-02
Tonawanda Motor Vehicle Co.
Tonawanda, New York
TOMLINSON—1901
D. W. Tomlinson Jr.
Batavia, New York
TOM THUMB—1910
Detroit Boat Works
Detroit, Michigan
TONE—1913
Tone Car Co.
Tone Car Corp.
Indianapolis, Indiana
TOOMEY—1913
S. Toomey Co.
Canal Dover, Ohio
TOQUET—1904-05
Toquet Motor Car & Construction Co.
Toquet Motor Co.
Boston, Massachusetts
Saugatuck, Connecticut
TORBENSON—1902-08
Torbenson Gear Co.
Bloomfield, New Jersey
Mostly running gear and delivery cars.
TORONADO (model)—1965 to date
See "Oldsmobile"
Oldsmobile Division of
General Motors Corporation
Lansing, Michigan
TORPEDO-KID—1903
TORRENCE—1904-05
William W. Torrence
Montrose, Colorado
TOURAINE—1907
Automobile Parts & Equipment Co.
2224 and 2234 Michigan Ave.
Chicago, Illinois
TOURAINE—1913-16
Touraine Co.
Philadelphia, Pennsylvania
Succeeded "Nance"
TOURIST—1902-10

Auto Vehicle Co.
Los Angeles, California
TOWANDA—1904
Towanda Motor Vehicle Co.
Towanda, Pennsylvania
Sold without motor.
Succeeded Centaur Motor Vehicle Co.
TOWER—1899
C. E. Tower
Syracuse, New York
TOWN CAR—1909
TOWNE SHOPPER—1948
International Motor Co.
San Diego, California
TOWNSEND—1903
Townsend Automobile & Piano Works
New York, New York
TRACTOBILE STEAM—1900-02
Pennsylvania Steam Vehicle Co.
Carlisle, Pennsylvania
An attachment for horse-drawn vehicles.
TRAIL BLAZER—1961 to date
Hickey Mfg. Co.
Downey, California
Four-wheel drive
TRANSIT STEAM—1899-1902
Steamobile Co. of America
W. S. Rogers Roller Bearing &
Equipment Co.
Keene, New Hampshire
Tonneau in front, driver in rear. Convertible to use on rails.
TRASK-DETROIT STEAM—1922-23
Detroit Steam Motor Corp.
Detroit, Michigan
Schlieder Mfg. Co.
Detroit, Michigan
TRASK-STEAM—1921-22
Trask-Kennedy Co.
(O. C. Trask)
Detroit, Michigan
TRAVELER—1906-08
Bellefontaine Automobile Co.
Bellefontaine, Ohio
Succeeded Zent Automobile Co. See "Zent"

TRAVELER—1913-14
Traveler Motor Car Co.
Detroit, Michigan
Also called "Traveler-Detroit"
TRAVELLER—1904
Neustadt-Perry Co.
St. Louis, Missouri
TRAVELLER HIGHWHEELER—1910-14
Traveller Automobile Co.
Single Center Buggy Co.
Evansville, Indiana
TRAVERSE CITY—1917-18
Traverse City Motor Car Co.
Traverse City, Michigan
Formerly Napoleon Motor Co.
November, 1916, 6 delivered and 18 under construction.
TREBERT—1904-08
Trebert Auto & Marine Motor Co.
Trebert Gas Engine Co.
Rochester, New York
TRIBUNE—1913-14
Tribune Motor Co.
Detroit, Michigan
TRIBUNE—1917
Tribune Engineering Co.
Owego, New York
TRI-CAR—1907
TRI-CAR THREE-WHEELER—1955
Lycoming Division, Avco Corp.
Williamsport, Pennsylvania
TRICOLET THREE-WHEELER—1905
Became "Pokorney"
H. Pokorney Automobile &
Gas Engine Co.
1704 Bellefontain St.
Indianapolis, Indiana
TRIDENT ELECTRIC—1959
Taylor Dunn Mfg. Co.
Anaheim, California
*TRI-MOTO—1896-1901
Believed to be "Tri-Motor" misspelled.
TRI-MOTOR THREE-WHEELER—1900-01
Western Wheel Works
(American Bicycle Co.)

Chicago, Illinois
TRINITY STEAM—1900-01
Trinity Mfg. Co.
Keene, New Hampshire
Became Keene Steamobile Co., then
Steamobile Co. of America.
TRIPLER LIQUID AIR—1901
Tripler Liquid Air Co.
Washington, D.C.
TRIPLEX—1905
TRIPLEX—1954-55
TRI-RICKSHA—1914-15
International Tri-Ricksha Co.
New York, New York
TRI-STATE—1903
Tri-State Automobile & Supply Co.
Memphis, Tennessee
TRITT ELECTRIC—1905
Tritt Electric Co.
South Bend, Indiana
TRIUMPH STEAM—1900-01
Triumph Motor Vehicle Co.
Chicago, Illinois
Steam and electric cars.
See "Ellis Electric" 1901
TRIUMPH—1906-07
Triumph Motor Car Co.
Chicago, Illinois
First cars placed on road November, 1905.
Firm dissolved May, 1908. See "Bendix"
TRIUMPH—1908-12
Christopher Bros.
Triumph Motor Car Co.
Chicago, Illinois
*TROMBLY—1911
Believed to be "Twombly" misspelled.
TROTT—1917
Trott Automobile Co.
Detroit, Michigan
TROTT & STUBBLEFIELD—1915
Trott & Stubblefield Co.
Bloomington, Illinois
TROY—1905
Troy Carriage Works
Troy, New York

*ASTERISK: Error corrected from previous list. See introduction to this section for complete code.

TRUE CYCLECAR—1914
    Badger Brass Mfg. Co.
    Kenosha, Wisconsin
(TRUE BLUE)—1910
    True Blue Motor Co.
    Detroit, Michigan
TRUMBULL—1899-1902
    Warren Machine Works
    Trumbull Mfg. Co.
    Warren, Ohio
TRUMBULL CYCLECAR—1913-16
    American Cyclecar Co.
    Trumbull Motor Car Co.
    Bridgeport, Connecticut
    First three cars shipped May 8, 1914.
TUCK—1904-05
    Tuck Petroleum Co.
    Brooklyn, New York
TUCKER—1947-48
    Tucker Corp.
    Chicago, Illinois
    Purchased Air-Cooled Motors Corp.
    (Franklin Air-Cooled Engines)
TUCKER MOBILE—1900-03
    J. O. Tucker
    Santa Clara, California
    Fewer than 20 made. 1894 and 1899 also
    claimed.
TUDHOPE—1906-13
    Tudhope Motor Car Co.
    Orillia, Ontario, Canada
TULCAR—1915
TULSA—1912-23
    Tulsa Auto & Mfg. Co.
    Tulsa Four Automobile Co.
    Tulsa Automobile Mfg. Co.
    Witt-Thompson Motor Co.
    Tulsa, Oklahoma
    Succeeded Dowagiac Motor Car Co.
TURBINE ELECTRIC—1904
    Turbine Electric Truck Co.
    New York, New York
TURNER—1900-01
    Turner Automobile Co. Ltd.
    Philadelphia, Pennsylvania

TURNER—1899-1900
    J. C. Turner
    Augusta, Georgia
TURNER-FRITCHLE—1903
TWEED-THOMAS—1906
    Tweed-Thomas Co.
    Wheatley, Minnesota
TWENTIETH CENTURY—1900
    Twentieth Century Mfg. Co.
    New York, New York
TWIN CITY—1912-15
    Twin City Motor Car Co.
    Twin City Four-Wheel Drive Co.
    St. Paul, Minnesota
TWIN CITY CYCLECAR—1914
    Twin City Motor Car Co.
    Minneapolis, Minnesota
TWOMBLY STEAM—1903-04
    Twombly Motor Carriage Co.
    New York, New York
TWOMBLY—1906-11
    Twombly Motor Car Co.
    Twombly Motors Co.
    New York, New York
TWOMBLY CYCLECAR—1913-15
    Twombly Car Corp.
    Nutley, New Jersey
    Experimental 1910
    Built by Driggs-Seabury Ordnance Co.
    Sharon, Pennsylvania
    Taxicabs 1915
TWYFORD—1899-1908
    Twyford Motor Vehicle Co.
    Pittsburgh, Pennsylvania
    Twyford Motorcar Company
    Brookville, Pennsylvania
    Four wheel drive.
TYRO—1912
    Tyro Mfg. Co.
    Detroit, Michigan

U

ULLRICH—1934

ULSTER—1939
(ULTRA)—1906
    Ultra Motor Car Co.
    New Haven, Connecticut
ULTRA—1918
UNDERWOOD—1900
    Frank M. Underwood
    Sandusky, Ohio
UNION ELECTRIC—1899
    Union Electric Vehicle Co.
    Portland, Maine
UNION—1902
    Springfield, Massachusetts
UNION—1902-05
    Union Automobile Co.
    Union City, Indiana
    Anderson, Indiana
    Subsidiary of Buckeye Mfg. Co.
    1905 reorganized with Lambert Gas &
    Gasoline Engine Co. in Buckeye Mfg. Co.
    See "Lambert" (1904-17)
    Over 300 cars built.
UNION—1905-09
    Union Automobile Mfg. Co.
    St. Louis, Missouri
UNION HIGHWHEELER—1908-09
    Union High Wheel Automobile Co.
    Union Carriage Co.
    St. Louis, Missouri
    Became Union Automobile Co.
UNION—1915-16
    Union Car Co.
    Los Angeles, California
UNION—1916-17
    Auburn Automobile Co.
    Auburn, Indiana
UNION CITY SIX—1916
    Union City Automobile Co.
    Union City, Ohio
UNION TWENTY-FIVE—1911-14
    Union Motor Car Co.
    Union Motor Sales Co.
    Columbus, Ohio
UNIQUE—1906
    C. B. Hatfield Jr.

CODE = ROMAN LETTERS: Complete entry. *ITALICS:* Unsubstantiated entry. (PARENTHESES): Production planned, but not realized.

Cortland, New York
UNITED—1900-01
United Power Vehicle Co.
Rutland, Vermont
UNITED—1902-04
UNITED—1904-05
See "Ormond"
United Motor & Vehicle Co.
Boston, Massachusetts
Both names apply to same vehicle.
UNITED cyclecar—1914
National United Service Co.
Detroit, Michigan
UNITED—1916-20
United Engine Co.
Greensburg, Indiana
UNITED MOTOR—1902-04
United Motor Corp.
Pawtucket, Rhode Island
See "Cameron"
UNITED STATES electric—1899-1900
United States Motor Vehicle Co.
New York, New York
Succeeded Wisconsin Auto & Machinery
Co. and Dey-Griswold Co.
UNITED STATES steam—1900-01
United States Carriage Co.
Rumford, Maine
U.S. Motor Carriage Co.
Andover, Maine
UNITED STATES—1909-15
United States Carriage Co.
Columbus, Ohio
UNITED STATES ELECTRIC—1899-1901
United States Automobile Co.
Attleboro, Massachusetts
UNITO MOTOR BUGGY—1908-10
Unito Motor Buggy Co.
Cleveland, Ohio
UNIVERSAL—1910
Universal Motor Co.
New Castle, Indiana
UNIVERSAL cyclecar—1914
Universal Motor Co.
Washington, Pennsylvania

UNIVERSAL—1917
Universal Service Co.
Detroit, Michigan
UNIVERSAL—1919
UNIVERSITY—1907-09
University Auto Co.
New Haven, Connecticut
See "Continental"
UNIVERSITY—1910
University Motor Car Co.
Detroit, Michigan
UNWIN—1921
Unwin Motor Car Co.
New York, New York
UPTON—1901-04
Upton Machine Company
Beverly, Massachusetts
UPTON—1905-07
Upton Motor Company (1905)
Lebanon Motor Works (1905-07)
Lebanon, Pennsylvania
UPTON—1903
Upton Pump Co.
New Castle, Indiana
UPTON—1914
J. L. Upton
Constantine, Michigan
Bristol, Indiana
U.S.—1907-08
United States Motor Co.
Upper Sandusky, Ohio
U.S. AUTO—1899-1918
U.S. CARRIAGE—1910-18
U.S. LONG DISTANCE—1900-04
United States Long Distance
Automobile Co.
Elizabethport, New Jersey
Became Standard Motor Construction Co.
U.S. MOBILE—1901
UTICA—1900
Utica Gas Engine Co.
Utica, New York
UTILITY—1910
Stephenson Motor Car Co.
Milwaukee, Wisconsin

UTILITY—1910
Utility Motor Car Co.
Ludington, Michigan
UTILITY—1918
Utility Car Co.
Richmond, Indiana
(UTILITY)—1921-22
See "Pagé"
Victor W. Pagé Motor Co.
Stamford, Connecticut
Both names apply to same vehicle.
UTILITY THREE WHEEL—1913
Utility Car Co.
New York, New York

𝒱

*VALCAN—1914
Valcan Mfg. Co.
Painesville, Ohio
Believed to be an error for "Vulcan"
VALLEY
Registered in two states before 1915.
VALIANT (model)—1960 to date
See "Plymouth"
Chrysler Corp.
Detroit, Michigan
A model of "Plymouth."
No "Plymouth" designation, 1960-61.
VALKYRIE—1967
Fiberfab Division of Velocidad, Inc.
Santa Clara, California
Sports car, also in kit form.
VALTRA—1917
VAN—1904
VAN—1906
Van Automobile Co.
St. Louis, Missouri
VAN—1910-11
Van Motor Car Co.
Grand Haven, Michigan
VAN—1911
L. C. Erbes
Waterloo, Iowa

*VANALL STEAM—1894-95
Believed to be "Vanell Steam Carriage" misspelled.

VAN BLERCK—1915
Van Blerck Motor Co.
Monroe, Michigan

(VANDERBILT EIGHT)—1921
Union Steel Manufacturing Co.
Brazil, Indiana

VANDEGRIFT—1906-07
Became "Autocycle"
Vandegrift Automobile Co.
Philadelphia, Pennsylvania

VANDEWATER—1911
Vandewater & Co.
Elizabeth, New Jersey
See "Correja"

VANELL STEAM CARRIAGE—1894-95
Frank Vanell
Vincennes, Indiana
Chicago Times-Herald Race entry.

VAN ETTEN SPECIAL—1912-13
S. Van Etten
Columbus, Ohio

VAN RUNABOUT—1909
H. F. Van Wambeke & Sons
Elgin, Illinois
See "Van Wambeke"

VAN STONE CYCLECAR—1914
Los Angeles, California
Cyclecar prototype; front-wheel drive.

VAN WAGONER—1899-1900
Saul & Van Wagoner Co.
Syracuse, New York
1900 became Century Motor Vehicle Co.

VAN WAMBEKE—1908-09
H. F. Van Wambeke & Sons
Elgin, Illinois
See "Van Runabout"

VAPOMOBILE STEAM—1903
Motor Construction Co.

VARSITY—1910
University Motor Co.
Detroit, Michigan

VAUGHAN—1909

Whiteside Wheel Co.
Indianapolis, Indiana

VAUGHAN—1914-15
Vaughan Motor Car Co.
Kingston, New York
November, 1915 reported sold to Remmington Motor Co. See "Guy Vaughan"

VAUGHAN—1921-23
American-Southern Motors Corp.
Irvine Automobile Co.
Greensboro, North Carolina
Designed by Hiram M. Browne.

VAUGHN RUNABOUT—1912
Marion E. Vaughn
Indianapolis, Indiana

VEERAC AIR COOLED—1905
Veerac Motor Car Co.
Springfield, Massachusetts

VELIE—1908-29
Velie Motor Vehicle Co.
Velie Motors Corp.
Moline, Illinois

VERA—1912
Vera Motor Car Co.
Providence, Rhode Island

VERACITY—1899-1904
Dr. L. Anton Smith
Topeka, Kansas
Later Smith Automobile Co.

VER LINDEN—1923
Edward Ver Linden
Detroit, Michigan

VERNON—1910
Vernon Motor Car Co.
Detroit, Michigan

VERNON—1916-23
Vernon Automobile Corp.
Mt. Vernon, New York

VERRETT MOTOR WAGON—1895
N. J. Verrett
Pine Bluff, Arkansas
Chicago Times-Herald Race entry.

VETTA VENTURA—1964-65
Vanguard Motors Corp.
Dallas, Texas

VIALL—1915-26
Viall Motor Car Co.
Chicago, Illinois
Mostly trucks, but some passenger cars.

VICEROY—1911

VICKERS—1910-11
Vickers Auto Car Co.
Vickers Motor Car Co.
Coshocton, Ohio

VICTOR STEAM—1899-1902
Victor Automobile Co.
Bridgeport, Connecticut
A. H. Overman
Chicopee Falls, Massachusetts
Became Overman Automobile Co. Absorbed by Locomobile Co. of America 1902.

VICTOR—1902
Victor Engine & Motor Carriage Co.
San Francisco, California

VICTOR—1906-09
Victor Automobile Co.
Ridgeville, Indiana
Also built "Senator"

VICTOR—1907-09
See "Sunset"
Both names are believed to apply to same vehicle.

VICTOR HIGHWHEELER—1907-11
Victor Motor Car Mfg. Co.
Victor Auto Mfg. Co.
Victor Automobile Co.
St. Louis, Missouri

VICTOR—1912-17
C. U. Stahl
Philadelphia, Pennsylvania
Victor Motor Car Co.
Greenville, South Carolina (1914-15)
Victor Motor Co.
Grubbs Landing, Delaware (1916)
Jenkintown, Pennsylvania (1916)
York, Pennsylvania (1917)

VICTOR CYCLECAR—1913-14
Victor Motor Car Co.
Philadelphia, Pennsylvania

VICTOR CYCLECAR—1914

CODE = ROMAN LETTERS: Complete entry. *ITALICS:* Unsubstantiated entry. (PARENTHESES): Production planned, but not realized.

Richmond Cyclecar Mfg. Co.
Richmond, Virginia
VICTORIA ELECTRIC—1900
Victoria Motor Vehicle Co.
Indianapolis, Indiana
VICTORIETTE—1901
Waltham Mfg. Co.
Waltham, Massachusetts
VICTORMOBILE—1901
Victormobile Co.
Omaha, Nebraska
(VICTOR PAGE)—1921-24
See "Pagé"
Victor Pagé Motors Corp.
Stamford, Connecticut
Both names apply to same vehicle.
VICTORS—1923
VICTOR STEAM—1908-09
*VICTORY
Believed to be "Victor" misspelled.
See "Sunset," Victor Motor Car Co. San
Jose, California. "Sunset" was also called
"Victor."
VICTORY—1913
VICTORY—1920-21
Victory Motor Car Co.
Boston, Massachusetts
Reworked Model T "Ford" using Raja
head, special roadster body and cycle
fenders.
*VICTORY STEAM—1900
Believed to be misspelling of "Victor"
steam, 1899-1902.
VICTRESS—1954
Victress Mfg. Co.
North Hollywood, California
VIDEX—1903
Videx Automobile & Carriage Co.
Marlborough, Massachusetts
VIKING—1908
Viking Company
Boston, Massachusetts
VIKING—1929-30
Olds Motor Works
Lansing, Michigan

Started April 13, 1929.
Companion car to "Oldsmobile."
VIKING—1966
Viking Corp.
Miami, Florida
VIM CYCLECAR—1914
Touraine Co.
Philadelphia, Pennsylvania
VIQUEOT—1905-06
Viqueot Co.
Long Island City, New York
French chassis with American coach work
VIRGINIA—1923
Virginia Motors Inc.
Lynchburg, Virginia
VIRGINIAN—1911-12
Richmond Iron Works Corp.
Richmond, Virginia
First car reported completed September,
1910.
Bankruptcy reported April, 1912
VIXEN CYCLECAR—1914
Davis Mfg. Co.
Milwaukee, Wisconsin
*VOCUR—1918
Believed to be "Vogue" misspelled.
VOGEL—1909
Vogel Car Mfg. Co.
St. Louis, Missouri
VOGHT—circa 1900
Voght Automobile Co.
Newark, New Jersey
VOGUE—1916-23
Vogue Motor Car Co.
Tiffin, Ohio
VOGUL—1918
VOITURETTE CYCLECAR—1914
American Voiturette Co.
Detroit, Michigan
See "Car-Nation"
VOLKSROD DUNE BUGGY—1968
Allied Industries Inc.
Lincoln, Nebraska
VOLOMOBILE STEAM—1902
New York Motor Vehicle Co.

New York, New York
VOLTACAR—1914-16
Cyco-Electric Car Co.
New York, New York
*VOLTRZ—1916
Believed to be misspelling of "Voltz."
VOLTZ—1912-13
Voltz Bros.
Chicago, Illinois
VULCAN—1909
Vulcan Motor Vehicle Co.
Pittsburgh, Pennsylvania
VULCAN—1911
Vulcan Motor Car Co.
Detroit, Michigan
VULCAN—1913-15
Vulcan Mfg. Co.
Vulcan Motor Car Co.
Painesville, Ohio
In hands of receiver January, 1915.

WABASH—1911
Michigan
W.A.C.—1905
Woodburn Automobile Co.
Woodburn, Indiana
WACHMAN—1908
Wachman Auto Mfg.
& Supply Co.
Detroit, Michigan
WACO—1915-17
Western Automobile Co.
Seattle, Washington
WADDINGTON—1904
Locke Regulator Co.
Salem, Massachusetts
WAGENHALS THREE-WHEELER—1910-15
W. G. Wagenhals
Wagenhals Motor Co.
St. Louis, Missouri
Detroit, Michigan
Also built electric cars 1914-15.

WAGNER—1902
Wagner Cycle Co.
St. Paul, Minnesota

WAHL—1913-14
Wahl Motor Car Co.
Detroit, Michigan
Streator, Illinois
Company bought by A. C. Barley in
December, 1914

WALDEN

WALDRON HIGHWHEELER—1909-12
Waldron Runabout Mfg. Co.
Kankakee, Illinois
Waldron Automobile Mfg. Co.
Waldron, Illinois

WALKER STEAM—1899-1903
John B. Walker
Tarrytown, New York

WALKER STEAM—1900-02
Marlboro Automobile & Carriage Co.
Marlboro, Massachusetts

WALKER STEAM—1901
Walker Bros.
New Albany, Indiana

WALKER—1905-06
Walker Motor Car Co.
Detroit, Michigan

WALKER SIX—1910
Walker Motor Car Co.
Detroit, Michigan
Not same as 1905-06 company.

WALKINS—1896
Bay State Motive Power Co.
Springfield, Massachusetts

WALL—1901-04
R. C. Wall Mfg. Co.
Philadelphia, Pennsylvania

WALL—1903
Oak Cycle Co.
Chicago, Illinois

WALLABUG DUNE BUGGY—1968
Hooker Industries
Ontario, California

WALLOF STEAM—1902
E. G. Wallof Machine Works

Minneapolis, Minnesota

WALSCHE ELECTRIC—1902
M. E. Walsche & Sons
Syracuse, New York

WALTER—1902-09
W. Walter
Walter Car Co.
New York, New York
American Chocolate Machinery Co.
New York, New York
Reorganized January 1, 1906´ as Walter
Automobile Co. Trenton, New Jersey. 1909
developed "Planche" car. Roebling Planche
Co. a subdivision.
Became "Mercer."

WALTERS—1900
J. W. Walters
New York, New York

WALTHAM—1900-08
Waltham Mfg. Co.
Waltham, Massachusetts
Became C. H. Metz Co. 1908.
Absorbed American Motors Co.

WALTHAM—1922-23
Waltham Motors Mfg. Inc.
Waltham, Massachusetts
Succeeded Metz Co. See "Metz"

WALTHAM-ORIENT AIR-COOLED—1905-08
Waltham Manufacturing Co.
Waltham, Massachusetts
"Waltham-Orient" succeeded "Orient."
Became "Metz"

WALTHAM STEAMER—1897-1902
Waltham Automobile Co.
Waltham Motor Carriage Co.
Waltham, Massachusetts

WALTHER—1903

WALTOMOBILE—1902
New York, New York

WALTON—1902
W. L. Walton
Neche, North Dakota

WALWORTH—1904-05
A. O. Walworth & Co.
Chicago, Illinois

*WANAMAKER—1893-1903
Wanamaker Stores in Philadelphia and
New York sold "De Dion," "Searchmont,"
"Cadillac," "Ford" and "Studebaker." They
did not build a car under their own name.

WARD CYCLECAR—1914
Ward Cyclecar Co.
Milwaukee, Wisconsin

WARD ELECTRIC—1914-16
Ward Motor Vehicle Co.
New York, New York
Trucks only before and after these dates.

WARD—1920

WARD BUTLER—1913
Ward Butler
Chicago, Illinois

WARD-LEONARD ELECTRIC—1898-1901
Ward-Leonard Electric Co.
Bronxville, New York
Became "Knickerbocker"

WARDWAY—1910-13
Montgomery Ward & Co.
Chicago, Illinois
See "Modoc"

WARNER ELECTRIC—1895

WARNER STEAM—1900
Warner Mfg. Co.
Cleveland, Ohio

WARREN—1905
Warren Automobile Co.
Warren, Pennsylvania

WARREN—1911-14
Rands Mfg. Co.
Detroit, Michigan
Successor to Warren Motor Car Co.
Formerly "Warren-Detroit"

WARREN-DETROIT—1909-11
Warren-Detroit Motor Car Co.
Detroit, Michigan
Became Warren Motor Car Co. 1911.
See "Warren"

WARREN ELECTRIC—1892
Holtzer Cabot Electric Co.
Brookline, Massachusetts
One car produced for Fiske Warren.

CODE = ROMAN LETTERS: Complete entry. *ITALICS:* Unsubstantiated entry. (PARENTHESES): Production planned, but not realized.

WARRINGTON THREE-WHEELER—1901
    Charles Warrington
    West Chester, Pennsylvania
WARRIOR—1963
    Vanguard Products Inc.
    Dallas, Texas
WARWICK—1901-04
    Warwick Cycle Co.
    Warwick Cycle & Automobile Co.
    Springfield, Massachusetts
    Engines supplied by De Dion-Bouton.
WASHBURN ELECTRIC—1896
WASHINGTON—1901
    Washington Auto Vehicle Co.
    Washington, D.C.
WASHINGTON—1907-17
    Carey A. Davis
    Washington, D.C.
    Carter Motor Car Co.
    Washington, D.C. and
      Hyattsville, Maryland
    Became Washington Motor Co.
WASHINGTON—1908-11
    Washington Mfg. Co.
    Washington, Indiana
WASHINGTON—1910
    Washington Motor Vehicle Co.
    Washington, D.C.
WASHINGTON—1921-24
    Washington Automobile Co.
    Cleveland, Ohio
    Washington Motor Car Co.
    Eaton and Middletown, Ohio
    Formerly Union Motor Car Corp.
WASHINGTON—1922-23
    Detroit Motor Co.
    (John A. Barr)
    Detroit, Michigan
WASHINGTON JR. (model)—1921-22
    See "Washington" (1921-24)
    Washington Motor Car Co.
WASHINGTON STEAM—1924
    Washington Motor Co.
    Middletown, Ohio
WASP—1921-25

Martin Wasp Corp.
    Bennington, Vermont
    Also referred to as "Martin-Wasp" but correct designation is "Wasp."
WASSON—1904
    Scott Iron Works
    Baltimore, Maryland
WATCH CITY STEAM—1903-04
    Watch City Automobile Co.
    Waltham, Massachusetts
    Steam racer also built for Louis S. Ross.
WATERLOO—1904-05
    Waterloo Gas Engine Works
    Waterloo Motor Works
    Waterloo, Iowa
    Built under "Duryea" patents.
WATERMAN & CHAMBERLAIN—1900
    Waterman & Chamberlain
    Medford, Massachusetts
WATERS—1899; 1903
    Gilbert Waters
    Newbern, North Carolina
    Two cars produced.
WATERVILLE—1911
WATROUS AIR-COOLED—1905
    Watrous Automobile Co.
    Elmira, New York
    The "Watrous" was a very light two-cylinder car with 85-inch wheel base. Company later built fire engines.
WATSON-CONOVER—1906
    Watson Machine Co.
    Paterson, New Jersey
WATT—1910
    Watt Motor Co.
    Detroit, Michigan
WATT STEAM—1910
    Not same as Detroit car.
WAUKESHA—1908
    Waukesha Motor Co.
    Waukesha, Wisconsin
WAVERLEY ELECTRIC—1899-1903
    Indiana Bicycle Co.
    Indianapolis, Indiana
    Became American Bicycle Co. Automobile

Dept. 1902; International Motor Car Co. 1902-03; Pope Motor Car Co. 1903.
WAVERLEY ELECTRIC—1908-16
    Waverley Company
    Indianapolis, Indiana
    Succeeded "Pope Waverley"
    1916 became Waverley Electric Vehicle Co.
WAYMAN & MURPHY—1903
    Wayman & Murphy
    Chicago, Illinois
    Runabout built from Lindsay-Russell parts.
WAYNE—1895
    Wayne Sulkeyette & Road Cart Co.
    Decatur, Illinois
WAYNE—1904-08
    Wayne Automobile Co.
    Detroit, Michigan
    Absorbed with Northern Motor Car Co. into "E.M.F."
WAYNE—1904-05
    Wayne Works
    Richmond, Indiana
    Became "Richmond"
WEALTHY-HEIGHTS—1917
WEATHERBEE—1907
WEBB—1904
    Webb Co.
    Newark, New Jersey
WEBBERVILLE—1920
WEBB-JAY STEAM—1908-10
    Webb-Jay Motor Co.
    Chicago, Illinois
WEBER—1900
    Weber Gas & Gasoline Engine Co.
    Kansas City, Missouri
WEBER—1905
    Orlando F. Weber Co.
    Milwaukee, Wisconsin
WEBFOOT
WEBSTER—1902
    Webster Automobile Co.
    New York, New York
WEEBER—1902
    C. F. Weeber Mfg. Co.
    Albany, New York

WEIDLEY—1922

*WEIDELY-ENTZ
  Believed to be company which built
  engines only.

WELCH—1904-09
  Welch Motor Car Co.
  Pontiac, Michigan

WELCH-DETROIT—1910-12
  Welch Co. of Detroit
  Welch-Detroit Car Co.
  Detroit, Michigan
  Absorbed by General Motors Corp.
  Became "Marquette"

WELCH-ESTBERG—1906
  Welch-Estberg Co.
  Milwaukee, Wisconsin

WELCH & LAWSON—1895
  Welch & Lawson
  New York, New York

WELCH-PONTIAC—1910-11
  Welch Motor Car Co.
  Pontiac. Michigan
  Formerly Welch Mfg. Co.
  Absorbed by General Motors Corp.

WELCH TOURIST (model)—1901-04
  Chelsea Mfg. Co.
  Chelsea, Michigan
  Reported in receivers hands February, 1904
  Became "Welch"

WELCO SIX

WEL-DOER CYCLECAR—1914
  Welker-Doerr Co.
  Berlin, Ontario, Canada

WELLS—1910-11
  L. J. Wells
  Des Moines, Iowa

WELLS-MEEKER—1900
  Wells-Meeker Motor Vehicle Co.
  Columbus, Ohio

WENTWORTH—1915
  E. E. Wentworth Corp.
  Springvale, Maine

WEST—1895
  H. B. West
  Rochester, New York

One car produced. Used balloon tires.

(WEST & BURGETT)—1899
  William S. West and C. E. Burgett
  Middleburg, New York

WESTBURY—1907

WESTCOTT—1909-25
  Westcott Motor Car Co.
  Richmond, Indiana
  New plant in Springfield, Ohio 1916.

WESTERN—1899-1900
  Western Motor Truck & Vehicle Co.
  Chicago, Illinois

WESTERN—1900
  Western Automobile Co.
  Chicago, Illinois

WESTERN—1917
  Western Motor Car Mfg. Co.
  Denver, Colorado

WESTERN RESERVE—1921
  Western Reserve Automobile Co.
  Warren, Ohio

WESTFIELD STEAM—1902-03
  Charles J. Moore
  Mechanical Tire Co.
  Westfield, Massachusetts
  Unassembled gasoline and steam vehicles.

WESTFIELD—1915
  Westfield Mfg. Co.
  Westfield, Massachusetts

WESTFIELD STEAM—1910

WESTINGHOUSE—1905-10
  Westinghouse Electric & Mfg. Co.
  East Pittsburgh, Pennsylvania
  First cars built in France.
  Receivers appointed October 23, 1907 and
  discharged March 31, 1908.

WESTINGHOUSE ELECTRIC—1901-02
  Westinghouse Electric & Mfg. Co.
  Pittsburgh, Pennsylvania

WESTON STEAM—1896
  Grout Bros.
  Orange, Massachusetts

WEST STEAMER—1897

W.F.S.—1911-12
  W.F.S. Motor Co.

Philadelphia, Pennsylvania

WHALEY-HENRIETTE—1900
  Whaley-Dwyer Co.
  St. Paul, Minnesota

WHARTON—1920-22
  Wharton Motors Co.
  Kansas City, Missouri
  Dallas, Texas
  Also listed in Johnstown, Pennsylvania October, 1922.

WHEEL—1902

WHEELER—1900-03
  E. O. Wheeler & Son
    (O. D. Wheeler)
  Marlboro, Massachusetts
  Three cars built 1900, 1901 and 1902.

WHIPPET—1926-30
  Willys-Overland Co.
  Toledo, Ohio
  See "Willys," "Overland" and "Jeep."

WHIPPLE—1902-03
  Whipple Cycle Co.
  Chicago, Illinois

*WHIT—1899
  Believed to be misspelling of "White" 1899.

WHITCOMB—1900
  G. A. Whitcomb
  Natick, Massachusetts

WHITE—1899
  White Motor Wagon Co.
  Kingston, New York

WHITE STEAM—1901-12
  White Sewing Machine Co.
  White Co.
  Cleveland, Ohio

WHITE GAS—1909-22
  White Co.
  Cleveland, Ohio
  Continued with trucks to date.

WHITE STEAM—1903
  White Steam Wagon Co.
  Indianapolis, Indiana

WHITE—1906-12
  George White Buggy Co.
  Rochelle, Illinois

WHITE—1909
White Motor Car Co.
Cleveland, Ohio
Former "French-American."
No relation to other Cleveland "White."
WHITE CYCLECAR—1914
White Manufacturing Co.
Waterloo, Iowa
WHITEMORE CYCLECAR—1914
Whitemore Co.
Dayton, Ohio
WHITE STAR—1909-11
White Star Automobile Co.
Atlanta, Georgia
Became Atlanta Motor Car Co.
WHITE SWAN CYCLECAR—1914
White Swan Cyclecar Co.
Marysville, California
WHITING—1906-07
Jackson, Michigan
WHITING—1909-12
Whiting Motor Car Co.
Flint Wagon Works
Flint, Michigan
WHITING-GRANT—1911-12
Whiting Motor Car Co.
Flint, Michigan
WHITNEY STEAM—1898-1905
Whitney Mfg. Co.
Lewiston, Maine
Moved to Brunswick, Maine 1902.
WHITNEY STEAM—1896-99
Whitney Motor Wagon Co.
East Boston, Massachusetts
Licensed by Stanley Mfg. Co.
See "Stanley-Whitney" and "McKay."
WHITNEY—1900
E. F. Whitney
Manchester, New Hampshire
WHITNEY—1901
R. S. Whitney
Brunswick, Maine
WHITNEY—1902-03
Whitney Automobile Co.
Whitney Point, New York

WHITNEY STEAMER—1899-1900
Stanley Mfg. Co.
Boston, Massachusetts
Absorbed Whitney Motor Wagon Co.
Boston, Massachusetts 1898-99.
WHYLAND CYCLECAR—1914
Whyland-Nelson Motor Co.
Buffalo, New York
WHYLAND-NELSON—1912-13
Whyland-Nelson Motor Car Co.
Buffalo, New York
WICHITA COMBINATION CAR—1920-21
Wichita Motor Co.
Wichita Falls, Texas
WICK—1902-05
Hugh B. Wick & Co.
Youngstown, Ohio
Used J. M. Quinby Co. bodies.
*WIEDLEY-ENTZ
See "Weidely Entz"
WIEMEYER—1901
J. L. Wiemeyer
St. Louis, Missouri
Built 6 cars.
WIFFLER—1903-05
Wiffler Automobile Co.
Detroit, Michigan
WILCOX—1909-11
H. E. Wilcox Motor Car Co.
Minneapolis Minnesota
Succeeded "Wolfe"
Continued with trucks after 1911.
WILCOX-BACHLE—1905
Church Mfg. Co.
Adrian, Michigan
WILDMAN—1902
Alfred F. Wildman
Morrisville, Pennsylvania
WILKENS—1895
V. H. Wilkens
Evanston, Illinois
WILKENS—1899-1900
Wilkens Automobile Co.
San Francisco, California
WILKINSON—1900-01

John Wilkinson Automobile Co.
Syracuse, New York
WILLARD ELECTRIC—1903-05
Jacob Hoffman Wagon Co.
Cleveland, Ohio
WILLARD STEAM—1905
H. L. Willard
Rutland, Vermont
WILLIAMS AIR-COOLED—1905
D. T. Williams Valve Co.
Cincinnati, Ohio
W. L. Casaday Manufacturing Co.
South Bend, Indiana
WILLIAMS—1906
Williams Motor Carriage Co.
Akron, Ohio
WILLIAMS ELECTRIC—1907-08
Williams Motor Carriage Co.
Williams Electric Vehicle Co.
Cleveland, Ohio
Succeeded "Blakeslee"
WILLIAMS—1914
W. A. Williams
Lima, Ohio
WILLIAMS STEAM—1960-68
The Williams Engine Co.
Ambler, Pennsylvania
Steam prototypes
WILLIAMSPORT—1907
Williamsport Engineering Co.
Williamsport, Pennsylvania
Became Imperial Motor Car Co.
WILLINGHAM—1916
Atlanta, Georgia
WILLOUGHBY-OWEN ELECTRIC—1902
Willoughby-Owen Electric Co.
Utica, New York
WILLS-LEE—1920-21
C. H. Wills & J. R. Lee
Detroit, Michigan
WILLS SAINTE CLAIRE—1921-26
C. H. Wills & Co.
Maryville, Michigan
1923 reorganized as Wills Sainte Claire
Motor Co. Inc.

*ASTERISK: Error corrected from previous list. See introduction to this section for complete code.

WILLYS—1909-42; 1952-63
  Willys-Overland Inc.
  Toledo, Ohio
  Became Kaiser-Jeep Corp.
  Models called "Aero Willys" 1952-54
WILLYS-KNIGHT—1914-33
  Willys-Overland Co.
  Toledo, Ohio
  Succeeded "Edwards-Knight" and
  "Garford-Knight"
WILLYS-KNIGHT—1932
  Willys-Overland Sales Co. Ltd.
  Toronto, Ontario, Canada
WILMOT—1907
  Wilmot Motor & Cycle Mfg. Co.
  Camden, New Jersey
WILSON—1902-05
  Wilson Automobile Mfg. Co.
  Wilson, New York
  Became "LaSalle-Niagara"
WILSON ELECTRIC—1895
  D. H. Wilson
  Chicago, Illinois
WINCHESTER—1909
  Winchester Repeating Arms Co.
  New Haven, Connecticut
WINDSOR—1906
  Windsor Automobile Corp.
  Chicago, Illinois
  Evansville, Indiana
  Became "Simplicity"
WINDSOR—1929-30
  Windsor Corp.
  St. Louis, Missouri
  Subsidiary of Moon Motor Car Co.
  See "Moon," "Diana" and "Hol-Tan."
WINDSOR STEAM CAR—1922-23
  Detroit Steam Motors Corp.
  Detroit, Michigan
  Prototypes for Canadian market only.
WINFIELD—1922
  Winfield Barnes Co.
  Philadelphia, Pennsylvania
  1922 model of "Adelphia."
WING—1896

L. J. Wing & Co.
  New York, New York
WING MIDGET—1922
  Chauncey Wing's Sons
  Greenfield, Massachusetts
  Wing Motors Corp.
  Binghamton, New York
WINNER—1899-1900
  Elgin Automobile Co.
  Chicago, Illinois
WINNER HIGHWHEELER—1907-09
  Winner Motor Buggy Co.
  St. Louis, Missouri
WINNIPEG—1921
  Winnipeg Motor Cars Ltd.
  Winnipeg, Manitoba, Canada
WINONAH—1912
  Bay City, Michigan
WINSLOW—1900-01
  Winslow Motor Carriage Co.
  Doylestown, Pennsylvania
WINTHER—1920-23
  The Winther Motor Co.
  Kenosha, Wisconsin
  Company primarily built trucks.
WINTON—1897-1923
  Winton Motor Carriage Co.
  Winton Motor Car Co.
  Winton Co.
  Cleveland, Ohio
  1896 experimental car. Reorganized as
  Winton Engine Co. (engines only).
WISCO—1909-10
  Wisconsin Carriage Co.
  Wisconsin Motor Co.
  Janesville, Wisconsin
WISCONSIN—1899
  Wisconsin Automobile & Machinery Co.
  Milwaukee, Wisconsin
WISCONSIN CYCLECAR—1914
  Wisconsin Cyclecar Co.
  Milwaukee, Wisconsin
WISNER—1903
  C. H. Wisner
  Flint, Michigan

WIZARD CYCLECAR—1914
  Wizard Motor Co.
  Indianapolis, Indiana
WIZARD—1920-21
  Wizard Automobile Co., Inc.
  Charlotte, North Carolina
  Very few, if any cars built.
  Receiver reported named February, 1921.
  Assets reported sold April, 1922.
WOLFE—1907-09
  H. E. Wilcox Motor Car Co.
  Minneapolis, Minnesota
  Became "Wilcox" April, 1909.
WOLVERINE—1896
  Wolverine Motor Works
  Grand Rapids, Michigan
WOLVERINE—1903-05
  Reid Mfg. Co.
  Detroit, Michigan
  1905 became Wolverine Auto. and Commercial Vehicle Co., Dundee, Michigan
  1906 became Maumee Motor Car Works.
WOLVERINE—1905-06
  Wolverine Automobile & Commercial Vehicle Co.
  Dundee, Michigan
  Became Maumee Motor Car Works, Detroit.
WOLVERINE—1910
  Wolverine Motor Car Co.
  Mt. Clemens, Michigan
  Absorbed by Alpena Motor Car Co.
  See "Alpena"
WOLVERINE (model)—1916-17
  Jackson Automobile Co.
  Jackson, Michigan
WOLVERINE—1916-20
  Wolverine Automobile Co.
  Toledo, Ohio
  1918 name changed to Wolverine Motors Inc. Kalamazoo, Michigan, again in 1919 to Wolverine Motor Car Co., Kalamazoo.
WOLVERINE—1917
  Wolverine Motor Co.
  Battle Creek, Michigan
WOLVERINE—1917

Wolverine Car & Tractor Co.
Wayne, Michigan
WOLVERINE—1927-28
Reo Motor Car Co.
Lansing, Michigan
WOLVERINE-DETROIT—1912-13
Pratt-Carter-Sigsbee Co.
Detroit, Michigan
WONDER—1909
Wonder Mfg. Co.
Syracuse, New York
WONDER—1909
See "Kansas City Wonder"
Wonder Motor Car Co.
Kansas City, Missouri
Both names apply to same vehicle.
WONDER—1917
Wonder Truck Co.
Chicago, Illinois
Touring car only.
WOOD STEAM—1902-03
Wood Vapor Vehicle Co.
Brooklyn, New York
WOOD STEAM—1902-03
J. C. Wood
Wood Vapor Vehicle Co.
Brooklyn, New York
WOODBURN—1912
Woodburn, Indiana
WOOD ELECTRIC—1902
F. R. Wood & Son
New York, New York
WOODILL—1952-58
Woodill Fiberglass Body Corp.
Tustin, California
Two models:
Wildfire sports car, Brushfire one-cylinder
juvenile car.
WOOD-LOCO STEAM—1901-02
Wood-Loco Vehicle Co.
Cohoes, New York
WOOD & MEAGHER—1896
Wood & Meagher
Richmond, Virginia
WOODRUFF—1901-04

Woodruff Automobile Co.
Akron, Ohio
Woodruff Motor Carriage Co.
Cleveland, Ohio
WOODS ELECTRIC—1899-1918
Woods Motor Vehicle Co.
Chicago, Illinois
1916 dual power cars, gasoline and electric.
WOODS ELECTRIC—1900-01
Clinton E. Woods
Woods-Waring Co.
Chicago, Illinois
See "Clinton E. Woods"
WOODS ELECTRIC—1901
Woods Motor Co.
New York, New York
WOODS—1905-07
Woods Motor Vehicle Co.
Chicago, Illinois
WOODS DUAL POWER—1916-18
Woods Motor Vehicle Co.
Chicago, Illinois
WOODS ELECTRIC—1898
Fischer Equipment Co.
Chicago, Illinois
WOODS MAGNETIC—1917
WOODS MOBILETTE CYCLECAR—1914-17
International Cyclecar &
Accessories Co.
Woods Mobilette Mfg. Co.
Woods Mobilette Co.
Chicago, Illinois (office)
Harvey, Illinois (factory)
WOOD STEAMER—1886
J. Elmer Wood
Beverly, Massachusetts
A steam tricycle with single front wheel.
WOODWORTH
WOOLVERTON—1895
G. C. Woolverton
Buffalo, New York
WOONSOCKET—1904
The Woonsocket Co.
Woonsocket, Rhode Island
WORLD—1905

Arnold Schwinn & Co.
Chicago, Illinois
WORLDMOBILE—1928
Service-Relay Motors Corp.
Lima, Ohio
Six-passenger sedan. Of the 7 made, one is
now in the Harrah Collection.
WORTH—1902
J. M. Worth Gas Engine Mfg. Co.
Chicago, Illinois
WORTH HIGHWHEELER—1907-10
Worth Motor Car Co.
Evansville, Indiana
Moved to Kanakee, Illinois 1908.
Reported October, 1910 creditors pressed
bankruptcy. S. R. Hunter, vice-president,
disappeared with car and machinery.
WORTHINGTON—1903-06
Worthington Automobile Co.
New York, New York
Absorbed Berg Automobile Co.
See "Berg" and "Meteor."
WORTHINGTON THREE-WHEELER—1957
Worthington Motor Co.
Stroudsburg, Pennsylvania
WORTHINGTON-BOLLEE—1903-06
See "Worthington"
Worthington Automobile Co.
New York, New York
Both names apply to same vehicle.
WORTHLEY STEAM—1897
C. A. Worthley
Boston, Massachusetts
Reportedly first car to use air brakes.
WOTTRING—1907
Wottring & Son Automobile Works
Prospect, Ohio
Made to order vehicles only.
W & R—1910
WRC—1906-09
WRC Auto Works
El Reno, Oklahoma
WREISNER—1901-04
Nels & Peter Wreisner
Dassel, Minnesota

One-cylinder vehicle started 1901, completed 1904.

WRIGHT—1900
Frederick C. Wright & Co.
Springfield, Massachusetts

WRIGHT—1904
Fred & Ralph Wright
Dayton, Ohio

WRIGHT—1912-13
C. E. Wright & Co.
Norfolk, Virginia

WRIGHT—1925

WRIGHT—1929
Benjamin Wright
Montreal, Quebec, Canada

WYETH—1911
Wyeth Motor Car Co.
Lynn, Massachusetts

*WYKOFF—1912
Company name, not name of vehicle. Company was "Wykoff, Church & Partridge," "Guy Vaughan" manufacturer.

WYLIE ELECTRIC—1894
W .W. Wylie
Ottawa, Illinois

WYMAN—1902
W. A. Wyman
Austin, Indiana

XANDER—1902
Xander Machine & Supply Co.
Reading, Pennsylvania
Gasoline and steam vehicles built to order.

XENIA CYCLECAR—1914-15
Hawkins Cyclecar Co.
Xenia, Ohio

X-RAY SPECIAL—1955
X-Ray Incorporated
Highland Park, Michigan

YALE—1900
Denison Electric Engineering Co.

New Haven, Connecticut

YALE—1902-05
Kirk Manufacturing Co.
Toledo, Ohio
First cars delivered June, 1902.
1903 became Consolidated Mfg. Co.

YALE—1916-18
Saginaw Motor Car Co.
Saginaw, Michigan

YALE FLYER—1913
Cameron Mfg. Co.
West Haven, Connecticut
Prototype only

*YALE-PULLMAN—1917
Believed to be "Yale," Saginaw Motor Car Co. Saginaw, Michigan.

YANK—1950
Custom Auto Works
San Diego, California
Sports cars

YANKEE HIGHWHEELER—1910
Yankee Motor Car Co.
Chicago, Illinois

YANKEE CYCLECAR—1914
Yankee Cyclecar Co.
Chicago, Illinois

YARIAN—1925
Yarian Motors Corp.
Syracuse, New York

YARLOTT—1920
Yarlott Bros. Motor & Car Co.
Ft. Wayne, Indiana

YATES—1914
Toledo, Ohio

YEAGER

YORK—1903-09
York Automobile Co.
York, Pennsylvania
Became York Motor Car Co.
Name changed to "Pullman."
Became Pullman Motor Car Co.

YORK-PULLMAN—1906-07
York Motor Car Co.
York, Pennsylvania

YOUNG—1921

YUKON CYCLECAR—1914
Yukon Automobile Co.
Seattle, Washington

Z

ZACHOW & BESSERDICH EXPERIMENTAL STEAM—1908
Otto Zachow & Wm. A. Besserdich
Clintonville, Wisconsin
Four wheel drive.
Became "Beaver" F.W.D.
Also called "Z & B."

ZEBEL—1909

ZEDER—1922
Zeder Motor Co.
Allyng-Zeder Motors Co.
Cleveland Tractor Co.
Cleveland, Ohio

ZENT—1905-16
Zent Automobile Mfg. Co.
Bellefontaine, Ohio
Name changed to Bellefontaine Automobile Co. 1907.

ZENTMOBILE—1901-02
S. W. Zent
S. W. Zent & Co.
Marion, Ohio

ZEPHYR (model)—1935-41
See "Lincoln"
Ford Motor Co.
Lincoln-Mercury Div.
Detroit, Michigan

ZIEBELL CYCLECAR—1914
A. C. Ziebell
Oshkosh, Wisconsin

ZIMMERMAN HIGHWHEELER—1908-14
Zimmerman Mfg. Co.
Auburn, Indiana
Also built "De Soto" 1913-16.

ZIP CYCLECAR—1913-14
H. A. Huebotter
Zip Cyclecar Co.
Davenport, Iowa

CODE = ROMAN LETTERS: Complete entry. *ITALICS:* Unsubstantiated entry. (PARENTHESES): Production planned, but not realized.

X

165 CARS THAT NEVER TURNED A WHEEL

A Listing of Incorporation Notices and Minor Trade Press Announcements of American Cars Planned but not Produced

● ●

BY STANLEY K. YOST

ACME: Acme Motor Car Co., Worcester, Massachusetts. Announced in *Horseless Age*, April 19, 1905.

ADAMS: Adams Vehicle Co., New York, New York. Announced in *Horseless Age*, November 22, 1905.

ALBANY: Albany Carriage Co., Albany, New York. Announced in *Horseless Age*, November 8, 1905.

ALBANY: Albany Vulcanizing Works, Albany, New York. Announced in *Motor Age*, February 11, 1909.

AMERICAN: American Wagon Co., Wilmington, Delaware. Announced in *Motor Age*, February 11, 1909.

AMERICAN: American Motor Car Co., Canton, Ohio. Announced in *The Automobile*, July 19, 1917.

AMERICAN ELECTRIC: American Electric Manufacturing & Power Co., Dayton, Ohio. Announced in *Horseless Age*, May 10, 1899.

ANSONIA: Ansonia Auto Service Co., New York, New York. Announced in *Motor Age*, February 18, 1909.

ATLANTA: Atlanta Motors Corp., Dover, Delaware. Announced in *The Automobile*, May 31, 1917.

ATLANTIC: Atlantic Automobile Co., Council Bluffs, Iowa. Announced in *Motor Age*, February 18, 1909.

AUTOCART: Autocart Co., Augusta, Maine. Announced in *The Automobile*, August 31, 1911.

AUTOCOACH: Autocoach Co., Wilmington, Delaware. Announced in *Automobile Topics*, December 20, 1913.

BARBER: Barber Auto-Cab & Repair Co., Brooklyn, New York. Announced in *The Automobile*, July 8, 1909.

BASSETT: W. H. Bassett Co., Bridgewater, Massachusetts. Announced in *The Automobile*, December 21, 1911.

BELL: Bell Automobile Corporation, New York, New York. Announced in *Automobile Topics*. April 21, 1917.

BLAKESLEE-BRITTON: Blakeslee-Britton Co., Jersey City, New Jersey. Announced in *Motor Age*, March 3, 1910.

BOURNVILLE: Bournville Motor Car Co., Wilmington, Delaware. Announced in *Automobile Topics*, May 31, 1924.

BROCKSHIRE: Brockshire & Robinson Co., St. Paris, Ohio. Announced in *The Automobile*, November 2, 1911.

BROWN: Brown Motor Vehicle Co., New York, New York. Announced in *Horseless Age*, July 8, 1903.

BUFFALO: Buffalo Specialty Co., Buffalo, New York. Announced in *Horseless Age*, June 7, 1905.

BUFFALO: Buffalo General Manufacturing Co., Buffalo, New York. Announced in *Motor Age*, February 25, 1909.

BUFFALO: Buffalo Motor Vehicle Co., Buffalo, New York. Announced in *The Automobile*, December 7, 1911.

CALIFORNIA: California Motor Car Co., Los Angeles, California. Announced in *Horseless Age*, March 23, 1904.

CARLISLE: Carlisle Body & Gear Co., New Bloomfield, Pennsylvania. Announced in *Motor Age*, November 24, 1904.

CASTLE: Announced in *Automobile Topics*, January 8, 1914.

CHALLENGE: Announced in *Automobile Topics*, January 8, 1914.

CHICAGO: Chicago Car Co., Chicago, Illinois. Announced in *Automobile Topics*, December 12, 1914.

CLIPPER: Announced in *Motor Age*, February 11, 1909.

CLUTS: Cluts Manufacturing Co., Cuba, Illinois. Announced in *Horseless Age*, October 28, 1903.

CONSOLIDATED: Consolidated Motor Co., Lafayette, North Carolina. Announced in *The Automobile*, October 19, 1911.

CROTON: Croton Motor Car Co., Washington, D.C. Announced in *The Automobile*, November, 1912.

CUSTEAD: Custead Motor Vehicle Co., New York, New York. Announced in *Motor Age*, June 17, 1909.

CUSTER: Custer Manufacturing Co., Marion, Indiana. Announced in *Motor Age*, June 3, 1909.

DAYTON: Dayton-Autoelectric Co., Jersey City, New Jersey. Announced in *The Automobile*, June 28, 1902.

DERIGHT: Deright Automobile Co., Omaha, Nebraska. Announced in *Horseless Age*, October 11, 1905.

DERMOT: Announced in *The Automobile*, July 22, 1915.

DETMAR: Detmar Auto Sales Co., New York, New York. Announced in *The Automobile*, December 14, 1911.

DILLARD: Dillard Delivery Co., Brooklyn, New York. Announced in *Motor Age*, January 28, 1909.

EBERMAN: Eberman Auto Appliance Co., Chicago, Illinois. Announced in *Motor Age*, February 11, 1909.

EDGAR: Edgar Motor Delivery, Chicago, Illinois. Announced in *The Automobile*, December 5, 1912.

EDISON: Edison Automobile Co., Washington, D.C. Announced in *The Automobile*, October 17, 1903.

ELEANOR: Eleanor Automobile Co., Washington, D.C. Announced in *Motor Age*, October 6, 1904.

ELGIN: Elgin Motor Co., Elgin, Illinois. Announced in *The Automobile*, November 28, 1912.

EMER: Emer Motor Livery Co., Chicago, Illinois. Announced in *Motor Age*, March 4, 1909.

ENGLAND: England Brothers Motor Car Co., Kansas City, Missouri. Announced in *The Automobile*, December, 1912.

FEDERAL: Federal Motor Car Co., Chicago, Illinois. Announced in *The Automobile*, November 23, 1911.

FEDERAL: Federal Motor & Manufacturing Co., Wilmington, Delaware. Announced in *The Automobile*, March 11, 1915.

FIELD & FEYDT: Field & Feydt Co., Waterbury, Connecticut. Announced in *The Automobile*, March 11, 1915.

FLEISCHMANN: Fleischmann Vehicle Co., New York, New York. Announced in *Motor Age*, March 3, 1910.

FLEXIBLE: Flexible Aeroplane Co., Newark, New Jersey. Announced in *The Automobile*, July 8, 1909.

FORD: Ford Automobile Co., Paterson, New Jersey. Announced in *Motor Age*, January 7, 1909.

FORTMAN: Fortman Manufacturing Co., Philadelphia, Pennsylvania. Announced in *The Automobile*, November 28, 1912.

FOTHERGILL: Fothergill Motor Co., Boston, Massachusetts. Announced in *The Automobile*, November 30, 1911.

GENERAL: General Automobile Co., Jersey City, New Jersey. Announced in *Motor Vehicle Monthly*, September 6, 1900.

GEYLER: Louis Geyler Co., Chicago, Illinois. Announced in *Motor Age*, April 18, 1909.

GLORIA: Gloria Motors Corp., Philadelphia, Pennsylvania. Announced in *Automobile Industries*, February 26, 1920.

GODSHALL: William H. Godshall, Philadelphia, Pennsylvania. Announced in *The Automobile*, October 19, 1911.

GRAND CENTER: Grand Center Motor Car Co., St. Joseph, Missouri. Announced in *Automobile Topics*, December 20, 1913.

GREENSBORO: Greensboro Motor Car Co., Greensboro, North Carolina. Announced in *The Automobile*, November 23, 1911.

GROSSMAN: Emil Grossman Co., New York, New York. Announced in *Motor Age*, March 4, 1909.

HALSEY: Halsey Automobile Co., St. Louis, Missouri. Announced in *The Automobile*, July 19, 1902.

HAMLIN-FOSTER: Hamlin-Foster Co., Portland, Maine. Announced in *The Automobile*, November 9, 1911.

HANOVER: Hanover Automobile Co., Hanover, Pennsylvania. Announced in *Horseless Age*, April 19, 1905.

HARMON: Harmon Manufacturing & Distributing Co., Chicago, Illinois. Announced in *Motor Age*, November 17, 1904.

HARRIS: Harris Car Co., Portland, Maine. Announced in *Motor Age*, April 15, 1909.

HARTFORD: Hartford Automobile & Boat Supply Co., Hartford, Connecticut. Announced in *The Automobile*, January 27, 1910.

HAYDEN: Hayden Automobile Co., Chicago, Illinois. Announced in *The Automobile*, February 6, 1904.

H-E: H-E Motors, Inc., Winston-Salem, South Carolina. Announced in *Motor Age*, June 30, 1927.

HENRICO: Henrico Car Co., Richmond, Virginia. Announced in *Horseless Age*, September 17, 1913.

HERRICK: William Herrick Co., Chicago, Illinois. Announced in *Motor Age*, November 24, 1904.

HOWARD: Howard Automobile Co., San Francisco, California. Announced in *Motor Vehicle Monthly*, September, 1923.

HUB: Hub Auto Carriage Co., Brookings, South Dakota. Announced in *Horseless Age*, August 1, 1900.

IDEAL STEAM: Ideal Steam Automobile Co., South Berwick, Maine. Announced in *Motor Age*, July 19, 1906.

INDEPENDENT: Independent Automobile Manufacturing Co., Sioux Falls, S. Dak. Announced in *Horseless Age*, December 30, 1903.

IRON CITY: Iron City Vehicle Co., Pittsburgh, Pennsylvania. Announced in *Horseless Age*, May 18, 1904.

JACKSON: Jackson Motor Car Co., Jackson, Tennessee. Announced in *The Automobile*, October 17, 1912.

JENNINGS: Jennings Automobile & Manufacturing Co., Jersey City, New Jersey. Announced in *Horseless Age*, December 30, 1903.

JUVENILE: Juvenile Vehicle Manufacturing Co., Chicago, Illinois. Announced in *Horseless Age*, September 23, 1914.

KEELEY-HUNTER: Keeley-Hunter Co., Chicago, Illinois. Announced in *Motor World*, November 9, 1905.

KENWOOD: Kenwood Cart & Garage Co., Beaver Falls, Pennsylvania. Announced in *Motor Age*, February 11, 1909.

KNICKERBOCKER: Knickerbocker Automobile Co., Wilmington, Delaware. Announced in *Motor Age*, April 29, 1909.

KRUPP: Krupp Motor Company, Pittsburgh, Pennsylvania. Announced in *The Automobile*, November 16, 1911.

LENOX: Lenox Motor Car Co., New York, New York. Announced in *Motor World*, July 19, 1906.

LUGREEN: Lugreen Motors Corp., Wilmington, Delaware. Announced in *Automotive Industries*, January 22, 1920.

LUMUND: Lumund Motor Car Corp., Rutherford, New Jersey. Announced in *Motor Age*, February 17, 1910.

LUXAMORE: Luxamore Co., New York, New York. Announced in *Automobile Topics*, May 8, 1915.

MARSHALL: William Marshall Inc., White Plains, New York. Announced in *The Automobile*, November 2, 1911.

McCLINTOCK: McClintock Automobile & Engine Co., Kansas City, Missouri. Announced in *Motor Age*, October 13, 1904.

McLAUGHLIN: McLaughlin & Ashley Motor Co., New York, New York. Announced in *Motor Age*, March, 1909.

M.C.M.: M.C.M. Motor Co., Muncie, Indiana. Announced in *The Automobile*, July 30, 1914.

MERCHANTS: Merchants Motor Car Co., Newark, New Jersey. Announced in *The Automobile*, October 26, 1911.

METEOR: Meteor Automobile Co., Mount Vernon, New York. Announced in *The Automobile*, November 23, 1911.

MEYER: Meyer Motor Car Co., Buffalo, New York. Announced in *Automobile Topics*, November 22, 1913.

MOOER: Mooer Automobile Co., New York, New York. Announced in *The Automobile*, December 14, 1911.

MORGAN: Morgan Manufacturing Co., Chester, Pennsylvania. Announced in *Motor World*, August 4, 1920.

MOSHER: Mosher Automobile Co., Anderson, Indiana. Announced in *Motor Age*, October 7, 1909.

MOULTON-JORDAN: Moulton-Jordan Motor Car Co., Minneapolis, Minnesota. Announced in *Horseless Age*, February 8, 1905.

NABOB: Announced in *The Automobile*, June 14, 1917.

NATIONAL: National Automobile Co., Jersey City, New Jersey. Announced in *Horseless Age*, December 7, 1904.

NATIONAL: National Auto & Motor Co., Portland, Maine. Announced in *Horseless Age*, May 15, 1901.

NATIONAL: National Automobile Co., Philadelphia, Pennsylvania. Announced in *Motor Vehicle Review*, July 17, 1900.

NATIONAL: National Motor Car Co., Jersey City, New Jersey. Announced in *Motor Age*, March 4, 1909.

NEWCOMB: Newcomb Engine Co., Harrison, New York. Announced in *Motor Age*, May 27, 1909.

NEW ERA: New Era Automobile Co., Portland, Maine. Announced in *Motor Vehicle Review*, May 22, 1900.

NEW YORK: New York Motor Works, New York, New York. Announced in *The Automobile*, December 7, 1911.

ORIGINATOR: Originator Manufacturing Co., Jersey City, New Jersey. Announced in *Motor Age*, April 29, 1909.

ORMOND: Ormond Motor Car Co., Brooklyn, New York. Announced

in *The Automobile*, December 21, 1911.

OVERBAUGH-MARTIN: Overbaugh-Martin Motor Car Co., New York, New York. Announced in *Motor Age*, February 25, 1909.

PACIFIC: Pacific Automobile Co., Los Angeles, California. Announced in *Motor Vehicle Review*, June 26, 1900.

PAIGE-TOLEDO: Paige-Toledo Co., Toledo, Ohio. Announced in *The Automobile*, July 30, 1914.

PALACE: Palace Automobile & Machine Co., New York, New York. Announced in *Horseless Age*, July 12, 1905.

PANTHER: Panther Motor Car Co., Kittery, Maine. Announced in *Motor Age*, April 29, 1909.

PARKER: Jerome P. Parker Co., Memphis, Tennessee. Announced in *Motor Age*, March 3, 1910. PARKER: Parker Motor Co., Hartford, Connecticut. Announced in *Motor Age*, September 2, 1909.

PELHAM: Pelham Motors, Inc., Queens, New York. Announced in *Automobile Topics*, January 24, 1914.

PERRING: Perring Manufacturing Co., Cleveland, Ohio. Announced in *The Automobile*, November 7, 1912.

PIQUA: Piqua Motor Co., Piqua, Ohio. Announced in *The Automobile*, September 14, 1911.

PITTSBURGH: Pittsburgh Motor Car Co., Pittsburgh, Pennsylvania. Announced in *The Automobile*, July 30, 1914.

PITTSBURGH: Pittsburgh Motor Car Co., Pittsburgh, Pennsylvania. Announced in *Motor Age*, January 6, 1910.

PREFERRED: Preferred Motor Car Co., Louisville, Kentucky. Announced in *Motor World*, April 21, 1920.

PREMIER: Premier Motor Co., Chicago, Illinois. Announced in *Motor Age*, April 15, 1909.

PRITCHARD-LYON: Pritchard-Lyon Motor Co., Rochester, New York. Announced in *The Automobile*, July 30, 1914.

PROGRESSIVE: Progressive Motor Car Co., Barker, New York. Announced in *The Automobile*, November 28, 1912.

RANTZ: Rantz Motor Co., Bridgeport, Connecticut. Announced in *Motor Age*, February 24, 1910.

RELIANCE: Reliance Automobile Co., Pierre, South Dakota. Announced in *Horseless Age*, September 23, 1903.

RICHARDSON: W. H. Richardson Co., Paterson, New Jersey. Announced in *The Automobile*, March 11, 1915.

RIGA: J. G. Riga & Sons Co., Springfield, Massachusetts. Announced in *Automobile Topics*, January 31, 1914.

SCHWARZ: Schwarz Motor & Truck Tire Co., Detroit, Michigan. Announced in *Horseless Age*, October 19, 1904.

SCRANTON: Scranton Automobile Co., Scranton, Pennsylvania. Announced in *Horseless Age*, September 2, 1914.

SENATOR: Senator Motor Car Co., Pittsburgh, Pennsylvania. Announced in *The Automobile*, August 3, 1911.

SILENT: Silent Motor Car Co., Dover, Delaware. Announced in *Motor Age*, March 3, 1910.

SIMKIN: Simkin Manufacturing Co., Chicago, Illinois. Announced in *The Automobile*, December 21, 1911.

SIMPLEX: Simplex Motor Vehicle Co., Kittery, Maine. Announced in *Motor Vehicle Review*, May 1, 1900.

SOUTHEASTERN: Southeastern Automobile & Machine Co., Hattiesburgh, Miss. Announced in *The Automobile*, December 21, 1911.

SPURR: Spurr Automobile Co., E. Orange, New Jersey. Announced in *Horseless Age*, August 1, 1900.

STANDARD: Standard Automobile Co. of America, Wabash, Indiana. Announced in *Motor Age*, January 20, 1910.

STANDARD: Standard Motor Manufacturing Co., Glen Cove, New York. Announced in *Horseless Age*, May 24, 1899.

STANDARD: Standard Automobile Co., Cleveland, Ohio. Announced in *Horseless Age*, October 11, 1905.

STANDARD: Standard Automobile Co., Louisville, Kentucky. Announced in *Horseless Age*, April 25, 1900.

STAR: Star Automobile Co., Buffalo, New York. Announced in *Horseless Age*, April 13, 1904.

STEARNS CAR: Dr. Stearn's Invalid Auto Co., New York, New York. Announced in *Motor Age*, August 11, 1910.

STERLING: Sterling Vehicle Co., Chicago, Illinois. Announced in *Motor Age*, February 11, 1909.

STEVENSON: William Stevenson Garage Co., Morristown, New Jersey. Announced in *Motor Age*, April 29, 1909.

STRANG: Strang Electro Gasoline Car Co., Kansas City, Missouri. Announced in *Horseless Age*, October 25, 1905.

SUMMIT: Summit Garage, Summit, New Jersey. Announced in *Horseless Age*, October 18, 1905.

SWAN: Swan Motor Car Co., Indianapolis, Indiana. Announced in *The Automobile*, June 10, 1915.

SYRACUSE: Syracuse Motor Car Co., Syracuse, New York. Announced in *Horseless Age*, December 7, 1904.

THIBERT: Thibert Manufacturing Co., Worcester, Massachusetts. Announced in *The Automobile*, May 3, 1917.

THOMPSON-SCHOEFFEL: Thompson-Schoeffel Co., New York, New York. Announced in *Horseless Age*, May 24, 1905.

TITUS: Fred J. Titus Co., Newark, New Jersey. Announced in *Motor Age*, May 27, 1909.

TURK & BROWN: Turk & Brown, Inc., Rochester, New York. Announced in *The Automobile*, December 14, 1911.

TUTTLE: D. M. Tuttle Co., Baldwinsville, New York. Announced in *Horseless Age*, September 23, 1903.

TYGARD: Tygard Engine Co., Plainfield, New Jersey. Announced in *Motor Age*, August 19, 1909.

UNION: Union Automobile Co., Baltimore, Maryland. Announced in *Horseless Age*, March 21, 1900.

UNION: Union Motor Car Co., Newark, New Jersey. Announced in *Motor Age*, August 26, 1909.

UNIVERSAL: Universal Automobile Co., E. Orange, New Jersey. Announced in *Motor Age*, August 5, 1909.

VERA: Vera Motor Car Co., Boston, Massachusetts. Announced in *The Automobile*, November 9, 1911.

VIKING: Viking Manufacturing Co., New York, New York. Announced in *The Automobile*, October 10, 1912.

VIRGINIA: Virginia Automobile Co., Norfolk, Virginia. Announced in *Horseless Age*, December 7, 1904.

VIRGINIA: Virginia Automobile Co., Alexandria, Virginia. Announced in *Motor Vehicle Review*, April 24, 1900.

WACO-SCHAFFER: Waco-Schaffer Motor Co., Detroit, Michigan. Announced in *Automobile Topics*, May 29, 1915.

WASHINGTON: Washington Automobile Co., Tacoma, Washington. Announced in *Motor Age*, November 17, 1904.

WEAVER-EBLING: Weaver-Ebling Automobile Co., New York, New York. Announced in *Motor Age*, February 18, 1909.

WEIT-HORTON: Weit-Horton Manufacturing Co., Detroit, Michigan. Announced in *The Automobile*, December 21, 1911.

WELLS: R. C. Wells Manufacturing Co., Fondulac, Wisconsin. Announced in *The Automobile*, November 28, 1912.

WHITEFIELD: Whitefield Motor Car Co., New York, New York. Announced in *Automobile Topics*, August 1, 1914.

WIDMAYER: F. B. Widmayer Co., Albany, New York. Announced in *Motor Age*, January 7, 1909.

XI

WHEELS FOR COMMERCE

A History of American Motor Trucks

BY JOHN MONTVILLE

INTRODUCTION: SOME DEFINITIONS

When viewed within the context of history, the birth and evolution of the commercial motor vehicle industry in the United States emerges as the product of both the technological advances and Yankee ingenuity that made it possible and the expanding sociological and economical factors that made it necessary. Like the railroad industry before it, the trucking industry grew out of a self-perpetuating cycle: Industrial advancement had led to the proliferation of manufacturing with its concomitant increase in the quality and quantity of goods, which in turn prompted the need for an effective transportation network for the conveyance of these goods locally and nationwide; automotive engineers set out to meet these needs, abetted by an informed public and government favorably disposed to the enacting of viable motor vehicle laws and to the building of an interlinking system of roads and highways. Thus the trucking industry was caused to be and was affected by a series of historical events. It, in turn, caused to be or affected other historical events. It is that which we shall explore here: the place of the truck in history.

Horses measure their opponent, the 1904 Moyea, prior to the Automobile Club Service Test of 1904. The Moyea won. (L)

The wry observation that, in the best Platonic tradition, the *idea* of trucks existed before a single commercial vehicle rumbled across American roads is rooted in fact. Indeed, the very word "truck" is derived from the Greek "trokhos," meaning "wheel." Although over the years it carried a number of other somewhat related meanings, the word became most widely used to define heavy horse-drawn wagons. Thus, with the advent of the motorized commercial vehicles in the late Nineteenth and early Twentieth Century, the word "motor" was placed in front of "truck" to distinguish the self-propelled from the horse-drawn type of vehicle. Interestingly, different words were used regionally to mean the act of transporting goods by truck — and some are used to this day. Midwesterners in the Detroit area use the word "cartage," while Californians refer to "drayage" — both obviously holdovers from horse-drawn days. The word "trucking," however, has become generally accepted in all parts of the country to mean the over-the-road shipment of general merchandise or freight.

Thus it is that from the simple Greek derivation, the word "truck" has evolved to embrace a multiplicity of vehicles and a gigantic industry which has risen to become a vital part of American life. This is the story of how it happened.

The 1901 Columbia Electric ambulance. (L)

EARLY DEVELOPMENTS

Probably the first American to demonstrate that a self-propelled road machine was a valid proposition was Oliver Evans of Philadelphia — and what he built was in essence a commercial vehicle, although admittedly not intended for the road. In 1804 he obtained a contract from the city fathers of Philadelphia for a dredging scow, all twenty tons of which he built. To convey this behemoth from his shops to the designated spot in the Delaware river, he cleverly added wheels and used its steam engine to propel it through the streets to river bank. Though he would spend the rest of his life vigorously promoting the idea of steam road transport, it was of little avail, the dredge being the only steam vehicle he built. Like so many forward-thinking inventors, he died practically penniless in 1819. But his ideas didn't die with him. Others would take up where he left off.

From 1829-1830 William T. James of New York built two experimental steam road vehicles, but he was to eventually turn his talents to the railway industry, becoming one of America's foremost locomotive designers. A couple of decades later, however, another New Yorker would confine his efforts strictly to the road. In the 1850's and 1860's Richard Dudgeon took the steam road vehicle several practical steps further, but despite his desire to go into manufacture he unhappily found no market. Only two versions of his steam carriage were built. Yet he remained adamant about the future of the road vehicle — and particularly its commercial applications, as witness his words in 1870: "Let no one suppose I intend to do without railways where there is business to sustain them. But this is not the case with most short lines and branches, and in such places I would use what would be far better — steam carriages."

Although Dudgeon rather trenchantly forecast the early development of motor truck transport, others in those days foresaw quite different commercial applications for the self-propelled vehicle. One of these, Major General Joseph R. Brown, Indian Agent for Minnesota, decided in the late 1850's that he could win the West with his New York-built steam tractor, designed to pull covered wagons across the plains. This tractor-cum-wagon-train was shipped to Nebraska City in 1862 where it undertook its maiden journey to Denver, but unfortunately it broke down seven miles outside of the Nebraska City limits and attempts to revive it proving hopeless, the project was abandoned and the tractor scrapped. Later a bronze tablet was attached to the Burlington Railroad station in Nebraska City to commemorate Brown's ambitious efforts.

Other efforts, equally ambitious, proved more practical. In the 1870's, for example, the Amoskeag Manufacturing Company of Manchester, New Hampshire, built and sold steam-powered fire fighting equipment which found service in the New England area up to the early 1900's. And, of course, steam traction engines developed in the late 1880's to handle plowing and threshing work became increasingly popular on farms between the years 1890 and 1910.

These early experiments — be they failures or successes — reflected an awareness of the growing need for viable methods of commercial transportation among enlightened inventors of the day. It would be, as Thomas A. Edison told the *New York World* in 1895 ". . . only a question of time when the carriages and trucks in every larger city will be run with motors."

And the time was drawing nigh. Indeed two events in 1895 offered a foretaste of what was to come. The first was the historic contest from Chicago to Evanston, Illinois, sponsored by the *Chicago Times-Herald*. Although this in itself did not change the national attitude toward the horseless contraption, it did indicate that the self-propelled vehicle might seriously be regarded as a potential solution to the nation's growing transportation needs. It was an effective beginning, and its repercussions were wide-reaching. The very announcement of the contest had been followed by another significant event. It was the publication of the first American automotive journals, devoted to recording the major and minor automotive news items of the day for the burgeoning ranks of inventors and mechanics who desired nothing more than to keep abreast of the latest developments in domestic and foreign automotive technology.

The most successful of these journals was *The Horseless Age* and glancing through its introductory November issue, it is apparent that already some three hundred self-propelled vehicles were under construction. Of these, the issue noted the progress of two experimental commercial vehicles. One, built by Richard F. Stewart of Pocantico Hills, New York, used a two horsepower Daimler motor and internal gear drive. The other, a "business wagon" under construction in the Stamford, Connecticut, shop of piano manufacturers Schleicher & Sons, was not described in detail, but the vehicle promised to be quite heavy, its rear wheels alone weighing almost one hundred pounds apiece. Later, of course, Schleicher & Sons would build heavy duty trucks in Ossining, New York, but in 1895 that idea could only have been a dream, though not a fanciful one. The market for commercial vehicles was but a few years away.

*This Nadig truck was built in 1901
by two brothers in Allentown, Pennsylvania.* (N)

The victorious Moyea during the five-day ACA Test of 1904. (B)

This 1905 Knox tower wagon
was used to repair trolley wires. (L)

This 1907 Model H 20 hp White
served the Glidden Tour that year. (L)

This two-cylinder 1907 Rapid
delivered newspapers during the 1909 Glidden Tour. (L)

The 1907 Torbenson. (L)

If the puff and clatter of self-propelled fire engines had already become a fact of life for citizens of some American cities by 1897, the idea of having one's goods delivered by self-propelled truck was still rather foreign to both supplier and consumer. But in the summer of that year a Chicago dry goods merchant took possession of two electric delivery wagons from the American Electric Vehicle Company, also of Chicago. This was apparently the first commercial vehicle sale in America. It did not lead immediately to an avalanche of others, but it was the beginning. By 1898 the Winton Motor Carriage Company in Cleveland had eight delivery wagons under construction, powered by six horsepower, single-cylinder gasoline engines. And in Brooklyn Andrew L. Riker proudly exhibited the electric delivery truck he had built for B. Altman & Company of New York City. A vigorous advocate of electric propulsion, having started in the electric motor business in the late 1880's and having built an electric tricycle in 1894, Riker soon had his Riker Electric Motor Company building what turned out to be the first real heavy duty trucks — in 1898 and 1899. About the same time the International Power Company was incorporated to produce compressed-air trucks for subsidiary companies in a few East Coast cities. The inventor of this unorthodox vehicle, Walter H. Knight, saw at least one of his ten-ton trucks tried in New York City before the scheme was shown to be impractical and abandoned.

The 1913 Knox-Martin three-wheeled tractor. (B)

The 1910 two-cycle three-cylinder Chase, a popular vehicle in rural areas. (B)

The 1911 Reliance at left sported the innovation of the year—pneumatic tires. (L)

The 1912 Alco stake-bodied truck (below left) was built by the American Locomotive Co. (B)

The four-cylinder 1912 Grabowsky (below) featured an engine removable from the front. (B)

The 1912 I.H.C. bookmobile pictured below right had an air cooled two-cylinder engine. (B)

Roll-up side curtains were a feature of this 1912 Argo electric. (L)

Like the automobile itself, the most successful commercial vehicles — insofar as sales were concerned — during this period were electrics, with gasoline vehicles demonstrating barely an inkling of their ultimate potential. In view of the earlier experimentation, it might seem rather surprising that steam did not power these earliest marketed trucks. But as time ran out for the Nineteenth Century, it would again come to the fore — briefly — as some American merchants rode part way to prosperity with a full head of steam.

Although steam was certainly the prime motive power for large trucks in England during this era, its development in America for commercial vehicles had been quite slow and rather unspectacular. A bit of impetus was provided in November of 1900 when the Mobile Company of America built a ramp on top of Madison Square Garden and demonstrated the power and flexibility of steam vehicles to the viewers of America's first automobile show. They followed this with three years' production of light steam trucks of 400 and 1000 pounds capaci-

ty. For a while, too, American steam proponents traded on the English experience. The British Thornycroft steam wagon was produced during the earliest years of the decade by the Cooke Locomotive Works of Paterson, New Jersey. The Coulthard six-ton steam truck also enjoyed a brief vogue, the vehicles being imported in 1903 and later, in 1905 and 1906, a few being built in Peabody, Massachusetts.

In retrospect, it seems that the American steam truck suffered growing pains commensurate with its very size and ungainliness. A case in point is that of the Herschmann steam truck built by the Columbia Engineering Works in Brooklyn, New York. Beginning in 1901 the Adams Express Company of Manhattan began testing the ponderous, coal-burning Herschmann on the streets of New York City to the shock and considerable outrage of the citizenry. In lurid prose the *New York Journal* of February 17, 1901, described how the vehicle "terrorizes New York," demanding that the owners of this "mechanical crazy-quilt" ". . . be requested that it be kept in the stable or else run it into the river."

The 1912 Little Giant—before it grew. (B)   *The 1913 FWD Model B.* (B)

Ford delivery trucks, ready to roll for Wanamaker's, 1912-13.

The 1914 Garford with Roman dashboard and cab-over-engine design. (B)

Such unfavorable conclusions did not bode well for the steam truck, nor undoubtedly did the fact that the large heavy duty versions probably did sound and perhaps perform like a derailed locomotive. The future of the steam truck was limited. No doubt many steam proponents shared the fate of Ralph L. Morgan of Worcester, Massachusetts. His ten-ton steam wagon of 1903-1904 was typical of its day, reflecting the British school of thought. By 1909, however, though externally the British influence was still there, an important change had occurred under the hood: the Morgan truck had become gasoline-powered.

The aforesaid Mr. Morgan, however, was nothing if not a forward-thinking man in another area. Early in 1903 he sent a letter to the Automobile Club of America in which he indicated that it was high time a public test was held to show the reliability of commercial motor vehicles. Given the temper of the times, it was a brave letter to write.

The concept of the automobile as a rich man's toy was so firmly rooted in public consciousness during the early 1900's that, inevitably, the commercial vehicle was affected as well. For if few besides doctors were willing to consider the automobile as a necessary adjunct to their work, even fewer business men were willing to gamble on buying a motorized truck. Only the most prominent merchants used them regularly, and even they appreciated trucks more for their advertising value than for any of the more practical considerations. Obviously, dramatic proof of the truck's virtues was needed before small businessmen would be convinced to part with some of their hard-earned capital to buy one. The 1903 Commercial Vehicle Trials, sponsored by the A.C.A., were intended to be just such a proof.

The 1913 Kelly, with its characteristic sloping hood. (L)

Although this type of test had been held in France as early as 1897, American truck manufacturers had not felt confident enough to stake their reputations on their products until this first two-day trial held on May 20-21, 1903. Moreover, some of the most prominent manufacturers of the day did not enter, though eight other hardy firms mustered eleven trucks between them for the event. Of these, six were propelled by steam, four by gasoline and one by electricity. The results of these tests were encouraging, if inconclusive. Many of the vehicles, including three light delivery trucks, the Waverley electric, the Knox gasoline and the Mobile steamer, performed to the satisfaction of their owners, and the huge Herschmann steamer belonging to Adams Express turned in a nearly flawless, if noisy, two-day run. Although some of the heavy

trucks ran into difficulties, the overall verdict was in favor of the truck as a pragmatic answer to America's transportation needs. Only the thorny problem of motive power remained to be settled, and that, too, appeared to be working itself out by the process of elimination: not one steam-propelled vehicle would participate in the succeeding truck trials.

Influenced either by the success of the previous year's truck trials or by continued pressure from some quarters of the incipient commercial motor vehicle industry, the National Association of Automobile Manufacturers decided to back the 1904 commercial vehicle tests sponsored by the A.C.A. Wisely, they appointed a committee to study the most efficient means of motor truck testing before awarding the

A 1914 Mack at work on New York's BMT subway at Herald Square. (L)

project their unqualified approval. The result of this study was the most equitable and practical method of testing the eight electric, eight gasoline and one gas-electric vehicles that entered.

The Automobile Club Service Test — as this year's trials were called — was one that placed competing trucks in actual service for the American and Wescott Express companies, hauling freight within the environs of New York City while a test committee kept careful records of cost and time. Accordingly, one work week of five days was allotted for completion of the test.

Few heavy duty trucks participated, leaving the field primarily open to

vehicles of one ton or less capacity. Most of these successfully completed the test, with the Oldsmobile, Columbia, Cantano, Consolidated (Moyea), Fischer gas-electric and Union trucks winning first prizes in various load-carrying classes. The Knox truck, too, though it did not qualify for a first prize, performed well, as it had in the 1903 event.

The test results verified the motorized truck's claim to supremacy over horse-drawn vehicles in the areas of speed and economy, but even in the face of such overwhelming success, manufacturers remained convinced of their imminent ruin if but a single truck ever failed in public trials. At the expense of reason, their fears prevailed — the 1904 event was the last one of this type held for a number of years.

The 1914 front-drive Walter, demonstrating its power and traction. (B)

The 1914 Saurer, with high-lift body for coal delivery. (L)

Somewhere between 1904 and 1907, when a growing segment of press and public ceased to regard the motorized truck merely as a mutation of the automobile, a proportional amount of attention began to be paid to this form of transport as a legitimate vehicular type in its own right. But gratifying as it was, this early recognition was not necessarily followed by a boom in the number of truck manufacturers. Far from it: The companies devoted exclusively to the manufacture of trucks rarely managed to keep afloat, developmental costs and limited demand most often accounting for their all-too-brief life spans.

But neither of those factors posed particular problems for the successful automobile manufacturer, and by 1906 such firms as Cadillac, Mitchell, Oldsmobile and Premier (among many others) found themselves successfully in pursuit of the commercial vehicle market. Indeed most automobile manufacturers offered at least one delivery body on a stock passenger car chassis — that was simple enough — and a few even came up with special truck designs, Packard being a notable example with its marketing of a truck chassis in 1905. Yet, if the realities of manufacture seemed to favor the automobile producer in the commercial vehicle field, at least one specialized truck and bus manufacturer managed to survive this period with a vengeance: The Mack Brothers Motor Car Company moved from Brooklyn, New York, to Allentown, Pennsylvania, in 1904. They needed more room.

Increased awareness of the motor truck's potential also prompted the appearance of the first truck shows and periodicals. Like many other publishing ventures of the day, the progress of truck periodicals was, at best, erratic: So significant was the March, 1906, publication of *The Commercial Vehicle*, a monthly, and the weekly *Power Wagon*, that the birth of the motor truck industry in America is often calculated from that date forward. But *Motor Traffic*, first published in April of 1906 lasted only until January of 1907.

Mixed results were also the consequence of the first motor truck shows. Encouraged by favorable public reaction to the separate grouping of trucks at the annual New York and Chicago auto shows, promoters arranged for the first exclusive showing of trucks to take place in Chicago from November 30 to December 7, 1907. Twenty-nine different commercial vehicle makes were displayed at this event, but attendance was so disappointingly low that nothing like it was attempted again until 1911, the year in which public approbation could no longer be doubted.

Logistical problems of the chicken-or-the-egg variety pose themselves when we try to determine whether mounting truck sales during the years of 1908-1910 contributed to standardization of truck design or if, conversely, a uniform application of good design principles boosted commercial vehicle sales during the same three-year period. In any case, it is obvious that manufacturers were now consolidating the knowledge and experience accrued in the early years of truck development.

One of the first systems to be found inadequate was the then-popular friction drive transmission. This and planetary transmission were replaced by the positive sliding gear system which had proved more

practical because of its non-slip features. But the major design innovation of the era was the adoption of a European idea. When a three-ton Packard appeared in 1909 with its engine jutting continental-style beyond the driver's cab, it marked the beginning of a trend away from the cab-over-engine fashion known as "American." Henceforth drivers would no longer be required to sit directly over the motor; for comfort and safety's sake it rode before the driver in most heavy duty trucks built after 1909. White adopted this style in the same year, followed by Peerless in 1910. Pierce-Arrow's worm-drive model also featured a protruding engine, but another company successfully bucked the growing trend for a number of years: A two-cylinder Autocar introduced in 1908 survived through 1926 with yearly power increases, but to the very end its cab remained firmly anchored above the engine.

The Jeffery "Quad" snowfighter, 1916. (L)

New three-ton Rikers, delivering army supplies in Texas, 1916. (L)

Another controversy was brewing between design-conscious truck companies of that era. This was over the comparative desirability of the "assembled" versus "manufactured" truck. The former made its impact felt in 1910 with the introduction of the popularly-priced Federal truck. Other "assemblers" quickly joined the fold, claiming as the advantages for their method of production the fact that their vehicles were built up of parts made by specialists and that the availability of those parts would never be a problem. The "assembled" Acme truck—Continental engine, Cotta transmission, Timken axles—for example, used the slogan "the truck of proved units." The motor truck "manufacturers," on the other hand, had a few telling arguments of their own; as the producers of most of the components that went into their vehicles, they could lay claim to quality control over all parts, as well as a balance of design in the construction of the complete vehicle. And so the argument went — and would go for some time to come.

It seems that in the history of any subject, there is always a point at which independent trends converge and consolidate themselves into a few, durable institutions. In the history of trucks, 1911 marks the point at which many small manufacturers began to merge, forming powerful trucking conglomerates to administer their production and sales.

The General Motors Truck Company led the field in that year by incorporating to market the Rapid and Reliance trucks. These, together with the Randolph name, had been acquired for them by William C. Durant in 1909 and 1910, and were joined by Lansden in 1911 when that Newark company added its seven-year-old electric truck to the infant GM combine. By 1912, all General Motors trucks were being marketed under the trade name GMC, including their electrics, which were built until 1916.

So significant did the amalgamation of trucking interests seem to financiers in 1911 that the International Motor Company was created by a bloc of Wall Street bankers who successfully engineered the merger of the Mack Brothers Motor Car Company and the American branch of the Saurer Motor Company. These same businessmen saw their investment pay off early in the following year when annexation of the Hewitt Motor Company, the first successful builders of ten-ton trucks, made IMC the producer of three outstanding heavy duty trucks: Mack, Saurer and Hewitt.

Corporate pride in these big three was more than justified. The Saurer, for example, a Swiss truck built in four and a half and six-ton models at Plainfield, New Jersey, completed a two-legged transcontinental run with unprecedented ease in 1911. Beginning in Denver on March 4, the truck reached the West Coast, was shipped by rail to Pueblo, Colorado, and started for New York on June 12. Less than two months later—on August 10—the Saurer arrived at its destination with barely a scratch.

Delivery trucks like the 1916 Vim shown above are often
restored and preserved by collectors. (B)
Below: a 1916 Ford, one of the last brass-radiator T's.
The 1917 two-cylinder engine-under-seat Autocar at top
right became popular with contractors. (B)
Center right: a 1917 U.S.A., nicknamed "Liberty." (B)
Originally an army truck, the 1918 Pierce-Arrow (below
right) was sold by the Government after the war. (B)

Soldiers called this 1918 Model AC Mack "The Bulldog." (L)

The 1920 Reo "Speedwagon"—with its gas tank over dashboard.

Attuned to the publicity potential of such runs, other manufacturers were quick to respond to the Saurer's implied challenge. A three-ton Packard was the first to take up the gauntlet, spanning the distance between New York and San Francisco in forty-seven days — from July 8th to August 24th of 1911. Like the Saurer before it, it did not carry an actual payload, but reserved its body space for camping, rigging, spare parts and other supplies needed for the trip. A three-ton load of silk soap, however, was the cargo an Alco truck carried the following year in its transcontinental trip from Philadelphia to Petaluma, California.

Although the transcontinental treks can certainly be viewed as meritorious and reasonable, even prudent methods of promotion for the truck industry, the same cannot be said for some of the practices initiated by the sales forces of many manufacturers. With the entrance of more and more automobile manufacturers into the commercial motor vehicle field, competition became quite fierce, and the result was a good many sales organizations utilizing such dubious sales techniques as extending one-day demonstrations to a month or more and guaranteeing a fifty percent over-load capacity for their vehicles. The former was simply not particularly good business, but the latter was potentially very dangerous. Finally the National Association of Automobile Manufacturers was forced to take a hard look at the sales practices of its member firms, and in 1912 that organization required its members to attach a plate to their trucks' dashboards reading in part: "Caution — overloading or overspeeding will void your warranty." No doubt the NAAM's intervention would ultimately improve the truck industry's image among potential buyers — obviously questionable sales practices had done nothing to enhance it — but they were too late to save forty-four truck makes from extinction in 1913. Such was the attrition in those days.

Significant as it was, the credibility gap was only one of many problems which beset commercial vehicle manufacturers at this time. There were engineering difficulties as well, with trouble developing from the inability of the then-current solid tires to support loads over six tons. Despite sales promises, it was a simple fact that truck tires tended to become squeezed along the rim when heavily laden, causing their rubber to fatigue and break up. Three solutions — the use of steel tires on large wheels (illegal on most highways), the invention of the Kelly-Springfield sectional block tire and finally molded solid tires on steel rims of sufficient size — did much to relieve the strain.

The problem of providing traction under off-highway conditions was met by the development of specialized trucks designed to absorb heavy loads with a minimum of wheel wear. The three-wheeled Knox-Martin tractor invented by C. H. Martin of Springfield, Massachusetts, for example, was built during the years of 1912 through 1915 to motorize heavy horse-drawn wagons. This same vehicle later proved invaluable in pulling the heavy horse-drawn steam pumping engines used by fire departments. The four wheel drive truck was also designed to meet the challenge of better-than-capacity loads; although some firms had experimented with all wheel drive trucks, it was not until the Four Wheel Drive Auto Company of Clintonville, Wisconsin, marketed their Model B three-ton truck in 1913 that such vehicles gained acceptance. Another truck, the Jeffery Quad, introduced in 1913, was capable of braking and steering with all four wheels.

Ironically, through these years and the transition from promise to productivity, truck manufacturers could but be unaware that their efforts would prove so vital to a challenge that lay just ahead of them. A few years later, Earl Curzon of the British War Cabinet would state flatly that the First World War could not have been won without the great fleets of motor vehicles supplied by the motor industries.

A fleet of 1918 Ward-Electric "Specials" in Baltimore. (B)

The 1922 Diamond T—an assembled truck with a reputation for quality. (L)

Yet if the truck played such a vital role in the war effort, it was commensurate with the far-reaching effects that the results of that war effort would have upon the development of motor freight transport itself. Some of these effects were immediate; others would influence the trucking industry for years to come.

Nineteen-fourteen had found the trucking industry faced with a business recession, a sufficient problem in itself, but compounded, too, by the continuous influx of new makes on the market which had resulted in the inevitable: overproduction. This situation was eased, however, just two months after the outbreak of war as the French and British war departments began placing truck orders with Packard, Pierce-Arrow, Peerless and White. In 1915 more orders followed for standard army trucks, special four wheel drive trucks and tractors to be used on the muddy wastes of the western and eastern fronts. The trucking industry boomed. So great was the domestic and foreign demand for trucks that models in stock and spare parts were soon depleted, requiring many plants to double their work shifts. At its peak in 1916, the stateside demand for motor trucks gave birth to a whole new industry devoted to the manufacture of specially-designed frame extensions to convert old passenger cars, especially Fords, into trucks. That industry was short-lived, however; the introduction of Ford's one-ton truck in 1917 effectively killed its reason for being. Helping, too, was the introduction the following year by Dodge of a lighter truck model of their own.

Following American involvement in the war in 1917, an Army plan to design two standardized truck models was formulated with support from the War Industry Board. The first five-ton "Class B" or "Liberty" truck was finished for testing by Gramm-Bernstein on Sunday, October 7, 1917. A "Class A" truck of two-tons capacity was also readied for action, but only the Liberty truck realized large-scale production. Although the government's influence on the trucking industry during these years was widespread, the most telling effect was no doubt the result of Washington's insistence upon uniformity in truck design. This forced many small manufacturers to cooperate in the design of interchangeable components, and the effects of this would soon be felt in civilian truck design as well.

The war and the now booming domestic economy caught the Iron Horse of America quite unprepared, and despite the fact that the railroads were taken over by the United States Railroad Administration after this country's entrance into the conflict, it was evident that neither military nor civilian needs for transport could be met by rail. The trucking industry drove right in.

The increased use of the motor truck for short haul freight between cities had as much effect on the truck as on the trucking industry itself. The importance of speed in the delivery of vital war materials was the principal impetus for the large-scale adoption of pneumatic tires on trucks during this period. Prior to about 1917 solid tires had been standard equipment on all truck models over one ton in capacity; a practical pneumatic had not been developed, nor really had there been much need for one. Since large trucks had rarely been sent far beyond city limits, the fact that solid tires restricted truck speed to about fifteen miles an hour was scarcely detrimental. What truck travelled faster than that within a city anyway? However, the increased range of travel demanded of heavier trucks, plus the need to protect the truck and its contents against bumpy rural roads, together with the urgent military requirement of quick delivery — all dictated a change in tires. By 1919 pneumatic tires were optional equipment on most two-ton trucks, and within a few years the solid-tired variety could be found on only trucks over three tons in capacity.

The rail car shortage which had put the trucking industry so dominantly into the short haul freight picture also saw the rapid development and use of the semi and full trailer. Originally designed to allow for the delivery of two loads — one in the truck itself and another in a trailer attached — it was soon found that the idea had a time-saving advantage as well. The driver with tractor could drop off loaded trailers and pick up empty ones without the wait for loading or unloading. Since speed in delivery was so vital to the war effort, this practice, needless to say, found quick favor.

The 1923 White. (L)

The 1923 MacDonald. (L)

The 1925 Doane low bed. (B)

397

This 1922 Packard, with utility body, was used for repairing power lines. (B)

The war had certainly proved the worth of the truck, and that worth had brought with it prosperity for the truck industry. How dearly they would have to pay for the brisk sales enjoyed during the war years could not have been foreseen by manufacturers before 1919. But between that year and 1921 the surfeit of heavy duty war trucks which glutted the market slowed production of new vehicles to a trickle. Despite this — and the fact that surplus army trucks were being offered cheaply by the U.S. government to state and local agencies for road maintenance, thus cutting off a potential lucrative market — optimistic new truck producers plunged into the already overcrowded field. They would not have an easy time of it. Domestically the situa-

tion was unpromising, and the widespread instances of foreign-owned army trucks being dumped on the U.S. market by speculators only made matters worse. Plainly, this situation coupled with the postwar business recession of 1921 spelled trouble for the truck industry.

In an effort to meet the unexpected competition, many truck producers cut their prices drastically only to face the grim prospect of receivership or, worse, total collapse. Peerless Motor Car Company was not the only prestigious firm to allow truck production to end simultaneously with the war in 1918. Maxwell and Paige, manufacturers of light trucks between 1917 and 1919, had discontinued this line by 1923 — the same year that the Packard truck disappeared. Only the White Motor Company escaped the general scourge, phasing out their automobiles in 1919 to concentrate upon the White truck which had achieved an enviable reputation during the previous decade.

Still, peacetime was the purveyor of hope to the majority of truck manufacturers who struggled to counter the sales squeeze with an improved product. A fast, one-ton "speed truck" introduced by many of these firms in 1920 and 1921 was symbolic of the Roaring Twenties era when a frantic pace became almost a way of life; the famous Reo Speed Wagon introduced in 1915 had been the grand-daddy of this new breed of truck.

Electric trucks were now virtually "out" despite the gains they had made prior to World War I. Their sedate pace plus the effects of two decades of successful gas truck development combined to keep them off the nation's major highways, although electrics continued to be produced through the Twenties and as late as 1941 for an in-city market. The largest manufacturer of electric trucks in 1916, the General Vehicle Company, had disappeared by the end of 1918. But more than enough producers of gasoline-engined trucks stepped forward to take their place during the following decade.

That legacy of the First World War, the quest for speed, had numerous ramifications in truck design during the Twenties. Wheels evolved as they revolved; the primitive wooden variety were obsolete by 1925 when most commercial vehicles were equipped with steel wheels as a matter of course. And pneumatics, as we have already noted, came into dominant use. Shortly after the war ended the Army Quartermaster Corps at Camp Holabird, Maryland, under the direction of Arthur W. Herrington, had begun experimentation with six-wheel trucks. During the early Twenties the Goodyear Tire and Rubber Company took up where the army left off. The six-wheel truck concept was attractive to Goodyear, naturally; two more wheels meant two more tires. But beyond that Goodyear was interested in expanding the market for the pneumatic to include the larger of the commercial vehicles which were still using solid tires to a great extent. The patents developed from the Goodyear experiment were used later in the design of many trucks, notably in that of the Safeway coach built in the late 1920's. The six-wheel concept proved advantageous in yet another regard. Naturally, six wheels spread the truck's weight over a greater extent of road surface than did four wheels, and it was not long before some states enacted laws to encourage the use of six-wheelers to lessen road damage inflicted by heavy trucks.

Another improvement, the introduction of the high speed, six-cylinder, low-slung bus chassis by many truck manufacturers in the mid-Twenties led to further refinements in heavy duty trucks. Not only were the special bus chassis used for moving van service, but more and more all-purpose trucks were equipped with six-cylinder engines and double-reduction rear axles instead of the slower worm-drive differential. Finally, air brakes gained wide acceptance because of their ability to effectively stop trailers moving at high speeds. Like the pneumatic tire and chassis development, this last modification enabled large trucks to move with the agility of smaller vehicles — a factor which was to play no small part in the buying decisions of truck users in the years of depression to come.

The 1926 Hug roadbuilders.

The 1929 Divco multi-stop delivery truck. (B)

The Pierce-Arrow's "Fleet Arrow" model of 1928. (L)

The 1931 Walker. (B)

The 1931 Ford Model A. (L)

The 1934 Linn half-track, an off-highway vehicle. (B)

The 1932 Fageol, with aluminum components. (B)

The 1933 model U.S.E. Autocar. (B)

THE TRUCK, THE DEPRESSION, WAR AGAIN

Spreading in concentric circles from Wall Street to assembly lines of the transport industry, the widespread business depression of the Thirties engulfed truck producers with a violence that ruined many firms altogether and left others crippled with severely curtailed production commitments.

The truck users, too, were caught in the eddy of the Depression, and to counteract the financial strain many of them bought larger and fewer trucks. Almost overnight great truck fleets disappeared, as the economy concept of fewer but heavier loads took hold. This led to the introduction of a number of so-called "super trucks" in the 1930 to 1932 period. The American-LaFrance Highway Mogul with V-12 engine developing 245 hp was one company's response to this trend — the Relay Duo-Drive with 275 hp and two Lycoming eight-cylinder engines was another. They were not to travel the roads long, however. Legislation restricting the maximum weight limit per axle on commercial vehicles was enacted in many states, and this, plus the increased use of tractor-trailer combinations, put most of the "super trucks" off the road.

Another innovation would, however, have a long-range impact on the truck industry, and it was heralded by the introduction of the Cummins automotive-type diesel engine in 1932. The lower cost of diesel fuel meant large savings for many fleet operators, and it was not long before many of them were buying new diesel engine trucks or replacing the gas engines in their old trucks.

As if economic depression was not enough to call attention to the passing of the old order, the traditional holdout of the horse-drawn era also gave way. The house-to-house milk wagon was largely retired from the American scene. Even the most stubborn of dairy owners finally conceded the merits of such multi-stop vehicles as the Walker and Ward electrics or Divco and Pak-Age-Car gasoline delivery trucks.

Although the Depression years were scarcely flourishing ones for the truck industry, it was not an era devoid of creative development, and some of these efforts would bear fruit in the decade ahead. Among the developments which deserve note are three: the construction of a lightweight aluminum truck by Fageol, the reintroduction of a modern cab-over-engine design by Autocar in 1933 which brought forth similar versions by most manufacturers within two years, and the pioneering work by Hug, Dart and Euclid on off-the-road highway trucks for mining and construction work.

And then, again, war. Small wonder if the transport industry regarded the outbreak of hostilities that preceded America's entry into World War II with a feeling of *déjà vu*. Once before — on the eve of the First World War — truck producers had mustered their forces to aid in the transportation of war materials, and a similar challenge lay before them in 1939 with the outbreak of war in Europe. This time there would be no hesitation: Those truck companies surviving the terrible years of the Depression were well prepared, with modern designs and excess plant capacity, to meet the influx of war orders to come.

When the fighting began in earnest, the American army was forced to seek an effective means of countering the "blitzkreig" or "lightning war," a method of attack which relied heavily upon mobile strike forces in specialized war vehicles. As in World War I, standardized trucks were built by independent producers to rigid army designs. But only two or three manufacturers built the various types of specialized trucks needed by the highly mechanized armed forces. Such light duty trucks as ambulances, jeeps and general cargo vehicles, for instance, were produced in quantity by Dodge, Ford, Willys and GMC, while the smaller demand for specialized vehicles — prime movers, wreckers and tank retrievers — was satisfied by Mack, Ward La France, Kenworth and

The 1935 White, designed by Alexis de Sakhnoffsky. (E)

Pacific Car & Foundry. For troop movement, there were half track personnel carriers manufactured by White and Autocar which resembled the Linn and Lombard vehicles used in off-highway logging and mining operations as far back as 1916.

Production of civilian trucks ended in March of 1943, with the Office of Defense Transportation assuming strict control over civilian vehicle users and producers. And although a limited number of civilian trucks were manufacturered again early in 1944, the O.D.T. could guarantee them only to the most essential industries. The others would have to wait the duration.

Peace came, and the restrictions over civilian truck production were lifted on August 20, 1946. But it would be 1948 before supply and de-

mand were reconciled, and truck production began to level off. Clearly this was not a replay of the situation that had followed the outbreak of peace after World War I. Why not? Several factors are involved here.

For one thing, the war surplus, or G.I. truck as it was known in the early postwar years, did not present a serious threat to domestic manufacturers. War vehicles had become so specialized in design — most having four or six wheel drive — that the majority of trucking firms found they could not use them economically. For the most part war surplus trucks were used as a stop-gap by smaller concerns who disconnected the drive shaft to the front axle and utilized only the conventional rear drive.

On the other hand, there were those in industry and farm work for

The 1940 model H.C. 175 Sterling with chain drive. (B)

whom the extra traction provided by all wheel drive vehicles was eminently suited. These users kept Willys busy after the war producing Jeeps, and even Dodge continued building a one-ton pickup with four wheel drive, the "Power Wagon" — foreshadowing the current trend toward four wheel drive trucks by contemporary manufacturers. Most civilian trucks, however, were of the familiar garden variety, and were gobbled up as quickly as they could be produced.

A number of wartime-inspired developments carried over to peacetime. Butyl, or synthetic rubber, was an early military-oriented discovery to find its way into commercial vehicle assembly lines, and the low-cost supply of aluminum which resulted when fighter-bomber construction ceased meant that more and more trucks sported aluminum bodies after the war. Too, the successful performance of six-wheel trucks during the

war ultimately convinced manufacturers that these vehicles could be produced for domestic consumption as dump trucks and highway tractors. Technology, it seems, had matured on the battlefield.

But not all the truck ideas nurtured during the battle years were to prove successful — indeed of the numerous new truck designs introduced after the war, most were not. Both the Marmon-Herrington and Lynn Coach & Truck Companies, for example, produced front-drive delivery trucks beginning in 1945 and 1946 respectively, but neither lasted for longer than a few years. A brilliant exception to the rule was the White Motor Company's highly successful "3000" truck with power-operated tilting cab for accessibility, a vehicle which led in the revival of the cab-over-engine design . . . and one which put White into a comfortable bargaining position for the era of mergers ahead.

For the truck industry the highlight of the Fifties was the Golden Anniversary of motor freight in 1953, fifty years after the first commercial vehicle trials in New York City. The Post Office issued a commemorative stamp to mark the occasion. Celebrations were overshadowed, however, by mergers, and the ultimate demise of several famous makes.

The levelling of truck production during 1949 and 1950 led almost inevitably to the amalgamation which took place in the decade that followed. The White Motor Company purchased Sterling Motors in 1951, Autocar in 1953, Diamond-T and Reo in 1956. Sterling, the last company to offer chain-drive models, was first to disappear, its last trucks being sold in 1953 as "Sterling-White." In 1956, Mack absorbed Brockway, as well as the C. D. Beck Company of Sidney, Ohio, builders of Ahrens-Fox fire apparatus and inter-city buses. By the mid-Sixties White had merged Reo and Diamond-T, whose products evolved into the Diamond-Reo in 1967. Two other West Coast trucks now linked together are Kenworth and Peterbilt, both owned by the Pacific Car and Foundry Company of Renton, Washington.

With the advent of state laws restricting the overall length of tractor-trailer combinations, the development of cab-over-engine trucks was measurably hastened. The concept spread to over-the-road tractors, with

*Kenworth tested the first truck
turbine engines. This is a 1950 model.* (B)

extremely tall versions whimsically nicknamed "cherry pickers" by truckers. Freightliner Corporation of Portland, Oregon, had produced a c-o-e tractor since the 1940's, which began being sold nationwide by White in 1951.

As the decade closed, truck manufacturing entered its second half century more prosperous and vibrant than ever — after massive government support of air and motor transportation. If the mergers had deprived consumers of some of the obvious benefits of competition, they had also strengthened and improved the surviving firms' resources for future research and development.

The Sixties marked several significant developments of considerable effect on truck manufacture. "Piggy-backing" — transporting highway trailers on railroad flat cars — was a novel marriage of two competing forms of transportation. This practice received wide-spread application after railroads introduced their low "all freight" rates, applying mainly to commodities shipped in containers or trailers which in turn could be quickly loaded onto flatcars. Today with railroads on the eve of possible fiscal recovery, thanks to new governmental efforts to treat them on even terms with their competitors, piggy-backing is taking on even greater potential for its users.

Of major changes facing truck design in the years ahead, the greatest challenge may well involve the growing problem of atmospheric pollution. Public concern over the gas emissions of internal combustion engines has placed as much pressure on truck manufacturers for an alternative as it has on the passenger car industry. At present, however, the diesel engine reigns supreme in heavy-duty trucks, and is even finding its way into middle- and smaller-sized commercial vehicles.

One of the largest roadblocks to a workable alternative power source is the nature of the diesel engine itself. Developing a powerplant with the same combination of power and economy will be a not easy task. Electric motors, thus far, have not provided sufficient power to match their physical bulk. Kenworth and the Boeing Company engineered a gas turbine truck in 1950, but it could not match the diesel's power/fuel ratio and is still not considered practical. The turbine offers tremendous power for its size and weight, but its only widespread vehicular application so far has been in fire engines, where sudden demands for power can justify uneconomical fuel consumption. On the other hand, the higher combustion rate of the turbine, and its consequently lower pollution level, is considered far more acceptable than those of the gasoline or diesel engines. This advantage, coupled with the general truck design trend to higher horsepower and lighter overall weight, may eventually spell success for the gas turbine in the Seventies.

The truck industry, one must conclude, has shown no sign yet of growing senile or obsolete, and without doubt vast changes and design breakthroughs are in the works which we'd have all considered impossible or impractical a few years ago. Even now, the automatic transmission has a place in truck design — it was considered completely inadequate for such applications just a few years ago. Greater creature comfort, too, will be produced by the trucks of the future. It seems assured that the industry, in years ahead, will continue to provide dramatic evidence of its traditional quest for efficient, practical commercial transportation.

The 1964 gas turbine Ford, a 600 hp experimental model.

XII

TITANS
OF
THE ROAD

BY JOHN MONTVILLE

Of all vehicles which have through history graced American roads, perhaps the most unappreciated has been the motor truck. The truck is largely taken for granted. Although it plays an incredibly vital role in the day-to-day lives of every American, probably few of those it serves ever accord it more than a fleeting thought. The automobile has drawn to it enthusiasts in the tens of thousands passionately devoted to collecting, restoring and lovingly caring for favored cars of good and even questionable vintage. Clubs devoted to the hobby proliferate, and the literature dedicated thereto is voluminous. Not so for the truck. There are, of course, problems of a logistics sort for a truck collector—a garage-full of Mack trucks would be quite a garage-full. And then, too, it has been said that the truck perhaps does not have either the glamour or the personal appeal of an automobile. Yet, try to convince a truck enthusiast of that. They're a small group, it is true, but as energetically devoted to their favored vehicles as any historic car enthusiast. And recently, too, in just the last few years, their ranks have begun to swell. The truck hobby is here to stay. This fortuitous fact is a source of satisfaction both for historians and for that hearty cadre of truck followers who long ago decided that the American motor truck was a subject eminently worthy of historical documentation. Among the most enthusiastic members of that latter group is John Montville. Since 1943 he has been avidly collecting truck literature and compiling a truck library. The list that follows—the most comprehensive ever published on the American motor truck—is the result of nearly three decades of research.

A few words are in order regarding the parameters of this list. Motor trucks are the subject—by definition, self-propelled commercial road vehicles used to haul goods. This definition runs the gamut from the largest vehicles which could be licensed for use over public roads to the smallest-type delivery vehicles within the automotive classification. Excluded, therefore, are those gargantuan vehicles built strictly for off-highway use which generally fall under the classification of construction equipment, as well as vehicles used predominately in messenger service operations which properly fall under the motorcycle classification. Also excluded are those varieties of commercial vehicle—fire engines, ambulances and hearses, buses, agricultural equipment, street sweepers, et al.—whose inherent purpose does not lie within the goods-carrying/road-use definition. Because of several factors particularly relevant to the motor truck industry, the roster comprises two listings and an index, as explained herewith.

MOTOR TRUCK MANUFACTURERS

This main listing comprises nearly 1000 entries and includes those manufacturers whose truck production has been fully documented. In addition to company literature and brochures, production by these manufacturers can be substantiated in the varied industrial publications which were founded to serve and report the motor truck industry. The periodicals researched in the compilation of this list include *Horseless Age* (1895 to 1907), *Power Wagon* (1906 to the mid-Twenties), *Commercial Vehicle* (1906 to 1923), *Motor Truck* (1910 to 1928) and *Commercial Car Journal* (1911 to date).

CROSS REFERENCE INDEX

This Index is explained in the introduction to Motor Truck Manufacturers. It is essentially a guide for the reader, so that he may have quick access to the full researched entries of that list.

A Listing of Motor Trucks Produced in the United States and Canada

SUPPLEMENT MOTOR TRUCK LIST

The preceding Motor Truck Manufacturers List includes those trucks which enjoyed serious or series production in the United States and Canada. This Supplement Motor Truck List comprises the others.

The truck historian's lot is a perplexing one. It would appear that everyone in America who had done anything automotively wanted also to build a truck. A good many of them did—or might be presumed to have done so—and should, therefore, not be overlooked in any listing of American motor trucks. However, for the sake of facility in research it seemed appropriate to separate these trucks from those which reached the full bloom of manufacture—and thus they appear here in the Supplement Motor List.

In theory, building a truck must have seemed a most logical extension of production for any automobile manufacturer during those salad days when automobile companies spanned this continent. Provided they had a chassis of sufficient size and heft, the addition of a delivery wagon or truck model was hard to resist. Numerous companies tried it, as automobile catalogues of this period will attest, but as often as not gave up the venture before getting into manufacture on any substantial scale. One might call these trucks "also-rans" —not to be meant detrimentally, but literally. They also ran, but research indicates that they enjoyed only the most limited of production. Sometimes, too, an automobile company, though not at all interested in truck manufacture, might have provided the chassis upon which a truck might be built, or even have built up a truck or trucks themselves on special order. And then, too, companies or individuals frequently built trucks for experimental purposes only, with no intention of manufacture. Such trucks are also the subjects of the Supplement Motor Truck List.

Featured in this list too are vehicles which do not properly fall into the motor truck classification (for example, the off-highway gargantuans), and companies frequently presumed to have built trucks but who instead devoted their production energies to truck-related equipment. Also included are Trucks-Which-Might-Have-Been and Trucks-Which-Never-Were. The former comprise those companies formed for the stated purpose of building trucks but who, research indicates, never got beyond the incorporation and prototype stage, as well as trucks indicated through the years as having been built but for which further corroboration has not yet been discovered. The Trucks-Which-Never-Were are just that, companies frequently referred to as having built trucks, but who, in reality, never did at all.

The Supplement Motor Truck List, then, seeks to bring together the varied efforts of truck builders which did not reach—so far as is now known—full-scale production. In large measure it provides groundwork for continuing research. In the months and years to come, it is hoped that the existence of those trucks presumed to have been built might be substantiated—and that the ranks of motor truck builders in this country might be augmented with trucks heretofore unknown. For that reason a tear-out form is appended to the back of this book so that interested readers might provide us with leads for further research. The motor truck is now claiming more followers than ever before, and the ranks are growing steadily. Its history, finally, is secure.

MOTOR TRUCK
MANUFACTURERS

This listing is arranged alphabetically by truck trade name, with each entry giving the dates of truck production, and, chronologically, the various companies or company names under which the truck was produced. All truck names mentioned within the text of an entry are set off in quotation marks. When the corporate name does not make the motive power clear, special note is made of those trucks powered by electric motor or steam engine. It should be stressed that the dates indicated on the list are those during which motor trucks were produced. In some cases the companies involved produced other varieties (e.g., fire engines) of commercial vehicle before and/or after the dates listed.

Immediately following the Motor Truck Manufacturers List is a Cross Reference Index. Trucks, it seems, have provided historians with a number of dilemmas, not the least of which is the fact that truck companies very frequently marketed their trucks under designations other than their corporate names. The reader, for example, might recall a truck made by Auburn Motor Chassis in Indiana before the First World War, or one made in the Twenties by an Ohio company called American Bus & Truck—but not recall what the truck was called. By checking the Cross Reference Index under "Auburn Motor Chassis" and "American Bus & Truck," one would discover that the former built the "Handy Wagon" and the latter the "Kelly" and could proceed to those references accordingly. In every case where a truck company built vehicles under a name other than its corporate title, that company is listed in the Cross Reference Index with a referral notation to the appropriate entry in this list.

The Cross Reference Index also includes a number of "see also" notations. These indicate that the truck is entered under that name in the Motor Truck Manufacturers List, but that the reader might check the other entries indicated for further information regarding, for example, additional trucks made, or corporate amalgamations or takeovers involving that particular truck or truck company.

A

A.&B.—1913-circa 1916
American & British Mfg. Co.
Charles & Cross Streets
Providence, Rhode Island

A.B.C.—1907-11
A.B.C. Motor Vehicle Mfg. Co.
3915 Morgan Street
St. Louis, Missouri

ABRESCH—1910-12
Abresch-Cramer Auto Truck Co.
Milwaukee, Wisconsin

ACASON—1915-24
Acason Motor Truck Co.
Brooklyn Ave. & Parry St.
Detroit, Michigan
Acason Motor Truck Co.
Wyandotte, Michigan
Acason Company
6401 Miller Avenue
Detroit, Michigan

ACE—1919-26
American Motor Truck Co.
16th Street & B.&O. RR.
Newark, Ohio

A.C.F.—1932-34
A.C.F. Motors Corporation
Brill Company, J.G.
62nd St. & Woodland Ave.
Philadelphia, Penna.

ACME—1915-31
Cadillac Auto Truck Co.
40 McKinnon Street
Cadillac, Michigan
Acme Motor Truck Co.
513 Mitchell Street
Cadillac, Michigan

ACME—1916-19
Acme Wagon Company
Emigsville, Penna.

ACME-DETROIT—1915-17
Acme Motor Truck Co.
808 Woodbridge St.
Detroit, Michigan

ACORN—1910-12
Acorn Motor Car Co.
Fifth & Lock Streets
Cincinnati, Ohio

ACORN—1924-31
Acorn Motor Truck Co.
3915 Armitage Avenue
Chicago, Illinois

ADAMS 1911-16
Adams Brothers Company
442 W. Main Cross Street
Findlay, Ohio
Adams Truck, Foundry & Machine Co.
442 W. Main Cross Street
Findlay, Ohio

ADMIRAL—1913-14
Admiral Motor Car Co.
St. Louis, Missouri

AETNA—1914-16
Aetna Motor Truck Co.
24-26 Richmond Ave.
Detroit, Michigan

A.I.C.—1912-14
American Ice Manufacturing Co.
New York, N.Y.

AIR-O-FLEX—1918-19
Air-O-Flex Automobile Corp.
519 Hilger Avenue
Detroit, Michigan

AJAX—circa 1921
Ajax Motors Corporation
Boston, Massachusetts
Taken over by Walker-Johnson Truck Co.

AKRON—1913-14
Ideal Commercial Car Co.
Akron Motor Car & Truck Co.
Akron, Ohio

AKRON MULTI-TRUCK—1920-21
Thomart Motor Co.
Kent, Ohio
Trade name changed to "Thomart."

ALCO—1908-13
American Locomotive Co.
Kinsley Avenue
Providence, R.I.

ALENA steam—1922-23
Alena Steam Products Co.
Indianapolis, Indiana

ALL-AMERICAN—1918-23
All-American Truck Co.
6501 W. Grand Avenue
Chicago, Illinois
Fremont Motors Corp.
Fremont, Ohio

ALLFOUR—1918-19
United Four Wheel Drive Truck Corp.
Madison St. & 47th Ave.
Chicago, Illinois

ALL-POWER—1919-20
All-Power Truck Company
372-380 W. Fort Street
Detroit, Michigan

ALMA—1911-13
Alma Mfg. Co. (1911-13)
Alma Motor Truck Co. (1913)
Alma, Michigan
Took over "Hercules" truck and changed name to "Republic."

ALTER—1914-16
Cincinnati Motors Mfg. Co.
1741-45 Central Avenue
Cincinnati, Ohio

AMERICAN electric—1897-1902
American Electric Vehicle Co.
56 & 58 W. Van Buren Street
Chicago, Illinois
American Electric Vehicle Co.
3rd & Clinton Streets
Hoboken, New Jersey

AMERICAN—1906-12
American Motor Truck Co.
Caledonia Street
Lockport, New York
Findlay Motor Company
Findlay, Ohio
Ewing-American Motor Co.
Findlay, Ohio

AMERICAN—1912-13
American Motor Truck Mfg. Co.
San Francisco, California

AMERICAN—1918-19
American Motor Truck Co.
16th Street & B.&O. RR.
Newark, Ohio
Trade name changed to "Ace."
AMERICAN—1920-circa 1923
American Motor Truck & Tractor Co.
Portland, Connecticut
AMERICAN AUSTIN—1930-35
American Austin Car Co.
Butler, Pennsylvania
Name changed to "Bantam."
AMERICAN-LaFRANCE—1921-31
American LaFrance Fire Engine Co.,
Inc.
100 E. LaFrance Street
Elmira, New York
American-LaFrance Fire Engine Co.,
Inc.
Bloomfield, New Jersey
American-LaFrance & Foamite Indus-
tries, Inc.
Bloomfield, New Jersey
LaFrance-Republic Corporation
Bloomfield, New Jersey
LaFrance-Republic Corporation
Alma, Michigan
AMERICAN-STANDARD—1910-11
American Motor Truck Co.
Battle Creek, Michigan
AMERICAN STEAMER—1921-23
American Steam Truck Co.
Elgin, Illinois
ANDOVER ELECTRIC—1915-16
Andover Motor Vehicle Co.
Andover, Mass.
APEX—1919-22
Panhard Motors Company
Grand Haven, Michigan
Hamilton Motors Company
Grand Haven, Michigan
A&R—1913-15
Abendroth & Root Mfg. Co.
Newburgh, New York
See also "Frontenac."

ARGO—1911-15
Argo Electric Vehicle Co.
Saginaw, Michigan
American Electric Car Co.
Saginaw, Michigan
ARMLEDER—1910-36
Armleder Company, O.
12th & Plum Streets
Cincinnati, Ohio
Armleder Motor Truck Co., O.
12th & Plum Streets
Cincinnati, Ohio
Armleder Truck Company
8th & Evans Streets
Cincinnati, Ohio
ATCO—1919-circa 1922
American Truck & Trailer Corp.
Kankakee, Illinois
ATLANTIC ELECTRIC—1912-circa 1918
Atlantic Electric Vehicle Co.
893-97 Frelinghuysen Ave.
Newark, New Jersey
ATLAS—1904-12
Knox Motor Truck Co. (1904-07)
Springfield, Mass.
Atlas Motor Car Co. (1907-12)
88 Birnie Avenue
Springfield, Mass.
ATLAS—1916-23
Martin Carriage Works
York, Penna.
Martin Truck & Body Corp.
York, Penna.
Martin-Parry Corp.
York, Penna.
Atlas Truck Corp.
York, Penna.
See "Martin."
ATTERBURY—1910-circa 1935
Atterbury Motor Car Co.
Elmwood & Hertel Aves.
Buffalo, New York
AUGLAIZE—1911-16
Auglaize Motor Car Co.
New Bremen, Ohio

AUTO-CAR—1903-08
Auto-Car Equipment Co.
77 Edward Street
Buffalo, New York
Trade name changed to "Buffalo."
AUTOCAR—1908 to date
Autocar Company
11th Street
Ardmore, Penna.
Purchased by White Motor Co. in 1953
Autocar Division
White Motor Company
Lancaster Ave.
Exton, Penna.
AUTOHORSE—1917-circa 1919
One Wheel Truck Co.
St. Louis, Missouri
AVAILABLE—1911 to date
Available Truck Co.
2334 Hamilton Ct.
Chicago, Illinois
Available Truck Co.
1539 No. 47th Street
Chicago, Illinois
Available Truck Co.
2501 Elston Avenue
Chicago, Illinois
Available Truck Co.
Div. Crane Carrier Corp.
Tulsa, Oklahoma
AVERY—1910-24
Avery Company
335 Iowa Street
Peoria, Illinois

BABCOCK—1911-13
Babcock Company, H.H.
Watertown, New York
BACKUS—1925-circa 1932
Backus Motor Truck Co.
East Rutherford, N.J.

BAKER ELECTRIC—1908-16
 Baker Motor Vehicle Co.
 Baker R&L Company
 Ft. of West 80th Street
 Cleveland, Ohio
Producers of industrial electric lift trucks
to date.
BANTAM—1936-41
 American Bantam Car Co.
 Bantam Ave. & Pillow St.
 Butler, Pennsylvania
BARKER—1912-16
 Barker, C. L.
 Norwalk, Conn.
BARROWS—1927-28
 Barrows Motor Truck Co.
 Indianapolis, Indiana
BATTRONIC ELECTRIC—1963 to date
 Battronic Truck Corp.
 5675 Rising Sun Ave.
 Philadelphia, Penna.
BEARDSLEY ELECTRIC—1914-16
 Beardsley Electric Company
 1250-60 W. 7th Street
 Los Angeles, Calif.
BECK—1912-22
 Cedar Rapids Auto Works
 901-913 First Avenue
 Cedar Rapids, Iowa
 Beck & Son
 901-913 First Avenue
 Cedar Rapids, Iowa
 Beck-Hawkeye Motor Truck Co.
 901-913 First Avenue
 Cedar Rapids, Iowa
BEECH CREEK—1915-circa 1917
 Beech Creek Truck & Auto Co.
 Beech Creek, Penna.
BELL STEAM—1913-15
 Bell Locomotive Works
 36 Morningside Ave.
 Yonkers, New York
BELL—1915-18
 Bell Motor Car Co.
 York, Pennsylvania

BELL—1919-23
 Iowa Motor Truck Co.
 Ottumwa, Iowa
BELMONT—1919-23
 Belmont Motors Corp.
 Harrisburg, Penna.
BESSEMER—1911-circa 1929
 Bessemer Motor Truck Co.
 Grove City, Pennsylvania
 Div. Bessemer-American Motors Corp.
 Holmesburg Junction
 Philadelphia, Pennsylvania
 Bessemer-American Motors Corp.
 Plainfield, New Jersey
BEST—1912-14
 Durant-Dort Carriage Co.
 South & Mason Streets
 Flint, Michigan
BETHLEHEM—1917-26
 Bethlehem Motors Corp.
 Bethlehem Motors Corp. of N.Y.
 Allentown, Penna.
BETZ—1920-circa 1928
 Betz Corporation
 Hammond, Indiana
 Betz Motor Truck Co.
 493 Lyman Avenue
 Hammond, Indiana
BEYSTER-DETROIT—1909-11
 Beyster-Detroit Motor Car Co.
 Detroit, Michigan
BIDDLE-MURRAY—1906-07
 Biddle-Murray Mfg. Co.
 Oak Park, Illinois
BIEDERMAN—1920-55
 Biederman Motors Corp.
 2131 Spring Grove Ave.
 Cincinnati, Ohio
BIMEL—1916-17
 Bimel Automobile Co.
 335 No. Miami Ave.
 Sidney, Ohio
BINGHAM—1914-15
 Bingham Mfg. Co.
 Cleveland, Ohio

BLACKER—1910-11
 Blacker & Co., John H.
 Chillicothe, Ohio
BLAIR—1911-18
 Blair Manufacturing Co.
 Newark, Ohio
 Blair Motor Truck Co.
 16th St. and B.&O. RR.
 Newark, Ohio
BOARD—1911-13
 Board Motor Truck Co.
 Alexandria, Va.
B-O-E—1911-circa 1913
 Motor Conveyance Company
 15th Ave. & Park Street
 Milwaukee, Wisconsin
BOLLSTROM—1920-22
 Bollstrom Motors, Inc.
 St. Louis, Missouri
BORLAND ELECTRIC—1913-14
 Borland-Grannis Co.
 324 E. Huron Street
 Chicago, Illinois
Merged into American Elec. Car Co.
BOURNE—1915-18
 Bourne Magnetic Truck Co.
 Sedgley Ave. & No. 17th St.
 Philadelphia, Penna.
 Bourne Magnetic Truck Co.
 5th Ave. & 142nd St.
 New York, New York
BOWMAN—1921
 Bowman Motor Car Co.
 Covington, Kentucky
BOYD—1916-18
 Boyd & Bro., Inc., James
 25th & Wharton Sts.
 Philadelphia, Penna.
BRIDGEPORT—1920-27
 Bridgeport Motor Truck Corp.
 1026-36 North Avenue
 Bridgeport, Conn.
 Morrisey Motor Car Co.
 653 Fairfield Ave.
 Bridgeport, Conn.

BRINTON—1913-26
  Brinton Motor Truck Co.
  5740 Cherry Street
  Philadelphia, Penna.
BRISCOE—1915-21
  Briscoe Motor Corp.
  Jackson, Michigan
BROCKWAY—1912 to date
  Brockway Motor Truck Co
  106 Railroad Street
  Cortland, New York
  Brockway Motor Truck Corp.
  106 Railroad Avenue
  Cortland, New York
  Brockway Motor Co., Inc.
  106 Central Avenue
  Cortland, New York
  Brockway Motor Trucks
  Div. Mack Trucks, Inc.
  106 Central Avenue
  Cortland, New York
BROCKWAY ELECTRIC—1933-37
  Brockway Motor Co., Inc.
  106 Central Avenue
  Cortland, New York
BRODESSER—1909-11
  Brodesser Motor Truck Co.
  Burleigh & Weil Streets
  Milwaukee, Wisconsin
  Trade name changed to "Juno."
BRONX ELECTRIC—1911-12
  Bronx Electric Vehicle Co.
  294 E. 135th Street
  Bronx, New York
BROOKS—1912-13
  Brooks Manufacturing Co.
  Saginaw, Michigan
BROWN—1912-14
  Brown Commercial Car Co.
  Peru, Indiana
BROWN—1922-24
  Brown Truck Company
  Duluth, Minnesota
BROWN—1939-53
  Brown Equipment & Mfg. Co.

829 So. Summit Avenue
  Charlotte, N.C.
BRUNNER—circa 1910
  Brunner Motor Car Co.
  988 Ellicott Street
  Buffalo, New York
BRUSH—1908-12
  Brush Runabout Company
  12 Rhode Island Ave.
  Detroit, Michigan
BUCK—1925-27
  Buck Motor Truck Co.
  Bellevue, Ohio
BUCKEYE—1910-11
  Buckeye Wagon & Motor Car Co.
  Dayton, Ohio
BUCKMOBILE—1905-circa 1906
  Black Diamond Automobile Co.
  700 Genesee Street
  Utica, New York
BUFFALO—1908-10
  Auto-Car Manufacturing Co.
  Elmwood & Hertel Avenues
  Buffalo, New York
  Atterbury Motor Car Company
  Elmwood & Hertel Avenues
  Buffalo, New York
BUFFALO ELECTRIC—1913-15
  Buffalo Electric Vehicle Co.
  1219-23 Main Street
  Buffalo, New York
BUFFALO—1920-25
  Buffalo Truck & Tractor Corp.
  Clarence, New York
  Buffalo Truck Corporation
  Clarence, New York
BUICK—1910-18
  Buick Motor Company
  Flint, Michigan
BURFORD—1916-17
  Burford Company, H.G.
  Fremont, Ohio
  Burford Motor Truck Co.
  Fremont, Ohio
  Taken over by Taylor Motor Truck Co.

BUTLER—1913-14
  Huselton Automobile Co.
  515 No. Washington St.
  Butler, Pennsylvania

C

CADILLAC—1904-08
  Cadillac Automobile Co.
  1343 Cass Avenue
  Detroit, Michigan
  Cadillac Motor Car Co.
  1343 Cass Avenue
  Detroit, Michigan
CAMERON—1911-13
  Cameron Car Co.
  Beverly, Mass.
CANTONO—1904-07
  Cantono Electric Tractor Co.
  Marion, New Jersey
  Cantono Electric Tractor Co.
  Newark, New Jersey
  Cantono Electric Fore Carriage Co.
CAPITOL ELECTRIC—1913-14
  Capitol Truck Mfg. Co.
  Denver, Colorado
CAPITOL CAR ELECTRIC—1912
  Washington Motor Vehicle Co.
  Washington, D.C.
CARHARTT—1911-12
  Carhartt Automobile Corp.
  Detroit, Michigan
CARLSON—1904-11
  Carlson Motor Vehicle Co.
  623 Bergen Street
  Brooklyn, New York
  Carlson Automobile Co.
  Brooklyn, New York
  Carlson Motor & Truck Co.
  Brooklyn, New York
CARTERCAR—1906-12
  Motorcar Company
  230 21st Street
  Detroit, Mich.

Cartercar Company
Pontiac, Michigan
Cartercar Motor Car Co.
Pontiac, Michigan
CASADAY—1905
Casaday Mfg. Co., W.L.
South Bend, Indiana
CASCO—1922-30
Casco Motors, Inc.
88 Oak Street
Portland, Maine
Sanford Automotive Corp.
2 Berwick Street
Sanford, Maine
CASE—1910-11
Case Motor Car Company
New Bremen, Ohio
Changed to Auglaize Motor Car Co.
CASE—1920-23
Case Plow Works, J.I.
Racine, Wisconsin
CASEY—circa 1915
Casey Co., Frank A.
River Street
Billerica, Mass.
CASS—1910-15
Cass Motor Truck Co. (1910-14)
1025 Lapeer Avenue
Port Huron, Mich.
Independent Motors Co. (1914-15)
Port Huron, Michigan
Trade name changed to "Independent."
C-B—1915-16
Downing Motor Car Co.
Detroit, Michigan
Downing Motor Truck Co.
Detroit, Michigan
CCC—circa 1949 to date
Crane Carrier Corp.
Tulsa, Oklahoma
Crane Carrier Co.
Div. C.C.I. Corporation
1150 No. Peoria St.
Tulsa, Oklahoma
CECO—1914-15

Continental Engineering Co.
1015 No. Halstead Street
Chicago, Illinois
CHAMPION ELECTRIC—1903-12
Champion Wagon Co.
Owego, New York
CHAMPION—1909-12
Mcgow Company, C. F.
Milwaukee Auto Truck Mfg. Co.
Milwaukee, Wisconsin
CHAMPION—1917
Champion Motors Co., Inc.
Fulton, Illinois
CHAMPION—1918-21
Direct Drive Motor Co.
Champion Motors, Inc.
Philadelphia, Penna.
CHAMPION—circa 1955 to date
Champion Carriers Inc.
65 No. Madison Street
Tulsa, Oklahoma
CHAMPION-ROTARY—1922-23
Champion Rotary Motors Co., Inc.
Buffalo, New York
CHASE—1907-circa 1917
Chase Motor Truck Co.
332 So. West Street
Syracuse, New York
CHESTER—1915-17
Chester County Motor Co.
Coatesville, Penna.
CHEVROLET—1918 to date
Chevrolet Motor Co.
Flint, Michigan
Chevrolet Motor Div.
General Motors Corp.
Flint, Michigan
CHICAGO—1905
Chicago Commercial Auto Mfg. Co.
Harvey, Illinois
CHICAGO—1911-12
Chicago Motor Wagon Co.
Chicago, Illinois
CHICAGO—1919-32
Chicago Motor Truck Inc.

335 West 28th Place
Chicago, Illinois
Cutting Co., Robert M.,
Chicago, Illinois
CLARK STEAM—1900-circa 1906
Clark, Edward S.
272 Freeport St.
Dorchester, Mass.
CLARK—1911-circa 1913
Clark, Edward S.
272 Freeport St.
Dorchester, Mass.
CLARK—1911-13
Clark Company, F. G.
Lansing, Michigan
Clark Power Wagon Co. (1911-13)
Lansing, Michigan
Changed to Kalamazoo Motor Vehicle Co.
CLARK—1910-15
Clark Delivery Car Co.
1035 E. 76th Street
Chicago, Illinois
CLARKSPEED—1927-31
Clarkspeed Truck Co.
Pontiac, Michigan
CLIMAX—1906-07
Hinde & Dauch
Sandusky, Ohio
Trade name changed to "Hinde & Dauch."
CLIMBER—1920-22
Climber Motors Corp.
Little Rock, Arkansas
CLINE—1953 to date
Cline Truck Company
1116 Campbell Street
Kansas City, Missouri
Cline Truck Company
3501 Gardner Avenue
Kansas City, Missouri
CLINTON—1920-33
Clinton Motors Corp.
336 Avenue B
New York, New York
Clinton Motors Corp.
Reading, Penna.

CLYDESDALE—1917-38
    Clyde Cars Company
    Clyde, Ohio
    Clydesdale Motor Truck Co.
    Amanda Street
    Clyde, Ohio
COLBY—1911-12
    Colby Motor Company
    Mason City, Iowa
COLEMAN—1911-16
    Coleman Carriage & Harness Co., F.
    Morgan & Main Streets
    Ilion, New York
    Coleman Motor Truck Company
    Ilion, New York
COLEMAN—1925 to date
    Coleman Motors Corp.
    Littleton, Colorado
    American Coleman Co.
    5801 So. Nevada Ave.
    Littleton, Colorado
COLLIER—1916-22
    Collier Motor Truck Co.
    Painesville, Ohio
    Collier Motor Truck Co.
    Bellevue, Ohio
COLUMBIA ELECTRIC—1899-1907
    Electric Vehicle Company
    Hartford, Connecticut
COLUMBIA—1915-26
    Columbia Motor Truck & Trailer Co.
    103 Columbia Road
    Pontiac, Michigan
COMET—1917-21
    Comet Automobile Co.
    815-69 Garfield Ave.
    Decatur, Illinois
COMMANDO—1959 to date
    Ottawa Steel Division (1959-64)
    Young Spring & Wire Corp.
    Ottawa, Kansas
    Ottawa Steel Products (1964 to date)
    Daybrook-Ottawa Corp.
    1313 No. Hickory St.
    Ottawa, Kansas

COMMER—1911-12
    Wyckoff, Church & Partridge, Inc.
    (1911)
    Kingston, New York
    Driggs-Seabury Ordnance Co. (1911-12)
    Sharon, Pennsylvania
COMMERCE—1906-08
    American Machinery Mfg. Co.
    Beaubien & Champlain Sts.
    Detroit, Michigan
COMMERCE—1911-32
    Commerce Motor Car Co.
    Solvay Avenue
    Detroit, Michigan
    Commerce Motor Truck Co.
    7424 Mackie Avenue
    Detroit, Michigan
    Commerce Motor Truck Co.
    Ypsilanti, Michigan
    Relay Motors Corporation
    Lima, Ohio
COMPOUND—1906
    Eisenhuth Horseless Vehicle Co.
    Middletown, Connecticut
CONCORD—1916-33
    Abbott & Downing Co.
    Concord, New Hampshire
    Abbott-Downing Truck & Body Co.
    80 So. Main Street
    Concord, New Hampshire
CONDOR—circa 1930-42
    Condor Motors, Inc.
    Chicago, Illinois
CONESTOGA—1917-20
    Conestoga Motor Truck Co.
    Lancaster, Penna.
CONRAD STEAM—1900-03
    Conrad Motor Carriage Co.
    1417 Niagara Street
    Buffalo, New York
CONTINENTAL—1912-14
    Continental Motor Truck Co.
    1435-39 Cleveland Place
    Denver, Colorado
CONTINENTAL—1912-18

Continental Truck Mfg. Co.
    1702 Sixteenth Street
    Superior, Wisconsin
CONTINENTAL—1915
    Continental Motor Truck Co.
    Chicago, Illinois
COOK—1920-circa 1923
    Cook Motors Corp.
    Kankakee, Illinois
COOK—1950 to date
    Cook Bros. Equipment Co.
    3330 San Fernando Road
    Los Angeles, California
COPPOCK—1907-09
    Coppock Motor Car Co. (1907)
    Marion, Indiana
    Coppock Motor Car Co. (1908-09)
    Decatur, Indiana
    Changed to Decatur Motor Car Co.
CORBITT—1913-52
    Corbitt Automobile Co. (1913-16)
    Corbitt Motor Truck Co.
    Corbitt Truck Company
    Henderson, N.C.
    Corbitt Company
    Henderson, N.C.
CORBITT—1957-circa 1958
    Corbitt Company, Inc.
    Henderson, N.C.
    Built to order only.
CORLISS—1917-18
    Corliss Motor Truck Co.
    Corliss, Wisconsin
CORTLAND—1911-12
    Cortland Motor Wagon Co.
    Cortland, New York
    Later Pittsfield, Mass.
COULTHARD STEAM—1905-06
    Corwin Manufacturing Co.
    Peabody, Massachusetts
    Made for American Coulthard Co.
COUPLE-GEAR ELECTRIC—1906-22
    Couple-Gear Freight Wheel Co.
    Couple Gear Electric Truck Co.
    1450 Buchanan Avenue

Grand Rapids, Michigan
COVERT—circa 1907
Covert Motor Vehicle Co.
57-61 Richmond Street
Lockport, New York
C.P.T.—circa 1912
Chicago Pneumatic Tool Co.
Chicago, Illinois
Trade name changed to "Little Giant."
CRAWFORD—1912-17
Crawford Automobile Co.
Surrey & Summit Avenues
Hagerstown, Maryland
CRESCENT—1912-13
Crescent Motor Truck Co.
Middletown, Ohio
Crescent Motor Truck Co.
Hamilton, Ohio
CREST—circa 1904
Crest Manufacturing Co.
Cambridge, Mass.
CROCE—1913-18
Croce Automobile Co.
First Avenue
Asbury Park, N.J.
CROSLEY—1939-52
Crosley Motors, Inc.
2530 Spring Grove Ave.
Cincinnati, Ohio
CROWN—1905-07
Detroit Auto Vehicle Co.
65 Catherine Street
Detroit, Michigan
CROWN—1907-11
Crown Commercial Car Co.
Philadelphia, Penna.
CROWN—1911-16
Crown Commercial Car Co.
North Milwaukee, Wisconsin
C-T ELECTRIC—1906-28
Commercial Truck Co. of America
13th and Hamilton Streets
Philadelphia, Penna.
Commercial Truck Co. of America
27th and Brown Streets

Philadelphia, Penna.
Commercial Truck Company
300 Hunting Park Avenue
Philadelphia, Penna.
Assets purchased by Walker Vehicle Co.
CUNNINGHAM STEAM—1900-01
Cunningham Engineering Co.
Boston, Massachusetts
Massachusetts Steam Wagon Co.
Boston, Massachusetts
CURTIS—1912-15
Pittsburgh Machine Tool Co.
Corey Avenue
Braddock, Penna.
CURTIS-BILL—1933-34
Bill Motors Company
1100 57th Avenue
Oakland, Calif.
Bill Motors Company
9601 San Leandro Blvd.
Oakland, Calif.
C-V ELECTRIC—1955-62
Cleveland Vehicle Co.
3949 Lakeside Avenue
Cleveland, Ohio
CYCLONE—1920-23
Cyclone Starter & Truck Co.
Greenville, S.C.
Cyclone Motors Corp.
Greenville, S.C.

𝒟

DAIMLER—1901-03
Daimler Manufacturing Co.
959 Steinway Avenue
Astoria, L.I., New York
DAIN—1912-13
Dain Mfg. Co.
Ottumwa, Iowa
DANIELSON—1911-18
Danielson Engine Works
335-41 E. 39th Street
Chicago, Illinois

DART—1910-58
Dart Manufacturing Co. (1910)
Anderson, Indiana
Dart Manufacturing Co. (1910-14)
Waterloo, Iowa
Dart Motor Truck Co. (1914-19)
Waterloo, Iowa
Dart Truck & Tractor Corp. (1919-24)
Waterloo, Iowa
Hawkeye Dart Truck Co. (1924)
Waterloo, Iowa
Dart Truck Company (1927-58)
27th & Oak Streets
Kansas City, Mo.
Name changed to "KW-Dart."
DAY-ELDER—1919-37
Day-Elder Motors Corp.
20 Coit Street
Newark, New Jersey
National Motors Mfg. Co.
464 Coit Street
Irvington, N.J.
Day-Elder Truck Co.
464 Coit Street
Irvington, N.J.
Day-Elder Motor Truck Co.
25 First Street
Newark, New Jersey
DAY UTILITY—1912-14
Day Automobile Co.
25 Milwaukee Ave.
Detroit, Michigan
DAYTON—1911
Dayton Auto Truck Co.
Dayton, Ohio
Trade name changed to "Durable Dayton."
D-E—1916-18
Day-Elder Motors Corp.
161-7 Ogden Street
Newark, New Jersey
Trade name changed to "Day-Elder."
DEARBORN—circa 1918-22
Dearborn Truck Co.
1301 So. Cicero Court
Chicago, Illinois

DECATUR—1909-14
    Decatur Motor Car Co. (1909-12)
    Decatur, Indiana
    Grand Rapids Motor Truck Co. (1912-13)
    Parcel Post Equipment Co. (1914-15)
    Grand Rapids, Michigan
    Taken over by United Motor Truck Co.
    Also marketed as "Decatur Hoosier Limited."
DEERE—1906-07
    Deere-Clark Motor Car Co.
    Moline, Illinois
DEFIANCE—1917-30
    Turnbull Motor Truck & Wagon Co.
    Defiance Motor Truck Co.
    Century Motor Truck Co.
    Defiance, Ohio
DE KALB—1914-21
    De Kalb Wagon Company
    110 Garden Street
    De Kalb, Illinois
DELAHUNTY—1913-15
    Delahunty Dyeing Machine Co.
    East Street
    Pittston, Pennsylvania
DELCAR—1947-49
    American Motors, Inc.
    Troy, New York
DeMARTINI—1915-circa 1950
    DeMartini, F. J.
    375-9 Bay Street
    San Francisco, Calif.
    DeMartini Motor Truck Co.
    435 Pacific Street
    San Francisco, Calif.
DENBY—1914-30
    Denby Motor Truck Co. (1914-15)
    Du Bois & Franklin Sts.
    Detroit, Michigan
    Denby Motor Truck Co. (1915-23)
    Denby Motor Truck Corp. (1923-30)
    Holbrook Ave. & G.T.RY.
    Detroit, Michigan
DENMO—1916-17

Denneen Motor Co.
12207 Euclid Ave.
Cleveland, Ohio
Absorbed by Grant Motor Car Co.
DENNISTON—1911-12
    Denniston Co., E. E.
    Buffalo, New York
DEPENDABLE—1918-23
    Dependable Truck & Tractor Co.
    233 Collinsville Avenue
    East St. Louis, Illinois
DESBERON STEAM—1900-03
    Desberon Motor Car Co. (1900-01)
    12 Rose Street
    New Rochelle, N.Y.
    Desberon Motor Car Co. (1901-03)
    51st St. & 12th Ave.
    New York, New York
DETROIT—1899-1900
    Detroit Automobile Co.
    1343 Cass Avenue
    Detroit, Michigan
DETROIT-ELECTRIC—1910-16
    Anderson Electric Car Co.
    450 Clay Avenue
    Detroit, Michigan
DETROIT-ELECTRIC—1924-circa 1927
    Detroit Electric Car Co.
    5860 Cass Avenue
    Detroit, Michigan
DETROIT MOTOR WAGON—1911-13
    Motor-Wagon Company of Detroit
    Detroit, Michigan
DEVON—1912-14
    Devon Engineering Co.
    512 Cherry Street
    Philadelphia, Penna.
DIAMOND REO—1967 to date
    Diamond Reo Trucks
    Div. White Motor Corp.
    1331 So. Washington Ave.
    Lansing, Michigan
DIAMOND T—1911-66
    Diamond T Motor Car Co.
    432 W. Superior Street

Chicago, Illinois
Diamond T Motor Car Co.
4501 W. 26th Street
Chicago, Illinois
Diamond T Motor Truck Co.
4401 W. 26th Street
Chicago, Illinois
Diamond T Division
White Motor Corp.
1331 So. Washington Ave.
Lansing, Michigan
Name changed to "Diamond Reo."
DIEHL—1918-circa 1927
    Diehl Motor Truck Works
    30th St. & Montgomery Ave.
    Philadelphia, Penna.
DIFFERENTIAL—1931-36
    Differential Steel Car Co.
    Findlay, Ohio
DISPATCH—1910-19
    Dispatch Motor Car Co.
    14th Ave. & Winter St.
    Minneapolis, Minn.
DIVCO—1925-35
    Detroit Industrial Vehicle Co. (1925-27)
    Detroit, Michigan
    Divco-Detroit Corp. (1927-34)
    2523 Merrick Avenue
    Detroit, Michigan
    Continental-Divco Co. (1934-35)
    12801 E. Jefferson Ave.
    Detroit, Michigan
    Name changed to "Divco-Twin."
DIVCO—1944 to date
    Divco Corporation (1944-56)
    Divco Truck Division (1957-67)
    Divco-Wayne Corp.
    22000 Hoover Road
    Detroit, Michigan
    Divco Truck Company (1968 to date)
    Delaware, Ohio
DIVCO-TWIN—1935-44
    Divco-Twin Truck Co.
    12801 E. Jefferson Ave.
    Detroit, Michigan

Name changed back to "Divco."

DIXON—1920-circa 1932
Dixon Motor Truck Co.
various addresses
Altoona, Penna.

DOANE—1912-circa 1948
Doane Motor Truck Co.
319 Jessie Street
San Francisco, California
Doane Motor Truck Co.
428 3rd Street
San Francisco, California
Graham-Doane Truck Co.
Oakland, California

DODGE—1935 to date
Dodge Division
Chrysler Corp.
7900 Jos. Campau Ave.
Hamtramck, Mich.

DODGE BROTHERS—1917-34
Dodge Brothers (1917-28)
7900 Jos. Campau Ave.
Hamtramck, Mich.
Dodge Brothers Corp. (1928-34)
Div. Chrysler Corporation
7900 Jos. Campau Ave.
Hamtramck, Mich.
Trade name changed to "Dodge."
See "Graham Brothers."

DOE-WA-JACK—1908-11
Dowagiac Motor Car Co., 1909
Dowagiac, Michigan
Tulsa Automobile & Mfg. Co.
Dowagiac, Michigan
Trade name changed to "Tulsa."

D-OLT—1922-24
D-Olt Motor Truck Co., Inc.
Lott & Jamaica Avenue
Woodhaven, L.I., New York

DOMINION—1916-17
Dominion Motor Truck Co.
Detroit, Michigan

DORRIS—1912-26
Dorris Motor Car Co.
4100 Laclede Avenue

St. Louis, Missouri

DOUBLE DRIVE—1917-28
Double Drive Truck Co. (1917-22)
Chicago, Illinois
Double Drive Truck Co. (1922-28)
Paw Paw Ave. & North Ave.
Benton Harbor, Mich.

DOUGLAS—1917-35
Douglas Motors Corp.
Omaha, Nebraska
Nebraska Auto & Truck Mfg. Co.
Omaha, Nebraska
Douglas Truck Mfg. Co.
30th & Sprague Sts.
Omaha, Nebraska

DOVER—1929-30
Hudson Motor Car Co.
12601 E. Jefferson Ave.
Detroit, Michigan

DOYLE—circa 1914
Doyle, James C.
Seattle, Wash.

DRAKE—1921-22
Drake Motor & Tire Mfg. Corp.
Knoxville, Tennessee

DUER—1910-11
Chicago Coach & Carriage Co.
Chicago, Illinois

DUNLAP ELECTRIC—1914-15
Dunlap Electric Truck Co.
Columbus, Ohio

DUNTLEY—circa 1910
Chicago Pneumatic Tool Co.
Chicago, Illinois

DUPLEX—1909 to date
Duplex Power Car Co. (1909-16)
Lovett & Pearl Streets
Charlotte, Michigan
Duplex Truck Company
2014 Washington Ave.
Lansing, Michigan
Duplex Truck Company
Hazel Street
Lansing, Michigan
Duplex Division (1955 to date)

Warner & Swasey Co.
830 E. Hazel Street
Lansing, Michigan

DURABLE—1917-18
Durable Motor Truck Co.
650 Hohman Street
Hammond, Indiana

DURABLE DAYTON—1912-17
Dayton Auto Truck Co. (1912-13)
Dayton, Ohio
Durable Dayton Truck Co. (1914-17)
First & Taylor Streets
Dayton, Ohio

DURO—1912-circa 1915
Amalgamated Motors Corp.
400 So. Raymond Avenue
Alhambra, California

DURYEA—1906-16
Duryea Power Co. (1906-09)
Stage Street
Reading, Penna.
Duryea, Chas. E. (1910-11)
Reading, Penna.
Duryea Auto Company (1911-12)
Saginaw, Michigan
Duryea Laboratories
Philadelphia, Penna.

DUTY—1920-21
Duty Motor Company
Greenville, Illinois

E

EAGLE—1919-28
Eagle Motor Truck Corp.
6150 Bartmer Avenue
St. Louis, Missouri

EARL—1921-22
Earl Motors, Inc.
Jackson, Michigan

ECKHARD—1912-circa 1913
Hercules Motor Truck Co.
Boston, Massachusetts

ECLIPSE—1911-13
Eclipse Truck Co.
Franklin, Penna.

ECONOMY—1908-11
Economy Motor Car Co.
Joliet, Illinois

ECONOMY—1916-19
Economy Motor Company
Washington & River Sts.
Tiffin, Ohio

EDISON ELECTRIC—circa 1913
Edison Electric Vehicle Co.
of America
Lawrence, Massachusetts

EHRLICH ELECTRIC—1920-26
Ehrlich Electric Truck Co.
710-20 So. Desplaines St.
Chicago, Illinois

EISENHAUER—1945-47
Eisenhauer Mfg. Co.
329 Center Street
Van Wert, Ohio

ELDRIDGE ELECTRIC—1911-17
Eldridge Mfg. Co.
178 Devonshire St.
Boston, Mass.

ELECTRUCK ELECTRIC—1914-23
Los Angeles Creamery, Auto & Machine
Works
1020 Towne Avenue
Los Angeles, California

ELECTRUCK ELECTRIC—1925-28
Electruck Corp. (1925-26)
536 W. 46th Street
New York, N.Y.
Commercial Truck Co. (1926-28)
300 Hunting Park Ave.
Philadelphia, Penna.

ELK—1913-14
Elk Motor Truck Co.
Charleston, W. Va.

ELLSWORTH—1916-21
Mills-Ellsworth Co.
Keokuk, Iowa

ELMIRA—1916-20
Elmira Commercial Motor Car Co.
Main Street
Owego, New York

ELWELL-PARKER ELECTRIC—1905-08
Elwell-Parker Electric Co.
Cleveland, Ohio

ELYSEE—1926-28
Moller Motor Car Co., M. P.
Pope Avenue
Hagerstown, Md.

EMPIRE STEAM—1901-03
Empire State Engineering Co.
533 & 555 E. 116th Street
New York, N.Y.

EPPERSON—1912-14
Epperson Commercial Truck Co.
St. Louis, Missouri

ERIE—1914-23
Erie Motor Truck Mfg. Co.
220 W. 12th Street
Erie, Pennsylvania

ESCO—1933-50
Esco Motor Company
Forbes, Magee & Gibbons Sts.
Pittsburgh, Pennsylvania
Esco Motor Company
W. Gen. Robinson Street
Pittsburgh, Pennsylvania

EUGOL—1921-22
Eugol Motor Truck Co.
Kenosha, Wisconsin

EUREKA—1905-06
Eureka Motor Car Co.
Allentown, Penna.

EVANS—1913-16
Merchant & Evans Co.
2035 Washington Ave.
Philadelphia, Penna.

EVANS LIMITED—1912-13
Evans Motor Car & Parts Mfg. Co.
Marine City, Michigan
Automobile Mfg. & En'g. Co.
Nashville, Tennessee

EWING—1909-circa 1912
Ewing Auto Co.
Geneva, Ohio
Findlay Motor Co.
Findlay, Ohio

FABCO—circa 1955 to date
F.A.B. Mfg. Co.
Fabco Mfg. Co.
1249 67th St.
Oakland, California

FACTO—1921-26
Facto Motor Trucks, Inc.
Springfield, Mass.
Facto Motor Truck Corp.

FAGEOL—1917-38
Fageol Motors Company (1917-32)
Fageol Truck & Coach Co. (1932-38)
107 Av. & Hollywood Blvd.
Oakland, California

FAGEOL—1950-54
Twin Coach Co.
Kent, Ohio

FAMOUS—1918-circa 1922
Famous Trucks, Inc.
St. Joseph, Michigan

FARGO—1913-22
Fargo Motor Car Co.
1164 W. 22nd Street
Chicago, Illinois

FARGO—1929-31
Fargo Motor Corp.
Div. Chrysler Corp.
Detroit, Michigan

F.C.S.—1910
Schmidt Bros.
Chicago, Illinois
Trade name changed to "Schmidt."

FEDERAL—1910 to date
Federal Motor Truck Co.
Leavitt & Campbell Sts.
Detroit, Michigan
Federal Motor Truck Co.
5800 Federal Avenue
Detroit, Michigan
Federal Motor Truck Div. (1952-54)
Federal Fawick Corp.
Detroit, Michigan

Federal Motor Truck Co. (1955-62)
Div. Napco Industries, Inc.
834 No. 7th Street
Minneapolis, Minn.
Federal Motor Truck Co. (1963 to date)
Div. Napco Industries, Inc.
1600 So. 2nd Street
Hopkins, Minnesota
FISCHER—1901-05
Fischer Motor Vehicle Co.
14th & Hudson Streets
Hoboken, New Jersey
FISHER—1925-30
Standard Motor Truck Co.
1111 Bellevue Avenue
Detroit, Michigan
Trade name changed to "Fisher-Standard."
FISHER-STANDARD—1930-33
Standard Motor Truck Co.
1111 Bellevue Avenue
Detroit, Michigan
FLINT—1913-15
Durant-Dort Carriage Co.
South & Mason Streets
Flint, Michigan
FORD—1912 to date
Ford Motor Company
Highland Park, Mich.
Ford Motor Company
Dearborn, Michigan
FORSCHLER—1914-22
Forschler Wagon & Mfg. Co., Philip
610-612 Montegut Street
New Orleans, Louisiana
Forschler Motor Truck Mfg. Co., Inc.
120 No. Claiborne Street
New Orleans, Louisiana
FORT WAYNE—1910-13
Fort Wayne Auto. Mfg. Co.
Fort Wayne, Indiana
FOSTORIA—1915-16
Fostoria Light Car Co.
Fostoria, Ohio
FOUR WHEEL DRIVE—1904-07
Four Wheel Drive Wagon Co.

3211 Vliet Street
Milwaukee, Wisconsin
FRANKLIN—1907-12
Franklin Company, H. H.
310 Geddes Street
Syracuse, New York
FRAYER-MILLER—1906-10
Lear Automobile Co., Oscar (1906-07)
Columbus, Ohio
Lear Automobile Co., Oscar (1907-10)
Springfield, Ohio
Taken over by Kelly Motor Truck Co.
FREEMAN—1928-34
Freeman Motor Co.
1217 Beaufait Ave.
Detroit, Michigan
Freeman Quadrive Corp.
5 W. Larned Street
Detroit, Michigan
FREIGHTLINER—1940-42
Freightliner Mfg. Co.
Salt Lake City, Utah
Revived after World War II.
FREIGHTLINER—1948-51
Freightliner Corp.
1925 N.W. Quimby St.
Portland, Oregon
Name changed to "White-Freightliner."
FREMONT-MAIS—1914-15
Lauth-Juergens Motor Car Co.
Fremont, Ohio
Purchased by H. G. Burford Co.
FRISBEE—1922-23
Frisbee Truck Company
Webberville, Michigan
FRITCHLE—1912-15
Fritchle Auto. & Battery Co.
1520 Clarkson Street
Denver, Colorado
FRONT DRIVE—1920-28
Double Drive Truck Co. (1920-22)
Chicago, Illinois
Double Drive Truck Co. (1922-28)
Paw Paw Ave. & North St.
Benton Harbor, Mich.

FRONTENAC—1907-12
Abendroth & Root Mfg. Co.
Newburgh, New York
Trade name changed to "A&R."
FRONTMOBILE—circa 1918
Camden Motors Corp.
Camden, New Jersey
F.S.—1912
F.S. Motors Company
1st & Oklahoma Aves.
Milwaukee, Wisconsin
FULLER—1910-12
Fuller Buggy Co.
Jackson, Michigan
FULTON—1917-23
Fulton Motor Truck Co. (1917-20)
Farmingdale, L.I., New York
Fulton Motors Corporation (1920-23)
Farmingdale, L.I., New York
FUL-TON—1937-circa 1938
Ful-Ton Truck Co.
Los Angeles, California
FWD—1912 to date
Four Wheel Drive Auto Co.
E. 12th Street
Clintonville, Wisc.
FWD Corporation
E. 12th Street
Clintonville, Wisc.

G

GABRIEL—1911-20
Gabriel Carriage & Wagon Co., W. H.
Cleveland, Ohio
Gabriel Auto Company
315 Prospect Avenue
Cleveland, Ohio
Gabriel Motor Truck Co.
315 Prospect Avenue
Cleveland, Ohio
GAETH—1906-10
Gaeth Automobile Works
2553 W. 25th Street
Cleveland, Ohio

GALE—1906-07
　Western Tool Works
　110-118 Kellogg St.
　Galesburg, Illinois
GARFORD—1909-34
　Garford Company (1909-15)
　Elyria, Ohio
　Garford Motor Truck Co. (1915-26)
　Wapakoneta Road
　Lima, Ohio
　Garford Truck Company (1926-27)
　Wapakoneta Road
　Lima, Ohio
　Relay Motors Corp. (1927-33)
　Lima, Ohio
　Consolidated Motors Corp. (1933-34)
　Lima, Ohio
GARY—1916-27
　Gary Motor Truck Co. (1916-22)
　Gary, Indiana
　Gary Motor Corp. (1922-27)
　9th Ave. & Taft St.
　Gary, Indiana
GASMOBILE—1900-01
　Automobile Co. of America
　West Side Ave. & Broadway
　Marion, New Jersey
GAY—1913-15
　Gay Company, S. G.
　Ottawa, Illinois
GENEVA—1911-20
　Geneva Wagon Co.
　60 Middle Street
　Geneva, New York
GERSIX—1915-22
　Gerlinger Motor Car Co.
　3011 So. Fifth Street
　Tacoma, Washington
　Gersix Manufacturing Co.
　Seattle, Washington
　Became "Kenworth" 1923.
GIANT—1918-22
　Chicago Pneumatic Tool Co.
　Chicago, Illinois
　Giant Truck Company

Chicago Heights, Illinois
GIBBS ELECTRIC—1903-05
　Gibbs Engineering & Mfg. Co.
　Glendale, L.I., New York
GIFFORD-PETTIT—1907-08
　Gifford-Pettit Mfg. Co.
　1217 Devon Street
　Chicago, Illinois
G&J—1921-22
　Gotfredson & Joyce Corp. Ltd.
　Walkerville, Ontario, Canada
　Trade name changed to "Gotfredson."
GLEASON—circa 1910-16
　Kansas City Vehicle Co.
　Bauer Machine Works Co.
　Kansas City, Missouri
　Bauer Motor Car Co.
　109-13 W. 18th Street
　Kansas City, Missouri
GLIDE—1911-13
　Bartholomew Co.
　Peoria, Illinois
GLOBE—1915-19
　Globe Truck Dept.
　Globe Furniture Co.
　Northville, Michigan
　Globe Motor Truck Co.
　1805 Brady Avenue
　East St. Louis, Illinois
GLOBE—1920-22
　Globe Motor Co.
　Cleveland, Ohio
GLOVER—1911-12
　Glover, George T.
　215 So. 43rd Avenue
　Chicago, Illinois
GMC—1912 to date
　General Motors Truck Co. (1912-25)
　Rapid Street
　Pontiac, Michigan
　General Motors Truck & Coach Div.
　　(1925-43)
　Yellow Truck & Coach Mfg. Co.
　Pontiac, Michigan
　GMC Truck & Coach Div. (1943 to date)

General Motors Corp.
　660 South Boulevard
　Pontiac, Michigan
GMC ELECTRIC—1912-16
　General Motors Truck Co.
　Rapid Street
　Pontiac, Michigan
GOLDEN GATE—1927-circa 1931
　Golden Gate Truck Co.
　1020 Folsom Street
　San Francisco, California
GOLDEN WEST—1914-15
　Golden West Motors Co.
　Sacramento, Calif.
　Trade name changed to "Robinson."
GOODWIN—1922-24
　Goodwin Car & Mfg. Co.
　Poughkeepsie, New York
　Succeeded by Guilder Engineering Co.
GOPHER—1911-circa 1912
　Robinson Loomis Motor Truck Co.
　Minneapolis, Minnesota
GOTFREDSON—1923-32
　Gotfredson Truck Corp. Ltd.
　Walkerville, Ontario, Canada
GOTFREDSON—1923-48
　Gotfredson Corp. (1923-29)
　3601 Gratiot Ave.
　Detroit, Michigan
　Gotfredson Truck Co., Robert (1929-48)
　3601 Gratiot Avenue
　Detroit, Michigan
　Became Cummins Diesel Ser. & Sales of
　Michigan.
GOULD ELECTRIC—1954-55
　Gould-National Batteries, Inc.
　35 Neoga Street
　Depew, New York
GOVE—1921-22
　Gove Motor Car Co.
　Detroit, Michigan
GRABOWSKY—1908-13
　Grabowsky Power Wagon Co.
　1812 Mt. Elliot Avenue
　Detroit, Michigan

Machinery and patents purchased by Seitz
Automobile & Transmission Co.

GRAHAM BROTHERS—1919-28
Graham Brothers Co.
Evansville, Indiana
Graham Brothers
1222 Meldrum Ave.
Detroit, Michigan
Dodge Brothers Corp.
7900 Jos. Campau Ave.
Detroit, Michigan

GRAMM—1911-13
Gramm Motor Car Co.
So. Lima Street
Lima, Ohio
Gramm Motor Truck Co.
So. Lima Street
Lima, Ohio
Purchased by John N. Willys.

GRAMM—1926-42
Gramm Motors, Inc.
Delphos, Ohio
Gramm Motor Truck Corp.
Delphos, Ohio

GRAMM-BERNSTEIN—1912-30
Gramm-Bernstein Co. (1912-16)
Lima, Ohio
Gramm-Bernstein Motor Truck Co.
(1916-23)
Lima, Ohio
Gramm-Bernstein Motor Truck Corp.
Lima, Ohio
Gramm-Bernstein Corp.
E. Wayne & Scott Sts.
Lima, Ohio

GRAMM & KINCAID—1925-26
Gramm & Kincaid Motors, Inc.
Lima, Ohio
Became Gramm Motors, Inc.

GRAMM-LOGAN—1908-10
Gramm-Logan Motor Car Co.
Bowling Green, Ohio

GRANT—1918-21
Grant Motor Car Co.
Cleveland, Ohio

GRASS PREMIER—1923-38
Grass Premier Truck Co.
Sauk City, Wisconsin

GRAY—1924-circa 1925
Gray Motors Corp.
Detroit, Michigan

GROUT STEAM—1901-05
Grout Brothers (1901-03)
Grout Bros. Auto. Co. (1903-05)
Orange, Mass.

GUILDER—1924-36
Guilder Engineering Co.
Poughkeepsie, New York

G.V. ELECTRIC—1906-18
General Vehicle Co., Inc.
Borden & Review Avenues
Long Island City, N.Y.

G. V. MERCEDES—1914-17
General Vehicle Co., Inc.
Borden & Review Avenues
Long Island City, N.Y.

G.W.W.—1920-26
Wilson Truck Mfg. Co.
Henderson, Iowa

H

HAHN—1908-48
William G. Hahn & Co.
Hamburg, Penna.
Hahn Motor Truck Co.
Hamburg, Penna.
Hahn Motor Truck & Wagon Co., Inc.
(1913-17)
South Fourth Street
Hamburg, Pennsylvania
Hahn Motor Truck Co. (1917-26)
So. 3rd St. & So. 4th St.
Hamburg, Penna.
Hahn Motor Truck Corp.
40 E. Walnut Street
Allentown, Penna.
Selden-Hahn Motor Truck Corp.
40 E. Walnut Street

Allentown, Penna.
Hahn Motors, Inc. (1931-48)
3rd & Windsor Sts.
Hamburg, Penna.
Specializing in fire apparatus since 1948.

HAL-FUR—1919-31
Hal-Fur Motor Truck Co.
1785 E. 21st Street
Cleveland, Ohio
Hal-Fur Motor Truck Co.
Canton, Ohio

HALL—1915-22
Lewis Hall Iron Works
Ferry Avenue
Detroit, Michigan
Lewis Hall Motors Corp.
6930 W. Jefferson Ave.
Detroit, Michigan

HALSEY STEAM—1901-06
Halsey Motor Vehicle Co.
27th & Brown Streets
Philadelphia, Penna.

HAMPDEN—circa 1922
Hampden Motor Truck Corp.
Holyoke, Massachusetts

HANDI-KAR—circa 1914
Handi-Kar Company
San Francisco, Calif.

HANDY WAGON—1912-13
Auburn Motor Chassis Co.
Auburn, Indiana
Changed to De Kalb Mfg. Co.

HANGER—1913-16
Hanger Carriage & Wagon Co., C. F.
6520-24 Carnegie Avenue
Cleveland, Ohio
Hanger Company, C. F.
6520 Carnegie Ave.
Cleveland, Ohio

HANNIBAL—circa 1916
Hannibal Wagon Works
So. 10th & Collier Streets
Hannibal, Missouri
Hannibal Motor Wagon & Body Co.
Hannibal, Missouri

HARDER—1909-14
Harder's Fire-Proof Storage & Van Co.
62nd & LaSalle Streets
Chicago, Illinois
Harder Auto Truck Co.
Chicago, Illinois
HARRISON—1911-circa 1915
Harrison Co., Robert
324-38 W. First Street
Boston, Massachusetts
HART-KRAFT—1907-13
Hart-Kraft Motor Co.
York, Pennsylvania
HARVEY—1911-32
Harvey Motor Truck Works
155th St. & Commercial Ave.
Harvey, Illinois
HATFIELD—1907-08
Hatfield Motor Vehicle Co.
Miamisburg, Ohio
HATFIELD—1910-14
Hatfield Company (1910-12)
25 Railroad Avenue
Elmira, New York
Hatfield Auto Truck Co. (1912-14)
25 Railroad Avenue
Elmira, New York
HATFIELD—1916-circa 1918
Cortland Cart & Carriage Co.
Sherman Avenue
Sidney, New York
HAWKEYE—1916-circa 1933
Hawkeye Mfg. Co.
313 Jennings St.
Sioux City, Iowa
Hawkeye Truck Co.
2700 Floyd Ave.
Sioux City, Iowa
HAYES—circa 1928 to date
Hayes Mfg. Co., Ltd.
225 W. Second Avenue
Vancouver, B.C., Canada
Also built "Hayes-Anderson" and "Hayes-Lawrence" trucks before World War II.
Joined Mack Trucks, Inc. in 1969.

HENDERSON BROS.—1914-circa 1925
Henderson Bros. Co., Inc.
2067 Massachusetts Ave.
Cambridge, Massachusetts
HENDRICKSON—1913 to date
Hendrickson Motor Truck Co.
1439 Carroll Avenue
Chicago, Illinois
Hendrickson Motor Truck Co.
3538 So. Wabash Avenue
Chicago, Illinois
Hendrickson Motor Truck Co.
Hendrickson Mfg. Co.
8001 W. 47th Street
Lyons, Illinois
HERCULES—1913
Hercules Motor Truck Co.
State Street
Detroit, Michigan
Rights to make "Hercules" truck purchased
by Alma Motor Truck Co.
HERRESHOFF—1911
Herreshoff Motor Co.
Detroit, Michigan
HERSCHMANN steam—1902-03
American Ordnance Co. (1902)
Bridgeport, Conn.
Columbia Engineering Works, Inc.
William & Imley Streets
Brooklyn, New York
Also called "Adams Express."
HERTNER electric—1934-36
Hertner Electric Co.
Cleveland, Ohio
HEWITT—1905-14
Hewitt Motor Co. (1905-09)
6 E. 31st Street
New York, N.Y.
Metzger Motor Car Co. (1909-11)
6-10 E. 31st Street
New York, N.Y.
Hewitt Motor Company (1911-12)
West End Ave. & 64th St.
New York, New York
International Motor Co. (1912-14)

West End Ave. & 64th St.
New York, New York
HEWITT-LUDLOW—1912-circa 1926
Hewitt-Ludlow Auto Co., Inc.
604 Mission Street
San Francisco, Calif.
Hewitt-Ludlow Auto Co., Inc.
149 11th Street
San Francisco, Calif.
Ralston Iron Works, Inc.
Indiana Street
San Francisco, Calif.
Hewitt-Ludlow Auto Co.
901-951 Indiana Street
San Francisco, Calif.
Hewitt-Ludlow Auto Co.
75 Fremont Street
San Francisco, Calif.
HEWITT-TALBOT—circa 1920
Hewitt-Ludlow Auto Co., Inc.
149 Eleventh Street
San Francisco, Calif.
HIGHWAY—1965-68
Highway Products, Inc.
Kent, Ohio
HIGHWAY-KNIGHT—1919-21
Highway Motors Co.
Chicago, Illinois
HIGRADE—1917-22
Higrade Motors Co.
Harbor Springs, Mich.
HINDE & DAUCH—1908
Hinde & Dauch
Sandusky, Ohio
H&M—1919
H&M Motor Truck Co., Inc.
Baltimore, Maryland
HOFFMAN—1912-15
Hoffman Motor Truck Co.
Minneapolis, Minn.
Hoffman Motor Car Co.
38th St. & University Ave.
Minneapolis, Minn.
HOLMES—circa 1920-24
Holmes Motors Mfg. Co.

Littleton, Colorado
Became Coleman Motors Corp.
HOLSMAN—1909-10
Holsman Automobile Co.
Chicago, Illinois
HOMER—1908-09
Homer Auto Truck Co.
Homer, Michigan
Changed to Homer Gas Engine Co.
HOOD—1917-20
Hood Manufacturing Co.
Seattle, Washington
HOOVER—1911; 1916-20
Hoover Wagon Co.
Wheatfield Street
York, Pennsylvania
HORNER—1913-18
Detroit-Wyandotte Motor Co.
Cedar Street
Wyandotte, Michigan
HOWARD—1903
Howard Automobile Co.
67 Dock Street
Yonkers, New York
HOWARD—1915-16
Howard Motor Truck Co.
87 Church Street
Boston, Massachusetts
H.R.L.—1920-22
H.R.L. Motor Company
3301 First Ave., South
Seattle, Washington
HUDSON—1939-47
Hudson Motor Car Co.
12601 E. Jefferson Ave.
Detroit, Michigan
HUFFMAN—1919-27
Huffman Bros. Motor Co.
Elkhart, Indiana
Valley Motor Truck Co.
1730 So. Main Street
Elkhart, Indiana
Trade name changed to "Valley."
HUG—1922-42
Hug Company

528 Cypress St.
Highland, Illinois
HUPMOBILE—1913-14
Hupp Motor Car Co.
1231 Milwaukee Ave.
Detroit, Michigan
HUPP-YEATS electric—1911-12
Hupp Corporation
131 Lycaste Street
Detroit, Michigan
R.C.H. Corporation
Detroit, Michigan
HURLBURT—1912-25
Hurlburt Motor Truck Co. (1912-15)
Fort George
New York, New York
Hurlburt Motor Truck Co. (1915-19)
3rd Ave. & Harlem River
Bronx, New York
Harrisburg Mfg. & Boiler Co. (1919-25)
19th & Manada Streets
Harrisburg, Penna.
HURON—1921-23
Huron Truck Co.
Bad Axe, Michigan

I

IBEX—1964 to date
Hafer-Ibex Corp.
Salt Lake City, Utah
Ibex Motor Truck Corp.
Salt Lake City, Utah
Ibex Division
Jelco Incorporation
847 West 17th South
Salt Lake City, Utah
IDEAL—1911-12
Ideal Commercial Car Co.
Detroit, Michigan
Trade name changed to "Akron."
IDEAL—1911-15
Ideal Auto Company
616 High Street
Fort Wayne, Ind.

I.H.C.—1907-13
International Harvester Co. (1907)
Chicago, Illinois
International Harvester Co. (1907-13)
Akron, Ohio
Trade name changed to "International."
INDEPENDENT—1911
Independent Harvester Co.
Plano, Illinois
INDEPENDENT—1914-21
Independent Motor Co.
Youngstown, Ohio
INDEPENDENT—1915-18
Independent Motors Co.
Port Huron, Michigan
INDEPENDENT—1917-circa 1927
Independent Motor Truck Co., Inc.
Second & Howell Streets
Davenport, Iowa
INDIANA—1911-39
Harwood-Barley Mfg. Co.
211 Indiana Avenue
Marion, Indiana
Indiana Truck Corp.
Indiana Park
Marion, Indiana
Indiana Motors Corp. (1932-33)
Indiana Park
Marion, Indiana
Indiana Motors Corp. (1933-39)
842 E. 79th Street
Cleveland, Ohio
Purchased by "White" 1932.
INTERBORO—1913-circa 1914
Interboro Motor Truck Co.
811 No. Taney Street
Philadelphia, Penna.
INTERNATIONAL—1914 to date
International Harvester Co.
Akron, Ohio
International Harvester Co.
Springfield, Ohio
International Harvester Co.
Fort Wayne, Indiana

INTER-STATE—1916-17
Inter-State Motor Co.
900 W. Willard St.
Muncie, Indiana
IROQUOIS—1906
Iroquois Iron Works
Buffalo, New York
ITALIA—1922-23
Italia Motor Truck Co.
1346 Folsom Street
San Francisco, California

J

JACKSON—1919-23
Jackson Motors Corp.
E. Main & Horton Streets
Jackson, Michigan
JARRETT—1933-35
Jarrett Motor Finance Co., J. C.
Colorado Springs, Colorado
JARVIS-HUNTINGTON—1911-12
Jarvis Huntington Auto Co.
Huntington, West Virginia
Jarvis Machinery & Supply Co.
Huntington, West Virginia
JEEP—1963 to date
Kaiser Jeep Corp.
Jeep Corp.
Toledo, Ohio
JEFFERY—1914-16
Jeffery Co., Thomas B.
Kenosha, Wisconsin
J.&J.—1920-21
Lorain Motor Truck Co.
Lorain, Ohio
JOERNS—1911-12
Joerns-Thiem Motor Car Co.
St. Paul, Minnesota
JOHNSON—1902-13
Johnson Service Co.
Milwaukee, Wisconsin
JOLIET ELECTRIC—1912
Joliet Auto Truck Co.
Joliet, Illinois

JOLY & LAMBERT ELECTRIC—1916
Joly & Lambert Elec. Auto Co.
Haverhill Street
Andover, Massachusetts
JONES—circa 1917-20
Jones Motor Car Co.
210-12 W. Douglas Ave.
Wichita, Kansas
JONZ—1911-13
American Automobile Mfg. Co.
New Albany, Indiana
JUMBO—1918-24
Saginaw Motor Car Co.
Saginaw, Michigan
Nelson Motor Truck Co.
Saginaw, Michigan
JUNO—1912-14
Brodesser Motor Truck Co.
Juneau, Wisconsin
Juno Motor Truck Co.
126 Fulton Street
Juneau, Wisconsin

K

KA DIX—1912-13
Newark Motor Truck Co.
East Orange, New Jersey
KALAMAZOO—1913-15
Kalamazoo Motor Vehicle Co.
Kalamazoo, Michigan
Became Columbia Motor Truck & Trailer.
KALAMAZOO—1919-23
Kalamazoo Motors Corp.
Reed & Fulford Streets
Kalamazoo, Michigan
Purchased by Sandow Motor Truck Co.
KANAWHA—1912
Kanawha Auto Truck Co.
Charleston, West Virginia
KANKAKEE—1919-24
Kankakee Automobile Co.
860 No. Greenwood Ave.
Kankakee, Illinois

Kankakee Truck Co.
860 No. Greenwood Ave.
Kankakee, Illinois
KANSAS CITY CAR—1905-07
Kansas City Motor Car Co.
310 West 9th Street
Kansas City, Missouri
Trade name changed to "Phoenix" truck.
KARAVAN—1920-circa 1923
Caravan Motors Company
E. 7th, Main & Salmon Sts.
Portland, Oregon
KASTORY—circa 1924
Kastory Mfg. Co.
301-9 Hillgrove Ave.
La Grange, Illinois
KATO—1909-13
Four Traction Auto Co.
Mankato, Minnesota
Purchased by Nevada Mfg. Co.
KEARNS—circa 1909-28
Kearns Motor Buggy Co.
Beavertown, Penna.
Kearns Motor Car Co.
Beavertown, Penna.
Kearns Motor Truck Co., Inc.
Beavertown, Penna.
Kearns-Dughie Motors Corp.
Danville, Penna.
KELDON—1919-20
House Cold Tire Setter Co.
St. Louis, Missouri
KELLAND ELECTRIC—circa 1915-25
Kelland Motor Car Co.
58 Elm Street
Newark, New Jersey
KELLY STEAM—1902-03
Kelly Company, O. S.
Springfield, Ohio
KELLY—1910-27
Kelly Motor Truck Co. (1910-12)
Burt Street
Springfield, Ohio
Kelly-Springfield Motor Truck Co.
(1912-26)

Burt & Sheridan Streets
Springfield, Ohio
American Bus & Truck Co. (1926)
Springfield, Ohio
Kelly Springfield Truck & Bus Corp.
  (1926-27)
Springfield, Ohio
KENEN—1913-15
  Kenen Mfg. Co.
  Broadway
  Long Beach, California
KENWORTH—1923 to date
  Kenworth Motor Truck Corp.
  506 Mercer Street
  Seattle, Washington
  Kenworth Motor Truck Corp.
  8801 E. Marginal Way
  Seattle, Washington
KEYSTONE—1919-23
  Keystone Motor Truck Corp.
  Oaks, Pennsylvania
  Purchased by Penn Motors Corp.
KIMBALL—1918-circa 1925
  Kimball Motors Corp.
  1700 East 9th Street
  Los Angeles, Calif.
KING—1912-17
  King Mfg. Co., A. R.
  Kingston, New York
KING-ZEITLER—1919-circa 1929
  King-Zeitler Co.
  315 No. Ada Street
  Chicago, Illinois
KISSEL—1910-30
  Kissel Motor Car Co.
  Kissel Avenue
  Hartford, Wisc.
KLEIBER—1914-37
  Kleiber & Company, Inc.
  1424-40 Folsom Street
  San Francisco, Calif.
  Kleiber Motor Truck Co.
  11th & Folsom Streets
  San Francisco, Calif.
  Kleiber Motor Company

1480 Folsom Street
San Francisco, Calif.
KLEMM—1916-circa 1921
  Klemm, E. R.
  1477 W. Austin Ave.
  Chicago, Illinois
KLINE—1910-12
  B.C.K. Motor Car Co.
  York, Penna.
KNICKERBOCKER—1911-17
  Knickerbocker Motor Truck Mfg. Co.
  Bronx, New York
  Knickerbocker Motors, Inc. (1916-17)
  151st Street & River Ave.
  Bronx, New York
KNOX—1901-circa 1921
  Knox Automobile Company
  Wilbraham Rd. & Waltham Ave.
  Springfield, Massachusetts
  Knox Motors Company
  53 Wilbraham Road
  Springfield, Mass.
  Semi-trailer tractor marketed as "Knox-
Martin" from 1912-21.
KNUCKEY—1943-circa 1955
  Knuckey Truck Company
  17th & Connecticut Sts.
  San Francisco, Calif.
  Knuckey Truck Company
  107 So. Linden Avenue
  So. San Francisco, California
KOEHLER—circa 1912-23
  Schlotterback Mfg. Co.
  Newark, New Jersey
  Koehler Sporting Goods Co., H. J.
  151 Ogden Street
  Newark, New Jersey
  Koehler Motors Corp., H. J.
  150 Ogden Street
  Newark, New Jersey
  Koehler Motors Corp., H. J.
  Llewellyn Avenue
  Bloomfield, New Jersey
KOPP—1911-circa 1915
  Kopp Motor Truck Co.

49 E. Utica Street
Buffalo, New York
KOSMATH—1913-16
  Kosmath Company
  1506 Fort St., West
  Detroit, Michigan
KREBS—1912-17
  Krebs Commercial Car Co.
  428 Amanda Street
  Clyde, Ohio
  Became Clyde Cars Company
KREBS—1922-25
  Krebs Motor Truck Co.
  Bellevue, Ohio
  Taken over by Buck Motor Truck Co.
KRICKWELL—1912-circa 1914
  Krickwell Motor Truck Co.
  1373 E. 55th Street
  Chicago, Illinois
KRIT—1913-14
  Krit Motor Car Co.
  East Grand Blvd.
  Detroit, Michigan
KUHN—1918-20
  Kuhn Tractor Truck Co.
  320 Terry Avenue, N.
  Seattle, Washington

L

LA CROSSE—1914
  La Crosse Motor Truck Co.
  106-8 No. Front Street
  La Crosse, Wisconsin
LA FRANCE—1917-18
  La France Motor Truck Co.
  Elmira, New York
  Changed to Ward La France.
LA FRANCE-REPUBLIC—1929-42
  La France-Republic Corp. (1929-32)
  Alma, Michigan
  La France-Republic Div. (1932-42)
  Sterling Motors Corp.
  Alma, Michigan

LAMBERT—1901-18
    Buckeye Mfg. Co.
    1801-99 Columbus Ave.
    Anderson, Indiana
LAMSON—1917-circa 1919
    Lamson Truck & Tractor Co. (1917-18)
    4646 W. Madison Street
    Chicago, Illinois
    United Four Wheel Drive Truck Corp.
    (1918-19)
    4638-48 W. Madison Street
    Chicago, Illinois
LANDSHAFT—1911-20
    Landshaft & Sons, Wm.
    2900 Darwin Terrace
    Chicago, Illinois
LANE—1916-19
    Lane Motor Truck Co.
    1812 Fulford
    Kalamazoo, Mich.
LANGE—1911-31
    Lange Wagon Works, H. (1911-12)
    Pittsburgh, Penna.
    Lange Motor Truck Co. (1912-18?)
    145 So. St. Clair Street
    Pittsburgh, Penna.
    Lange Motor Truck Co.
    6633 Hamilton Avenue
    Pittsburgh, Penna.
LANPHER—1910
    Lanpher Motor Buggy Co.
    Carthage, Missouri
LANSDEN ELECTRIC—1904-circa 1927
    Lansden Company
    54 Lackawanna Ave.
    Newark, New Jersey
    Lansden Company
    233-5 High Street
    Newark, New Jersey
    Lansden Company
    394-400 Frelinghuysen Ave.
    Newark, New Jersey
    Lansden Company, Inc.
    Flatbush & Nostrand Aves.
    Brooklyn, New York

    Lansden Company, Inc.
    Danbury, Connecticut
LAPEER—1916-circa 1920
    Lapeer Tractor Truck Co.
    Lapeer, Michigan
LARRABEE—1916-32
    Larrabee-Deyo Motor Truck Co., Inc.
    27 Washington Street
    Binghamton, New York
LAUTH-JUERGENS—1908-14
    Lauth-Juergens Motor Car Co.
    1345 Rawson Street
    Chicago, Illinois
    Lauth-Juergens Motor Car Co.
    Fremont, Ohio
    Trade name changed to "Fremont-Mais."
L.A.W.—1912-13
    L.A.W. Motor Truck Co.
    Findlay, Ohio
LEASE—circa 1921
    Lease Motors Co., Inc.
    Long Island City, N.Y.
LEHIGH—1925-27
    Lehigh Company
    Allentown, Penna.
    Merged with Bethlehem Motors Corp. of
    N.Y.
LE MOON—1910-39
    Nelson & Le Moon
    851 No. Kedzie Ave.
    Chicago, Illinois
    Nelson-Le Moon Truck Co.
    849 No. Kedzie Avenue
    Chicago, Illinois
LENOX—1914-16
    Lenox Motor Car Co.
    60 Factory Street
    Hyde Park, Mass.
LEWIS—1912-15
    Lewis Motor Truck Co.
    932 Folsom Street
    San Francisco, California
    Lewis Motor Truck Co., Inc.
    12th & Oak Streets
    Oakland, California

LIGHT—1913-14
    Light Commercial Car Co.
    Wilmington, Delaware
LIMA—1915
    Lima Light Car Co.
    Lima, Ohio
LINCOLN—circa 1907
    Lincoln Automobile Co.
    Lincoln, Illinois
LINCOLN—1910-14
    Lincoln Motor Car Works
    1352 W. Harrison Street
    Chicago, Illinois
LINCOLN—1916-17
    Lincoln Motor Truck Co.
    Pontiac, Michigan
    Joined Krebs Commercial Car Co.
LINDSLEY—circa 1908
    Lindsley Co., J. V.
    Indianapolis, Indiana
LINN—1916-circa 1950
    Linn Mfg. Corp.
    Lake Street
    Morris, N.Y.
LINN—1945-52
    Linn Coach & Truck Corp.
    Oneonta, New York
LIPPARD-STEWART—1911-18
    Lippard-Stewart Motor Car Co.
    237 West Utica Street
    Buffalo, New York
LITE WAY—1953-55
    McBright Incorporated
    Lehighton, Penna.
LITTLE GIANT—1912-18
    Chicago Pneumatic Tool Co.
    Chicago, Illinois
    Trade name changed to "Giant."
    See also "C.P.T."
L.M.C.—1919-21
    Louisiana Motor Car Co.
    Shreveport, Louisiana
LOCOMOBILE STEAM—1899-1902
    Locomobile Co. of America
    Bridgeport, Conn.

LOCOMOBILE—1912-16
  Locomobile Co. of America
  Bridgeport, Conn.
LOGAN—1903-circa 1908
  Motor Storage & Mfg. Co. (1903-04)
  Chillicothe, Ohio
  Logan Construction Co. (1905-08?)
  Chillicothe, Ohio
  Taken over by John H. Blacker & Co.
LONE STAR—1920-21
  Lone Star Motor Truck & Tractor Assn.
  515 Roosevelt Avenue
  San Antonio, Texas
LONGEST—1910-16
  Longest Brothers Co.
  725-729 S. Third St.
  Louisville, Kentucky
LORD BALTIMORE—1911-14
  Lord Baltimore Motor Car Co.
  Baltimore, Maryland
  Lord Baltimore Truck Co.
  Bank & Fifth Streets
  Baltimore, Maryland
LOWELL—1918-19
  Lowell Motor Truck Co.
  Lowell, Indiana
LOYAL—1918
  Loyal Motor Truck Co.
  Erie, Pennsylvania
LOZIER—1911-12
  Lozier Motor Co.
  Detroit, Michigan
LUCK—1911-14
  Cleburne Motor Car Mfg. Co.
  Cleburne, Texas
LUEDINGHAUS—1920-33
  Luedinghaus-Espenschied Wagon Co.
  1721 West Broadway
  St. Louis, Missouri
LUVERNE—1912-circa 1920
  Luverne Automobile Co.
  Luverne, Minnesota
  Luverne Motor Truck Co.
  Maple & McKenzie Streets
  Luverne, Minnesota

Building only fire apparatus since early
1920's
LYON—1911
  Lyon Motor Truck Co.
  Pittsburgh, Penna.

M

MACCAR—1914-35
  Maccar Truck Co.
  Providence Ave.
  Scranton, Penna.
  Maccar-Selden-Hahn Truck Corp.
  40 East Walnut Street
  Allentown, Pennsylvania
MACCARR—1912-13
  Maccarr Company
  Allentown, Penna.
  Changed to Maccar Truck Co.
MacDONALD—1920-circa 1952
  MacDonald Truck & Tractor Co.
  Fifth & Harrison Streets
  San Francisco, Calif.
  Union Construction Co.
  351 California Street
  San Francisco, Calif.
  MacDonald Truck & Mfg. Co.
  757 Folsom Street
  San Francisco, Calif.
  MacDonald Truck & Mfg. Co.
  Div. Peterbilt Motors Co.
  107th Ave. & MacArthur Blvd.
  Oakland, California
MACK—1911 to date
  International Motor Co. (1911-36)
  Mack Manufacturing Corp. (1937-56)
  Mack Trucks, Inc. (1956 to date)
  Allentown, Penna.
MACK JR.—1936-37
  Reo Motor Car Co.
  1331 Washington Ave.
  Lansing, Michigan
MADSEN—circa 1958 to date
  Madsen Equipment Co., Jay
  120 Wilson Avenue

Bath, New York
MAIBOHM—1919-20
  Maibohm Motors Co.
  Racine, Wisconsin
MAIS—1911-16
  Mais Motor Truck Company
  So. LaSalle St. & Belt Ry.
  Indianapolis, Indiana
  Absorbed by Premier Motor Mfg. Co.
MANHATTAN—1905-10
  Mack Bros. Motor Car Co.
  Allentown, Penna.
  Trade name changed to "Mack."
MANLY—1917-19
  Manly Motor Corp.
  Waukegan, Illinois
  Trade name changed to "Super Truck."
MANSUR—1912-14
  Mansur Motor Truck Co.
  204 Main Street
  Haverhill, Mass.
  May have been marketed under name
  "Salvador" as well.
MARATHON—1912-13
  Marathon Motor Works
  Nashville, Tennessee
MARION—1905
  Marion Motor Car Co.
  Indianapolis, Indiana
MARMON—1912-14
  Nordyke & Marmon Co.
  Indianapolis, Indiana
MARMON—1964 to date
  Marmon Motor Company
  Shiloh Rd. & Fairdale Ave.
  Garland, Texas
MARMON-HERRINGTON—1931-64
  Marmon-Herrington Co., Inc.
  1001 York Street
  Indianapolis, Indiana
  Marmon-Herrington Co., Inc.
  Washington & Harding Sts.
  Indianapolis, Indiana
  Rights to build "M-H" trucks acquired by
  Marmon Motor Co.

MARQUETTE—1910-12
  Marquette Motor Vehicle Co.
  3626-28 So. Halstead St.
  Chicago, Illinois
MARTIN—1909-15
  Martin Carriage Works
  York, Pennsylvania
  Trade name changed to "Atlas."
MASON—1912-14
  Mason Motor Co.
  Waterloo, Iowa
MASON ROADKING—1922-25
  Mason Motor Truck Co.
  Ossington Avenue
  Flint, Michigan
  Became "Flint Roadking."
MASTER—1917-circa 1929
  Master Trucks, Inc.
  3132 S. Wabash Ave.
  Chicago, Illinois
  Master Motor Corp.
  2381 Archer Avenue
  Chicago, Illinois
  Master Motor Truck Mfg. Co.
  2381 Archer Avenue
  Chicago, Illinois
  Master Motor Truck Co.
  3919 S. Michigan Ave.
  Chicago, Illinois
MATHESON—1906
  Matheson Motor Car Co.
  Wilkes Barre, Penna.
MAXFER—1917
  Maxfer Truck & Tractor Co.
  5025 S. Wabash Avenue
  Chicago, Illinois
MAXIM—1914
  Maxim Motor Company
  Wareham Street
  Middleboro, Mass.
  Still building fire apparatus.
MAXIM TRICAR—1911-14
  Bushnell Co., G. H.
  Thompsonville, Conn.
MAXWELL—1905-09

Maxwell-Briscoe Motor Co.
  35 Highland Avenue
  Tarrytown, New York
MAXWELL—1917-24
  Maxwell Motor Corp.
  12300 Oakland Ave.
  Detroit, Michigan
McCARRON—1927-28
  McCarron Corp., W. E.
  2369 Milwaukee Ave.
  Chicago, Illinois
McINTYRE—1909-15
  McIntyre Company, W. H.
  Auburn, Indiana
McKAY STEAM—1901
  Stanley Mfg. Co.
  Lawrence, Mass.
MEISELBACH—1904-09
  Meiselbach Motor Wagon Co., A. D.
  North Milwaukee, Wisconsin
MENGES—1920-22
  Menges Motor Co.
  Greenville, Miss.
MENOMINEE—1911-36
  Poyer Company, D. F. (1911-15)
  Broadway & Saxon Ave.
  Menominee, Michigan
  Menominee Motor Truck Co. (1916-20)
  Broadway & Saxon Ave.
  Menominee, Michigan
  Menominee Motor Truck Co. (1920-29)
  East 12th Street
  Clintonville, Wisconsin
  Utility Supply Company (1929-36)
  East 12th Street
  Clintonville, Wisconsin
  Speed truck model (1922-26) marketed un-
  der the name "Hurryton."
MERCHANTS—1911-14
  Merchants Automobile Co.
  Chicago, Illinois
MERCURY—1911-circa 1915
  Mercury Mfg. Co.
  4108 S. Halstead St.
  Chicago, Illinois

MERIT—1911
  Waterville Tractor Co.
  Waterville, Ohio
MESERVE STEAM—1901-02
  Meserve, W. F.
  Canobie Lake, N.H.
MESERVE—1902-03
  Meserve Autotruck Co.
  Methuen, Mass.
METROPOLITAN—1916-17
  Metropolitan Motors, Inc.
  585-7 Jackson Avenue
  Bronx, New York
METZ—1916-17
  Metz Company
  Rumford Avenue
  Waltham, Mass.
MIDDLEBORO—1913-14
  Middleboro Auto Exchange
  Middleboro, Massachusetts
MIDLAND—1918
  Midland Motor Car Co.
  Oklahoma City, Okla.
MILBURN ELECTRIC—1915-17
  Milburn Wagon Co.
  3134 Monroe St.
  Toledo, Ohio
  Production suspended 1918 to 1921
MILBURN ELECTRIC—1922-26
  Milburn Wagon Co. (1922-23)
  3134 Monroe St.
  Toledo, Ohio
  Milburn Truck Co. (1924-25)
  740 E. 51st Street
  Chicago, Illinois
  Nelson-LeMoon Truck Co. (1925-26)
  849 N. Kedzie Avenue
  Chicago, Illinois
MILFORD—1945-52
  Milford Crane & Machine Co.
  143 Buckingham Avenue
  Milford, Connecticut
MISSION—1914-15
  Mission Motor Car Co.
  1310-12 So. Grand Ave.

Los Angeles, Calif.
MITCHELL—1905-08
  Mitchell Motor Car Co.
  62 Mitchell Street
  Racine, Wisconsin
MOBILE STEAM—1901-03
  Mobile Company of America
  North Tarrytown, N.Y.
MODERN—1910-12
  Modern Motor Truck Co.
  St. Louis, Missouri
MODERN—1911-18
  Bowling Green Motor Truck Co.
  500 Lehman Avenue
  Bowling Green, Ohio
MOELLER—1911-17
  New Haven Truck & Auto Works
  166-168 Saint John Street
  New Haven, Connecticut
MOGUL—1911-16
  Mogul Motor Truck Co. (1911-13)
  4060 Princeton Avenue
  Chicago, Illinois
  Mogul Motor Truck Co. (1913-16)
  6148 Maple Avenue
  St. Louis, Missouri
MOLINE—1920-22
  Moline Plow Co.
  Moline, Illinois
MONARCH—1916
  Monarch Light Truck Co.
  932 Becher Street
  Milwaukee, Wisconsin
MONITOR—1908-14
  Monitor Automobile Works
  220 N. Academy Street
  Janesville, Wisconsin
MONTPELIER—1958-59
  Montpelier Mfg. Co.
  Montpelier, Ohio
  Taken over by White Motor Co.
MOON—1912-18
  Moon Buggy Co., Jos. W.
  Main & Douglas Streets
  St. Louis, Missouri

MOORE—1910-16
  Moore Company, F. L.
  Moore Motor Truck Co., F. L.
  Los Angeles, Calif.
  Pacific Metal Products Co. (1913-16)
  Carson Street
  Torrance, California
MOORE—1911-13
  Moore Motor Truck Co.
  Toledo, Ohio
MORA—1911-14
  Mora Power Wagon Co.
  5320 St. Clair Avenue
  Cleveland, Ohio
MORELAND—1911-41
  Moreland Motor Truck Co.
  1701 North Main Street
  Los Angeles, Calif.
  Moreland Motor Truck Co.
  E. San Fernando Blvd.
  Burbank, California
MORGAN STEAM—1902-03
  Morgan Motor Co.
  Barber's Crossing
  Worcester, Mass.
MORGAN—1908-12
  Morgan, Ralph L. (1908-09)
  Worcester, Mass.
  Morgan Company, R. L. (1909-11)
  Lincoln Square
  Worcester, Mass.
  Morgan Motor Truck Co. (1911-12)
  677 Cambridge St.
  Worcester, Mass.
MORSE—1909-15
  Easton Machine Company
  Washington & Central Sts.
  South Easton, Mass.
MORTON—1912-16
  Morton Truck & Tractor Co., Inc.
  19th & Manada Streets
  Harrisburg, Penna.
MOTOKART—1913-14
  Tarrytown Motor Car Co.
  Tarrytown, New York

MOYEA—1904
  Consolidated Motor Co.
  175 N. 9th Street
  Brooklyn, New York
M&P ELECTRIC—circa 1912
  M&P Electric Vehicle Co.
  Franklin & DuBois Streets
  Detroit, Michigan
  Trade name changed to "Victor."
M.P.C.—1926-circa 1927
  Milwaukee Parts Corp.
  271-275 First Avenue
  Milwaukee, Wisconsin
MURTY—circa 1949 to date
  Murty Brothers
  906 N.E. Third Street
  Portland, Oregon
MUSKEGON—1917-circa 1919
  Muskegon Engine Co.
  Muskegon, Michigan
  Muskegon Truck Corp.
  Muskegon, Michigan
MUTUAL—1919-21
  Mutual Truck Co.
  Sullivan, Indiana
MYERS—1918-20
  Myers Company, E. A.
  Pittsburgh, Penna.

N

NAPOLEON—circa 1916-22
  Traverse City Motor Car Co.
  Traverse City, Michigan
  Napoleon Motors Company
  Traverse City, Michigan
NASH—1916-circa 1929; 1947-49
  Nash Motors Company
  Kenosha, Wisconsin
NATCO—1911-16
  National Motor Truck Co.
  Bay City, Michigan
NATIONAL—circa 1920
  National Steel Car Co. Ltd.
  Hamilton, Ontario, Canada

NETCO—1914-38
New England Truck Co.
86 Lunenburg Street
Fitchburg, Mass.
NEVADA—1913-16
Nevada Mfg. Company
Nevada, Iowa
Nevada Truck & Tractor Co.
Nevada, Iowa
See also "Kato."
NEWARK—1911-12
Newark Automobile Mfg. Co.
Frelinghuysen Ave. & Bigelow St.
Newark, New Jersey
NEW YORK—1912-21
Tegetmeier & Riepe Co.
771-773 First Avenue
New York, New York
NIELSON—1906-07
Nielson Motor Car Company
Woodbridge & Randolph Sts.
Detroit, Michigan
NILES—1916-23
Niles Car & Mfg. Co. (1916-17)
Niles, Ohio
Niles Motor Truck Co.
207-219 So. Main St.
Pittsburgh, Penna.
South Main Motor Co.
207 So. Main Street
Pittsburgh, Penna.
NOBLE—1917-31
Noble Motor Truck Co.
Wayne Street
Kendallville, Indiana
NORTHERN—1906-08
Northern Motor Car Co.
Detroit, Michigan
NORTHWAY—1919-circa 1925
Northway Motors Corp.
Natick, Massachusetts
Speed truck model (1925) marketed under
the name "Rocket."
NORTHWESTERN—1913-circa 1933
Star Carriage Company

First Ave. & Stacy St.
Seattle, Washington
NORWALK—1917-22
Norwalk Motor Car Co.
Martinsburg, W. Va.
NYBERG—1912-13
Nyberg Automobile Works
Anderson, Indiana

O

O.B. ELECTRIC—circa 1921-31
O.B. Electric Vehicles, Inc.
Harris Ave. & Sherman St.
Long Island City, N.Y.
O.B. Electric Truck, Inc.
578-582 Washington St.
New York, New York
OFELDT STEAM—1901
Ofeldt & Sons, F. W.
Foot of 25th Street
Brooklyn, New York
OGDEN—1919-circa 1928
Ogden Motor & Supply Co.
3854-60 Ogden Avenue
Chicago, Illinois
Ogden Truck Company
3848 Ogden Avenue
Chicago, Illinois
O.K.—1913-15
Star-Tribune Motor Sales Co.
Detroit, Michigan
O.K. Motor Truck Co.
Flint, Michigan
O.K.—1917-28
Oklahoma Auto Mfg. Co.
North Muskogee, Okla.
O.K. Truck Manufacturing Co.
Muskogee, Oklahoma
OLD HICKORY—1914-23
Kentucky Wagon Mfg. Co.
Third & K Streets
Louisville, Kentucky
OLD RELIABLE—1911-circa 1927
Lee Power Co., Henry

5230-36 Evanston Ave.
Chicago, Illinois
Old Reliable Motor Truck Co.
3921 Michigan Avenue
Chicago, Illinois
Reliable Trucks Inc.
Chicago, Illinois
OLDSMOBILE—1904-07
Olds Motor Works
Lansing, Michigan
OLDSMOBILE—1919-23
Olds Motor Works
Lansing, Michigan
OLIVER—1910-13
Oliver Motor Car Co.
464 Lawton Avenue
Detroit, Michigan
Oliver Motor Truck Co.
Detroit, Michigan
OLYMPIAN—1918-19
Olympian Motors Co.
Pontiac, Michigan
OLYMPIC—1921-29
Olympic Motor Truck Co.
1856 East 28th Street
Tacoma, Washington
OMORT—1926-34
Greenville Mfg. Works
Div. American Aggregates Corp.
Greenville, Ohio
Omort Truck Division
American Aggregates Corp.
Greenville, Ohio
ONEIDA—1917-circa 1930
Oneida Motor Truck Co. (1917-23)
1800 So. Broadway
Green Bay, Wisconsin
Oneida Manufacturing Co.
Green Bay, Wisconsin
Oneida Truck Company
Green Bay, Wisconsin
ONEIDA ELECTRIC—1920-22
Oneida Motor Truck Co.
1800 So. Broadway
Green Bay, Wisconsin

OREN—1956-58
    Oren-Roanoke Corp.
    1201 W. Salem Avenue
    Roanoke, Virginia
ORIENT BUCKBOARD—1906
    Waltham Mfg. Co.
    Waltham, Massachusetts
    Trade name changed to "Waltham."
ORLEANS—1920-21
    New Orleans Motor Truck Mfg. Co.
    New Orleans, Louisiana
OSHKOSH—1918 to date
    Oshkosh Motor Truck Mfg. Co.
    Oshkosh, Wisconsin
    Oshkosh Motor Truck, Inc.
    23rd & Oregon Streets
    Oshkosh, Wisconsin
    Oshkosh Truck Corp.
    Oshkosh, Wisconsin
OVERLAND—1908-26
    Overland Automobile Co. (1908-09)
    Indianapolis, Indiana
    Willys-Overland Co.
    Toledo, Ohio
    Willys-Overland Inc.
    Toledo, Ohio
OWOSSO—1910-12
    Owosso Motor Truck Co.
    Owosso, Michigan

𝒫

PACIFIC—circa 1960 to date
    Pacific Truck & Trailer Ltd.
    1460 Franklin Street
    Vancouver, B.C., Canada
PACKARD—1904-23
    Packard Motor Car Co.
    E. Grand Blvd. & Belt Line
    Detroit, Michigan
PACKERS—1910-13
    Packers Motor Truck Co. (1910-11)
    Pittsburgh, Penna.
    Packers Motor Truck Co. (1911-13)
    Wheeling, West Virginia

PACKETT—1916-17
    Packett Motor Car Mfg. Co.
    2743-45 Lyndale Ave., S.
    Minneapolis, Minnesota
PAIGE—1918-23
    Paige-Detroit Motor Car Co.
    Fort & McKinstry Streets
    Detroit, Michigan
PAIGE—1930-31
    Graham-Paige Motors Corp.
    Detroit, Michigan
PAK-AGE-CAR—1926-42
    Package Car Corp. (1926-32)
    Union Stock Yards
    Chicago, Illinois
    Stutz Motor Car Co. of America, Inc.
    10th Street & Capitol Avenue
    Indianapolis, Indiana
    Pak-Age-Car Corporation
    Connersville, Indiana
    Sales and service taken over by Diamond-T.
PALMER—1912-18
    Palmer-Meyer Motor Car Co.
    5027-35 McKissock Ave.
    St. Louis, Missouri
PALMER-MOORE—1911-17
    Palmer-Moore Co.
    100 No. Geddes St.
    Syracuse, N.Y.
PANHARD—1917-19
    Hamilton Motors Company
    Grand Haven, Michigan
    Panhard Motors Company
    Grand Haven, Michigan
PARKER—1918-circa 1933
    Parker Motor Truck Co. (1918-24)
    606 Linus Street
    Milwaukee, Wisconsin
    Parker Motor Truck Service Co.
        (1925-26)
    Milwaukee, Wisconsin
    Parker Truck Company, Inc. (1926-33?)
    Milwaukee, Wisconsin
PARR—1909-10
    Parr Wagon Company

Pittsburgh, Penna.
PATRIOT—1918-26
    Hebb Motors Co. (1918-20)
    Patriot Motors Co. (1920-22)
    1405 P Street
    Lincoln, Neb.
    Patriot Mfg. Co. (1922-26)
    Havelock, Neb.
    Trade name changed to "Woods."
PAULDING—1914-circa 1915
    St. Louis Motor Truck Co.
    4274-76 Easton Avenue
    St. Louis, Missouri
PEERLESS—1911-18
    Peerless Motor Car Co.
    Quincy Ave. & E. 93rd St.
    Cleveland, Ohio
PEET—1923-24
    Peet Motor Corp.
    Hollis, L.I., New York
PENDELL—1926-circa 1928
    Mechanics Mfg. Co.
    1237 E. Eighth St.
    Los Angeles, California
PENN—1922-26
    Penn Motors Corp.
    Bridgeton, N.J.
PENNSY—1916-17
    Pennsy Motors Company
    901 Pennsylvania Ave.
    Pittsburgh, Penna.
PENN-UNIT—1910-circa 1913
    Penn-Unit Car Co.
    Allentown, Penna.
PENTON—1927
    Penton Motor Co.
    Cleveland, Ohio
PERFECTION—1923
    Perfection Truck Co.
    1519 So. 7th Street
    Minneapolis, Minn.
PERFEX—1912-17
    Perfex Company, The
    52nd & Santa Fe Ave.
    Los Angeles, Calif.

PETERBILT—1939 to date
Peterbilt Motors Company
107th Ave. & Hollywood Blvd.
Oakland, California
Peterbilt Motors Company
107th Ave. & MacArthur Blvd.
Oakland, California
Peterbilt Motors Company
38801 Cherry Street
Newark, California
PETREL—1911-12
Petrel Motor Car Co.
Milwaukee, Wisconsin
Became FS Motors Co.
PHILADELPHIA—1911-12
Philadelphia Truck Co.
Philadelphia, Penna.
PHOENIX—1909-10
Phoenix Auto Works
Phoenixville, Penna.
P.H.P.—1911-12
P.H.P. Motor Truck Co.
Westfield, Mass.
Became Westfield Motor Truck Co.
PIEDMONT—1917-21
Piedmont Motor Car Co.
Cleveland Avenue
Lynchburg, Virginia
PIERCE—1955 to date
Pierce-Portland Crane Carrier Co.
1306 S.E. Ninth Avenue
Portland, Oregon
PIERCE-ARROW—1911-circa 1934
Pierce-Arrow Motor Car Co.
1695 Elmwood Avenue
Buffalo, New York
PIGGINS—1911-16
Piggins Motor Car Co.
Racine, Wisconsin
Piggins Motor Truck Co.
1113 Sixth Street
Racine, Wisconsin
Became "Reliance" in 1917.
PIONEER—1919-circa 1925
Pioneer Truck Company

4638-48 W. Madison St.
Chicago, Illinois
PITTSBURGH ELECTRIC—1904-10
Shady Side Motor Vehicle Co. (1904-05)
5708-10 Walnut Street
Pittsburgh, Penna.
Pittsburgh Motor Vehicle Co. (1905-10)
Ellsworth Ave. & Summerlea St.
Pittsburgh, Penna.
Changed to Ward Motor Vehicle Co.
PITTSBURGHER—1919-circa 1924
Pittsburgh Truck Mfg. Co.
609 Neville Street
Pittsburgh, Penna.
PLAINS—1923
Plains Motor Corp.
Larimer & 8th Streets
Denver, Colorado
PLYMOUTH—1906-14
Commercial Motor Truck Co. (1906)
So. Erie Street
Toledo, Ohio
Commercial Motor Truck Co. (1906-08)
Plymouth, Ohio
Plymouth Motor Truck Co. (1909-14)
Price & Bell Streets
Plymouth, Ohio
PLYMOUTH—1935-41
Plymouth Motor Corp.
6334 Lynch Road
Detroit, Michigan
PONTIAC—1926-27
Oakland Motor Car Co.
Pontiac, Michigan
PONTIAC—1949-54
Pontiac Motor Division
General Motors Corp.
Pontiac, Michigan
PONY—1919-20
Minnesota Machine & Foundry Co.
Talmage & 33rd Avenues, S.E.
Minneapolis, Minnesota
POPE-HARTFORD—1906-14
Pope Manufacturing Co.
Hartford, Connecticut

POPE-WAVERLEY ELECTRIC—1904-08
Pope Motor Car Co.
So. East Street
Indianapolis, Ind.
Changed to Waverley Co.
POSS—1911-12
Poss Motor Co.
504-8 Howard St.
Detroit, Michigan
POWER—1918-24
Power Truck & Tractor Co.
Beard & Goldsmith Sts.
Detroit, Michigan
Power Truck & Tractor Co.
Goodfellow Ave. & Wabash RR.
St. Louis, Missouri
PREMIER—1905-06
Premier Motor Mfg. Co.
1007 Georgia Street
Indianapolis, Ind.
PREMOCAR—1922
Preston Motors Corp.
18th Ave. & Vanderbilt Rd.
Birmingham, Alabama
PROGRESS—1912-13
Universal Machinery Co.
1916 St. Paul Avenue
Milwaukee, Wisconsin
PULLMAN—1916-17
Pullman Motor Car Co.
No. George Street
York, Pennsylvania
PULL-MORE—1917-18
Pull-More Motor Truck Co.
New Castle, Penna.
PURITY ELECTRIC—circa 1914
Saint Paul Bread Co.
St. Paul, Minnesota

QUADRAY—1904-05
Commercial Motor Vehicle Co.
259 to 267 Franklin Street
Detroit, Michigan

R

RAINIER—1916-26
  Rainier Motor Corporation (1916-24)
  Bayside Ave. & Long Island R.R.
  Flushing, L.I., New York
  Rainier Trucks, Incorporated (1924-26)
  Farrington St. & Bayside Ave.
  Flushing, L.I., New York
RANDOLPH—1908-13
  Randolph Motor Car Co.
  175 E. Randolph Street
  Chicago, Illinois
  Randolph Motor Car Co.
  Flint, Michigan
  Randolph Motor Truck Co.
  Flint, Michigan
RANGER—1920-22
  Southern Motor Mfg. Assn., Ltd.
  Houston, Texas
RAPID—1903-11
  Max Grabowsky (1903-04)
  380 Woodward Ave.
  Detroit, Michigan
  Rapid Motor Vehicle Co. (1904-05)
  302-4 Woodward Ave.
  Detroit, Michigan
  Rapid Motor Vehicle Co. (1905-11)
  Rapid Street
  Pontiac, Michigan
  Changed to "GMC" in 1912.
RASSEL—1911-12
  Rassel Mfg. Co., E. C.
  Toledo, Ohio
  Rassel Motor Car Co.
  Toledo, Ohio
  Taken over by Toledo Motor Truck Co.
R&B—1929-41
  Reiland & Bree Truck Mfg. Co.
  Northbrook, Illinois
RED BALL—1924-27
  Red Ball Motor Truck Corp.
  401-437 W. Barnard St.
  Frankfort, Indiana

RED SHIELD HUSTLER—1912
  Red Shield Hustler Power Car Co.
  Detroit, Michigan
REHBERGER—1923-33
  Rehberger & Son, Arthur
  310-320 Ferry Street
  Newark, New Jersey
RELAY—1927-circa 1934
  Relay Motors Corp. (1927)
  Wabash, Indiana
  Relay Motors Corp. (1927-33)
  Lima, Ohio
  Consolidated Motors Corp. (1933-34?)
  Lima, Ohio
RELIANCE—1906-11
  Reliance Motor Car Co. (1906-08)
  67-89 Fort Street, E.
  Detroit, Michigan
  Reliance Motor Truck Co. (1909-11)
  Owosso, Michigan
  Changed to "GMC" in 1912.
RELIANCE—1917-circa 1927
  Racine Motor Truck Co. (1917)
  Racine, Wisconsin
  Reliance Motor Truck Co. (1918-22)
  1161 Spencer Street
  Appleton, Wisconsin
  Appleton Motor Truck Co. (1922-27?)
  924 W. Spencer Street
  Appleton, Wisconsin
REMINGTON—1912
  Remington-Standard Motor Co.
  New York, New York
RENNOC—1918-19
  Rennoc-Leslie Motor Co.
  Philadelphia, Penna.
RENVILLE—circa 1911
  Renville Motor Buggy Mfg. Co.
  Minneapolis, Minnesota
REO—1908-67
  Reo Motor Car Company (1908-39)
  1331 Washington Ave.
  Lansing, Michigan
  Reo Motors, Incorporated (1940-57)
  1331 So. Washington Ave.

Lansing, Michigan
  Reo Division (1957-60)
  White Motor Company
  1331 So. Washington Ave.
  Lansing, Michigan
  Reo Motor Truck Div. (1961-66)
  White Motor Company
  1331 So. Washington Ave.
  Lansing, Michigan
REPUBLIC electric—1901
  Republic Motor Vehicle Co.
  Minneapolis, Minnesota
REPUBLIC—1913-29
  Alma Motor Truck Co. (1913-14)
  Alma, Michigan
  Republic Motor Truck Co. (1914-16)
  Alma, Michigan
  Republic Motor Truck Co., Inc.
    (1916-29)
  Alma, Michigan
  Became La France-Republic Corp.
REX—1922-23
  Royal Rex Motors Co.
  4649 Grand Boulevard
  Chicago, Illinois
REYA—1917-18
  Reya Motor Co.
  Napoleon, Ohio
REYNOLDS—1919-23
  Reynolds Truck Company
  Grand Ave. & Wilson Blvd.
  Mt. Clemens, Michigan
RIKER electric—1898-1901
  Riker Electric Motor Co. (1898-99)
  45 & 47 York Street
  Brooklyn, New York
  Riker Electric Vehicle Co. (1899-1901)
  Elizabethport, N.J.
  Absorbed by Electric Vehicle Co.
RIKER—1916-21
  Locomobile Co. of America
  Bridgeport, Connecticut
ROAD KING—1956-circa 1957
  McCullough Motor Corp.
  Lehighton, Penna.

ROAMER—1927-29
Roamer Motors, Inc.
Kalamazoo, Mich.
Roamer Consolidated Corp.
1902 Reed Street
Kalamazoo, Michigan

ROBINSON—circa 1914-16
Robinson Motor Truck Co.
Second Ave. & Seventh St.
Minneapolis, Minn.
Robinson Motor Truck Co.
141 Ninth Street
Minneapolis, Minn.

ROBINSON—1915-circa 1920
Golden West Motors Co.
Riverside Road
Sacramento, Calif.
Formerly "Golden West."

ROCK FALLS—circa 1915-20
Rock Falls Mfg. Co.
Third St. & Third Ave.
Sterling, Illinois

ROCKFORD—1913-14
Rockford Motor Truck Co.
Rockford, Illinois

ROCKLIFF—1902-06
Rockliff, Chas.
Brooklyn, N.Y.
Rockliff Motor Truck Co.
446 Hudson Avenue
Brooklyn, New York

ROCKNE—1932-33
Studebaker Corporation
Main & Bronson Streets
South Bend, Indiana

ROGERS—1912
Rogers Motor Car Co.
Omaha, Nebraska

ROGERS-UNA-DRIVE—1919-circa 1922
Rogers-Una-Drive Motor Truck Corp.
Sunnyvale, California

ROLAND—1914-15
Roland Gas-Electric Vehicle Corp.
20th Street & Avenue B
New York, New York

ROTO—1916-17
Roto Motor Car Corp.
Hannibal, Missouri

ROUSTABOUT—1961
Roustabout Truck Mfg. Co.
Niles, Ohio
Trade name changed to "Trivan."

ROVAN—1910-circa 1914
Kinnear Mfg. Co.
Columbus, Ohio
Boyd & Bro., Inc., James
25th & Wharton Streets
Philadelphia, Penna.

ROWE—1909; 1911-25
Rowe Motor Company (1909)
Waynesboro, Penna.
Rowe Motor Company (1911)
Coatesville, Penna.
Rowe Motor Mfg. Co. (1912-13)
Coatesville, Penna.
Rowe Motor Mfg. Co. (1914-18)
Wallace Avenue
Downington, Penna.
Rowe Motor Mfg. Co. (1918-25)
Lancaster, Penna.

ROYAL—circa 1914-20
Royal Motor Truck Co.
112 Eighth Avenue
New York, New York

RUGBY—1928-32
Durant Motors, Inc.
Lansing, Michigan
Durant Motor Co. of Michigan
Lansing, Michigan

RUGGLES—1921-28
Ruggles Motor Truck Co.
109 N. Washington Ave.
Saginaw, Michigan

RUMELY—1920-28
Advance-Rumely Co.
La Porte, Indiana

RUSH—1915-18
Rush Delivery Car Company
1007-11 No. Front Street
Philadelphia, Penna.

RUSSELL—1906
Canada Cycle & Motor Co.
Toronto Junction, Ontario, Canada

S

SAFEWAY—1926-27
Six Wheel Company
1800 W. Lehigh Avenue
Philadelphia, Penna.

ST. LOUIS—1899-1905
St. Louis Motor Carriage Co.
1211 No. Vandeventer Ave.
St. Louis, Missouri

SALTER—1914-circa 1916
Salter Motor Mfg. Co.
1516-18 Oakland Avenue
Kansas City, Missouri

SAMPSON—1907-13
Sampson Mfg. Co., Alden (1907-11)
Hawthorne & Mill Streets
Pittsfield, Massachusetts
Alden-Sampson Mfg. Co. (1911-13)
1312 Rhode Island Ave.
Detroit, Michigan

SAMSON—1920-22
Samson Tractor Company
Div. General Motors Co.
Janesville, Wisconsin

SANBERT—1911-12
Sanford-Herbert Co.
Syracuse, New York

SANDOW—1913-circa 1929
Sandow Truck Company (1913-14)
3751-55 Wentworth Ave.
Chicago, Illinois
Sandow Truck Company (1915-16)
2916-20 W. Lake Street
Chicago, Illinois
Sandow Motor Truck Co. (1917-21)
3330-50 W. Grand Ave.
Chicago, Illinois
Moses & Morris Motors Corp. (1922-?)
Chicago Heights, Ill.

Sandow Motor Truck Co.
17th St. & Center Ave.
Chicago Heights, Ill.
SANDUSKY—1910-14
Sandusky Auto Parts & Motor Truck Co.
Sandusky, Ohio
Taken over by Dauch Mfg. Co.
SANFORD—circa 1910-37
Sanford Motor Truck Co.
W. Fayette St. & St. Marks Ave.
Syracuse, New York
SAURER—1911-16
Saurer Motor Company (1911-12)
Plainfield, New Jersey
International Motor Co. (1912-16)
1325 W. Front Street
Plainfield, New Jersey
SAUTTER—1910-11
Brown-Sautter Motor Truck Co.
Newark, New Jersey
SAXON—1915
Saxon Motor Company
Beaufait & Waterloo Sts.
Detroit, Michigan
SAYERS & SCOVILL—1907-12
Sayers & Scovill Co.
2261 Colerain Ave.
Cincinnati, Ohio
SCHACHT—1910-38
Schacht Manufacturing Co. (1910)
2727 Spring Grove Ave.
Cincinnati, Ohio
Schacht Motor Car Co. (1911-13)
2843 Spring Grove St.
Cincinnati, Ohio
Schacht Motor Truck Co., G.A. (1913-27)
Leblond-Schacht Truck Co. (1927-38)
Eighth & Evans Streets
Cincinnati, Ohio
SCHLEICHER—1895; 1910-18
Schleicher & Sons
Schleicher Motor Vehicle Co.
Ossining, New York
SCHMIDT—1911-15
Schmidt Brothers Co.

7100 So. Chicago Ave.
Chicago, Illinois
SCHURMEIER—1907-circa 1911
Schurmeier Wagon Co.
29 Western Avenue
Minneapolis, Minn.
SCHWARTZ—1918-23
Schwartz Motor Truck Corp.
Reading, Pennsylvania
Taken over by Clinton Motors Corp.
SECURITY—1921-circa 1923
Freeman Motor Co.
Omaha, Nebraska
SEITZ—1908-13
Seitz Auto. & Transmission Co.
225 Beecher Street
Detroit, Michigan
SELDEN—1913-circa 1932
Selden Motor Vehicle Co. (1913-19)
Probert Street
Rochester, New York
Selden Truck Corporation (1919-28)
Rochester, New York
Selden-Hahn Motor Truck Corp. (1929-32?)
Allentown, Pennsylvania
SENECA—1916-21
Seneca Motor Car Co.
Fostoria, Ohio
SERVICE—1910-32
Service Motor Car Co. (1910-11)
Kankakee, Illinois
Service Motor Car Co. (1911-14)
4226 Grant Street
Wabash, Indiana
Service Motor Truck Co. (1914-23)
Wabash, Indiana
Service Motors, Inc. (1923-26)
Garfield Street
Wabash, Indiana
Relay Motors, Inc. (1927-32)
Lima, Ohio
SHARON—1912
Driggs-Seabury Ord. Corp.
Sharon, Pennsylvania

SHAW—1916-20
Shaw Livery Co., Walden W.
1006 So. Wabash Ave.
Chicago, Illinois
SHELBY—1918-circa 1921
Shelby Tractor & Truck Co.
Shelby, Ohio
SHERIDAN—1916-circa 1917
Sheridan Commercial Car Co.
Harvey, Illinois
SICARD—circa 1936 to date
Sicard Industries
Montreal, Quebec, Canada
SIEBERT—1911-circa 1916
Siebert, The Shop of
614-18 Southard Ave.
Toledo, Ohio
Siebert Motor Truck Co.
Toledo, Ohio
SIGNAL—1914-24
Signal Motor Truck Co.
672-74 Commonwealth Ave.
Detroit, Michigan
Signal Truck Corporation
Connors Rd. & Charlevoix Ave.
Detroit, Michigan
SMITH-MILWAUKEE—1912-13
Smith Company, A. O.
27th St. & Keefe Ave.
Milwaukee, Wisconsin
SOULES—1905-08
Soules Motor Car Co.
Grand Rapids, Michigan
SOUTH BEND—1913-16
South Bend Motor Car Works
Monroe & Emerick Streets
South Bend, Indiana
SOUTHERN—1918-circa 1925
Southern Truck & Car Corp.
Greensboro, N.C.
Carolina Truck & Body Co.
Greensboro, N.C.
SOWERS—1913
Sowers Motor Truck Co.
Boston, Massachusetts

SPANGLER—1947-49
Spangler Engrg. & Sales Co.
Hamburg, Pennsylvania
SPAULDING—1912-13
Spaulding Mfg. Co.
Grinnell, Iowa
SPEEDWELL—1911-15
Speedwell Motor Car Co.
655 Essex Avenue
Dayton, Ohio
SPHINX—1916
Sphinx Motor Car Co.
Hay & Duke Streets
York, Pennsylvania
SPOERER—1912-14
Spoerer's Sons Co., Carl
Baltimore, Maryland
SPRINGER—1903-04
Springer Motor Vehicle Co.
242-244 W. 41st Street
New York, New York
STANDARD—1912-30
Standard Motor Truck Co.
496 Bellevue Avenue
Detroit, Michigan
Trade name changed to "Fisher-Standard."
STANDARD—1913-15
Standard Motor Truck Co.
Warren, Ohio
Taken over by Warren Motor Truck Co.
STANLEY STEAM—1912-16
Stanley Motor Carriage Co.
44 Hunt Street
Newton, Massachusetts
STAR—1914-15
Star Motor Car Company
Summit & Wildt Streets
Ann Arbor, Michigan
STAR—1922-27
Durant Motors, Inc.
Lansing, Michigan
STARBUCK—1913-14
Starbuck Automobile Co.
5223-25 Market Street
Philadelphia, Penna.

STAR SIX COMPOUND FLEETRUCK
—1927
Durant Motors, Inc.
Lansing, Michigan
Trade name changed to "Rugby."
STEAMOTOR—1917-18
Steamotor Truck Co.
Chicago, Illinois
STEARNS STEAM—1901-03
Stearns Steam Carriage Co.
Syracuse, New York
STEARNS—1911-16
Stearns Co., F. B.
12963 Euclid Ave.
Cleveland, Ohio
STEELE, W. M.—1914-16
Steele, W. M.
100 Beacon Street
Worcester, Mass.
STEGEMAN—1910-17
Stegeman Motor Car Co. (1910-12)
1148-60 Holton Street
Milwaukee, Wisconsin
Stegeman Motor Car Co. (1912-17)
Linus Street
Milwaukee, Wisconsin
STEINKOENIG—1925-27
Steinkoenig Motors Co.
Cincinnati, Ohio
Name changed to "World" in 1927.
STEINMETZ ELECTRIC—1920-circa 1927
Steinmetz Elec. Motor Car Corp.
Grantley Ave. & W.M. RR.
Baltimore, Maryland
STEPHENSON—1910-13
Stephenson Motor Car Co.
South Milwaukee, Wisconsin
Stephenson Motor Truck Co.
South Milwaukee, Wisconsin
STERLING—1909-10
Sterling Vehicle Co.
Harvey, Illinois
STERLING—1916-51
Sterling Motor Truck Co. (1916-33)
46th Ave. & Rogers St.

Milwaukee, Wisconsin
Sterling Motors Corp. (1934-51)
So. 54th St. & W. Rogers Sts.
Milwaukee, Wisconsin
Changed to "Sterling-White."
STERLING-WHITE—1951-53
Sterling Division (1951-52)
White Motor Company
2021 So. 54th Street
Milwaukee, Wisconsin
Sterling Division (1952-53)
White Motor Company
842 E. 79th Street
Cleveland, Ohio
STERNBERG—1908-15
Sternberg Motor Truck Co. (1908-13)
Burleigh & Weil Streets
Milwaukee, Wisconsin
Sternberg Manufacturing Co. (1913-14)
820 46th Avenue
Milwaukee, Wisconsin
Sternberg Motor Truck Co. (1914-15)
820 46th Avenue
Milwaukee, Wisconsin
Trade name changed to "Sterling."
STEWART—1912-42
Stewart Motor Corp.
Superior & Randall Sts.
Buffalo, New York
Stewart Motor Corp.
93 Dewey Avenue
Buffalo, New York
Stewart Motor Corp. (1940-42)
201 Urban Street
Buffalo, New York
STEWART—1913-14
Stewart Iron Works
Covington, Kentucky
STODDARD—1911
Dayton Motor Car Co.
Dayton, Ohio
STOUGHTON—1920-31
Stoughton Wagon Co. (1920-26)
Motor Truck Division
Stoughton, Wisconsin

Stoughton Truck Co. (1927-31)
Stoughton, Wisconsin
STUDEBAKER ELECTRIC—1905-10
Studebaker Automobile Co.
South Bend, Indiana
STUDEBAKER—1913-18
Studebaker Corporation
Main & Bronson Streets
South Bend, Indiana
STUDEBAKER—1927-64
Studebaker Corporation (1927-54)
Main & Bronson Streets
South Bend, Indiana
Studebaker Division (1955-64)
Studebaker-Packard Corp.
635 So. Main Street
South Bend, Indiana
STURGIS—1900-circa 1901
Sturgis & Bros., S. D.
Fifth Street
Los Angeles, Calif.
SUBURBAN—1912
Suburban Truck Co.
Philadelphia, Penna.
SUCCESS—1918-21
Four Wheel Drive Truck Co. (1918-19)
Webberville, Michigan
Webberville Truck Co. (1919-21)
Webberville, Michigan
SULLIVAN—1910-23
Sullivan Motor Car Co.
1703 East Avenue
Rochester, New York
Sullivan Motor Truck Corp.
1703 East Avenue
Rochester, New York
SUPERIOR—1911-13
Superior Motor Car Co.
691 Mack Avenue
Detroit, Michigan
SUPERIOR—1915-circa 1925
Willingham's Sons, E. G.
Atlanta, Georgia
Superior Motor Truck Co.
Whitehall St. & Stewart Ave.

Atlanta, Georgia
Superior Company
101 Wells Street
Atlanta, Georgia
SUPER-TRACTION—1922-23
Six-Wheeled Truck Co.
Fox Lake, Wisconsin
Taken over by Wisconsin Truck Co.
SUPER TRUCK—1919-36
Manly Motor Corp.
O'Connell Motor Truck Co.
Waukegan, Illinois
SYNNESTVEDT ELECTRIC—1903-07
Synnestvedt Machine Co.
4117 Liberty Avenue
Pittsburgh, Penna.

T

TAYLOR—1917-19
Taylor Motor Truck Co.
Fremont, Ohio
TECHNO—1962
Techno Truck Company
1908 E. 66th Street
Cleveland, Ohio
TEC TRAILER MOTOR—1920-21
Truck Engineering Co.
3533 Cedar Avenue
Cleveland, Ohio
TEEL-WOODWORTH—1912-14
Teel Manufacturing Co.
Medford, Massachusetts
TERRAPLANE—1934-38
Hudson Motor Car Co.
12601 E. Jefferson Ave.
Detroit, Michigan
TEXAN—1919-22
Texas Motor Car Association
Fort Worth, Texas
THOMART—1922-23
Thomart Motor Co.
Kent, Ohio
THOMAS—1906-circa 1908
Thomas Wagon Co.

Vernon, New York
THOMAS—1916-17
Thomas Auto Truck Co.
639 West 51st Street
New York, New York
Consolidated Motors Corp.
639 West 51st Street
New York, New York
THOMPSON STEAM—1902
Thompson Automobile Co.
Olneyville Square
Providence, R.I.
THORNE—1929-circa 1938
Thorne Motor Corp.
6147 W. 65th Street
Chicago, Illinois
THORNYCROFT—1900-02
Cooke Loco. & Mach. Co.
Paterson, New Jersey
Thornycroft Steam Wagon Co. of
America
Paterson, New Jersey
THREE POINT—1919-circa 1924
Three Point Truck Corp.
Watertown, New York
THRIFT-T—1947
Tri-Wheel Motor Corp.
Oxford, North Carolina
TIFFIN—1913-23
Tiffin Wagon Co.
40 Harrison St.
Tiffin, Ohio
TITAN STEAM—1916-17
Titan Motor Car Co.
Newark, Delaware
American Machine Co.
82 E. Cleveland Ave.
Newark, Delaware
TITAN—1917-circa 1927
Titan Truck Company
25th St. & St. Paul Ave.
Milwaukee, Wisconsin
TOLEDO—1912-13
Toledo Motor Truck Co.
Toledo, Ohio

TORBENSON—1904-11
    Torbenson Gear Co. (1904-05)
    Bloomfield, New Jersey
    Torbenson Motor Car Co. (1905-11)
    610 Bloomfield Avenue
    Bloomfield, New Jersey
TOURIST—1903-circa 1907
    Auto Vehicle Company
    943 No. Main Street
    Los Angeles, California
TOWER—1915-23
    Tower Motor Truck Co.
    Foot of Grove Street
    Greenville, Michigan
TRABOLD—1911-32
    Trabold Truck Mfg. Co. (1911-23)
    810-12 Railroad Ave.
    Johnstown, Penna.
    Trabold Motors Company (1923-32)
    Ferndale and Johnstown, Penna.
TRAFFIC—1918-circa 1928
    Traffic Motor Truck Corp. (1918-19)
    3807-19 Laclede Ave.
    St. Louis, Missouri
    Traffic Motor Truck Corp.
    5200 N. Second Street
    St. Louis, Missouri
    Traffic Motors
    5200 N. Second Street
    St. Louis, Missouri
TRANSIT—1911-16
    Transit Motor Car Co.
    Louisville, Kentucky
    Transit Motor Truck Co.
    18th & Burnett Streets
    Louisville, Kentucky
TRANSPORT—1915-17
    Transport Tractor Co.
    87-93 Sunswick St.
    Long Island City, N.Y.
TRANSPORT—1918-25
    Transport Truck Co.
    Mt. Pleasant, Michigan
    Transport Motor Truck Co.
    Pickard Avenue

Mt. Pleasant, Michigan
TRAYLOR—1920-28
    Traylor Engineering & Mfg. Co.
    Truck & Tractor Division
    Cornwells, Pennsylvania
    Traylor Engineering & Mfg. Co.
    Allentown, Pennsylvania
TRIANGLE—1917-24
    Triangle Motor Truck Co.
    St. Johns, Michigan
TRI-CAR—1955
    Tri-Car Incorporated
    Wheatland, Penna.
TRIUMPH—1911-12
    Triumph Motor Car Co.
    Chicago, Illinois
TRIUMPH—1919-23
    Triumph Truck & Tractor Co.
    110 South West Boulevard
    Kansas City, Missouri
TRIVAN—1962-circa 1963
    Roustabout Company
    Frackville Industrial Park
    Frackville, Penna.
    Formerly "Roustabout."
TROJAN—1914-20
    Toledo Carriage Woodwork Co.
        (1914-15)
    1001 Water Street
    Toledo, Ohio
    Commercial Truck Co. (1916-20)
    5320-28 St. Clair Ave.
    Cleveland, Ohio
TROJAN—1937-40
    Trojan Truck Co.
    Alhambra, Calif.
TRUCTOR—1917-18
    Highway Tractor Co.
    Indianapolis, Indiana
TULSA—1912-circa 1913
    Tulsa Auto. & Mfg. Co.
    Tulsa, Oklahoma
TUTTLE—1913
    Tuttle Motor Company
    Canastota, New York

TWIN CITY—1913-15
    Brasie Motor Truck Co. (1913-14)
    2743-45 Lyndale Ave.
    Minneapolis, Minn.
    Brasie Motor Car Co. (1914-15)
    2743-45 Lyndale Ave.
    Minneapolis, Minn.
    Became Packett Motor Car Mfg. Co.
TWIN CITY—1915-19
    Twin City Four Wheel Drive Co., Inc.
    2482-96 University Avenue
    St. Paul, Minnesota
TWIN CITY—1920-28
    Minneapolis Steel & Machinery Co.
    29th Street & Minnehaha Ave.
    Minneapolis. Minnesota
TWIN COACH—1929-35
    Twin Coach Company
    850 W. Main Street
    Kent, Ohio

U

ULTIMATE—1919-23
    Vreeland Motor Co., Inc.
    Chestnut Ave. & L.V. RR.
    Hillside, New Jersey
UNION—1901-04
    Union Motor Truck Co.
    106 Tasker Street
    Philadelphia, Penna.
UNION—1911-13
    Union Motor Truck Co.
    San Francisco, Calif.
UNION—1916-26
    Union Motor Truck Co.
    2nd & Water Streets
    Bay City, Michigan
UNITED—1915-30
    United Motor Truck Co. (1915-16)
    Grand Rapids, Michigan
    United Motors Company (1916-22)
    675 North Street
    Grand Rapids, Michigan
    United Motors Products Co. (1922-26)

675 Richmond Street
Grand Rapids, Michigan
Acme Motor Truck Co. (1927-30)
Cadillac, Michigan
UNIVERSAL—1911-18
Universal Motor Truck Co. (1911-15)
503 Theodore Street
Detroit, Michigan
Universal Service Co. (1915-18)
1120 Grand River Ave.
Detroit, Michigan
UPTON—1902-03
Upton Machine Co.
Beverly, Mass.
URBAN ELECTRIC—1912-16
Kentucky Wagon Mfg. Co., Inc.
Third St. & Eastern Parkway
Louisville, Kentucky
URSUS—1920-21
Ursus Motor Co.
Chicago, Illinois
U.S.—1909-30
United States Motor Truck Co.
(1909-14)
216-220 Webster Street
Cincinnati, Ohio
United States Motor Truck Co., Inc.
(1914-30)
17th Street & Madison Street
Cincinnati, Ohio
UTILITY—1911-12
Stephenson Motor Car Co.
South Milwaukee, Wisconsin
See also "Stephenson."

V

VALLEY—1927-30
Valley Motor Truck Co.
1730 So. Main Street
Elkhart, Indiana
VAN—1908-09
Van Wambeke & Sons, H. F.
501 Jefferson Ave.
Elgin, Illinois

VAN AUKEN ELECTRIC—1913-15
Connersville Buggy Co.
Connersville, Indiana
VAN DYKE—1910-12
Van Dyke Motor Car Co.
13 Leavitt Street
Detroit, Michigan
VAN WINKLE—1910-circa 1915
Van Winkle & Machine Co.
Atlanta, Georgia
Van Winkle Motor Truck Co.
Atlanta, Georgia
V-C—1912-13
V.C. Motor Truck Co.
Lynn, Massachusetts
V.E. ELECTRIC—1901-06
Vehicle Equipment Co.
Church Ave. & 36th St.
Brooklyn, New York
Vehicle Equipment Co. (1905-06)
Borden & Review Avenues
Long Island City, N.Y.
Purchased by General Vehicle Co.
VEERAC—1909-14
Veerac Motor Co.
Anoka, Minnesota
VELIE—1911-23
Velie Motor Vehicle Co. (1911-15)
3rd Ave. & 3rd Street
Moline, Illinois
Velie Motors Corporation
3rd Avenue & 3rd Street
Moline, Illinois
VELIE—1927-circa 1930
Velie Motors Corp.
3rd Ave. & 3rd St.
Moline, Illinois
VERSARE—1926-30
Versare Corporation
103 Washington Ave.
Albany, New York
VIALL—1913-19
Viall Motor Car Co.
19-21 E. 111th Street
Chicago, Illinois

VICTOR—1910-13
Victor Motor Truck Co.
Military & Beaver Roads
Buffalo, New York
VICTOR ELECTRIC—1913-14
M&P Electric Vehicle Co.
Franklin & DuBois Streets
Detroit, Michigan
Formerly "M&P."
VICTOR—1918-20
Victor Motor Truck & Trailer Co.
Chicago, Illinois
Became Waltham Motors Corp. (1920)
VICTOR—circa 1920
Victor Truck Company
St. Joseph, Michigan
VICTOR—1923-circa 1928
Victor Motors, Inc. (1923-25)
28th & Locust Streets
St. Louis, Missouri
Victor Motors, Inc. (1925-28?)
24th & McCasland Ave.
East St. Louis, Mo.
VIM—1913-circa 1923
Touraine Company (1913-15)
Broad & Huntingdon Sts.
Philadelphia, Penna.
Vim Motor Truck Company (1916-20)
23rd & Market Streets
Philadelphia, Penna.
Vim Motor Truck Company (1921-23?)
Roberts Ave. & Fox St.
Philadelphia, Penna.
VOLTZ—1914-17
Voltz Brothers
840 S. Halstead St.
Chicago, Illinois
VULCAN—1913-16
Driggs-Seabury Ordnance Corp.
81 Sharpsville Street
Sharon, Pennsylvania
VULCAN—1920-22
Vulcan Manufacturing Co.
Pine & Bellevue Streets
Seattle, Washington

W

WACHUSETT—1922-circa 1929
 Wachusett Motors, Inc.
 300 Lunenburg Street
 Fitchburg, Mass.
WADE—1912-16
 Wade Commercial Car Co.
 Holly, Michigan
WAGENHALS—1910-15
 Wagenhals Commercial Motor Car Co.
 St. Louis, Missouri
 Wagenhals Motor Car Co.
 668-70 Grand River Ave.
 Detroit, Michigan
 Wagenhals Motor Co.
 668 Grand River Ave.
 Detroit, Michigan
WALDRON—1911
 Waldron Runabout Mfg. Co.
 Waldron, Illinois
WALKER ELECTRIC—1906-42
 Automobile Maint. & Mfg. Co. (1906-11)
 217 So. Green Street
 Chicago, Illinois
 Walker Vehicle Company (1911-20)
 531-45 West 39th Street
 Chicago, Illinois
 Walker Vehicle Company (1921-42)
 101 West 87th Street
 Chicago, Illinois
WALTER—1909 to date
 Walter Auto Truck Mfg. Co. (1909-11)
 49-51 West 66th Street
 New York, New York
 Walter Motor Truck Co. (1911-17)
 49-51 West 66th Street
 New York, New York
 Walter Motor Truck Co. (1918-23)
 227 West 61st Street
 New York, New York
 Walter Motor Truck Co. (1923-35)
 Queens Blvd. & Hulstead St.
 Long Island City, N.Y.
 Walter Motor Truck Co. (1935-57)

1001-19 Irving Avenue
 Ridgewood, L.I., N.Y.
 Walter Motor Truck Co. (1957 to date)
 School Road
 Voorheesville, N.Y.
WALTER ELECTRIC—1921-24
 Walter Motor Truck Co. (1921-23)
 227 West 61st Street
 New York, New York
 Walter Motor Truck Co. (1923-24)
 Queens Blvd. & Hulstead St.
 Long Island City, N.Y.
WALTHAM—1907-08
 Waltham Mfg. Co.
 Waltham, Mass.
WALTHAM—1920-21
 Waltham Motors Corp.
 Chicago, Illinois
WARD—1911-13
 Ward Motor Vehicle Co.
 Concord Ave. & E. 143rd St.
 Bronx, New York
WARD ELECTRIC—1911-18
 Ward Motor Vehicle Co. (1911-14)
 Concord Ave. & E. 143rd St.
 Bronx, New York
 Ward Motor Vehicle Co. (1915-18)
 718 So. Fulton Avenue
 Mt. Vernon, New York
 Trade name became "Ward-Electric."
WARD-ELECTRIC ELECTRIC—1918-35
 Ward Motor Vehicle Co.
 718 So. Fulton Avenue
 Mt. Vernon, New York
 Built truck bodies until 1965.
WARD LA FRANCE—1918 to date
 Ward La France Truck Co., Inc.
  (1918-20)
 Elmira, New York
 Ward La France Truck Corp. (1920-22)
 Elmira, New York
 Walker La France Motors, Inc.
 (1922-24)
 Elmira, New York
 Ward La France Truck Corp.

(1924 to date)
 Grand Central Ave. & 11th St.
 Elmira Heights, N.Y.
Has concentrated on fire apparatus since
1955.
WARE—1912-15
 Ware Motor Vehicle Co.
 771 Raymond Avenue
 St. Paul, Minnesota
Taken over by Twin City Four Wheel Drive
Co.
WARE—circa 1918-20
 Ware Twin Engine Truck Co.
 201 Harvard Street, S.E.
 Minneapolis, Minnesota
WARFORD—1937-circa 1940
 Baumis-Warford Co., Inc.
 Townsend, Massachusetts
Rebuilt "Ford" truck with dual axle drive.
WARREN—1911-13
 Warren Motor Car Co.
 Detroit, Michigan
WARREN—1915-16
 Warren Motor Truck Co.
 Dana Avenue
 Warren, Ohio
WASHINGTON ELECTRIC—1910-11
 Washington Motor Vehicle Co.
 Washington, D.C.
Trade name changed to "Capitol Car."
WATSON—1917-25
 Watson Wagon Co. (1917-19)
 48 W. Centre St.
 Canastota, N.Y.
 Watson Products Corp. (1919-22)
 121 W. Center Street
 Canastota, N.Y.
 Watson Truck Corp. (1923-25)
 121 W. Center St.
 Canastota, N.Y.
WAVERLEY ELECTRIC—1899-1903
 Indiana Bicycle Co. (1899)
 Indianapolis, Indiana
 American Bicycle Co. (1899-1901)
 Indianapolis, Indiana

International Motor Car Co. (1902-03)
Waverley Department
Indianapolis, Indiana
Changed to "Pope-Waverley."
WAVERLEY ELECTRIC—1908-16
Waverley Company
139 South East Street
Indianapolis, Indiana
WEEKS—1907-08
Weeks Commercial Vehicle Co.
Aldine Square
Chicago, Illinois
WEST COAST—1914-16
West Coast Wagon Co.
1948-52 Pacific Ave.
Tacoma, Washington
WESTERN—1917-24
Western Truck Mfg. Co.
122 No. Curtis Street
Chicago, Illinois
Western Truck Mfg. Co.
3546 Ogden Avenue
Chicago, Illinois
WESTFIELD—1912-circa 1913
Westfield Motor Truck Co.
Westfield, Massachusetts
WESTMAN—1911-12
Westman Motor Truck Co.
Cleveland, Ohio
WEYHER—1910
Weyher Mfg. Co.
Whitewater, Wisconsin
WHARTON—1922-circa 1923
Wharton Motors Co., Inc.
Johnstown, Penna.
WHATTOFF—1960
Whattoff Motor Co.
Ames, Iowa
WHIPPET—1929
Willys-Overland, Inc.
Toledo, Ohio
WHITE STEAM—1900-03
White Engineering Works (1900-01)
Indianapolis, Indiana
White Steam Wagon Co.

15th Street & Big Four RR.
Indianapolis, Indiana
WHITE STEAM—1901-09
White Sewing Mach. Co.
Cleveland, Ohio
White Company, The
Cleveland, Ohio
WHITE—1909 to date
White Company, The (1909-15)
E. 79th St. & St. Clair Ave.
Cleveland, Ohio
White Motor Company (1916-65)
E. 79th St. & St. Clair Ave.
Cleveland, Ohio
White Trucks (1966 to date)
Div. White Motor Corp.
842 E. 79th Street
Cleveland, Ohio
WHITE-FREIGHTLINER—1951 to date
Freightliner Corp.
5400 No. Basin St.
Portland, Ore.
WHITE HICKORY—1916-21
White Hickory Wagon Mfg. Co.
Atlanta, Georgia
WHITESIDES—1911-12
Whitesides Commercial Car Co.
New Castle, Indiana
WHITE STAR—1911-16
White Star Motor & Engineering Co.
118-20 Henry Street
Brooklyn, New York
Taken over by Metropolitan Motors, Inc.
WHITING—1904-05
Whiting Foundry Equip. Co.
Harvey, Illinois
Business sold to Chicago Commercial Auto
Mfg. Co.
WHITWOOD—1914
Whitwood Corp.
Weedsport, N.Y.
WICHITA—1911-32
Wichita Falls Motor Co.
Arthur Boulevard
Wichita Falls, Texas

WILCOX—1910-27
Wilcox Motor Car Co., H. E.
1030 Marshall Street
Minneapolis, Minn.
Wilcox Motor Co., H. E.
1030 Marshall Street
Minneapolis, Minn.
Wilcox Trux. Inc. (1921-27)
1030 Marshall Street
Minneapolis, Minn.
Taken over by C. H. Wills. See "W.M.C."
WILL—1928-30
Will Corporation, C. H.
Minneapolis, Minn.
WILLET—1913-14
Willet Engine & Truck Co., Inc.
6-8 Lock Street
Buffalo, New York
WILLYS—1930-62
Willys-Overland, Inc.
Toledo, Ohio
Willys-Overland Motors, Inc.
Walcott Boulevard
Toledo, Ohio
Willys Motors, Inc. (1953-62)
940 No. Cove Blvd.
Toledo, Ohio
Trade name changed to "Jeep."
WILLYS-KNIGHT—1928-29
Willys-Overland, Inc.
Toledo, Ohio
WILLYS UTILITY—1913-14
Gramm Motor Truck Co.
South Lima Street
Lima, Ohio
WILSON—1914-23
Wilson Company, J. C.
Warren Ave. & 15th St.
Detroit, Michigan
WINKLER—1910-11
Winkler Bros. Mfg. Co.
South Bend, Indiana
WINTER & HIRSCH—1922-23
Winter & Hirsch Motor Truck Co.
Chicago, Illinois

WINTER-MARWIN—1918-21
Marwin Truck Co.
Kenosha, Wisconsin
WINTHER—1917-26
Winther Motor Truck Co. (1917-18)
Winthrop Harbor, Ill.
Winther Motor Truck Co. (1918-21)
Kenosha, Wisconsin
Winther Motors, Inc. (1921-26)
Kenosha, Wisconsin
Became Kenosha Fire Engine & Truck Co.
WINTON—1898-1906
Winton Motor Carriage Co.
Belden & Mason Streets
Cleveland, Ohio
WISCONSIN—1912-circa 1923
Wisconsin Motor Truck Works
(1912-15)
Baraboo, Wisconsin
Myers Machine Company (1916-18)
Sheboygan, Wisconsin
Wisconsin Truck Company (1919-23)
Loganville, Wisconsin
WITTENBERG—circa 1966 to date
Wittenberg Motor Co.
27454 Pacific Highway So.
Midway, Washington
WITT-WILL—1911-32
Witt-Will Co., Inc.
52 N Street, N.E.
Washington, D.C.
W.-J—1921-24
Walker-Johnson Truck Co.
Montvale Avenue
Woburn, Massachusetts
W.M.C.—1927-28
Wills Motor Corp., C. H.
1030 Ramsey Street
Minneapolis, Minn.
Changed to Will Corp.
WOLFE—1909
Wilcox Motor Car Co., H. E.
1030 Marshall St., N.E.
Minneapolis, Minn.
Trade name changed to "Wilcox."

WOLFWAGON—1956-circa 1964
Wolf Engineering Corp. (1956-60)
1201 Main Street
Dallas, Texas
St. Louis Car Company
8000 No. Broadway
St. Louis, Missouri
St. Louis Car Division
Gen. Steel Industries Inc.
8000 Hall Street
St. Louis, Missouri
WOLVERINE—1918-circa 1923
American Commercial Car Co.
Gratiot Ave. & Detroit Term. RR.
Detroit, Michigan
Wolverine Motor Truck & Coach Co.
Gratiot Ave. & Detroit Term. RR.
Detroit, Michigan
WOLVERINE-DETROIT—1912-13
Pratt, Carter, Sigsbee & Co.
Detroit, Michigan
WONDER—1917
Wonder Motor Truck Co.
Chicago, Illinois
WOOD steam—1903-05
Wood Vapor Vehicle Co.
Brooklyn, New York
Wood, J. C.
784 Madison St.
Brooklyn, N.Y.
WOODS—1927-31
Patriot Mfg. Co.
Havelock, Neb.
WOODS MOBILETTE—1913-16
Woods Mobilette Company
147th St. & Marshfield Ave.
Harvey, Illinois
Became Sheridan Commercial Car Co.
WORLD—1927-31
World Motors Company
3289 Spring Grove Ave.
Cincinnati, Ohio
WORTH—1907-09
Worth Motor Car Mfg. Co.
Evansville, Indiana

Worth Motor Car Mfg. Co.
Kankakee, Illinois
Became Service Motor Car Co.
W-S—1913-18
Weier-Smith Truck Co.
Birmingham, Michigan
W-S Truck Company
110 Brownell Street
Birmingham, Michigan

YALE—1920-22
Yale Motor Truck Co.
10-12 Bassett St.
New Haven, Conn.
YELLOW CAB EXPRESS—1921-22
Yellow Cab Mfg. Co.
5801 W. Dickens Ave.
Chicago, Illinois
YELLOCAB TRUCK—1923-27
Yellow Cab Mfg. Co.
5801 W. Dickens Ave.
Chicago, Illinois
Yellow Truck & Coach Mfg. Co.
5801 W. Dickens Ave.
Chicago, Illinois
YELLOW-KNIGHT—1926-27
Yellow Truck & Coach Mfg. Co.
5801 W. Dickens Avenue
Chicago, Illinois
YOUNG—1920-23
Young Motor Truck Co.
Geneva, Ohio

ZEITLER & LAMSON—1914-16
Zeitler & Lamson Motor Truck Co.
Chicago, Illinois
ZIMMERMAN—circa 1909
Zimmerman Mfg. Co.
Auburn, Indiana

CROSS REFERENCE INDEX
TO MOTOR TRUCK MANUFACTURERS

A

A.A.
  See "All-American"
ABBOTT & DOWNING
  See "Concord"
ABENDROTH & ROOT
  See "A&R"
ACE
  See also "American" (1918-19)
ACME (Michigan)
  See also "United"
ADAMS EXPRESS
  See "Herschmann"
ADVANCE-RUMELY
  See "Rumely"
AKRON
  See also "Ideal" (1911-12)
ALDEN-SAMPSON
  See "Sampson"
AMALGAMATED (California)
  See "Duro"
AMALGAMATED (New Jersey)
  See "Bessemer"
AMERICAN (Indiana)
  See "Jonz"
AMERICAN ARGO
  See "Argo"
AMERICAN BICYCLE
  See "Waverley" (electric)
AMERICAN & BRITISH
  See "A&B"
AMERICAN BUS & TRUCK
  See "Kelly" (1910-27)
AMERICAN COLEMAN
  See "Coleman"
AMERICAN COMMERCIAL CAR
  See "Wolverine"
AMERICAN COULTHARD
  See "Coulthard"
AMERICAN ELECTRIC CAR
  See "Argo"—"Borland"

AMERICAN ICE
  See "A.I.C."
AMERICAN LOCOMOTIVE
  See "Alco"
AMERICAN MACHINE
  See "Titan"
AMERICAN MACHINERY
  See "Commerce" (1906-08)
AMERICAN MOTORS
  See "Delcar"
AMERICAN MOTOR TRUCK
  See "Ace"
AMERICAN ORDNANCE
  See "Herschmann"
ANDERSON ELECTRIC
  See "Detroit Electric"
APPLETON
  See "Reliance" (1917-circa 1927)
ATTERBURY
  See "Buffalo" (1908-10)
AUBURN MOTOR CHASSIS
  See "Handy Wagon"
AUGLAIZE
  See also "Case" (1910-11)
AUTOMOBILE MAINTENANCE
  See "Walker" (electric)
AUTO VEHICLE
  See "Tourist"

B

BANTAM
  See also "American Austin"
BARTHOLOMEW
  See "Glide"
BAUER
  See "Gleason"
BAUMIS-WARFORD
  See "Warford"
B.C.K.
  See "Kline"

BEST-ON-EARTH
  See "B.O.E."
BETHLEHEM
  See also "Lehigh"
BILL
  See "Curtis-Bill"
BLACK DIAMOND
  See "Buckmobile"
BLACKER
  See also "Logan"
BOWLING GREEN MOTOR TRUCK
  See "Modern" (1911-18)
BOYD
  See also "Rovan"
BRASIE
  See "Twin City"
BRILL
  See "A.C.F."
BROWN-SAUTTER
  See "Sautter"
BUCK
  See also "Krebs" (1922-25)
BUCKEYE (Indiana)
  See "Lambert"
BUFFALO (1908-10)
  See also "Autocar" (1903-08)
BURFORD
  See also "Fremont-Mais"
BUSHNELL
  See "Maxim Tricar"

C

CADILLAC AUTO TRUCK
  See "Acme" (1915-31)
CAMDEN
  See "Frontmobile"
CANADA CYCLE
  See "Russell"
CAPITOL CAR
  See also "Washington" (electric)

CARAVAN
See "Karavan"
CAROLINA TRUCK
See "Southern"
C.C.I.
See "CCC"
CEDAR RAPIDS
See "Beck"
CENTURY (Ohio)
See "Defiance"
CHICAGO COACH
See "Duer"
CHICAGO COMMERCIAL AUTO
See also "Whiting"
CHICAGO PNEUMATIC
See "C.P.T."
"Duntley"—"Giant"
CINCINNATI
See "Alter"
CLEBURNE
See "Luck"
CLEVELAND
See "C-V"
CLINTON
See also "Schwartz"
CLYDE
See "Clydesdale"
"Krebs" (1912-17)
COLEMAN MOTORS
See also "Holmes"
COLUMBIA MOTOR TRUCK
See also "Kalamazoo" (1913-15)
COLUMBIA STEAM
See "Herschmann"
COMMERCIAL MOTOR TRUCK (Ohio)
See "Plymouth"
COMMERCIAL MOTOR VEHICLE (Michigan)
See "Quadray"
COMMERCIAL TRUCK (Ohio)
See "Trojan"
COMMERCIAL TRUCK (Pennsylvania)
See "C.T."
"Electruck"
CONNERSVILLE BUGGY
See "Van Auken"
CONSOLIDATED MOTOR (New York)
See "Moyea"
CONSOLIDATED MOTORS (New York)
See "Thomas"
CONSOLIDATED MOTORS (Ohio)
See "Garford"—"Relay"
CONTINENTAL-DIVCO
See "Divco"

CONTINENTAL ENGINEERING
See "Ceco"
COOKE
See "Thornycroft"
CORTLAND CART & CARRIAGE
See "Hatfield" (1916-circa 1918)
CORWIN
See "Coulthard"
CRANE
See "CCC"
CRESTMOBILE
See "Crest"
CUMMINS DIESEL
See "Gotfredson"
CUTTING
See "Chicago" (1919-32)

D

DAUCH
See "Sandusky"
DAYBROOK-OTTAWA
See "Commando"
DAY-ELDER
See also "D-E"
DAYTON MOTOR CAR
See "Stoddard"
DECATUR
See also "Coppock"
DE KALB MFG.
See "Handy Wagon"
DENNEEN
See "Denmo"
DETROIT AUTO VEHICLE
See "Crown"
DETROIT INDUSTRIAL VEHICLE
See "Divco" (1925-35)
DETROIT-WYANDOTTE
See "Horner"
DIAMOND REO
See also "Diamond T"
DIAMOND T
See also "Pak-Age-Car"
DIRECT DRIVE
See "Champion" (1918-21)
DOUBLE DRIVE
See also "Front Drive"
DOWAGIAC
See "Doe-Wa-Jack"
DOWNING
See "C-B"
DRIGGS-SEABURY
See "Commer"—"Sharon"—"Vulcan"

DURABLE DAYTON
See also "Dayton"
DURANT
See "Rugby"—"Star"
DURANT-DORT
See "Best"—"Flint"

E

EASTON
See "Morse"
EISENHUTH
See "Compound"
ELECTRIC VEHICLE
See "Columbia" (electric)
"Riker" (electric)
EWING-AMERICAN
See "American" (1906-12)

F

FAWICK
See "Federal"
FINDLAY MOTOR
See "American" (1906-12)
"Ewing"
FISHER-STANDARD
See also "Standard"
FLINT ROADKING
See "Mason Roadking"
FORD
See also "Warford"
FOUR TRACTION
See "Kato"
FOUR WHEEL DRIVE AUTO (Wisconsin)
See "F.W.D."
FOUR WHEEL DRIVE TRUCK (Michigan)
See "Success"
FREEMAN (Nebraska)
See "Security"
FREMONT
See "All-American"
F-S
See also "Petrel"

G

GENERAL MOTORS
See "GMC"—"Samson"
GENERAL STEEL
See "Wolfwagon"

GENERAL VEHICLE
  See "G.V."
GERLINGER
  See "Gersix"
GIANT
  See also "Little Giant"
GMC
  See also "Rapid"—"Reliance"
GOTFREDSON
  See also "G&J"
GOTFREDSON & JOYCE
  See "G&J"
GRABOWSKY (Max)
  See "Rapid"
GRAHAM-DOANE
  See "Doane"
GRAHAM-PAIGE
  See "Paige"
GRAMM (Lima, Ohio)
  See also "Willys Utility"
GRAND RAPIDS MOTOR TRUCK
  See "Decatur"
GRANT
  See also "Denmo"
GREENVILLE
  See "Omort"
GUILDER
  See also "Goodwin"

H

HAMILTON MOTORS
  See "Apex"
      "Panhard"
HARRISBURG
  See "Hurlburt"
HARWOOD-BARLEY
  See "Indiana"
HAWKEYE DART
  See "Dart"
HEBB
  See "Patriot"
HERCULES (Massachusetts)
  See "Eckhard"
HERCULES (Michigan)
  See also "Alma"
HIGHWAY TRACTOR
  See "Tructor"
HINDE & DAUCH
  See also "Climax"
HOOSIER
  See "Decatur"

HOUSE COLD TIRE SETTER
  See "Keldon"
HUDSON
  See also "Dover"
               "Terraplane"
HURRYTON
  See "Menominee"
HUSELTON
  See "Butler"

I

INDEPENDENT (Michigan)
  See also "Cass"
INDIANA BICYCLE
  See "Waverley" (electric)
INTERNATIONAL (Indiana)
  See "Waverley" (electric)
INTERNATIONAL (New Jersey)
  See "Saurer"
INTERNATIONAL (New York)
  See "Hewitt"
INTERNATIONAL HARVESTER
  See also "IHC"
IOWA MOTOR TRUCK
  See "Bell"

J

JEEP
  See also "Willys"
JUERGENS
  See "Fremont-Mais"
JUNO
  See also "Brodesser"

K

KAISER-JEEP
  See "Jeep"
KALAMAZOO MOTOR VEHICLE
  See "Clark" (1911-13)
KANSAS CITY VEHICLE
  See "Gleason"
KELLY MOTOR TRUCK
  See also "Frayer-Miller"
KENOSHA
  See "Winther"
KENTUCKY WAGON
  See "Old Hickory"
      "Urban" (electric)

KENWORTH
  See also "Gersix"
KINNEAR
  See "Rovan"
KLINE KAR
  See "Kline"
KNOX MOTOR TRUCK
  See "Atlas" (1904-12)
KREBS COMMERCIAL CAR
  See also "Lincoln" (1916-17)
KW-DART
  See "Dart"
K-Z
  See "King-Zeitler"

L

LA FRANCE-REPUBLIC
  See also "American LaFrance"
               "Republic"
LAMSON
  See "Zeitler & Lamson"
LEAR
  See "Frayer-Miller"
LEBLOND-SCHACHT
  See "Schacht"
LEE
  See "Old Reliable"
LESLIE
  See "Rennoc-Leslie"
LEWIS-HALL
  See "Hall"
LOCOMOBILE
  See also "Riker"
LOOMIS
  See "Gopher"
LORAIN
  See "J&J"
LOS ANGELES CREAMERY
  See "Electruck"
LOUISIANA
  See "L.M.C."

M

MACK
  See also "Manhattan"
MARTIN-PARRY
  See "Atlas" (1916-23)
MARWIN TRUCK
  See "Winter-Marwin"
MASSACHUSETTS STEAM
  See "Cunningham"

MCBRIGHT
 See "Lite Way"
MCCULLOUGH
 See "Road King"
MECHANICS MFG.
 See "Pendell"
MEGOW
 See "Champion"
MERCHANT & EVANS
 See "Evans"
METROPOLITAN
 See also "White Star"
METZGER (New York)
 See "Hewitt"
M-H
 See "Marmon-Herrington"
MILLS-ELLSWORTH
 See "Ellsworth"
MILWAUKEE
 See "M.P.C."
MILWAUKEE AUTO TRUCK
 See "Champion" (1909-12)
MINNEAPOLIS STEEL
 See "Twin City" (1920-28)
MINNESOTA MACHINE
 See "Pony"
MOLLER
 See "Elysee"
MORRISEY
 See "Bridgeport"
MOSES & MORRIS
 See "Sandow"
MOTOR CONVEYANCE
 See "B.O.E."
MOTOR STORAGE
 See "Logan"
MYERS (Wisconsin)
 See "Wisconsin"

N

NATIONAL MOTORS (New Jersey)
 See "Day-Elder"
NATIONAL MOTOR TRUCK (Michigan)
 See "Natco"
NEBRASKA AUTO & TRUCK
 See "Douglas"
NELSON
 See "Jumbo"
NELSON-Le MOON
 See "Le Moon"
   "Milburn"

NEWARK MOTOR TRUCK
 See "Ka Dix"
NEW ENGLAND TRUCK
 See "Netco"
NEW HAVEN TRUCK
 See "Moeller"
NEW ORLEANS
 See "Orleans"
NORDYKE & MARMON
 See "Marmon" (1912-14)

O

OAKLAND
 See "Pontiac"
O'CONNELL
 See "Super Truck"
OKLAHOMA
 See "O.K." (1917-28)
ONE WHEEL TRUCK
 See "Autohorse"
OTTAWA
 See "Commando"

P

PACIFIC METAL PRODUCTS
 See "Moore" (1910-16)
PACKAGE CAR
 See "Pak-Age-Car"
PACKETT
 See also "Twin City"
PANHARD
 See also "Apex"
PARCEL, PARCEL POST
 See "Decatur"
PENN MOTORS
 See also "Keystone"
PHOENIX (Missouri)
 See "Kansas City Car"
PITTSBURGH MACHINE TOOL
 See "Curtis"
POPE-WAVERLEY
 See also "Waverley"
POYER
 See "Menominee"
PRATT, CARTER, SIGSBEE
 See "Wolverine-Detroit"
PREMIER
 See also "Mais"
PRESTON
 See "Premocar"

RACINE MOTOR TRUCK
 See "Reliance" (1917-circa 1927)
RALSTON IRON WORKS
 See "Hewitt-Ludlow"
R.C.H.
 See "Hupp-Yeats"
REILAND & BREE
 See "R&B"
RELAY
 See also "Commerce"
   "Garford"—"Service"
RELIABLE
 See "Old Reliable"
RELIANCE (Wisconsin)
 See also "Piggins"
REO
 See also "Diamond Reo"—"Mack Jr."
REPUBLIC
 See also "Alma"
ROBINSON LOOMIS
 See "Gopher"
ROCKET
 See "Northway"
ROYAL REX
 See "Rex"
RUGBY
 See also "Star Six Compound Fleetruck"

S

SAGINAW
 See "Jumbo"
ST. LOUIS CAR
 See "Wolfwagon"
ST. LOUIS MOTOR TRUCK
 See "Paulding"
SALVADOR
 See "Mansur"
SANDOW
 See also "Kalamazoo" (1919-23)
SANFORD (Maine)
 See "Casco"
SANFORD-HERBERT
 See "Sanbert"
SCHLOTTERBACK
 See "Koehler"
SCHMIDT
 See also "F.C.S."
SEITZ
 See also "Grabowsky"

SELDEN-HAHN
See "Hahn"
SERVICE
See also "Worth"
SHADY SIDE
See "Pittsburgh"
SIX WHEEL
See "Safeway"
SIX WHEELED TRUCK
See "Super-Traction"
SOUTHERN MOTOR
See "Ranger"
SOUTH MAIN MOTOR
See "Niles"
STANLEY
See also "McKay"
STAR (Washington)
See "Northwestern"
STAR-TRIBUNE
See "O.K." (1913-15)
STEARNS-KNIGHT
See "Stearns" (1911-16)
STERLING (Wisconsin)
See also "Sternberg"
STUDEBAKER
See also "Rockne"
STUTZ
See "Pak-Age-Car"
SUPER TRUCK
See also "Manly"

𝒯

TARRYTOWN
See "Motokart"
TAYLOR
See also "Burford"
TEGETMEIER & RIEPE
See "New York"
THOMART
See also "Akron Multi-Truck"
TOLEDO CARRIAGE
See "Trojan"
TOLEDO MOTOR TRUCK
See also "Rassel"
TOURAINE
See "Vim"
TRAVERSE CITY
See "Napoleon"
TRI-WHEEL MOTOR
See "Thrift-T"
TRUCK ENGINEERING
See "TEC Trailer Motor"

TULSA (Michigan)
See "Doe-Wa-Jack"
TURNBULL
See "Defiance"
TWIN CITY FOUR WHEEL DRIVE
See also "Ware"
TWIN COACH (1950-54)
See "Fageol"

𝒰

UNION CONSTRUCTION
See "MacDonald"
UNITED FOUR WHEEL DRIVE
See "Allfour"
    "Lamson"
UNITED MOTOR TRUCK
See also "Decatur"
UNITED STATES MOTOR TRUCK
See "U.S."
UNIVERSAL MACHINERY
See "Progress"
UTILITY SUPPLY
See "Menominee"

𝒱

VALLEY
See also "Huffman"
VAN WAMBEKE
See "Van"
V.E.C.
See "V.E."
VEHICLE EQUIPMENT
See "V.E."
VREELAND
See "Ultimate"

𝒲

WALKER
See also "C-T"
WALKER-JOHNSON
See "Ajax"
    "W-J"
WALTHAM
See also "Orient Buckboard"
WALTHAM MOTORS
See also "Victor" (1918-20)
WALTHAM-ORIENT
See "Waltham" (Massachusetts)

WARD ELECTRIC
See also "Pittsburgh"
WARD La FRANCE
See "La France"
WARNER & SWASEY
See "Duplex"
WARREN (Ohio)
See also "Standard"
WATERVILLE
See "Merit"
WAVERLEY
See also "Pope-Waverley"
WEBBERVILLE TRUCK
See "Success"
WEIER-SMITH
See "W-S"
WESTERN TOOL
See "Gale"
WESTFIELD
See also "P.H.P."
WHITE
See also "Autocar" (1908 to date)
    "Diamond Reo"—"Diamond T"
    "Indiana"—"Montpelier"
    "Reo"—"Sterling-White"
WHITE-FREIGHTLINER
See also "Freightliner"
WILCOX
See also "Wolfe"
WILLINGHAM
See "Superior"
WILLS (C.H.) MOTOR
See "Wilcox"
    "W.M.C."
WILLYS
See also "Gramm"
    "Overland"—"Whippet"
WILSON (Iowa)
See "G.W.W."
WINTHER-KENOSHA
See "Winther"
WISCONSIN
See also "Super-Traction"
W-J
See also "Ajax"
WOLF
See "Wolfwagon"
WOODS (Nebraska)
See also "Patriot"
WORLD
See also "Steinkoenig"
WYCKOFF, CHURCH & PARTRIDGE
See "Commer"

SUPPLEMENT
MOTOR TRUCK LIST

Because the entries in this Supplement Motor Truck List comprise such a wide variety of vehicles, truck companies and truck-related companies, as noted in the introduction to the motor truck section, a code has been provided as a guide to the reader. The entries herein are listed alphabetically by either corporate or trade name. The corporate name is used generally; frequently it served also as the trade name for the truck or might be so presumed until further evidence indicates otherwise. The trade name is used only when it differed from the corporate name and was reported as such, and cross references to the manufacturing company are provided in these cases. Included with each entry is such pertinent data as the geographical location of the company, the dates of truck construction, as well as explanatory notes where these would be useful to the reader. Entries are coded by Roman Numerals—(I) through (VIII)—as follows:

(I) A number of references appeared in contemporary truck journals indicating that the reference company planned to manufacture a truck, or that the company had recently been incorporated for that purpose. Undoubtedly a prototype or prototypes were built, but no further references could be found regarding actual production. Until further evidence can be presented, one must assume that the truck company did not proceed beyond the prototype(s) stage. Sometimes, however, these companies evolved into or merged with another company which did get into serious manufacture. For example, Franklin Commercial Truck Co., indicated on this list as having planned truck production in 1910, evolved into the Eclipse Truck Co. by 1911 and were forthwith building the "Eclipse" truck. The "Eclipse" is, of course, entered in the Motor Truck Manufacturers section, and the reader is referred to the main listing. This sample Code (I) entry is given below:

FRANKLIN COMMERCIAL TRUCK CO.
—1910 (I)
Franklin, Pennsylvania
Changed to Eclipse Truck Co. which appears in the main listing.

(II) Truck production was limited. The companies involved here were frequently automobile manufacturers who added a delivery wagon or truck model to their line but, research indicates, did not proceed into truck manufacture on any extensive scale, frequently discontinuing the truck idea after it was found to be financially unsound. Oftentimes the company literature—brochures, catalogues, et al.—included a truck model among their vehicles, but such production, as followed, was not recorded in any of the motor truck periodicals of the day. As with Code (I) entries, occasionally these companies did evolve into or merge with other companies who did get into series truck production, and appropriate cross references to the main listing of Motor Truck Manufacturers are given in each case. A sample Code (II) entry appears below:

BAILEY MOTOR CAR CO.—1910 (II)
Detroit, Michigan
Became Federal Motor Truck Co. which appears in main listing.

(III) These trucks were experimental only. The company or individual involved made no serious attempt to proceed into truck manufacture at the date indicated. In some cases, truck manufacture was begun at a later date, as, for example, the American LaFrance Fire Engine Co., who in 1910-11 built a number of experimental gasoline hydraulic trucks carrying a "LaFrance" name and who a decade later did get into actual manufacture of trucks under the trade name "American LaFrance." In other cases, the company never did proceed into manufacture, as indicated in the sample Code (III) entry below:

SHADBOLT MFG. CO. steam
—1902-03 (III)
Brooklyn, New York
Built a few experimental steam trucks for various inventors.

(IV) Truck production is very doubtful. The company was a manufacturer of passenger cars only—or ambulances, hearses and other related vehicles. References have appeared indicating that the company did build trucks, but such trucks might be presumed to have been produced on special order. A sample Code (IV) entry is given below:

> S&S—1924-30 (IV)
> Sayers & Scovill Co.
> Cincinnati, Ohio
> Believed to have built ambulances primarily during these years.

(V) Truck production is very doubtful. The company specialized in truck-related equipment as, for example, the Step-N-Drive Truck Corp. who converted Fords and other delivery trucks for multi-stop service, but who were themselves not truck producers. Another example is given below in a sample Code (V) entry:

> FRONT DRIVE MOTOR CO.—1912-18 (V)
> Hoboken, New Jersey
> Built "Christie" front drive power unit attachment for use in motorizing horse-drawn fire apparatus.

(VI) Truck production is very doubtful. The company specialized in off-highway construction equipment or small motorcycle-type vehicles not generally considered in the motor truck category. A sample Code (VI) entry is given below:

> LECTRA-HAUL—1959 to date (VI)
> Unit Rig & Equipment Co.
> Tulsa, Oklahoma
> Off-highway construction vehicles.

(VII) References have often indicated these companies as truck manufacturers, but in reality they were not—as, for example, the American Steam Wagon Co. who built no trucks themselves but instead licensed other manufacturers to build Herschmann steam trucks. A further example is given in the sample Code (VII) entry below:

> COMMERCIAL MOTOR CAR CO.
> —1906-11 (VII)
> New York, New York
> Not a manufacturer, but transportation and sales engineering company. Also importers of the Swiss Safir truck.

(VIII) References have appeared through the years indicating that these trucks were built during the dates noted, but no corroborative evidence has been discovered. A sample Code (VIII) entry is given below:

> STANDARD GAS & ELECTRIC POWER
> CO.—1911 (VIII)
> Philadelphia, Pennsylvania

Code (VIII) entries will be the most intriguing to truck historians, simply because so little now is known about these trucks. The entry above is an interesting example. The Standard Gas & Electric Power Co., as noted in the 5000 Marques listing in this book, built passenger cars from 1908 through 1910. Did that company perhaps decide to switch over to what they hoped might be a more lucrative enterprise—truck manufacture? With the facilities on hand, assuredly they might have built a truck in 1911, conceivably may have marketed some of them too, and then, like so many of their contemporaries, failed before year's end. Unfortunately, at this point, we simply do not know. Further research will perhaps some day uncover the truck-manufacturing status of Code (VIII) entries. And it is hoped that interested readers might provide information about these trucks—on the tear-out form appended to the back of this book—to assist in this research.

A

ACME MOTOR CAR CO.—1905 (II)
    Reading, Pennsylvania
ADVANCE MOTOR TRUCK CO.
    —1918 (I)
    Wilmington, Delaware
AETNA MOTOR CORP.
    —1920 (I)
    New York, New York
A-G TRUCK MFG. CO.—1907 (I)
    New York, New York
ALLEN & CLARK CO.—1908 (I)
    Toledo, Ohio
ALLEN-KINGSTON MOTOR CAR CO.
    —1907-09 (IV)
    Kingston, New York
ALLIANCE MFG. CO.—1917 (I)
    Streator, Illinois
ALLIANCE MOTORS CORP.—1916 (I)
    New York, New York
ALLIED TRUCK & TRACTOR CO.
    —1920 (I)
    Minneapolis, Minnesota
ALPENA MOTOR CAR CO.
    —1910-14 (IV)
    Alpena, Michigan
AMALGAMATED MACHINERY CORP.
    —1917 (VIII)
    Chicago, Illinois
A-M-C TRUCK CO.—1919 (I)
    Chicago, Illinois
AMERICAN BRASS CO.
    —1907-08 (VIII)
    Waterbury, Connecticut

AMERICAN CYCLECAR CO.
    See "Trumbull."
AMERICAN EAGLE MOTOR CAR CO.
    —1912 (I)
    Brooklyn, New York
AMERICAN ELECTROMOBILE CO.
    —1906-07 (II)
    1571 River Street
    Detroit, Michigan
AMERICAN FOUNDRY CO.
    —1906 (II)
    Leipsic, Ohio
AMERICAN MOTOR TRUCK CO.
    —1917-18 (I)
    Detroit, Michigan
AMERICAN STEAM WAGON—1903 (VII)
    New York, New York
    Not a manufacturer; license agency for
    Herschmann steam truck.
AMERICAN WHEELOCK ENGINE CO.
    See "Pneumatic."
AMHURST—1912 (II)
    Two-in-One Co.
    Amhurstburg, Ontario, Canada
    Seven-passenger touring car convertible to
    a pickup truck. No more than 6 made.
AMS STERLING—1917 (VIII)
    Sterling Automobile Co.
    Amston, Connecticut
AMTORG—1930-35 (VIII)
ANDERSON CARRIAGE & MFG. CO.
    —1910 (I)
    Anderson, Indiana
ANHEUSER-BUSCH CO.—1911-12 (VIII)
    Milwaukee, Wisconsin

ANN ARBOR—1912 (II)
    Huron River Mfg. Co.
    Ann Arbor, Michigan
APEX MOTOR CORP.—1923 (I)
    Ypsilanti, Michigan
APPERSON BROS. AUTOMOBILE CO.
    —1905-20 (II)
    Kokomo, Indiana
ARANDSEE CO.—1920 (I)
    Brooklyn, New York
ARBENZ MOTOR CAR CO.
    —circa 1916 (I)
    Chillicothe, Ohio
ARGO MOTOR CO.—1916 (II)
    Jackson, Michigan
ARTANA & SON, L.
    —circa 1913 (I)
    San Jose, California
ATLAS ENGINE WORKS—1907 (II)
    Indianapolis, Indiana
ATLAS MOTOR TRUCK CO.—1918 (I)
    Creston, Iowa
AURORA MOTOR WORKS
    —1908 (II)
    Aurora, Illinois
AULTMAN & CO. STEAM
    —1901 (II)
    Canton, Ohio
AUTO-DYNAMIC ELECTRIC
    —1901 (VIII)
    The Auto-Dynamic Co.
    140 West 39th Street
    New York, New York
AUTO MFG. CO.—1911 (I)
    Fort Wayne, Indiana

AUTOMATIC ELECTRIC
—1915-25 (I)
Automatic Transportation Co.
Buffalo, New York
AUTOMOBILE TRUCK CO.—1899 (I)
New York, New York
AUTOMOTIVE DEVELOPMENT CORP.
See "Fairfield."
AUTOMOTOR CO.—1911 (I)
Columbus, Ohio
AUTO-TRI MFG. CO.—1909 (I)
Buffalo, New York
AUTO-TRUCK CO.—1915 (I)
Bangor, Pennsylvania

ℬ

BAILEY MOTOR CAR CO.—1910 (II)
Detroit, Michigan
Became Federal Motor Truck Co. which appears in the main listing.
BAILEY-PERKINS AUTO CO.
—1915 (VIII)
Springfield, Massachusetts
BAKER-BELL MOTORS CO.—1912 (I)
Philadelphia, Pennsylvania
BAKER STEAM MOTOR CAR & MFG. CO.
—circa 1922 (II)
Pueblo, Colorado
BALDNER MOTOR VEHICLE CO.
—1901-03 (IV)
Xenia, Ohio
BALDWIN MOTOR WAGON CO. STEAM
—1899-1901 (II)
Providence, Rhode Island

BANTA MOTOR TRUCK CO.—1911 (I)
Detroit, Michigan
BARBER MOTORS CORP.—1917 (I)
Brooklyn, New York
BARGER TRUCK CO.—1918 (I)
Indianapolis, Indiana
BARKER MOTOR TRUCK CO.
—circa 1915 (I)
Los Angeles, California
BARRON, JAMES J.—1918 (I)
New York, New York
BATTON—1898-99 (VII)
Batton Motor Vehicle Corp.
Chicago, Illinois
Incorrect spelling for "Patton."
BEARDSLEY & HUBBS MFG. CO.
—1902-03 (II)
Shelby, Ohio
BEAVER MFG. CO.—1911 (I)
Milwaukee, Wisconsin
BEAVER STATE MOTOR CO.
—1915-20 (IV)
Gresham, Oregon
BEAVER TRUCK CORP., LTD.
—circa 1925 (I)
Wilson Street
Hamilton, Ontario, Canada
BECK—1947 (VIII)
BEGGS MOTOR CAR CO.—1918-28 (II)
Kansas City, Missouri
BENDIX CO.—1908 (II)
Chicago, Illinois
BERGDOLL MOTOR CAR CO., LOUIS J.
—1908-13 (IV)
Philadelphia, Pennsylvania

BERKSHIRE AUTOMOBILE CO.
—1906 (II)
Pittsfield, Massachusetts
BESTEVER TRUCK CO.—1917 (I)
Chicago, Illinois
BEST MFG. CO.—1912 (I)
San Leandro, California
BIG FOUR TRUCK CO.
—circa 1920 (I)
Sacramento, California
Formerly Golden West Motors Co. which appears in the main listing.
BIGGAM TRAILER CORP.—1917 (I)
Corunna, Michigan
BINGHAMTON MOTOR CAR CO.
—1912 (I)
Binghamton, New York
BINNEY & BURNHAM STEAM
—1902 (II)
Boston, Massachusetts
BIRCH MOTORS CORP.
—circa 1918 (II)
Chicago, Illinois
BLACK CROW—1910 (II)
Black Mfg. Co.
Chicago, Illinois
BLACK MFG. CO., C. H.—1899 (II)
Indianapolis, Indiana
BLAISDELL & CO.—1903 (II)
Brooklyn, New York
BLEVNEY, JOHN C. STEAM—1902 (II)
Newark, New Jersey
BOBBICAR—1946-47 (IV)
Keller Motors Corp.
Huntsville, Alabama

BOIS CAR & TRUCK CO.—1913 (I)
New York, New York
BOLLSTROM PRODUCT SALES CO.
—1916 (I)
Battle Creek, Michigan
BOSTON COMMERCIAL CAR CO.
—1910 (I)
Boston, Massachusetts
BOYLE AUTOMATIC TRUCK CO.
—1911 (VII)
Portland, Oregon
Incorrect spelling for Doyle Automatic
Truck Co.
BRADFORD MOTOR CAR CO.
—1919-20 (IV)
Haverhill, Massachusetts
BRAZIER, H. BARTOL—1904 (I)
Philadelphia, Pennsylvania
BRECHT AUTOMOBILE CO.—1901-03 (I)
1207 Cass Avenue
St. Louis, Missouri
Steam and electric vehicles.
BRISTOL ENGINEERING CORP.
See "Rockwell."
BRITTON-STEVENS MOTORS CORP.
—circa 1915 (I)
56-62 Binney Street
Cambridge, Massachusetts
BROC CARRIAGE & WAGON CO.
—1909-15 (I)
Cleveland, Ohio
Merged with "Argo" and "Borland" into
American Electric Car Co.
See main listing.
BROMFIELD MFG. CO.—1930 (VIII)
Boston, Massachusetts
BROWN CARRIAGE CO.—1916 (IV)
Cincinnati, Ohio
BUCKLEN MOTOR TRUCK CO., H.E., JR.
—1912 (I)
Elkhart, Indiana
BUFFALO GASOLINE MOTOR CO.
—1901 (I)
Buffalo, New York
BUGGYCAR CO.—1908-09 (IV)
Cincinnati, Ohio
BUGMOBILE CO. OF AMERICA
—1907-09 (IV)
Chicago, Illinois

BULL DOG MOTOR TRUCK CO.
—1924-25 (VIII)
Galena, Ohio
BURLINGTON MOTOR TRUCK CO.
—1917 (I)
Burlington, Wisconsin
BURROWS CYCLECAR CO.—1914 (I)
Ripley, New York
BYRON CO., E. W.—1933 (VIII)
New Haven, Connecticut
BYRON MOTOR CAR CO.—1912 (I)
Pueblo, Colorado

C

CALEY & NASH—1912 (I)
Canastota, New York
CANNON MOTOR CO.—1912 (I)
Des Moines, Iowa
CANTON BUGGY CO.—1912 (I)
Canton, Ohio
CAPITAL MOTORS CORP.—1917 (I)
Fall River, Massachusetts
CAPITOL TRUCK CO.—1917 (I)
Indianapolis, Indiana
CARL ELECTRIC VEHICLE CO.
—1914 (I)
Toledo, Ohio
CARLTON-HILL MOTOR CAR CO.
—circa 1915 (I)
Rutherford, New Jersey
CARROLL MOTOR CAR CO.
—circa 1913 (I)
Strasburg, Pennsylvania
CATASAUQUA MOTOR CAR CO.
—1914 (VIII)
Catasauqua, Pennsylvania
CATERPILLAR TRACTOR CO.
—1963 to date (VI)
100 N.E. Adams Street
Peoria, Illinois
Off-highway construction vehicles.
C&D—1907 (VIII)
C. de L. ENGINEERING WORKS
—1913 (I)
Nutley, New Jersey
CEDAR—1921 (VIII)
CENTURY ELECTRIC MOTOR CAR CO.

—1915 (IV)
Detroit, Michigan
CENTURY MOTOR VEHICLE CO. ELECTRIC
—1902 (I)
519 East Water Street
Syracuse, New York
CHADWICK—1905-17 (IV)
Fairmount Engineering Works
Chadwick Engineering Works
Philadelphia, Pennsylvania
Pottstown, Pennsylvania
CHAIN BELT CO.
See "Rex."
CHALMERS MOTOR CO.—1907-23 (II)
Detroit, Michigan
Named "Chalmers-Detroit" 1907-10.
CHAMPION—circa 1910 (II)
Famous Mfg. Co.
East Chicago, Indiana
CHAUTAUQUA MOTOR CO.—1912 (I)
Dunkirk, New York
CHICAGO COACH & CARRIAGE CO.
See "Webster."
CHICAGO COMMERCIAL CAR CO.
—1911 (I)
Chicago, Illinois
CHICAGO ELECTRIC MOTOR CAR CO.
—1912 (I)
Chicago, Illinois
CHICAGO MOTOR BUGGY CO.
—1908 (IV)
Chicago, Illinois
CHICAGO MOTOR VEHICLE CO.
—1900 (I)
Harvey, Illinois
CHILDS CO., O. J.—1909 (I)
Utica, New York
CHRISTIE
See "Front Drive Motor Co."
CHRYSLER—1925-28 (IV)
Chrysler Motor Corp.
Detroit, Michigan
CINO—1912 (I)
Haberer & Co.
Cincinnati, Ohio
CITY CARRIAGE WORKS—1910 (VIII)
Fort Wayne, Indiana
CLARK-CARTER AUTOMOBILE CO.
See "Cutting."

CLARK EQUIPMENT CO.
See "Michigan."
CLASSIC MOTOR CAR CORP.
—1916 (I)
Chicago, Illinois
CLEMIC-HIRSCH CO.—1905 (II)
Milwaukee, Wisconsin
CLEVELAND—circa 1913 (I)
Paxson, C.D.
Cleveland, Ohio
May also be referred to as "Paxson."
CLEVELAND-GALION MOTOR TRUCK
CO.—1912 (I)
Cleveland, Ohio
Galion, Ohio
Later Galion Dynamic Truck Co.
CLEVELAND MOTOR CAR CO.
—1903-07 (I)
Cleveland, Ohio
CLEVELAND MOTOR TRUCK CO.
—1910 (I)
Cleveland, Ohio
CLIFFORD—1905 (VIII)
CLOVER LEAF MILLING COMPANY
—1914 (I)
Ontario Street & Cloverdale Road
Buffalo, New York
CLUB CAR COMPANY—1911 (I)
New York, New York
CLYDE MOTOR TRUCK CO.—1916 (II)
Farmingdale, Long Island, New York
Changed to Fulton Motor Truck Co. which
appears in the main listing.
COATES TRI-CAR CO.—1912 (I)
Goshen, New York
COGGSWELL MOTOR CAR CO.
—1912 (I)
Grand Rapids, Michigan
COLERIDGE COMMERCIAL CAR CO.
—1911 (I)
Detroit, Michigan
COLLINS ELECTRIC VEHICLE CO.
—1900 (II)
Scranton, Pennsylvania
COLONIAL MOTORS CORP.—1920 (I)
Boston, Massachusetts
COLUMBUS BUGGY CO. ELECTRIC
—1902-07 (II)
Columbus, Ohio

COMMERCIAL CAR CO.—1912 (I)
Detroit, Michigan
COMMERCIAL CAR UNIT CO.
—1917 (I)
Philadelphia, Pennsylvania
COMMERCIAL MOTOR CAR CO.
—1906-11 (VII)
New York, New York
Not a manufacturer, but transportation and
sales engineering company. Also importers
of the Swiss Safir truck.
COMMERCIAL MOTOR CO. STEAM
—1903-04 (I)
Jersey City, New Jersey
COMMERCIAL MOTOR TRUCK
CONSTRUCTION CO.—1911 (I)
Newark, New Jersey
COMMERCIAL TRUCK CO.
See "Pole."
COMMERCIAL TRUCK & POWER CO.
—1906 (II)
Rahway, New Jersey
CONSOLIDATED MOTOR CAR CO.
—1922 (I)
New London, Connecticut
CONTINENTAL CAR & EQUIPMENT CO.
—1911 (I)
Louisville, Kentucky
CORBIN MOTOR VEHICLE CO.
—circa 1905 (II)
New Britain, Connecticut
COURIER CAR CO.—1911 (I)
Dayton, Ohio
COVEL MFG. CO.—circa 1916 (I)
Benton Harbor, Michigan
CRAM & SOVERIGN—1912 (I)
Geneva, New York
CRANE & BREED MFG. CO.—1911 (I)
Cincinnati, Ohio
CRESCENT—1914-15 (I)
Mission Motor Car Co.
Los Angeles, California
CRESCENT MOTOR TRUCK CO.
—1917 (I)
New York, New York
CROSS FRONT DRIVE TRACTOR
CO., C. J.—1914 (V)
Newark, New Jersey
Conversion unit for horse-drawn fire ap-

paratus. No known production of trucks.
CROW MOTOR CAR CO.—1912 (I)
Elkhart, Indiana
CROWN CARRIAGE CO.—1923 (I)
Los Angeles, California
CROXTON MOTOR CO.—1912 (I)
Washington, Pennsylvania
CRUICKSHANK STEAM ENGINE WORKS
—1896 (II)
Providence, Rhode Island
CRUISER MOTOR CO.—1917-19 (VII)
Madison, Wisconsin
Not a truck, but rather a convertible tour-
ing-camping car.
CUMBACK MOTOR CO.—1910 (VIII)
Detroit, Michigan
CUNNINGHAM SON & CO., JAMES
—1916 (I)
Rochester, New York
CURTIS MOTOR CAR CO.—1919 (I)
Little Rock, Arkansas
CUSHMAN—1950 to date (VI)
Cushman Motor Works Inc.
Cushman Motors
Division of Outboard Marine Corp.
North 21st Street
Lincoln, Nebraska
Around 1950 the term "Truckster" began
to be used for certain Cushman models,
and small four-wheelers are produced to-
day, but these are vehicles which are not
generally termed motor trucks.
CUTTING—1909-12 (IV)
Clark-Carter Automobile Co.
Jackson, Michigan
CYCO-LECTRIC CAR CO.—1914 (I)
New York, New York

𝒟

DAIRY EXPRESS—1926-30 (VIII)
Eastern Dairies Inc.
General Ice Cream Corp.
Springfield, Massachusetts
DARBY MOTOR CO.—1910 (I)
St. Louis, Missouri
DAVENPORT—1902-03 (VIII)
Davenport, Iowa

DAVIS CAR CO.—1916 (I)
 Seattle, Washington
DAVIS MFG. CO.—1905 (I)
 Milwaukee, Wisconsin
DAVIS MFG. CO.—1914-15
 See "Vixen."
DAY AUTOMOBILE CO. STEAM—1902 (II)
 Kansas City, Missouri
DAYTON ELECTRIC CAR CO.
 —1911-15 (IV)
 Dayton, Ohio
DAYTON MOTORS—1924 (I)
 Monaca, Pennsylvania
DECKER AUTOMATIC TELEPHONE
 EXCHANGE CO.—1902-03 (IV)
 Owego, New York
DECOSMO
 See "Delia."
DE DION-BOUTON MOTORETTE CO.
 —1901 (II)
 Church Lane & 37th Street
 Brooklyn, New York
DELIA—1915 (III)
 Michael Decosmo
 San Francisco, California
 Experimental amphibious truck.
DELMORE MOTORS CORP.—1924 (I)
 New York, New York
DE LOACH MFG. CO.—1911-12 (VIII)
 Bridgeport, Alabama
 Atlanta, Georgia
DE MOTTE MOTOR CAR CO.
 —1904 (IV)
 Philadelphia, Pennsylvania
DENISON THREE WHEELER
 —1899-1903 (IV)
 Denison Motor Carriage Co.
 New Haven, Connecticut
DE SCHAUM MOTOR SYNDICATE CO.
 —1909 (I)
 Buffalo, New York
DE SOTO
 Export name for "Dodge" trucks from 1950
 to date.
DETROIT COMMERCIAL CAR CO.
 —1911 (I)
 Detroit, Michigan
DETROIT MOTOR WAGON
 See "Motor Wagon."

DETROIT TRANSPORTATION TRUCK
 CO.—1920 (I)
 Monroe, Michigan
DIAMOND MATCH CO.—1908 (III)
 Barberton, Ohio
DILE MOTOR CO.—1916 (I)
 721 North Eighth Street
 Reading, Pennsylvania
DOBLE STEAMER—1918-19 (II)
 Doble Laboratories
 San Francisco, California
 Trucks built by W. T. Garratt & Co.
DOBLE STEAM MOTORS—1930 (VIII)
 Emeryville, California
 Presumed to be experimental only.
DORT MOTOR CAR CO.—1915 (I)
 Flint, Michigan
DOWNE TRACTOR CO.—1911 (I)
 St. Louis, Missouri
DOYLE AUTOMOBILE TRUCK CO.
 —1911 (VIII)
 Portland, Oregon
 May be predecessor to James C. Doyle.
 See "Doyle" in main listing.
DRAYMASTER—1931-33 (VIII)
DRIER—1929 (VIII)
DRUMMOND MOTOR CO.—1916 (I)
 2568-72 Farman Street
 Omaha, Nebraska
DUDLY TOOL CO.—1909 (I)
 Menominee, Michigan
DUER
 See "Webster."
DUMORE—1917 (I)
 American Motor Vehicle Co.
 Lafayette, Indiana
DUMPTOR—1907, 1912 (VIII)
 This is also the name currently used by the
 Koering company for their off-highway
 dump truck, built since the 1930's.
DUNMORE—1917 (VII)
 Probably a misspelling of "Dumore."
DUQUESNE MOTOR CAR CO.—1912 (I)
 Pittsburgh, Pennsylvania
DUROCAR MFG. CO.—1907-09 (IV)
 Los Angeles, California
DUSSEAU FORE & REAR DRIVE
 AUTO CO.—1913 (I)
 Toledo, Ohio

DYKE—1900-04 (VII)
 St. Louis Motor Carriage Co.
 St. Louis, Missouri
 Trade name should be "St. Louis."

𝓔

EAGLE MACOMBER MOTOR CAR CO.
 —1915 (I)
 Chicago, Illinois
EAST DAVENPORT MACHINE SHOP
 —1912 (I)
 Davenport, Iowa
EASTERN DAIRIES, INC.
 See "Dairy Express."
EASTERN POWER TRUCK CO.—1912 (I)
 Providence, Rhode Island
ECONOMY CAR CO.—1913 (I)
 Indianapolis, Indiana
EDWARDS MOTOR CAR CO.
 —1912 (I)
 New York, New York
EDWIL—1934-40 (VIII)
EIGHT WHEEL MOTOR VEHICLE CO.
 —1923 (III)
 San Jose, California
 Built at least one experimental bus.
ELBERT MOTOR CAR CO.—1914 (I)
 Seattle, Washington
ELECTRA—1913-15 (VIII)
 Electric Storage Battery Power Co.
 Chicago, Illinois
ELGIN—1916-24 (IV)
 Elgin Motor Car Corp.
 Chicago, Illinois
 Elgin Motors Inc.
 Indianapolis, Indiana
ELITE AUTO WAGON CO.—1913 (I)
 Woodside, New York
ELKHART MOTOR TRUCK CO.—1930 (I)
 Elkhart, Indiana
ELMORE MFG. CO.—1901-12 (IV)
 Clyde, Ohio
EMERSON & FISHER CO.—1896 (I)
 Cincinnati, Ohio
EMPIRE MOTOR CO.—1896 (I)
 Pittsburgh, Pennsylvania
ENKEL—1915 (VIII)

EQUITABLE AUTOMOBILE & TRUCK CO.
—1901-03 (VIII)
Boston, Massachusetts
ERBES—1917 (I)
Erbes, L. C.
St. Paul, Minnesota
Erbes Motor Car Co., L.C.
Waterloo, Iowa
ERIE MOTOR CAR CO.—1917 (I)
Painesville, Ohio
ERSKINE—1927-30 (IV)
Studebaker Corp.
South Bend, Indiana
ESSEX—1918-32 (IV)
Essex Motors
Hudson Motor Car Co.
Detroit, Michigan
ESSEX MOTOR TRUCK CO.—1916 (I)
New York, New York
Changed to Rainier Motor Corp. which ap-
pears in the main listing.
ETNYRE CO., E. D.—1917 (I)
Oregon, Illinois
EUCLID—1933 to date (VI)
Euclid Road Machinery Co.
1361 Chardon Road
Cleveland, Ohio
Euclid Division
General Motors Corp.
1361 Chardon Road
Cleveland, Ohio
Off-highway construction vehicles.
EUREKA AUTOMOBILE CO.—1903 (VIII)
Jersey City, New Jersey
EVANS TRUCK & AXLE CO.—1919 (I)
Auburn, Indiana
EVERETT MOTOR CAR CO.—1912 (I)
Detroit, Michigan
EWBANK—1916-17 (I)
EX-CEL MOTOR TRUCK CO.—1912 (I)
Jamesburg, New Jersey
EXETER MACHINE WORKS
—1909-13 (VIII)
Exeter, New Hampshire

FAIRBANKS-MORSE CO.
—1909-circa 1921 (VIII)

Chicago, Illinois
FAIRFIELD—1927 (VIII)
Automotive Development Corp.
Stamford, Connecticut
FAIRMAN MOTOR IMPLEMENT CO.
—1915 (I)
Davenport, Iowa
FALCON CYCLECAR CO.—1915 (VIII)
Cleveland, Ohio
FALCON MOTOR TRUCK CO.—1915 (I)
Detroit, Michigan
F.A.L. MOTOR CO.—1912 (IV)
Chicago, Illinois
FAMOUS MFG. CO.
See "Champion."
FARGO
Export name for "Dodge" truck, used since
the mid-Thirties.
See "Dodge" in the main listing.
FARMERS AUTO SALES CO.—1920 (I)
Columbus, Indiana
FARMERS HIGHWHEEL—1910-11 (I)
Oklahoma City, Oklahoma
FAUBER, W. H.—1914 (I)
New York, New York
FAWICK MOTOR CAR CO.—1912 (I)
Sioux Falls, South Dakota
FEDERAL AUTOMOBILE & SUPPLY CO.
—1917 (I)
Camden, New Jersey
FIDELITY MOTOR CAR CO.—1909 (I)
Chicago, Illinois
FIELD MFG. CO.—1920 (VIII)
Owosso, Michigan
FINNAGAN, CHARLES A.—1913 (VIII)
Buffalo, New York
FLANDERS MOTOR CAR CO.—1912 (I)
Detroit, Michigan
FLINT WAGON WORKS
See "Whiting."
FLYING DUTCHMAN—1915 (I)
N. C. Gauntt
FOLEY BROS. CO.—1913 (I)
St. Paul, Minnesota
FORSYTHE MFG. CO.
—circa 1914 (I)
Third Street & Kentucky Avenue
Joplin, Missouri

FOSTER AUTOMOBILE MFG. CO.
—1900 (II)
297 State Street
Rochester, New York
FOSTORIA WAGON WORKS—1913 (I)
Fostoria, Ohio
FRANKLIN BOILER WORKS—1912 (I)
Troy, Ohio
FRANKLIN COMMERCIAL TRUCK CO.
—1910 (I)
Franklin, Pennsylvania
Changed to Eclipse Truck Co. which ap-
pears in the main listing.
FRANKLIN MACHINE CO.—1912 (I)
Brooklyn, New York
FREEMAN—1928-31 (VII)
Chicago, Illinois
This truck make, often listed as having
been built in Chicago, was built in Detroit.
See the main listing.
FRONT-AWAY—1917 (II)
Millington Motor Car Co.
Chicago, Illinois
FRONT DRIVE MOTOR CO.—1912-18 (V)
Hoboken, New Jersey
Built "Christie" front drive power unit at-
tachment for use in motorizing horse-drawn
fire apparatus.
FRONT DRIVE MOTOR CO.
—1921-circa 1929 (VIII)
Kansas City, Missouri
FULLER POWER TRUCK CO.
—1910 (VIII)
Delphos, Ohio
FULLER POWER VEHICLE CO.
—1906 (II)
Detroit, Michigan
FULTON MOTORS—1916 (I)
Fulton, Illinois
FURNAS OFFICE & BANK FURNITURE
CO.—1912 (I)
Indianapolis, Indiana

GALION DYNAMIC TRUCK CO.
—1914 (I)
Galion, Ohio
Former Cleveland-Galion Motor Truck Co.

GALLOWAY CO., WM.—1916 (I)
Waterloo, Iowa
GARFORD CORPORATION
—circa 1939 (I)
Marion, Indiana
GAUNTT, N. C.
See "Flying Dutchman."
GAYLORD MOTOR CAR CO.—1912 (I)
Gaylord, Michigan
GEARLESS STEAM AUTO MFG. CO.
—1921 (VIII)
Denver, Colorado
GEM AUTO TRUCK CO.—1921-22 (VIII)
Watervliet, New York
GEM MOTOR CAR CO.—1917 (I)
Grand Rapids, Michigan
GENERAL AUTOMOBILE & MFG. CO.
—1903 (II)
Cleveland, Ohio
GENERAL INDUSTRIAL MFG. CO.
—1912 (I)
Indianapolis, Indiana
GENEVA STEAM—1901-03 (IV)
Geneva Automobile & Mfg. Co.
Geneva, Ohio
GILL & SONS, P. H.—1913 (I)
Brooklyn, New York
GOLDEN STATE—1928-35 (VII)
Probable misspelling of "Golden Gate"
—produced by the Golden Gate Truck
Co.—which appears in main listing.
GOLDMAN AUTO CO.—1918 (VIII)
Chicago, Illinois
GOODYEAR TIRE & RUBBER CO.
—1919-20 (III)
Akron, Ohio
Built at least two experimental six-wheel
trucks and buses.
GRAHAM EQUIPMENT CO.—1899 (I)
170 Summer Street
Boston, Massachusetts
GRANT-FERRIS CO.—1901 (II)
Troy, New York
GREAT-EAGLE—1910-14 (IV)
United States Carriage Co.
Columbus, Ohio
GREAT SOUTHERN AUTOMOBILE CO.
—1912 (I)
Birmingham, Alabama

GREENE MOTOR CAR CO.—1907 (II)
Newark, New Jersey
GRINNELL ELECTRIC CAR CO.—1912 (I)
Detroit, Michigan
GUMPRICE MOTOR TRUCK CO.
—1912 (I)
Chicago, Illinois

𝓗

HABERER & CO.
See "Cino".
HALL MOTOR CAR CO.—1914 (I)
Waco, Texas
HALL SAFE CO.—1901 (VII)
Purchased electric winch truck from vehi-
cle equipment company in 1901 for use in
the delivery of safes. Did not build any
trucks themselves.
HAMBRICK MOTOR CAR CO.
—1906 (VIII)
Washington, Indiana
HANNAY—1917 (VIII)
HARGER STEAM TRUCK CO.—1911 (I)
New York, New York
HARLEY-DAVIDSON MOTOR CO.
—1915 (VI)
Milwaukee, Wisconsin
Motorcycle-type vehicles.
HARROUN MOTORS CORP.—1921 (IV)
Wayne, Michigan
HASBROUCK—1899-1901 (IV)
Hasbrouck Motor Co.
Newark, New Jersey
Hasbrouck Motor Works
Piermont, New York
HASCALL MOTOR TRUCK CO.—1916 (I)
Painesville, Ohio
HATHAWAY-PURINTON
—1924-25 (VIII)
Peabody, Massachusetts
HAUBER WAGON WORKS—1912 (I)
St. Marys, Pennsylvania
HAULPAK—1958 to date (VI)
LeTourneau-Westinghouse Co.
2301 North Adams Street
Peoria, Illinois
Off-highway construction vehicles.

HAWKEYE CARRIAGE & AUTO CO.
—1911 (I)
Cedar Rapids, Iowa
HAYNES AUTOMOBILE CO.
—1904-14 (IV)
Kokomo, Indiana
HAYWOOD WAGON CO.—1912 (I)
Newark, New York
HENDY IRON WORKS, JOSHUA
—circa 1915 (I)
75 Fremont Street
San Francisco, California
HENNEGIN—1908 (I)
Commercial Automobile Co.
Chicago, Illinois
HERCULES MOTOR TRUCK CO.
—1913-circa 1914 (I)
First & L Streets
Boston, Massachusetts
HEWITT-LINDSTROM ELECTRIC CO.
—1900-01 (I)
Chicago, Illinois
HEXTER, P. K.—1913 (II)
New York, New York
Later built as the "Roland." See main
listing.
HICKS-PARRETT TRACTOR CO.
—1922 (VIII)
Chicago Heights, Illinois
HOADLEY BROS.—1916 (I)
Gasport, Indiana
HODGETTS MFG. CO.—1916 (I)
Wallingford, Connecticut
HOMER MOTOR CO.—1914 (I)
Los Angeles, California
HORNER HANDY WAGON CO.
—1912 (VIII)
Detroit, Michigan
HOUGHTON MOTOR CAR CO.
—1916 (I)
Marion, Ohio
HOUGHTON SULKY CO.—1915 (I)
Marion, Ohio
HOWARD AUTOMOBILE CO. STEAM
—1900-01 (VIII)
Trenton, New Jersey
HUBER AUTOMOBILE CO.—1903 (II)
248 Jefferson Avenue
Detroit, Michigan

HUB MOTOR CO. ELECTRIC
—1917 (VIII)
Chicago, Illinois
HUB MOTOR TRUCK CO.—1916 (I)
325 South High Street
Columbus, Ohio
See "Piercy."
HUNTER-WECKLER BOAT CO.
—1909 (I)
McHenry, Illinois
HUNTINGDON—1912 (VIII)
HURON RIVER MFG. CO.
See "Ann Arbor."
HYDRAULIC TRUCK CO.—1916 (I)
Los Angeles, California

I

IDEAL ELECTRIC VEHICLE CO.
—1911 (I)
Chicago, Illinois
IDEAL MFG. CO.—1907 (I)
Portsmouth, Ohio
IDEAL MOTOR CAR CO. ELECTRIC
—1905-06 (VIII)
1238 West 11th Street
Cleveland, Ohio
IMMEL & SONS, JOHN—1911 (I)
Columbus, Ohio
IMP—1913-14 (IV)
W. H. McIntyre Co.
Auburn, Indiana
IMPERIAL—1904 (IV)
Rodgers & Co.
Columbus, Ohio
INDIAN MOTORCYCLE CO.—1930 (VI)
Springfield, Massachusetts
Motorcycle-type vehicles.
INDUSTRIAL TRUCK CO.—1921 (VIII)
Holyoke, Massachusetts
INTERNAL GEAR DRIVE CO.
—1913 (I)
Detroit, Michigan
INTERNATIONAL MOTOR CAR CO.
—1908 (VIII)
Philadelphia, Pennsylvania
This may be the International Motor Co.
incorporated in Philadelphia in 1908 to
produce the "Lea" truck. See "Lea."

IOWA MOTOR CAR CO.—1908 (IV)
Kellogg, Iowa
IVEY MOTOR TRUCK CO.—1913 (I)
Buffalo, New York

J

JACKSON AUTOMOBILE CO.—1904 (I)
Jackson, Michigan
JAMES & MEYER MOTOR CAR CO.
—1909-11 (VIII)
Lawrenceburg, Indiana
JANNEY, STEINMETZ & CO. STEAM
—1901 (VIII)
Philadelphia, Pennsylvania
JEFFERY CO., THOMAS B.
See "Rambler."
J.L.B. MOTOR CO.—1916 (I)
Dayton, Ohio
JOHNS MOTOR TRUCK CO.—1912 (I)
Detroit, Michigan
JOHNSTOWN MOTOR CAR CO.
—1913 (I)
Johnstown, Pennsylvania
JONES CO., S. H.—1904 (VIII)
Toledo, Ohio

K

KARBACH AUTOMOBILE & VEHICLE
CO.—1905 (II)
Omaha, Nebraska
KARDELL—1918 (VIII)
KAWS QUALITY—1922-25 (VIII)
Kaws Truck & Bus Mfg. Co.
Indianapolis, Indiana
KEATING AUTOMOBILE & WHEEL CO.
—1899 (I)
Middletown, Connecticut
KELLER CYCLECAR CO.—1914-15 (IV)
Chicago, Illinois
Wilmington, Delaware
KELLER MOTORS CORP.—1947 (II)
Huntsville, Alabama
KELLEY CONVERTIBLE AUTO TRUCK
CO.—1917 (VIII)
Chicago, Illinois

KELSEY THREE-WHEELER
—1910-12 (I)
Kelsey Mfg. Co., C. W.
Hartford, Connecticut
KEYSTONE MOTOR CO.—1900 (I)
Philadelphia, Pennsylvania
KIBLINGER CO., W. H.
—1907-09 (IV)
Auburn, Indiana
KIDDER MOTOR VEHICLE CO.
—1901 (I)
New Haven, Connecticut
KIMBALL CO., E. S. ELECTRIC
—1917-18 (VIII)
New Haven, Connecticut
KLONDIKE—1918-20 (VIII)
F. W. Kohlmeyer
Logansville, Wisconsin
KNUCKLEY TRUCK CO.
See "Western."
KOENIG & LUHRS WAGON CO.
—circa 1916 (I)
320 South Sixth Avenue
Quincy, Illinois
KOERING
See "Dumptor."
KOHLMEYER
See "Klondike."
KRATZNER AUTOMOBILE CO.
—1912 (I)
Allentown, Pennsylvania
KRUEGER MFG. CO.—1905 (I)
Milwaukee, Wisconsin
KUGEL AUTO CO.—1913 (I)
Indianapolis, Indiana
KW-DART TRUCK CO.
—1958 to date (VI)
2623 Oak Street
Kansas City, Missouri
1301 North Manchester Trafficway
Kansas City, Missouri
Off-highway construction vehicles.

L

LAFAYETTE MOTOR TRUCK CO.
—1917 (I)
Lafayette, Indiana

LA FRANCE—circa 1910-11 (IV)
American LaFrance Fire Engine Co.
Elmira, New York
Built experimental gasoline-hydraulic trucks during these years.

LAMBERT-MORIN MOTOR VEHICLE CO.
—1912 (I)
Lawrence, Massachusetts

LAMMERT & MANN CO.—1922 (I)
Chicago, Illinois

LANDOVER—1917-18 (VIII)

LANE & DALEY STEAM—1902 (VIII)
Barre, Vermont

LAUREL MOTORS CORP.
—circa 1922 (I)
Anderson, Indiana

LAVIGNE CYCLECAR CO.—1914-15 (IV)
Detroit, Michigan

LEA—1908 (VIII)
International Motor Co.
Philadelphia, Pennsylvania
Possibly this should be International Motor Car Co., also listed as having been incorporated in Philadelphia in 1908.

LEACH MOTOR CAR CO.
—1920-23 (VIII)
Los Angeles, California

LEACH MOTOR VEHICLE CO. STEAM
—1899-1901 (IV)
Everett, Massachusetts

LECTRA-HAUL—1959 to date (VI)
Unit Rig & Equipment Co.
Tulsa, Oklahoma
Off-highway construction vehicles.

LEITNER MOTOR TRUCK CO.—1912 (I)
Kenton, Ohio

LENDE AUTOMOBILE MFG. CO.
—circa 1909 (I)
Minneapolis, Minnesota

LENGERT CO.—1896 (II)
12th & Locust Streets
Philadelphia, Pennsylvania

LESLIE MOTOR CAR CO.—1918 (VIII)
Detroit, Michigan

LeTOURNEAU, INC., R. G.
—1954-circa 1957 (VI)
2399 South MacArthur
Longview, Texas
Off-highway construction vehicles.

LeTOURNEAU-WESTINGHOUSE
See "Haulpak."

LIBERTY—1917-circa 1930 (VII)
Gramm-Bernstein Co.
Lima, Ohio
Not a trade name. Class A & B Liberty trucks had "U.S.A." cast into radiator.

LIBERTY AUTO TRUCK CO.—1919 (I)
Chicago, Illinois

LIBERTY MOTOR VEHICLE CO.
—1926 (I)
Cleveland, Ohio

LINCOLN—1921-30 (IV)
Lincoln Motor Co.
Division of Ford Motor Co.
Detroit, Michigan

LINCOLN MOTOR TRUCK CO.—1914 (I)
San Francisco, California

LION MOTOR CO.—1907-12 (VIII)
Philadelphia, Pennsylvania
Adrian and Detroit, Michigan

LOMBARD AUTO TRACTOR TRUCK CORP.
—circa 1917 (VI)
Waterville, Maine
Half-track type vehicle used mostly in off-highway logging operations.

LONG ISLAND MOTOR VEHICLE CO.
—1901 (II)
Brooklyn, New York

LOOMIS AUTOMOBILE CO.—1902 (IV)
Westfield, Massachusetts

LORRAINE CAR CO.—1919-22 (VIII)
Richmond, Indiana

LOVELACE ENGINEERING CO. INC.
—1916 (I)
New Brunswick, New Jersey

LUDLOW AUTO ENGINEERING CO.
—1914 (I)
Philadelphia, Pennsylvania

LYONS MOTOR WORKS—1919-21 (VIII)
Manchester, New Hampshire

M

MAPLELEAF
Canadian export name for "Chevrolet" truck.

MARINETTE MOTOR CAR CO.
—1912 (I)
Marinette, Wisconsin

MARKEY MFG. CO.—1912 (I)
Mt. Clemens, Michigan

MARKS—1901 (VII)
Name of truck designer, not make. Harry J. Marks designed steam vehicle for Empire State Engineering Co. See "Empire" in main listing.

MARSHALL MFG. CO.—1919 (I)
Chicago, Illinois

MARTIN MOTOR TRUCK CO.—1930 (I)
Waverly, New York

MARVEL—1912 (VIII)

MARWIN MOTOR TRUCK CO.—1918 (I)
Kenosha, Wisconsin
Merged with Winther Motor Truck Co., producers of the "Winther" truck, which appears in main listing.

MARYLAND STEAM—1900-01 (VIII)
Maryland Automobile Mfg. Co.
Luke, Maryland

MASTER MOTOR CAR CO.
—1907-circa 1920 (VIII)
Cleveland, Ohio

MAUMEE—1906 (VIII)
Wolverine Automobile & Commercial Vehicle Co.
Dundee, Michigan
Maumee Motor Car Works
Detroit, Michigan

MAXI—1940-42 (VI)
Six Wheels Inc.
1572-84 East 20th Street
Los Angeles, California
Off-highway construction vehicles.

MAYTAG-MASON MOTOR CO.
—circa 1908 (I)
Des Moines, Iowa

McCREA MOTOR TRUCK CO.
—1906 (VII)
Cleveland, Ohio
Not a truck manufacturer.
Sales Agent for Champion Wagon Co. of Owego, New York.

McFARLAN MOTOR CO.—1916 (I)
Connersville, Indiana

MEECH-STODDARD—1922-27 (VIII)

MEISTER & SONS CO., A.
—circa 1951 (I)
Ninth & D Streets
Sacramento, California
MERCURY CYCLECAR CO.—1913-14 (IV)
Detroit, Michigan
MERCURY MOTOR TRUCK CO.
—1911 (VIII)
Boston, Massachusetts
MESSERER, S.—1898 (II)
15 Springfield Avenue
Newark, New Jersey
MESSINGER MFG. CO.—circa 1914 (I)
Tatamy, Pennsylvania
METROPOLITAN AUTOMOBILE WORKS
—1912 (I)
Chicago, Illinois
METROPOLITAN MOTOR CAR CO.
—1903 (I)
New York, New York
METZGER MOTOR CAR CO.
—circa 1909 (I)
Detroit, Michigan
MEYERS MOTOR TRACTOR CO.
—1913 (V)
Philadelphia, Pennsylvania
Front conversion unit for cars.
MICAMPBELL—1915 (VIII)
MICHIGAN—1963-65 (VI)
Clark Equipment Co.
Construction Machinery Division
2439 Pipestone Road
Benton Harbor, Michigan
Off-highway construction vehicles.
MICHIGAN HEARSE & AUTOMOBILE CO.
—circa 1913 (I)
Grand Rapids, Michigan
MICHIGAN STEAM MOTOR CO.
—1909-11 (VIII)
Detroit, Michigan
MIDDLEBY AUTO CO.
See "Reading."
MID-WEST STEAM MOTOR CO.
—1924 (I)
Laramie, Wyoming
MILLER CAR CO.—1914 (IV)
Detroit, Michigan
MILLINGTON MOTOR CAR CO.
See "Frontaway."

MILWAUKEE AUTOMOBILE CO.
—1901 (I)
19th St. & St. Paul Avenue
Milwaukee, Wisconsin
MINNEAPOLIS MOTOR CO.—1914 (IV)
Minneapolis, Minnesota
MINNEAPOLIS MOTOR CYCLE CO.
—1912 (I)
Minneapolis, Minnesota
MISSION MOTOR CAR CO.
See "Crescent."
MISSOURI MOTOR CAR CO.—1912 (I)
108 North Eighth Street
St. Louis, Missouri
MITCHELL MFG. CO., J. HENRY
—1906 (II)
Philadelphia, Pennsylvania
MODEL AUTOMOBILE CO.—1906 (VIII)
Peru, Indiana
MOHAWK CYCLECARS—1914-16 (IV)
New Orleans, Louisiana
MOHAWK MOTOR TRUCK CO.
—1916 (I)
Ravenna, Ohio
MOHICAN MOTOR CORP.—1921 (VIII)
New York, New York
MOORE MOTOR VEHICLE CO.
—1916-21 (IV)
Minneapolis, Minnesota
Danville, Illinois
MOR-POWER—1921 (VIII)
MOTOR TRUCK & VEHICLE CO.
—1901 (I)
Columbus, Ohio
MOTOR VEHICLE & MARINE
CONSTRUCTION CO.—1912 (I)
Sewarren, New Jersey
MOTOR WAGON CO.—1910 (I)
Detroit, Michigan
Later may have used name "Detroit Motor
Wagon."
MUEHLHAUSER MACHINE CO.
—1912 (I)
Cleveland, Ohio
MUNCIE MOTOR TRUCK CO.—1912 (I)
Muncie, Indiana
MUNSON GAS-ELECTRIC—1899 (VIII)
Munson Electric Motor Co.
La Porte, Indiana

MYERS CARRIAGE CO.
—circa 1914 (I)
Franklin, Pennsylvania

NATIONAL MOTOR TRUCK & MFG. CO.
—1913 (I)
Gibsonburg, Ohio
NEUSTADT COMPANY, J. H.—1905 (II)
826 South 18th Street
St. Louis, Missouri
NEVIN—1927-circa 1934 (VIII)
NEWCOMB—1921 (VIII)
NEWCOMER—1926-30 (VIII)
NEW DEPARTURE MFG. CO.
See "Rockwell."
NEW ENGLAND MOTOR CARRIAGE CO.
—1898-1900 (VIII)
Waltham, Massachusetts
NEW ERA AUTO CYCLE CO.
—1911-12 (VIII)
Dayton, Ohio
NEW ERA ENGINEERING CO.
—1917 (VIII)
Joliet, Illinois
NEW HAVEN CARRIAGE CO.
—1911-14 (VIII)
New Haven, Connecticut
NEW YORK MOTOR WORKS
—1910 (II)
East Nutley, New Jersey
NUCAR FORWARDING CORP.
—1930 (VIII)
Trenton, New Jersey
NUSCO—1916 (VIII)

O

O'BRIEN & O'CONNELL
—circa 1914 (I)
318-21 Cherry Street
Terre Haute, Indiana
OGREN MOTOR CAR CO.—1922 (I)
Milwaukee, Wisconsin
OHIO ELECTRIC CAR CO.—1912 (II)
Toledo, Ohio

OHIO MFG. CO.—1912 (VIII)
Upper Sandusky, Ohio
OHIO MOTOR TRUCK CO.—1909 (I)
Warren, Ohio
OHIO UNIVERSAL TRUCK CO.
—1911 (I)
Warren, Ohio
OLDS-McCOMB MOTOR WAGON CO.
—1907 (II)
Detroit, Michigan
OLSEN—1921 (VII)
Swedish Crucible Steel Co.
Detroit, Michigan
Converted Ford Model T trucks from one
to two tons capacity.
OMAHA MOTOR CAR CO.—1912 (I)
Omaha, Nebraska
OMASKA TRACTOR MFG. & FOUNDRY
CO.—1911 (VIII)
Omaha, Nebraska
OTTO-MOBILE CO.—1912 (I)
Mt. Holly, New Jersey
OWENS WAGON & AUTOMOBILE
WORKS—1912 (I)
Charlotte, North Carolina

𝒫

PACE, A. G.—1901 (I)
New York, New York
PACIFIC CAR & FOUNDRY CO.
—1942-45 (VI)
Renton, Washington
Specialized in military trucks for heavy du-
ty tank recovery work.
PACO—circa 1905-10 (VIII)
Pietsch Auto & Marine Co.
Chicago, Illinois
PAGE BROS. BUGGY CO.—1916 (I)
Marshall, Michigan
PAN AMERICAN MOTORS CO.
—1919-22 (IV)
Decatur, Illinois
PANTHER—1920 (I)
Fremont Motors Corp.
Fremont, Ohio
Fremont did build the "All-American"
which appears in the main listing.

PARAGON MOTOR TRUCK CO.—1916 (I)
Auburn, Indiana
PARRY AUTOMOBILE CO.—1910-11 (IV)
Indianapolis, Indiana
PARSONS ELECTRIC CARRIAGE CO.
—1905 (I)
Cleveland, Ohio
PARSONS TRUCK WAGON CO.—1912 (I)
Newton, Iowa
PATERSON CO., W. A.
—circa 1908-24 (IV)
Flint, Michigan
PATHFINDER MOTOR MFG. CO.
—1913-15 (IV)
Indianapolis, Indiana
PATRICK CORP.—1916 (I)
Spokane, Washington
PATTERSON-GREENFIELD
—1916-18 (IV)
C. R. Patterson & Sons
Greenfield, Ohio
PATTON MOTOR VEHICLE CO.
ELECTRIC—1899 (I)
Chicago, Illinois
PAXSON
See "Cleveland."
PENN MOTOR CAR CO.—1912 (VIII)
New Castle, Pennsylvania
PEOPLES AUTOMOBILE CO.
—1901-02 (IV)
Cleveland, Ohio
PHIPPS-GRINNELL ELECTRIC
—1911 (I)
Phipps-Grinnell Auto Co.
Detroit, Michigan
PHOENIX MOTOR CAR & TRUCK CO.
—1911 (I)
Brooklyn, New York
PHOENIX MOTOR VEHICLE CO.
—1900-01 (VIII)
Cleveland, Ohio
PIERCY—1916 (I)
Hub Motor Truck Co.
Columbus, Ohio
PIERSON, INC., A. N.
—1912-18 (VIII)
Cromwell, Connecticut
PIETSCH AUTO & MARINE CO.
See "Paco."

PIONEER CAR CO., INC.—1909-11 (IV)
El Reno, Oklahoma
Pioneer Car Mfg., Co.
Oklahoma City, Oklahoma
PITTSBURGH MODEL ENGINEERING
CO.—1920-25 (VIII)
Pittsburgh, Pennsylvania
PITTSBURGH MOTOR TRUCK CO.
—circa 1912 (I)
Pittsburgh, Pennsylvania
PNEUMATIC—1896-1905 (VIII)
Pneumatic Carriage Co., Inc.
American Wheelock Engine Co.
Worcester, Massachusetts
POLE ELECTRIC
—1913-circa 1920 (VIII)
Commercial Truck Co.
Philadelphia, Pennsylvania
PONTIAC MOTOR CAR CO.—1906 (I)
East Huron Street
Pontiac, Michigan
POPE-TOLEDO—1904-09 (IV)
Pope Motor Car Co.
Toledo, Ohio
PORT ALBANY FOUNDRIES, INC.
—1929 (I)
Coxsackie, New York
POWELL ENGINEERING CO.—1911 (I)
Brooklyn, New York
POWER VEHICLE CO.—1912 (I)
Milwaukee, Wisconsin
PRATT MFG. CO., WM. E.—1912 (VIII)
Joliet, Illinois
PRIGG, PAUL H.—1914 (I)
Converse, Indiana
PRUDENCE—1912 (VIII)
PUBLIC MOTOR TRUCK CO.
—1914 (VIII)
PURITAN MOTOR CO.—1914 (IV)
Chicago, Illinois

𝓡

RAE ELECTRIC VEHICLE CO.—1909 (IV)
Boston, Massachusetts
Springfield, Vermont
RAMBLER—1904-13 (IV)
Thomas B. Jeffery Co.
Kenosha, Wisconsin

RANGER MOTOR WORKS
—1907-11 (VIII)
Chicago, Illinois
RAUCH & LANG ELECTRIC
—1905-30 (IV)
Rauch & Lang Carriage Co.
Baker, Rauch & Lang Co.
Cleveland, Ohio
Chicopee Falls, Massachusetts
RAVENNA MOTOR TRUCK CO.—1912 (I)
Ravenna, Ohio
READING STEAM—1902 (II)
Steam Vehicle Co. of America
753-755 Cherry Street
Reading, Pennsylvania
READING—1920 (VIII)
Middleby Auto Co.
Reading, Pennsylvania
READING TRUCK CO., H. J.
ELECTRIC—1903 (II)
Detroit, Michigan
READ MOTOR CAR CO.—1913 (I)
Detroit, Michigan
RED ARROW AUTOMOBILE CO.
—circa 1916 (I)
East Main Street
Orange, Massachusetts
REDCLIFF MOTORS CO., LTD.
—circa 1917 (I)
Redcliff, Alberta, Canada
RED STAR MOTOR TRUCK CO.
— 1912 (I)
St. Louis, Missouri
RED WING—1912 (VIII)
Wallof Motor Truck Co.
Red Wing, Minnesota
REEDSBURG MOTOR TRUCK CO.
—1914 (I)
Reedsburg, Wisconsin
REEVES-THOMPSON MOTOR CO.
—1899 (I)
Columbus, Ohio
RELIABLE DAYTON MOTOR CAR CO.
—1909 (II)
Chicago, Illinois
REPUBLIC MOTOR VEHICLE CO.
—1902 (I)
Minneapolis, Minnesota
RESEARCH ENGINEERING CO.

See "Spencer."
REX—1963 to date (VI)
Chain Belt Company
4701 West Greenfield Avenue
Milwaukee, Wisconsin
Construction equipment vehicles.
REX MACHINE WORKS
—circa 1914 (I)
90 Eldert Street
Brooklyn, New York
REXROAD ENGINEERING CO.—1916 (I)
705-707 South Main Street
Hutchinson, Kansas
REX-WATSON CORP.—1925 (VIII)
Canastota, New York
RHODE ISLAND AUTOMOBILE TRUCK
CO.—1900 (VIII)
Providence, Rhode Island
RICHARD AUTO MFG. CO.
—circa 1914 (I)
Cleveland, Ohio
ROCKFORD AUTOMOBILE & ENGINEER-
ING CO.—1908-12 (VIII)
Rockford, Illinois
ROCK HILL BUGGY CO.—1915 (I)
Rock Hill, South Carolina
ROCK-OLA TRIVAN—1938 (VIII)
Rock-Ola Mfg. Corp.
Chicago, Illinois
ROCKWELL—1909-12 (IV)
New Departure Mfg. Co.
Bristol Engineering Corp.
Bristol, Connecticut
RODEFELD MFG. CO.
—circa 1915 (I)
96 West Main Street
Richmond, Indiana
RODGERS & CO.
See "Imperial."
ROMER MOTOR CORP.—1922 (I)
Taunton, Massachusetts
ROSS AUTOMOBILE CO.—1915-18 (IV)
Detroit, Michigan
ROSS AUTOMOBILE CO.—1921 (I)
Chicago, Illinois
ROSS CARRIER CO.—1933 (VII)
New York, New York
A straddle-carrier industrial vehicle, not a
motor truck.

RUGGLES AUTOMOBILE CO.—1905 (II)
Ware, Massachusetts
RULER MOTOR CAR CO.—1916 (I)
Sixth & Chestnut Streets
St. Louis, Missouri

S

ST. CHARLES MOTOR TRUCK CO.
—1914 (I)
St. Louis, Missouri
SALENTINE-LIBBY & CO.—1912 (I)
Milwaukee, Wisconsin
SCHLEICHER & SONS—1896 (I)
Stamford, Connecticut
SCHLOSSER MFG. CO.—1909 (I)
151 East 126 Street
New York, New York
SCHOEPFLIN CO., L. G.—1914 (I)
Buffalo, New York
SCHOONMAKER MOTOR TRUCK CO.
—1921 (I)
Hudson, Michigan
SCHURMEIER WAGON CO.—1910 (I)
St. Paul, Minnesota
SCOTT AUTOMOBILE CO. ELECTRIC
—1904-05 (VIII)
St. Louis, Missouri
S&D MOTOR VEHICLE CO.—1912 (I)
Oakland, California
SEARS, ROEBUCK & CO.—1909-11 (II)
Chicago, Illinois
Succeeded by Lincoln Motor Car Works
which appears in the main listing.
SEFRIN MOTOR CARRIAGE CO., CHAS.
—1905 (I)
90 Cornelia Street
Brooklyn, New York
SEXTON TRACTOR CO.—1917 (I)
Asbury Park, New Jersey
SHADBOLT MFG. CO. STEAM
—1902-03 (III)
Brooklyn, New York
Built a few experimental steam trucks for
various inventors.
SHAFER-DECKER CO.—1916 (I)
Rochester, New York
SHERWOOD—1914 (VIII)

SHILLITO STEAM—1901 (VIII)
    The John Shillito Co.
    Cincinnati, Ohio
SIGMUND AUTO TRUCK CO.—1912 (I)
    Milwaukee, Wisconsin
SIMONDS-LA FRANCE—1905-06 (VIII)
    Marlboro, Massachusetts
SING SING—1912 (VII)
    Ossining, New York
    Plan to make trucks at Sing Sing Prison
    abandoned after a few months.
SIX WHEELS INC.
    See "Maxi."
SKOOTMOBILE INC.—1939 (VIII)
    Chicago, Illinois
SMITH FLYER FIVE-WHEELER
    —1917-20 (IV)
    Smith Co., A. O.
    Milwaukee, Wisconsin
SOUTHERN AUTOMOBILE MFG. CO.,
    INC.—1922 (I)
    Memphis, Tennessee
SPACKLE MACHINE & TOOL CO.
    —circa 1920 (I)
    Indianapolis, Indiana
SPENCER—1922 (VIII)
    Research Engineering Co.
    Dayton, Ohio
SPENCER AUTO-VEHICLE CO.
    STEAM—1902 (II)
    Hartford, Connecticut
SPOKANE AUTO MFG. CO.
    —circa 1916 (I)
    Sinto & Cedar Streets
    Spokane, Washington
SPRINGFIELD MOTOR VEHICLE CO.
    —1901 (II)
    Springfield, Massachusetts
S&S—1924-30 (IV)
    Sayers & Scovill Co.
    Cincinnati, Ohio
    Believed to have built ambulances primarily during these years.
STANDARD GAS & ELECTRIC POWER
    CO.—1911 (VIII)
    Philadelphia, Pennsylvania
STANDARD TRACTOR CO.—1916 (II)
    120 Waverly Avenue
    Brooklyn, New York

STANLEY BROTHERS—1899 (I)
    Newton, Massachusetts
STANLEY POWER WAGON CO.—1910 (I)
    Detroit, Michigan
STAPF & CO., JOHN M.—1915 (VIII)
    Dunkirk, New York
STATES MOTOR CAR MFG. CO.
    —1916 (I)
    Kalamazoo, Michigan
STAVER CARRIAGE CO.—1912 (I)
    Chicago, Illinois
STEAMOBILE—1922 (VIII)
    Winslow Boiler & Engineering Co.
    Chicago, Illinois
STEAMOBILE CO.—1902 (VIII)
    Keene, New Hampshire
STEAM-O-TRUCK—1920 (VIII)
STEAM VEHICLE CO. OF AMERICA
    See "Reading Steam."
STEP-N-DRIVE TRUCK CORP.—1928 (V)
    1255 Niagara Street
    Buffalo, New York
    Converted Fords and other delivery trucks
    for multi-stop service.
STERLING AUTOMOBILE CO.
    See "AMS Sterling."
STERLING POWER VEHICLE CO.
    —1902 (I)
    New York, New York
    Had plans to build plant in Cleveland.
STEWART, RICHARD F.—1895 (III)
    Pocantico Hills, New York
    Experimental business wagon with Daimler
    engine and internal gear drive.
STUART COMMERCIAL CAR CO.
    —1910 (I)
    Detroit, Michigan
STUDEBAKER
    See "Erskine."
STURTEVANT MILLS CO.—1906-08 (IV)
    Boston, Massachusetts
SWAB WAGON CO.—circa 1916 (I)
    Elizabethville, Pennsylvania
SWANSON MOTOR CAR CO.—1912 (I)
    Chicago, Illinois
SWEDISH CRUCIBLE STEEL CO.
    See "Olsen."
SYMONDS AUTO TRUCK CO.—1912 (I)
    Chicago, Illinois

T

THEIM MOTOR CAR CO.—1911 (I)
    St. Paul, Minnesota
THOMAS MOTOR CAR CO., E.R.
    —circa 1905-17 (IV)
    Buffalo, New York
THRESHER ELECTRIC CO.—1900 (I)
    Dayton, Ohio
TOEPPINGER—1910 (VIII)
TOEPPNER BROS.—circa 1915 (I)
    Bay City, Michigan
TOLEDO STEAM—1901 (II)
    American Bicycle Co.
    Toledo, Ohio
    Built large steam truck for plant use.
TOLEDO ELECTRIC VEHICLE CO.
    —1909 (I)
    Toledo, Ohio
TOPPINS TRACTOR TRUCK CO.
    —1923 (I)
    Milwaukee, Wisconsin
TORRANCE, E.A.—circa 1915 (I)
    1324 Cedar Street
    Spokane, Washington
TRACTION CO. STEAM—1901 (VIII)
    Elizabethport, New Jersey
TRANSCONTINENTAL MOTOR TRUCK
    CORP.—1917 (I)
    Buffalo, New York
TRIPLE MOTOR TRUCK CO.—1916 (I)
    Minneapolis, Minnesota
TROY WAGON WORKS—1914-16 (VIII)
    Troy, Ohio
TRUCKSTELL INC.
    —1937-circa 1950 (V)
    Cleveland, Ohio
    Converted Chevrolet trucks to dual rear axle drive.
TRUMBULL—1914-15 (II)
    American Cyclecar Co.
    Trumbull Motor Car Co.
    Bridgeport, Connecticut
TURBINE ELECTRIC TRUCK CO.
    —1904 (II)
    Union, New Jersey
    A steam-electric vehicle.
TWO-IN-ONE-CO.
    See "Amhurst."

TWOMBLY—1913-16 (II)
Driggs-Seabury Ordnance Corp.
81 Sharpsville Street
Sharon, Pennsylvania
TWYFORD MOTOR CAR CO.—1907 (IV)
Brookville, Pennsylvania

U

ULTRA TRUCK CORP.—1917 (I)
Philadelphia, Pennsylvania
UNION CAR CO.—1916 (I)
Los Angeles, California
UNITED STATES CARRIAGE CO.
See "Great-Eagle."
UNIT RIG & EQUIPMENT
See "Lectra-Haul."
UNWIN MOTOR CAR CO.—1922 (I)
New York, New York
U.S.A.—1917-circa 1930
Class A and B trucks — nicknamed
"Liberty" — built exclusively for the U.S.
Army in World War I by various manufac-
turers, including Gramm-Bernstein,
Bethlehem and Selden. Also a few ex-
perimental Army trucks built at Camp
Holabird, Maryland, by the Quarter Master
Dept. after World War I carried "U.S.A."
on the radiator.
U.S. LONG DISTANCE AUTO CO.
—1904 (II)
Jersey City, New Jersey
UTAH MOTOR TRUCK CO.—1913 (I)
Salt Lake City, Utah

V

VAN-L COMMERCIAL CAR CO.
—1912 (I)
Grand Rapids, Michigan
VESTAL MOTOR CAR CO.—1914 (I)
Pittsburgh, Pennsylvania
VETERAN—circa 1920 (VIII)
Sherbrook, Quebec, Canada
VIDEX AUTOMOBILE CO.—1903 (VIII)
Boston, Massachusetts
Steam and gasoline trucks.
VIRGINIA—1932-34 (VIII)

VIXEN—1914-15 (IV)
Davis Mfg. Co.
Milwaukee, Wisconsin
VULCAN MOTOR TRUCK CO.—1912 (I)
Detroit, Michigan

W

WACO—1915-17 (IV)
Western Automobile Co.
Seattle, Washington
WALLOF MOTOR TRUCK CO.—1912 (I)
Minneapolis, Minnesota
See "Red Wing."
WASHINGTON AUTO TRUCK MFG. CO.
—1912 (I)
Milwaukee, Wisconsin
WASHINGTON AUTO VEHICLE CO.
—1901 (I)
511 Ninth Street
Washington, D.C.
WASHINGTON MOTOR CAR CO.
—circa 1915 (I)
Hyattsville, Maryland
WASHINGTON MOTOR VEHICLE CO.
—1908-10 (VIII)
Washington, Indiana
WAYNE LIGHT COMMERCIAL CO.
—1912 (I)
New York, New York
WEBER MOTOR VEHICLE CO.—1910 (I)
Louisville, Kentucky
WEBSTER—1910-12 (IV)
Chicago Coach & Carriage Co.
Chicago, Illinois
Also called "Duer."
WEGE—1917 (VIII)
WERNER MOTOR TRUCK CORP.
—1935 (II)
Eastport, L.I., New York
WESTERN—circa 1939-42 (VI)
Knuckey Truck Co.
200 Paul Avenue
San Francisco, California
Off-highway construction vehicles.
WESTERN AUTOMOBILE CO.
See "Waco."
WESTERN MOTOR TRUCK CO.

—1911-28 (VIII)
Cleveland, Ohio
WESTERN MOTOR TRUCK CO.—1913 (I)
Oakland, California
WESTERN MOTOR TRUCK & VEHICLE
WORKS—circa 1906 (I)
Chicago, Illinois
WEST MOTOR CO., INC.—1919 (I)
New York, New York
WHITCOMB WHEEL CO.—1927-35 (VIII)
Kenosha, Wisconsin
WHITING—1910-11 (VIII)
Flint Wagon Works
Flint, Michigan
WILSON BROS. STEAM—1902 (I)
Easton, Pennsylvania
WINCHESTER—1909 (VIII)
WINSLOW BOILER & ENGINEERING
See "Steamobile."
WISCONSIN DUPLEX AUTO CO.
—1918 (I)
Oshkosh, Wisconsin
Changed to Oshkosh Motor Truck Mfg. Co.
which appears in main listing.
WISCONSIN FARM TRACTOR CO.
—circa 1922 (II)
Sauk City, Wisconsin
WISHART-DAYTON AUTO TRUCK CO.
—1912 (VIII)
501 Fifth Avenue
New York, New York
WOLVERINE AUTOMOBILE &
COMMERCIAL VEHICLE CO.—1905 (I)
Dundee, Michigan
See also "Maumee."
WOOD-LOCO VEHICLE CO. STEAM
—1901-03 (VIII)
Cohoes, New York
WOOD & SON, FRED R.—1900-02 (I)
219 West 19th Street
New York, New York
W.S.M. TRUCK MFG. CO.—1912 (I)
Newark, New Jersey

Y

YPSILANTI MOTOR TRUCK CO.
—1917 (I)
Ypsilanti, Michigan

XIII

LICENSING THE MOTORCAR

BY KEITH MARVIN

Of the many accessories attendant to motor vehicles and motoring, one of the least heralded but most important is the ubiquitous license plate. During its seven decades of existence, it has served as an effective system of identification for a variety of vehicles and, for the governmental agencies issuing them, has provided a source of revenue totalling into the billions. At the same time, the license plate's varied and colorful appearance has given birth to the national pastime known as plate-spotting.

Although number plates in the modern sense are relatively new, they have existed in various forms since the time of the Romans for registration of all kinds of vehicles — from ancient chariots to the hansom cabs of Nineteenth Century London. In the United States, automobiles were registered on a statewide basis in 1901, as California and New York began registering and taxing vehicles. Assigned registrations were first displayed in New York, where the initials of the car owner were carried at the rear of the motor vehicle. This was the forerunner of the modern license plate.

The first state-issued plates appeared in Massachusetts in 1903; with each passing year more and more states adopted the practice of providing tags for automobilists. Since 1918, when Florida joined the other states in issuing official plates, home-made tags of tin, brass, aluminum, steel, wood, leather or wire screening have disappeared.

The first officially-issued markers were constructed of various types of metals, sometimes with flat surfaces and occasionally with numbers and letters embossed or recessed. Popular during these early days were plates of porcelain-enameled iron which were expensive to make and handsome to view. Unfortunately, they also suffered from a tendency to chip when struck by such hard objects as flying stones and gravel. Porcelain plates reached the zenith of their popularity in 1913 and faded rapidly thereafter, replaced by more durable embossed metal tags which have endured to the present time.

There were exceptions to this rule, however, such as the flat fibreboard

*1905 tag issued to K. I. Harrison
of Brooklyn for his Columbia electric.*

License Plates in the United States, Its Possessions and Neighboring Countries

plates used in Quebec between 1911 and 1924 and again in 1944. Rubber tags were used in Ontario from 1905 through 1910 and a compressed paper variety was used in several states during World War II. Even a plastic plate appeared in Utah in 1944.

A variety of designs, as well as materials, has characterized official plates as well. Many of the earliest plates carried state seals or provincial coats-of-arms and later a plethora of symbols appeared — from the steer's head on 1917 Arizona tags to the keystone favored in Pennsylvania and the bear, poppy, bell and star employed in California. Even more detailed insignias became common, notably the codfish in Massachusetts, pelican in Louisiana, potato in Idaho and bucking bronco in Wyoming.

License plate advertising slogans first appeared in Prince Edward Island where the 1928 plates called attention to two of the island's distinguishing features, "SEED POTATOES" and "FOXES." South Carolina's "IODINE" slogan appeared in 1930, and from this time on, the name of a product or tourist attraction for which the state or province is well-known has been carried proudly on plates. Today no fewer than twenty-eight states and the District of Columbia, as well as six Canadian provinces and both territories carry some sort of advertising slogan or symbol on their markers.

Systems for numbering license plates have also varied through the years. Some states, provinces and territories use straight numbers while others use a series of letters or numbers denoting counties of issuance. Letter and number combinations can also indicate the Congressional District of the issuing offices or the weight of the vehicle being registered. The county name is included on current plates in Georgia, Kentucky, Mississippi and Tennessee. Many states have also adopted the "vanity plate"—combinations of up to six letters or fancy letter-number combinations may be obtained upon payment of an extra fee.

Plate colors have been selected, for the most part, with an eye to choosing the most legible combinations. Most tags used throughout North America today are reflectorized to expedite nighttime identification.

Since 1957 the size of all plates in the United States, Canada, Mexico and most U.S. possessions has been standardized to twelve by six inches, eliminating the confusion caused by the diversity of plate sizes and shapes prior to this date.

Another important development should be noted: Since World War II, when the wartime metal shortage forced many states and provinces to use their plates for more than one year at a time, there has been a growing tendency to revalidate an existing series of plates for a number of years by stickers which can be applied to the plates themselves or to windshields. But the most interesting development in recent license plate history concerns the wedding of antique plates to antique cars. Some years ago, antique automobile collectors in several states were successful in their efforts to introduce legislation resulting in the issuance of special antique automobile plates for use on their old cars under special stipulations. The idea soon spread to other states and today antique auto plates are issued in virtually every state, the District of Columbia and eight Canadian provinces. How the plates may be used varies from place to place: Some may be used only on vehicles of a certain age while others may be used for off-highway purposes only for attending parades, meetings and historical or educational events. Recently, two states have issued a second series of plates to owners of classic cars, and state officials are hoping that this series will prove as successful as the antique car plates.

And what of the future? We can safely predict that if current trends continue, plates of tomorrow will remain the same size, will be reflectorized and will carry highly developed numbering systems. The issuance of more permanent and semi-permanent plates, too, is probable in the future. One factor can be predicted with certainty: License plates will always reflect the individuality of the regions they represent. As long as motor vehicles are registered by state or province rather than federal government, a variety of license plates will prevail.

THE UNITED STATES

ALABAMA—1903 or later

On October 9, 1909, the Alabama State Legislature approved an act requiring automobile owners to register with the probate judge of their county. But few — if any — of these counties required any sort of numerical display on motor vehicles. By 1910 the cities of Birmingham, Mobile and presumably others were providing number plates to automobile owners. These annually-issued plates were porcelain-enameled iron and dated.

The first state-issued license plates in Alabama appeared in 1912 and were attached to the nearly 5000 motor vehicles in the state. The only difference between these annually-issued plates and earlier local plates was that these state plates carried no date. In 1916 these enameled iron plates were replaced by an embossed metal type, and in 1917 the first dated markers appeared.

From that day to this, Alabama plates have been issued annually, with the exception of 1943 when, due to the metal shortage caused by World War II, 1942 plates were reused with the addition of windshield stickers in a variety of color combinations.

From 1922 to 1927 license plates on privately-owned vehicles carried the word "PRIVATE," and since 1955 the plates have carried a heart-shaped design bearing the motto "HEART OF DIXIE."

ALASKA—1917

The first number plates issued in Alaska were red on white and considerably smaller in size than plates used in other possessions and states. Their size increased somewhat for 1932, but until 1949 they were still smaller than most plates in the U.S.

Undeterred by the World War II metal shortage, Alaska issued new license plates in 1943, revalidating them by means of tabs for the following year. A steel shortage in 1945-48, however, caused the Alaskans to manufacture plates of flat, compressed paper during those years.

Starting in 1949, a small Alaskan flag insignia appeared to the left of the numbers on passenger car markers, and even today this device is incorporated into the basic design of the plate. Only in the 1966-67 series was the flag omitted, and the motto "NORTH TO THE FUTURE" was substituted. Another legend, "THE GREAT LAND," appeared in 1968-69, and the current series notes "NORTH TO THE FUTURE" as well as "ALASKA — U.S.A."

Alaska is the only state which has never used the dash or hyphen on its passenger car tags. Instead, a straight numeric system of one to five numerals is employed.

ARIZONA—1910

As a territory, Arizona never issued or assigned license plates, but at least one community, the city of Tucson, used a porcelain-enameled iron variety between 1910 and 1912. Individual automobile owners sup-

plied the first state plates in Arizona in 1912, the number 1 plate and registration going to Dr. W. H. Fenner of Tucson for his Stoddard-Dayton "Savoy" Roadster. Most of these plates were metal numbers mounted on leather or metal backgrounds and identified by the abbreviation "ARIZ" or simply "ARZ." This practice continued through 1913.

In 1914 the first plates were issued by the state. They were white on blue embossed metal, and annual issues appeared thereafter until 1943 when, because of the metal shortage, the 1942 series was repeated. Since that time most Arizona plates have been used for two years or more, with revalidation effected by means of windshield stickers, plate tabs or plate stickers.

Perhaps the most noteworthy plates issued in Arizona at any time were those of 1932-34 which were made of copper, Arizona being the top copper-producing state. An imitation copper coloring was also used on those plates for 1916, 1925, 1927, 1928, 1935-37, 1939 and 1941.

Arizona plates featured a steer's head motif on its 1917 plate, carried the county names from 1936 through 1938, and commemorated its 400th anniversary of discovery in 1939 by adding the name of the explorer Marcos de Niza on that issue. In 1940 the plates included the slogan "GRAND CANYON STATE" and, with the exception of 1945 plates which were also used in 1946, have retained it.

ARKANSAS—1909 or earlier

The first state-issued plates in Arkansas, porcelain-enameled iron tags, appeared in 1911; however, there are known registrations on a local basis previous to that date in a number of Arkansas communities.

These porcelain-enameled types were used for three years until 1914 when the state switched to the embossed metal variety. Natural aluminum was used in 1939, 1940, 1941 and 1947-49. In 1944, as an answer to the World War II metal shortage, flat compressed paper tags were used. The plates changed annually until 1967 with the exception of 1949 when the 1948 plate was revalidated with a date tab.

In 1968 a permanent series, red on white, was introduced, and these are revalidated on a staggered basis by means of monthly and annual stickers placed either side of the state name. For the last several years only a single rear plate has been used.

To mark its first hundred years, Arkansas advertised its "CENTENNIAL CELEBRATION" on the 1935 tags; on the 1938 plate, just below the numbers and date, the state name in a winged motif was enclosed in a small outline of the state. The motto, "OPPORTUNITY LAND" or "LAND OF OPPORTUNITY" was included in 1940-42 and 1948-67.

CALIFORNIA—circa 1901

Under a California State Legislature act approved March 16, 1901, counties, cities, incorporated towns and chartered and incorporated cities were authorized to tax and license motor vehicles. Unfortunately, it is not exactly known when the first numbers were carried on motor vehicles under this act.

However, under another act approved March 22, 1905, registrations

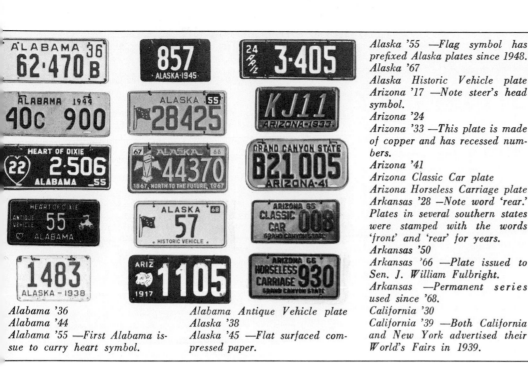

Alaska '55 —Flag symbol has prefixed Alaska plates since 1948.
Alaska '67
Alaska Historic Vehicle plate
Arizona '17 —Note steer's head symbol.
Arizona '24
Arizona '33 —This plate is made of copper and has recessed numbers.
Arizona '41
Arizona Classic Car plate
Arizona Horseless Carriage plate
Arkansas '28 —Note word 'rear.' Plates in several southern states were stamped with the words 'front' and 'rear' for years.
Arkansas '50
Arkansas '66 —Plate issued to Sen. J. William Fulbright.
Arkansas —Permanent series used since '68.
California '30
California '39 —Both California and New York advertised their World's Fairs in 1939.

Alabama '36
Alabama '44
Alabama '55 —First Alabama issue to carry heart symbol.
Alaska '38
Alaska '45 —Flat surfaced compressed paper.
Alabama Antique Vehicle plate
California Horseless Carriage
California pre-1914 —Issued to members of the Auto Club of Southern California.

---

went on a statewide basis under the authority of the Secretary of State. Each automobile owner was assigned a number and assumed responsibility for carrying that number three inches high with the abbreviation of the state in a black on white combination. Like most other early state registrations, certain liberties were taken. The abbreviation was often omitted and black on silver, silver on black or white on black was often used — a minor violation of the law, perhaps, but if any violators were asked to conform to the specifications, it is not a matter of record.

Materials were optional, and most of the plates up to and including 1913 were made of metal, leather, wood, metal mounted against a square frame with inset screen, or, for those who could afford to have their plates made by a manufacturer, porcelain-enameled iron.

By 1907 or 1908 most of the plates in use conformed to the required colors and the abbreviation was usually carried vertically or diagonally to the right of the numbers. The Auto Club of Southern California had special porcelain-enameled plates made, black on white and carrying the state abbreviation, and issued them to its members. These plates are frequently referred to as "Mickey Mouse" plates because of the resemblance their semicircular sides bore to the ears of the famous Walt Disney character.

The first state-issued plates appeared in 1914. They were white on vermillion porcelain-enameled iron and were the first California issues to carry a date. A similar plate with black numbers on a yellow background was used the following year.

In 1916 a four-year plate was issued. This was a blue on white variety and considerably smaller in size than the earlier issues. It featured a bear-shaped removable insignia which carried the date located to the left of the numbers The plate was renewed in 1917 with a yellow poppy insignia, in 1918 with a green mission bell and, in 1919, a red star.

The first embossed annual tags appeared in 1920, and from that date until 1941 California plates were issued annually The 1941 plate was revalidated in 1942 with a date strip and again in 1943 with a red on white date tab comprising a red letter "V" (for "Victory") on a white background. The series was continued in 1944 with a windshield sticker. New plates were issued for 1945 and revalidated for 1946 with a date tab. In 1947 another new series appeared, and the 1947 plates were revalidated annually through 1950.

In similar fashion the 1951 series was used through 1955, and since then only three other series have appeared — the black on yellow plates of that date, revalidated annually by plate stickers through 1962, a similar yellow on black type used from 1963 to 1970 and a yellow on blue variety similar to the others which has been assigned since 1970. This latest series differs from the previous two by using a three letter suffix combination instead of the earlier prefix placement of the letters.

California's only advertising venture using its license plates occurred in 1939 when the state, not to be outdone by New York's "WORLD'S FAIR" legend appearing the year before on New York plates, added its own World's Fair notice to their plates to entice all comers.

COLORADO—1913

Although this state did not begin to issue license plates until 1913, a number of municipalities within the state registered motor vehicles prior to this date by means of plates ranging in material and design from the porcelain-enameled iron variety adopted in Salida to the home-made leather and wooden types common in other cities. Most of the latter carried neither identification nor a prefix letter.

Porcelain-enameled plates prevailed between 1913 and 1916, but the most flamboyant issue of the period, the black on pink plates of 1917, appeared in embossed metal. Dates appeared on the first state-issued series in 1913, and upon every series issued thereafter.

A statewide re-registration of automobiles took place in 1920, with previously registered vehicles using the existing 1919 plates with date inserts. New registrants were issued new 1920 plates similar in color to those of 1919 but of a different design and minus the date tabs.

The adjective "COLORFUL" appeared on all plates from 1950 through 1959, joined by a ski jumper insigne in 1958. Since 1960, a fitting device has appeared on all Colorado passenger car plates: a jagged upper border depicts the mountain peaks for which the state is known.

CONNECTICUT—1903

An act adopted by the Connecticut General Assembly caused the first automobile registrations in the state to be listed in May of 1903. Vehicle owners were required to furnish their own plates and to display an assigned number upon them. Most often, these early markers were constructed of leather with metal numbers attached thereon, and the mandatory letter "C" prefix was displayed prominently. Nearly all of them carried silver-colored letters and numerals on a black background, although brass numbers were not unknown. The first registration ("C1") was assigned to the Woodruff family of Litchfield.

The state issued its first official plates in 1905 and the switchover to the new white on black porcelain-enameled iron plates was complete by September 1 of that year. Logically, the prefix "C" was retained as part of the design. This series was used through 1909 with increasingly high numbers appearing each year; the last of the 1909 plates, for example, carried numbers from about 8451 through the low 9000's! The size of the plate increased too, for legibility's sake.

The first dated plates in Connecticut appeared in 1914, two years before porcelain-enameled plates disappeared. Flat metal plates replaced them from 1917 through 1919, with embossed steel used for the 1920 series.

Straight numeric sequences were used on plates until 1932, when the plates were also sharply reduced in size. One or two prefix letters and from one to three numbers replaced the earlier "C" prefix in that year. A "permanent" plate adopted in 1937 was a black on natural aluminum tag carrying the state abbreviation. A space was allotted on the bottom for a metal date insert, and the first of these dates appeared in yellow. This series was used through 1956 although many of them were made of steel rather than aluminum during and after World War II.

The "Vanity Plate" was introduced during this series, and in order to

obtain one an automobile owner in good standing paid a fee which entitled him to show as many as four letters on his plate and to subtract numbers. Certain four-letter combinations, of course, were not issued, but their possibilities are provocative.

In 1957 a second "permanent" series was issued. These plates were white on blue and larger than the previous "permanent" ones because they conformed to the 12 x 6 inches adopted by all the states, provinces and Mexico in that year. Currently, this series includes combinations of straight numbers of one to six digits, as well as a single, dual or triple letter prefix. The "Vanity Plate," of up to four letters, is still obtainable.

DELAWARE—1905

The first numbered plates used in Delaware were "do-it-yourself" affairs, and the owner provided his own plates with an assigned number displayed thereon. These plates were made of leather, metal, wood or any other serviceable material, and although no identification was required most of them carried the prefix letter "D" or the state abbreviation.

But a law which took effect May 1, 1907, required future plates to carry numbers five inches high, the abbreviated name of the state and the date. No color was stipulated, but the few which have been seen by this writer were either white on red or white on blue, made of porcelain-enameled iron, and resembled the design of those used in the neighboring state of Pennsylvania. Indeed, some Delaware plates were made by using the reverse side of expired Pennsylvania tags.

Cars being registered for the first time in 1909 were provided with state-issued white on black porcelain-enameled plates, but previously registered automobiles were allowed to retain their old tags. This practice ceased in the following year, however, when all motor vehicles were required to carry a standard tag.

Porcelain plates were generally used until 1916 when annually-issued embossed steel tags became the rule. In mid-1941 Delaware followed Connecticut's example by issuing "permanent" plates; these white on black porcelain-enameled steel plates (with locations provided for quarterly and annual date inserts) were manufactured by the Baltimore Enamel & Novelty Company, a firm which manufactured many of the earlier plates for a number of states.

A second "permanent" type of plate appeared in 1946 with silver numbers attached to a black metal plate. Since that time, three other "permanent" series have been issued, two of them featuring yellow reflectorized numbers attached to a metal plate against a medium blue background. The third bore reflectorized yellow numbers on a dark blue background, minus the metal-plate prop for the numbers; it was instead a single, embossed metal unit. Oddly enough, examples of *all* "permanent" license plates are still in legal use in Delaware.

The legend "THE FIRST STATE" has remained untouched on Delaware plates for some years, but a recent license plate change substituted stickers for the metal date attachments. As long as the car owner removes the date sticker, a second, or front plate may be attached to his car for a fee, even though the state requires only a rear license plate.

DISTRICT OF COLUMBIA—1904

Each automobile owner in the District of Columbia between the years of 1904 and 1907 provided his own number plates with a number assigned to him by the Police Department. Most of these plates were made of leather and carried metal numbers plus the letters "DC." Silver or white on a black background was the accepted color combination, although this color scheme was occasionally reversed.

In 1907, the District issued standard, undated plates of white on black porcelain-enameled iron with "DISTRICT OF COLUMBIA" placed above the numbers. This series was used through 1917.

From 1918, when the first steel embossed plates appeared, through 1923, the abbreviation "D.C." was employed, but it was later expanded to "DIST. COL." or its fullest form, "DISTRICT OF COLUMBIA." The "D.C." abbreviation was used again for a while after World War II, but then reverted to the full name of the District. Since 1965, the plate reads simply "WASHINGTON, D.C." Also, the legend "NATION'S CAPITOL" has appeared on the plates since 1953.

A curious situation arose involving car owners in Washington, D.C. during the 1914-24 period. Since most of them commuted daily between the nation's capital and Maryland, officials of Maryland passed a law requiring dual registration for Washingtonians — and this meant that prosecution awaited those who failed to register their cars in both Washington and Maryland. To make matters worse, the state of Virginia passed similar legislation, and although it was revoked shortly

thereafter, it increased the discomfort of Washington motorists proportionately. It may be noted, as one looks at photographs of the era, that dual plates appeared on the front and rear of motorcars, and during the period when Virginia required D.C. vehicle registration, many Washingtonians sported a total of *six plates* on their cars — District of Columbia, Maryland and Virginia plates both fore and aft.

Not even the President was exempt from the law. The State cars of Presidents Wilson, Harding and Coolidge, for a time, carried D.C. numbers "100," "101" and "102" as well as Maryland registrations "100-000," "100-001" and "100-002." Presidential car registration, by the way, began with President William Howard Taft, whose White Steamer carried plate Number 4515. In the late 1920's, White House cars were assigned numbers starting with "100" as a protective measure, but this practice was abandoned as impractical years ago. Today White House cars carry general numbers, selected at random.

Perhaps the most interesting series of D.C. plates is the one issued every four years since 1933 to mark the inauguration of a President and Vice-President. Colored red, white and blue, these plates are emblazoned with a flag, coat-of-arms or U.S. Capitol insigne, and sometimes the plates bear pictures of the President-elect and his Vice-President. They are assigned to those officially connected with the Inaugural ceremonies and to those of the public who wish to purchase them from the Inaugural Committee. Although these markers are official D.C. plates, good for a two-month period, certain states do not recognize their validity. Despite this, nearly 10,000 sets of the plates are displayed on automobiles in all states every four years.

Connecticut '14 —This enameled plate was the last of Connecticut's undated tags.
Connecticut '23
Connecticut '37 —This series marked the beginning of the 'permanent' tag.
Connecticut Antique Automobile plate
Delaware '31
Delaware '43 —Although this 1941-45 porcelain-enameled plate was replaced with another series, a number of them are still in legal use.
Delaware —Current permanent series.
District of Columbia '07-'17
District of Columbia '30
District of Columbia '57 —This plate was assigned to the White House bubble-topped limousine during President Eisenhower's administration.
District of Columbia '60 —This

plate identified the car of the then-Vice-President, Richard M. Nixon.
District of Columbia '65 —This red, white and blue plate, valid through February 28, 1965, appeared on the author's car while he attended the inauguration of President Johnson.
District of Columbia Antique Car plate

lorado '20
lorado '32
lorado '55
lorado '62 —Note plate bor-

der's mountain range motif.
Colorado Horseless Carriage plate
Connecticut '03-'05 —Leather plate with metal numbers.

469

Florida Horseless Carriage plate
Georgia '27
Georgia '34
Georgia '41 —Large decal peach advertises an important state product. Numbers and letters are reflectorized.
Georgia '42 —This tri-colored marker sports a red state name and date plus white numbers on a blue background.
Hawaii '26
Hawaii '32 —'TH' on this government plate stands for 'Territory of Hawaii.'
Hawaii '49
Hawaii —Current series used since 1969.
Idaho '28
Idaho '32
Idaho '47
Idaho '65 —Gubernatorial plate.
Idaho '66 —Congressional plate.
Idaho Old Timer plate
Illinois '13 —Plate was attached so that air circulated around

auto's radiator.
Illinois '27
Illinois '31
Illinois '43 —Flat surfaced compressed paper.
Illinois Antique Vehicle plate

Florida '15-'16 —This type was used when registrations were under county authority.
Florida '24 —Note provision of plate designating weight of vehicle.

Florida '35 —The famous 'grapefruit' plate; grapefruits in upper corners resemble small bombs.
Florida '62 —This special series is assigned without fee to Seminole Indian motorists.

FLORIDA—1905

The history of motor vehicle registration in Florida is somewhat confused since registration started under state aegis, passed for several years to city and county control and finally reverted again to the state.

Car owners provided their own plates between 1905 and 1911. Most of these were metal numbers attached to the conventional leather pads and included the abbreviation of the state.

In 1912 counties and cities became responsible for registrations, and between that year and 1917 hundreds of varieties of plates were issued. Some cities bowed to county authority in registrations, but in other instances where city plates were issued, those motorists were exempt from county registration.

In the six years of local registrations nearly every imaginable material and color scheme was noted on Florida plates as well as a great diversity in size, some being no larger than motorcycle tags. Oddly enough, nearly all of them carried the designation "AUTO," the "FLA" abbreviation as well as their local designation and, in a few cases, the county seal.

A flat metal plate appeared in 1918 after the state again became the enforcing and issuing agency, and from 1919 to the present all plates have been made of embossed metal.

For a few years in the Twenties the plates were embellished with an outline of the state's shape, and in 1934 and 1935 the design in-

corporated a separate plate in reversed colors on which the date and vehicle classification was noted.

A particular oddity was the 1935 series on which Florida attempted to get in a plug for its grapefruit and accordingly added two small symbols intended to convey the shape of the fruit. If the plates had been yellow on black instead of black on yellow, this might have been beneficial, but as it was the insignias resembled small bombs as they appeared to caricaturists in their cartoons of anarchists.

Florida plates have included the legend "SUNSHINE STATE" on them for many years, and in 1965 they noted the "400TH ANNIVERSARY" of discovery.

For the last thirty years Florida plates have carried prefix numbers designating the county of registration with some also carrying a small letter denoting weight classification.

A unique series of Florida passenger car plates are those issued to members of the Seminole Indian tribe. These plates bear the designation "SEMINOLE INDIAN."

GEORGIA—1910

The first license plates in Georgia appeared in 1910, and through 1914 they were made of metal and not embossed. Dated plates began with the 1914 issue, and subsequent to a single porcelain-enameled iron issue of 1915 all plates have been of the conventional embossed metal type.

Georgia is known as the "PEACH STATE," And this first appeared on the plates in 1940. The legend was continued in 1941 and has been included as an integral part of the tag design since 1947. A peach insignia was also employed in the design of the 1940 and 1941 plates.

The 1942 plates were tri-colored, white numbers against a dark blue background with the date and state name appearing in red.

Like Florida, Georgia used a prefix numerical combination plus a letter to denote the county of registration and the weight classification of the vehicle through 1970. The current series employs a three letter-three number combination plus county designation. This series will be valid for five years.

HAWAII—1906

Automobile registrations in Hawaii date back to 1906 when the first one was issued to Gerrit Parmile Wilder who painted his number on the rear of his Autocar. From that time until the issuance of the first territorial plates in 1914, the only stipulation was that the numbers had to be painted on a black background in white paint. The material was optional. No date or any other identification appeared, and if the motorcar happened to be black, painting the number on the car itself was condoned.

The first territorial plates were issued in 1914. At first they were made of porcelain-enameled iron, then, starting in 1917, they were changed to embossed metal. Since the chief issuing office, if not the only one, was in Honolulu, the plates carried the abbreviation "HON." The first plates to carry the name "HAWAII" appeared in 1922.

Plates were issued annually until World War II. The 1942 plate was used until 1946, revalidated annually by means of a windshield sticker. These semi-permanent types have been in use for many years. The last three series, white on red from 1957 through 1960, white on green from 1961 through 1968, and black on yellow since 1969 have carried no date and include the legend "ALOHA" or "ALOHA STATE."

IDAHO—before 1913

Before 1913 Idaho car owners registered their motor vehicles or did not depending on where they happened to live. Certain communities such as Boise, Emmett, Nampa and Weiser, to name a few, had local ordinances and issued number plates; however, many communities failed to utilize this ready means of taxation until the state stepped in.

Under an act of the Idaho General Assembly approved March 13, 1913, the Secretary of the State Highway Commission was required to issue plates. The first were white on blue embossed steel.

The plates were prosaic enough through the years until 1928 when the ubiquitous Idaho potato came into its own. At that time a potato was incorporated into the actual plate design, realistic to the extent that even the "eyes" were included and the color, appropriately enough, was potato brown on a green background.

For some reason or another the potato lobby failed to exert itself, for the spud wasn't to reappear again until the plates of 1948 and 1949 when the space situated between banks of numbers featured a colored decal of a baked Idaho, complete with melting butter. Although after 1949 the potato insignia disappeared, the words "FAMOUS POTATOES" were incorporated on plates in 1953 and from 1956 to the present.

Idaho has sported other advertising on its plates, however, including a plug for its 50th year of statehood in 1940, its claim to being "SCENIC" from 1941 through 1946 and an advertisement for its ski resorts in 1947, a ski-jumping figure, poised in flight.

ILLINOIS—1907

Although the first number plates required on a statewide basis in Illinois date back to 1907, local plates were in use before that date in Chicago. The first registered auto owner in Chicago was Arthur J. Eddy of 1635 Sheridan Road. This registration dates back to September 1, 1902.

A General Assembly act effective July 1, 1907 required automobile owners to provide their own number plates, stipulating that they be black on white and include the abbreviation, "ILL." for both front and rear of the vehicle. Most of the plates were constructed of tin, wood or leather, with numbers either attached or painted on.

Four years later the state began issuing plates. The first series was black on white embossed metal plates which were undated.

In 1912 the plates were dated. The rear tag was the conventional embossed steel type, and the front one had numbers cut out of a rectangle of mesh or screenlike design. This unique plate expedited cooling of the car. At this time, the majority of front plates were carried against the honeycomb front of the radiator, and the Illinois plate was designed to let a maximum of air pass through the plate. The front plates for 1913 handled the problem somewhat differently. The numbers were held in place by the edges of a frame. From 1914 through 1917 the problem was solved by having vertical slits between the numbers. The practice was dropped altogether in 1918, presumably because of improved cooling systems and provision of brackets on which to attach the plates.

Illinois carried the shape of the state on its license plates for 1927, but little other novelty appeared through the years other than the legend "LAND OF LINCOLN." This motto has appeared on Illinois plates since 1954.

Because of its large number of registrations, Illinois plates exceeded six-digit combinations by the mid-1920's; because a straight numeric system was employed, plates above 1-000-000 were difficult to read.

The state augmented its numeric series with a new one in 1962 which utilized two letters and four numbers, with letters appearing taller and thicker than numbers.

During World War II and for a few years thereafter, plates were flat surfaced and made of a compressed paper material. In production of this plate, a soybean solution was added. Strangely enough, this appealed to animals, and between 1943 and 1948 several cases were reported of cows and horses eating the license plates right off of cars. One can only suppose that these incidents took place as the cars stood stationary.

INDIANA—1905

The first Indiana registrations date back to 1905, and through 1907 numbers were provided by the automobile owner. These plates varied in material, color, shape and basic design, although the state abbreviation "IND" was mandatory.

In 1907 although the responsibility of registration numbers still rested with the owners, the state stipulated that thereafter all number plates should be white on black and carry the numbers four inches high followed by the abbreviation. The numeric sequence was uninterrupted. About 1910, the numeric sequence was changed to include a prefix letter, number, hyphen and two additional numbers.

In 1913 the state issued black on yellow porcelain-enameled iron plates. These were the first dated markers. From 1914 to the present all Indiana plates have been constructed of the conventional embossed steel. The 1915 issue was outstanding in color alone with green numbers on a pink background.

From 1956 through 1958 the state urged its motorists to "DRIVE SAFELY" on its plates, and in 1959 to commemorate the 150th birthday of one of the state's most illustrious former citizens, the legend "LINCOLN YEAR" appeared on plates. Safety considerations returned in 1960 with the reminder that "SAFETY PAYS." This slogan continued through 1962. In 1963 the state advertised its "150TH YEAR" on its plates.

IOWA—1904

From 1904 through 1910 Iowa automobile owners were assigned numbers and provided their own registration plates. Most of these were made of metal numbers attached to leather pads and colored silver on black. The abbreviation of the state "IA" was mandatory, and this usually appeared either vertically or in one-half size horizontally to the right of the numerical sequence.

Dated embossed metal plates first appeared in 1911 but, due to the steel restrictions of the period immediately preceding America's entry into World War I, an undated plate was issued for 1916 and continued through 1918.

In 1922 Iowa adopted the county system wherein a number or pair of numbers preceding the basic number indicated the county of issuance. The prefix number 77 has been assigned to the capitol area since then. This area has the greatest concentration of registered motor vehicles, so the plates run into eight numbers.

The only advertising plug to appear on Iowa plates was "THE CORN STATE" which was incorporated into the plates issued in 1953 and revalidated for 1954 and 1955.

KANSAS—1913

It is frustrating to speculate on the date of the first registrations in Kansas because so many municipalities, towns and counties registered motor vehicles during the early part of the century, and a great variety of number plates from this era exist today which cannot be accurately dated. Porcelain-enameled plates were used in Kansas City and Great Bend, with metal and leather types known in Wichita, Wellington, Staunton and Topeka. Some were dated and some were not.

Kansas '16 —All plates issued by Kansas from 1913 through 1920 were undated.
Kansas '18
Kansas '32
Kansas '44 —Small plate made necessary by World War II metal shortage.
Kansas Antique plate
Kentucky '28 —County name has been used on Kentucky plates since the 1930's.
Kentucky '31 —Front plate.
Kentucky '31 —Rear plate.
Louisiana '32 —The first appearance of the pelican symbol on Louisiana plates.
Louisiana '40 —Small map of the state was used on Louisiana plates 1940-41.
Louisiana '50 —Pelican symbol was dropped in 1964.
Maine '05-'11

Indiana pre-1913 —Aluminum numbers attached to metal.
Indiana '43 —Small metal plate attached to 1942 tag.
Indiana '44 —Wartime issue restricted use of metal.
Iowa '16-'17 —Three-year plate.
Iowa '29
Iowa '34
Iowa Antique plate

Maine '27
Maine '44 —'Vacationland' has appeared on Maine plates since 1936.
Maine Antique Auto plate

The first statewide registration went into effect on July 1, 1913 with black and white undated embossed metal plates provided by the state. Subsequent issues through 1920 saw the continuation of the dateless plates with the first dated ones assigned for the 1921 calendar year.

Kansas plates have been issued on an annual basis without lapse with the exception of 1943 when a date tab was attached to the 1942 type because of the wartime metal shortage.

The plates of 1942-43 carried two sunflower insignias on them and the motto "THE WHEAT STATE" appeared from 1949 through 1959. The state's "CENTENNIAL" was noted in both 1960 and 1961 and its geographic location has been celebrated by the inclusion of "MIDWAY U.S.A." between 1965 and 1970. The current series carries the expiration date below the numbers.

The shape of the state itself has been reproduced on Kansas plates since 1955.

KENTUCKY—before 1910

It is uncertain when the first number plates were issued in this state although certain cities were known to have used local plates as early as 1910 and presumably plates were used even earlier than this.

The first state registration became mandatory July 1, 1910, when white on black porcelain-enameled iron plates were manufactured and assigned to motorists. These were undated and carried the state abbreviation "KY" vertically on the right.

There is an air of mystery surrounding these plates, however, for directly below the abbreviation a red device was placed in a number of shapes. In the form of a circle, square, diamond, pyramid or triangle, a letter was placed within the shape and its meaning is still being sought. The letters "B," "G," "L," "M" and "N" are known to have been used. Some feel that the letters stood for the names of state officials by whom registrations had been assigned; others believe that the letters stood for geographical areas of assignment. The plausibility of the latter hypothesis, though, is thwarted by the existence of one plate showing a square surrounding the number "13" instead of the expected letter.

In addition, a number of these white on black plates appeared with red horizontal borders whereas others were issued without borders.

The white on black enameled plates continued to be used on an annual basis, i.e. after the fee was paid the tags were good for one year of service before renewal of the fee became due.

By an act of the Kentucky General Assembly effective June 12, 1914 license plates were required to be issued annually. In order to establish a January 1 expiration date, the law caused licenses issued before January 1, 1915, to expire at that time. Licenses expiring after that date were good until January 1, 1916. A new series of plates, dated, red on white embossed steel, were issued for the cars renewing their registrations January 1, 1915. Those which expired a year later retained the old white on black tags.

In 1927 it became the policy of the state to include the county designation on its license plates and this policy has lasted to the present day.

The 1930 issue included the words "FOR PROGRESS," and from 1952 through 1957 the tags advertised the state by urging spotters to "TOUR KENTUCKY."

Front and rear plates differed in design in the early Thirties, with the front ones carrying the state abbreviation, year and county name. The rear ones carried the state's name in full flanked by the date.

Blue and white colors have been alternated since 1953.

LOUISIANA—circa 1906

Although the date when numbers were first used in Louisiana registrations is unknown, numbers were carried on motorcars in Shreveport as early as 1906; several cities and a few parishes required registrations annually after that time including Baton Rouge and New Orleans.

Between 1915, when the first dated and embossed metal state-issued plates appeared, and 1942, plates were issued annually. The 1942 series was continued through 1943 with revalidation by windshield sticker. A compressed-paper marker was used in 1944 and the embossed metal type reappeared in 1945 destined to last till the present time. Since 1964, plates have been issued every other year with a windshield sticker used for revalidation purposes.

Two differently colored plates were issued in Louisiana between 1922 and 1929; one went to owners of cars developing less than 23 hp and the other plate was issued to owners of cars developing more than 23 hp.

The first pelican insigne was used on Louisiana plates in 1932, replacing the conventional hyphen between numbers. It was omitted from the design of 1940 and 1941 plates which featured instead a small map of the state, but the pelican reappeared in 1942, continuing until 1964 when passenger-car registrations exceeded a million. Then a code letter was substituted for the insigne. An interesting feature of the pelican device itself is the bird's open bill on plates used between 1942 and 1958. On all other plates carrying the pelican insigne, the bird's bill is closed.

Louisiana plates advertised one of the state's primary crops in 1954 with the motto "LOUISIANA YAMS." In 1960 tabs paid respect to one of the state's leading educational institutions by including the legend "LSU CENTENNIAL" in its plate design. Louisiana has used its number plates to advertise "SPORTSMEN'S PARADISE" in 1958-59 and from 1961 to date.

MAINE—1905

The first license plates used in Maine were the white on scarlet porcelain-enameled ones which were issued by the state in 1905. These were used each year thereafter until January 1, 1912, when the numbers had reached the 8000's. The plates were dateless as were subsequent issues in 1912 and 1913.

Dated porcelain-enameled types were issued for 1914 and 1915 and the first embossed metal ones appeared in 1916. With the exception of 1918 when the state used a flat metal type, the embossed plates were issued annually from 1916 to 1942. The 1942 series were used for 1943 also with a windshield sticker for revalidation.

For the last several years each series of Maine plates has been used for several years at a time, yearly revalidated first by means of a metal insert and more recently by plate stickers.

Since 1936 passenger plates in Maine have carried the motto "VACATIONLAND."

MARYLAND—1904

Automobile owners were responsible for their own plates between 1904 and July 1, 1910, when the first state-issued plates made their debut. The first homemade plates were required to display numbers at least three inches high but no further stipulation regarding color, material or inclusion of state abbreviation was made.

By an act approved April 3, 1906, the state required that all plates be white on black, so the majority of Maryland automobilists continued to make their plates of metal numbers or black leather pads. The majority of these pre-1910 tags carried the state abbreviation.

The first state-issued tags were black on deep yellow embossed metal, and these were replaced by porcelain-enamel markers from 1911 through 1914. Maryland reverted to embossed metal in 1915. All state plates since 1910 have been dated.

The state advertised its "TERCENTENARY" in 1934 and in 1941 issued semi-permanent tags with base plates revalidated annually by means of date tabs. It returned to annual plates again in 1953.

MASSACHUSETTS—1903

To Massachusetts goes the credit for the first officially-issued state license plates (undated white on blue, of porcelain-enameled iron) issued on September 1, 1903, to Frederic Tudor of 17 Regent Circle, Brookline. These earliest plates were identified by the placement of "MASS. AUTOMOBILE REGISTER" immediately above the numbers.

This same series continued through 1907, but the blue on white 1908 series was the first in Massachusetts to carry the date. Porcelain-enameled plates were used through 1915, flat metal ones prevailed from 1916-19 and the embossed metal variety was introduced in 1920. Tags were alternately colored blue or white until 1923.

From 1917 through 1937, Massachusetts plates differed from those of other states and provinces in that a comma was used to separate groups of numbers instead of the conventional dash or hyphen.

The Commonwealth attempted to promote its fishing industry in 1928 by placing a small fish insigne under the numbers on the plate between the date and state abbreviation. Sheerly by chance, the illustrated fish swam in the direction of the date and away from "MASS," causing trepidation among the superstitious, and this is presumably the reason why the fish insigne was dropped from passenger car plates after this date. Commercial tags, however, bore a detailed fish insigne during the following year — swimming determinedly toward "MASS"— but even this emblem vanished in 1930.

When metal became scarce during World War II, Massachusetts elected to follow the practice of many other states by revalidating 1942 tags for 1943 by means of a windshield sticker. In 1944 the 1942 series was continued with a revalidated windshield sticker, but those who purchased new vehicles in that year were issued plates still imprinted with the 1942 date, painted white on green. Annual plates were again issued from 1945 through 1949.

In 1950, the 1949 plates were used with a windshield sticker, and new plates were issued every other year until 1966 — with one notable exception: When faulty black paint on the new 1963 series peeled off within a matter of weeks, exposing the plates to the vagaries of the weather, a whole new series had to be introduced in 1964. These new plates were held over in 1965 with a new series appearing for the following year.

The current blue on white plates, issued first in 1967, are the first to carry the full name of the state. They will be replaced in 1973 by another semi-permanent type showing cranberry red numbers and letters against a white background, and the numeric sequence of future plates will probably follow the example of the present one: Straight numbers from 1 to 999,999, numbers prefixed by a letter, numbers with a letter used as a suffix or "Vanity Plates" allowing the car owner to choose from one to six letters without numbers.

MICHIGAN—1905

Michigan number plates were owner-provided between 1905 and January 1, 1910, a state law providing that all markers be white on black carrying either the state name or its abbreviation in addition to the numbers. Like those of many states with similar laws, some Michigan plates featured silver metal numbers against a black background and apparently these aberrations were tolerated despite their nonconformity to the law. The majority of pre-1910 Michigan plates were made of leather; none were dated.

From 1910 through 1914, dated porcelain-enameled iron plates were the rule and their design included the state seal. After the advent of embossed metal plates in 1915, the seal remained a part of the design through 1919.

The words "WATER WONDERLAND" appeared on the plates from 1954 until 1965 when "WATER-WINTER WONDERLAND" was substituted. This was replaced in 1968 by the present motto "GREAT LAKE STATE."

Interesting early Michigan plates are those enameled, dated ones for 1907, 1908 and 1909 in the collection of H. Bogart Seaman of Long Island, New York. They closely resemble plates of 1910-14 — but it is almost certain that they are counterfeits.

MINNESOTA—1903

The first motor vehicle registrations in Minnesota date back to 1903 when, under an act of the State Legislature, the State Boiler Inspector was empowered to register all automobiles. He was also required to exempt those motorists who were registered under any other state municipality from Minnesota registration. The act further called for the display of an assigned number on the rear of each motor vehicle in figures "not less than 4½ inches high and of proportionate width." These state registrations prevailed — except for communities issuing local plates — until the first state plates were issued on May 15, 1909.

In that year, silver on red flat metal plates were issued to motorists. Similar plates in gold on black colors appeared in 1910, and white on blue porcelain-enameled iron tags made their debut in 1911.

Triennial plates were issued between 1912 and 1920, but annual plates reappeared for 1921. Annuals were issued until 1943, when a date tab was used to revalidate the 1942 series. Annual tags were used again between 1944 and 1956. Since that time, Minnesota markers have been used for more than one year at a time.

Minnesota plates have carried the motto "10,000 LAKES" since 1949.

MISSISSIPPI—1912

Mississippi is unique among all the states in that its first officially-issued number plates turned out to be illegal!

Effective June 1, 1912 the first Mississippi plates appeared as dated, black on white embossed markers of soft metal. A new series, also black on white but undated was scheduled to be issued April 30, 1914. Until then, it was reasoned, the original issue would have to serve for 1913 as well as 1912.

But controversy brewed over the legality of the first, 1912-13 plates, and under an act of the Mississippi State Legislature of February 19, 1914, some $28,040 was ordered refunded to automobile owners for registration fees paid in 1912 and 1913. The law which had required said registrants to pay had been declared unconstitutional by the Supreme Court!

The new, undated 1914 plates were used through 1918. During the following year annual plates began to be issued, a practice which continues to today.

Since 1941, the county of issuance has appeared on Mississippi passenger car plates.

MISSOURI—1903

Under an act of the Missouri General Assembly approved March 23, 1903, motorists were required to register their automobiles with the license commissioner of their city. In cities where such an office did not exist, registrations were made with the county clerk who assigned each registrant a number which was to be displayed conspicuously on the automobile.

Notable among the early local plates in this state were the annually-issued porcelain-enameled types provided both by the city of St. Louis and St. Louis County. They were issued through 1911, despite the first state-issued plates which appeared in that year.

The state took over the actual assignment of registration numbers in 1907 and even though motorists were still obliged to provide their own plates, they were obliged to be sure that said plates were white on black as well — and that the state abbreviation "MO" was displayed.

The first state-issued tag was a silver on yellow embossed aluminum type. Its metal became steel a year later.

Missouri markers of 1942 were continued again in 1943 with a white on green metal date strip attached to previously registered cars for revalidation purposes. For new registrations, a compressed paper tag was issued.

Starting in 1948, Missouri plates were revalidated for several years at a time, although in 1968 the state returned to annually-issued markers.

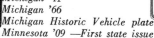

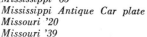

Massachusetts '03-'07 —This was the first state-issued series in the country.
Massachusetts '28 —The famous 'sacred codfish' plate.
Massachusetts —Current series, 1967-72.
Massachusetts Antique Auto plate
Michigan '10
Michigan '38
Michigan '41
Michigan '66
Michigan Historic Vehicle plate
Minnesota '09 —First state issue in Minnesota.
Minnesota '12-'14
Minnesota '37
Minnesota Pioneer plate
Minnesota Classic Car plate
Mississippi '31
Mississippi '35
Mississippi '45 —County names appear on Mississippi plates.

Maryland '11
Maryland '21
Maryland '34
Maryland Antique Motor Vehicle plate
Maryland '57 —Gubernatorial

Mississippi '65
Mississippi Antique Car plate
Missouri '20
Missouri '39
Missouri '42 —Compressed paper
Missouri Historic Motor Vehicle

475

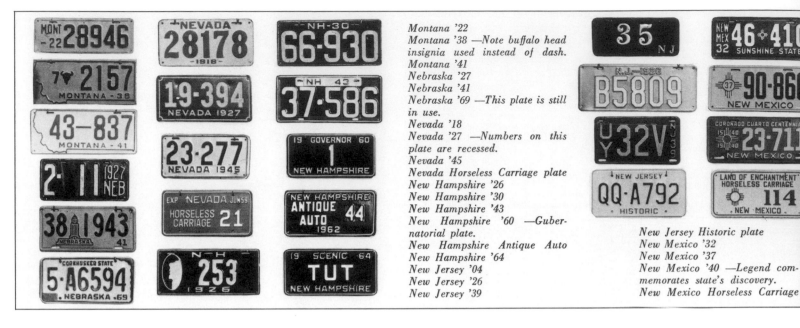

Montana '22
Montana '38 —Note buffalo head insignia used instead of dash.
Montana '41
Nebraska '27
Nebraska '41
Nebraska '69 —This plate is still in use.
Nevada '18
Nevada '27 —Numbers on this plate are recessed.
Nevada '45
Nevada Horseless Carriage plate
New Hampshire '26
New Hampshire '30
New Hampshire '43
New Hampshire '60 —Gubernatorial plate.
New Hampshire Antique Auto
New Hampshire '64
New Jersey '04
New Jersey '26
New Jersey '39

New Jersey Historic plate
New Mexico '32
New Mexico '37
New Mexico '40 —Legend commemorates state's discovery.
New Mexico Horseless Carriage

MONTANA—1913

The first auto registrants in Montana were required to receive a number from the Secretary of State, and then to attach that number, in black figures, to a white background. Generally the letter "M," the state abbreviation, appeared after the number.

A new act in 1915 required auto owners to register with the Secretary of State and then to supply their own plates in colors specified by the Secretary's office. They were also allowed to buy embossed metal plates from the Secretary for 75¢. Since few auto owners chose to do-it-themselves, the commonest plate seen during that year was the regulation 1915 plate, white on black, dated and carrying the abbreviation "MON."

The "MON" abbreviation was used through 1917 and was replaced during the following year with "MONT." The state name appeared in full in 1927, and remains so to this day.

The shape of the state was incorporated into the design of license plates in 1933 which depicted the outer border of the state. Montana plates retained this attractive and distinctive feature except during 1944 and 1957-58. For many years, the imprinted words "PRISON MADE" appeared in embossed form under the lower border of all Montana plates. Montana plates, like those of most other states, are made by inmates of the state prison, but Montana is the only state which ever advertised the fact openly on its plates. Interesting too is the fact that in this state the motor vehicle bureau is located at Deer Lodge, site of the prison, rather than in the capital, Helena.

Montana obtained surplus 1943 Illinois compressed-paper plates in 1944, painted them over and issued them anew. Close scrutiny, however, sometimes reveals the previous numbers and "ILLINOIS 1943" under the new paint.

Plates included the motto "THE TREASURE STATE" in 1950-56 and 1963-66. This motto has been dropped since 1967 in favor of "BIG SKY COUNTRY."

The only insigne to appear on Montana tags was the bison's skull used in lieu of a hyphen on 1938 plates.

NEBRASKA—1905

Between 1905 and 1911, Nebraska motorists were obliged to provide their own number plates with numbers three inches high and a two-inch-high state abbreviation. Neither color nor material was specified by law, but the majority of owners provided black leather pads with white painted or natural metal numbers. From 1911 to the advent of the first state-issued markers in 1915, numbers of four inches and an abbreviation of three inches were required. Further, a white on black combination was stipulated (although many motor vehicle owners still attached natural silver metal numbers to the black pads.)

The first state-issued tags, appearing in 1915, were made of embossed metal as were all subsequent Nebraska plates. A state capitol motif was featured on plates in 1940 and 1941, and Nebraska advertised itself as "THE BEEF STATE" in 1956 and 1957.

The plates for 1966, revalidated for 1967 and 1968, advertised the state's "CENTENNIAL" and they carried the shape of the state itself by depicting its border. Since 1969, the motto "THE CORNHUSKER STATE" has been included in the plate's design.

NEVADA—1913

The first motor vehicle registrations in Nevada were accomplished under the direction of the Secretary of State who stipulated that all automobile owners were required to provide their own plates of a light color on a dark background (preferably white or silver on black), carrying numbers at least 3 inches high. The abbreviation "NEV" was also required.

This system was enforced for three years and a purchased-tag option was also offered to owners who didn't want to provide their own plates. Most of these plates were flat or embossed metal, carrying the state abbreviation and, in many cases, the date.

The first state-issued plates were yellow on green undated embossed metal tags issued in 1916. Dated tags appeared officially for 1917 and the plates used between that year and 1922 were made of flat surfaced metal. Markers used from 1923 through 1927 featured recessed numbers and letters.

Annual plates were issued for many years, although plates have been used for a few years at a time during the last several years. These have been revalidated annually by stickers.

NEW HAMPSHIRE—1905

Like Maine, Connecticut and Vermont, the state of New Hampshire issued its first plates as undated porcelain-enameled iron types; these white on green New Hampshire plates were used until January 1, 1912. The first number was assigned to Governor John McLane of Milford on April 4, 1905, for his 20 hp Franklin.

The 1912 series was made of embossed steel, but plates for 1913 reverted to the porcelain type. Porcelain prevailed until 1919 when flat metal plates were issued. In 1922, embossed metal tags were reintroduced, and these have been in use since that time.

New Hampshire has alternated green and white on its plates since 1905 with two exceptions: In 1914, a white on green type similar to that of 1913 was used, and from 1945 through 1948, black and white was alternated. A green on white date strip was attached to the previous year's tags for revalidation in 1943.

The "OLD MAN OF THE MOUNTAIN" or "OLD STONE FACE" was carried on the plates for 1926 and the state has been advertised as "SCENIC" from 1957 to the present time except for 1962 when the word was dropped. In 1963 the motto "PHOTO-SCENIC" appeared.

On its vanity plate series, the words "LIVE FREE OR DIE" was in use in New Hampshire in 1970-71.

NEW JERSEY—1903

Until 1908, New Jersey automobile owners provided their own identification, making their markers in most cases of leather or metal with attached or painted metal numbers. Between 1903 and mid-1905, these homemade plates were required for the rear of motor vehicles, and

from 1905-07 plates were obliged to appear on both front and rear of vehicles. The initials "N.J." were also generally included in the design, although there were exceptions to the rule—especially in the earlier days.

In 1908 the first state-issued annual plates appeared. These were made of flat metal with the numbers printed on individual metal sections crimped into place by a frame. Also included was the date, state abbreviation and manufacturer's seal. Their colors were white on blue. Although they were similarly designed, plates used between 1909 and 1915 were made of porcelain-enameled iron; embossed metal types were issued in 1916.

Until 1925, New Jersey plates employed from one to six numbers without hyphens or dashes, but in 1926 a prefix letter was added with up to five numbers, the letter designating the county of registration.

New and smaller plates were introduced in 1939 which used two prefix letters before the numbers. Frequently a suffix letter appeared. Annual issues were employed until 1952 with the exception of 1943: In this year, 1942 plates were revalidated by means of date tabs.

The aforesaid date tabs appeared on the 1952 series until about 1960. Orange on black, this series was augmented in 1955 by a small new orange on black series carrying the state abbreviation minus date. Windshield stickers revalidated this mini-series annually.

In 1959, a black on cream series employing the legend "GARDEN STATE" was issued, and for another year all three types — the original 1952-60 series, the 1955-60 mini-series and the new 1959 black on cream plates — were in legal use. The latter are the only ones which have been used since the early 1960's.

NEW MEXICO—1912

Under an act of the State Legislature approved June 8, 1912, automobile registration became compulsory under the direction of the Secretary of State in New Mexico. Green on white embossed metal plates were provided without dates and lasted through the following year.

The first annual and dated tags appeared in 1914, and these were issued through 1919. The 1920 plate was a blue on white porcelain-enameled iron type, revalidated for three years by means of a special insigne attached to the plate.

Embossed metal plates appeared again in 1924 and were in use until recently. New Mexico, however, has used semi-permanent plates since 1961 which have been revalidated by plate stickers.

The "zia" symbol was adopted as a part of the plate design in 1927. This is the Zuni Indian sun emblem and the date of the plate was carried within the orb of the symbol for many years.

The state used its plates in 1940 to proclaim a bit of ancient New Mexico history: The motto for that year, "CORONADO QUARTO CENTENNIAL," honored Coronado's discovery of the area four centuries ago.

New Mexico plates advertised "THE LAND OF ENCHANTMENT" in 1941, a motto which has been retained on the plates ever since then.

NEW YORK—1901

Automobile registrations in New York state became effective April 25, 1901, and owners were responsible for the provision of their own registrations which cost $1 per car. The owners' initials were used on the earliest markers in lieu of numbers. Most of these plates were made of leather with attached metal letters, wood or tin with letters painted on the plate. The state abbreviation was not required. By the end of 1901, a total of 954 motor vehicles had been registered.

Effective May 15, 1903, initial tags were abandoned in favor of number plates, with number 1 being assigned to G. P. Chamberlain of Harrison, Westchester County. A black on white combination was stipulated, and although the state abbreviation wasn't required, most motorists added the state letters anyway. As usual, material was optional and although the law forbade it, another option was frequently exercised: White or silver on black plates appeared. By May 3, 1904, the inclusion of the state abbreviation became mandatory.

These "do-it-yourself" tags were retained until August 1, 1910, when the first state-issued plates appeared. These included white metal numbers and the state abbreviation attached to a blue metal background. Like their predecessors, these carried no date. White on maroon embossed metal plates were issued for 1911 and white on vermillion porcelain-enameled ones were introduced in 1912. Both, like the earlier series, were undated. Plates since 1913 have been dated (by plate stickers, in recent years) and all have been made of embossed metal since that date. The first use of the hyphen to expedite identification in New York occurred in 1916, an idea of Secretary of State Francis M. Hugo. Registrations were controlled by the State Department until 1924, the year in which the Bureau of Motor Vehicles was formed.

Empire State plates appeared in a variety of color schemes until 1927 when black and deep yellow prevailed. That color combination lasted until 1967 when the current deep yellow and blue tags were issued. Perhaps the black and yellow colors were settled upon after the white on French gray series was found to be difficult to read. It was rumored that the latter combination was picked by a high state official who wanted plates to match the color scheme of his wife's car!

New York State advertised its "WORLD'S FAIR" on 1938-40 plates, using the "EMPIRE STATE" legend from 1951 to 1965.

In 1942, only one plate instead of two was issued to each motorist; although plates had been manufactured in pairs, the second plate was withheld until 1944 when motorists received it with the "44" date stamped over the original "42." In the interim, 1943 plates were merely the old, 1942 ones revalidated with a black on yellow strip carrying state abbreviation and date.

The current series, which has been in use since 1966, expires during 1972; then it will be replaced by a new series.

NORTH CAROLINA—1907

North Carolina's license plate history is unique in that only three of its counties — Guilford, Wake and Wayne — were affected by the state's first registration laws. A North Carolina General Assembly act approved March 5, 1907, required automobile owners in these counties to register with the clerk of the Superior Court and to display assigned numbers both on the front and rear of their vehicles.

A subsequent act, approved March 6, 1909, and effective the following July 1, empowered the Secretary of State to register all automobiles except those in New Hanover County where motorists were required to register with the Superior Court. White on black or black on white plates were provided by owners and carried the state abbreviation. No material was stipulated by law.

Under the provisions of a General Assembly act approved March 10, 1913, and effective April 1 of that year, the Secretary of State was required to register and issue license plates to all auto owners. According to this law plates and registrations were to expire on June 30. Because 1913 certificates had already been issued, they were allowed to remain in effect through June 30, 1913, and motorists registering vehicles between April 1 and June 30 of 1913 were issued a white on black porcelain-enameled plate with "EXP. JUNE, 1913" across the bottom.

Annual enameled plates were issued through a series expiring June 30, 1916 when an embossed metal series for 1916-17 appeared. Annual plates issued for the fiscal year appeared until the 1926-27 white on black series. Then it was decided to adopt the calendar year for plates. To complete 1927, a red on gray plate was issued for the remaining six-month period. Since 1928, North Carolina has followed the calendar year plan for registration of automobiles.

License plates have appeared annually in North Carolina with the exception of 1943 when the 1942 tags were tabbed for revalidation. Plates carried the words "DRIVE SAFELY" from 1956 through 1963.

NORTH DAKOTA—1911 or earlier

The first state registrations in North Dakota became law under an act of the State Legislative Assembly approved March 17, 1911. At that time the Secretary of State was empowered to issue two plates annually to all automobile owners. Before this time, local registrations were in effect in various communities of the state.

The first plates, issued for 1911, were made of flat metal and painted gold on black. The design included the state initials "N.D." and the date. These appeared on the left and right-hand sides of the tags respectively, and this design prevailed through the 1947 series. The state name appeared in full on plates between 1948 and 1961 and the abbreviation "N. DAKOTA" has been in effect since 1962. Since 1956, all passenger car plates in North Dakota have carried the motto "PEACE GARDEN STATE" to honor the 2200 acre park which extends across the Canadian border into Manitoba, symbolizing the friendly relations between the two countries.

Due to the wartime steel shortage, all previously issued plates were revalidated in 1943 by a windshield sticker. For new registrations, similarly-colored yellow on red plates imprinted "1943" were issued. The same situation occurred in 1949 when 1948 plates were tabbed for the new year and new plates were issued for new registrations.

OHIO—1906

Although number plates weren't required in Ohio before 1906, it is a matter of record that the first registration in Cleveland was assigned to C. E. Burke of 813 Prospect St. on June 15, 1901. At that time, a total of 282 motor vehicles were reported in that city.

Auto owners were required to register with the Secretary of State effective June 1, 1906, and to provide themselves with a number plate displaying assigned numbers and the abbreviation "OH." Materials were optional and the required colors were white on black. This same year, the first municipal registrations went into effect. Local plates were frequently used in a number of Ohio cities through 1908.

The Secretary of State was required to register cars and issue license plates to all automobile owners under state law effective May 11, 1908. The Secretary exempted those who had been previously registered by a municipality from registration until January 1, 1909.

These first state plates were undated white on dark blue markers. Number 1 was assigned to Thomas B. Paxton Jr., Fourth and Main Streets, Cincinnati, for his Franklin. Numbers assigned in the first year ran from 1 through 10649. The series was continued in 1909, beginning with number 10650.

Dated plates were introduced for 1910. These and the 1911 series were also made of porcelain enamel. The markers issued from 1912 through 1917 were made of flat metal. Plates are manufactured at the Lebanon Correctional Institute and Ohio State Penitentiary.

From the time of the first annually-issued dated tags, Ohio has issued dated tags on an annual basis except for two years when windshield stickers were used to revalidate plates for a second year's use.

Ohio plates carried a motif depicting a covered wagon and the motto "150 ANNIV. N.W. TERR." in 1938 and in 1953 tags proclaimed "1803-1953" to mark the state's 150th anniversary of statehood.

OKLAHOMA—1911 or earlier

The first registration of motor vehicles by the state of Oklahoma dates back to March 16, 1911, when the State Legislature required owners to register their vehicles with the State Highway Commissioner. This act failed to provide for the issuance of license plates, however, and did not usurp the right of cities or towns to tax or license automobile owners. Until 1915 a number of local communities registered cars. Oklahoma City and Tulsa issued dated types and El Reno used undated porcelain plates.

The first state-issued markers were the blue on white dated tags appearing in 1915. A variety of designs and color schemes have been employed on plates since that time.

"VISIT OKLAHOMA" was inscribed on plates from 1955 through 1964, although wags were frequently tempted to paint the word "DON'T" above the "VISIT." This practice may have had something to do with the discontinuance of the motto on plates after 1964.

Since 1967, plates have advertised that "OKLAHOMA IS OK."

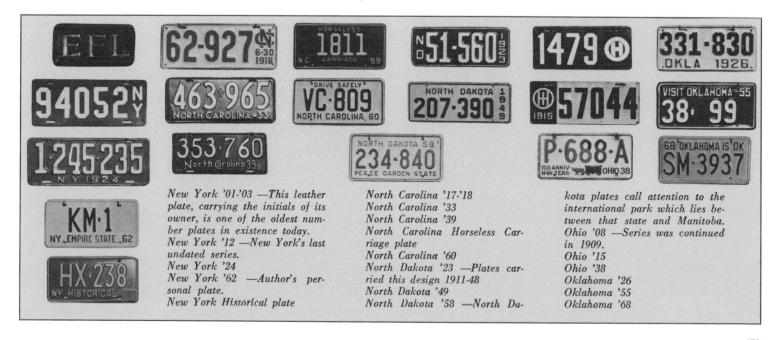

New York '01-'03 —This leather plate, carrying the initials of its owner, is one of the oldest number plates in existence today.
New York '12 —New York's last undated series.
New York '24
New York '62 —Author's personal plate.
New York Historical plate

North Carolina '17-'18
North Carolina '33
North Carolina '39
North Carolina Horseless Carriage plate
North Carolina '60
North Dakota '23 —Plates carried this design 1911-48
North Dakota '49
North Dakota '58 —North Da-

kota plates call attention to the international park which lies between that state and Manitoba.
Ohio '08 —Series was continued in 1909.
Ohio '15
Ohio '38
Oklahoma '26
Oklahoma '55
Oklahoma '68

479

OREGON—1905

The first registrations in Oregon were provided by motor vehicle owners who displayed their numbers according to law in figures at least three inches high in a light color against a dark background. The initials "ORE" also appeared in similarly-sized letters. Material was not specified by law although a stamping company issued many a white on red embossed steel tag with the state abbreviation preceding the number to fanciful motorists.

The first state-issued plates were the black on yellow embossed metal dated ones issued in 1911. Annual plates were the rule thereafter until 1933 when two series were employed.

Registrations employed a fiscal year expiration date in 1930, so the 1929 series was continued to June 30, 1930, when an orange on black 1930-31 plate appeared.

In 1933, however, a decision to return to the calendar year issue was made, and upon expiration of the 1932-33 series, a black on yellow series was issued with a December 31 expiration date.

Oregon plates for 1942 were revalidated three times and were not replaced until 1946. Annual plates were used until 1950 when that year's series was revalidated annually until 1955. In that year a new yellow on blue type was issued.

Some of these plates are still in use and consist of two types: one without a motto and the other bearing the legend "PACIFIC WONDERLAND." In 1963 a new yellow on blue type appeared without legend employing a numeric system of three letters and three numbers. This plate has gradually been replacing the earlier yellow on blue markers revalidated annually on a staggered basis by stickers.

PENNSYLVANIA—1903

The first state registrations of motor vehicles in Pennsylvania were enacted under provisions of a Pennsylvania General Assembly act of April 23, 1903, which required automobile owners to register with a county official. The law also decreed that any motorist otherwise licensed by any city or municipality under local ordinance would be exempt from such registrations.

The majority of markers in use between 1903 and 1906 were provided by owners who chose the conventional metal house numbers attached to leather pads. In almost all cases, the suffix letter "P" (or occasionally the abbreviation "PA") appeared.

Notable exceptions to these rules were the annual tags issued motor vehicle owners in the city of Philadelphia between 1903 and 1906 and the undated ones used during the same period in Pittsburgh. With the exception of a number of 1903 Philadelphia local plates which were made of embossed steel, all were of porcelain-enameled iron.

The first annual and dated license plates, white on blue enameled markers, were issued on January 1, 1906. The porcelain-enameled tags were issued annually thereafter through 1915.

On all 1906 through 1909 plates consisting of one to three numbers and on all passenger plates of any number from 1910 through 1915, a small metal seal in the shape of a keystone containing the manufacturer's number was incorporated into the plate design. With the advent of embossed steel plates in 1916, the keystone emblem was retained as an integral part of the plate design. This design was abandoned for the 1920 series when the practice of placing the state abbreviation and date below the numbers was adopted. Keystone insignias, however, flanked these on either side and were retained in the basic plate design until 1937 when they were replaced by the shape of the state. This shape was effected by the border of each plate.

In 1933 (and possibly in other years of the period), two different dies were used in Pennsylvania plate manufacture creating two types: those which had "PENNA 1933" above the numbers and the ones which carried the identification as "1933 PENNA."

The state issued plates annually — with the exception of 1944 when 1943 markers were tabbed and used again until 1958. Then a seven-year type was issued, revalidated annually by a sticker. A six-year tag appeared in 1965 and a 1971 series includes the Liberty Bell (complete with crack) and the phrase "BICENTENNIAL STATE" in its design. Since 1922, the state has alternated the same blue and yellow-orange colors.

RHODE ISLAND—1904

The first license plates in Rhode Island, like those of most of her sister states, were issued by the state itself. These were undated white on porcelain-enameled iron tags carrying the notice "REGISTERED IN R.I." Plate Number 1 was issued to Rolland R. Robinson of Wakefield for his 20 hp Cadillac.

These were undated plates, and numbers issued in 1904 spanned 1 through 850. The same series was continued through 1908, with numbers 851-1407 issued in 1905; 1408-2115 in 1906; 2116-2971 in 1907 and 2972-3263 in 1908.

The first series was replaced by a second white on black enameled type on June 1, 1908. The new series carried the letters "R.I." after the numerals in similar size. This series was continued through 1911.

For 1912, a black on white series appeared with the state abbreviation listed vertically on the lefthand side of the plate. This series was continued through 1917, the flat metal tag of 1918 being the state's first dated marker. Flat metal plates were also issued in 1919 and 1920.

Since 1921, all Rhode Island plates have been made of embossed metal. White and black were alternated until mid-1946 and these colors have been used again since 1948. Rhode Island noted its "300TH YEAR" on 1936 tags but no legend has appeared since then.

In 1943, the 1942 plates were used again with a windshield sticker and from 1944 through 1946 the same series was retained with orange, green and red plate inserts attached for revalidation.

The tabbed 1942 plates were replaced with a brand new series in August of 1946. These were black on natural aluminum with date inserts and the series was continued in 1947 with a white insert bearing the new date.

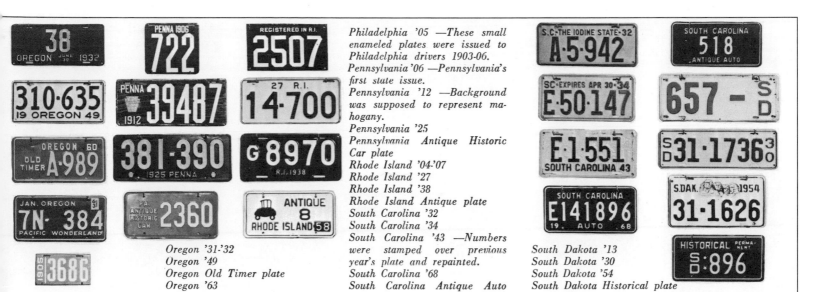

Philadelphia '05 —These small enameled plates were issued to Philadelphia drivers 1903-06.
Pennsylvania '06 —Pennsylvania's first state issue.
Pennsylvania '12 —Background was supposed to represent mahogany.
Pennsylvania '25
Pennsylvania Antique Historic Car plate
Rhode Island '04-'07
Rhode Island '27
Rhode Island '38
Rhode Island Antique plate
South Carolina '32
South Carolina '34
South Carolina '43 —Numbers were stamped over previous year's plate and repainted.
South Carolina '68
South Carolina Antique Auto

Oregon '31-'32
Oregon '49
Oregon Old Timer plate
Oregon '63

South Dakota '13
South Dakota '30
South Dakota '54
South Dakota Historical plate

For the last two decades, it has been the general policy of the state to use number plates for more than one year at a time, using stickers for revalidation.

SOUTH CAROLINA—1906

Registration of automobiles in South Carolina was assigned to county authority in 1906 and the first number plates were most often provided by the owners who displayed their assigned numbers in metal upon leather pads. The county abbreviation was often included.

The first uniform plates, still under county authority, were black on white porcelain-enameled types with the county name imprinted above the numbers and the prefix letters "s.c." immediately preceding the numbers. There were exceptions; certain counties didn't subscribe to the standard type and issued their own markers in various colors and materials, although the black on white type predominated.

Authority for registration was transferred to the state in 1917, and from this date on plates have been issued on an annual basis with the exception of 1944 when the 1943 tags were revalidated by a date strip.

A palmetto tree insigne was used on the plates for 1926-27 and in 1930 the word "IODINE" was included in the plate design. "THE IODINE STATE" appeared in 1931-32 and "THE IODINE PRODUCTS STATE" was used in 1933. In the Depression-ridden 1930's, half-year registrations were also marked by special number plates which carried reversed colors of the regulation full-year types.

In 1943 South Carolina license plates were made by flattening out plates from earlier issues and re-embossing them. Despite a new paint job which made the plates readable, the imprint of the originals could be easily discerned.

The plates noted the state's anniversary in 1970 by including the motto "1670 300 YEARS 1970."

For many years, passenger car registrations have been categorized according to car weight. One or two prefix letters ranging from "A" (for the lightest cars) to "G" (indicating the heaviest ones) are used.

SOUTH DAKOTA—1906

When the first state-issued number plates were issued from 1906 to 1913, automobile owners provided their own plates in South Dakota, nearly all of which were black leather pads with aluminum numbers attached. Some carried the state abbreviation and some omitted this identification.

Embossed metal plates appeared in 1913 and the first dated tags came out for 1916. The abbreviation "S.D." was used through 1932 and again in 1939. "S. DAK." appeared on plates from 1933 through 1938. Since 1952 "S. DAK" has appeared again. The full state name was used between 1940 and 1951 on plates.

South Dakota advertised the "RUSHMORE MEMORIAL" on its license plates in 1939 to honor the mountain on which Gutzon Borglum carved the gigantic heads of Presidents Washington, Jefferson, Lincoln and Theodore Roosevelt.

Since 1952, the actual portrayal of the heads by decal have appeared on South Dakota plates.

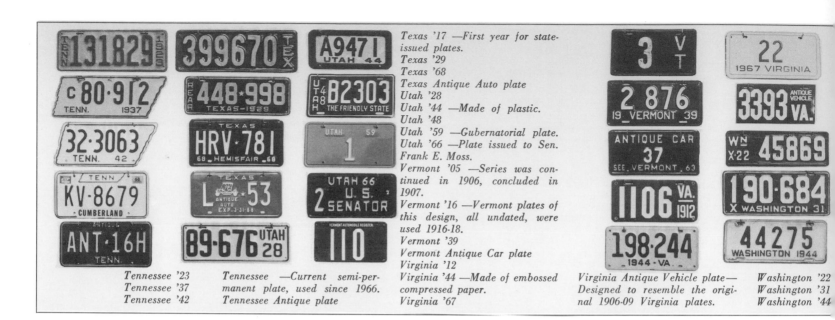

Texas '17 —First year for state-issued plates.
Texas '29
Texas '68
Texas Antique Auto plate
Utah '28
Utah '44 —Made of plastic.
Utah '48
Utah '59 —Gubernatorial plate.
Utah '66 —Plate issued to Sen. Frank E. Moss.
Vermont '05 —Series was continued in 1906, concluded in 1907.
Vermont '16 —Vermont plates of this design, all undated, were used 1916-18.
Vermont '39
Vermont Antique Car plate
Virginia '12
Virginia '44 —Made of embossed compressed paper.
Virginia '67

Tennessee '23
Tennessee '37
Tennessee '42
Tennessee —Current semi-permanent plate, used since 1966.
Tennessee Antique plate

Virginia Antique Vehicle plate— Designed to resemble the original 1906-09 Virginia plates.

Washington '22
Washington '31
Washington '44

TENNESSEE—1905

All motorists in Tennessee were required to register with the Secretary of State after May 4, 1905, to receive their assigned numbers from him. Motorists were obliged to provide their own plates carrying numbers at least three inches high and one and a half inches wide mounted on a background measuring 7 by 4 inches. No state identification, date or material was stipulated by law, nor was a single color mandatory.

Certain Tennessee municipalities were issuing their own plates by 1911, and a variety of these were in use until 1915, notably the white on blue undated porcelain-enameled iron type used in Memphis and surrounding communities.

The first state-issued plates, embossed metal dated types, appeared July 1, 1915, and plates were issued annually thereafter until 1942 when that year's plate was revalidated by a tab and used through 1943.

Tennessee plates were cut to resemble the shape of the state itself from 1936 through 1956, and in 1957, when the 12 x 6 inches plates became mandatory, the state shape was preserved as a small motif within the plate's rectangular shape.

The state issued a semi-permanent type of tag in 1966 which is still in effect. At the bottom of this tag a reflectorized section appears carrying the name of the registering county.

TEXAS—1907

Effective July 11, 1907, automobile owners in Texas were required to register their motor vehicles through the clerk of the county in which they resided. Their assigned numbers were to be displayed on their vehicles in figures not less than six inches high. Although no set colors were stipulated, most of these markers were either made of leather with metal numbers attached or of base metal with numbers of aluminum fastened on the plates in any number of ways. Often numbers were simply painted on. The state name or the abbreviation "TEX" appeared on many tags although such identification wasn't required. After 1912 or 1913, several counties began issuing embossed plates of porcelain-enameled iron, incorporating the county name into the plates' design. Most of these were white on a dark blue background.

After a new law was enacted requiring state registration after July 1, 1917, the first state-issued plates appeared. These were made of embossed metal and carried the state abbreviation without a date. White on blue, they were accompanied by a round metal seal bearing the words "REGISTERED MOTOR VEHICLE," the state name and the date. Only the date was required to be atttached to the front of the car. The plates were continued in 1918 and 1919 with seals issued for revalidation.

Texas plates were dated from 1920 through 1922, carrying the "REGISTERED MOTOR VEHICLE" notice which had heretofore been confined to small metal tags on the base plates.

Plates once again were dateless in 1923 and the name "TEXAS" was placed vertically on both the left and right hand sides of the plates. A year later the date and the "REGISTERED MOTOR VEHICLE" notice reappeared, but the latter was dropped soon thereafter. All Texas plates have been dated since 1924.

Markers for 1928 through 1930 were marked "FRONT" or "REAR," and in 1936 they noted the state's "CENTENNIAL." In 1943 and 1944 the 1942 plates were retained with date tabs. Texas also noted its "HEMISFAIR" on the tags of 1967.

A significant feature of Texas license plates since the 1920's has been a small star insigne which replaces the conventional dash. By this means, legibility is served, and a tangible reminder of Texas' fame as the "Lone Star State" is offered to observers.

UTAH—1909

Utah's first registrations date back to 1909 when all automobile owners were required to display their assigned numbers in figures four inches high along with a one-inch letter "U." Most of these early Utah markers were black on white flat metal, with numbers and letter painted on despite the availability of commercially-issued embossed silver on black plates.

The first state-issued tags appeared for 1915 and these, like all subsequent issues until recently, were assigned annually and carried the date.

During several years in the Forties, the state heralded itself as "CENTER SCENIC AMERICA." Because of the wartime metal shortage, 1942 plates were used in 1943 with a revalidating windshield sticker. The 1944 tags were smaller, flat-surfaced plastic affairs.

"THIS IS THE PLACE," a phrase supposedly spoken by Brigham Young at the site of Salt Lake City to his Mormon followers at the end of his famous trek to the West, was proclaimed on 1947 license plates.

VERMONT—1905

Imitating the example of its neighboring state of Massachusetts, the first Vermont license plate series carried the notice "VERMONT AUTOMOBILE REGISTER" above the numbers on the white on blue porcelain-enameled iron tags. These plates became effective May 1, 1905, when the first number was assigned to Charles C. Warren of Waterbury for his Packard touring car. Approximately 220 cars were registered during 1905 with the same tag series continuing through number 373 in 1906. This series ended in 1907 with numbers approaching (and perhaps slightly exceeding) 1000.

All annual plates of this state between 1908 and 1916 were black on white porcelain-enameled iron tags; all were dated except those of 1908.

Tags used for 1916, 1917 and 1918 were undated and made of embossed metal, as were all subsequent Vermont plates. They were colored white on black, blue on white and yellow on green respectively.

Annual plates were issued through 1943 when a date tab revalidated the 1942 plates. Annual plates were issued again until 1957 when two-year tags were introduced. The 1969 series was revalidated in 1970 and again in 1971.

Since 1957, Vermont plates have carried the motto "SEE VERMONT."

VIRGINIA—1906

The first license plates in Virginia were issued by the state in 1906 as white on black porcelain-enameled iron carrying the state abbreviation without date. They were used continually through 1909 with the first assigned to Carl LeRoy Armentroud of Staunton for use on his Oldsmobile.

Dated tags were issued in 1910 and the porcelain-enameled type was replaced by an embossed metal variety for 1914.

Since that time, Virginia plates have been issued on an annual basis with the exception of 1943 and 1952 when the preceding years' series were continued with date tabs.

Although the state had most often used black and white plates, black on yellow ones were issued in 1944 made of embossed compressed paper. They were unique among plates of the period, for other states, similarly deprived of metal during the war years, issued compressed paper tags with flat, rather than embossed surfaces.

WASHINGTON—1905

Statewide automobile registration became compulsory in 1905 and between that year and 1916 all plates were the owners' responsibility. Soon a law called for the display of numbers at least four inches high preceded by the abbreviation "WN" in light colored letters on a dark background. In most instances number plates were of painted or metal numbers on metal rectangles or leather pads and the colors were invariably white or silver on black. Later, front plates were required. In case an owner simply preferred to paint the mandatory numbers on the back of his car, this too was permitted.

The first state-issued markers appeared in 1916 and from then until 1925 all plates officially carried the "WN" abbreviation. The state name appeared in full from 1925 through 1962, and since 1963 a green on white permanent plate has been used with earlier issues of this series carrying the identification "WASH." Recently, plates have carried the full state name.

All Washington plates since 1916 have been made of embossed metal. An interesting designation which appeared between 1917 and 1935 was a small letter "x" to denote a passenger car.

In 1920, the previous year's plates were used again, revalidated by a porcelain-enameled iron tab carrying the state abbreviation, the date, the ubiquitous "x" and a number corresponding to that of its accompanying plate.

Plates carried the legend "STATE OF WASHINGTON" and noted the state's "GOLDEN JUBILEE" in 1939. Since 1942 plates have been used for more than a year at a time with various tabs, inserts or stickers used to update them. In 1944, while 1942 plates were in use, similarly colored and designed tabs carrying the date "1944" were issued for new registrations.

WEST VIRGINIA—1906

The first number plates in West Virginia were dated, embossed metal tags issued by the state in 1906. They were superseded in 1907 by a larger, undated porcelain-enamel type, and this series was carried through the following year when, for congruity's sake, an attached brass

West Virginia '26
West Virginia '50-'51
West Virginia —*Two plates issued for 1960-61. No. 39-718 is representative of the earlier, white on maroon embossed type of the series, whereas 217-618 is a later, reflectorized example.*
West Virginia Antique Car plate

Wisconsin '13
Wisconsin '40
Wisconsin '45 —*Note rounded corners, also used in Arizona and California in the early 1940's.*
Wisconsin Antique plate
Wyoming '18
Wyoming '32
Wyoming '41

tag carried the number of the 1907 marker.

Plates were issued annually each January 1 until 1913 when it was decided to adopt a fiscal year date for registrations. Because of this decision, the 1912 plates were used until July 1, 1913, when they were replaced by a series dated "July 1914"— the expiration date. The next two series were dated "1914-1915" and "1915-1916" respectively, and for many years West Virginia markers maintained the dual dates, covering June to June periods.

Porcelain-enameled iron plates were used through the 1915-16 series. The 1916-17 plates were made of flat metal and since then all plates in this state have been of the embossed steel type. The state reverted to the calendar year for its 1921 plates, and in that year through the following one the state abbreviation appeared in a monogram design.

To compound the confusion, it was decided to readopt June 30 as an expiration date in 1934 and, consequently, the 1933 license plates were used until June 30, 1934, when the 1934-35 series was issued.

In 1960 the 1960-61 plates appeared in the conventional embossed metal colored white on maroon. But shortly after sales commenced it was decided to employ reflectorization. And so, because plates with lower numbers had already been issued, only plates with numbers above about 145-000 were reflectorized, with recessed numbers and letters. These also appeared with crimson rather than maroon backgrounds.

The state began alternating yellow and blue with its 1962-63 series. All of the plates were reflectorized, the yellow on blue types having recessed characters and the blue on yellow carrying embossed characters. The basic 1969-70 series, revalidated by a sticker, is in current use.

West Virginia plates carried the word "CENTENNIAL" on its 1962-63 and 1963-64 plates and "MOUNTAIN STATE" during years since then.

WISCONSIN—1905

The first license plates in Wisconsin were state-issued in July of 1905. These undated, black metal plates with attached aluminum numbers were suffixed with the letter "W" and used through 1911 — although new car registrants after July 7, 1911, were required to attach silver on green plates to their vehicles, similar in design to the previous type ex-

cept for their left-side dates.

Plates for 1912 and 1913 looked much the same; the 1912 series had aluminum numbers set on a zinc plate and 1913 tabs carried numbers on a lighter metal background. Embossed plates appeared in 1914. All Wisconsin plates through 1920 carried "W" for their identification with "WIS" substituted for the 1921 series and retained through 1931.

In 1940, the legend "AMERICA'S DAIRYLAND" appeared for the first time; it is still in use. Two types of plates were used that year, the initial group carrying the identity and date ("WISCONSIN 1940") above the numbers, and later plates carrying the abbreviation and date between sets of considerably larger numbers.

Several types of plates have been used since 1942. They have been revalidated by inserts, tabs, stickers and, because Wisconsin employs the staggered registration system, the abbreviation of the month of expiration is included in the plate design.

WYOMING—before 1913

Undoubtedly the most famous of all U.S. license plate insigne is that which has appeared on Wyoming tags since 1936, depicting a cowboy astride a bucking bronco. This insigne was created at the suggestion of Lester C. Hunt, then Secretary of State in Wyoming and later governor of the state. He not only copyrighted the insigne, but then assigned the copyright to the state of Wyoming. The rider on the horse was claimed to be A. G. "Stub" Farlow and the bronc was named "Deadman."

Wyoming, incidentally, along with Illinois and Mississippi, has issued annual plates to automobile owners since the first issue. No passenger car plates have ever been revalidated by tabs or stickers.

Although a few local communities registered automobiles prior to 1913, the state plates only date back to that year. For several years the design included the state seal, and all Wyoming plates through 1917 were undated.

With the exception of the 1916 plates (which were porcelain-enameled iron) and those used in 1944 (which were of flat compressed paper), all Wyoming markers have been constructed of embossed metal.

U.S. TERRITORIES, CANAL ZONE AND PUERTO RICO

AMERICAN SAMOA—1925

At last count American Samoa only registered 1568 passenger cars, but the islands' license plates date back to 1925 when the first plates carried the date and a number prefixed by the letters "A.S."

The abbreviation was discarded in the early 1930's in favor of the words "AMERICAN SAMOA AUTOMOBILE LICENSE" and the date was retained. Like the first tags, these were made of embossed metal — just as they are today.

All dated, plates changed annually until 1943 and 1944 when the 1942 series was continued because of the wartime metal shortage.

Current American Samoa number plates are manufactured in Japan, attractively designed with a palm tree motif placed to the left of the numerals. The Polynesian legend "PAGO PAGO MOTU O FIAFIA" ("Pago Pago is a place of happiness") also appears as a tribute to American Samoa's capital.

The 1970 plate series is currently in use revalidated by plate stickers.

CANAL ZONE—1910

Although the first automobile registrations in the Panama Canal Zone were effected by law on October 31, 1910, it was not until December 3 of that year that the first registration was assigned to Natalio Ehrman of Panama. Even so, Mr. Ehrman was not the first car owner living in the Canal Zone proper; that honor goes to Capt. C. Nixon of Mont Hope, Canal Zone, who was assigned Number 5.

The first plates were small, undated porcelain-enameled iron ones carrying the abbreviation "CZ." In use for many years, they were carried on cars along with Panama plates. The first annual plates probably date back to the World War I period.

As late as the early Forties, residents of the Canal Zone were obliged to carry their Canal Zone plate on the rear of their cars with a Panama tag on the front — with the exception of the City of Colon where the front Panama tag gave way to the Colon city plate obsolete since 1937.

In 1943 and 1944, the 1942 plates were used with date tabs. Since 1955, yellow and black have been alternated, and for the last several years all Canal Zone plates have carried the legend "FUNNEL FOR WORLD COMMERCE."

GUAM—circa 1924

Because early records are missing, the history of Guam motor vehicle registrations is clouded in mystery. But dated plates can be traced with certainty to 1924. These, like the rest of this region's plates through 1947, were flat metal affairs cut square at the corners and were either

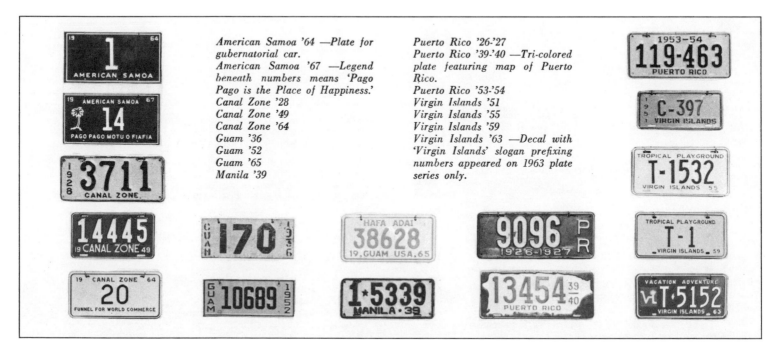

American Samoa '64 —Plate for gubernatorial car.
American Samoa '67 —Legend beneath numbers means 'Pago Pago is the Place of Happiness.'
Canal Zone '28
Canal Zone '49
Canal Zone '64
Guam '36
Guam '52
Guam '65
Manila '39

Puerto Rico '26-'27
Puerto Rico '39-'40 —Tri-colored plate featuring map of Puerto Rico.
Puerto Rico '53-'54
Virgin Islands '51
Virgin Islands '55
Virgin Islands '59
Virgin Islands '63 —Decal with 'Virgin Islands' slogan prefixing numbers appeared on 1963 plate series only.

hand painted or stenciled until 1946 when numbers were stamped on their surfaces. The first embossed plates appeared in 1948.

The 1965 series was revalidated annually by stickers and retained through 1969. The current yellow on green series will be revalidated in similar fashion through 1974.

PUERTO RICO—1906

Historic information about Puerto Rican license plates is sparse but it is known that the first motor vehicle law was established in 1906, stipulating that an owner was responsible for providing an assigned number in black on white at the rear of his vehicle. Annual plates came into being around World War I.

Because Puerto Rico used June 30 as an expiration date, all tags until the early 1960's carried dual dates, the first representing the year of issue and the second indicating the date of expiration. Plates carried the abbreviation "P.R." until the mid-1930's when the full name of the island was used.

In 1939, Puerto Rico issued the first of its two tri-colored tags: This displayed red numbers against a white background with a blue border. The white background resembled the shape of the island. The second tri-color tag, the 1940-41 series, retained the blue border but carried black numbers on an orange background. The 1941-42 series was continued through June 30, 1944, revalidated by windshield stickers.

The 1959-60 series was yellow on dark blue. Although the date appeared on the first plates, it was soon eliminated as the plates were made permanent and were revalidated annually by plate stickers. This series was replaced in mid-1970 by a new permanent type with the shape of the island emphasized by a colored border. The black on bright orange plates carry, in addition to the numbers, a letter which designates the area of registration.

VIRGIN ISLANDS—1927

License plates were hand-painted in the Virgin Islands until 1939 when the highest numbers of that year's issue appeared as the embossed metal type which has been in use since then.

Initially, this region's plates carried the abbreviation of the island and the date, but in 1932 the initials "V.I." were substituted. The island designation appeared again in 1935 and continued on plates until 1940 when "VIRGIN ISLANDS" appeared in full on all plates. Letter prefixes were used to designate the island of registration.

The previous year's issue was continued in 1943 with a revalidating plate tab, and in 1944 a windshield sticker revalidated the plates.

The words "TROPICAL PARADISE" appeared on plates from 1952 through 1962, but "VACATION ADVENTURE" replaced the motto in 1963. This, in turn, was replaced by "AMERICAN PARADISE" in 1968, and plates from that year were retained through 1969 and 1970. A new white on blue series was issued for 1971.

In 1963 a special decal carrying the letters "V.I." was used as a prefix to the numbers on all Virgin Islands plates.

CANADA

ALBERTA—1912

The first Alberta plates of 1912 were white on blue porcelain-enameled tags; this material was used again during the following year when the provincial coat-of-arms also appeared on the now white on crimson plates. The use of the coat of arms was short-lived, however, and was dropped a few years later. Flat metal plates were also used, but most of Alberta's markers have been fashioned of the conventional embossed metal.

In addition to the provincial name and date, 1942 Alberta plates also carried the word "CANADA" as did Prince Edward Island markers of 1927 and Yukon Territory tags of the early 1950's.

Plates have been issued annually in Alberta except during 1944 and 1953 when plates of the previous years were revalidated by windshield sticker and insert respectively.

In 1967 plates carried the dates "1867" and "1967" plus a small maple leaf insigne to commemorate Canada's Centennial.

BRITISH COLUMBIA—1905

Registrations between 1905 and the year in which the first official provincially-issued plates made their debut (1912) were on a do-it-yourself basis, and the majority of plates during this period consisted of metal numbers attached to black leather pads. The abbreviation "B.C." also appeared.

During the first two years of provincial issues, plates were made of porcelain-enameled iron; flat metal tags sporting the provincial coat-of-arms replaced them for a brief time, but these tags were short-lived.

Plates for 1918 were used again in 1919 with date tabs and the 1920 tags were continued in 1921 and 1922 in similar fashion. Markers of 1950 were retained in the following year with metal plate strips. The 1952 series, with its elaborately-designed maple leaf and inset totem pole insigne, was re-tabbed for use in 1953 and 1954. Otherwise, plates have appeared annually through 1970. This series will be continued in the future with revalidation by means of stickers.

The oddly-colored green on gold tags of 1958 carried a reminder of the "CENTENARY" observance and, although the motto was dropped for 1959, peculiar color schemes prevailed for the next four years; maroon and robin's-egg blue was used in 1959 and 1960 with maroon and pink following in 1961 and 1962.

The name of the province has been prefixed by the adjective "BEAUTIFUL" since 1964.

MANITOBA—1908

The first automobile registrations occurred in Manitoba during 1908 with some 408 motor vehicles being assigned legal numbers. Generally of flat metal or metal numbers against leather backgrounds, plates were provided by auto owners. The provincial abbreviation "MAN" or even the prefix letter "M" was occasionally added.

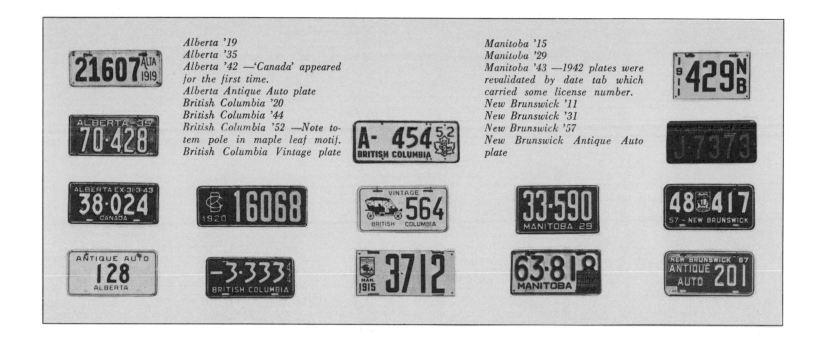

Alberta '19
Alberta '35
Alberta '42 —'Canada' appeared
for the first time.
Alberta Antique Auto plate
British Columbia '20
British Columbia '44
British Columbia '52 —Note totem pole in maple leaf motif.
British Columbia Vintage plate

Manitoba '15
Manitoba '29
Manitoba '43 —1942 plates were revalidated by date tab which carried some license number.
New Brunswick '11
New Brunswick '31
New Brunswick '57
New Brunswick Antique Auto plate

Provincial issues began in 1911 and all Manitoba tags have been dated since that time. Plates from 1911 through 1914 were made of porcelain-enameled iron and from 1915 through 1918 of flat metal. All carried the provincial coat-of-arms. In 1919 the previous year's plates were revalidated by metal date tabs which carried numbers corresponding to those which appeared on the base plates.

The previous year's series was continued in 1943 with tabs being attached carrying the license plate number; in 1944 the same series was retained for yet another year through the use of revalidating windshield stickers.

In 1949 and 1951, plates of the previous years were used with plate inserts, but the province inaugurated a policy of using plates for six-year periods in 1952.

The 1958-63 and 1964-70 series have shown slight differences in the designs of front and rear markers, with the front ones carrying a small bison insigne plus the name of the province and the rear ones carrying the bison emblem, provincial name and date on the initial base plates. Annual date strips thereafter noted the provincial name and date. These strips left the bison insigne only exposed in the space below the numbers.

The current series, introduced in 1971, heralds the province as "SUNNY MANITOBA," the home of "100,000 LAKES" — contrasting sharply with the "10,000 LAKES" motto on markers of Minnesota, Manitoba's neighbor to the south.

NEW BRUNSWICK—1905

Registrations began in the Province of New Brunswick in 1905 with a total of twelve motor vehicles assigned numbers. The provincial coffers netted a grand total of $84 as a result of this transaction. Black on white was the approved color scheme, but many owners preferred reverse colors and made their tags accordingly without interference from the authorities. The letters "N.B." were mandatory.

Automobiles were uncommon in New Brunswick, and despite the first issuance of provincial plates in 1911, registrations failed to exceed 1000 until the spring of 1914.

From the outset of the provincial issues, all plates were dated. From 1911 through 1917 they were made of porcelain-enameled iron; flat metal prevailed from 1918 through 1921 and embossed metal has endured since then. The abbreviation "N.B." was retained through 1927 although the full provincial name has appeared since 1928.

New Brunswick plates carried the provincial coat of arms from 1954 through 1961 and the motto "PICTURE PROVINCE" has appeared since 1958.

Revalidation in recent years has been common: The 1960 plates were used again in 1961 with windshield stickers while 1962 plates were used in 1963 with plate stickers. Plates from 1964 were used again the following year with stickers, as were the '66 tags which were continued through 1968. The 1969 issue is still in use.

NEWFOUNDLAND—1906

The Dominion (now Province) of Newfoundland registered automobiles as early as 1906 when motorists were required to carry their assigned number in white on a black background at the rear of their automobiles. Most, and perhaps all of these were provided by the owner. No identity was required and the motorist had the option of painting his number on the rear of the car itself.

This custom was replaced in the mid-1920's by conventional embossed metal plates carrying the date, but other identifying characteristics were omitted. The abbreviation "NFLD." was added in the late 1920's; by 1930 the full name "NEWFOUNDLAND" appeared. The name of Newfoundland's mainland, Labrador, has also appeared on all plates since 1965.

To honor the coronation year of King George VI and Queen Elizabeth, Newfoundland plates carried a crown insigne in 1937. In 1944, because of the prevailing wartime steel shortage, extra 1942 plates were issued to the islanders. Originally orange on black, these were repainted red on black. Flat metal plates were used in 1945.

"CANADA CENTENNIAL" was included on the 1967 tags and in 1968 the province was heralded as "CANADA'S HAPPY PROVINCE." As a plug for Newfoundland's main river, "THE MIGHTY CHURCHILL" appeared on 1969 markers.

The 1970 plates have been continued in use for 1971 with a revalidation sticker.

NORTHWEST TERRITORIES—1941

Despite the fact that approximately 5000 automobiles are currently registered in the Northwest Territories, the remoteness of the area and its lack of motor vehicles made registrations unnecessary until 1941.

There were some motor vehicles in this region as long ago as 1920 when a Ford truck was brought there by the Hudson's Bay Company, but registrations were unknown before the first green and white license plate series was issued in 1941.

The 1942 series was retained for use both in 1943 and 1944 due to the wartime metal shortage, but from 1945 until 1966 plates were issued annually, carrying the abbreviation "N.W.T." and the date. From 1964 on, the legend "CANADA'S NORTHLAND" has appeared on the tags.

"NORTHWEST TERRITORIES" was spelled out in full on the 1966 series, and the territorial coat-of-arms was also used. This series was continued through 1969 with date tabs, the final numbers exceeding 10-000.

In observance of its centennial, 1970 and 1971 plates were issued in the shape of a polar bear.

NOVA SCOTIA—1907

Auto owners provided their own plates from the time of the first registrations in this province in 1907. The first number was assigned to W. M. Black of Wolfville on May 9, 1907.

Until the advent of provincially-issued markers in 1918, laws pertaining to number plates specified black on white as the legal color combination and called for the inclusion of the letters "N.S." Most of the pre-1918 tags were made of flat metal, although more expensive porcelain-enameled iron types were available on special order for fanciful motorists. These could be ordered from two stamp concerns in Halifax.

The first plates issued by the government were made of flat metal carrying the provincial coat-of-arms, but they were soon replaced by embossed metal tags.

The 1943 plates were used in 1944 again with windshield stickers; the 1952 series was used through 1956 with date strips attached to base plates.

Since 1960, Nova Scotia has used its plates for a minimum of two years.

ONTARIO—1903

The first province to register motor vehicles, Ontario assigned its first two numbers to John C. Eaton of Toronto for his Winton and National Electric cars. For 1903 and 1904 each car owner provided his own plates with aluminum numbers and a black leather background. Although no name or abbreviation was required, most — if not all — of the early tags included a small metal provincial coat-of-arms placed immediately above the numbers. A total of 178 motor vehicles were registered during 1903.

The first provincial number plates were issued for 1905 when some 553 automobiles were registered. The plates were white on black and made of pliable rubber; they were devoid of either identification or date and the series was continued through 1910. The design of the last plates of this series was augmented by a long white rectangle above the numbers — this is believed to have carried the date of expiration, but no one can be certain of this.

A white on blue porcelain-enameled series was issued in 1911, alike in design and color to the plates issued in Alberta for 1912, in British Columbia for 1913 and in Manitoba in 1911.

All Ontario plates were made of flat metal from 1912 through 1920 and they carried the provincial coat-of-arms. Embossed metal tags appeared for 1921.

The British crown has been incorporated into the plate design since 1937 and 1967 tags carried the word "CONFEDERATION."

PRINCE EDWARD ISLAND—1913

Prior to April 24, 1913, automobiles were not allowed to operate on Prince Edward Island, but a Provincial law which allowed their use was finally passed and the secretary of the Province was designated as registrar. To make it official, a pair of black on white number plates was issued to all owners. The aforementioned law also stipulated that numerals not less than four inches high and not less than one-half inch in stroke be used — plus the initial letters of the province appearing not less than two inches high. No material was stipulated.

It is doubtful that any official plates were issued until 1916, and a few examples of these early markers have turned up in both black on white and white on black, all made of painted tin without dates.

Dated embossed metal plates were issued in 1916, but tags remained dateless in the years following until 1923. A variety of plates was used during this dateless period including flat fiberboard in 1917, flat metal in 1918, porcelain-enameled iron in 1919 and embossed metal from 1920 through 1922.

Plates carried the province abbreviation "P.E.I." through 1925. "P.E. ISLAND" in 1926 and the island's full name since then.

Quick to recognize the advertising potential of its license plates, the provinces plugged "SEED POTATOES AND FOXES" in 1928, switching to "GARDEN OF THE GULF" in 1929-30 and 1962-65. Since 1966 the legend "GARDEN PROVINCE" has appeared on P.E.I. plates, and the province's coat-of-arms was included in the plates' design from 1938 through 1961.

An interesting feature of the island's plates is its numeric system: Beginning at 30,000, no lower numbers are used on plates, nor are official tags of special design known. Also noteworthy is a license plate experiment currently underway to test the reflectorized surfaces of tags: Approximately 250 of the lowest-numbered tags issued are dark blue on a red-orange reflectorized background rather than the conventional blue on tan regulation issue. Time will tell whether or not the bizarre reflectorized colors aid visibility.

If a motorist loses one of his plates in Prince Edward Island he must apply to the motor vehicle authorities who retain a stock of "blanks," or unnumbered plates. Upon payment of a fee, the motorist is issued a replacement plate — a "blank" with his number freshly painted upon it.

QUEBEC—1906

The earliest Quebec number plates were provided by the automobile owners themselves; the majority of these plates were constructed of tin with numbers painted on or of leather pads with metal house numbers attached. Most of them carried either the prefix letter "Q" or the provincial abbreviation "P.Q."

A Provincial law of 1910 required numbers to be carried, black on white, above the word "QUEBEC." Letters had to correspond in height to the numbers. Automobilists had their plates made for them in many instances and some of these manufactured plates were made of porcelain-enameled iron.

Newfoundland '37
Newfoundland '63
Newfoundland '69 —Plates advertised Churchill river.
Northwest Territory '41
Northwest Territory '69
Northwest Territory '70
Nova Scotia pre-1918 —Owners provided their own plates in Nova Scotia prior to 1918.

Nova Scotia '20
Nova Scotia '42
Nova Scotia Antique Auto plate
Ontario '05-'10 —This 1910 rubber plate was issued near the end of the series.
Ontario '20
Ontario '37
Ontario Historic Vehicle plate
Prince Edward Island '17

Prince Edward Island '26
Prince Edward Island '39
Prince Edward Island '62—Blank plates are kept on hand by the Motor Vehicle Bureau and assigned to motorists whose original plates have been lost or damaged. Numbers are then stenciled or painted by hand on blanks.

Prince Edward Island Antique plate
Quebec '22 —Quebec plates were constructed of flat-surfaced fiberboard through 1924.
Quebec '36
Quebec '67 —Front and rear plate design differed, with the front plate carrying an advertisement for 'Expo 67.'

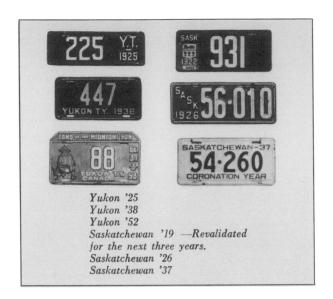

Yukon '25
Yukon '38
Yukon '52
Saskatchewan '19 —Revalidated
for the next three years.
Saskatchewan '26
Saskatchewan '37

Baja California, Mexico '24
State of Mexico, Mexico '28
Chihuahua, Mexico '28
Mexico (national plate) '38 —
National plates which carried no
state name or abbreviation were
used 1937-46.

State of Mexico, Mexico '50 —
Small plate with number corresponding to that on base plate
indicates vehicle owner paid full
registration fee and tax.
Baja California, Mexico '58-'59
Campeche, Mexico '68-'69 —

All motorcar owners except the Premier, Lieutenant-Governor, Motor Vehicle Registrar and Cardinal were required to register their automobiles; thus, in 1911, the first provincially-issued flat fibreboard plates appeared. These dateless markers included the "P.Q." abbreviation and were carried on both the front and rear of each motor vehicle. In 1915 the name "QUEBEC" was substituted for "P.Q." Fibreboard plates were in use through 1924 and plates were first dated a year earlier in 1923.

The first embossed metal tags replaced fibre plates in 1925; these have been issued annually ever since with the sole exception of 1944 when the Province returned to flat fibreboard tags because of the wartime metal shortage.

In 1945 the fleur-de-lys emblem, the lily of France and emblem of the Province of Quebec were incorporated into the plates' design. The words "LA BELLE PROVINCE" were added in 1963 and have been retained in the plates' design since then — with the exception of 1967 when the province promoted its Expo '67.

The Expo plates were perhaps the most complicated sets issued in either Canada or the U.S. because their designs differed in the front and rear markers: In addition to the date, "QUE" abbreviation, tiny number and fleur-de-lys emblem, the "EXPO '67" notice appeared on the front tags in large figures. Site of Expo, "MONTREAL" was also included. Rear plates carried the numbers in conventional size plus the dates "1867" and "1967," the word "CONFEDERATION" and a maple leaf insigne.

SASKATCHEWAN—1906

Although registrations were in effect as early as 1906 in Saskatchewan,

the first provincially-issued series only dates back to 1912 when porcelain-enameled iron plates were assigned to motorists, replacing the hand-made varieties in use at that time.

Porcelain plates were in use for 1912, 1913 and 1914, and the next series, made for 1915 through 1918, appeared in flat metal. The province returned to the porcelain-enameled type in 1919; this was a white on black plate sporting the provincial coat-of-arms revalidated with annual metal date tabs for three years.

Saskatchewan has issued annual tags since 1923 with the exception of 1944 when 1943 plates were used again. Plates of this province bore the words "CORONATION YEAR" in 1937 and in 1955 "GOLDEN JUBILEE" appeared on plates. Saskatchewan reminded plate spotters of its fame as the "WHEAT PROVINCE" between 1951 and 1959 and "CANADA CENTENNIAL" was added to its tags in 1967.

YUKON TERRITORY—1917

The first plates issued in the Yukon Territory in 1917 were made of flat metal and were hand painted black on white; they carried the abbreviation "Y.T." as well as the date. The colors, material and design were continued through 1923 without change other than the date which, of course, changed annually.

Although similar in design to these first plates, markers were made of embossed metal between 1924 and 1930. In 1931 the "Y.T." abbreviation was abandoned in favor of "YUKON TY." which was retained through 1955. Since 1956 the single name "YUKON" has been used.

The now-famous insigne depicting a miner panning for gold was added to the plates' design in 1952 and between that year and 1970 this insigne was accompanied by the legend "LAND OF THE MIDNIGHT SUN."

490

MEXICO

The history of Mexican license plates is a complicated one because, prior to the first national registrations in 1933, each state and territory — not to mention the Federal District — issued plates of their own design. Predictably, colors, shapes and sizes of these plates varied wildly; to complicate the matter further, different types of vehicles were assigned different color schemes, a Mexican custom which has been retained to this day.

Standardization came in 1933 when the first national plates were issued. These were black on orange (for passenger cars) and carried the name of the state or territory on them. They were also revalidated in 1934 with a plate tab.

A new and similarly designed series was issued in 1935 and again in 1936, but the latter series was distinguished by its glass numerals which represented a sort of experiment in reflectorization.

Individual state names were dropped with the 1937 series and from that year through 1946 the plates carried only the name "MEXICO" and the date. Series plates of 1937 and 1938 were abnormally large, measuring 13⅝ x 7¾ inches; ironically, plate sizes were gradually reduced after 1938 until Mexico could claim, by 1947, some of the smallest markers in North America: 11 x 4¾ inches. These mini-plates were used through 1949, gradually assuming standard North American proportions by 1958.

Mexico's first two-year plates were issued in 1954 and these have been in use ever since. Host for the World Olympics in 1967-68, Mexico advertised the event by carrying the Olympics insigne — five intertwined rings — on its plates. Current plates include the dates "70" and "71," the state or territorial abbreviation ("D.F." for Distrito-Federal) and a second abbreviation, "MEX."

PASSENGER CAR REGISTRATION FOR THE YEAR 1970

Preliminary Figures by State

State	Registration	State	Registration
Alabama	1,510,000	Missouri	1,890,000
Alaska	96,000	Montana	321,000
Arizona	832,000	Nebraska	689,000
Arkansas	677,000	Nevada	261,000
California	9,964,000	New Hampshire	327,000
Colorado	1,099,000	New Jersey	3,281,000
Connecticut	1,534,000	New Mexico	455,000
Delaware	265,000	New York	5,978,000
District of Columbia	230,000	North Carolina	2,235,000
Florida	3,570,000	North Dakota	272,000
Georgia	2,088,000	Ohio	5,331,000
Hawaii	349,000	Oklahoma	1,206,000
Idaho	333,000	Oregon	1,123,000
Illinois	4,648,000	Pennsylvania	5,185,000
Indiana	2,304,000	Rhode Island	425,000
Iowa	1,398,000	South Carolina	1,112,000
Kansas	1,134,000	South Dakota	290,000
Kentucky	1,375,000	Tennessee	1,618,000
Louisiana	1,418,000	Texas	5,224,000
Maine	407,000	Utah	482,000
Maryland	1,638,000	Vermont	188,000
Massachusetts	2,250,000	Virginia	1,899,000
Michigan	4,045,000	Washington	1,716,000
Minnesota	1,752,000	West Virginia	684,000
Mississippi	819,000	Wisconsin	1,775,000
		Wyoming	159,000

SOURCE: U.S. Department of Transportation, Bureau of Public Roads

TOTAL PASSENGER CAR REGISTRATIONS IN THE UNITED STATES 1900-1970

Year	Registrations
1900	8,000
1905	77,400
1910	458,377
1915	2,332,426
1920	8,131,522
1925	17,439,701
1930	22,972,745
1935	22,494,884
1940	27,372,397
1945	25,694,926
1950	40,190,632
1951	42,530,935
1952	43,659,062
1953	46,258,305
1954	48,293,457
1955	51,960,532
1956	54,013,753
1957	55,704,636
1958	56,664,435
1959	59,213,993
1960	61,430,862
1961	63,153,425
1962	65,824,939
1963	68,755,848
1964	71,663,851
1965	79,903,163
1966	77,750,764
1967	80,013,724
1968	83,276,317
1969	86,861,334
1970*	89,861,000

*preliminary figure

XIV

ROSTER OF AUTOMOBILE CLUBS & REGISTERS OF THE UNITED STATES & CANADA

BY AUTOMOBILE QUARTERLY

The idea of automobilists banding together in common cause is scarcely a new one. In the United States it can be traced back to the American Motor League, which was founded for "the general advancement of the new fledged motor interest in America" and whose first meeting was attended by such motor enthusiasts as Charles E. and J. Frank Duryea, Charles B. King, Elwood Haynes, Henry G. Morris and Pedro G. Salom. That was November of 1895. Four decades later—in November of 1935 —a handful of individuals gathered in Philadelphia to join forces in appreciation of the Motor League pioneers and all those who followed them, by creating the first American car club dedicated to the history of the motorcar: the Antique Automobile Club of America. Two years later the Horseless Carriage Club of America was founded, and in 1938 the Veteran Motor Car Club of America.

The success of these car clubs paved the way for a proliferation of others with interests in varied types of cars: the Sports Car Club of America, founded in 1944; the Classic Car Club of America, organized in 1952; the Vintage Sports Car Club of America in 1959. The Fifties, too, saw a flourishing of single-marque clubs—Auburn, Cord and Duesenberg devotees, Packard, Franklin and Model T enthusiasts, all joining forces in the cause of their favored automobiles. Their ranks have swelled impressively.

Significant in recent years has been the growth of clubs dedicated to automobiles or types of automobiles not generally included in the antique, classic or sports classifications. These have sometimes been referred to as "special interest" cars. Single-marque clubs devoted to such varied automobiles as the Lincoln Zephyr and the Corvair thrive. Multi-marque clubs of this genre include the Contemporary Historical Vehicle Association and the Milestone Car Society. The emergence of clubs such as these is an encouraging sign that the significant automobiles of today will not be lost tomorrow. What that small band of automobilists began in 1935 has become a nationwide enthusiasm.

The list that follows is confined to clubs of the United States and Canada: first, the general clubs—those devoted to all makes of automobile within a particular period or classification. This is followed by American marque clubs—those organizations dedicated to specific American cars.

The car club movement is, of course, an international one. Indeed the British movement preceded America's by five years, with the founding of the Veteran Car Club in 1930—and in Germany the Allgemeiner Schnauferl Club has been flourishing since 1900. The number of clubs overseas has increased with the self-same rapidity as it has in North America—and there's arisen an international comraderie among enthusiasts which we've been delighted to enjoy through correspondence undertaken in the compilation of our international roster of clubs included in AUTOMOBILE *Quarterly's* Cumulative Indexes. Just as Great Britain has a number of thriving clubs devoted to American cars, and Australian enthusiasts have joined together in clubs to perpetuate the Model T, the Packard and the Cadillac, so too in America there have been founded dozens of clubs dedicated to foreign marques such as Bugatti, Alfa Romeo and Porsche. Significantly, interest in the automobile knows no borders.

ANTIQUE AUTOMOBILE CLUB OF AMERICA
501 West Governor Road, Hershey, Pennsylvania 17033

ANTIQUE AND CLASSIC AUTOMOBILE CLUB OF THE
WABASH VALLEY, INC.
c/o Charles Hilton, Jr., 2011 Barton Avenue, Terre Haute,
Indiana 47802

ANTIQUE AND CLASSIC CAR CLUB OF BUTLER
COUNTY
6 Court Street, Hamilton, Ohio 45011

ANTIQUE COMMERCIAL VEHICLE CLUB OF AMERICA
c/o Milton S. Hill, 3616 Coronado Avenue, Farmington, New
Mexico 87401

ANTIQUE MOTOR CLUB
c/o Harold Akers, R.D. 3, Box 30, Rockville, Indiana 47872

ANTIQUE TRUCK CLUB
Lyons Transportation Company, Erie, Pennsylvania

ARKANSAS ANTIQUE CAR CLUB
c/o William J. Harris, 2005 Edgewood Drive, Jonesboro,
Arkansas 72401

AUTO ENTHUSIASTS INTERNATIONAL
Box 2379, Dearborn, Michigan 48123

AUTOMOBILISTS OF THE UPPER HUDSON VALLEY
c/o Keith Marvin, Record Newspapers, Troy, New York 12181

AUTOMOTIVE OLD TIMERS, INC.
P.O. Box 62, Warrenton, Virginia 22186

CAPITOL CITY OLD CAR CLUB, INC.
1225 Edward, Lansing, Michigan 48910

CENTRAL INDIANA OLD CAR CLUB
c/o Jack Burroughs, 717 Vermillion Court, Anderson, Indiana
46012

CERCLE CONCOURS D'ELEGANCE, LE
9476 Readcrest Drive, Beverly Hills, California 90210

CLASSIC AND ANTIQUE RESTORERS CLUB
c/o Harold J. Carr, 212 E. Chicago Road, White Pigeon,
Michigan 49009

CLASSIC CAR CLUB OF AMERICA, THE
Box 443, Madison, New Jersey 07940

CLINTON COUNTY ANTIQUE AND CLASSIC CAR CLUB
151 Oak Street, Wilmington, Ohio 45177

CLUB DE LA CARROSSERIE
249 East 50th Street, New York, New York 10022

COLES COUNTY OLD CAR CLUB
c/o Herman Briggerman, R.R. 1, Charleston, Illinois 61920

CONTEMPORARY HISTORICAL VEHICLE ASSOCIATION,
INC.
71 Lucky Road, Severn, Maryland 21144

CORTLAND ANTIQUE AUTOMOBILE CLUB
c/o Richard McKnight, Box 375, Tully, New York 13159

FORT WAYNE HISTORICAL AUTO ASSOCIATION
c/o Ann Staadt, 9955 Wayne Terrace, Fort Wayne, Indiana

FREMONT ANTIQUE AUTO CLUB
c/o E. W. Hancock, 1635 North Broad Street, Fremont,
Nebraska 68025

FRONT-WHEEL DRIVE CLUB
P.O. Box 22, San Marcos, California 92069

HISTORIC AUTO ASSOCIATION OF MICHIGAN
R.F.D. 2, 117 U.S. #12-W, Sturgis, Michigan 49091

HISTORICAL AUTOMOBILE CLUB OF THE BLACK HILLS
c/o Dorothy Ostrander, 2115 Sioux Avenue, Rapid City,
South Dakota 57701

HORSELESS CARRIAGE CLUB OF AMERICA
9031 East Florence, Downey, California 90240

HORSELESS CARRIAGE CLUB OF NEVADA
P.O. Box 5414, Reno, Nevada 89502

HUNTERTOWN PIONEER CLUB, INC.
c/o M. E. Koester, 7022 Stellhorn Road, Fort Wayne,
Indiana 46085

ILIANA ANTIQUE AUTO CLUB
P.O. Box 245, Danville, Illinois 61833

INDIANA CLASSIC CAR CLUB
c/o J. Dougherty, R.R. 1, Box 764, Indianapolis, Indiana
46227

INTERNATIONAL TRUCK RESTORERS ASSOCIATION
2026 Beyer Avenue, Fort Wayne, Indiana 46805

KALAMAZOO AUTO RESTORERS CLUB
c/o Norman Knight, 7383 North 12th Street, Kalamazoo,
Michigan 49001

KOKOMO PIONEER AUTO CLUB
c/o Mrs. Jayne McLure, 1810 South Union Street, Kokomo,
Indiana 46902

LAFAYETTE INDIANA HISTORIC AUTO CLUB
P.O. Box 191, Lafayette, Indiana 47902

MADISON AVENUE SPORTS CAR DRIVING
& CHOWDER SOCIETY
234 West 44th Street, New York, New York

MAINE OBSOLETE AUTOMOBILE LEAGUE
c/o Robert J. Dingley, Box 12, Naples, Maine 04055

METRO-EAST ANTIQUE AUTOMOBILE CLUB
c/o B. Serni, 1927 Third Street, Madison, Illinois 62060

MID-AMERICA OLD TIME AUTOMOBILE ASSOCIATION
1749 Mignon, Memphis, Tennessee 38107

MIDWESTERN COUNCIL OF SPORTS CAR CLUBS
1812-R N. Kennicott Avenue, Arlington Heights, Illinois
60004

MILESTONE CAR SOCIETY
P.O. Box 1166, Pacific Palisades, California 90272

MISSISSIPPI VALLEY HISTORIC AUTOMOBILE CLUB
c/o Quinsippi Island Antique Auto Museum, All America
City Park, Front and Cedar, Quincy, Illinois 62301

NORTH SHORE ANTIQUE CLUB OF NEW JERSEY
141 Clark Avenue, Ocean Grove, New Jersey 07756

NORTH SHORE OLD CAR CLUB
8 Pierce Street, Marblehead, Massachusetts 01945

OLD CAR CLUB, INC.
30 Hudson Street, Northborough, Massachusetts 01532

OLYMPIC VINTAGE AUTO CLUB
P.O. Box 2023 Sheridan Park Station, Bremerton, Washington
98310

PIONEER AUTOMOBILE ASSOCIATION
c/o James R. Cerney, 17445 Battles Lane, South Bend,
Indiana 46614

PIONEER AUTOMOBILE CLUB OF NORTHWESTERN
OHIO
410 North Main Street, Dunkirk, Ohio 45836

PIONEER AUTOMOBILE TOURING CLUB
252 North 7th Street, Allentown, Pennsylvania 18102

PIONEER ENGINEER CLUB OF INDIANA, INC.
c/o Eldon Myers, 5349 Guion Road, Indianapolis, Indiana
46254

SCIOTO ANTIQUE MOTOR CLUB
P.O. Box 463, Portsmouth, Ohio 45662

SOCIETY FOR THE PRESERVATION AND
APPRECIATION OF ANTIQUE MOTOR FIRE
APPARATUS IN AMERICA
184 Jasper Street, Syracuse, New York 13203

SOCIETY OF AUTOMOTIVE HISTORIANS
460 Ridgewood Crescent, London 63, Ontario

SOUTH BEND PIONEER AUTOMOBILE ASSOCIATION
c/o Harold D. Fairchild, 160 North Main Street, Nappanee,
Indiana 46550

SOUTH SHORE ANTIQUE AUTO CLUB
P.O. Box 266, Holbrook, Massachusetts 02343

SOUTHEAST IOWA ANTIQUE CAR CLUB
Box 1, Mount Pleasant, Iowa

STEAM AUTOMOBILE CLUB OF AMERICA, INC.
1937 East 71st Street, Chicago Illinois 60649

SPORTS CAR CLUB OF AMERICA
P.O. Box 791 Westport, Connecticut 06880

SPORTS CAR COLLECTORS SOCIETY OF AMERICA
Box 1855, Quantico, Virginia 22134

TERRE HAUTE ANTIQUE & CLASSIC AUTO CLUB
c/o James A. Shaw, 1500 Lafayette Avenue, Terre Haute,
Indiana 47804

VETERAN MOTOR CAR CLUB OF AMERICA
15 Newton Street, Brookline, Massachusetts 02146

VINTAGE SPORTS CAR CLUB
4350 North Knox Avenue, Chicago, Illinois 60641

VINTAGE SPORTS CAR CLUB OF AMERICA
61 Boxwood Lane, Hicksville, New York 11801

WINAMAC OLD AUTO CLUB
c/o Mrs. Elouise Hollenbaugh, 11 Rimbach Street, Hammond,
Indiana 46320

Canada

ALBERTA PIONEER AUTO CLUB
c/o Gordon R. Campbell, 10447 Brackenridge Road, S.W.
Calgary 14, Alberta

ANTIQUE AUTO ASSOCIATION OF REGINA
P.O. Box 501, Regina, Saskatchewan

ANTIQUE AUTOMOBILE CLUB OF OTTAWA, INC.
Box 2525, Ottawa, Ontario

ANTIQUE AUTO CLUB OF SASKATCHEWAN
P.O. Sub 1, Box 106, Moose Jaw, Saskatchewan

ANTIQUE AND CLASSIC CAR CLUB OF CANADA
P.O. Box 1304, Postal Terminal 'A', Toronto 1, Ontario

CENTRAL NEWFOUNDLAND ANTIQUE CAR CLUB
Main Street, Windsor, Newfoundland

EDMONTON ANTIQUE CAR CLUB
Box 102, Edmonton, Alberta

HALIFAX ANTIQUE CAR CLUB
P.O. Box 2302, Halifax, Nova Scotia

HISTORICAL AUTOMOBILE SOCIETY OF CANADA
c/o Donald F. Warren, 72 South Street W., Dundas, Ontario

HISTORIC VEHICLE SOCIETY OF ONTARIO
c/o S.H. Scratch, 3790 Riberdy Road, Windsor, Ontario

LAKEHEAD ANTIQUE AUTO CLUB
c/o J. D. Squirrell, 1 Squirrell Drive, R.R. 12, Thunder Bay 'N', Ontario

MANITOBA CLASSIC AND ANTIQUE AUTO CLUB
53 Moore Avenue, Winnipeg 8, Manitoba

NEW BRUNSWICK ANTIQUE AUTO CLUB
P.O. Box 115, Fredericton, New Brunswick

PRINCE EDWARD ISLAND ANTIQUE AUTO CLUB
P.O. Box 534, Charlottetown, Prince Edward Island

ROARING TWENTIES ANTIQUE AUTO CLUB
Box 188, Yarmouth, Nova Scotia

SASKATCHEWAN ANTIQUE AUTO CLUB
201 Avenue 'G' North, Saskatoon, Saskatchewan

VEHICLE RESTORERS ASSOCIATION
Box 761, Regina, Saskatchewan

VINTAGE AUTOMOBILE CLUB OF MONTREAL
c/o S. Macbeth, P.O. Box 246, N.D.G. Station Montreal 260, Quebec

VINTAGE CAR CLUB OF CANADA
Box 2070, Vancouver, British Columbia

YORKTON ANTIQUE CAR CLUB
137 Smith Street, Yorkton, Saskatchewan

American Marque Clubs

AHRENS-FOX
AHRENS-FOX FIRE BUFFS CLUB
R.D. 2, Box 233, Schwenksville, Pennsylvania 19473

AMERICAN AUSTIN
AMERICAN AUSTIN-BANTAM CLUB
P.O. Box 328, Morris, New York 13808

PACIFIC BANTAM AUSTIN CLUB
3315 Viscount Street, Alhambra, California 91803

AMERICAN MOTORS
JAVAMX, INC.
P.O. Box 2191, Costa Mesa, California 92626

AUBURN
AUBURN-CORD-DUESENBERG CLUB, INC.
Box 1614, Chico, California 95925

AVANTI
AVANTI OWNERS ASSOCIATION INTERNATIONAL, INC.
Box 2626, Cincinnati, Ohio 45201

BARRACUDA
NATIONAL BARRACUDA OWNERS CLUB
P.O. Box 478, Detroit, Michigan 48232

BUICK
BUICK CLUB OF AMERICA
P.O. Box 853, Garden Grove, California 92642

McLAUGHLIN BUICK CLUB OF AMERICA
409 Tecumseh Street, Newmarket, Ontario, Canada

CADILLAC
CADILLAC AUTOMOBILE CLUB
(For all Cadillacs over ten years old)
P.O. Box 2842-D, Pasadena, California 91105

CADILLAC-LASALLE CLUB, INC.
3340 Poplar Drive, Warren, Michigan 48091

CHEVROLET
NATIONAL CHEVROLET RESTORERS CLUB
P.O. Box 311, La Mirada, California 90638

NATIONAL NOMAD CLUB
50 Teller, Lakewood, Colorado 80226

1911 CHEVROLET REGISTER
c/o Larry Burke, 6528 South Main, Anderson, Indiana 46013

VINTAGE CHEVROLET CLUB OF AMERICA, INC.
2812 Garfield, Box 152, Orange, California 92667

CHRYSLER
AIRFLOW CLUB OF AMERICA
(for Chrysler and DeSoto Airflow automobiles)
1475 President Street, Yellow Springs, Ohio 45387

CHRYSLER AUTO CLUB
Western Division: c/o Ray Doeon, 4614 S.E. 32nd, Portland, Oregon 97202

CHRYSLER RESTORERS CLUB
(Eastern Region of the W.P.C. Club)
5986 Irishtown Road, Bethel Park, Pennsylvania 15102

CHRYSLER 300 OWNERS CLUB
c/o Robert Dupin, 3033 Curran Road, Louisville, Kentucky 40205

DODGE, CHRYSLER, PLYMOUTH, DESOTO AND MAXWELL CLUB
928 East 81st Street, Brooklyn, New York 11236

GOLDEN LIONS
909 Edgewood Terrace, Wilmington, Delaware 19809

W.P.C. CLUB
(Walter P. Chrysler Club)
17916 Trenton Drive, Castro Valley, California 94546

CORVAIR
CORVAIR SOCIETY OF AMERICA (CORSA), INC.
209 Lyndhurst, Piqua, Ohio 45356

CORVETTE
NATIONAL COUNCIL OF CORVETTE CLUBS, INC.
c/o G.A. Gross, 6672 Balsam Drive, Reynoldsburg, Ohio 43068

VINTAGE CORVETTE CLUB OF AMERICA
2359 West Adams, Fresno, California 93706

CROSLEY
CROSLEY AUTOMOBILE CLUB
15 Westminster Drive, Montville, New Jersey 07045

MIAMISBURG CROSLEY CAR CLUB
10 Bradstreet Road, No. 8-B, Centerville, Ohio 45459

DESOTO
DESOTO CLUB OF AMERICA
Box 4912, Columbus, Ohio 43202

DURANT
DURANT OWNERS CLUB
7614 Langdon Street, Philadelphia, Pennsylvania 19111

EDSEL
EDSEL OWNERS CLUB OF AMERICA, INC.
P.O. Box 7, West Liberty, Illinois 62475

INTERNATIONAL EDSEL CLUB
P.O. Box 304, Bellevue, Ohio 44811

ERSKINE
ERSKINE REGISTER
441 East St., Clair Street, Almont, Michigan 48003

FAIRTHORPE
FRIENDS OF THE FAIRTHORPE
182 Menands Road, Londonville, New York 12211

FORD
EARLY FORD V-8 CLUB OF AMERICA, INC.
P.O. Box 2122, San Leandro, California 94577

FORD AND MERCURY RESTORERS CLUB
P.O. Box 2133, Dearborn, Michigan 48123

FORD MOTORSPORTS ASSOCIATION
12263 Market Street, Livonia, Michigan 48150

FORTIES LTD.
(For 1939, 1940, 1941 Fords)
16752 Huggins Avenue, Yorba Linda, California 92686

LONG BEACH MODEL T CLUB, INC.
c/o E. Enyeart, 5608 Keynote, Long Beach, California

MEADOWLARK MODEL A FORD CLUB
c/o William Sprague, 713 East 7th Street, Papillion, Nebraska 68046

MODEL A FORD CLUB OF AMERICA
Box 2564, Pomona, California 91766

MODEL A FORD CLUB OF PEMBROKE
624 Bruham Avenue, Pembroke, Ontario

MODEL A RESTORERS CLUB
P.O. Box 1930A, Dearborn, Michigan

MODEL T FORD CLUB OF AMERICA
P.O. Box 711, Tarzana, California 91356

MODEL T FORD CLUB INTERNATIONAL
c/o The Allerton, 701 North Michigan Avenue, Chicago, Illinois 60611

OLD FORD CLUB OF MIAMI
11635 N.W. 58th Court, Hialeah, Florida 33012

RETRACTABLE FORD CLUB
1761 National Road, Dayton, Ohio 45414

FRANKLIN

H. H. FRANKLIN
P.O. Box 66, Onondaga Branch, Syracuse, New York 13215

FRONTENAC

FRONTENAC CLUB
45 Greenwood Street, Tamaqua, Pennsylvania 18252

GENERAL MOTORS

GENERAL MOTORS RESTORERS CLUB
P.O. Box 143, Highland Station, Springfield, Massachusetts 01109

GRAHAM-PAIGE

GRAHAM-PAIGE REGISTRY
c/o Andrew Wittenborn, 109 Edgemont Road, Scarsdale, New York 10583

HAYNES

HAYNES AND APPERSON OWNERS CLUB
409 East Walnut Street, Kokomo, Indiana 46901

HUDSON

HUDSON-ESSEX-TERRAPLANE CLUB
R.D. #3, Box 289, Warren, Indiana 46792

HUPMOBILE

THE HUPMOBILE CLUB
Box AA, Rosemead, California 91770

JEEPSTER

MIDSTATES JEEPSTER ASSOCIATION
312 South Sterling Street, Streator, Illinois 61364

WILLYS-OVERLAND JEEPSTER CLUB
c/o Jay Sherwin, 395 Dumbarton Boulevard, Cleveland, Ohio 44143

KAISER

KAISER-FRAZER OWNERS CLUB INTERNATIONAL, INC.
4015 South Forest, Independence, Missouri 64052

KISSEL

KISSEL KAR KLUB (INTERNATIONAL)
546 North Main Street, Hartford, Wisconsin 53027

LINCOLN

LINCOLN CONTINENTAL OWNERS CLUB
Box 549, Nogales, Arizona 85621

LINCOLN OWNERS CLUB
P.O. Box 189, Algonquin, Illinois 60102

LINCOLN ZEPHYR OWNERS CLUB
Box 185, Middletown, Pennsylvania 17059

MARMON

MARMON OWNERS CLUB
5364 Stuart Avenue S.E., Grand Rapids, Michigan 49508

MERCER

MERCER ASSOCIATES
MGT Department, Texas Tech, Lubbock, Texas

METZ

METZ OWNERS CLUB
c/o Franklin E. Tucker, 216 Central Avenue, West Caldwell, New Jersey 07006

NASH

NASH CAR CLUB OF AMERICA
c/o James F. Dworschack, 1006 North 3rd Street, Clinton, Iowa 52732

NASH CLUB
c/o Robert Sohl, Star Route, Box 28, Woodside, California 94062

NASH-HEALEY CAR CLUB
c/o Richard M. Kauffman, R.D. 2, Boyertown, Pennsylvania 19512

OLDSMOBILE

CURVED DASH OLDS OWNERS CLUB
c/o C. C. Green, 61 York Street, Lambertville, New Jersey 08530

OLDSMOBILE CLUB OF AMERICA
Box 1498, Samp Motar Station, Fairfield, Connecticut 06430

PACKARD

PACKARD AUTOMOBILE CLASSICS, INC.
P.O. Box 2808 Oakland, California 94611

PACKARDS INTERNATIONAL MOTOR CAR CLUB, INC.
P.O. Box 1347, Costa Mesa, California 92626

PIERCE-ARROW

PIERCE-ARROW SOCIETY, INC.
135 Edgerton Street, Rochester, New York 14607

PLYMOUTH

PLYMOUTH 4 & 6 CYLINDER OWNERS CLUB
c/o Robert Bender, R.D. 1, Box 305, Jeanette, Pennsylvania 15644

PONTIAC

PONTIAC OWNERS CLUB INTERNATIONAL
c/o Donald A. Bougher, Box 612, Escondido, California 92025

SAFARI CLUB OF AMERICA
220 17th Avenue S., Seattle, Washington 98144

REO

REO-OLDS CLUB
c/o N. B. Horsfall, 319 Templeton Avenue, Winnipeg 17, Manitoba

RICKENBACKER

RICKENBACKER CLUB
c/o Michael McBride, 13572 Appoline, Detroit, Michigan 48227

SIMPLEX

SIMPLEX AUTOMOBILE CLUB
Meadow Spring, Glen Cove, New York 11542

STEVENS-DURYEA

STEVENS-DURYEA ASSOCIATES
3565 Newhaven Road, Pasadena, California 91107

STUDEBAKER

ANTIQUE STUDEBAKER CLUB
175 May Avenue, Monrovia, California 91016

STUDEBAKER DRIVERS CLUB
Box 3044, South Bend, Indiana 46619

STUDEBAKER OWNERS CLUB
Box 5294, Pasadena, California 91107

STUTZ

STUTZ NUTS
c/o C. McCord Purdy, 3856 Arthington Boulevard, Indianapolis, Indiana 46226

THUNDERBIRD

CLASSIC THUNDERBIRD CLUB, INTERNATIONAL
48 Second Street, San Francisco, California 94105

VINTAGE THUNDERBIRD CLUB OF AMERICA
147 S. 117 East Avenue, Seattle, Washington

TUCKER

TUCKER REGISTER
c/o W. B. Hamlin, 229 East Rosewood Court, Ontario, California 91762

WILLS SAINTE CLAIRE

THE WILLS CLUB
705 South Clyde Avenue, Kissimmee, Florida 32741

WILLYS-KNIGHT, WILLYS-OVERLAND

WILLYS-OVERLAND-KNIGHT REGISTRY
2754 Lullington Drive, Winston Salem, North Carolina 27103

CROSS REFERENCES TO MARQUE CLUB LIST

APPERSON, see "Haynes"
BUICK, see also "General Motors"
CADILLAC, see also "General Motors"
CHEVROLET, see also "Corvair," "Corvette," "Frontenac," "General Motors"
CONTINENTAL, see "Lincoln"
CORD, see "Auburn"
DODGE, see "Chrysler"
DUESENBERG, see "Auburn"
ESSEX, see "Hudson"
FLINT, see "Durant"
FORD, see also "Edsel," "Thunderbird"
FRAZER, see "Kaiser"
FRONTENAC, see also "Durant"
GENERAL MOTORS, see also "Buick," "Cadillac," "Chevrolet," "Pontiac," "Oldsmobile"
HENRY J, see "Kaiser"
JAVELIN, see "American Motors"
LASALLE, see "Cadillac"
MAXWELL, see "Chrysler"
MERCURY, see "Ford"
OLDSMOBILE, see also "General Motors," "Reo"
PLYMOUTH, see also "Barracuda," "Chrysler"
WILLYS-OVERLAND, see also "Jeepster"

XV

•

LISTING OF AUTOMOBILE MUSEUMS & COLLECTIONS IN THE UNITED STATES & CANADA

BY AUTOMOBILE QUARTERLY

We once observed that a museum is a place where artifacts go to die. No longer able to fulfill the function intended by their creator, they languish, depersonalized and disused—or unusable. But an automobile museum, that's something else again. One feels that an automobile hasn't arrived there to die, but rather to be put out to pasture to enjoy a well-deserved rest. If called upon, it would be happy to demonstrate that it not only once could—and did—but that it still can.

This curious immortality which the automobile enjoys may be partly responsible for the fact that only recently has it become an object of historic value, worthy of being meticulously studied and documented, and most important, collected and preserved. Interestingly, this didn't begin to happen on a significant scale until after the Second World War, although the automobile had long before made its impact upon us. Prior to that the idea of collecting and preserving venerable old cars had been the pursuit of but a handful of farsighted enthusiasts, among them, in this country, Lindley Bothwell, James Melton, D. Cameron Peck, George H. Waterman and Kirkland Gibson. At the time the concept of a museum devoted exclusively to the automobile was virtually unheard of. A pacesetter in this regard was Albert B. Garganigo who opened his personal collection to the public in 1939. Even public or institutional museums devoting a part of their exhibition space to automobiles were the exception, not the rule. There were probably less than a dozen throughout the world. In America these included the Smithsonian Institution, the Thompson Auto-Album and Aviation Museum, the Chicago Museum of Science and Industry, and the now closed New York Museum of Science and Industry and Stevens Institute of Technology.

Happily all this changed during the Fifties and Sixties. Phenomenal is a word too often casually used, but it is certainly appropriate to describe the postwar proliferation of museums devoted to the automobile, as this list will attest. And just as happily, that growth shows no sign of retarding. Every four years AUTOMOBILE *Quarterly* includes in its Cumulative Index an international roster of museums. Between the first such index and the second—a scant four years—we learned of no fewer than fifty new museums and collections throughout the world. And we expect that four years hence the list will have grown just as dramatically.

The AUTOMOBILE *Quarterly* list that follows, in keeping with the subject of this book, is confined to museums in the United States and Canada. Predominately, it concentrates upon public museums, that is, museums open to the general public at scheduled hours. In some cases—because of their historic importance—private collections which may be viewed by appointment have been included as well. Also featured is a capsule description of what one may expect to find at these museums, the number of cars on display, a sampling of noteworthy American cars in the collection and the availability of literature about the museum for those readers who might wish to write for it. Admission charges, dates and scheduled hours for viewing are also given. These latter, of course, are subject to change and it is suggested that planned visits be confirmed in advance.

The automobile has really come into its own. Its social and technological aspects are a continuing subject of interest, but now it is being looked upon aesthetically as well. The automobile as a work of art has been the focus of exhibitions, for example, at New York's Museum of Modern Art, the Rhode Island School of Design's Museum of Art and at the Louvre in Paris. The automobile—technically, socially and aesthetically—commands attention. It is altogether reassuring that there are so many museums to demonstrate to us why.

Arkansas

THE MUSEUM OF AUTOMOBILES
Petit Jean Mountain, Morrilton 72110
Director: Buddy Hoelzeman
Number of Cars: 50
Noteworthy Features: 1933 Chrysler Imperial phaeton; 1933 Stutz Super Bearcat; 1905 Model B Ford.
Status: Open to the public 10 a.m. to 5 p.m. daily.
Admission: Adults $1.00; children 12-16 $.50, under 12 free if accompanied by parent.

California

BRIGGS CUNNINGHAM AUTOMOTIVE MUSEUM
250 Baker Street, Costa Mesa, 92627
Director: John W. Burgess, Sr.
Number of Cars: 90
Noteworthy Features: Automobiles from 1898 to 1969, Automotive artwork. 1910 American Underslung; 1917 Cunningham boattail speedster; 1926 Duesenberg racer; Duesenberg J and SSJ; 1932 KB Lincoln; 1924 Locomobile; 1931 V-16 Marmon; 1933 V-12 Packard; 1915 Model 48 Pierce-Arrow; 1932 DV-32 Stutz; 1922 Wills Sainte Claire.
Status: Open to the public 10 a.m. to 5 p.m. daily
Admission: Adults $2.00; children 5-12 $.50; students and military personnel $1.50 with proper I.D.
Publications: Brochure available.

LOS ANGELES COUNTY MUSEUM OF NATURAL HISTORY
900 Exposition Boulevard, Los Angeles 90007
Director: Dr. Herbert Friedmann
Number of Cars: 32
Noteworthy Features: 1907 Studebaker-Garford; 1965 Chrysler gas turbine car. Extensive automobile research and photographic library.
Status: Open to the public 10 a.m. to 5 p.m. daily except Monday. Closed Thanksgiving and Christmas.
Admission: Free.
Publications: Catalogue.

MILLER'S CALIFORNIA RANCH HORSE & BUGGY DISPLAY
Route #9, Yosemite Boulevard, Modesto
Director: Mrs. Pierce A. Miller
Number of Cars: 8
Noteworthy Features: 1901 curved dash Olds; 1906 Sears; 1907 single-cylinder Reo; 1915 Pierce-Arrow; 1912 Studebaker; 16-cylinder Cadillac ambulance; 1900 Success auto buggy; 1911 Hudson. Extensive horse-drawn carriage collection.
Status: Open to the public during daylight hours; other times by appointment.
Admission: Adults, $.50; children $.25.
Publication: Flyer.

JACK PASSEY JR. AUTOMOBILE COLLECTION
3210 South Bascom Avenue, San Jose 95124
Director: Jack Passey, Jr.
Number of Cars: 65
Noteworthy Features: Largest known Lincoln collection. 1913 Pope-Hartford; 1915-1925 Locomobiles; 1920 Milburn electric; 1913-1931 Pierce-Arrows; Duesenberg Models A and J; 1922 Cunningham; Packard Super Eight and Twelve; 1913 Pierce-Arrow; 1921 Wills Sainte Claire; 1906 Maxwell.

Status: Open by appointment.
Admission: Adults $1.00; children $.25.

Colorado

COLORADO CAR MUSEUM
Business Route 24 and Midland Expressway, Manitou Springs
Noteworthy Features: 1903 Cadillac, 1907 Sears high wheeler, Presidential limousines, Count Ciano's Lancia.
Status: Open to the public weekdays at 9 a.m. Sundays at 10:30 a.m., evenings during summer season
Admission: Adults $1.00; children 5-12 $.35, children under 5 free.
Publications: Brochure available.

RAY DOUGHERTY COLLECTION
Route 2, Box 253-A, Longmont
Number of Cars: 40
Noteworthy Features: 1903 Cadillac Model A; 1908 Waverley Electric victoria phaeton; 1914 Stanley Model 607; 1908 International; 1906 Stevens-Duryea; 1908 "30" Packard; 1909 Reo; 1912 E.M.F.; 1912 Case; 1914 Metz; 1916 Franklin; 1916 Packard Twin-Six; 1917 Studebaker; 1917 White truck; 1910 Lozier Briarcliff; 1918 Kissel truck. Antique horse-drawn equipment, farm machinery, guns, musical instruments.
Status: Private collection; open by appointment only.
Admission: Free.

FORNEY TRANSPORTATION MUSEUM
1416 Platte Street, Denver 80202
Director: J. D. Forney
Number of Cars: 200
Noteworthy Features: 1899 Locomobile; 1915 Cadillac; 1914 Detroit Electric; Amelia Earhart's Gold Bug Kissel. World's largest collection of Kissels.
Status: Open to the public 9 a.m. to 6 p.m. daily; 1 to 7 p.m. Sundays. Closed Christmas.
Admission: Adults $1.00; high school students $.50; junior high and grade school students $.30. Group rates available.
Publications: Brochure available.

THE VETERAN CAR MUSEUM
2030 South Cherokee Street, Denver 80223
Director: Arthur G. Rippey
Number of Cars: 36
Noteworthy Features: Exhibits on loan from Colorado collectors.
Status: Open to the public 9 a.m. to 5 p.m. daily except Sunday and holidays.
Admission: Adults $1.00; children $.50.

Connecticut

ANTIQUE AUTO MUSEUM
Slater Street and I-86, Manchester
Director: Edgar H. Clarke
Number of Cars: 26
Noteworthy Features: 1906 Stevens-Duryea; 1926 Kissel; 1915 Pullman Gentleman's Roadster; 1922 Cadillac; 1924 Lincoln opera coupe; 1930 Buick; 1939 Bantam.
Status: Open to the public 10 a.m. to 8 p.m. daily, June 15 through September 1.
Admission: Adults $1.00; children $.50.

District Of Columbia

NATIONAL MUSEUM OF HISTORY AND TECHNOLOGY
Smithsonian Institution, Washington 20560
Director: Dr. Robert P. Multhauf
Number of Cars: 45
Noteworthy Features: Pioneer vehicles such as the Duryea, Haynes, Balzer and Winton experimental and racing cars.
Status: Open to the public 10 a.m. to 5:00 p.m.; open to 9 p.m. summer evenings. Closed Christmas.
Admission: Free.
Publications: "The Smithsonian Collection of Automobiles and Motorcycles," $4.95.

Florida

BELLM CARS & MUSIC OF YESTERDAY
5500 North Tamiami Trail, Sarasota 33580
Director: Walter Bellm
Number of Cars: 160
Noteworthy Features: 1897 Duryea Buggyaut, 1899 Locomobile Steamer, 1902 Stanley Steamer, 1922 Pierce-Arrow, 1936 V-12 Packard. Also antique bicycles, motorcycles.
Status: Open to the public 8:30 a.m. to 6 p.m. daily; 9:30 a.m. to 6 p.m. Sunday.
Admission: Adults $2.00; children 6-12 $.75, under 6 free.
Publications: Brochure available.

EARLY AMERICAN MUSEUM
P.O. Box 188, Silver Springs
Director: Sidney Strong
Number of Cars: 50
Noteworthy Features: Automobiles from 1897 to 1955. Steam, electric and gasoline antiques and classics.
Status: Open to the public 9 a.m. to 9 p.m. daily.
Admission: Adults $1.50; children $.50, under 6 free.
Publications: Accordion postcard. Catalogue.

MUSEUM OF SPEED
U.S. 1, South Daytona—P.O. Box 4157, Daytona Beach 32021
Director: William R. Tuthill
Number of Cars: 7
Noteworthy Features: Fireball Roberts' No. 22 Pontiac stock car; Art Afrons' Green Monster racer; Don Garlits' world championship fuel dragster. Also motorcycles, engines.
Status: Open to the public 9 a.m. to 6 p.m. daily; February, March, June, July and August to 9 p.m.
Admission: Adults $1.25; children 10-16 $.75, under 10 free if accompanied by adult.
Publication: Brochure available.

Georgia

ANTIQUE AUTO & MUSIC MUSEUM
Stone Mountain
Director: Tommy Protsman
Number of Cars: 32
Noteworthy Features: Large brass collection.
Status: Open to the public 10 a.m. to 5 p.m. during winter months; 9 a.m. to 9 p.m. during summer.
Admission: Adults $.75; children $.35. Group rates available.

MUSEUM OF AUTOMOBILES
Hamilton On The Square, Hamilton 31811
Director: Allen M. Woodall, Jr.
Number of Cars: 12
Noteworthy Features: Largest U.S. collection of motometers (over 150) and marble gearshift knobs (over 250).
Status: Open to the public 10 a.m. to 6 p.m. Monday through Saturday; noon to 6 p.m. Sunday.
Admission: Adults $.85; children $.50; under six free.
Publications: Brochure available.

Illinois

MUSEUM OF SCIENCE & INDUSTRY
57th Street & South Lake Shore Drive, Chicago 60637
Director: Daniel M. MacMaster
Number of Cars: 32
Noteworthy Features: 1908 Brush Runabout; 1911 Simplex; 1924 Marmon; 1909 Gleason tourer; 1905 Orient Buckboard; 1900 Locomobile steamer; 1903 McIntyre; 1913 National; 1904-05 Stevens-Duryea; 1907 Stoddard-Dayton.
Status: Open to the public daily. Summer hours: 9 a.m. to 5.30 p.m. Monday-Saturday; 10 a.m. to 6 p.m. Sundays and holidays. Winter hours: 9:30 a.m. to 4 p.m. Monday-Saturday; 10 a.m. to 6 p.m. Sundays and holidays. Closed Christmas.
Admission: Free.
Publications: "Progress" magazine, bimonthly.

QUINSIPPI ISLAND ANTIQUE AUTO MUSEUM
All America City Park, Front & Cedar, Quincy 62301
Director: Rowen J. Zander
Number of Cars: 45
Noteworthy Features: Owned and operated by the Mississippi Valley Historic Auto Club.
Status: Open to the public 11 a.m. to 8 p.m. daily June 1 to September 1. Open weekends only Sept. 1 to November 1 and April to June 1.
Admission: Adults $.75; children $.35, with parents free.

TIME WAS VILLAGE MUSEUM
U.S. 51, Mendota 61342
Director: Ken Butler
Number of Cars: 30.
Noteworthy Features: Gasoline, electric and steam vehicles from 1902 to 1961. Extensive memorabilia collection.
Status: Open to the public 9 a.m. to 6 p.m. daily May 1 to October 1.

Indiana

EARLY WHEELS MUSEUM
817 Wabash Avenue, Terre Haute 47807
Number of Cars: 34
Noteworthy Features: Car exhibition owned by Indianapolis Motor Speedway. Also bicycles, wagons and locomotives.
Status: Open to the public 10 a.m. to 4 p.m. Monday through Friday.
Admission: Free.

GOODWIN MUSEUM
200 South Main Street, Frankfort 46041
Director: J. William Goodwin
Number of Cars: 24
Noteworthy Features: 1905 Gatts, one of five made; 1904 Haynes-Apperson; 1932 Duesenberg; 1948 Tucker; 1918

Stutz Bulldog; 1907 Stanley; 1909 Buick; 1901 Frisbie; 1939 LaSalle; 1915 National hearse.
Status: Open to the public 10 a.m. to 6 p.m. daily.
Admission: Free.

ELWOOD HAYNES MUSEUM
1915 South Webster Street, Kokomo 46901
Director: John O. Cupp
Number of Cars: 3
Noteworthy Features: 1905 and 1920 Haynes, 1923 Apperson. Artifacts, papers and records pertaining to the career of Mr. Haynes. The museum is the former home and estate of the pioneer inventor.
Status: Open to the public 1 to 4 p.m. Tuesday through Saturday, 1 to 5 p.m. Sunday
Admission: Free.

INDIANAPOLIS MOTOR SPEEDWAY MUSEUM
4790 West 16th Street, Indianapolis 46224
Director: Karl Kizer
Number of Cars: 18
Noteworthy Features: Race car exhibits featuring 11 Indy 500 winners, including Ray Harroun's 1911 Marmon Wasp. Early Speedway trophies, hpotos, and memorabilia.
Status: Open to the public 9 a.m. to 5 p.m. daily.
Admission: Free.
Publications: Brochure available.

Iowa

HARRY E. BURD COLLECTION
828 West 4th Street, Waterloo
Director: Harry E. Burd
Number of Cars: 8
Noteworthy Features: 1908 Holsman; 1908 Sears surrey; 1919 Maytag; 1911 Brush.
Status: Private collection, open by appointment.

Kansas

ABILENE AUTO MUSEUM
Abilene
Number of Cars: 40
Noteworthy Features: 1920 Buick; 1937 V-12 Packard limousine; 1929 Reo Royal; 1936 Buick hearse; 1922 Franklin; 1932 V-12 Cadillac; 1937 La France fire truck.
Status: Open to the public.
Admission: Adults $.50; children $.25.
Publications: Brochure available, $.15.

Maine

BOOTHBAY RAILWAY MUSEUM
Route 87, Boothbay 04537
Director: George H. McEvoy
Number of Cars: 25
Status: Open to the public Memorial Day through early October.
Admission: Adults $.50; children $.25.
Publications: Brochure available.

H. E. MUCKLER'S HIGHWAY OF MEMORIES MOTORAMA
Route 128, North Woolwich
Status: Open to the public.

SEAL COVE AUTOMOBILE MUSEUM
Box 37, Seal Harbor 04675 (mailing); Seal Cove, Mount Desert Island (buildings)
Number of Cars: 105
Status: Open to the public daily 10 a.m. to 5 p.m. June 20th through September 10th.
Admission: Adults $1.50; children $.50.

Maryland

FIRE MUSEUM OF MARYLAND
1301 York Road, Lutherville 21093
Number of Cars: over 40 fire apparatus vehicles.
Noteworthy Features: 1881 Hayes aerial ladder, 1897 American steamer, 1905 Hale water tower, 1922 Ahrens-Fox pumper.
Status: Open to the public April through October on Saturdays 10 a.m. to 5 p.m., on Sundays 1 p.m. to 5 p.m. Other times by appointment.
Admission: Adults $2.00, students $1.00, children under 12 $.50.

Massachusetts

ANTIQUE AUTO MUSEUM OF MASSACHUSETTS
Larz Anderson Park, 15 Newton Street, Brookline 02146
Director: Charles Broderick
Number of Cars: 75
Noteworthy Features: Franklin Roosevelt's Twin-Six Packard; 1867 Dudgeon. Also 75 bicycles and many early carriages and sleighs.
Status: Open to the public 1 to 5 p.m. daily except Mondays.
Admission: Adults $1.00; children $.50.

EDAVILLE RAILROAD MUSEUM
P.O. Box 7, South Carver
Director: John R. Bryden
Number of Cars: 11
Status: Open to the public daily June 13 through Columbus Day, weekends and holidays in the spring.
Admission: Adults $1.75, children $.70, includes 5½-mile steam train ride.
Publications: Brochure available.

HERITAGE PLANTATION OF SANDWICH
Grove and Pine Streets
Sandwich, Massachusetts
Director: Josiah K. Lily III
Number of Cars: 35 on display
Noteworthy Features: Sears High Wheeler; Mercer; Stutz Bearcat; Olds Autocrat racer; Auburn; Franklin; Kissel; LaSalle; Lincoln; Model J Duesenberg; sixteen-cylinder Cadillac; Cord.
Status: Open to the public 10 a.m. to 5 p.m. daily June to October.
Admission: Adults $1.00; children under 12 $.75.
Publications: Brochure available.

STURBRIDGE AUTO MUSEUM
Route 20, Sturbridge 01566
Director: Harold J. Kenneway
Number of Cars: 30
Noteworthy Features: Cars and carriages, 1897-1939.
Status: Open to the public, 10:30 a.m. to 9:30 p.m. daily

June through August; 10:30 a.m. to 5:30 p.m. daily September and October. Open week-ends 12:30 to 5:30 p.m. April, May and November. Closed December through March.
Admission: Adults $1.00; children $.50.
Publications: Brochure available.

Michigan

HENRY FORD MUSEUM AND GREENFIELD VILLAGE
Dearborn
Director: Dr. Donald A. Shelly
Number of Cars: 200
Noteworthy Features: 1863 Roper steam carriage; 1896 Ford; Ford "999"; 1903 Packard "Old Pacific"; 1912 Baker Electric of President Taft; 1913 Scripps-Booth cyclecar prototype; Edison-built car; among numerous vehicles of historic interest. Comprehensive collection of Americana dating from the 1600's. An old car festival each September.
Status: Open to the public 9 a.m. to 5 p.m. daily; open until 6:30 p.m. June 15 through Labor Day.
Admission: (Museum) Adults $1.50; children 6 to 14 years $.50; special rates for educational groups.
Publications: Brochure available.

GILMORE CAR MUSEUM
Rt. 43, Hickory Corners
Director: Dr. P. Bernard
Number of Cars: over 50
Noteworthy Features: horse-drawn fire engine, 1910 Rolls-Royce Silver Ghost, English lake steam yacht, 27 cars over fifty years old.
Status: Open to the public Sunday afternoons, 1 to 5 p.m.
Admission: modest charge, children under 12 free.
Publications: Brochure available

POLL MUSEUM
U.S. 31 & New Holland Street, Holland 49423
Director: Henry Poll
Number of Cars: 28
Noteworthy Features: Antique and classic cars, five trucks, bicycles, engines and carriages.
Status: Open to the public daily except Sunday 9 a.m. to 5:30 p.m. May, June and September. 8 a.m. to 8 p.m. July and August.
Admission: Adults $.50; children 10-12 $.25, under 10 free.
Publications: Brochure and post cards available.

SLOAN PANORAMA OF TRANSPORTATION
1221 E. Kearsley Street, Flint 48503
Director: Roger VanBolt
Number of Cars: 29, plus about 16 on loan. Twenty cars on display in changing exhibit program.
Noteworthy Features: Classic Six Chevrolet; Buick "Bug"; Flint Roadster; Whiting; Flint Six; Paterson. A community museum, with predominant emphasis on the industrial history of the region.
Status: Open to the public 10 a.m. to 5 p.m. Tuesday through Friday, 12 to 5 p.m. weekends. Closed holidays.
Admission: Adults $.50; children $.10; students $.25.

WOODLAND CARS OF YESTERDAY
6504—28th Street S.E. Grand Rapids 49506
Directors: Ralph and Dawn Grooters
Number of Cars: 25
Noteworthy Features: 1898 Krastin; 1906 Cadillac tulip touring car; 1910 Brush.
Status: Open to the public 10 a.m. to 8 p.m. daily.

Admission: Adults and children over 11, $.50; children 10 and 11, $.25, under 10 free with parent.
Publications: Brochure available.

Minnesota

HEMP OLD VEHICLE MUSEUM
Rochester
Director: Paul L. Hemp
Number of Cars: 40
Noteworthy Features: 1905 Model F Ford. Also old steam engines and tractors; antique carriages.
Status: Open to the public, March to November.
Admission: Adults $.50; children $.25.
Publications: Pamphlet available.

Missouri

KELSEY'S ANTIQUE CAR COLLECTION
Highway 57, Camdenton 65020
Director: Paul Kelsey
Number of Cars: 44
Status: Open to the public 8 a.m. to 8 p.m. daily May through October; other months as weather permits.
Admission: Adults $.75; children $.30.

Montana

MONTANA HISTORICAL SOCIETY—
ED TOWE ANTIQUE FORD COLLECTION
225 North Roberts, Helena 59601
Director: Sam Gilluly
Number of Cars: 40
Noteworthy Features: Ford collection from 1903 Model A runabouts to 1935 Standard Fordor.
Status: Open to the public daily 8 a.m. to 8 p.m. Memorial Day through Labor Day. Winter hours: 8 a.m. to 5 p.m. weekdays; 12 noon to 5 p.m. weekends and holidays.
Admission: Free.
Publications: Brochure available.

Nebraska

HOUSE OF YESTERDAY
1330 North Burlington, Hastings 68901
Director: Burton R. Nelson
Number of Cars: 6
Noteworthy Features: 1903 Cadillac Runabout; 1905 Buick; 1907 Reo; 1909 Sears; 1910 Brush; 1914 Model T Ford.
Status: Open to the public daily, 8 a.m. to 5 p.m. September through May; 8 a.m. to 8 p.m. June through August. Sundays, 1 to 5 p.m.; holidays 2 to 5 p.m.
Admission: Adults $.50; children under 12 $.25, under 6 free.
Publications: "Yester News," 9 months per year.

SANDHILLS MUSEUM
Highway U.S. 20, Valentine
Director: G. M. Sawyer
Number of Cars: 26
Noteworthy Features: 1903 Schacht; 1908 Brush; 1908 Firestone Columbus; 1911 Chalmers; 1913 Imperial; 1914 Jef-

fery; 1916 Paterson; 1910 Flanders.
Status: Open to the public Memorial Day to Labor Day.
Admission: Adults $.75; school-age children $.50.
Publications: Brochure available.

THE HAROLD WARP PIONEER VILLAGE
Highway U.S. 6 & 34—Nebraska 10, Minden
Director: T. C. Jensen
Number of Cars: 150
Noteworthy Features: Early examples of a Milwaukee and Mobile steamer; Duryea; Cadillac; Reo; Regal. Excellent collection of early farm tractors. Also fire wagons, airplane and locomotive exhibits.
Status: Open to the public 8 a.m. to sundown daily.
Admission: Adults $1.35; children $.50; special group rates.
Publications: Brochure available.

Nevada

HARRAH'S AUTOMOBILE COLLECTION
P.O. Box 10, Reno 89504
Number of Cars: over 1400, 750 on display
Noteworthy Features: Largest known collection of antique, vintage and classic automobiles. Includes the New York to Paris Thomas Flyer; more than 100 Fords from 1903 to 1951; more than fifty models of both Packard and Franklin. Over 325 cars on display; restoration facilities open to the public.
Status: Open to the public 10 a.m. to 5 p.m. daily.
Admission: Adults $1.50; children $.75.

New Hampshire

MEREDITH AUTO MUSEUM
Route 3, Meredith 03253
Director: Glen C. Gould, Jr.
Number of Cars: 50
Noteworthy Features: Stanley; Stutz; Maxwell; Metz; Overland. Nickelodeon (all playable) and iron toy collection.
Status: Open to the public 9 a.m. to 6 p.m. daily, July 1 through Labor Day. Evenings by appointment.
Admission: Adults $.50; children $.35. Group rates available.
Publications: Brochure available.

New Jersey

ROARING 20 AUTOS
East Highway 37, Toms River 08753
Director: Irving Rothman
Number of Cars: 50 to 80
Status: Open to the public 10 a.m. to 5 p.m. daily.
Admission: Adults $1.25; children 6-12 $.50.

New York

ELLENVILLE MOTOR MUSEUM
46 Canal Street, Ellenville 12428
Director: Richard Joel Pettingell
Number of Cars: 60
Status: Open to the public 10 a.m. to 5 p.m. daily
Admission: Adults $1.50; children $.75.

LONG ISLAND AUTOMOTIVE MUSEUM
Route 27, Southampton
Director: Henry Austin Clark, Jr.
Number of Cars: 180
Noteworthy Features: The oldest U.S. automotive museum. Special collections of early sport and racing cars and commercial vehicles. Collection of early automotive art.
Status: Open to the public 9 a.m. to 5 p.m. daily June through September; weekends only in May and October.
Admission: Adults $1.30; children $.65. Group rates available by advance appointment.

MURCHIO'S MUSEUM OF ANTIQUE CARS
Jersey Avenue, Greenwood Lake 10925
Director: Helena M. Murchio
Number of Cars: 25
Status: Open to the public June 1 through October 15, 11 a.m. to 5 p.m. daily except Tuesdays; 1 to 3 p.m. Sundays. Other months by appointment.
Admission: Adults $.50; children $.25.

North Carolina

O. A. CORRIHER COLLECTION
Box 92, Landis
Directors: O. A. Corriher, B. E. Efird, Hal T. and Earl Allen
Number of Cars: 40
Noteworthy Features: 1904 Thomas Flyer; 1916 Stutz Bearcat; 1910 National Speedway Roadster; and the 1941 Indianapolis winner.
Status: Private collection, open by appointment.

Ohio

ALLEN COUNTY MUSEUM
620 West Market Street, Lima 45805
Director: Joseph Dunlap
Number of Cars: 5
Noteworthy Features: 1909 Locomobile Sports Roadster; 1941 Packard sedan.
Status: Open to the public 1:30 to 5 p.m. daily except Mondays and major holidays.
Admission: Free.
Publications: "The Allen County Reporter," quarterly.

FREDERICK C. CRAWFORD AUTO-AVIATION MUSEUM OF THE WESTERN RESERVE HISTORICAL SOCIETY
10825 East Boulevard, Cleveland 44106
Director: Mrs. Philip L. Sommerlad
Number of Cars: 145
Noteworthy Features: Extensive automobile collection, with emphasis on Ohio-built cars; large auto-aviation library and research service. "Main Street"—at the turn of the century—includes a general store, blacksmith shop, music shop, pharmacy, cigar store, barber shop and saloon—all completely furnished.
Status: Open to the public 10 a.m. to 5 p.m. daily except Mondays and legal holidays; 1 to 6 p.m. Sundays.
Admission: Adults $.75; children $.35. No charge for groups when appointment has been made.
Publications: Brochure available.

Oklahoma

HORSELESS CARRIAGES UNLIMITED
Highway 62, Muskogee
Director: James C. Leake
Number of Cars: 40
Noteworthy Features: 1919 Pierce-Arrow; 1925 Locomobile; 1934 Packard; 1929 Model A Ford Town Car; 1929 Model A Ford Popcorn Wagon.
Status: Open to the public 9 a.m. to 6 p.m. daily except Thanskgiving, Christmas and New Year's Day.
Admission: Adults $1.50; children under 12 free. Special group rates.

WILLIAM STEWART COLLECTION
300 East Federal, Shawnee
Director: William Stewart
Number of Cars: 41
Noteworthy Features: Devoted particularly to luxury vehicles.
Status: Private collection, open by appointment.
Admission: Adults (single) $1.00; (more than one) $.50 each; children free.

Pennsylvania

AUTOMOBILORAMA
Holiday West, U.S. 15 and Pennsylvania Tpke., Exit 17, Harrisburg
Director: E. W. Zimmerman
Number of Cars: 250
Noteworthy Features: 1898 Malden Steamer; 1902 Studebaker electric; Fords from 1903 to 1932; Chevrolets from 1914 to 1939; Cadillacs from 1903 to 1957; Buicks from 1906 to 1933; Sig Haughdahl racer; Doris Duke Duesenberg; Clark Gable Packard.
Status: Open to the public 9 a.m. to 10 p.m. daily.
Admission: Adults $1.50; children $.75.
Publications: Brochure available. Catalogue, $1.50.

BOYERTOWN AUTO BODY WORKS HISTORICAL VEHICLES MUSEUM
P.O. Box 30, Warwick & Laurel Streets, Boyertown
Director: Paul R. Hafer
Number of Cars: 57
Noteworthy Features: Devoted to vehicles built in Berks County, Pennsylvania, such as: 1902 Duryea phaeton; 1903 Boss Steam Car; 1912 "SGV" roadster; 1914 Dile; 1919 Daniels touring; 1924 Walker Electric Truck; 1928 Cadillac limousine.
Status: Open to the public 1 to 4 p.m. weekdays, Saturday and Sunday by appointment.
Admission: Free.
Publications: Brochure available.

POLLOCK AUTOMOTIVE COLLECTION
70 South Franklin Street, Pottstown 19464
Director: William Pollock
Number of Cars: 55
Noteworthy Features: Only two Chadwicks known to exist today. Also vintage motorcycles, antique typewriters and bicycles.
Status: Open by appointment only.

PAUL H. STERN'S ANTIQUE CARS
121 South Main Street, Manheim 17545

Number of Cars: 40-50
Noteworthy Features: Extensive Chrysler products collection, 1926-55. Many classic phaetons and antiques.
Status: Open to the public 9 a.m. to 5 p.m. daily, April through October.
Publications: Brochure available.

SWIGART MUSEUM
Box 214, Museum Park, Huntingdon 16652
Director: Mrs. Mardell Glosser
Number of Cars: 40 on display
Noteworthy Features: Large collection of automobile nameplates and license plates; extensive library.
Status: Open to the public 9 a.m. to 5 p.m. daily in June; 9 a.m. to 8 p.m. daily July and August; 9 a.m. to 5 p.m. weekends May, September and October
Admission: Adults $1.35; children $.65. Special group rates available.

South Carolina

JOE WEATHERLY STOCK CAR MUSEUM
Box 500, Highway 34 W. Darlington 29532
Director: Floyd N. Lane
Number of Cars: 10
Noteworthy Features: Stock car exhibit, trophies, engines and parts.
Status: Open to the public 9 a.m. to noon and 2 to 5 p.m. weekdays; 2 to 5 p.m. Sundays. Closed Saturdays.
Admission: Free.

WINGS & WHEELS
Highway 301 (and I-95), Santee
Number of Cars: 25
Noteworthy Features: Large antique aircraft collection, together with automobile exhibits, illustrating how development of the automobile and airplane closely paralleled each other.
Status: Open to the public.
Publications: Brochure available.

South Dakota

HORSELESS CARRIAGE MUSEUM
U.S. 16, Keystone Rte., Box 255, Rapid City
Director: LeRoy Healey
Number of Cars: 100
Noteworthy Features: 1905 Stanley Steamer; 1918 V-8 Chevrolet, Americana collections.
Status: Open to the public year-round, weather permitting
Admission: Adults $1.00; children $.25.
Publications: Brochure available.

PIONEER AUTO MUSEUM
Highways U.S. 16 and 83, Murdo
Director: A. J. Geisler
Number of Cars: 130
Noteworthy Features: 1902 Jewel; 1904 Fuller; 1913 Spacke cycle car; 1913 R.C.H.; 1913 Argo electric; 1919 Velie; 1921 Case; 1918 Marmon; 1928 Cunningham.
Status: Open to the public 6:30 a.m. to 9 p.m. May 15 through October 1; 7:30 a.m. to 6:30 p.m. October 2 through May 14.
Admission: Adults $1.00; children under 12 $.25.
Publications: Brochure available.

Tennessee

SMOKY MOUNTAIN CAR MUSEUM
U.S. Highway 441, Pigeon Forge
Number of Cars: 30
Noteworthy Features: Early models of Reo, Brush, Ford, Cadillac, Hupmobile, Overland, Marathon. Also Duesenberg, Cord L-29.
Status: Open to the public daily May through October; open evenings until 9 p.m. July through Labor Day.
Admission: Adults $1.00; children 6 to 12 years $.50, under 6 free with adult.
Publications: Brochure available.

Texas

CLASSIC CAR SHOWCASE
3009 South Post Oak Road, Houston 77027
Director: R. L. Atwell, Jr.
Number of Cars: 15 on display; 40 in collection
Noteworthy Features: Classic cars in scenes representative of the era 1925-1940.
Status: Open to the public 10 a.m. to 5 p.m. weekdays; 10 a.m. to 6 p.m. Saturday; noon to 6 p.m. Sunday.
Admission: Adults $1.50; children $.50. Group rates available.

PATE MUSEUM OF TRANSPORTATION
P.O. Box 711, Highway 377 South, Fort Worth 76101
Director: A. M. Pate, Jr.
Number of Cars: 33
Noteworthy Features: 1904 Schacht; 1912 Paige touring; 1917 Premier touring; 1924 Franklin; 1933 Studebaker touring; 1938 V-16 Cadillac limousine; 1913 American LaFrance fire truck. Locomotive and aircraft exhibits.
Status: Open to the public 9 a.m. to 5 p.m. daily except Monday.
Admission: Free.

Vermont

BOMOSEEN AUTO MUSEUM (CARS OF YESTERDAY)
Castleton Corners
Director: B. F. Smith
Status: Open to the public.

Virginia

CAR AND CARRIAGE CARAVAN
P.O. Box 389, at Luray Caverns, Luray 22835
Director: H. T. N. Graves
Number of Cars: 75 on display; 138 in collection
Noteworthy Features: 1907 International Autowagon; 1915 Dodge roadster; 1930 Cord front wheel drive phaeton; 1914 Locomobile Gentleman's Speedster; 1912 Hudson tourer.
Status: Open to the public daily, March 1 through April 15, 9 a.m. to 5 p.m.; April 16 through June 15, 9 a.m. to 7 p.m.; June 16 through Labor Day, 9 a.m. to 9 p.m.; Labor Day through October 15, 9 a.m. to 7 p.m.; October 16 through December 24, 9 a.m. to 5 p.m. Closed December 25 through February 28.
Admission: Adults $1.00; children 7-13 $.50, under 7 free. Special group rates.
Publications: Brochure available.

THE PETTIT COLLECTION
P.O. Box 8, Louisa 23093

Director: William A. C. Pettit, III
Number of Cars: 75
Noteworthy Features: 1906 Reo; 1922 Wills Sainte Claire; 1917 Rauch & Lang electric; 1928 Chrysler Imperial; 1931 Stutz DV-32; 1947 Tucker Torpedo; the Bauer Duesenbergs. Collection of license plates and display engines.
Status: Private collection.

Wisconsin

BERMAN'S AUTO & ANTIQUE MUSEUM
U.S. Highway 14, Oregon 53575
Director: Eugene F. Berman
Number of Cars: 18
Noteworthy Features: Vehicles from 1902 to 1931. 1916 Chevrolet touring; 1918 Model T snowmobile. Farm equipment displays; household antiques; money and coin collection; blacksmith shop; fire fighting equipment.
Status: Open to the public 7 a.m. to 9 p.m. daily March 1 through December 1.
Admission: Adults $.98; children under 10 free.
Publications: Brochure and post card available.

FOUR WHEEL DRIVE MUSEUM & HISTORICAL BUILDING
FWD Corporation, Clintonville
Director: Walter A. Olen
Noteworthy Features: 1909 "Battleship" (first successful fwd car in America); 1932 Miller Special racing car; Butterworth FWD/ASB race car; four-wheel drive trucks.
Status: Open to the public 9 a.m. to 5 p.m. weekdays May 15 through Labor Day. Open to groups by appointment.
Admission: Free

BROOKS STEVENS AUTOMOTIVE MUSEUM
Port Washington and Donges Bay Roads, Milwaukee
Director: Brooks Stevens
Number of Cars: 50
Noteworthy Features: Luxury, sports and racing cars ranging from a 1905 Cadillac roadster to the last model built by Howard Marmon in 1933 at a cost of $380,000.
Status: Open to the public 10 a.m. to 5 p.m. daily.
Admission: Adults $.50; children under 15 $.25.
Publications: Brochure available.

SUNFLOWER MUSEUM OF ANTIQUE CARS
Between "Big" and "Little" Tomahawk lakes
Director: F. A. Woodzicka
Number of Cars: 60
Status: Open to the public May 1 to October 1.
Admission: Adults $1.00; children under 10 free.

WARVEL VINTAGE CAR MUSEUM
Gillett 54124
Director: H. S. Warvel
Number of Cars: 35
Status: Open to the public 9 a.m. to 5 p.m. (during plant hours) Monday through Friday.
Admission: Adults $1.00; children $.50.

Canada

ANTIQUE AUTO MUSEUM
1871 Falls Avenue, Niagara Falls, Ontario
Director: Peter Stranyes
Number of Cars: 55
Noteworthy Features: Charles Lindbergh's 1927 Packard Sport Phaeton and numerous other cars of dignitaries and celebrities.

Admission: Adults $1.00; children $.50. Family plan rate, $3.00. Special group rates.

ARMSTRONG'S ANTIQUE AUTO MUSEUM
Harvey Station, New Brunswick
Directors: Gordon and Cecilia Armstrong
Number of Cars: 12
Noteworthy Features: Two of the first automobiles to appear in New Brunswick and Nova Scotia.
Status: Open to the public most of the year.
Admission: Free

CANADIAN AUTOMOTIVE MUSEUM
99 Simcoe Street South, Oshawa, Ontario
Number of Cars: Approx. 40
Noteworthy Features: Tudhope, Durant, McLaughlin, Gray Dort and Guy.
Status: Open to the public 9 a.m. to 5 p.m. Monday through Saturday; 10 a.m. to 6 p.m. Sunday; open evenings until 9 p.m. during summer months.
Admission: Adults $.75; students $.35; children under 11 free with adult.
Publications: Brochure available.

CAR LIFE MUSEUM
Trans Canada Highway, between Charlottetown & Bordon Ferry, Prince Edward Island.

ELKHORN MANITOBA AUTOMOBILE MUSEUM
Provincial Trunk Highway No. 1, Elkhorn, Manitoba
Director: Isaac Clarkeson
Number of Cars: 110
Noteworthy Features: 1912 Flanders 20 & 30; 1908 Reo; 1909 McLaughlin Buick; 1913 Russell Knight.
Status: Open to the public May 1st through fall.
Admission: Adults $1.00; children free with adult.
Publications: Brochure available.

MUSEE DE L'AUTO LTEE
12470 rue Lachapelle, Montreal 9, Quebec

MUSEUM OF SCIENCE AND TECHNOLOGY
(National Museum of Canada) Ottawa
Number of Cars: 23
Noteworthy Features: 1899 Locomobile; 1929 Durant; 1933 Pierce-Arrow; 1921 Gray Dort.
Status: Open to the public.

REYNOLDS MUSEUM
Highway 2A, Wetaskiwin, Alberta
Number of Cars: 412
Noteworthy Features: 1907 Maxwell; 1912 Locomobile; 1911 Overland; 1917 National. Also antique tractors, steam engines, fire engines, cycles and aircraft.
Status: Open to the public 10 a.m. to 5 p.m. daily May 1 to October 1.
Admission: Adults $1.00; children $.35.
Publications: Brochure available.

WESTERN DEVELOPMENT MUSEUM
1839 11th Street, Saskatoon, Saskatchewan (branches at Yorktown and North Battleford)
Director: Gordon A. Wilson
Number of Cars: 40 at each branch
Noteworthy Features: Holsman Rope Drive; Brush roadster; Russell touring; plus collection of gas and steam tractors.
Status: Open to the public daily. Yorkton and North Battleford branches open during summer months only.
Admission: Adults $.50; children free.
Publications: Brochure available.

AUTOMOBILE *Quarterly's*

LIBRARY SERIES

THE **american**
car
since
1775